NATIONAL
GEOGRAPHIC

T R A V E L E R

mexico

NATIONAL GEOGRAPHIC

TRAVELER

mexico

by Jane Onstott

National Geographic
Washington, D.C.

CONTENTS

Pages 2–3: Catedral, San Cristóbal de las Casas; Left: Cactuses, Baja California

TRAVELING WITH EYES OPEN

Alert travelers go with a purpose and leave with a benefit. If you travel responsibly, you can help support wildlife conservation, historic preservation, and cultural enrichment in the places you visit. You can enrich your own travel experience as well.

To be a geo-savvy traveler:

- Recognize that your presence has an impact on the places you visit.

- Spend your time and money in ways that sustain local character. (Besides, it's more interesting that way.)

- Value the destination's natural and cultural heritage.

- Respect the local customs and traditions.

- Express appreciation to local people about things you find interesting and unique to the place: its nature and scenery, music and food, historic villages and buildings.

- Vote with your wallet: Support the people who support the place, patronizing businesses that make an effort to celebrate and protect what's special there. Seek out shops, local restaurants, inns, and tour operators who love their home—who love taking care of it and showing it off. Avoid businesses that detract from the character of the place.

- Enrich yourself, taking home memories and stories to tell, knowing that you have contributed to the preservation and enhancement of the destination.

That is the type of travel now called geotourism, defined as "tourism that sustains or enhances the geographical character of a place—its environment, culture, aesthetics, heritage, and the well-being of its residents." To learn more, visit National Geographic's Center for Sustainable Destinations at *www .nationalgeographic.com/travel/sustainable.*

mexico

ABOUT THE AUTHOR

Jane Onstott earned a bachelor of arts degree in Spanish language and Hispanic literature from San Diego State University, with a year's study at Spain's Universidad Complutense de Madrid. Since that time she has lived and traveled extensively in Mexico and throughout Latin America. She worked as Director of Communications and Information for the Charles Darwin Research Station in the Galápagos Islands, Ecuador, and as a Spanish-language interpreter and translator in Mexico and the United States. Since 1986 Onstott has contributed to travel guides covering Mexico, Ecuador, and the United States. Her website, *www.mexicoguru.com,* has information about Mexico's destinations, history, and culture.

Charting Your Trip

Easy to stereotype but harder to comprehend, Mexico is nothing if not diverse. Spanish invaders, European immigrants, and indigenous people from a wide variety of ethnic traditions have over the centuries created a complex national character and cultural lexicon. From this diversity have emerged folk art and music, paintings and poetry.

Possessing a capital city with alluring cultural and historical sites, facing tropical seas east and west, Mexico is a magnet for vacationers. Many people spend a couple of days in Mexico City, then choose between a resort vacation or exploration of the country's colonial interior. For a traditional beach vacation, you can choose between a high-octane (and high-end) resort like Cancún or Los Cabos, a diverse resort city like Puerto Vallarta, or a lower-key destination such as Ixtapa or Huatulco. Less touristy towns and villages await RVers and travelers pursuing cheaper prices and fewer tourists.

An emerging nation with a reasonably sophisticated infrastructure, Mexico has an excellent bus system (see "Buses in Mexico," p. 10) and a growing network of toll-roads connecting major cities. A number of smaller airlines have sprung up to serve destinations without the need for a stopover in Mexico City, making internal plane travel cheaper and more convenient than ever.

NOT TO BE MISSED:

Petting a gray whale in Laguna San Ignacio **68–69**

Riding the train through the Copper Canyon **90–91**

Sportfishing in the Sea of Cortés **72**

Attending a Day of the Dead festival **225**

Mexico City's fantastic Museo Nacional de Antropología **198–201**

Visiting the less-crowded Maya sites of Uxmal and the Ruta Puuc **341–344**

Snorkeling or diving in a crystalline cenote (sinkhole) in the Yucatán **324**

Mexico City & Around

Today, most international flights stop in **Mexico City.** Mexico's overcrowded, highly charged capital has a lot to offer, and you should plan on spending at least three days here, and, if you have the time, four more days in the surrounding area. With the city's fabulous restaurants, colonial churches, excellent museums, and the ruins of the Aztec capital of Tenochtitlán directly behind its vast main plaza, you will be both entertained and educated about this diverse country and its fascinating history.

Tucked away among the gorgeous peaks of the central Sierra surrounding Mexico City, you'll discover the lovely towns of **Puebla, Cholula, Tlaxcala,** and **Tepoztlán,** founded early on by the Spanish, as well as fascinating archaeological sites from pre-Aztec civilizations. Visit the enigmatic archaeological site of **Teotihuacán,** just north of Mexico City, or the Toltec ruins at **Tula,** 61 miles

When to Visit

When you visit depends largely on what you want to do and see, and your tolerance for wet, hot, or humid weather. June through October is the wettest time, and if you don't mind late afternoon showers, consider booking your vacation during this low season. Rain during this time may put a damper on beach vacations, however, though

Mexicans love to travel to beach resorts during the hottest months of the year, July and August. Most folks avoid the coast in September and October because of the hurricane threat. If you want to avoid both the rainy season and the high season, choose late spring (after Easter) or late fall. Book well in advance during Easter, Christmas, and regional holidays.

(98 km) to the northwest. Explore the enormous pyramid of **Tepanapa** at Cholula, about 81 miles (130 km) due east of the city. Even **Xalapa,** the mountain-straddling capital of the Gulf-embracing state of Veracruz, is four hours away. It's east of Mexico City on the toll Highway 190 (via Puebla) or on Highway 136.

Most sites can be seen on guided tours from Mexico City, or by taxi or with a rental car. Consider staying in Mexico City and taking day or overnight trips, or, for longer stays, combining a trip to the capital city with one or more forays to Mexico's coastal resorts or heartland.

The Beach

If relaxing at the beach is as much a part of your program as cultural forays, **Cancún** and the **Riviera Maya** along the Yucatán's Caribbean coast are Mexico's most popular tourist destinations. Base yourself in Cancún if you enjoy major resorts with varied (albeit pricey) restaurants and fancy discos. Forty miles (68 km) south, **Playa del Carmen** is a smaller and somewhat more sophisticated city. Resorts such as the luxurious Maroma Resort & Spa and bare-bones Cabañas Paamul (with adjacent dive shop) cater to those looking for more isolated digs facing the beach along the Caribbean coast. Among the region's things to see are **Xcaret,** a Maya-theme nature park on a beautiful cove just south of Playa del Carmen; and the pre-Hispanic archaeological sites of **Tulum,** 80 miles (130 km) south of Cancún, and **Chichén Itzá,** 112 miles (179 km) west. It's about a two-hour flight from Mexico City to Cancún; direct flights

Beach statue of
Chac Mool, Cancún

Buses in Mexico

Buses are a good option for travel around Mexico. The country's first-class buses have bathrooms, reclining seats, and air-conditioning. Some provide a snack. Executive-class buses offer roomier seats and foot rests. The following companies accept credit cards and advance reservations.

ADO/GL/UNO (Gulf coast, south and southeast Mexico), www.ticket bus.com.mx

Grupo Flecha Amarilla/Primera Plus (Pacific and central Mexico), www.primeraplus.com.mx

TAP (northern and central Mexico), www.gruposenda.com

are available from the United States, Canada, and sometimes Europe.

On the other side of the country, Pacific sojourns can be based on any of the major beach resorts from Mazatlán to Huatulco, accessible via one-hour (or so) flights from Mexico City. Some, including **Puerto Vallarta,** have direct flights from the United States and, in high season, Canada. Each town has its own personality—**Mazatlán,** with its recently restored early 20th-century downtown; **Huatulco,** with its nine beautiful bays; modern but diminutive **Ixtapa;** the quintessential Mexican beach village of **Zihuatanejo;** and alluring **Puerto Vallarta,** with its excellent location on a beautiful bay backed by big, green mountains. All along the Pacific Coast, you'll revel in excellent sunsets, shopping, and fine dining, as well as opportunities for getting away to more remote and lonely beaches.

Relatively isolated from Mexico City and the rest of mainland Mexico, **Baja California** lures desert rats who love the sea. Baja's main tourist destination is **Los Cabos,** at the tip of the peninsula, which offers excellent fishing as well as shopping, golfing, and an energetic nightlife scene. There are direct flights from Mexico City, as well as from most major U.S. gateways.

If You Have More Time

Lovely **Oaxaca city,** 280 miles (450 km) south of Mexico City, is the place to visit excellent museums and impressively restored baroque churches, as well as to shop for

Using a Cell Phone in Mexico

With some exceptions, cell phone technologies in North America and Europe are not compatible. You can use a cell from Canada or the United States in Mexico, although roaming charges are high and coverage is variable. If you do need to use or call a cell phone while in Mexico, follow these guidelines.

Cell to cell, local call: area code (in Spanish, "LADA") + local number

Land line to cell, local call: 044 + area code + local number

Cell to land line, local call: local number

Cell to cell, long distance within

Mexico: 01 + area code + local number

Land line to cell, long distance within Mexico: 045 + area code + local number

Cell to land line, long distance within Mexico: 01 + area code + local number

To Cell from outside Mexico: Add 1 before the area code

Cell to U.S. & Canada (cell or land line): 001 + area code + local number

Cell to other countries: 00 + country code + area code + local number

Emergencies: 065 or 060

Toll-free numbers (Mexico) 01800 + seven-digit number

Safety in Mexico

Certain areas, especially border cities like Tijuana and Ciudad Juárez, are experiencing such heightened violence among drug cartels that tourism has all but evaporated, leaving business owners and their employees in desperate straits.

The interior is generally safe, although certain precautions are advised in Mexico City. Standard procedure includes not wearing expensive jewelry or flashing cash. Check with locals or hotel staff about any areas or cab companies to avoid. Don't drive at night, and use toll roads when available. Daytime bus rides are also safer both because drivers are more alert and there's little probability of a roadblock robbery, which are uncommon but unpleasant.

folk art and fine art. Learn about one of Mesoamerica's earliest civilizations at the hilltop archaeological site of **Monte Albán.** At nearby **Mitla,** ancient artisans produced exquisite geometric mosaics from the area's fine limestone. A flight between Mexico City and Oaxaca takes less than an hour, while a bus ride takes about five hours. Many people combine a visit to Oaxaca with a couple of days at its beaches—

from Huatulco to Puerto Escondido, and miles of beach in between. They're located well away from the city, about a 30-minute flight, or an eight-hour bus ride.

Squeezed between Oaxaca and Guatemala, **Chiapas** is an undervalued state. It's 391 miles (630 km) east of Oaxaca City to Chiapas' most popular tourist destination, the colonial city of **San Cristóbal de las Casas,** with beautiful churches, inexpensive hotels, and loads of handcrafts for sale. Visit more highland towns and myriad natural attractions by taxi, tour, or rental car, and don't overlook the excellent Maya ruins at **Palenque,** 110 miles (177 km) away on Highway 199.

Also much overlooked is **Campeche**. If you eschew overcrowded Maya ruins like Tulum and Chichén Itzá, seek out this state's fantastic, little visited ruins of **Calakmul.** This, and smaller Maya sites, lie within the Calakmul Biosphere Reserve, nearly two million acres of tropical forest providing haven for jaguars, spider monkeys, and howlers. Visit Calakmul from Mexico's prettiest capital city, Campeche, or after visiting the Riviera Maya, or Mérida, the capital of Yucatán State.

Acapulco's divers have impressed onlookers for decades.

History & Culture

A Mixtec priest.
Opposite: Parroquia de San Pedro
church in charming Tlaquepaque

Mexico Today

In *The Labyrinth of Solitude,* Nobel Prize–winning poet and essayist Octavio Paz calls his countrymen defensive, reticent, and remote. Yet most visitors characterize their Mexican hosts as congenial and helpful, just one example of Mexico's many contradictions. Intense and passionate, Mexicans hide their emotions under a mask of serenity and indifference.

The Land

Mexico radiates from its physical and political heart in the highland Valley of Mexico (Valle de Anáhuac), into which more than one-fifth of the nation's population crowds. Built from the remains of the ancient Aztec capital, Tenochtitlán, in 1521, Mexico City is surrounded by some of the nation's most fertile farmlands. While at least half of its acreage is arid or semiarid, Mexico produces corn, wheat, soybeans, rice, beans, coffee, cacao, fruit, and vegetables.

This geographically diverse country is, nonetheless, dominated by mountains. Marching south from the U.S. border for around 700 miles (1,120 km) are the eastern and western ranges of the Sierra Madre (literally, "mother mountain"): the Sierra Madre Oriental and the Sierra Madre Occidental. In between, the Mexican Plateau cradles a series of lesser ranges and highland valleys, and in the north, the Chihuahua and Sonora Deserts.

> **Mexico radiates from its ... heart in the highland Valley of Mexico, into which more than one- fifth of the nation's population crowds.**

Surrounded by the Pacific Ocean and the Sea of Cortés, the Baja California peninsula is equal parts desert and mountain, with eight main mountain ranges, dozens of islands, and a combined coastline of about 3,000 miles (4,800 km). One of the world's longest and most isolated peninsulas, it was linked top to tip by road only in the 1970s.

A mother lode of precious minerals in the Sierra Madre Occidental and Sierra Madre Oriental made these rugged and frequently inhospitable mountains among the first places explored and settled by the Spaniards, and minerals are still an important source of revenue. Mexico leads the world in silver mining; copper, lead, zinc, and salt are important commodities. Mahogany, walnut, rosewood, and other hardwoods are harvested, especially in the central and northwestern forests, as are pines for paper and pulp. Despite legislation in 1988 to promote sustainable development, the practice of cattle ranching, slash-and-burn agriculture, and cutting of trees as a domestic fuel source contribute to deforestation, especially in the poorer southern region. Nature-based tourism, although still in its infancy, may be the solution to providing poor communities with viable alternatives to such destructive ecological practices.

Mountaineers are inspired by some of the continent's tallest peaks—including Pico de Orizaba, Iztaccíhuatl, and La Malinche—that cluster around the 19th parallel in the Cordillera Neo-Volcánica, at the southern edge of the Sierra Madre Oriental. Like El Nevado de Colima, on the Pacific coast, Popocatépetl volcano is active and closed to climbers; villages on its slopes and in surrounding valleys have been sporadically evacuated.

A mariachi musician gets his shoes polished in El Jardín, San Miguel de Allende.

Traffic orbits el Monumento a la Independenica at Paseo de la Reforma in Mexico City.

Mexico's few lowland areas include the Yucatán Peninsula, an unusual limestone shelf of underground rivers and cenotes (sinkholes) jutting into the Caribbean Sea. Extending north and west from the Yucatán along the Gulf of Mexico is a broad expanse of steamy tropical and semitropical lowlands laced by rivers, swamps, and estuaries. Between that and the narrower, longer Pacific littoral, Mexico has 5,320 miles (8,560 km) of coastline.

Along the Pacific coast and into southern Mexico and Guatemala, the Sierra Madre del Sur and Sierra Madre de Chiapas are two mountain ranges whose isolation has preserved the indigenous cultures of their peoples but at the cost of such basic services as potable water, sewage systems, schools, hospitals, and electricity.

The People

Few countries in the hemisphere have a greater degree of both *mestizaje* (fusion of indigenous and European blood) and indigenous identity. Nearly 30 percent of Mexicans are indigenous, while about twice that number are *mestizos*. (Some sources put the number of mestizos higher, with fewer indigenous people.) More than seven million Mexicans speak an indigenous language or dialect, especially Mayan, Mixtec, Náhuatl, Otomí, Purépecha, and Zapotec. Although it cannot be said that whites (9 percent) make up Mexico's rich elite exclusively, it is safe to say that mestizos and Indians compose the poor—about 40 percent of the population.

In the 16th century, Spanish invaders brought draft animals and the wheel along with Renaissance-era Romanticism and religious zeal. Dozens of independent and unique cultures were eventually conquered and catechized, although pockets of resistance held out until the 20th century. But many native peoples do retain their indigenous identities. Cultural groups such as the Lacandón and the Huichol, who fled to the dense tropical forests and inhospitable mountains, avoided significant contact with mainstream society until well into the 20th century. Even today, the Huichol people living in the western Sierra Madre include few Catholic rituals into their spiritual belief system, retaining their traditional gods and ceremonies.

Most indigenous people, though, have blended their ancient gods and customs with saints and religious rites introduced by the Spaniards. Catholicism is practiced—influenced by modern indifference and indigenous dogma—by 88 percent of the population. Around half of the remainder are evangelical Christians, whose form of Christianity sometimes produces conflict with their neighbors. In highland Chiapas, traditional Tzotzil Indians have in recent decades clashed with large populations of villagers who have been converted to evangelical sects. In larger, more mainstream communities, Protestants and Catholics live and work together peacefully.

Fascinating customs and cultures have attracted adventure travelers for centuries. Writer John Lloyd Stephens's (1805–1852) and artist Frederick Catherwood's (1799–1854) published accounts of buried Maya ruins intrigued the Western world in the 19th century. Since then, writers have praised and scoffed, but rarely remained indifferent to, Mexico's charms and idiosyncrasies.

Modern Challenges

Born in the aftermath of the revolution, the Institutional Revolutionary Party, or PRI (Partido Revolucionario Institucional), was the official government party from 1929 on. Polls before the 2000 elections showed that people in the most rural areas believed the PRI and the government to be synonymous, and indeed they had every reason to do so. The party won every presidential election, and most governorships, between 1929 and 1994. Beginning in 1978, opposition parties were admitted in the Lower House, or Cámara de Diputados, to promote an illusion of democratic debate but with no chance to effect real change. However, in the 1997 elections, opposition parties actually won more seats in Congress than the PRI. That same year, leftist candidate Cuauhtémoc Cárdenas, of the Democratic Revolutionary Party, the PRD (Partido de la Revolución Democrática), became the first elected mayor of Mexico City.

A series of significant events in the 1990s continued to mobilize the public for political change. Popular presidential candidate Luis Donaldo Colosio was assassinated in 1994. Outgoing president Carlos Salinas de Gortari—credited during his six-year tenure (1988–1994) with a host of economic advances—left behind a trail of scandal and economic chaos, including devaluation of the peso and a bank bailout costing upward of $93 billion. That same year, a guerrilla army calling itself the Zapatista Army for National Liberation, or EZLN (Ejército Zapatista de Liberación Nacional), seized control of several strategic cities in highland Chiapas. Although they quickly retreated to the forest, their Internet postings and media

EXPERIENCE:
Lend a Hand

Opportunities to volunteer for good causes in Mexico are plentiful. You can teach English in Oaxaca (www.travel-to-teach.org/mexico/san_isidro.html) or help build homes with **Habitat for Humanity** (see p. 227). If you find yourself along either of the coasts, you can spend some time to help save sea turtles (see p. 317). Some organizations offer both short- and long-term volunteer opportunities, including **Global Volunteers** (www.globalvolun teers.org) and **Cross-Cultural Solutions** (www.crossculturalsolutions.org). No matter what you decide to do, make arrangements before arriving so you are prepared for your volunteer jobs.

communiqués have drawn world attention to the plight of the nation's disenfranchised peasant populations.

The prudent economic policies of Salinas's successor, Ernesto Zedillo Ponce de León (1994–2000), helped restore the economy, but more surprising were the political reforms started by the Yale-educated economist. Ahead of the 2000 presidential elections, extensive reforms of electoral institutions and a large presence of foreign observers eliminated many of the usual election day "irregularities" and encouraged the electorate to participate. And instead of picking the presumed successor, a traditional practice since the party's formation, the PRI under Zedillo held a nationwide primary election. The result of these groundbreaking reforms was the election of opposition party candidate Vicente Fox, of the National Action Party, or PAN (Partido de Acción Nacional), in July 2000. Accepting defeat with good grace, PRI candidate Francisco Labastida helped maintain calm and encouraged a peaceful transition to the historic opposition party government.

Mexico has emerged as an important player in the world economy. In 2008, it was considered the second most dynamic economy of Latin America.

But the country's divided government (none of the three major parties had a majority in Congress, and the constitutional presidency is inherently weak) hindered positive change during the Fox administration, and the giant from Guanajuato did not control his party as his PRI predecessors did. Campaign promises remained largely unfulfilled, and most Mexicans became dissatisfied with Fox's performance. Trade with Canada and the United States has doubled since the North American Free Trade Agreement (NAFTA) went into effect in 1994, but expanded industrialization has fouled rivers and created smog and hazardous-waste disposal problems, traffic congestion, and housing challenges, especially in the cities along the U.S. border, where industrial growth is greatest.

Powerful drug cartels fight among themselves and intimidate, kill, and corrupt police and judges who refuse collusion or attempt to restrict their spheres of influence. The demands of small but significant guerrilla movements must be addressed to ensure future stability.

Despite these and other difficulties, Mexico has emerged as an important player in the world economy. In 2008 it was considered the second most dynamic economy of Latin America, after Brazil, with a GDP of more than 17,000 USD per capita (although distribution among rich and poor is terribly unbalanced). Perhaps most important, Mexico has avoided a coup since 1920, longer than any other Latin American nation, and, after years of political demagoguery, is enjoying ever increasing political freedoms.

Festivals & Fiestas

As a predominantly Catholic country, Mexico celebrates saints' days and other religious holidays with elaborate festivities. Mexicans are great admirers of pyrotechnics and incorporate fireworks

whenever possible into their high days and holidays, creating great towers of shooting sparks and rockets that boom throughout the night. They rarely retire early on
the night of a fiesta or, for that matter, on the nights preceding it.

Mexico's coastal peoples are especially known for their exuberant fiestas and love
of music and dance. The country's most famous Carnaval (pre-Lenten celebration) is
held in Veracruz with masked balls, lavish parades with floats and costumes, and lively
all-night street parties. Those of Campeche, Mazatlán, Cozumel, and an increasing
number of other communities are also animated, well-attended events. Easter is
celebrated with much ceremony; especially moving rituals take place in Oaxaca, San
Miguel de Allende, San Luis Potosí, and Taxco. Christmas represents an entire season of
family gatherings and special foods, processions, and music.

For All Saints' Day and All Souls' Day, families clean and decorate their loved ones'
tombs, and in some regions, hold graveside vigils and create lavish home altars in honor
of their departed relatives. In Pátzcuaro, Oaxaca, Mérida, and other cities, cultural events
and public altars make the family-oriented holiday accessible to visitors. ■

Celebrating the Festival of the Virgin of Guadalupe, Mexico City

History of Mexico

Great civilizations were born and buried in ancient Mexico, some existing in isolation, but most with contacts as far off as the Great Plains of the United States and the mountains of Peru. No less fascinating is the history of colonial and modern Mexico, which has blended European and indigenous world views to forge one of the most important developing nations.

Early Humans

Many scholars agree that some 30,000 or even 40,000 years ago, during the late Pleistocene, humans crossed the Bering Sea from northeastern Asia to North America. Fanning across the continents, family units occupied caves and other available shelters, hunting small game and gathering food.

In the pre-Hispanic era (before the Spanish Conquest), two distinct zones composed the land we now call Mexico. Roughly north of Tampico and the tip of Baja California, extending into today's central United States, were the great, hot deserts and sweeping plains referred to as la Gran Chichimeca. Long after the arrival of European explorers, individual tribes of nomadic hunter-gatherers, collectively referred to as Chichimeca, eked out an existence in this harsh environment. In times of scarcity and drought, they were likely to rain down on the farming villages to the south in a storm of chaos and destruction.

Extending south of la Gran Chichimeca all the way to northern Honduras and El Salvador was a geographic and cultural zone now referred to as Mesoamerica. By the Archaic period (7000–1500 B.C.), many tribes had abandoned the nomadic lifestyle and established sedentary villages. By about 3000 B.C., while still seasonally gathering seeds and fruit, clans had domesticated corn, which they cultivated along with squash, chili peppers, avocados, and a wide variety of other foods. By 1500 B.C., simple agricultural societies existed throughout the region.

Compelling archaeological evidence demonstrates that early Mesoamericans had contact with South American tribes. Seafaring peoples from around Ecuador and Peru brought new and improved varieties of corn, which were successfully crossed with native species. These itinerant traders also introduced fired pottery to the west coast peoples, as well as metallurgy, which was practiced only among the Purépecha (Tarascan) and the Mixtec (based, respectively, in modern-day Michoacán and Oaxaca). Even the Purépecha language, which is unlike any in North America, has been linked to Quechua, the language of Peru.

Among the earliest known examples of ... public architecture is a massive artificial plateau, or early pyramid, built around 1350 B.C. in Veracruz.

During the early Preclassic, or Formative, period (1500 B.C.–A.D. 150), certain societies became sufficiently large and differentiated by class to bring about the construction of impressive public buildings. These edifices required an enormous commitment of man-hours, since neither beasts of burden nor the wheel were available. Among the earliest known examples of this public architecture is a massive artificial plateau, or early pyramid, built around 1350 B.C. at San Lorenzo in Veracruz.

A giant Olmec head, one of 11 discovered in 1946 in southern Mexico

Battle scenes like those in this fresco at Bonampak helped disprove early theories of Maya pacifism.

The Mother Culture

The San Lorenzo pyramid was built by the Olmec, the oldest known civilization in North America. Olmec society was stratified, with an elite class governing non-farming priests and artisans and a vast plebeian majority. Fertile tropical lowlands with extreme rainfall easily supported slash-and-burn agriculture, and the region's many rivers, lagoons, and estuaries provided an extensive transportation system.

Although there is some early evidence of Olmec culture on the southern Pacific coast, the first great centers were built along the Gulf, in southern Veracruz and Tabasco. For years the origins of the Olmec language eluded linguists, until clues carved in hieroglyphic writings showed it to be derivative of that of the Mixe-Zoque, whose descendants still inhabit the Pacific coast of Oaxaca and Chiapas states.

San Lorenzo was the first known Olmec city, at its apogee between about 1150 and 900 B.C. Other nearby cities later gained preeminence, including La Venta, Tres Zapotes, and Laguna de los Cerros. At San Lorenzo, drains of basalt diverted rainwater from the pyramid. Quarried in the Tuxtla Mountains near Laguna de los Cerros and at other sites, the stone was rolled, dragged, and floated to San Lorenzo in uncanny feats of engineering. Thrones, stelae, and other monumental works of artistry were created, including immense stone heads thought to honor important rulers.

Other characteristic Olmec art forms include exquisite masks and statuettes. Many of them portray deities such as the jaguar and the half-man, half-jaguar being that may have represented a bridge between the feline god and the ruling dynasty. The Olmec imported jade, greenstone, obsidian, and other materials, as well as agricultural products. Exports, including carved axheads of jade and wooden and stone masks and figurines, have been found as far north as Tlatilco, in the Valley of Mexico, and south in the highlands of El Salvador. Although highland and Gulf coast cultures borrowed from one another, the major artistic, intellectual, and political contributions came from the Olmec.

As the Olmec culture waned in importance in the tenth century B.C., other cities and city-states emerged in Oaxaca and the highland valleys of central Mexico. Strategically perched above the confluence of three valleys in Oaxaca, Monte Albán prospered from about 500 B.C. At Cuicuilco, south of Mexico City, the round, terraced pyramid built around 400 B.C. (and engulfed by lava from the nearby Xitle volcano some 500 years later) was one of the earliest and most unusual structures of the Preclassic period.

In the Soconusco region of Chiapas, Izapa forms an important link between Olmec and Maya cultures. This large city peaked in size and artistic achievement between about 300 and 50 B.C., when its inhabitants carved a great number of stelae in a highly narrative, pictorial style similar to those produced in early Maya art. Scattered throughout the region, these monuments demonstrate a devotion to rituals tied to astronomy, agricultural cycles, fertility, and other natural events.

Significant similarities between the Maya and the Olmec include representations of a "Long-Lipped God" (precursor to the Maya rain god Chac, also spelled Chaac) and the use of Long Count (see below) date glyphs. Some experts attribute the latter to the Maya; equally reputable scholars credit the Olmec. The same debate surrounds the earliest hieroglyphic writing system.

Classic Civilizations

One of Mexico's earliest and most fascinating civilizations was that of the ancient Maya, who occupied the Yucatán Peninsula, as well as the highlands and lowlands of Chiapas and Central America. (With 3 million people, the Maya today constitute Mexico's largest indigenous population, and many still practice ancient ways.)

Maya culture began to blossom just before the Christian era. Its cities produced learned mathematicians as well as artists and architects. With none of the instruments known to the modern world, the Maya achieved great accuracy in astronomy. They had a place-value system of numbers and used several different calendars, including a 365-day solar calendar and a 260-day ritual calendar. The two calendars were meshed to produce a 52-year cycle in which each day had prophetic significance. Although other ancient civilizations used these cyclical calendars, only the Olmec and the Maya used the Long Count, a noncyclical calendar. It had a definite start date (by Western reckoning August 11, 3114 B.C.) and was used to record historical events. The Maya also used the most sophisticated system of writing in Mesoamerica: a phonetic script often employing rebuses or written puns.

Temazcal Steam Ritual

Like the Lakota and Iroquois, pre-Hispanic Mesoamericans used the steam ritual, or temazcal (house of heat). Although some sources say the ritual was more physically restorative than metaphysical, modern ceremonies often incorporate ritual blessings.

In Puerto Escondido, Temazcalli (www.temazcalli.com) leaders study under Maestro Tlakaelel, elder, teacher, and guardian of Tolteca-Chichimeca traditions. More and more high-end hotel and spas have built the igloo-shape edifices on their grounds, including the Four Seasons at Punta de Mita, Nayarit (www.fourseasons.com/puntamita); the Maroma (see p. 381) and Ceiba del Mar (www.ceibadelmar.com/English) on the Riviera Maya; and Puerto Vallarta's Marriott (see p. 369). Just south of Tulum, Posada Dos Ceibas (www.dosceibas.com) also offers yoga and shamanistic cleansings, or limpias. Dos Palmas (www.dospalmas.info) gives visitors a chance to enjoy a ritual sweat and go for a swim in a crystalline cenote (sinkhole).

The Maya made their exquisite palaces and temples of quarried limestone faced with brightly painted plaster. Where stone was plentiful, elaborate pictorial and hieroglyphic messages were carved into limestone lintels and stelae. Elsewhere the Maya used modeled and carved stucco to glorify births, marriages, deaths, victories in battle, and other momentous events involving the royal families.

While most Preclassic Maya cities were isolated and autonomous, extensive communication characterized the Classic Maya civilizations. "White roads" (sacbeób), highways elevated up to 15 feet (4.5 m) above the surrounding jungle, gleamed white in the night, possibly to aid couriers who traveled between cities during the cooler hours. Paved with flat stones and stucco, these roads facilitated commerce and transportation and may have served military and religious purposes. They not only joined one city to another but also linked the most important buildings within a city, possibly to help transport icons between temples.

> **Hundreds of years after the demise of the great city of Teotihuacán, Aztec lords made pilgrimages to the ruins to consult with the gods and to bring home relics.**

Early on, the Maya established trade with Teotihuacán, in central Mexico, built by a Totonac-speaking people from the Gulf coast. Teotihuacán, in turn, traded as far north as the Oasis America tribes of northern Mexico and the southwestern United States. Like the Maya, the Teotihuacanos were mathematicians and astronomers. Hundreds of years after the demise of the great city of Teotihuacán, Aztec lords made pilgrimages to the ruins to consult with the gods and to bring home relics for their own palaces and altars. According to Aztec legends, the gods gathered there to bring about the current era—the Fifth Sun—sacrificing themselves and in the process creating the sun and the moon. These celestial bodies, honored in two of the largest pyramids in the Western Hemisphere—the Pirámide del Sol and Pirámide de la Luna—would, along with all else in the world, disappear in the inevitable demise of the Fifth Sun, as the previous four worlds had been cataclysmically undone. Mesoamericans expected the world to end and begin anew with each successive era, or "sun." The epoch of the Fifth Sun was expected to be wiped out by earthquakes at the end of one of the 52-year cycles.

Teotihuacán fell into ruin around A.D. 600, when some of its most important buildings appear to have been purposefully burned or dismantled. In Oaxaca, Monte Albán was abandoned around 700, and the decline of the great Maya cities began about a hundred years later. For no obvious reason, ceremonial centers were left to crumble, often to be reused later by others as places of worship or as burial grounds.

Postclassic Mesoamerica

While previously accepted theories held that Classic Maya cities were brought down by peasant revolts, there was actually a relatively smooth and seamless transition to the Postclassic phase between approximately A.D. 900 and 1200. The most important distinction between the Classic and Postclassic eras was the substitution of tribal councils for the kingdoms that had previously ruled. After 1200, monumental art depicting the glories of kings and queens was replaced with more utilitarian public art and architecture.

Another popular misconception regarding the Postclassic era (900–1521) in general is that it was characterized by a breakdown of society and increased warfare. Upon reexamining the evidence, however, most archaeologists agree that warfare and ritual sacrifice continued more or less apace during the period preceding the Spanish Conquest (1521). The clearest example of this is shown in the rise of the Mexica, or Aztec (see pp. 184–185), an extremely warlike people who sacrificed victims in truly astonishing numbers.

Ritual sacrifice took place throughout Mesoamerica. The standard practice was to rip out the victim's heart with a ceremonial flint knife. Other unfortunates were trussed and rolled down steep pyramids, shot with arrows, or slow roasted on a Divine Hearth. Prior to crop planting, children were sacrificed to appease Tláloc; their frantic cries were thought to please the rain god. In acts of self-sacrifice, nobles bled their arms, tongues, earlobes, and genitals for penitence and purification.

Later a spectator sport, pre-Hispanic ball games originated as one-on-one contests of life and death between rival lords. Important captives taken in war were subjected to a ritual ball game in which death to the loser assured continued success for the winning tribe. The games, played on a rectangular court, had variations, but usually involved using the hips, legs, and arms to pass a small, solid rubber ball through a stone hoop.

Statue of the lesser god Chac Mool at Chichén Itzá

Fearing the threat of sacrifice less than a tortuous death during drought, Chichimec tribes periodically migrated south. The result of one such incursion was the settlement of Tula, north of the Valley of Mexico. The Chichimeca-Tolteca (more commonly called the Toltec) soon established themselves as people of culture and learning.

For years archaeologists theorized, excavated, and debated to determine whether the Toltec had, through trade or conquest, come to influence the important Maya site of Chichén Itzá on the Yucatán Peninsula. Conclusive evidence has shown, however, that Tula was actually a trading outpost of Chichén Itzá, and that Maya influence traveled north to the central plateau as much as, if not more than, it flowed south.

The last of the important Chichimec tribes to migrate south were the Aztec, or Mexica, who wandered from a place they called Aztlán (meaning "place of herons") to found a city in the middle of Lake Texcoco, in the Valley of Mexico, in the late 13th century. In a few hundred years, the Aztec rose from illiterate nomads from the north to the dominant force in Mesoamerica. With its extensive marketplaces, fine palaces filled with richly dressed lords and ladies, and impressive temples housing a panoply of gods, the city of Tenochtitlán astounded the invading Spaniards. Well-engineered causeways linked the island city to the mainland, and "floating" gardens surrounding the city (see p. 208) provided a ready source of food.

In 1487, when Hernán Cortés, the future conqueror of New Spain, was two years

old, up to 80,000 people may have been sacrificed during the dedication of a new temple in Tenochtitlán. Beaten nonstop during the four-day bloodbath, snakeskin drums marked the rise and fall of flint knives as black-painted priests, their long hair matted with blood, sacrificed victims to the war god Huitzilopochtli.

During the reign of Moctezuma Ilhuicamina (Moctezuma I, R.1440–1469), Flower Wars were introduced with the purpose of providing rival armies with soldiers for sacrifice. Although the Flower Wars were sham conflicts (a fact the soldiers were not privy to), most of the battles unleashed by the Aztec were thoroughly real and rarely lost. The Aztec controlled some 370 cities and had a standing army of 150,000 soldiers, with more in reserve.

One kingdom the Aztec never conquered was that of the Purépecha, or Tarascan, of Michoacán in the Central Highlands. One of the few Mesoamerican peoples to use metallurgy, the Purépecha had a definite edge in battle with their bronze weapons. They also differed in religion. Ignoring the rain god Tláloc and other deities so important to their neighbors, the Purépecha worshipped a family of related gods and goddesses linked to creatures of the heavens, Earth, and the underworld.

The long and triumphant reign of Moctezuma II was ended by Hernán Cortés.

Conquest & Early Colonization

Into this world of power, conflict, and beauty burst a new (and in many ways equally violent) enemy: Spain. In the name of Emperor Charles V, Hernán Cortés (1485–1547) and his troops brought the supposed salvation of Christianity and the undeniable curse of serfdom. The Europeans also introduced the wheel, firearms, and beasts of burden, and spread the concept of metallurgy.

An inspired military leader and fervent Catholic, Cortés was driven nearly as much by a love of adventure and a sincere motivation to Christianize the Indians as by a desire for gold and other treasures. Cortés was initially commissioned to explore and chart new lands to the west by the governor of Cuba. Ignoring orders to return to Cuba and relinquish his command, he and his relatively small army were soon involved in skirmishes with native peoples who had been tested and hardened by internal wars and conflicts with the Aztec. During these early battles, the foes and vassals of the Aztec were impressed with the Spaniards' horses and firearms, and other previously unknown accoutrements of combat. All of this was reported to Emperor Moctezuma II (R. 1502–1520) in Tenochtitlán.

The emperor had cause for concern. Ancient prophecy predicted the year 1 Reed, during which Cortés appeared from the east, as the year in which the god-king Quetzalcóatl would return to reclaim his throne, abandoned several centuries before. Wielding booming cannon and commanding strange, armored beasts (horses), Cortés was initially thought to be Quetzalcóatl, and Moctezuma sent gifts of gold, fine garments, and rich food to the Spaniards bivouacked on the coast, while also begging them to return from wherever they came.

Bent on finding the source of the golden treasures and meeting the legendary Aztec leader, Cortés and his most trusted captains scuttled their ships to dispel any thoughts of retreat. They preserved sails and hardware, however, which were used to outfit boats built two years later during a four-month siege that demolished Tenochtitlán.

> **Cortés was initially thought to be [the god-king] Quetzalcóatl, and Moctezuma sent gifts of gold, fine garments, and rich food.**

Details of the Spanish battles, alliances, and eventual conquest were recorded by Bernal Díaz, a soldier, who later described them in a fascinating narrative entitled *True History of the Conquest of New Spain.* One detail not overlooked by the sagacious soldier was the importance of the two translators—Jerónimo de Aguilar and la Malinche. The former was a Spanish soldier shipwrecked on a previous expedition and enslaved by the Maya. When returned to Cortés, he spoke Mayan and Spanish. A young girl of noble descent, la Malinche had been sold into slavery in Tabasco and thus spoke Maya and classical Náhuatl, the Aztec tongue.

La Malinche, baptized and renamed doña Marina by the Spaniards, proved especially helpful to them, with her well-worded translations, grasp of politics, and ability to turn potential foes into allies. Despite horses, cannon, and other military advantages, the Spanish Conquest would not have been possible without the allied strength of Aztec foes: the Tlaxcalan, Totonac, and, as the end drew near, some of the subject kingdoms that surrounded Tenochtitlán.

Before waging outright war on the Aztec, a large contingency of Spanish soldiers was entertained for months in the fortified city of Tenochtitlán, almost as captive guests. Emperor Moctezuma wavered between friend and foe as an increasingly indignant retinue of nobles and priests urged him to sacrifice the Spaniards to Huitzilopochtli, god of war. Soon held hostage by his guests and dismissed by his detractors, Moctezuma was killed by his own people during a battle. Afterward, Cortés, la Malinche, and some of the remaining soldiers fled the capital in a daring nighttime exodus.

The last Aztec emperor, Cuauhtémoc (R. 1520–1521), was captured and, when he refused to reveal a cache of gold and treasure, subsequently tortured and hanged. La Ciudad de México, or Mexico City, was raised from the rubble of Tenochtitlán using the forced labor of the conquered people. Favored by fate, his own cunning, and the bravery of his Spanish soldiers, Cortés had crushed the mighty Aztec empire just two years after landing in the New World.

In the chaotic early years of the colony, plebeians who had suffered under the Aztec regime saw one harsh reality replaced with another. And while they would avoid the dreaded sacrificial slab, they were statistically more likely to be worked to death in a mine or dispatched by smallpox, measles, or some other imported disease. Millions of Indians died in the first hundred years of Spanish domination, possibly more than 90 percent of the indigenous population.

The New World was ruled by a viceregal system. Under the viceroy (answerable only to the king of Spain) were *audiencias* (judicial bodies) in Mexico City and Guadalajara, which controlled a hierarchy of officials, each serving at the whim of his superior. Enormous land grants (*encomiendas*) were awarded to some individuals (*encomendados*), and despite regulations their word was virtually law. Unlike the New England settlers, who drove the indigenous people from their lands (and much later herded them into reservations), Mexico's conquerors interacted with the native people, depending on Indian labor to work the mines and fields and help run their households.

The conquerors were given girls and women by the tribes they bested in battle, and by the Aztec who initially treated them as honored guests, producing a caste called *mestizos* (part European, part Indian). The settlers kept concubines, or less often, took Indian women as legitimate wives.

Unlike the Aztec nobles, who accepted the offspring of their mistresses and raised them in privilege, most Spaniards refused to recognize their bastard children. Consequently, the first generations of mestizos enjoyed no legal status whatsoever. Largely spurned by both Indians and whites, a renegade class was created, with no cultural group and no place within the emerging colony.

> In the ... early years of the colony, plebeians who had suffered under the Aztec regime saw one harsh reality replaced with another.

Although Indians and mestizos generally suffered ignoble lives, indigenous lords and other lucky individuals who swore fealty to the king were named local strongmen, or caciques, and ruled over their former dominions. Both caciques and encomendados demanded large amounts of tribute from the peasants, and, whenever possible, usurped Indian lands.

To escape virtual slavery, some Indians fled to the stark deserts or the most inhospitable mountain ranges. Many of those who remained flocked for Catholic baptism, encouraged by the appearance in 1531 of the dark-skinned Virgin of Guadalupe near a shrine to the Indian goddess Tonántzin (see p. 193).

For nearly three centuries of colonial rule, enormous mineral wealth and free or nearly free labor brought great riches to Spain. In the Sierra Madre, gold, silver, iron, zinc, and other minerals also created fabulous personal fortunes. In the wake of the miners, or sometimes leading the way, religious orders established mission churches to convert the people to Christianity. First to arrive were the Franciscans followed shortly by the Dominicans, Augustinians, and others. The Jesuits and Franciscans braved the hinterlands of the north and (with the Dominicans) the difficult terrain of Baja California. The Jesuits were expelled from New Spain in 1767 by King Charles III, who was convinced by rival orders that they were becoming too influential.

Independence

Rich in land and prosperous mines, the Catholic Church was a powerful force in colonial Mexico. Government was weak and largely controlled by the church and rich, influential families. Despite the wealth and power of some *criollos* (people of Spanish descent born in Mexico), their class did not enjoy all the privileges afforded

Enraged Aztecs attack Spaniards after the death of Moctezuma II. The Spanish lost so many men they later called this the *Noche Triste* or Night of Sorrows.

A native Zapotec speaker, Benito Juárez studied for the priesthood before switching to law.

peninsulares, Spaniards born in Spain. Inspired by the American Revolution and the ideals of the Enlightenment—the 18th-century movement rejecting traditional European agendas in favor of more pragmatic approaches to society's problems—dissatisfied criollos and priests bent on social reform began to plot independence in the early 19th century.

Royalist forces learned of a conspiracy in 1810, and the Independence Movement was launched a bit sooner than planned under priest Miguel Hidalgo y Costilla (1753–1811) and intellectuals from Morelia and Querétaro. Not all of Mexico was united in the cause. Isolated Yucatán, for example, had more ties to Europe than to Mexico City. And most peninsulares, having little if anything to gain from independence, remained loyal to Spain.

After initial rebel victories, the Royalists regrouped. The war dragged on with isolated insurgent attacks and little chance of full-scale success on either side. Also called the Plan of Three Guarantees (which were for Mexico to remain Catholic, to be headed by a constitutional monarch, and to guarantee the same rights to those born in the New World as those born in Spain), the Plan de Iguala was signed by Agustín de Iturbide (1783–1824) and rebel leader Vicente Guerrero in 1821. Spain barely opposed losing the colony, and signed the Treaty of Córdoba the same year, through which the conditions set forth in the Plan de Iguala were implemented. According to the agreed-upon covenant, the rich resumed their lives of privilege while the poor remained chattel. Catholicism continued as the official religion of Mexico.

What followed was a half century of reconstruction and political and economic chaos. Agustín de Iturbide reigned for less than a year as head of the new constitutional monarchy before being forced into exile. After his ousting, a succession of feeble and impoverished governments took turns overthrowing one another. Antonio López de Santa Anna (1794–1876), an energetic general from Veracruz, acted as president on multiple occasions, in between starting and stopping various rebellions throughout the nation. In the countryside, the campesinos were ruthlessly exploited as large landholders stole communal lands and the caciques terrorized anyone who was bold enough to complain.

The weak central government invited foreign intervention. In 1838 the French blockaded the port of Veracruz during the Pastry War, a dispute over damages suffered by a baker and other French nationals during earlier riots in Mexico City. In 1846 the United States declared war on Mexico on trumped-up complaints in order to annex Texas and coveted lands to the west. Landing at Veracruz, U.S. troops soon captured the Mexican garrison at Chapultepec Castle, Mexico City. As a result of the Mexican-American War (1846–1848), the United States gained Texas, New Mexico, Arizona, and Alta California; Mexico lost half of its territory, retaining the Baja California peninsula and lands south of the Río Bravo (called the Rio Grande in the United States).

In the ensuing political chaos, Zapotec lawyer Benito Juárez (1806–1872) helped promulgate the Reform Laws, intended primarily to separate Church and state and reduce the influence of the church. The ensuing Reform Wars (1858–1861) were eventually won by the liberals under Juárez. But empty national coffers forced him to default on international debts, giving France an excuse to invade Mexico and install (with the approbation of the conservatives) the Austrian Maximilian of Habsburg (1832–1867) as emperor. A short-lived but symbolically important victory against the French invaders was won on May 5, 1862. Young and poorly armed, the defenders routed the French military in a battle that is reenacted each year in Puebla and celebrated throughout the country.

The Second Empire, as it was called, lasted only three years (1864–1867). A just man, Maximilian angered conservatives by refusing to retract liberal reforms. Still, a foreign king ruling Mexico suited nearly no one. After French troops were recalled to fight Prussia, the emperor was captured and executed in Querétaro in 1867. President-in-exile Benito Juárez returned to rule the nation for nearly five years before dying of a heart attack in 1872.

Despite his intentions, Juárez's policy of confiscating church property had a disastrous effect on indigenous people. Church lands communally worked by campesino farmers were auctioned and snatched up by wealthy hacienda owners. Many indigenous and mestizo campesinos were then forced to work for slave wages on fields they had formerly tilled for their own families.

The Porfiriato

While Juárez is nonetheless lauded as a hero, Porfirio Díaz, who came to power in 1876, is a more controversial figure. Under Díaz, Mexico finally achieved economic and political stability. Construction of an extensive railway system moved goods for national and international consumption, mining and other industries prospered, and foreign investment boomed. A great admirer of European art and architecture, the Oaxaca-born mestizo commissioned luxurious public buildings during his 33-year presidency, which was in reality a thinly veiled dictatorship.

The Porfiriato (era of Porfirio Díaz) revived the economy, restored order out of chaos, and created public works. However, journalistic freedom and political dialogue were strongly repressed, and a national police force, *los rurales,* snuffed out any protest in the countryside. Although an emerging middle class did benefit from a form of trickle-down economics, the peasantry suffered the usual indignities: their lands were illegally confiscated and their people tied to large haciendas by debt-peonage. In a situation that was tantamount to slavery, poor peasants were paid a pittance and bound to the estate on which they worked by debts incurred from purchases such as soap, corn, and coffee from

Maya Uprising

During the Mexican-American War, fearful whites in the isolated Yucatán Peninsula formed a Maya army, which immediately turned its weapons on the wealthy elite who had so incautiously armed it. Unsophisticated in waging war, the Maya, after launching bloody raids that struck fear into the rich Spanish landholders, succeeded in taking the most important cities and towns of the peninsula.

The Maya merely wanted revenge and the return of their ancestral lands. They had no desire to rule and after their few successes simply laid down their weapons to return to the seasonal planting. But they had not calculated the consequences of their actions. The whites and mestizos reorganized and counterattacked. About half of the Yucatán Maya population was murdered in the ensuing reprisals.

the plantation store. Subsequent generations were held responsible for their forefathers' debts and so remained trapped by the hacienda system.

Revolution & Reconstruction

Under the banner of "Effective suffrage, no reelection!" the wealthy, reserved Francisco I. Madero (1873–1913) mobilized the Mexican public against the patriarch Díaz, who was exiled to Europe in 1911. Despite early hopes for a peaceful transition to a more egalitarian system, a lack of consensus on reform agendas soon divided military leaders with wildly disparate goals. Madero's agenda was political reform. In Morelos, south of Mexico City, Emiliano Zapata (1879–1919) fervently demanded the return of stolen communal lands and other agrarian reforms to benefit dispossessed peasants.

Treachery characterized the long and bloody Revolutionary War (1911–1917). As president of the republic, Madero was jailed and then assassinated by dissatisfied generals. Zapata was killed in a perfidious ambush arranged by the rival revolutionary (and landowner) Venustiano Carranza (1859–1920). Charismatic (but often unduly violent) military tactician Pancho Villa (1878–1923) was murdered in an ambush several years after the end of fighting.

> **Emiliano Zapata fervently demanded the return of stolen communal lands and other agrarian reforms to benefit ... peasants.**

The revolution cost approximately two million lives, and many of the victims were unarmed civilians. The conflict dragged on until 1920, when the ideals of the Constitution of 1917 were adopted. The country was economically devastated by years of war. Political unrest reigned, and subsequent transfers of presidential power through nominal elections were accompanied by revolts and instability.

The constitution promised agrarian reform, but redistribution of land was ignored until General Lázaro Cárdenas del Río (1895–1970) was elected president in 1934. Truly committed to the poor, the mestizo from Michoacán expropriated and redistributed nearly 50 million acres (20 million ha), creating 180,000 *ejidos,* or communal farms. Alarming foreign investors and governments and conservative nationals, Cárdenas's most sweeping reforms were to nationalize the railroads and the oil companies. While encouraging unions and labor organizations, he eliminated the cronies of his predecessor, Plutarco Elías Calles, who had—as tradition dictated—chosen him as successor to the presidency.

It was Calles who enforced previously ignored articles of the new constitution limiting the power of the church. When the clergy urged boycotts of church services, enraged Catholics began fighting detractors in grisly street battles. Even after the insurgency, later dubbed the Cristero Revolt, was put down, temples were ransacked and colonial art stolen. The church's long-standing influence in affairs of state had ended, although most of Mexico's population remained staunchly Catholic.

20th-century Mexico

Before 1910, Mexico City was a quiet capital with colonial churches, surrounded by traditional indigenous villages. The revolution's unrest brought country people to the safety of the capital, where many remained. During World War II, Mexico was launched into the industrial era, and waves of workers relocated to the capital to fill factory jobs. President Miguel Alemán (1946–1952) encouraged development of infrastructure and attracted foreign and national investment in industry.

Created in 1929 as the National Revolutionary Party, or PNR, the Institutional Revolutionary Party (PRI) became the official government party, adopting the tricolor of the Mexican flag and ruling with virtual impunity. Internal squabbles and an inability to capitalize on the discontent of campesinos and the middle classes rendered the opposition parties totally ineffective and enabled the PRI to maintain the status quo. From 1929 until 2000, the PRI never lost a presidential election.

World War II brought industrialization to Mexico, after which the country's economy continued to grow. But a population explosion resulted in an ever increasing number of poor, and reforms by Adolfo Ruiz Cortines (1952–1958) and others never truly eased their burden. Heavy investment in petroleum production left the economy vulnerable to fluctuations in the world market for this commodity, and the drop in oil prices in the early 1980s led to recession and huge foreign debt. But although discontent was manifested to one degree or another under various PRI presidencies, the country's system of one-party politics was never seriously challenged.

So Mexicans were stunned, and many jubilant, when in 2000 former Coca-Cola executive and Guanajuato state governor Vicente Fox Quesada was elected president for slightly-right-of-center PAN, the National Action Party.

Political reform has come about slowly but, considering the depth of cronyism and corruption, remarkably peacefully. Despite Fox's lack of accomplishment, it was a historic administration. Fox was succeeded in 2006 by PAN candidate Felipe Calderón, who narrowly won against firebrand Andrés Manuel López Obrador, a left-leaning coalition candidate of the Convergence and Labor parties. The next presidential election is in 2012. ■

Independence Day parade, San Cristóbal de las Casas

Food & Drink

For 5,000 years, corn has reigned as Mexico's most important food, and the plant has religious significance for the Maya, Huichol, and other indigenous groups. Mesoamericans introduced the world to squash, beans, chilies, turkey, avocados, tomatoes, sweet potatoes, and chocolate. To this the Spanish added wheat (and bread), sugar, rice, and domestic animals: beef and dairy cattle and goats.

A woman prepares fresh produce for market day in Tlacolula, outside Oaxaca city.

With goats and dairy cows came cheese. Many varieties are made today, from tangy, crumbly *cotija* to soft, creamy *panela*. Somewhat salty *queso fresco* is crumbled over savory dishes and served with high-sugar desserts to cut the sweet. From Oaxaca comes *quesillo*, a ball of mild but tangy string cheese. It's used to make *queso fundido,* a delicious cheese fondue served with a stack of flour tortillas and often loaded with

mushrooms, chorizo sausage, or strips of mild or hot chilies.

Although tasty flour tortillas typically accompany some dishes, corn tortillas are the traditional staple. Conquistador Hernán Cortés called them "maize cakes": flat disks of corn milled with lime and cooked on a hot griddle. Today, neighborhood "factories" produce fresh tortillas throughout the day, although many restaurants and rural women make their own. Bread rolls are served in both homes and restaurants, yet to many Mexicans, a traditional meal without tortillas is unthinkable. This said, it's true that the less affluent the family, the more tortillas it probably consumes. For a very poor family, a meal might consist of nothing more than tortillas and salt.

Masa (finely ground cornmeal) is used to make tamales: dense, rectangular cakes wrapped in corn husks or banana leaves and then steamed. Subtly sweet, plain tamales are served as a light evening meal with coffee or hot chocolate; dessert tamales might surround sweet pineapple chunks; and savory tamales enclose pieces of meat cooked in a chili sauce.

A wide selection of savory snacks is made with tortillas or masa. Loosely translated as "appetizers," these *antojitos* are the dishes familiar to most foreigners. They include enchiladas (tortillas smothered in chili sauce) and stuffed tacos and *taquitos,* as well as chalupas, gorditas, and *memelas* (griddle-cooked or fried disks of masa topped with crumbled cheese, salsa, onions, and often cilantro).

If each region has its favorite antojitos, each neighborhood has its favorite *taquería.* Specializing in tacos, taquerías range from comfortable restaurants to takeout-only storefronts and bicycle-powered carts. Soft tacos consist of warm tortillas filled with grilled meats and served with a variety of condiments. In a variation, tacos (in this case often called *taquitos)* are rolled around meat or chicken, deep fried, and served with guacamole (avocado sauce) or spicy fresh salsa.

The chili pepper is the tortilla's great companion. From Yucatán's fiery habanero to the relatively mild chile poblano, dozens of varieties are used fresh, roasted, or dried. Drying chilies changes their flavors. For example, when dried, the blistering jalapeño produces the distinctive, smoky-tasting chile chipotle; the light orange *chile manzano* becomes *chile cascabel.*

Used blended or chopped, raw or cooked, chilies are combined with onion, garlic, cilantro, and tomatoes (both green and red) to make salsas that accompany almost every meal. Jalapeño and serrano chilies are also served pickled *(en escabeche)* with carrots and onions.

Ground chilies were a key ingredient in *chocolate,* one of the favorite drinks of Aztec royalty. Today, steaming pots of this delicious hot drink are made from bars of bitter chocolate mixed with ground almonds, cinnamon, and sugar. Beaten until frothy, with water or milk, chocolate is a popular accompaniment to a plateful of *pan dulce,* or sweet bread. Coffee lovers should try wonderfully aromatic *café de olla,* boiled with cinnamon and *piloncillo* (crude brown sugar). It is definitely more satisfying than the weak *café americano* sold in U.S.-style coffee shops and diners.

If you strictly avoid buying food from market restaurants, street stands, and itinerant vendors, your experience of Mexico will be less than authentic, yet no one wants to risk digestive upset or more serious ailments. There's no guarantee, however, that a prosperous-looking restaurant will be more hygienic than a humble taco stand or a faded yet well-scrubbed market

Keeping Healthy with Food & Drink

Avoid tap water even for brushing teeth. In tourist-oriented restaurants, however, avoiding salads, ice, and fruits that cannot be peeled is not normally necessary. Ice cubes with holes in the middle are factory made with bottled water.

Seafood is the most common culprit for food poisoning, even in expensive restaurants. If you order something that tastes or smells funky, don't swallow any of it, since it doesn't take much to make a person seriously ill.

If you choose to eat from taco carts or other vendors, choose one popular with locals where food is prepared to order rather than left sitting out or reheated.

kitchen. If you decide to go native, head for the most popular stands and check out the vendor and his wares for cleanliness. It's also wise to eat during peak hours, when food is still being freshly prepared. Tap water should be strictly avoided. While most vendors use bottled water in their coffee and other water-based drinks, it's worth investigating if you are in any doubt.

Markets are a great place to shop for Mexico's huge variety of tropical and semitropical fruits, from which juices and their watered-down counterparts, delicious and refreshing *aguas frescas,* are made. Tourist-oriented restaurants often inexplicably offer only canned or boxed orange, grapefruit, and tomato juices instead of regional favorites such as delightful mango, papaya, guava, and watermelon.

Other popular beverages include *atole* and *horchata.* The former is a thick, filling, slightly sweet drink made of ground rice or cornmeal sweetened with sugar and served warm or at room temperature. The latter is a refreshing cool drink commonly made of filtered rice

water, sugar, and cinnamon, sometimes spiked with fresh fruit and almond slivers. Unless the quality of the water is questionable, it's a shame to drink anything out of a can or bottle—with the exception of beer!

Many fine beers are brewed in Mexico. Some are regional, such as Pacífico from Mazatlán, and Montejo and León Negro from the Yucatán, while others are seasonal (Noche Buena is sold only around Christmas). Fortunately most are ubiquitous. Baja California's wineries produce wine and brandies of fair to good quality. Cultivated since before the Spanish Conquest, the agave plant produces pulque, a rather gooey, fermented alcoholic beverage. More palatable are the distilled agave products mescal and tequila (see p. 154).

With thousands of miles of coastline, Mexico is known for fresh seafood, and in places such as Cabo San Lucas, at the tip of Baja, chefs have finally gone beyond simple grilling or pan-frying with garlic (*al mojo de ajo*) to add sashimi, sushi, and inspired sauces to their menus. Still, dishes such as *huauchinango a la veracruzana* remain universally popular. Grilled whole with tomato, chili, onion, garlic, parsley, capers, and green olives, Veracruz's version of red snapper is a Mexican standard. Also popular is *ceviche,* any firm, white fish marinated in lime juice and served with fresh chopped onion, chili, tomato, and cilantro. (To make it more hygienic, many cooks briefly boil the fish before "cooking" it in lime.) Depending on the local catch, conch, octopus, or shrimp may be used as well.

Meat is the mainstay of the northern diet, often accompanied by *frijoles charros* (beans cooked with pork rind) and flour tortillas. As well as various types of dried, grilled, and shredded beef, northerners are fond of *cabrito,* or barbecued goat. From the north also come *huevos rancheros:* sunny-side-up eggs served on a lightly fried corn tortilla and smothered in a mild cooked salsa. This breakfast favorite is often accompanied by beans and a basket of fresh tortillas.

Some of the most unusual dishes come from central and southern Mexico. Seven vastly different mole sauces are made in the state of Oaxaca

What Hernán Cortés called "maize cakes" are still eaten in many forms.

EXPERIENCE: Wine-tasting in Mexico

Mexico's wine-making tradition was established by the friars who accompanied the conquistadores. The monks planted vineyards in the dry northern climes of mainland Mexico and Baja California. The first vintages (originally from native grapes, soon imported vines) were bottled in Coahuila's Parras Valley in the 16th century.

In the Parras Valley, in fact, you can visit the oldest vineyard in the Americas, **Casa Madero** (tel 842/422-0111, www.casamadero.com.mx), where winemaking from native grapes began in 1597. Today, vintners produce Cabernet Sauvignon, Merlot, and Shiraz, as well as Chardonnay, Chenin Blanc, and Semillón. The winery offers free tours and tastings daily between 9 a.m. and 5 p.m.

Most of Mexico's wineries, however, are found in Baja California just a few hours south of the U.S. border. **Bodegas de Santo Tomás** (see p. 57) is the oldest vineyard on the peninsula. The largest winery, **L.A. Cetto** (tel 646/155-2179, www.lacetto.net), offers tours and tastings at its vineyards on Highway 3 in the Guadalupe Valley (daily 10:30–3:30). L.A. Cetto also offers tastings at its Tijuana and Ensenada wine cellars (closed Sun.).

More than a dozen wineries operate in the Guadalupe Valley stretching between Tecate and Ensenada. The second largest producer, **Pedro Domecq** (tel 646/155-2249) is just across from L.A. Cetto and offers free tastings daily except Sunday.

Smaller, family-run businesses like **Vinos Liceaga** (tel 646/155-3091, www.vinosliceaga.com) sell table wine as well as grappa; they welcome tastings by appointment.

Harvest festivals (Fiestas de la Vendimia) provide an excuse for exuberant celebrations. That of the Ensenada wine country (see p. 57) lasts for three weeks in August and includes concerts, dinners, and cultural events along with wine tastings and gastronomical events held at venues both in Ensenada and the surrounding countryside.

alone. Among the principle ingredients of mole verde are pumpkin seeds (pipián) and chilies, which give it a green color. Fruits and raisins make mole mancha manteles bright red. Thought to have been invented by a Puebla nun, mole negro (black mole, or in Puebla, mole poblano) represents Mexican cuisine at its most complex. This classic dish combines stale tortillas, sesame seeds, chilies, chocolate, nuts, peppercorns, and cloves, among about a dozen others. Cooks from Tlaxcala, Puebla, and Oaxaca compete to create the most savory adaptation.

The Yucatán Peninsula has its share of unusual and flavorful recipes, especially those from Mérida, where French, Spanish, and Lebanese cultures come together. Locally grown sour oranges are the key to marinated poc chuc, savory pork grilled with onions, tomatoes, and garlic. Pollo (chicken) and cochinita (pork) pibil are seasoned with pungent achiote paste and cooked in a traditional pit.

Worms from the agave fields (gusanos de maguey), and highly salted and seasoned grasshoppers (chapulines) from Oaxaca, are fried and sold by the scoop in markets, but also appear in expensive restaurants serving nouvelle Mexican cuisine. Other delicacies include escamoles (ant eggs) and huitlacoche (black corn fungus), the latter found in crêpes and quesadillas (flour tortillas with melted cheese).

With so many unusual foods to try, why settle for a hamburger and soft drink from the inevitable chain restaurant? Right down the road you might find freshly grilled prickly-pear cactus pads (spines removed) served with a cool glass of cantaloupe juice.

The Arts

Mexican culture is as expressive and varied as the landscape. Inspired by Spanish and indigenous themes alike, Mexican baroque architecture displays a passion for abundance and flamboyance. Modern folk-dance troupes re-create pre-Hispanic dances, while *mestizo* culture is evident in the nation's regional dances, many of which attuned immigrants' instruments and dance steps to an entirely Mexican sensibility.

Architecture

Before the Spanish Conquest, Mesoamerica's oldest cities and ceremonial centers were laid out much like modern towns. Temples and palaces framed a central plaza, or *zócalo,* in the heart of town. Along one side was a church; along another the most important public buildings, including the seat of local government. Nearby plazas held open-air markets, and side roads led to businesses and residential neighborhoods. Stone, adobe, and mortar were the main building materials, supplemented by wood and natural fibers such as straw. Important buildings boasted elaborate painted murals and stone carvings; ornamentation and color were key themes.

European tastes and techniques have influenced Mexico's architecture since the 16th century, when the Spanish conquistadores employed indigenous slaves to build palaces and churches from the stones of ruined temples. European images quickly replaced indigenous ones; paintings of warriors in feathered headdresses disappeared and instead conquerors in helmets stood out on walls and in bold relief on carved stone pillars. Fragments of ancient carvings, however, can still be seen in churches and city halls from Mexico City to Mérida.

> **European images quickly replaced indigenous ones. ... Fragments of ancient carvings, however, can still be seen in churches and city halls from Mexico City to Mérida.**

The Spaniards concentrated their construction efforts in populated areas where labor was easy to exploit. Churches and monasteries were among the earliest colonial-era structures, designed in the prevailing European styles. Many of the finest cathedrals were built over several centuries and consist of baroque, Gothic, and plateresque (richly ornamented, suggesting silverware) elements with Mexican influences. Flying buttresses, gargoyles, stained glass, and wooden ceilings carved in the Mudejar style (a blending of Spanish and Arabic artistic elements) were all used in the more ornate cathedrals. In the 17th century, facades were covered with decorative high-relief carvings and multiple religious statues characteristic of the Churrigueresque style (Spanish baroque, named after Spanish architect Benito Churriguera). Moorish-style domes were covered with tiles from Puebla in the 18th century. A flurry of construction in the neoclassical style took place in the late 18th and early 19th centuries, until the War for Independence brought a halt to building.

Some of the first colonial-era residences were monasteries and convents, with

A dancer at a Virgin of Guadalupe feast day celebration sports an ornate headdress.

cavernous domed-ceiling rooms and elaborately tiled kitchens. European architects and engineers designed palaces for the elite, with multiple patios framed by one- or two-story wings. A similar pattern emerged at haciendas from the Yucatán to Chihuahua. Mexico's colonial-era buildings have survived earthquakes, floods, and gun battles, and UNESCO now considers entire colonial cities, such as San Miguel de Allende in Guanajuato, national historic treasures. Massive monasteries have been restored in Querétaro and Oaxaca, and some of the Yucatán's finest haciendas now house first-class hotels.

Modern Mexican architecture incorporates design elements introduced by pre-Hispanic, colonial, and Mexican builders. Office towers, government buildings, and resort hotels mimic the pyramids of Teotihuacán and Chichén Itzá; tiles such as those seen covering 17th- and 18th-century buildings in Puebla appear in modern stairways, bathrooms, and kitchens. Craftsmen in Guanajuato have become famous for their *bóvedas,* domed ceilings made entirely of brick.

The first significant skyscraper in Mexico City was designed by Leonardo Zeevaert and erected in 1956 near the frothy art nouveau Palacio de Bellas Artes. The sleek glass Torre Latinoamerica is surrounded by traditional colonial structures, including the exuberantly Churrigueresque Iglesia de San Francisco (1524) and the Casa de los Azulejos, which was built in 1596 and completely covered in hand-painted tiles in 1737.

Juxtapositions of old and new styles can be seen in the work of architect Pedro Ramírez Vázquez, who designed the Museo Nacional de Antropología, in Chapultepec

Bright colors mark Ricardo Legorreta's Camino Real hotel, Mexico City.

Park. With a layout similar to that of an ancient Aztec city, stately buildings face a central patio dominated by an enormous open shelter of carved stone and aluminum. Similar use of natural and fabricated elements are characteristic of the sleek structures of German-born Mathias Goeritz, who immigrated during the rise of Nazism and taught at both the University of Guadalajara and UNAM, the National Autonomous University, in Mexico City. But far and away the most influential architect of the 20th century was Luis Barragán (1902–1988). His use of clean lines and vivid colors in monumental structures emphasized the importance of the natural elements, including sunlight, in the overall architectural design.

Of the many architects to follow in Barragán's footsteps, one of the most prolific and highly successful is Ricardo Legorreta (1931–). Like that of his friend and predecessor Barragán, Legorreta's innovative style combines massive walls painted in vivid colors to reflect the movement of light. Collaboration between these two greats produced the Camino Real hotel in Mexico City, with walls and niches painted hot pink, marigold yellow, and deep lavender. This achievement led to many commissions for Legorreta, who is considered one of today's top architects, and who has designed more than a hundred buildings in Mexico and abroad.

The use of brilliant color is, in fact, one of the defining elements of the Mexican aesthetic sense. Plain adobe or stucco structures are painted cobalt blue with marigold trim, lime green, canary yellow, or *rosa mexicano*–a deep pink. Advertisements, public service messages, and campaign slogans in bright colors compete for attention on the facades of homes and businesses, retaining walls, and any other available surface.

EXPERIENCE: Play Ball!

Although *béisbol mexicano* began in Mexico City in the 1920s, today it is most popular outside central Mexico. Mazatlán loves its Venados (Deer). Part of the Liga Mexicano del Pacífico, or LMP *(www.ligadelpacifico.com.mx)*, they play October through December. The larger Liga Mexicana de Béisbol *(www. MiLB.com)* is affiliated with American Minor League baseball and plays March through July. Tickets *($–$$$$$)* are available at the stadiums or at *www.ticket master.com.mx*. Over the years, Mexico has had some 90 minor league teams. See *www.mexonline.com/sports.htm* for stats and information.

Art

Mexico's artistic heritage far predates the European invasion. In 790, Maya artists covered the walls of the Temple of the Paintings at Bonampak, in southeast Chiapas, with murals depicting fierce battles and harmonious tableaux of the royal family. Olmec sculptors carved gigantic round heads in basalt around 1150 B.C., and some of the cave paintings found in Baja California are believed to be 5,000 years old.

The arrival of Spanish conquistadores drastically changed Mesoamerican art. The Catholic Church became the dominant force in everyday life. Saints and Virgins replaced pantheistic gods and goddesses, and Indian artists were made to paint and sculpt foreign images. European artisans in New Spain took on indigenous apprentices, who learned to paint biblical scenes on magnificent *retablos,* the ornate altarpieces that adorned colonial churches. Sixteenth-century religious art replaced the murals and serpentine sculptures, though Indian artists never completely ignored their origins. Angels drifting through murals sometimes show Maya, Mixtec, and Zapotec features; scrollwork incorporates ancient symbols for wind and fire. The finest Mexican painters studied in Seville and

Florence, and Mexican viceregal art retained a primarily Eurocentric tone.

As *criollo* and mestizo artists emerged in the 17th century, Mexican art began to take on a distinct flavor. The dark-skinned Virgin of Guadalupe, who purportedly appeared in 1531 to the Indian convert Juan Diego, was a purely Mexican creation whose image spread throughout the country. Mexicans looked back to indigenous history for inspiration, and painters began portraying scenes depicting Spanish and Aztec warriors in battle.

Mexico's first formal art school, the Real Academia de las Bellas Artes de México, was established in Mexico City in 1731, and European sculptors and painters were commissioned to instruct Mexican artists. Art was superseded by war during the early 19th century as Mexicans battled for independence, though a few of the country's most famous artists and sculptors emerged in the midst of conflict. The portraits of José María Estrada (1830–1862) and landscape paintings of José María Velasco (1840–1912) are cited in particular as evidence of an established Mexican art scene in the 1800s. Velasco is considered the master of 19th-century academic painting; he specialized in landscapes, skillfully depicting the lakes and volcanoes in the Valley of Mexico and the candelabra cactus of Oaxaca. Several of his finest works can be seen at the Museo Nacional de Arte in Mexico City.

> As *criollo* and mestizo artists emerged in the 17th century, Mexican art began to take on a distinct flavor.

The early 20th century was Mexico's belle époque—at least for the wealthy. Under the dictatorship of Porfirio Díaz, who idolized all things European, Mexicans schooled in European styles and fashions began to celebrate an emerging sense of identity. While still heavily influenced by European training, Mexican artists used their exposure to impressionism, symbolism, and art nouveau styles to embrace Mexican themes. Young artists focused on the iniquities of the dictatorship and demanded a revitalization of Mexican culture. Gerardo Murillo (1875–1964), one of the most influential painters and intellectuals of the era, protested the European influences in Mexico by changing his surname to Atl, which in the Náhuatl language of the Aztec means "water." Atl's work consists mainly of landscape paintings; his view of volcanoes serves as the design for the glass-and-metal curtain at the Palacio de Bellas Artes. Many of Mexico's most famous 20th-century artists studied under Atl, who was as much a spiritual leader as a teacher of art. He first proposed the idea of covering public buildings with murals by Mexican artists in the early 1900s; the revolution of 1910 put his plans on hold.

This episode in history solidified the young artists' passion for their country and their desire to create truly Mexican works of art. In 1921, Education Minister José Vasconcelos

Diego Rivera's "A Dream of a Sunday Afternoon in Alamada Park," at Mexico City's Museo Mural Diego Rivera

asked Atl to paint murals (now destroyed) at the Escuela Nacional Preparatoria (National Preparatory School). In 1922, Vasconcelos initiated the muralist movement, which dominated the art scene for nearly 50 years. Atl's students, including Diego Rivera (1886–1957) and José Clemente Orozco (1883–1949), began tracing the entire history of Mexico on the walls of the country's most significant buildings, incorporating pre-Hispanic themes, the Spanish Conquest, and the revolution into massive storyboards.

The muralists quickly became Mexico's most famous artists and politics their favorite theme. "We repudiate so-called easel-painting," David Alfaro Siquieros (1896–1974) declared in 1922. "Art should no longer be the expression of individual satisfaction, which it is today, but should aim to become a fighting, educative art for all." The most famous muralists also painted on canvas, but even then they seemed captivated by the tragedies of the revolution. After training in Europe, painter Francisco Goita (1882–1980) joined Pancho Villa's army as an artistic chronicler of the struggle for freedom and equality. His paintings are gruesome reminders of war.

Mexico's 20th-century artists were devoted to the concept of *mexicanidad*, the celebration of their native origins, natural surroundings, and cultural quirks. Much of their work was violent, inflammatory, and highly emotional, but even the most political artists paused from time to time to depict the beauty in their surroundings. Diego Rivera's paintings of tortilla makers and flower sellers portray Mexico's indigenous peoples with beauty and dignity. Rivera's wife, artist Frida Kahlo (1907–1954), known for her anguished self-portraits, often dressed in gorgeous indigenous costumes. The lesser known painter Antonio M. Ruíz (1895–1964) focused on scenes of daily life, often filled with humor.

The outside world began to appreciate Mexican art with the work of the muralists, who became virtual folk heroes and spokespersons for their country. Orozco, Siquieros, and Rivera all created murals in the United States. Miguel Covarrubias (1904–1957), who contributed to some of Mexico City's most famous murals, worked as an illustrator and cartoonist for *The New Yorker* and *Vanity Fair* in the 1920s and '30s. Rufino Tamayo (1899–1991), one of a small group of painters who preferred to create modern art rather than focus on politics, spent much of his life in New York City.

Today, Mexico has a thriving art scene, as shown by the multitude of galleries and art schools in Mexico City, Oaxaca, San Miguel de Allende, and other centers. Cutting-edge art is displayed at Mexico City's Museo José Luis Cuevas, where a few Picassos and the works of other contemporary artists are displayed with Cuevas's erotic sculptures.

Oaxaca state is rich in crafts, including embroidery, jewelry, and many styles of pottery.

Folk Art

Weavers, potters, wood-carvers, and glass-blowers all feel at home in Mexico, where everyday items are often works of art. Early Mesoamerican civilizations created decorated clay water vessels; the Mixtec crafted fabulous jade and gold pendants and other jewelry—some of the finest in the world. Indigenous artisans quickly learned European techniques after the Spanish Conquest, and a new form of folk art emerged from the blend of natural materials, native talents, and foreign influences. Today, popular art is one of Mexico's richest treasures, and craftsmen and women are among its most famous artists.

Mexican folk art is both functional and fanciful, and often reflects patterns and themes handed down for centuries. Weavers in Oaxaca incorporate the highly stylized fret designs from the ruins of Mitla in their woolen rugs. Huichol Indians in Nayarit painstakingly reproduce ancient symbols of lizards, suns, peyote, and stars in shoulder bags and beaded ceremonial bowls. Enterprising craftsmen and women throughout the country create inexpensive paintings in Day-Glo colors on paper made from the amate tree, used since pre-Hispanic times to make ledgers and important books.

Religious themes appear in all forms, from painted tin portraits of the Virgin of Guadalupe to handpainted tile groupings of the Stations of the Cross. Nativity scenes, called *nacimientos,* are created from almost any material, from fragile blown glass to woven straw. The Mexican fascination with all things macabre emerges in multiple forms, from miniature dioramas of skeletons at play to papier-mâché *judases*—garish, larger-than-life-size devils and other characters used in Semana Santa (Holy Week) processions.

Every imaginable material may become art in the hands of a Mexican artisan. In Oaxaca, a whole celebration is devoted to carved radishes. The earth itself has always been a source of inspiration; museums throughout the country are filled with clay vessels and figurines created by the Olmec, Maya, Mixtec, and Aztec cultures. Pottery is one of Mexico's oldest art forms, and one of its most popular.

Clay is molded and fired into imaginative shapes. The Lancandón Indians in remote Chiapas model red clay into crocodiles and birds; Nahua Indians in Guerrero create water vessels with human shapes. Certain regions are known for their exquisite, fragile pieces. Mata Ortíz pottery, from the Casas Grandes region in Chihuahua, is treasured by knowledgeable collectors, as is the glossy black pottery from San Bartolo Coyotepec, Oaxaca.

The Spanish conquistadores were responsible for some of Mexico's finest ceramics. With very few exceptions, pre-Hispanic potters were unfamiliar with glazing, and the Spaniards imported artisans from their homeland to create fine majolica tiles and tableware. These artists set to work in Puebla, where they created delicate blue-and-white talavera pieces (so named because they resembled pottery from the town of Talavera de la Reina in Spain). While native artisans added more color, classic talavera designs remained popular, and the majolica technique is still used today to create vases, dishes, jars, and tiles in the states of Puebla, Tlaxcala, Guanajuato, and Jalisco.

Clay is often the favored medium for musical instruments, toys, dolls, and fantastical figurines. Nearly every early civilization played clay flutes and whistles. Modern artisans let their imaginations soar, creating elaborate scenes of miniature figures in vividly colored tableaux. Adam and Eve, the Virgin of Guadalupe, angels, devils, and regular human beings are portrayed in realistic and absurd situations. Some dioramas are as tiny as matchboxes; others as large as a young child. Some of the best painted-clay artists work in Michoacán and Puebla. Potters in Oaxaca make life-size terra-cotta dolls called *muñecas bordadas;* some in Toluca and Puebla specialize in enormous polychrome tree of life figurines stacked with tiny figures and symbols.

Playfulness exerts itself in wood carving as well. Dragon-like *alejibres* carved from soft wood and painted in almost garish colors started appearing in Oaxaca in the 1980s,

Books About Mexican Art

In Mexico, museums and public venues associated with the arts often have wonderful government-sponsored bookstores called Librerías Educal. Many of the books are in Spanish, but Artes de Mexico—which celebrated its 20th year in 2008—publishes slender bilingual volumes dedicated to individual topics of interest. You can learn all there is to know about Mexican Talavera, Huichol art, mask making, or ancient cultures. Buy the softcover books individually, or purchase a subscription for 6, 8, 10, or 12 issues at *www.artesdemexico.com.*

along with more lifelike animal characters called *animalitos*. The most elaborate creations now command hundreds of dollars in upscale galleries. Primitive dolls are common among most indigenous groups. The native people of the Sierra Tarahumara fashion small wooden figures wearing traditional white shirts and trousers, while Otomí artisans in Puebla and Hidalgo create sweet-faced cloth dolls wearing the full, lace-edged skirts of their makers.

Wood is frequently employed to create masks, which have been used in religious ceremonies since pre-Hispanic times. The mask makers of Guerrero, Tlaxcala, Morelia, Chiapas, and Oaxaca are especially talented and prolific. Used in folk dances and religious processions, their masks represent saints and demons, poets and politicians, animals and pink-cheeked conquistadores. Some even have realistic glass eyes that open and shut at the tug of a string.

Glass beads were the first gifts and objects of barter of the Spaniards, who later introduced glass blowing to native artisans. Exceptional hand-blown glassware and miniatures are today produced in small family workshops as well as large factories, especially in the states of Puebla and Mexico, and around Guadalajara, Jalisco.

Chiapas is home to brilliantly woven and embroidered *huipiles* (blouses) covered with Maya designs. The residents of indigenous villages throughout the state shun modern fashion in favor of woolen ponchos and cotton huipiles covered with vivid embroidered

EXPERIENCE: Speak Spanish

Opportunities abound to study Spanish in Mexico. Things to consider include class size (ratio of students to teacher) and the ratio of grammar lessons to conversation. Many schools offer opportunities for one-on-one face time with Mexicans, who will trade time speaking Spanish with you for the same opportunity to practice their conversational English on topics of mutual interest.

Research whether the school you're considering offers classes in subjects that interest you, because you'll learn with less effort if you study something meaningful to you—for example, cooking or archaeology. Some schools offer university credit or continuing education credits (CEUs).

Select a part of the country you'd like to visit because many schools offer field trips as part of the immersion experience. It's best to choose a city or town where English is not widely spoken. Thus you'll get more opportunities to develop your Spanish in Veracruz or Chiapas than you will in Cancún.

A homestay can immerse you in Spanish, but make sure your host family isn't boarding other English-speaking students or you may get less practice than you'd want.

Among many offerings by many different organizations, the **Language Immersion School** *(tel 520/903-0574, www .veracruzspanish.com)* at Veracruz offers the opportunity to study in the tiny village of Villa Rica. This is an excellent opportunity for students with some skill already to maximize exposure to spoken Spanish. The school also offers business Spanish, cooking classes, and excursions.

Querétaro Language School *(tel 339/499 4390 from U.S., tel 442/171-1306 from Mexico, www.quere tarolanguageschool.com)* offers cooking classes, "survival Spanish," and classes geared to older folks as well as kids. It also provides students opportunities to use their Spanish as community volunteers.

designs. The intricate patterns represent Maya legends and lore. Villagers are identified by their dress, be it the distinctive blue shawls of San Juan Chamula or the beribboned hats worn for special ceremonies in Zinacantán. Villagers in some parts of Oaxaca still wear indigenous dress and create shawls, belts, huipiles, and blouses that are true works of Mexican art.

Religious themes play an important role in Mexican folk art. Many of the masks and costumes used in regional dances represent saints and sinners. Small paintings called ex-votos, often on metal, are used to express gratitude for a religious figure's assistance in solving some problem. Ex-votos first appeared in the late 18th century and picture the devotee in pain or injury praying to a saint or to the Virgin or Jesus Christ. The story of the miraculous cure or resolution to a problem is detailed in script below the scene. A chapel at the Basílica de Nuestra Señora de Guadalupe in Mexico City is filled with ex-votos praising the Mexican saint.

Skeletons, like this one of papier-mâché, pervade Mexican folk art.

Milagros—small tin (or occasionally silver) charms shaped as various body parts, houses, cows, or cars—are also used as pleas for divine intercession. Penitents pin these charms to the robes of statues of favorite saints and pray for relief from pain or the appearance of a cow or a new car. In recent years, some artists have incorporated milagros into jewelry, creating silver chains draped with tiny hearts, legs, and heads.

Mexico's silver tradition began with the Mixtec: formidable pre-Hispanic metalsmiths whose gold and silver jewelry adorned the ruling elite. During the colonial period, huge quantities of gold and silver were used in the interior decoration of Catholic churches and in religious artifacts. Silver and other precious metals are still mined, and modern artisans take inspiration from traditions both old and new to produce jewelry and other handicrafts, mainly of silver. Much of it comes from Taxco, Guerrero—an entire city dedicated to silversmithing.

Printmaking became a popular means of expression in the late 19th century under the hand of José Guadalupe Posada (1852–1913), long considered Mexico's greatest lithographer. Posada's engravings and highly detailed etchings in metal and wood were used to print broadsheets distributed by street vendors. A whole genre of broadsheets called *calaveras* (skulls) was created for Day of the Dead celebrations. They satirized everyone and everything with mocking verse and illustrations. Originally created for the masses, Posadas's broadsheets and calaveras caught the attention of artists of the early 20th century. Some nearly deified him as the originator of a truly Mexican art movement. His calaveras certainly provided inspiration to future artists and have become synonymous with modern Day of the Dead celebrations.

Papier-mâché is one of the most popular mediums in Mexican folk art and is used for everything from masks to the ubiquitous piñatas. The Linares family of Mexico City is famous for its papier-mâché skeletons, skulls, dragons, and life-size devils. Glamorous papier-mâché dolls from Guanajuato wear exaggerated makeup and glittery jewelry.

Everything from gold to gourds is used to create art in Mexico. Collectors crave items as simple as a wooden spoon and as intricate as a beaded mask. Certain parts of the country—especially Oaxaca, Chiapas, and Michoacán—are veritable living museums with markets that feel like galleries.

Music

Every Mexican is a musician in his or her soul. As the saying goes, *"También de dolor se canta cuando llorar no se puede."* ("Sorrow also sings, when it runs too deep to cry.")

The most famous and familiar tunes are the *rancheras,* typically played and sung by mariachi musicians with violins, trumpets, and a variety of guitar-like instruments. Some of these songs of lost loves and defeat date back to the Mexican Revolution, when roving musicians carried the ballads of the war-torn northern regions to Mexico City. The *charro* (Mexican cowboy) movies of the 1930s and '40s spread ranchera music throughout the country, and the composer José Alfredo Jiménez added dozens of new songs to the mariachi repertoire.

Until the rise of mariachis and rancheras, most Mexican music was regional, based on indigenous and religious traditions. The advent of radio, film, and television spread mariachi music around the country, until it became a national emblem. The popularity of regional music grew as well, and Mexicans came to appreciate the marimbas of Chiapas and the romantic boleros of composer Agustín Lara, who added the sensual rhythms of Veracruz.

> **The most famous and familiar tunes are the *rancheras,* typically played and sung by mariachi musicians with violins, trumpets, and a variety of guitar-like instruments.**

Soulful, passionate ballads are at the core of most of the music played in Mexico. Singers stand out for their ability to evoke all the emotions of even the most common tunes such as "Cielito Lindo" ("Beautiful Little Sky") and "La Paloma" ("The Dove"). Lola Beltrán's (1932–1996) passionate singing made her the long-reigning queen of rancheras from the 1950s, while María Félix carried the romantic lyrics of tropical ballads to the sands of Acapulco in the 1940s, captivating the international artsy set with the rhythms of Mexico. Today's balladeers, including Juan Gabriel, Luis Miguel, and Alejandro Fernández, rely on old favorites to enhance their modern repertoires and bring cheers from their fans.

Romance and loss still inspire Mexico's modern musicians. Even Mexico's rock 'n' rollers love a good heartbreaker, although they also combine traditional instruments with electronics and political themes. Carlos Santana, raised near the border in Tijuana, was the first artist to bring Mexican influences into the international mainstream. Others have garnered fanatical followings within Mexico and beyond. The pop-rock group Maná and alternative rock band Café Tacuba are well-known outside Mexico,

Pueblos Mágicos

The Mexican government has designated as "magic villages" places that embody the spirit of Mexico in their art, culture, or traditions. Otherwise unremarkable Papantla, Veracruz, received the designation for its Papantla "flyers" (voladores de Papantla), an ancient tradition associated with the harvest; Taxco, Guerrero, for its silver-smithing traditions; Tepotzlán and Izamal for their churches; and San Cristóbal de las Casas and Pátzcuaro for their well-maintained historical centers.

Here is a sampling of the towns currently designated Pueblos Mágicos. For a full list, see www.pueblomagicodemexico.com.mx.

Álamos, Sonora
Coatepec, Veracruz
Creel, Chihuahua
Izamal, Yucatán
Pátzcuaro, Michoacán

Real de Catorce, San Luis Potosí
Real del Monte, Hidalgo
San Cristóbal de las Casas, Chiapas
San Miguel de Allende, Guanajuato
Tapalpa, Jalisco
Taxco, Guerrero
Tepotzotlán, Estado de México
Tepoztlán, Morelos
Todos Santos, Baja California Sur

and new sounds are emerging from a burgeoning underground music scene. Versatile and eclectic Oaxaca singer Lila Downs performed several moving songs in the movie *Frida* (2002), one of which was nominated for an Academy Award.

Each part of the country has a particular sound. *Norteño* bands combine accordion, bass, and guitar with polka and ranchera melodies to create a rousing country and western sound popular in the northern regions of Mexico. The lyrics often touch on themes of immigration and national politics. *Cumbia,* salsa, and marimba music, with a tropical beat, bring dancers to their feet in Veracruz, home of the overplayed "La Bamba." The brassy *banda*, or band music, of Sinaloa has a German undertone, which was contributed by immigrants in the 1920s. Familiar and unusual sounds travel the air waves all over the country.

Dance

Dance in Mexico dates back to Indian cultures and forward beyond *La Macarena*. Catholic ritual and indigenous tradition have fused to create dances such as those celebrated during the Easter season by the Yaqui and Maya of Sonora. Deer masks and flowers are elements that remain from an important pre-Hispanic ritual asking that the deer sacrifice itself for the good of the people. Today, deer dancers join with others representing Jesus and the Marys to defend the church from evil men (represented by the Pharisees) in elaborate dances that are held throughout the land.

Ballet folklórico dance groups abound in all parts of the country; some of the finest appear in the most popular tourist destinations. Young children perform in central plazas large and small and grow up to compete for spots in professional troupes. The reigning favorite is ruled by Amalia Hernández at Mexico City's Palacio de Bellas Artes; watching the theater's Tiffany curtain rise to reveal gorgeously costumed dancers is a necessary ritual for any fan of Mexican dance.

Traditional folkloric dancing began in the 1800s. Today, regional dances echo the music of immigrants and the rhythms of nature. In San Luis Potosí, dancers perform the *huapango,* a variation of the Spanish fandango. In Veracruz, couples dance the disciplined *danzón,* of Cuban origins. Even the most famous of all Mexican dances, *el jarabe tapatío* (the Mexican hat dance), originated among mestizos.

The states of Oaxaca, Michoacán, Yucatán, Jalisco, Chiapas, and Veracruz are renowned for their numerous folk dances. In Oaxaca, dancers from throughout the state perform at the annual Guelaguetza, a two-week-long celebration of ethnic heritage held in July. The costumes for dances from Oaxaca and Chiapas are among the most gorgeous imaginable works of art that enhance the beauty of the movements and of the wearers. The Dance of the Old Men (Danza de los Viejitos), which originated in Michoacán, provides the humorous interlude in performances around the country.

Less familiar dances are performed during religious holidays, especially around Semana Santa (Holy Week). The Cora Indians of Nayarit dance in hallucinogenic agitation for days on end, while the Tarahumara of the Copper Canyon engage in tumultuous, eerie mock battles between soldiers and the Pharisees.

Dancing is part celebration, from birthday parties to formal fiestas. Mexicans of all ages show up at dance halls and clubs to waltz, dance salsa and merengue, or move to the beat of pop or *rock en español.* Mexican discos are typically elegant places where clients dress to impress and dance till dawn.

> *El Laberinto de la Soledad (the Labyrinth of Solitude),* published in 1950, stands out as the definitive portrait of the Mexican psyche.

Literature

Mexico's first books were codices made of bark paper and animal skin and filled with pictures and symbols. The Maya were particularly prolific and created two of pre-Hispanic Mexico's most important books, along with several codices relating historical events. The *Popol Vuh,* written between 1554 and 1558, is an epic account of supernatural legend and lore, while the *Chilam Balam,* written during the 17th and 18th centuries, offers a more realistic account of astronomical observations and historic events. Books in the Náhuatl and Mixtec languages have also remained intact, as have many more stone and stucco carvings relating stories of battle, birth, death, and royal succession.

Although some Spaniards worked to preserve native books and writings, others were equally successful in their post-conquest campaign to destroy documents they considered works of Satan. One of the most important records of the Spanish Conquest itself is *La Historia Verdadera de la Conquista de la Nueva España (True History of the Conquest of New Spain)* by Bernal Díaz del Castillo (ca 1492–1581), a conquistador who later in life related the events of the Conquest with startling clarity.

As might be expected, the ruling Spaniards stuck to European and religious themes in poetry, theater, and literature. The first printing press, which arrived in Mexico in 1537, was used primarily to disseminate information about science, nature, and the country's settlement. A Mexican style of literature began emerging late in the 16th century, as mestizos and criollos began drawing on themes of more local significance. The most famous writer of the colonial era was Sor Juana Inés de la Cruz (1651–1695), a nun and prolific poet. Her theme was frequently the plight of the citizens of New Spain, who suffered under Spanish restraints as Mexico's wealth was plundered for the motherland. In one of her most famous poems she wrote:

Señora, I was born in the land of plenty . . .
to no other land on Earth is Mother Nature so generous.
Europe knows this best of all
for this many years, insatiable,
She has bled the abundant veins
of America's rich mines.

Although the printed word was largely used for political campaigns and social causes in the 19th century, the first novel with a Mexican theme, *El Periquillo Sarniento (The Itching Parrot)* by José Joaquin Fernández de Lizardi (1776–1827), appeared in the early 1800s. Francisco I. Madero (who later became Mexico's president) wrote one of the first significant pieces of political nonfiction. His *The Presidential Succession of 1910* was instrumental in the downfall of Porfirio Díaz.

Of all the literature produced in the 20th century, *El Laberinto de la Soledad (The Labyrinth of Solitude),* published in 1950, stands out as the definitive portrait of the Mexican psyche. Author and Nobel laureate Octavio Paz (1914–1998) attempted to analyze and describe the character of his countrymen and capture the essence of *mexicanidad.* Though controversial, his book is considered a masterpiece, and Paz was revered as the elder statesman of Mexican writers. Carlos Fuentes, author of *La Región Más Transparente (Where the Air Is Clear)* and *El Gringo Viejo (The Old Gringo),* is another modern master.

Many young people practice folk dancing, like those in this University of Guadalajara troupe.

Film

Mexico's earliest films helped popularize mariachi music and the lifestyle of the northern Mexico cowboys. Pancho Villa's exploits were a popular theme, as were the trials and tribulations of urban families. They united Mexicans unaccustomed to the music and culture of distant regions, and by the 1930s Mexican film was receiving worldwide attention.

Mexican filmmakers and actors benefited from Hollywood's fascination with Mexico's topography. Many early U.S. Westerns were filmed in northern Mexico, and Hollywood stars frequented the resorts of Acapulco in the 1940s. Dolores del Río (1905–1983), who regularly partied with the Hollywood elite on Playa Caleta, was beginning to gain fame outside Mexico when she caught the eye of the international press at the 1946 Cannes Film Festival. As the star of *María Candelaria* (1944), the hit film directed by Emilio Fernández (1904–1986), Del Río helped popularize Mexican cinema, as did Mario Moreno (1911–1993), better known as Cantinflas, "the Charlie Chaplin of Mexico," and Germán Valdés (also known as Tin Tan). Actress María Félix and actors Jorge Negrete and Pedro Infante were also idolized by fans in the 1940s. Films including *Enamorada* (directed by Fernández) and *Distinto Amanecer* (Julio Bracho) became instant classics. Mexico's most famous director of the 1950s, Luis Buñuel (1900–1983), was a Spaniard who fled his country during the Civil War. His *Los Olvidados* (1950) is another Mexican masterpiece.

In the 1950s and 1960s a flurry of schlock horror films—including Jerry Warren's 1963 *Attack of the Mayan Mummy,* adapted from the 1957 Mexican film *La Momia Azteca*—drew a loyal following. The greatest cult film of all appeared in 1970, when Alejandro Jodorowsky came out with *El Topo,* a violent hodgepodge of surrealism and Western cowboy images. More serious themes emerged in the 1980s. Director Gregory Nava delved into the miseries of illegal immigration in the acclaimed 1983 film *El Norte* (1984). Roberto Rodríguez portrayed modern northern Mexico in his 1993 *El Mariachi* and again in *Desperado (*1995) and *Once Upon a Time in Mexico (2003).*

The most famous film to come out of Mexico in the 1990s was *Like Water for Chocolate (Como Agua Para Chocolate),* the soulful interpretation of Laura Esquivel's best-selling novel. Today, more and more movies, documentaries, and soap operas are being filmed in Mexico. Mexican filmmakers compete for funding and awards with peers around the world, while Mexican actors are gaining fame in their own country and abroad.

EXPERIENCE: Enjoy Carnival

Mexico's festivities preceding Lent are called *carnaval.* Participating towns host parades and music. Mazatlán *(www. maztravel.com)* adds poetry contests and ballet. In Cozumel, the lively fiesta (http://cozumelinsider.com/carnival) attracts floats and dance troupes from throughout the Yucatán. Playa del Carmen's celebration is growing in popularity and sophistication. Guaymas,

Sonora (www.go2sancarlos.com), crowned its first carnival queen in 1888. Most travelers simply make hotel reservations a year in advance then enjoy the street parties and other inexpensive activities without advance planning. For travelers who would rather not worry about details, **My Mexico Tours** *(http:// mymexicotours.com)* and other tour companies can plan itineraries for groups.

An isolated finger of mountains and desert between the Pacific Ocean and the Sea of Cortez

Baja California

Barnacle-encrusted gray whale

Baja California

Though superficially barren and desolate, the Baja California peninsula has long entranced scientists and adventurers. "The very air here is miraculous, and outlines of reality change with the moments," wrote author John Steinbeck (1902–1968). "A dream hangs over the entire region." A similar feeling inspires a more modern cadre of adventurers, dedicated to exploring every crevice and cove of Baja.

Baja's desert wilderness offers plenty of solitude for those seeking to get away from it all.

Long and lean, the Baja California peninsula gradually separated from the mainland five million years ago along the San Andreas Fault, bringing with it a series of mountain ranges. At its widest, it stretches just 120 miles (193 km) along the U.S. border. The bulk of Baja's tourists visit Los Cabos, 860 miles (1,300 km) from the U.S. border. Between the two extremes lie rugged, dramatic, and often lonely, yet lovely, desert-and-ocean landscapes. Recently, tourism in the Tijuana–Ensenada corridor has dropped off because of news reports of border-area violence among drug cartels and law enforcement.

At least five indigenous groups lived in Baja when Padre Juan María Salvatierra established the mission church in Loreto in 1697. As missionaries and European adventurers made their way up the peninsula, the native population was decimated by battles or disease. Only about a thousand indigenous people now live in Baja, some still following their forefathers' traditions.

The Pacific side of Baja's coastline is renowned for its awesome waves, massive billfish, and migrating whales; the Gulf of California (also called the Sea of Cortez) is a biologist's dream. Here, thousands of species of marine creatures flourish in protected coves and open waters. Nearly every environmental group in the world has an interest in protecting the Gulf of California from commercial fishing and any development that threatens its natural balance. Such concern led to its designation in 2005 as a UNESCO World Heritage site.

Despite the harshness of Baja's terrain, its plant and animal life is surprisingly abundant and varied. Stately cardón cactuses, bizarre

NOT TO BE MISSED:

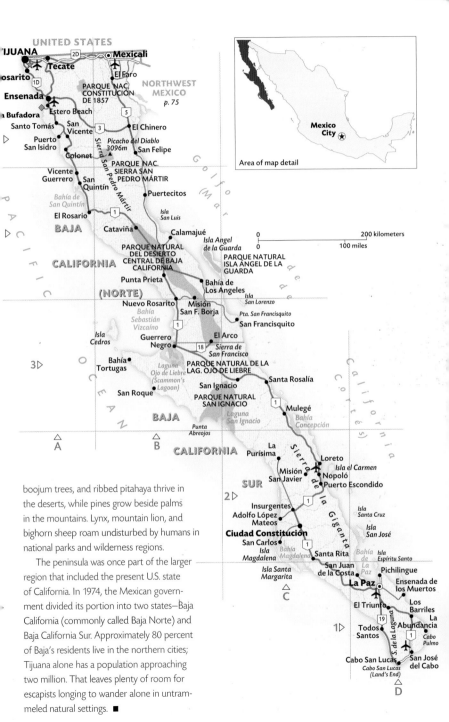

UNITED STATES

TIJUANA
Mexicali
2D
Tecate
El Faro
osarito
1D
NORTHWEST
MEXICO
Ensenada
PARQUE NAC.
CONSTITUCIÓN
DE 1857
p. 75
a Bufadora
Estero Beach
Santo Tomás
San
Vicente
5
El Chinero
Puerto
San Isidro
3
Picacho del Diablo
3096m
San Felipe
Colonet
Vicente
Guerrero
San
Quintín
PARQUE NAC.
SIERRA SAN
PEDRO MÁRTIR
Puertecitos
Bahía de
San Quintín
El Rosario
1
Isla
San Luis
BAJA
Cataviña
Calamajué
Isla Angel
de la Guarda
PARQUE NATURAL
DEL DESIERTO
CENTRAL DE BAJA
CALIFORNIA
PARQUE NATURAL
ISLA ÁNGEL DE LA
GUARDA
CALIFORNIA
Punta Prieta
Bahía de
Los Angeles
(NORTE)
Nuevo Rosarito
Misión
San F. Borja
Isla
San Lorenzo
Bahía
Sebastián
Vizcaíno
1
Guerrero
Negro
Pta. San Francisquito
San Francisquito
Isla
Cedros
El Arco
18
Sierra de
San Francisco
3
Bahía
Tortugas
Laguna
Ojo de Liebre
(Scammon's
Lagoon)
PARQUE NATURAL DE LA
LAG. OJO DE LIEBRE
Santa Rosalía
San Roque
San Ignacio
1
Mulegé
PARQUE NATURAL
SAN IGNACIO
Laguna
San Ignacio
Bahía
Concepción
BAJA
Punta
Abreojos
A
B
CALIFORNIA
La
Purísima
Loreto
Isla el Carmen
SUR
Misión
San Javier
Nopoló
Puerto Escondido
2
Insurgentes
Adolfo López
Mateos
1
Isla
Santa Cruz
Ciudad Constitución
San Carlos
Isla
Magdalena
Bahía
Magdalena
1
Santa Rita
Isla
San José
Bahía
de
Isla
Espíritu Santo
Isla Santa
Margarita
San Juan
de la Costa
La
Paz
Pichilingue
C
La Paz
Ensenada de
los Muertos
El Triunfo
Los
Barriles
19
La
Abundancia
1
Todos
Santos
Cabo
Pulmo
1
Cabo San Lucas
Cabo San Lucas
(Land's End)
San José
del Cabo
D

Mexico
City
Area of map detail

0   200 kilometers
0   100 miles

boojum trees, and ribbed pitahaya thrive in the deserts, while pines grow beside palms in the mountains. Lynx, mountain lion, and bighorn sheep roam undisturbed by humans in national parks and wilderness regions.

The peninsula was once part of the larger region that included the present U.S. state of California. In 1974, the Mexican government divided its portion into two states—Baja California (commonly called Baja Norte) and Baja California Sur. Approximately 80 percent of Baja's residents live in the northern cities; Tijuana alone has a population approaching two million. That leaves plenty of room for escapists longing to wander alone in untrammeled natural settings. ■

Tijuana to Ensenada

Between Tijuana, Mexico's fourth largest city, and Ensenada, Baja California's largest port, lies an ever multiplying number of hotels, businesses, and oceanfront rentals that has grown steadily in recent decades, engulfing once isolated fishing villages and resort hotels alike. But tourism to this region is not new. Since the days of U.S. Prohibition, Tijuana has attracted day- and night-trippers with its dance halls and discos, raucous bars, and bullfights.

One of Tijuana's more picturesque corners

Tijuana

🗺 55 A5

Visitor Information

✉ Av. Revolución bet. Calles 3 & 4

☎ 664/685-3117, 01800/025-0888 toll-free, 888/775-2417 from U.S. For tourist assistance, dial 078.

www.seetijuana.com

Tijuana

For some, Tijuana is a shopping destination or a chance to get a glimpse of Mexico while vacationing in Southern California. For others, it's the gateway to adventure farther south. Tourists wary of wandering too far on their own—and those who like a good deal—take advantage of two-hour, on-and-off bus tours (*$$$*). The double-decker buses make 13 stops, including the L.A. Cetto winery, the cultural center, and Tijuana's legendary main street—**Avenida Revolución.**

At Tijuana's bullring, sequined bullfighters divert 1,000-pound (450 kg) bulls with a flourish of their heavy silk capes. But more palatable to most folks is a visit to **L.A. Cetto winery** (*Av. Cañón Johnson 2108, Col. Hidalgo, tel 664/685-3031, www.lacetto.com, closed Sun., $*), where you can sample a variety of vintages and tour the facilities.

East of downtown looms the **Centro Cultural Tijuana** (*Paseo de los Héroes at Mina, tel 664/687-9600, www.cecut.gob. mx*). In its dome is the thousand-seat **Omnimax theater** (*$$*). The adjacent museum has a restaurant and two floors of exhibits. The **Museo de las Californias** (*tel 664/687-9650, closed Mon., $$*) highlights the peninsula's history.

Rosarito

Just 18 miles (29 km) south of Tijuana lies Rosarito. Today, this tourist-oriented city heads its own municipality boasting 20 miles (32 km) of coastline with many decent beaches. It's known for its shops, stores, and stalls selling glazed and unglazed pottery, wrought-iron hardware, hand-carved furniture, and handicrafts. Most shops are along **Boulevard Benito Juárez,** a jumble of bars, hotels, and restaurants.

Just down the coast, **Fox Studios** *(Km 32.8 Carr. Libre a Ensenada, tel 661/612-4294 or 866/369-2252 from U.S., www.foxploration.com, closed Mon.–Tues., $$$$)* was built as the set for the 1997 film *Titanic.* Since then more movies have been produced there, including *The Weight of Water* and *Pearl Harbor.* Visitors can explore sets and learn about film production.

Ensenada

About 32 miles (51 km) south of Rosarito, Ensenada hugs the northern end of **Bahía de Todos Santos.** Its proximity to the U.S. border, seafood restaurants, and water sports make this town a favorite weekend getaway. Shopping is concentrated along **Avenida López Mateos.**

Whale-watching excursions leave from the **Sportfishing Pier** *(Blvd. Costero near Av. Macheros)* from December to March. Overnight fishing trips are also available. The best fishing is June through September.

South of Ensenada, a blowhole called **La Bufadora** shoots ocean water 80 feet (24 m) high. Below, the rocky cove at **Punta Banda** is popular with divers, fishermen, and kayakers. Kayaks are more easily launched at **Estero Beach,** an estuary halfway up the bay.

Taste local wines at **Bodegas de Santo Tomás** or one of the wineries tucked into **Valle de Guadalupe,** about a 30-minute drive east. The largest of these wineries, **L.A. Cetto** *(Hwy. 3 Km 73.5 toward Tecate, tel 646/155-2179),* offers tastings and tours daily from 10 a.m.to 3:30 p.m.; smaller wineries like **Monte Xanic** *(tel 646/174-7055)* require an appointment. (See also "Wine-tasting in Mexico," p. 37.) ■

Rosarito
🗺 55 A5
Visitor Information
✉ Blvd. Juárez 907-14 at Oceana Plaza mall
☎ 661/612-3078 or 01800/962-2252 (toll-free within Mexico)

Ensenada
🗺 55 A5
Visitor Information
✉ Blvd. Lázaro Cárdenas 609-5
☎ 646/178-8588 or 800/310-9687 (from U.S.)
www.enjoyensenada .com

EXPERIENCE: Sailing Down Mexico Way

Several fun races provide yacht enthusiasts with the opportunity to sail south of the border. The **Newport Harbor Yacht Club** (www.nhyc.org) has a point-to-point race from Newport, California, to Cabo San Lucas, usually held in early March. Visit the club's website for details on entering the race. Proceeds of the 800-mile (1,287 km) regatta benefit the Casa Hogar orphanage for boys.

Marina del Rey Yacht Club (www.dryc .org) in Los Angeles co-hosts an annual race from Southern California to the tip of Baja California with the **San Diego Yacht Club** (www.sdyc.org). The multi-leg race's first stop is Los Cedros Island, about a 2.5-day sail from San Diego. The second leg ends at Magdalena Bay, where you might be running next to a gargantuan gray whale. Check the club's website for more information on entering the race. The overall champ is fêted at the **Paradise Village Marina** (www.vallarta yachtclub.org) in Nuevo Vallarta, Nayarit.

Baja Peninsula Drive

Until 1974, mostly die-hard naturalists, explorers, and anglers bumped down rutted dirt and sand roads to the tip of the Baja Peninsula. Then the government paved Highway 1, opening Baja to a wider audience. Fortunately, the drive is still arduous enough to discourage crowds. The road meanders from the Pacific to the Gulf of California, passing by and through several mountain ranges.

The towering peaks of Baja's Sierra de la Giganta, near Loreto

Angeles Verdes (Green Angels; see sidebar p. 244) patrol the highway to assist stranded travelers, and local mechanics are ingenious, but drivers should be prepared for heat, potholes, arroyos (watercourses), and wandering cows. Fuel up frequently, and always carry plenty of water, a jack and good spare tire, maps, and spare parts. Forget about speeding past the scenery—many of the crosses at the roadside mark the spot where incautious drivers have died. Instead, take the time to enjoy Baja's extraordinary landscape of cactuses, canyons, and coves.

Highway 1 begins just after the San Ysidro border crossing (open 24 hours), connecting

NOT TO BE MISSED:

San Ignacio • Bahía de la Concepción • Loreto • Cabo Pulmo

San Diego County with **Tijuana ❶** (see p. 56). Some travelers stop to shop and sightsee in Tijuana; others head south to **Rosarito** (see pp. 56–57) and the shore break at **Cantamar.** Nearby **Puerto Nuevo** (also known as Newport)—once a clutch of friendly lobster shacks—has grown. Today this seaside town is an enclave of liquor stores, shops, and

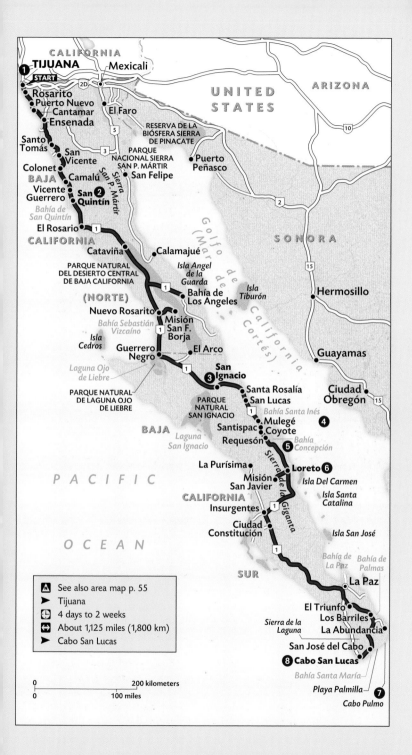

CALIFORNIA

1 TIJUANA Mexicali
START
2D
Rosarito
Puerto Nuevo
Cantamar   El Faro
Ensenada
5
Santo
Tomás   San
3   Vicente
Colonet
BAJA   Camalú
Vicente
Guerrero   **San 2
Quintín**
Bahía de
San Quintín
El Rosario   1
CALIFORNIA
Cataviña   Calamajué
PARQUE NATURAL
DEL DESIERTO CENTRAL
DE BAJA CALIFORNIA   Isla Angel
de la
Guarda
(NORTE)   1
Bahía de
Los Angeles
Nuevo Rosarito
Misión
Bahía Sebastián   San F.
Vizcaíno   1   Borja
Isla
Cedros   Guerrero   El Arco
Negro
Laguna Ojo   1   **San 3
de Liebre   Ignacio**
PARQUE NATURAL   Santa Rosalía
DE LAGUNA OJO   San Lucas
DE LIEBRE   PARQUE   1   Bahía Santa Inés   **4**
NATURAL
SAN IGNACIO   Mulegé
Santispac   Coyote
BAJA   Laguna   Requesón   Bahía
San Ignacio   **5**   Concepción
La Purísima   **Loreto 6**
Misión   Isla Del Carmen
San Javier
PACIFIC   CALIFORNIA   Isla Santa
Insurgentes   1   Catalina
Ciudad
Constitución   Isla San José
OCEAN   1
Bahía de   Bahía de
SUR   La Paz   Palmas
La Paz
El Triunfo
Los Barriles
Sierra de la   La Abundancia
Laguna
San José del Cabo
8 Cabo San Lucas
Bahía Santa María
Playa Palmilla   **7**
Cabo Pulmo

UNITED
STATES   ARIZONA

RESERVA DE LA
BIÓSFERA SIERRA
DE PINACATE
PARQUE
NACIONAL SIERRA   Puerto
SAN P. MÁRTIR   Peñasco
San Felipe
2
GOLFO DE
(Mar de   SONORA
Golfo de
California
15
Isla
Tiburón   Hermosillo

Mar de
Cortés)   Guaymas

Ciudad
Obregón   15

Sierra de la Giganta

See also area map p. 55
▶ Tijuana
🕐 4 days to 2 weeks
↔ About 1,125 miles (1,800 km)
▶ Cabo San Lucas

0   200 kilometers
0   100 miles

restaurants specializing in refried beans, rice, tortillas, and, of course, lobster.

After the frequently congested stretch of Highway 1 from Tijuana to Ensenada, the true Baja experience begins. The road descends into the undulating wine country around **Santo Tomás,** then ascends a steep grade and evens out as it passes remote ranches and vineyards at **San Vicente.** Serious agriculture occupies the land around **Colonet, Camalú,** and **Vicente Guerrero.** Side roads lead from Colonet to the formidable peaks of the **Sierra San Pedro Mártir,** far out of sight to the east.

INSIDER TIP:

If you drive on Mexico highways, use your left-turn signal only if you want someone to pass you.

—DENISE PRICHARD
National Geographic Film

Restaurants (try the local pismo clams), grocery stores, hotels, and beaches make **San Quintín ❷,** 115 miles (185 km) south of Ensenada, a sensible place to break for lunch or the night. Asphalt and dirt streets lead to **Bahía de San Quintín** (79 miles/129 km south of Colonet), where a late 19th-century English wheat-farming venture quickly succumbed to drought. Clamming and bird-watching are popular pursuits here, along with sportfishing.

Some of northern Baja's best beaches lie along the 36-mile (58 km) stretch of Highway 1 between San Quintín and **El Rosario,** which has grocery stores and a gas station. South of El Rosario, Highway 1 jogs abruptly east to enter Baja's eerie central desert. Most travelers stop to pose beside one of the many towering cardón cactuses or wavy branched cirio trees. Some are tempted to camp beside the spooky, flat-top mesas that would make ideal UFO landing strips. The mesas and low hills give way to fields of enormous boulders around

Cataviña. A sign indicates the turnoff, 65 miles (105 km) south of Cataviña, to a paved road heading east to **Bahía de Los Angeles** (see p. 73). Later, other signs point to another turnoff 32 miles (53 km) south at **Nuevo Rosarito,** where high-clearance vehicles can detour 22 miles (35 km) to **Misión San Francisco Borja** (see p. 73).

The next important stop is **Guerrero Negro,** 145 miles (234 km) south of Cataviña, at the Baja California Sur state line. Important as a supply stop but otherwise unexceptional, the bleak, windy town is headquarters for whale-watching expeditions (*Dec.–March;* see pp. 68–69). Nearby **Laguna Ojo de Liebre** (also known as Scammon's Lagoon) is a mating and birthing ground for gray whales and has a large salt-evaporation plant, which produces around a million tons of salt annually.

South of Guerrero Negro the highway cuts inland and up into the mountains for 88 miles (142 km) to **San Ignacio ❸,** a true high-desert oasis (see p. 62). The highway swoops downhill, first touching the Gulf of California at **Santa Rosalía.** Short detours to the south bring you to **Caleta San Lucas,** a mangrove-lined cove with good snorkeling and fishing, and to **Bahía Santa Inés ❹,** where the long, eponymous bay provides great shelling, diving, fishing, and sailboarding.

A riverbed thick with lush palms marks the entrance to **Mulegé** (see p. 63), and it becomes increasingly difficult to keep your eyes on the road. Beautiful **Bahía de la Concepción ❺,** a narrow bay scalloped with coves containing clear, aquamarine water, appears like a glistening mirage. Take a break and go for a swim at **Coyote, Santispac,** or **Requesón Beaches,** and join the campers and kayakers for a cool drink at one of the simple palm-thatched restaurants.

The next stop along Highway 1 is **Loreto ❻** (see p. 63), 84 miles (136 km) south of Mulegé. **Misión San Javier** (see pp. 73–74), an hour inland up a passable dirt road, may well be Baja's most impressive historic church.

After Loreto, Highway 1 climbs into the rusty red **Sierra de la Giganta** in a series of switchbacks and hairpin turns to the Santo Domingo Valley, **Insurgentes,** and **Ciudad Constitución,** Baja Sur's third largest town. Gas up, and replenish your water supply here. Wheat, alfalfa, cotton, and corn farms nourished by water from deep wells are the only distractions during the next leg of the journey.

It's almost impossible to keep from speeding through the barren moonscape of dull desert during the 134 miles (216 km)

region. Fishing camps and semi-luxurious hotels are tucked away on the beach or the hills above.

Sailboarding is very popular at nearby **Bahía de Palmas,** while a detour 11 miles (17 km) south of Los Barriles accesses the East Cape beach road. The pavement ends at La Abundancia. After that, rough travel over washboard roads rewards with sugar-fine beaches dotted with strange rock formations. There's great fishing and reef diving at **Cabo Pulmo ❼,** an underwater preserve.

Mulegé, among Baja Sur's greenest oases, attracts many winter visitors.

between Constitución and **La Paz.** The road edges **Bahía La Paz** before entering Baja California Sur's busy state capital, a good place to pass the night (see pp. 66–67).

Passing forests of organ and cardón cactuses, Highway 1 crosses the **Sierra de la Laguna** range south of La Paz and travels through **El Triunfo,** a quirky old mining town. The Gulf of California beckons at **Los Barriles,** the entrance to the fast-growing **East Cape**

From Los Barriles, the road swings inland and widens into a four-lane, divided highway near the airport. It passes **San José del Cabo** (see p. 71) and skirts the coast, passing surf spots at **Costa Azul** and **Acapulquito. Playa Palmilla** is good for swimming, while **Bahía Santa María** is a perfect snorkeling and diving spot. The journey ends at **Cabo San Lucas ❽** and Baja California's best known rock: the natural arch at Land's End (see p. 72).

San Ignacio to Loreto

After crossing into Baja Sur at Guerrero Negro, Highway 1 heads east toward the Sea of Cortez. Ninety sun-baked miles (145 km) later, the road meets spring-fed San Ignacio. With its well-preserved mission church poking above the date palms, San Ignacio offers a glimpse into traditional Baja. Santa Rosalía presents a 19th-century mining town hardly improved by modern trappings, while Mulegé and Loreto echo historic mainland Mexican villages.

San Ignacio
🗺 Map p. 55
Visitor Information
✉ Calle Hidalgo 6
☎ 615/154-0150

San Ignacio

The sleepy mountain town of San Ignacio greets the traveler like a heat-induced mirage. Its Jesuit founders planted date palms and orange and fig trees at this desert oasis, and

Dominicans completed the lava-stone **Iglesia de San Ignacio de Loyola** adjacent to the main plaza. Stop in for Sunday Mass, or visit its small **museum** *(closed Sun.).*

Although inland, San Ignacio serves as a base for whale-watching excursions to **Laguna San Ignacio** (see p. 69) and treks to prehistoric rock paintings (see "Visiting Cave Paintings," p. 64) in the mountains.

Santa Rosalía

Highway 1 first kisses the gulf 46 miles (74 km) southeast of San Ignacio at Santa Rosalía, established by German copper-mining entrepreneurs in the late 19th century, then run by the French. The cast-iron **Iglesia de Santa Bárbara** *(Calle Obregón near plaza)* was designed by Gustave Eiffel and shipped in pieces from France.

Arrow-straight streets lined with wooden houses (built as homes for immigrant miners) give Santa Rosalía a "company town" feel. The mine's French managers lived on the mesa north of town, overlooking the railroad tracks and the sea. Check out the view from the restored 19th-century **Hotel Francés** *(Av. 11 de Julio 15 at Jean M. Cousteau, Col. Mesa Francia, tel 615/152-2052).*

Built in 1687, Our Lady of Loreto was the first California mission church.

Visitors not using Santa Rosalía as a base for visiting nearby sites usually move on after a visit of a few hours or an overnight stay.

Mulegé

Lush Mulegé, 38 miles (61 km) south of Santa Rosalía, attracts U.S. and Canadian snowbirds escaping the northern winter and sports enthusiasts who revel in the town's slow pace, tourist facilities, and green river valley by the sea. Visitors trek into the surrounding mountains to see cave art at **San Borjitas, Trinidad,** or **Piedras Pintas,** or fish, kayak, snorkel, or sailboard along the rocky coast of Bahia Conceptión.

Mulegé is centered among orange trees and date palms; small hotels, adventure-tour companies, and restaurants cluster near the plaza. Established in 1705, damaged by a hurricane in 1770, and abandoned in 1828, the town's restored mission church, **Santa Rosalía de Mulegé,** lies south of the center on Calle Zaragoza. A former prison at the north end of town houses the uninspiring **Museo de Mulegé** (closed Sat.– Sun.), with local memorabilia.

Loreto

Tucked between the golden sierras and the languid Gulf of California, Loreto was once the religious and political center of the Baja peninsula. Its **Misión Nuestra Señora de Loreto** (Salvatierra at Misioneros) was built in 1687 and restored in the 1970s. Check out the gilded altar and the statue of the Virgin believed by some to perform miracles.

Loreto was Baja's capital for

one hundred years before a devastating 1829 hurricane. After that the seat of government was moved to La Paz, and Loreto drifted into obscurity. In 1974 the Mexican government pegged the town as a major tourist destination and installed telephones, electricity, paved streets, and an international airport. Neighborhoods rose beside a resort hotel at **Bahía Nopoló;** an 18-hole golf course followed. Nearby **Puerto Escondido** got a new marina and an expanded RV park and hotel.

INSIDER TIP:

In central Baja, stop by the town of San Ignacio. It is a little oasis in the desert with a beautiful mission and museum that features a reproduction of some of the area's rock art.

—AMY GUSICK
National Geographic field researcher

Today, few planes land at the airport and Loreto retains its provincial air. A handful of hotels and restaurants cater to Loreto's loyal followers and sightseers, who cherish its isolation. Rich feeding grounds around **Isla Coronado,** seahorse-shaped **Isla El Carmen,** and tiny **Isla Danzante** lure fishermen to schools of dorado, tuna, roosterfish, and billfish, while snorkelers and divers swim with rays and tropical fish, and kayakers paddle around the islands. ∎

Loreto

🄼 55 C2

Visitor Information

✉ Palacio del Municipio, Av. Federico I. Madero s/n

☎ 613/135-0411

www.gotoloreto.com

Cave Paintings of Baja California

Prehistoric mural paintings are found throughout central Baja California, most at an elevation of more than 1,000 feet (305 m). Some are on exposed rocks, while others crowd the walls and ceilings of caves both small and large. Red and black pigments were most commonly used, in addition to yellow, orange, pink, and white. Some images appear to have been sketched first in white chalk, charcoal, or paint.

Favorite subjects were humans and deer (the latter often pierced with arrows), but artists depicted all the creatures that shared their world, including birds, reptiles, rabbits, squids, fish, turtles, whales, and manta rays.

Paintings found within each of the main mountain ranges exhibit a characteristic style. Human figures (monos) predominate in the Sierra de Guadalupe near San Ignacio. These are stiff, often bulb-shaped figures with vertical stripes and outstretched arms and legs. In the Sierra de San Borja, large, red figures were painted on huge granite boulders, while to the south, in the Sierra de San Juan and Sierra San Francisco, artists chose the walls and ceilings of caves up to 30 feet (9 m) high as their canvases. Figures from the San Francisco range tend to be red on one half,

black on the other, with elaborate head gear.

North and south of this central region, other artistic innovations are seen. Figures in the south tend toward abstraction: Some are filled in with a checkerboard pattern. Northwest of San Borja, paintings tend to be of a more whimsical nature and employ a broader range of colors, including more pinks and yellows.

But who created these paintings, why, and when? Jesuit priests noted them in the 17th century. The priests' indigenous converts, the Cochimí, attributed the paintings to "giants from the north." Today, experts disagree as to the paintings' provenance, but radiocarbon tests from the **Cueva del Ratón** site in the San Francisco range date them at nearly 5,000 years old. (Previous estimates had set the newest paintings at 500 to 2,000 years old.) Scholars agree, however, that newer images are superimposed on older ones, indicating that the authors valued the act of creation more than the artistic result.

Several factors determine the quality of surviving paintings, including the rock surface's durability, location, and exposure to the elements. One of the most magnificent and often visited sites is **Cueva Pintada**, north of San Ignacio in the San Francisco range. Five hundred feet (150 m) of walls and ceilings are covered with paintings of men, women, birds, and sea creatures. How the artist reached the ceiling is not known, but palm trunks or the fibrous skeleton of the cardón cactus may have served as ladders or scaffolding.

UNESCO designated the Sierra de San Francisco and its cave paintings a World Heritage site in 1993, and government and private organizations are collaborating to preserve the sites, involve local communities, and make the art more accessible to visitors.

EXPERIENCE:
Visiting Cave Paintings

In San Ignacio, Baja California Sur, **INAH** (the national government research agency; tel 615/154-0222) will help with paperwork and arrange Spanish-speaking guides and burros to visit cave paintings in remote mountain areas. The office is next door to the mission. In the same town, **Ecoturismo Kuyima** (tel 615/154-0070, www.kuyima. com) leads groups to cave paintings. In Guerrero Negro, at the juncture of Baja California and Baja California Sur, **Malarrimo** (www.malarrimo.com) is also recommended. The best (coolest) time to visit the cave paintings is between November and February.

Depictions of fish, birds, and people cover the walls of Cueva Pintada, Baja California Sur.

La Paz

Despite a fabulous location on the Gulf of California and beautiful nearby beaches, La Paz's character is defined by its busy port and university. Seated at the bottom of a C-shaped bay, this sophisticated capital city is famous for its streaky vermilion sunsets, observed equally well from a solitary, sandy beach on a turquoise inlet or an open-sided restaurant along the bayfront promenade. Nearby are excellent deep-sea fishing and diving.

View of the Sea of Cortez from the *malecón* in La Paz

The Spaniards briefly explored the area in the 16th century, for the most part leaving the cactus-strewn peninsula in peace until the founding of a Jesuit mission in 1720. In a sad irony, the mission was abandoned less than 30 years later, after introduced diseases such as smallpox wiped out almost all of the potential converts. Today a cathedral of the same name, **Nuestra Señora de la Paz,** Our Lady of Peace *(Revolución de 1910 at 5 de Mayo)*, occupies the site of the original mission.

The cathedral faces **Plaza Constitución,** which along with the 3-mile (5 km) seawalk,

the *malecón,* is one of La Paz's favorite meeting spots. Interesting exhibits on the geology, history, and folklore of the region can be found at the **Museo Regional de Antropología e Historia** *(Altamirano at 5 de Mayo, tel 612/122-0162, $)*. Although the exhibits are labeled in Spanish only, the museum's photographs of the area's natural beauty don't require any translation.

Whale-watching trips can be arranged December through March with larger hotels and tour operators in the area.

The best beaches are found to the north of town on the thumb of land that separates La Paz Bay from the Gulf of California. Simple, beachfront restaurants overlook the turquoise bay at **Playa Pichilingue,** near the docks where daily ferries depart for the mainland at Topolobampo and Mazatlán. Lovely **Playa Balandra** has calm water great for

INSIDER TIP:

Numerous outfits offer kayaking trips or dives with hammerhead sharks around Isla Espíritu Santo, but my favorite is Baja Expeditions.

—AMY GUSICK
National Geographic field researcher

swimming or snorkeling (bring your own gear). There are firepits, and primitive camping is allowed. For sustenance, you will have to go a mile or two north to popular El Tecolote beach, which has rest rooms, restaurants, and water-sports equipment for rent.

Boats are available for rental to travel to **Isla Espíritu Santo,** about 5 miles (8 km) offshore. One of the best dive spots at La Paz, the Island of the Holy Spirit offers great visibility almost all year long. Kayakers can explore the coves and inlets off the 14-mile-long (22.5 km) island, and off smaller **La Partida** and **Los Islotes** to the north, both of which have large colonies of sea lions. July through September are the best months to dive with hammerhead sharks and manta rays near **El**

Bajo (Marisla) Seamont, off the north shore of the island.

More isolated beaches such as Punta Coyote and San Evaristo are accessible from La Paz via dirt roads, and **La Ventana** and **Ensenada de los Muertos** can be reached as a day-long excursion south along Highway 286. As you climb into the Sierra de la Laguna you'll pass cactus fields and cattle ranches soon replaced by the rolling hills around **San Juan de los Planes.** Beyond this small agricultural town, dirt and gravel roads lead to excellent fishing, swimming, and boating beaches. ■

La Paz

🗺 55 D1

Visitor Information

✉ Tourist wharf, Paseo Alvaro Obregón, 16 de Septiembre

☎ 612/124-0103

Baja Expeditions

✉ La Paz

☎ 800/843-6967 from U.S.; 800/221-2252 or 612/125-3828 from Mexico

www.bajaex.com

The Pearls

Inspired by tales of fierce, independent women to the west, Spanish conquistador Hernán Cortés led an expedition to the Baja Peninsula, which he presumed to be an island. The Spaniards named it California after an island in Garci Ordóñez de Montalvo's popular Spanish novel *Las Sergas de Esplandian (The Exploits of Esplandian),* published in 1510. During his visit, Cortés is said to have obtained some of the area's precious white, pink, and black pearls from the island of Espíritu Santo. By the time author John Steinbeck published his allegorical novel about the misfortunes of a poor oyster-diving family, *The Pearl,* in 1947, La Paz's oysters were history, finished off by a mysterious blight.

Whales Great & Small

Whether books, movies, television, or actual close encounters have influenced your idea of whales, it's doubtful that these beautiful creatures will leave you indifferent. Orcas, with their large, conical teeth and the misleading moniker "killer whale," command respect. As the largest mammal on record, the blue whale is nearly mythical—it's difficult to imagine an animal that weighs nearly two tons at birth.

A gray whale at San Ignacio Lagoon. The whales migrate to Baja from the northern Bering Sea to mate and give birth; they are generally seen January to early April.

Intelligent and curious, whales are mammals whose ancestors returned to the water millions of years ago, retaining the lungs developed on land but adapting well to aquatic life. Today scientists acknowledge approximately 40 different species. These include baleen whales, which feed on krill (planktonic crustaceans and larvae) and small fish strained through horny plates descending from the upper jaw; and toothed whales, which include orcas, sperm whales, porpoises, and dolphins.

There is no better destination for whale spotting than the Baja California peninsula. Of the ten (some scientists say eleven) surviving baleen whale species, eight are found in the Gulf of California—more than anywhere else on Earth. Visitors may sight the streamlined

INSIDER TIP:

After you see a spout, do not narrow your focus because the next one will be in a different location.

—DON MANKIN
National Geographic author

A diving whale shows off its broad, flat fluke.

finback whale, second in size only to the blue. The humpback is often spotted breaching (hauling its gargantuan body completely out of the water) or slapping the surface with a flipper or scalloped tail. Less often seen are Bryde's, minke, sei, and northern right whales. Bottlenose dolphins bodysurf the translucent waves near the shore, while common dolphins perform astounding acrobatics that make them seem anything but common. Although less gregarious than the humpback, barnacle-encrusted gray whales may approach kayaks or *pangas* (skiffs), allowing thrilled observers the occasional caress.

Gray whales tarry in the protected lagoons of Baja's Pacific coast; prime breeding grounds include **Laguna Ojo de Liebre** (also called Scammon's Lagoon) and **Laguna San Ignacio,** as well as **Bahía Magdalena** (Mag Bay), the latter protected from the open ocean by a 40-mile-long (64 km) barrier island. Each year an estimated 18,000 to 24,000 gray whales migrate south from summer feeding grounds in the northern Bering Sea. Of these, an unknown number complete the marathon migration to give birth or mate in the relatively warm, shallow, and inviting lagoons and estuaries off the Baja Peninsula. The journey—one of the most ambitious undertaken by any mammal—is an astonishing 5,000 miles (8,045 km).

EXPERIENCE: See the Whales

Many reputable tour operators lead excursions of 4 to 14 days; a good number (including some of those listed below) depart from San Diego, California, just across the Mexican border. Cruises focusing on the Pacific coast (where primarily gray whales are spotted) depart San Diego for Scammon's and San Ignacio Lagoons, and may stop at Todos Santos, Cedros Islands, or other locations. Trips to Bahía Magdalena often begin and end in La Paz, Baja California Sur. Land-based excursions charter small planes to camp at San Ignacio or other locations. Passengers board *pangas* to get closer to the marine mammals and their babies. Whale-watching excursions are less common in the species-rich Gulf of California.

Recommended operators include: **Baja Expeditions** *(2625 Garnet Ave., San Diego, CA 92109, tel 858/581-3311 or 800/843-6967);* **Natural Habitat Adventures** *(2945 Center Green Court, Suite H, Boulder, CO 80301, tel 800/543-8917);* and **Searcher Natural History Tours** *(2838 Garrison St., San Diego, CA 92106, tel 619/226-2403),* all of which whale-watch on the Pacific side. Local operators **Ecoturismo Kuyima** *(San Ignacio, BCS, tel 615/154-0070, www.kuyima.com)* and **Malarrimo** *(Guerrero Negro, BC, www.malarrimo.com)* are also recommended.

Los Cabos

Dramatic desert scenery, beautiful beaches, and plenty of action draw visitors to the tip of Baja's narrow peninsula, where the Gulf of California's turquoise waters meet the Pacific Ocean. The deep-sea fishing is world-renowned. Today less than three hours from several major U.S. airports, and also easily accessible from La Paz via the transpeninsular highway (completed in 1974), Cabo has lost its isolation, but not its desert-by-the-sea allure.

Boats stream past Land's End at Cabo San Lucas.

Cabo San Lucas
🔺 55 D1

In the 1940s, John Wayne, Ernest Hemingway, and others came in small private planes to hunt and fish, when Cabo San Lucas consisted of a scattering of humble homes opening onto dusty, nameless streets. By the 1960s, a handful of comfortable, seaside hotels had sprung up among the organ cactuses and spindly ocotillos. Several decades and many millions of investment dollars later, **Cabo San Lucas** has grown up, although not necessarily matured: At night spots like Squid Roe and The Giggling Marlin, the mainly American crowd tends to down lots of tequila shooters and dance on the bar. Warm weather, a relaxed atmosphere, and excellent sports facilities lure all types of travelers to the tip of one of the world's longest peninsulas.

Posh resort hotels and more than half a dozen high-priced golf courses line the 23-mile (37 km) beachfront corridor north of Cabo San Lucas. (To avoid confusion, Cabo San Lucas, San José del Cabo, and the corridor in between have been dubbed "Los Cabos.") Resorts along the corridor have their own beaches and cater to those content to stay put—not a bad idea, since cab rides in this relatively isolated area begin at around $20. With multiple swimming pools, hot tubs, and restaurants, as well as European-style spas and gym facilities, these vacation spots offer a variety of activities to entertain their guests. If you plan to do much exploring beyond your hotel's swim-up bar, you might consider renting a car.

San José del Cabo was established by the Jesuits in the 18th century. Fronting its plain, recently remodeled plaza is San José's simple yet winning church, its whitewashed interior decorated with rather naively drawn gilded accents. Boutiques and restaurants in restored 19th-century houses fan out from the plaza; galleries line Calle Alvaro Obregón and surrounding streets but are often closed (or close early) off-season. While Cabo San Lucas offers proximity to the marina and boisterous nightlife, San José has a more subdued, more Mexican attitude. It also has its own marina: Puerto Los Cabos. Now Mexico's largest private marina, it has a cactus sanctuary as well as housing developments.

Heading south toward San Lucas, **Playas Costa Azul** and Acapulquito are favored by surfers, while just beyond, **Playa Palmilla** (at the Hotel Palmilla) is the closest recommended swimming beach. Go on your own or join an organized tour to **Chileno Bay** or **Santa María Bay,** the two best places to snorkel. Shade umbrellas and snorkel equipment are usually available.

Placid **Playa Médano,** on the bay at Cabo San Lucas, is popular for its unlimited water sports. Waverunners, Jet Skis, catamarans, and banana boats crowd the bay, while those lounging

San José del Cabo

🅐 55 D1

Visitor Information

✉ Plaza San Jose, Local 3, Carr. Transpeninsular s/n

☎ 624/142-3310

Currying Favor with Heavenly Benefactors

Why does Mexico's most popular saint hang upside down? Single women in Mexico pray to St. Anthony of Padua *boca abajo* in the hope that he will produce a suitable mate; if the saint does, the woman turns the image rightside up.

If a woman already has a boyfriend but needs a piece of land, a new truck, or an expensive medical procedure, she also needs a *milagro*. These tiny tin or silver icons of houses, children, and other hearts' desires are pinned to the tunics of saints to petition favors. Those whose prayers are answered may leave an ex-voto, a pictorial acknowledgment of the saint's benevolent intervention.

Among the more unusual manifestations of sainthood in Mexico is Jesús Malverde, patron saint of drug traffickers. Although not recognized by the Vatican, this Robin Hood–style character is thought to have lived in the late 19th and early 20th centuries. His icon is found on the altars of homes of *narcos* in Sinaloa and Jalisco, and in at least one chapel in Mexico City.

The arch at Land's End, seen here from Playa del Amor, is accessible only by boat.

INSIDER TIP:

Playa Los Cerritos is a nice beach north of Los Cabos. Bring a picnic and a surfboard.

—LUZ MARIA MEJIA
National Geographic field researcher

on the sand or in shoulder-to-shoulder beach restaurants enjoy views of **Land's End.** Underneath Cabo's trademark rock arch, **El Arco,** is **Playa del Amor,** a sandy beach accessible by water taxi or inexpensive glass-bottomed boat tour. More secluded beaches can be reached in ATVs or four-wheel-drive vehicles.

The bay's rocky outcrops make for good diving. At a depth of 90 feet (27 m) are the mysterious **sand falls,** a seemingly endless cascade created as the current drags fine sand over an undersea crag and into deeper water. Sportfishing, however, remains Los Cabos' most enduring draw; more marlin and swordfish are caught here than anywhere else in the world. Each October hundreds of serious anglers gather for **Bisbee's Black & Blue Marlin Tournament,** a three-day event with a purse exceeding $1 million. Although the best billfishing (except for marlin) is generally June through September, the fishing is excellent year-round, for wahoo, tuna, dorado, and others.

Increasingly popular with expats, the old mission town of **Todos Santos,** 40 miles (65 km) north of Cabo San Lucas, has a good bookstore and several worthwhile hotels, restaurants, and art galleries. Hikes into the as yet relatively untouched Sierra de la Laguna can be arranged through area hotels or tour operators throughout Los Cabos. ∎

More Places to Visit in Baja California

Bahía de Los Angeles

Surrounded by the stark peaks of the eastern San Pedro Mártir mountains, "L.A. Bay" is a beautiful base for fishing, diving, kayaking, and relaxing up and down the Gulf of California, more often referred to as the Sea of Cortez. Offshore, 45-mile-long (72 km) **Angel de la Guarda** island serves as a barrier for the town's bay, which is subject to 22-foot (7 m) tidal surges. To the south is a string of smaller islands, including **Isla Raza,** a sanctuary for seabirds as well as sportsmen and -women.

Increasingly popular with all sorts of visitors, Bahía de Los Angeles offers accommodations from rustic camping to beach-front **Los Vientos,** with a pool, wonderful restaurant, and Internet access. The town's small museum, on the west side of the plaza, displays peninsular fauna, marine life, and Indian artifacts. Beachfront camping and RV sites abound, including **Guillermo's** at the south end of town.

A bit farther north and down a washboard road, La Gringa beach is an ideal spot for beachcombing or putting in a kayak. It's just a 20-minute paddle from there to **Smith Island,** great for fishing. www.bahiadelosangeles.info 🅐 55 B4

Misión San Francisco Borja

This isolated mission was established by the Jesuits in 1759, farmed by the Franciscans, and completed by the Dominicans. The fine stone church—surrounded by fig, olive, and date orchards—was abandoned in 1818 after disease decimated the local Indian converts. Located 22 miles (35 km) east of Rosarito (not to be confused with the beach resort north of Ensenada), near Guerrero Negro, the active church holds Sunday services. Hire a local to guide you to the area's rock art. Only sturdy vehicles with high clearance should attempt the drive.
🅐 55 B4

Misión San Javier

Considered the loveliest and best preserved of all Baja's missions, San Javier, west of Loreto, was the second to be built on the

---

EXPERIENCE: Be Pro-Nature with Pronatura

Established in 1981, the non-profit Pronatura promotes conservation and sustainable tourism. Regional offices around the nation work with communities and volunteers to prevent climate change and deforestation, protect endangered species, and maintain pollution-free rivers and lakes.

Visit Pronatura regional offices *(www.pronaturane. org)* to find out about hiring local guides or purchasing eco-friendly souvenirs such as shade-grown, fair-trade coffee. Pronatura gratefully accepts donations and occasionally accepts long-term volunteers. But one of the best and most enjoyable ways to show support is by visiting Pronatura's ecotourism projects. For example, at Bahía de los Angeles, Baja California, you can kayak and hike at the **Reserva Natural La Única;** while snorkeling or diving you may meet the whale shark that your visit helps to protect.

Across the Gulf of California at El Palmito in the state of Sinaloa, stay at eco-cabins built within the **Reserva Chara Pinta.** Nature hikes or horseback rides are the thing to do here, as well as bird-watching for species like the tufted jay, the bird for which the nature reserve was named.

peninsula (between 1699 and 1759). This Moorish-style church, located in a deep valley, contrasts with the thatch-roofed adobe huts found in this region of the Sierra de la Giganta. Admire the stained-glass windows, the 18th-century wooden altar covered in gold leaf, and the statue of St. Francis. High-clearance vehicles can make the rocky, three-hour drive from Loreto in dry weather, but a four-wheel-drive vehicle is best. Hire a guide in Loreto or the town of San Javier to lead you to rock paintings in the region. The town swells with pilgrims around its feast day, December 3, and celebrates the onion harvest, one of its most important crops, August 15.

▲ 55 C2

Parque Nacional Sierra San Pedro Mártir

The granite peaks, high meadows, and fragrant forests of this 49,000-acre (20,000 ha) national park are little visited. Fishing, camping, and hiking are permitted. Experienced climbers tackle Picacho del Diablo (Devil's Summit)—the peninsula's highest peak, at 10,154 feet (3,100 m) above sea level. If you prefer to photograph rather than scale the rocky mountain, don't miss the terrific view of the peak from the National Autonomous University of Mexico's observatory on a packed granite road. Hikers should take adequate water and supplies, as well as a map and compass; the national park has no facilities and few rangers.

▲ 55 B4/B5 ✉ Entrance 47 miles (75 km) off Hwy. 1 on paved road. Ranger station at Corona de Abajo 💲 $

San Felipe

Until 1951, San Felipe was a sleepy fishing village on the northwestern shore of the Gulf of California, but this resort town of more than 25,000 now counts tourism as its main source of revenue. It is also the shrimp capital of Baja California. Hugging the northern shore of a wide, relatively shallow

natural bay, the relaxed desert town squats in the shadow of Punta San Felipe, a twin-peaked headland nearly 1,000 feet (305 m) high. With less than 2 inches (5 cm) of rain a year, vegetation is scant, and in summer temperatures may soar to 115°F (46°C). In the winter, U.S. and Canadian snowbirds fill area RV parks and cruise the beach on ATVs.

South of town, shrimp boats depart from the marina that also accommodates private craft. Fresh seafood—including a giant *campechana,* a cocktail of shrimp, clams, and octopus—is the main draw of the many casual restaurants along the *malecón,* or seawalk. Extreme tidal fluxes here send beachcombers searching for shells along 12 miles (19 km) of wide, grainy sand beaches south of town, many nearly deserted.

www.sanfelipe.com.mx ▲ 55 A5 ✉ Calle Manzanillo 300 at Av. Mar de Cortés ☎ 686/577-1155

Tecate

Set in a bowl-shaped valley at 1,690 feet (515 m), Tecate has none of the raucous flavor of most border towns. It thrives on light industry and agriculture, with outlying fields of grain, olives, and grapes. Visitors can tour the **Tecate Brewery** (*Av. Dr. Arturo Guerra 70, tel 665/654-9490*). It's free, with a five-person minimum. Arrive at 10 a.m. weekdays or 11 a.m. Saturday to inquire about the day's tours, or call ahead. **Railway tours** (*www.sdrm.org, $$$$*) are a good way to see the countryside. They run between Campos, California (in the U.S.), and Tecate. An hour each way, the trip goes through open country and ranchlands. The 1930s train is from the original San Diego & Arizona Railway. In Tecate visitors have free time plus a brewery visit if desired. Reservations are required. Highway 3 between Tecate and Ensenada winds through the rolling hills of the Guadalupe Valley, famous for its wineries.

▲ 55 A5 ✉ Calle Lázaro Cárdenas 83, centro ☎ 665/654-5892

Huge tracts of high and low desert, more than 1,000 miles (1,600 km) of coast, and the world's largest volcanic field

Northwest Mexico

Barrel cactus

Northwest Mexico

Harsh yet imposing, Mexico's vast northwest comprises the states of Sonora, Chihuahua, Durango, and Sinaloa. Seldom visited by tourists, it offers 10,000-foot (3,050 m) peaks clothed in pine-oak forests, North America's first and third largest deserts, and a 1,300-mile (2,090 km) coast. Explorers head for Sierra Tarahumara's extensive system of canyons, where it's easy to organize hiking, horseback riding, or vehicular tours to spectacular waterfalls and lost Jesuit missions.

Roughly following the Gulf of California, the formidable Sierra Madre Occidental runs northwest to southeast. The range's steeper, more dramatic eastern escarpment drops down to Chihuahua's high desert, while to the west, valleys, canyons, and peaks finally give way to the foothills and then the coast. A dozen major rivers drain into the narrow, fertile coastal plain, creating land that is prime for farming.

In the 16th century, European and *criollo* (Mexican-born Spanish) explorers, adventurers, and Jesuit friars began to infiltrate the harsh northern areas. Along with the elements, they faced the Chichimeca, fierce northern tribes, most of whom even the Aztec could not conquer. Over the centuries, vast numbers of indigenous peoples, and even entire tribes, succumbed to disease, slavery, deportation, and capital punishment, although sporadic rebellions and wars lasted until the 20th century.

Despite this resistance, the Jesuits founded dozens of mission villages before their expulsion in 1767, while entrepreneurs established incredible mining empires along the western flanks of the Sierra Madre Occidental. Vast ranches supplied the mines, missions, and *presidios* (military posts) with beef, creating immense individual fortunes in the process. Today, ranching is still important, as are forestry, farming, and fishing.

Great distances between sights and a limited tourist infrastructure notwithstanding, the northwest offers an awesome variety of scenery and experiences. Explore the ruins of Oasis America culture at Paquimé or the surreal moonscapes of silent, solitary Pinacate, with its impossibly wide craters, underground lava tubes, black cinder cones, and shifting sand dunes. Access and services for the Sierra Tarahumara (Copper Canyon) and Sonora's low-key

NOT TO BE MISSED:

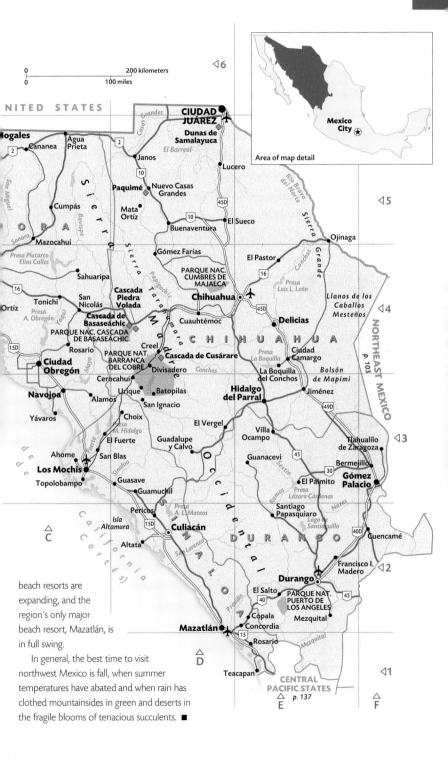

0   200 kilometers
0   100 miles

Area of map detail

Mexico City

NITED STATES

Nogales
Cananea
Agua Prieta
2

CIUDAD JUÁREZ
Dunas de Samalayuca
El Barreal
Janos
10
Lucero

Paquimé
Nuevo Casas Grandes
45D
Cumpás
Mata Ortíz
Buenaventura
El Sueco
10

Mazocahui
Gómez Farías
El Pastor
Ojinaga

Presa Plutarco Elías Calles
16
Presa Luis L. León

Sahuaripa
PARQUE NAC. CUMBRES DE MAJALCA
16

Llanos de los Caballos Mesteños

Tonichi
San Nicolás
Cascada Piedra Volada
Chihuahua
45D
Delicias

Ortíz
Presa A. Obregón
Cascada de Basaseáchic
Cuauhtémoc
CHIHUAHUA

Rosario
PARQUE NAC. CASCADA DE BASASEÁCHIC
Creel
Cascada de Cusárare
Presa La Boquilla
Ciudad Camargo

Ciudad Obregón
PARQUE NAT. BARRANCA DEL COBRE
Divisadero
La Boquilla del Conchos
Bolsón de Mapimí

Cerocahui
Conchos
Navojoa
Urique
Batopilas
Hidalgo del Parral
Jiménez

Alamos
San Ignacio
49D

Yávaros
Choix
El Vergel
Villa Ocampo
Tlahualilo de Zaragoza

El Fuerte
Guadalupe y Calvo
45

Ahome
San Blas
Guanacevi
Bermejillo
30
Gómez Palacio

Los Mochis
Guasave
El Palmito

Topolobampo
Guamuchil
Santiago Papasquiaro
Lago de Santiaguillo
40D
Cuencamé

Isla Altamura
Pericos
15D
DURANGO

Culiacán
Francisco I. Madero

Altata
Presa A. L. Mateos
Durango
45

El Salto
PARQUE NAT. PUERTO DE LOS ANGELES
40
Copala
Mezquital
Concordia

Mazatlán
15
Rosario

Teacapan
CENTRAL PACIFIC STATES
p. 137

NORTHEAST MEXICO
p. 103

beach resorts are expanding, and the region's only major beach resort, Mazatlán, is in full swing.

In general, the best time to visit northwest Mexico is fall, when summer temperatures have abated and when rain has clothed mountainsides in green and deserts in the fragile blooms of tenacious succulents. ∎

El Pinacate

Lunar-like and otherworldly, the landscape of El Pinacate is as beautiful as it is barren. Huge, craggy craters rise in startling contrast to the flatness of the surrounding desert, and in the western portion of the 1.8-million-acre (728,460 ha) park, winds build shifting dunes hundreds of feet high. Geologists and photographers are especially drawn to the rich textures and striking hues of this arid region.

Cerro Colorado is one of the many craters that rise above the Gran Desierto de Altar.

Reserva de la Biósfera Sierra de Pinacate

🗺 76 A6

Visitor Information

✉ Hwy. 8 Km 51

☎ 638/384-9007 (in Puerto Peñasco)

Designated a UNESCO Man and the Biosphere Reserve in 1993, this unique ecosystem in the Gran Desierto de Altar (Mexico's Sonora Desert) has the largest concentration of volcanic cones and craters on Earth. Volcanic activity that began three or four million years ago created miles of jagged lava beds so unforgiving that colonial-era wayfarers called it the Sea of Broken Glass.

More than 400 cinder cones (conical mounds formed around a volcanic vent) jut in dramatic waves along the desert floor within a 30-mile-wide (48 km) field. The tallest are raven-colored **Cerro del Pinacate** and **Cerro del Carnegie,** at 4,000 (1,219 m) and 3,700 feet (1,128 m) respectively.

Huge maars, or craters, were probably created when bubbling magma hit groundwater, initiating explosions of steam and blasting rock and lava into the air.

One of the most spectacular examples of these black behemoths is **Cráter Elegante,** about 16 miles (27 km) north of the main (east) park entrance. Rising 165 feet (50 m) from the desert floor, the crater's uneven walls are the product of prevailing winds at the time of eruption. Peering over the edge of the mile-wide (1.5 km), 800-foot-deep (245 m) crater inspires nothing short of awe. In addition to the park's ten maars, underground lava tubes and other extraordinary formations provide unlimited opportunities for exploration.

Despite its bleak and desolate first impression, the reserve sustains a variety of plants and animals. Endangered desert bighorn sheep, Sonoran pronghorn

evening primroses, yellow desert marigolds, and colorful skeleton weeds to bloom.

Visitors must register at the park's main entrance, 32 miles (51 km) south of the Lukeville, Arizona/Sonoyta border crossing, on Highway 8. There are no facilities at the park; bring your own water and food, and take away all trash. The best time to visit is spring, when temperatures are least extreme and wildflowers most abundant. From late April to September, daytime temperatures may soar to 120°F (49°C); nighttime temperatures in winter can dip below freezing. Sunscreen, sunglasses, water, and a hat are essential. A high-clearance vehicle is advised; four-wheel drive is recommended but not required.

Of the park's two basic campgrounds, **El Tecolote,** 5 miles

Cactuses

There are about 1,650 species of cactus worldwide, but Mexico has more species and more specimens than any other country. The Sonora, driest and hottest of North America's four deserts, has the greatest diversity of species. Adaptations such as a lack of leaves, shallow wide-ranging roots, and the ability to store water for more than a year allow cactuses to thrive in the uncompromising desert.

Historically, cactuses have provided food, water, building materials, and inspiration for the desert's hardy inhabitants. The Huichol and other indigenous peoples employ the hallucinogenic *peyote* cactus to commune with the divine, seek visions, and heal disease. Prickly pear, saguaro, and organ cactuses provide sweet fruits. Barrel cactuses are a source of water, while other species are burned as fuel or used as living fences.

antelope, and desert tortoises share the unforgiving desert with the park's namesake, the endemic pinacate beetle. Roadrunners and rattlers are abundant, and more than 550 plant species have been identified. In spring, brief rains encourage white dune

(8 km) northeast of Elegante, has the best access to hiking trails and the craters. **Cono Rojo,** 14 miles (22 km) northwest of the information center, is a better bet for hiking up to the volcanic peaks. Backcountry camping is permitted with a few restrictions. ∎

Sonora's Beaches

Backed by cliffs ranging from rust to red to gold, the simple fishing villages and unpretentious towns from Puerto Peñasco to Guaymas have long provided fresh seafood and a relaxing atmosphere. Time-shares, hotels, condos, and private residences are popping up fast, as are restaurants and services geared mainly toward U.S. and Canadian visitors. Spring and fall see fewer tourists and more competitive prices than in the peak winter months.

Puerto Peñasco
🄰 76 A5
Visitor Information
✉ Blvd. Juárez 320 at V. Estrella
☎ 638/383-6122 or 800/476-6672 (from the U.S.)
www.gotosonora.com

Puerto Peñasco

Just 60 miles (97 km) from the border at Lukeville, Arizona, Puerto Peñasco is the first seaside town on Sonora's 600-mile (965 km) coastline. Sandy beaches, rocky coves, and extreme tidal variation attract shell collectors and lovers of long walks. The town was established in the 1920s as a shrimp camp, but long before that British explorers had named the place Rocky Point, a designation still used by most English speakers today. Overfishing in recent years has significantly reduced the shrimp harvest, once the mainstay of the economy. Now, tourism and foreign-owned real estate are the most important industries. Building is booming, and there are two full-service marinas with shops, restaurants, hotels, and condos.

Bahía Kino

South of Puerto Peñasco is Bahía Kino, named for Padre Chini (1645–1711), the Italian-born Jesuit priest and adventurer known as Padre Kino. **Kino Viejo,** a simple fishing village, hugs the bay with its fine, sandy beaches, while to the north **Kino Nuevo** is an enclave of Canadian and U.S. vacationers and retirees. Once dominated by RV parks, the 8-mile (13 km) beachfront road that constitutes the town has an increasing number of condos, time-shares, hotels, and private residences. The **Museo de los Seris** (*Blvd. Mar de Cortés at Progreso, closed Mon., $*) highlights the Seri culture (see pp. 84–85). The Seri themselves come to town to sell grass baskets, pottery, ironwood statuettes, and necklaces of seashells, seeds, and animal bones. Across the channel from Bahía Kino are **Isla Tiburón** (see p. 85) and

Sandy beaches and lush verdure at Bahía Kino

EXPERIENCE:
Explore Ocean & Desert Ecosystems

Northern Mexico is vast, and infrastructure outside tourist towns like Puerto Peñasco is limited. Based in Tucson, Arizona, **CEDO** (the Intercultural Center for the Study of Deserts and Oceans; tel 520/320-5473, www.cedointercultural.org) makes it easy to explore the area's unique, fragile ecosystems by offering fun and educational outdoor excursions throughout Sonora state. Join scheduled events or form your own group to visit the Pinacate lava flows, amazing sand dunes ecosystems, or tide pools. Kayak through estuaries or take a boat trip to an offshore island. Take a hands-on tour at a local oyster farm (including cooking and eating the mollusks) and learn about ecologically correct area restaurants that support sustainable tourism. Offerings range from a walk through CEDO's on-site botanical gardens ($$$$) to full-day expeditions to Gran Desierto del Altar (part of the Sonoran Desert). There's summer camp, too, for the kids.

tiny **Isla San Esteban,** which have been protected as an ecological reserve since 1963.

Bahía San Carlos

The carmine-colored peaks of the **Sierra de Bacochibampo** —including the town's symbol, craggy Tetakawi, or "goat teat hill"—form a magnificent backdrop for **Bahía San Carlos,** one of northern Mexico's fastest-growing tourist destinations. Spindly ocotillo cactuses with spidery red blooms brighten the surrounding desert in the fall, while snorkelers seek out colorful fish among the rocky outcroppings separating Bahía San Carlos and **Bahía Bacochibampo.** Divers are drawn to the 5,000-foot-deep (1,500 m) **Guaymas Trench,** which attracts an estimated 700 species of marine life. Half- and full-day fishing boat trips go after yellowtail, sailfish, marlin, and grouper; closer to shore, anglers catch triggerfish and sea bass. The well-protected bay has two full-service marinas, an 18-hole golf course, and tennis courts at the country club. A few major resorts line **Playa los Algodones,** on the west end of San Carlos, offering kayaking, jet skiing, and windboarding.

Guaymas & Miramar

A mountainous peninsula separates San Carlos from more commercial **Guaymas,** about 10 miles (16 km) to the southeast. Bolstered by a significant canning industry and a PEMEX oil refinery, Guaymas is Sonora's main port. Vermilion peaks crouch above its fine natural harbor, crowded with vessels of all shapes and sizes, including oil tankers and shrimp boats. For a tour of a working pearl farm, visit **Perlas del Mar de Cortés** (tel 622/221-0136, www.perlas.com.mx) on the campus of the "Tec" (Monterrey Technical University).

Nearby, **Playa Miramar** beach attracts local families on weekends, and around the pleasant plaza are several attractive 19th-century churches. Travelers who choose Guaymas over neighboring San Carlos prefer a more Mexican, less touristy enclave. ∎

Bahía San Carlos
- 76 B4

Visitor Information
- Blvd. Escénico Km. 9.2
- 622/226-0202
- www.gotosancarlos .com

Guaymas
- 77 B4

Visitor Information
- Malecón Malpica, bet. Calles 22 & 23

Paquimé

Paquimé, the most important archaeological site in northern Mexico, was built by the Oasis America cultural group, who lived in an area extending from northwest Chihuahua and northeast Sonora to the southwestern United States. Its inhabitants lived in rammed-earth, multiple-story houses. Unlike ancient Pueblo villages, however, Paquimé had fixed, interior stairways and an elaborate system of water collection, filtration, distribution, and disposal.

The massive sun-washed plazas and ruined walls of Paquimé

Inhabited since about A.D. 700, this historic site overlooking the Casas Grandes River began to blossom some time after 1150, reaching its apogee between 1300 and 1450 before being abandoned. Some anthropologists think it was abandoned earlier, possibly after attacks by Apache from the north. Five-foot-thick (1.5 m) walls provided insulation from the desert's intense heat and bitter cold.

Aspects of Paquimé's culture show the influence of central Mexico, such as organization of artisans by neighborhood, veneration of the god Quetzalcoatl (Feathered Serpent), and use of ceremonial plazas and I-shaped ball courts.

Today, for the most part, only the first-floor exterior walls and myriad room dividers survive. "We have to restore the crumbling walls at least twice a year," explained Paquimé's former director, archaeologist Mercedes Jiménez. "Sun, wind, snow . . . everything harms these very fragile structures." The *montículos*, or temple mounds, can still be visited. **Montículo del Pájaro, Montículo de las Ofrendas,** and **Montículo de los Héroes** are named for birds, offerings, and heroes. **Montículo de la Cruz** is a cross-shaped, raised adobe structure roughly oriented toward the four cardinal points and surrounded by four circular platforms. It was most likely used in agricultural or celestial rituals.

To the south, vestiges of a second floor can be seen at the **Casa del Pozo,** along with partially reconstructed flooring, wooden columns, and beams. A stairway leads up to a section of the stone aqueduct that carried water throughout the city. It

human bones found here), more than 90 grave sites were found beneath the **Casa de los Muertos** (House of the Dead). Birds—probably macaws imported from the south—were kept in adobe cages in the adjacent structure, and in the **Casa de la Serpiente;** their feathers were used in ceremonies.

South of the Casa de los Muertos is the **Casa de los Pilares—**originally four to five stories high and today one of the few buildings with walls more than one story tall. To the west, the **Montículo de la Serpiente** is thought to have been dedicated to Quetzalcóatl, revered in central Mexico since the days of Tula (see p. 231).

The **Museo de las Culturas del Norte** *(tel 636/692-4140, closed Mon.)* highlights the Oasis America culture in general and Paquimé in particular. Examples of the city's

Paquimé
🅰 77 D5
Visitor Information
✉ 0.5 mile (1 km) outside Nuevo Casas Grandes
☎ 636/692-4140
💲 $$

Mata Ortíz Pottery

Pottery produced in the small village of Juan Mata Ortíz, 12.5 miles (20 km) south of Casas Grandes, is exquisite with extremely thin walls and a soft, bright luster. The techniques originated with Juan Quezada. He spent 15 years experimenting with clay, pigments, and firing techniques before producing his first pots. In 1976, Spencer MacCallum found a few of these unsigned pots in a secondhand shop in New Mexico and traced Quezada to his village. A quarter century later, about half of the town's population makes this internationally collected pottery without the use of a potter's wheel or kiln. While they use Quezada's techniques, many artisans have their own motifs and designs.

is not possible to wander the rooms of most of the former dwellings. However, they can still be appreciated from the outside. (The multimedia exhibit in the museum gives a 360-degree, virtual tour.)

Beyond the **Casa de los Cráneos** (named for the skulls and

pottery are displayed, as are a scale model of the site and artifacts from the mission church built near Casas Grandes in 1660.

Most people visit Paquimé from Nuevo Casas Grandes, 3 miles (5 km) north. This small agricultural town has a few comfortable, if simple, hotels and restaurants. ∎

The Seri

Historically, the pantheistic Seri revered the sun and the moon as well the marine turtle, the pelican, and other divine manifestations. However, their lack of totems and monuments led icon-bearing Jesuit priests to consider them godless. The Seri were one of the last indigenous cultures in North America to integrate into European-derived culture and to accept Christianity.

Burning bark off sticks used in the traditional practice of basketweaving

The Seri paid a high price for their resistance to mission life and Spanish rule. In 1662, a violent rebellion by a band of Seri was quelled only when every last man and woman had been slain and their children whisked off to the mission. Hanged as cattle rustlers, deported, and decimated by introduced disease, the Seri numbered a mere 150 by the early 20th century. Today, roughly 800 individuals speak the native language; most of them live in the towns of Punta Chueca and El Desemboque, located north of Bahía Kino on Sonora's Gulf of California coastline.

Autonomous and proud, the Seri roamed the stark deserts, plains, coasts, and offshore islands long before the arrival of the Spaniards. Surviving with the ebb and flow of the seasons, they foraged for food in the Desierto de Altar and fished for shellfish. Their annual marine turtle harvest provided not only a source of food but also a ceremonial link with traditional culture.

A long history of storytelling in narrative song is an important part of the Seri heritage; this lyrical recital is passed from generation to generation. Songs are sung in praise of animals that provide food or to protect their people from natural phenomena, including navigating the sometimes treacherous passage to Isla Tiburón. Deprived of their traditional turtle harvest since 1991, when a government ban on hunting turtles and collecting their eggs was put in effect, the Seri struggle to maintain their cultural identity.

Despite pressure to acculturate, the Comcaac, as the Seri call themselves, continue to sing their songs. They support themselves by fishing and by the sale of handicrafts, particularly shell jewelry and carved ironwood statues of lizards, dolphins, and other animals. Working with the Arizona-Sonora Desert Museum in Tucson and a government agency protecting the Gulf of California, the Seri have extensively catalogued natural food and herbs used traditionally as both food and medicine to solve modern ecological problems with ancestral knowledge.

Isla Tiburón

Isla Tiburón (Shark Island), ancestral homeland to the Seri, once provided refuge
from Spanish military expeditions and
aggressive cattle ranchers. Mexico's largest
island has been protected as an ecological
reserve since 1963, but it's owned by the
Seri themselves, who also have exclusive
fishing rights to el Canal del Infernillo,
between the island and mainland. Knowledgeable Seri guides accompany visitors
to the biologically diverse island to camp,
hike, kayak, and snorkel.

Bighorn sheep, threatened by widespread
poaching on the mainland, now freely roam
the island's two mountain ranges. Peregrine
falcons, owls, and frigate birds patrol the skies.
Blue-footed boobies show off their powder
blue appendages along lovely, secluded sandy
beaches, and red, black, and white mangroves
shelter a wide variety of marine fauna. There is
good anchorage in the south at Kun Kaak Bay.

It's often difficult to contact the Gobierno
de la Comunidad Seri by cell phone *(tel
662/279-2535 or 662/115-3776)*. Instead
arrange your trip in Punta Chueca.

A stingray is caught in the waters near Punta Chueca.

Chihuahua

Born of a silver mine, bathed in the blazing light of Mexico's huge northern desert, and surrounded by mountains rich in resources, Chihuahua was destined for success. Although today industry and cattle ranching have replaced mining as the mainstays of the economy, the city continues to prosper. Elegant colonial buildings, precocious Victorian mansions, and self-confident modern sculptures make Chihuahua a city to be admired.

Ornate facade and copper-tile roof of the cultural center at Quinta Gameros

Known as the Cradle of the Revolution, Chihuahua looms large in Mexican history. Independence hero Miguel Hidalgo y Costilla and three of his lieutenants were executed here in 1811. At different times during the French Intervention and the Second Empire (see p. 31) the city served as Benito Juárez's provisional capital. And Pancho Villa—once governor of Chihuahua—based his División del Norte (Northern Division) army here for a number of years during the Mexican Revolution. Today it is the capital of Mexico's largest state.

Although the city's outer limits sprawl, the historic district is attractive and diverse. Remains of an 18th-century aqueduct give portions of the city an old European air. Well-tended gardens surround the wrought-iron bandstand, imported from Paris in 1893, at **Plaza de Armas,** the city's principal square.

At one end of the plaza stands the Churrigueresque **Catedral**

Metropolitana *(Libertad at Independencia),* dedicated to St. Francis of Assisi. Indian raids and the expulsion of the Jesuits—who began construction in 1735—delayed the cathedral's completion for nearly a hundred years. Its facade, adorned with statues of the 12 Apostles, is topped by two slender, ocher-colored towers. Inside, note the Venetian chandeliers and the monumental German organ. The late 18th-century main altar of carved limestone is almost obscured by a neoclassical altar of Carrara marble. In the back of the church, the **Museo de Arte Sacro** *(closed Sat.–Sun., $)* has 17th- and 18th-century religious objects and paintings.

The revolutionary history of Chihuahua figures largely in its museums. North of the main square within the former federal building, **Casa Chihuahua** *(Calle Libertad bet. Guerrero & Carranza, tel 614/410-4888, closed Tues., $$)* has exhibits about local cultures and ecosystems. On the first floor is the cell where independence hero Miguel Hidalgo was imprisoned. Across the street, see where Hidalgo was shot by firing squad in the patio of the **Palacio de Gobierno** *(Plaza Hidalgo, Aldama at Guerrero, tel 614/429-3596),* now surrounded by murals depicting the region's history.

The revolution and the role of Chihuahua's adoptive son, General Francisco "Pancho" Villa, are detailed at the **Museo de la Revolución Mexicana** *(Calle 10a 3010 at Méndez, tel 614/416-2958, closed Mon., $).* The museum is located within

Quinta Luz, a mansion named for Villa's legal wife, Luz Corral de Villa. The stately house has original furnishings, as well as photos, documents, firearms, and the black Dodge that Villa was driving when he was assassinated in 1923. A few blocks north, **Quinta Gameros** *(Paseo Bolívar 401 at Calle 4, tel 614/416-6684, closed Mon., $)* is a wonderfully restored, two-story mansion with a so-so collection of paintings and some elegant art nouveau furnishings. You can see these and other downtown sights

INSIDER TIP:

From Chihuahua City, a cheap bus ride takes you to the historic mining town of Santa Eulalia, where a rock shop sells quartz and other local mineral specimens.

—MARAEL JOHNSON
National Geographic author

on a one-hour **guided bus tour** *(each hour 9–12 & 3–5, closed Mon., $).* The double-decker bus departs from Calles Aldama and Guerrero at the main plaza.

On Sundays, Chihuahuans like to visit the **Museo de Arte Contemporánea Casa Redonda** *(Av. Colón at Escudero, Col. Santo Niño, tel 614/414-9061, closed Mon., $).* Or they might admire the restored buildings of historic **Santa Eulalia,** 15 miles (9 km) southeast of town, or wonder at the beauty of **Las Grutas Nombre de Dios,** a system of caves en route to the airport. ∎

Chihuahua
▲ 77 E4
Visitor Information
✉ Palacio de Gobierno, Plaza Hidalgo, Aldama at Guerrero
☎ 614/429-3596 or 01800/508-0111 (toll-free within Mexico)
www.chihuahua.gob .mx/turismoweb

Sierra Tarahumara (Copper Canyon)

The dramatic series of canyons collectively known as the Copper Canyon (or more accurately, la Sierra Tarahumara) are immense and impressive. Of the six major canyons composing Las Barrancas del Cobre system, four are deeper than the Grand Canyon in Arizona. In addition to their natural beauty, the gorges are dotted with Jesuit missions, abandoned mines, early 20th-century mansions, and indigenous cave dwellings.

Dwarfed by Sierra Madre peaks, a train trundles across one of the Copper Canyon's 37 major bridges.

La Sierra Tarahumara

During 10 million to 15 million years of the Tertiary era, volcanic activity and shifting tectonic plates created this mountain range, with peaks up to 12,000 feet (3,650 m). Working on surface fissures, time plus rain and underwater currents carved out the series of deep canyons known collectively as Las Barrancas del Cobre. The hard igneous strata resist erosion, causing dramatic rock formations. Among the six main canyons of the Sierra Tarahumara, depth varies from 4,986 feet (1,520 m) at **Barranca Oteros** to 6,135 feet (1,870 m) at **Barranca Urique. Barranca Sinforosa** has the highest elevation, at 8,293 feet (2,528 m); **Chínipas,** at 6,555 feet (1,998 m), is lowest.

Missionaries and miners were the first non-Indians to settle in the pine-scented mountains and deep, scrubby gorges of the Sierra Tarahumara, part of the Sierra Madre Occidental west of Chihuahua. In the 17th and 18th centuries, the Jesuits established simple yet beautiful churches throughout this canyon country—despite drawn-out and widespread local resistance.

EXPERIENCE: Riding in the Canyon

Copper Canyon is one of the last really wild places in Mexico that's suited for both cultural and adventure tourism. A descent into some of North America's deepest gorges is not for the faint of heart, but you can count on a safe, comfortable ride on one of **Rancho del Oso**'s horses (*www.mexicohorse.com*), outside the colonial village of Cerocahui.

A horseback ride to Batopilas (see p. 94) is typically oneway and includes two days at Rancho del Oso to acquaint riders with horse, saddle, and mountain riding. Then it's usually four 3- to 7-hour days in the saddle to Batopilas, with a day more there for touring. All treks are accompanied by a bilingual guide. Out of Creel, **Noriberto Padillo** *(tel 656/456-0557, www.ridemexico.com)*, a professional cowboy, leads canyon tours. **EcoTravel** *(tel 614/179-0392, www.ecotravel-mexico. com)* and **Conexión a la Aventura** *(tel 614/413-7929, www.conexionalaaventura .com)* are two recommended horse tour outfitters in Chihuahua City. October through March is the best time for deep canyon rides. Rain is unlikely; days are usually sunny, and nights around the campfire cool. Trips during the Easter season provide unique opportunities to see the synergistic rituals of the Tarahumara Indians.

INSIDER TIP:

The Tarahumara Indians believe men have three souls and women four, and that, dying, they become nighttime stars.

−CYNTHIA GORNEY
National Geographic *magazine writer*

At the same time, a wealth of copper gave the Copper Canyon (part of Urique Canyon) and the region its name, and large deposits of gold and silver were discovered in Batopilas.

Forced to labor in the Spaniards' mines and toil on railroads built by Americans and Mexicans, the Indians later lost access to much of their traditionally held lands. Only 10 of the 50 indigenous groups living in the Sierra Tarahumara and Chihuahua Desert in the 1600s survive today.

The stalwart Tarahumara (who call themselves Rarámuri, or people who run) number 50,000 to 60,000. Living on a simple diet of corn and beans, they are as rugged as the mountains in which they live. They can run vast distances carrying heavy loads, and team races organized as social events last days.

Some Rarámuri women dress in a melee of flowered and polka-dotted clothing, with long, flowing skirts, ruffled blouses, and head scarves of contrasting prints. Near tourist areas, they sell sweet-smelling pine baskets, homemade dolls, and simple pottery. Most of the Rarámuri men have traded the traditional white cotton breechcloths *(tagoras)* and blousey shirts for more Western-style clothing.

Some Rarámuri follow traditional migratory patterns, living in caves, along cliffs, or in houses of wood and stone near the

100 feet (30 m) above sea level. Corn is the staple crop, though fruits are also grown.

Chihuahua al Pacífico Railway

Visitors first gained access to this breathtaking canyon world in 1961 with the completion of the Chihuahua al Pacífico Railway. Connecting Chihuahua with Los Mochis on Sinaloa's coast, the narrow-gauge, 415-mile (670 km) line passes 87 tunnels. Of its 37 major bridges, the longest stretches nearly a third of a mile (0.5 km) over a dizzying gorge. To pass the best canyon scenery during daylight hours, travel from west to east.

canyon's rim in summer months, when temperatures at the canyon bottom may reach 113°F (45°C). The rest of the year, they move to caves or small wooden houses within the canyon. Crops are generally raised

Sixty miles (96 km) into the journey, the train begins an

A Tarahumara woman weaves a pine-needle basket.

0   60 kilometers
0   30miles

—— Railroad

Los Mochis

⬛ 77 C3

Visitor Information

✉ Palacio de
Gobierno,
Degollado &
Cuauhtémoc

☎ 668/816-4000
Train Station:
668/824-1167

Chihuahua Train Station

✉ Méndez at Calle
24

☎ 614/439-7210
or 01800/122-
4373 (toll-free
within Mexico)

www.chepe.com.mx

impressive ascent, climbing more than 7,500 feet (2,286 m) in just over 150 miles (241 km). Along the way, and at the all-too-brief station stops, you'll be rewarded with magnificent canyon views. East of Creel, the canyons give way to alpine mountains and high valleys backed by tremendous peaks. The train begins a gradual descent through fertile farmland and high meadows down to the city of Chihuahua.

To get the most out of your rail adventure, spend one or more nights along the train route. The cost of the journey, *(SS, first-class, one way),* allows three stops, which must be scheduled when you buy the ticket. Creel has the most hotels, restaurants, and services and is the most convenient departure point for trips into the canyons. Divisadero has excellent canyon views and several comfortable hotels. At the floor of its eponymous canyon, Batopilas is a long journey from Creel but, once reached, is another good departure point for canyon exploration.

West to East

If you start your tour in the west, consider bypassing Los Mochis and spending a day in charming **El Fuerte,** 50 miles

(80 km) to the east, built as a fort and later used as a major trading post for gold and silver miners. The town still functions as a commercial center for the surrounding farms and ranches. Like nearby Alamos, El Fuerte is an engaging town with cobblestone streets and 18th- and

Sangre de Cristo gold mines (1.8 miles/3 km) and **Wicochic Falls** (2 miles/3.25 km), or go on a two- to three-day trek to Batopilas (see p. 94).

Twenty-four miles (38 km) south of Cerocahui, Urique affords excellent views of its namesake canyon and refresh-

The Case of the Disappearing Burro

Sure-footed and stoic, the burro (small donkey) doesn't deserve its bad rap. In Mexico the word "burro" also means "idiot," "a losing horse," or "a drudge." In English, the burro's ancestor, the ass, is also a stupid, stubborn, or perverse person. Despite the negative anthropomorphisms, *campesinos* from Baja to the Yucatán have traditionally depended on donkeys to carry themselves and their loads.

Especially useful in rocky, steep terrain, donkeys can carry more weight per pound than horses and survive with less water. They also eat thorny brush, making them well suited to desert and mountain environments. Unfortunately for fans of this stalwart beast, Mexican burros are in short supply today. Four out of five Mexicans queried will jokingly place them on the endangered species list.

19th-century mansions near its center. Visit the 1854 **Iglesia del Sagrado Corazón de Jesús**, the **Palacio Municipal**, and the **Casa de la Cultura**, all on or around the main square, **Plaza de Armas** *(Degollado at Rosales).* The area's lakes are well known for their plentiful largemouth bass.

Lovely **Cerocahui** is tucked in a deep gorge at 5,000 feet (1,525 m) and surrounded by apple orchards (about 10 miles/16 km south of Bahuichivo station). The gateway to the Urique Canyon, this small mountain town was founded by Jesuit priests in 1680. Here, as throughout the sierra, the Tarahumara dance traditional *matachines* during Easter week and other holy days. Rent a horse or go on foot to visit the

INSIDER TIP:

In the language of the Tarahumara Indians, the word for anyone not a Tarahumara translates as "person with spiderwebbing across the face."

—CYNTHIA GORNEY
National Geographic *magazine writer*

ing walks along the river. The abandoned mine of **Chiflón,** a 20-minute walk away, is a good place to swim. It's best to hire a local guide when exploring within the canyon.

There are breathtaking views of Urique Canyon from **Divisadero,** where many people choose to spend the night in one of several hotels. There is no actual town, so each hotel provides meals. You can usually arrange a guided tour or horseback riding with a fellow stationed outside **Hotel Divisadero Barrancas.** More magnificent canyon views are seen on a horseback ride to **Wacajipare,** a Tarahumara village about 2.5 miles (4 km) into the gorge.

The train continues to **Creel,** about 36 miles (58 km) from Divisadero and definitely worth a visit. Thirty years ago, there were many horses but few hotels along the packed-earth main street. Today Creel is connected by paved highway to Chihuahua (see pp. 86–87), and visitors benefit from a range of amenities, although the town retains its cowboy charm. Guides, pack animals, horses, and organized tours can be arranged.

A few miles south of Creel, **San Ignacio de Arareko** and its mission church are now accessible by paved road. Outside town, you can rent a rowboat for fishing in **Lago Arareko,** a 100-acre (40 ha) reservoir with woodland campsites and simple cabins. The surrounding valleys are named for their unique rock formations: **Valle de los Hongos** (mushrooms), **Las Ranas** (frogs), **Las Chichis** (breasts), and **Bisabírachi** (penises). About 15.5 miles (25 km) from Creel, **Cascada de Cusárare** waterfall can be visited on a long day or an overnight camping trip.

About 75 miles (120 km) northwest of Creel, in **Parque Nacional Basaseáchic,** are Mexico's first- and second-highest waterfalls. The 1,486-foot (453 m) **Cascada Piedra Volada** was only recently discovered (at least by outsiders), in 1995. The national park was named for **Cascada Basaseáchic,** best seen during or right after the rainy season *(June–Oct.),* when the falls plunge 800 feet (243 m) into a rocky pool.

Creel
 77 D4

Visitor Information

✉ Casa de las Artesanías, zócalo

☎ 635/456-0080

A yucca plant thrives at an altitude of 8,000 feet (2,440 m).

Tiny **Batopilas** perches beside a jade green river of the same name on the canyon's floor. Connected to the world by a paved road only for the last 25 years, the town was originally established in the early 17th century by Spaniards looking for precious metals. These they found in abundance, sometimes as polished silver rocks strewn along the riverbed. Wealth earned from mining paid for some of the elegant Porfiriato-era mansions that today enliven this remote town.

From Batopilas, hike or ride to the abandoned, fired-brick mission at **Satevó** (4 miles/6.5 km), or take a shorter hike to abandoned **Hacienda San Miguel** or to the stone dam that still supplies the town's aqueduct. Satevó is a "dry" town, gas is expensive, and most restaurants serve just the basics. There are half a dozen simple lodgings. An alternative to the magnificent but hair-raising 87-mile (140 km) trip from Creel is a several-day horse or mule trek from Cerocahui. ∎

Sierra Tarahumara Flora & Fauna

The highest mountains of the Sierra Tarahumara, above 8,000 feet (2,440 m), support conifer forests, with Douglas-fir and ponderosa pine. In winter these peaks may be cloaked in snow. Down to 5,900 feet (1,800 m), live oak, juniper, and twisted red *madroño* (strawberry tree) mingle with the still predominant pine, notably the pinyon pine. Between 5,900 feet and 4,265 feet (1,800 m and 1,300 m), the pine-oak forest gives way to the arid tropical deciduous thorn forest, with scrub oak, succulents, mesquite, and some species of cactus. Below 4,265 feet (1,300 m) are the tropical and subtropical riparian forests. Here you will find fan palms next to evergreens, orchids, and wild figs, and, in the humid areas, ceiba, bamboo, and river cane.

About 30 percent of Mexico's mammals can be found in the Sierra Tarahumara, many increasingly rare. At the higher elevations live black bear, mountain lion, and rattlesnake. Deer, bobcat, coyote, wild boar, white-tail deer, and collared peccary are wide-ranging but elusive and rarely sighted. Most frequently seen are raccoons, skunks, hare, gray foxes, squirrel, and bats. Coral snakes and beaded lizards, both poisonous, inhabit the arid tropical thorn forest, while near the canyon bottom live jaguar, jaguarundi, and boa constrictor. Wandering cattle, goats, and pigs upset nature's delicate balance, stripping vegetation traditionally eaten by other species. Throughout the region there are around 50 species of freshwater fish, including catfish, rainbow trout, carp, mullet, and mojarra.

Many species of birds (there are more than 360 in the region) can be seen along the canyon's rim, among them the vermilion flycatcher, black vulture, crested caracara, thick-billed parrot, zone-tailed hawk, and hairy woodpecker. At the canyon's base live the colorful violet-crowned and Lucifer hummingbirds, oriole, tanager, and the magnificent, endangered military macaw. Near rivers look for lilac-crowned parrot and elegant trogan.

Hidalgo del Parral

Snuggled in an isolated valley between the foothills of the Sierra Madre and the Chihuahua Desert, Hidalgo del Parral is among the country's richest mining towns. Parral (as it's usually called) produced lead, copper, and silver for more than 350 years before being exhausted in the 1980s. The city also gained fame as the place where Pancho Villa was assassinated.

The Casa de Alvarado, built in the Italian Renaissance style

During the 16th and 17th centuries, indigenous slaves worked Parral's mines, suffering huge loss of life due to unsafe conditions and overwork. They created altars within the tunnels, frequently dedicated to their patron saint, Nuestra Señora de Fátima. Above ground, the wealthy metal barons built churches and cathedrals, often encrusting columns and walls with crude or refined ore.

The **Parroquia de San José** (Francisco Moreno at General Benítez) is decorated with chunks of ore, and its baroque pink quarrystone altarpiece is edged in gold. Built three centuries later, the **Templo de Nuestra Señora de Fátima** overlooks the city near La Prieta mine. It has a plain facade and single bell tower, but its interior walls are also encrusted with silver, gold, copper, and zinc ore.

Silver mining peaked in the mid- to late 19th century, and many palatial homes date from that era. The home of the town's founder, mining entrepreneur Pedro Alvarado, restored as **Museo Palacio de Alvarado** (Lic. Verdad & Riva Palacio, tel 627/522-0290, closed Mon.), has a neobaroque portal and carved limestone facade.

The remodeled **Museo del General Francisco Villa** (Barreda at Juárez, tel 627/525-3292) displays Revolution-era artifacts and personal effects of Pancho Villa. ∎

Hidalgo del Parral

🗺 77 E3

Visitor Information

✉ Calle Estaño s/n at Fátima, Col. Fátima

☎ 627/525-4400

www.parral.org

Durango

Nestled in the fertile Guadiana Valley, near the eastern foothills of the Sierra Madre Occidental, the city of Durango is an important agricultural and industrial center. Friendly people, a mild climate, clean, well-signed streets, and a dearth of tourists make Durango an ideal stop for those seeking a bite of "real" Mexico off the tour-bus trail. Its colonial-era city center has been designated a national historic monument.

Moonrise over the Sierra de Organos, a popular film set for Hollywood Westerns

Founded in 1563, Durango began as an outpost in the wilds of Nueva Vizcaya, New Spain's huge northern province. Both the city and the surrounding region developed slowly, plagued by extreme hostilities between the Spaniards and the Tepehuán and Acaxe Indians. The city flourished in the early 1900s, when the completion of a railroad to Mexico City established it as a shipping center for lumber and minerals from the productive mountains nearby.

The surrounding hills still produce substantial amounts of silver, gold, copper, and iron. One of the world's largest iron ore deposits can be found at **Cerro del Mercado,** just north of the city. Hundreds of tons of iron ore are transported from this virtual mountain of metal every day.

Durango's historic buildings cluster downtown near the main square, the **Plaza de Armas** (*Av. 20 de Noviembre at Juárez*). On Thursday and Sunday afternoons around 5 p.m., the state band serenades from the bandstand, which is surrounded by gardens and fountains. The **catedral,** with its impressive baroque facade, commands the plaza to the north. Locals tell of a young girl who killed herself after learning of the death of her lover, a French soldier. The girl's ghost is said to hover near sunset in the west bell tower, from which she jumped. Among the cathedral's most precious icons is its gilded *sillería* (row of choir stalls), adorned with bas-relief carvings of saints and Apostles.

One block west of Plaza de Armas is the multi-arched **Palacio de Gobierno** (*Bruno Martínez bet. Coronado & Aquiles Serdán, tel 618/827-0800*). It was built by a Spanish mining tycoon, then seized by the state after the end of colonial rule. Now government headquarters, its interior features colorful murals depicting Durango's history.

Handsome colonial-era houses are sprinkled throughout the historic district. An excellent example of 18th-century Churrigueresque architecture is the

Casa del Conde de Suchil (*5 de Febrero at Madero, tel 618/813-2601, closed Sun.*), originally the region's mint and now a Banamex bank. The beautiful, neoclassical **Teatro Ricardo Castro** (*Av. 20 de Noviembre at Bruno Martínez, tel 618/811-4694*) hosts opera, orchestra, and dance, and is a film venue.

For an overview of local culture and art, visit the **Museo de las Culturas Populares** (*Av. 5 de Febrero 1107 Pte. between Independencia & Nogal, tel 618/825-8827, closed Mon., $*), which displays a collection of folk art made by local Mennonites as well as Huichol, Acaxe, and Tepehuán Indians. Modern handiwork, including leather goods and typical wool *sarapes* (blankets), can be found at the **Mercado Gómez Palacio** (*Av. 20 de Noviembre at Pasteur*). The **Museo Regional de Durango** (*Victoria 100 Sur & Aquiles Serdán, tel 618/813-1094, closed Mon., $*), known locally as "El Aguacate," has paintings by colonial master Miguel Cabrera (1695–1768) as well as exhibits on regional history and archaeology. ■

Durango
🅰 77 E2

Visitor Information
✉ Calle Florida 1106 Pte., Barrio del Calvario
☎ 618/811-2139 or 01800/ 624-6567 (toll-free within Mexico)
www.visitadurango .com.mx

EXPERIENCE: Visiting Film Sets

Since the 1950s, hundreds of films have been shot on location outside Durango, most of them Westerns. Clear blue skies, a temperate climate, and the absence of power lines and other trappings of modern society make the region well suited to the role of outdoor film set. *Romancing the Stone* (1984) was filmed here, as were *The Mask of Zorro* (1997) and *Bandits* (2005).

About 8 miles (12 km) north of Durango, **Villa del Oeste** (*Carr. a Parral Km 12,*

tel 618/149-3390, closed Mon., $) shimmers like a mirage on the dusty horizon. Built in the 1950s, it was for decades one of Durango's most important sets.

Film production here is sporadic today, but you can see some action. On weekends and holidays, actors present skits (2:30 & 4:30 Sat.; 1:30, 3:30, & 5:30 Sun.). Buses ($) leave from Durango's cathedral about 30 minutes before each show. On weekdays, the site, which has a restaurant and gift shop, is open 11 a.m. to 7 p.m.

Mazatlán & Environs

Despite its famous pre-Lenten Mardi Gras celebration, its world-class billfishing, and some of the tastiest seafood on the planet, Mazatlán is not one of Mexico's most sought-after seaside resorts. But admirers of this bayside city of nearly 700,000 couldn't care less if it's spurned by the masses. Fifteen miles (24 km) of beaches stretch north and south of downtown, and hotel and restaurant prices are about half of those in Cancún or Los Cabos.

In Mazatlán, a hill rises between the Old Town and the newer Zona Dorada.

Just 12 miles (19 km) south of the Tropic of Cancer, Mazatlán enjoys a semitropical climate. Warm year-round, it is hottest and steamiest at the height of the rainy season, in August and September, but even then the humidity doesn't compare to that of resorts farther south.

Most visitors come for the sand, sun, and nighttime fun. The **Zona Dorada** (Golden Zone), north of **Punta Camarón** (Shrimp Point), has some of Mazatlán's most popular beaches. Crowded throughout this bustling hotel zone are shell and souvenir shops, sidewalk bars, and beachfront restaurants. Resort hotels rent water sports equipment, and the bay has gentle breakers. Vendors stroll the sand, selling cases of silver jewelry, striped blankets, Talavera pottery, and hammocks. Just offshore lie three islands: **Isla de Pájaros, Isla de Venados,** and **Isla de Lobos.** Of the birds, deer, and sea lions for which they are respectively named, only the first are in evidence.

The north end of the Golden Zone is home to **El Cid Mega**

Resort, a hotel and time-share complex with a marina and 27-hole golf course. Surfers catch good waves at **Playa las Brujas** (Witches Beach), where thatched restaurants sell fresh seafood and host live dance bands on Sunday afternoons. Walkers and joggers tend to favor **Playa Cerritos** (Little Hills Beach) around the point north of Playa las Brujas. These and other beaches are accessible by public buses, taxis, and *pulmonías* (open-air taxis).

The city's long *malecón* (beach-front promenade) begins at Valentine's Disco, at the south end of the Golden Zone, and continues south (toward downtown) past **Playa Norte.** One block inland is the **Acuario Mazatlán** *(111 Av. de los Deportes, tel 669/981-7815, $$),* where you can see hundreds of marine species in aquariums, as well as the sea lion, bird, or dive shows. In addition to gift shops and a snack bar, there are botanical gardens and a small aviary.

A large statue of a naked fisherman and his female companion—known to the locals as "los Monos Bichis," or "the Naked Monkeys"—presides over the south end of the bay. Fishing boats depart from **Playa los Pinos,** where an informal fish market is held daily just after dawn. Farther south, during high tide, young men dive into the shallow water from a 45-foot (15 m) platform at **El Mirador.**

Walk inland to admire the streets of historic downtown, its 19th- and 20th-century homes in various states of repair and disarray. Many of the one- and two-story, brick-and-stucco buildings are painted in bright pastel colors with white trim, their windows and doors protected by intricate wrought-iron grillwork. A 21st-century restoration project has infused the area with new life in the form of bars, cafés, shops and boutique hotels.

The civic and religious heart of the city is **Plaza Revolución** *(Bet. Calles Flores, Nelson, 21 de Marzo, & Juárez).* Mango and watermelon vendors sit in the shade of tall coconut palms and shiny leafed Indian laurels, while in the cool, dark, subterranean diner underneath the gazebo bandstand, teenagers linger over burgers and soft drinks. On the north side of the square, two distinctive, yellow-tiled spires top the **Catedral.**

INSIDER TIP:

When in the Mazatlán region, sample the mango liqueur.

—ERIC RAMIREZ BRAVO
National Geographic field researcher

A few blocks north of the square is the **Mercado Pino Suárez** *(Juárez & Aquiles Serdán),* a typical market selling clothing and souvenirs, in addition to skinned cow's heads and other victuals. Mazatlán's oldest square, **Plazuela Machado** *(Constitución bet. Frías & Carnaval)* is surrounded by sidewalk cafés. The 19th-century plaza was a gift from Filipino-born Juan Machado, who made a fortune in commerce and mining. Surrounding streets are closed to traffic Thursday through Sunday, when various

Mazatlán

▲ 77 D2

Visitor Information

✉ Carnaval at M. Escovedo Centro

☎ 669/981-8883

Estrella del Mar

✉ Isla de la Piedra
Km 10

☎ 669/982-3300
ext. 3010

**www.estrellademar
.com**

genres of live music are played.

Back at the beach, the road winds south past lookout points with views of the bay as well of the world's highest lighthouses (500 feet/152 m) at **Cerro de la Crestería,** accessed by a steep, rocky path. From here you will see **Isla de la Piedra** (Stone Island, but really a peninsula), popular with families for weekend picnics. Take a water taxi there, and enjoy a walk on the beach and a meal or a cold beer at one of the many seafood shanties. Also here is the 18-hole **Estrella del Mar golf course.** Small boats ($) ferry

passengers over from the east side of downtown Mazatlán (save ticket for the return trip).

Mazatlán is one of Mexico's premier billfishing destinations. Near the base of Cerro de la Crestería, the city's **sportfishing fleet** has a dozen boats eager to help you catch sailfish, marlin, yellowfin tuna, and sea bass. Nearby, at **La Puntilla,** ferry boats depart for La Paz, in Baja California Sur.

Organized tours are the primary vehicle for visiting the agricultural town of Quelite and the former mining hamlets of Concordia and Copala. The **Quelite** tour includes a colorful graveyard, an exhibition of the pre-Hispanic ball game *ulloa,* and a rooster farm, after which lunch is served. Just outside **Concordia** (30 miles/48 km from Mazatlán), chunky carved furniture and unglazed ceramic pottery are for sale. In Concordia itself, admire the baroque **Catedral de San Sebastián,** on the main plaza, and take a walk around town before continuing another 15 miles (24 km) to smaller, more isolated **Copala,** winding up into the mountains off Highway 40.

Copala's single street leads to the rustic **Catedral de San José,** where young men sell miniature churches carved from the region's thorny *pochotla* tree. Visit the church and walk about to admire the colorful adobe houses dressed in peach and red-violet bougainvillea, organ cactuses, and flowering trees. Set aside some time to dine in one of the town's three pleasant restaurants before heading back to civilization. ∎

Carnival

Mazatlán's Carnaval, among the world's most unusual pre-Lenten parties, began as friendly battles between 19th-century stevedores, who hurled flour-filled eggshells and *comparsas* **(rhyming verses) at each other. When rhymes and eggs turned to insults and rocks, officials replaced the free-for-all with organized parades, regional bands, and a reigning queen and king.**

Today's revelers toss confetti as well as flour, and the rhyming tradition continues as a poetry competition. Friday night Flower Games consist of a ballet and orchestral and *tambora* **music at the baseball stadium. Saturday night's Batalla Naval is a mock naval battle and stirring fireworks display on Olas Altas Bay.**

More Places to Visit in Northwest Mexico

Alamos

Begun as a mountain mining town, Alamos was among the most lucrative in the 19th century. Yaqui Indian rebellions and the Mexican Revolution eventually put the mines out of business. In the 1940s, crumbling yet still elegant Andalusian-style mansions were discovered and renovated by wealthy foreigners who have created many social clubs and organized activities. During high season you can take a Saturday morning **house and garden tour** *($$$)*. At other times, seek out a guide for a tour of the town *($$$)* at the friendly tourism headquarters.

On the smart **Plaza de Armas** you'll find the modest **Museo Costumbrista de Sonora** *(tel 647/428-0053, closed Mon.–Tues., $)*, which highlights Sonora's history, and the **Iglesia de la Purísima Concepción,** a Spanish colonial stone church with a three-tiered bell tower. Locals and tourists promenade around poplar-shaded **Parque Alameda** and shop in the surrounding stores and the municipal market. For a good view of the town, walk or drive south on Calle Juárez up to **El Mirador** (The Lookout). If you want to go farther afield, most hotels can arrange visits to abandoned silver mines and Mayo villages (where artisans make traditional wooden masks).

Little-visited but nevertheless worthwhile, **Cuchujaqui Ecological Reserve** *(tel 647/428-0875, $)* comprises pine-oak, low deciduous, and semitropical forests and has more than 200 species of birds, including the endangered spotted owl, pygmy cactus owl, and peregrine falcon. Canyons, dry riverbeds, and riparian environments also attract about a hundred species of migratory birds to the area. This 92,000+-acre eco-reserve bumps up against Alamos and smaller Aduana ejido.

Just east of Alamos, the **Arroyo Cuchujaqui** has a pretty pond for swimming or fishing for large-mouth bass, as does nearby

Presa Adolfo Ruíz Cortines Mocuzarit, off the Alamos-Navojoa road. The mining town of **Aduana**—its 17th-century church with a much venerated statue of the Virgin—is also worth a visit.

◭ 77 C3 ✉ Guadalupe Victoria 5
☎ 647/428-0450

Cuauhtémoc

Although established in Chihuahua state since 1921, the Mennonite communities living north and south of Cuauhtémoc still speak their Low German dialect and wear traditional farmer clothing. This large Mennonite group has found peace in Mexico's northern desert, having first fled Europe in search of religious freedom, and later Canada after refusing military service during World War II.

The Mennonites' tidy looking villages, called *campos menonitas,* are numbered, and the wood-frame, pitched-roof houses contrast with the typical Mexican towns in the surrounding plains. Agencies such as **Turismo Almar** *(tel 614/410-9232, www.copper-canyon.com)* lead day tours out of Chihuahua to see these homes and cheese factories and to visit the **Museo Menonita** *(Carr. Cuautémoc–Alvaro Obregón Km 10.5, tel 625/583-1895, closed Sun., $)* to see a typical pioneer house with furnishings.

◭ 77 D4

Cumbres de Majalca

About 37 miles (60 km) north of Chihuahua's eponymous capital (the last half on a good dirt road), this 12,000-acre (4,770 ha) park offers accessible hiking and mountain biking, mainly on fire roads. Beginning at 5,250 feet (1,600 m) above sea level, the national park is home to grasslands and pine-oak forests. Rock climbers appreciate the rock formations carved by wind and water erosion. The weather here is generally dry in late winter to early summer. July through September brings afternoon showers (and

brilliant cloud formations). Late fall and winter precipitation brings snow to the higher elevations. Primitive camping is permitted, and there are basic cabins, too.
🏔 77 D4

Hermosillo

Four hours south of the U.S. border at Nogales is Hermosillo, Sonora's midsize state capital, surrounded by golden plains and backed by jagged mountain peaks. It makes a convenient stopping place for travelers headed south. Walk around the battered yet appealing historic district, admiring the **plaza** (*Pino Suárez, P.E. Calles, Yáñez, & Monterrey*), where the neoclassical **Catedral de la Asunción** indulges a few neo-Gothic whims. The crest of the **Cerro de la Campana** affords a fine view of the city; at its base, the **Museo Regional de Sonora** (*Jesús García at Calle Esteban Sarmiento, tel 662/217-2714, closed Mon., $*) has exhibits on Sonora's history, geology, and anthropology.

South of town, the government-run **Centro Ecológico de Sonora** (*Carr. a Guaymas Km 2.5, tel 662/250-1225, closed Mon., $*) is a center for ecological research and preservation.

Ferry Crossing

Ferries connect Baja California Sur with mainland Mexico, and when taking into account gas prices and tolls, they represent a good value. The Mazatlán-La Paz route takes 12 hours, while the shorter crossing from La Paz to Los Mochis, also in Sinaloa state, takes just five. Passengers can choose an inside or outside deck seat, a basic cabin, or a small suite with a toilet and tiny tub. Both the *Chihuahua Star* and *California Star* accommodate vehicles; the Los Mochis run is once daily, and the Mazatlán route is six days a week. For more information see *www.baja ferries.com* or call 612/123-6600 in La Paz, Baja California Sur.

A 2-mile-long (3 km) path meanders past exhibits of some 300 plant and 240 animal species, many of them endemic to the region. If you come to town in mid-July, join wine lovers in an annual celebration of the grape harvest at **Fiesta de la Vendimia.** www.sonoraturismo.gob.mx 🏔 77 B4 ✉ Edificio Estatal, Calle Comonfort & Paseo del Canal ☎ 662/217-0076 ext. 122

El Rosario

If you haven't had your fill of former mining towns, visit sun-baked El Rosario, whose mines churned out gold and silver for nearly 300 years. Much of the gold seems to have ended up on the baroque altarpiece of **Iglesia de Nuestra Señora del Rosario.** Unlike many of northern Mexico's plain Jesuit mission churches, this 18th-century temple is deliciously baroque. After excessive tunneling of nearby mines caused the original church to sink, it was moved, stone by stone, to its present location near the town square. El Rosario is best known among Sinaloans as the birthplace of Mexican mariachi singer and actress Lola Beltrán.
🏔 77 E1

Teacapán

Near Sinaloa's rural southern border, Teacapán and its environs are famous for their plums, shrimp, and mangoes. Cattle ranches and coconut plantations line the 18-mile-long (28 km) peninsula. For now you can stop at one of the area's peaceful, white-sand beaches, including **La Tambora, Las Lupitas, Las Cabras,** and **Los Angeles,** but this entire coastline is slated for Cancún-style development. Day tours from Mazatlán explore Teacapán's estuaries, where you can see white and pink herons, and many other migratory and resident bird species. Within the mangroves is a remarkable pre-Hispanic pyramid of shells accessible only at high tide.
🏔 77 E1

An arid land whose people–like the area's vanguard Franciscan missionaries–are hardy and independent

Northeast Mexico

Juan Soriano sculpture
in Monterrey

Northeast Mexico

As in neighboring Texas, things in northern Mexico just seem *bigger*. Distances in the northeast are certainly vast. This factor, combined with a dearth of mineral wealth (Zacatecas excepted) led to minimal immigration in colonial times. However, the late 20th century saw a change in the region's fortune, and the Monterrey-Saltillo corridor has emerged as the nation's leading manufacturing region.

A storm brews in the Sierra del Carmen behind the sun-baked town of Boquillas.

In 1547, the discovery of a rich silver mine in Zacatecas encouraged exploration to the north. But unlike its western counterpart, the Sierra Madre Oriental contained relatively few precious metals. To encourage settlement in the mid-18th century, the Spanish crown granted huge landholdings for sheep and cattle ranches. A wealth of available land and lax Mexican immigration policies led many U.S. citizens to settle the area; by the time Texas declared itself independent of Mexico in 1836, the ratio of U.S. immigrants to Mexicans living there was four to one.

Below the border at the Río Bravo (known as the Rio Grande in the United States), sheep and cattle ranching continue to contribute to northern Mexico's economy and culture. Meat is the mainstay of the northern diet, usually served with bread rolls or flour tortillas instead of the corn tortillas ubiquitous in central and southern Mexico. Along with *machaca* (dried, shredded beef) and barbecued kid, a favorite meal is *carne*

a la tampiqueña—thin, grilled or charbroiled steak accompanied by rice, *frijoles charros* (beans cooked with pork rind and cilantro), grilled green onions, fresh salsa, and avocado.

NOT TO BE MISSED:

Fishing and shrimping form the base of the coastal economy, although petroleum rules in Tampico. Meanwhile, manufacturing in border cities and along the Monterrey–Saltillo corridor continues to grow. The inhabitants of inland valleys in the Sierra Madre Oriental practice subsistence agriculture, harvesting apples, prickly pears, nuts, and pine nuts.

Outside the major population centers, northeastern Mexico's wilderness areas invite exploration by adventurous travelers. Appearing like mirages in the scrubby desert are ancient archaeological sites, small towns with gold- and silver-studded churches, and productive vineyards. Despite limited infrastructure, backpacking, canyoneering, and rock climbing are gaining popularity in the rugged and still wild mountain ranges. ■

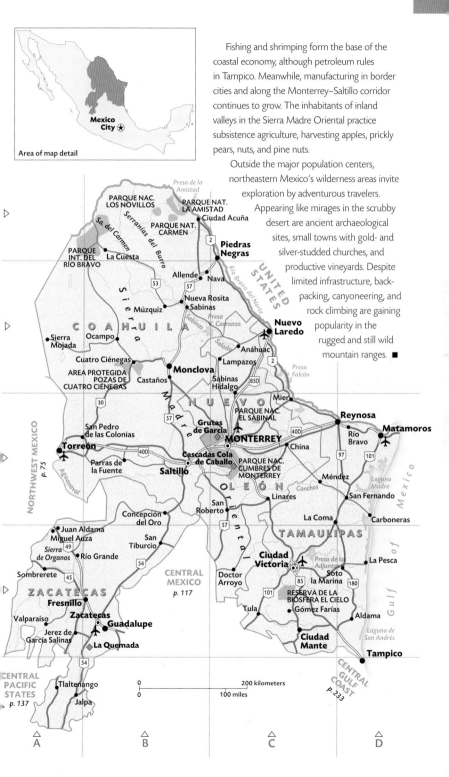

Area of map detail

Mexico City ✴

Saltillo

Saltillo, capital of the state of Coahuila and the oldest city in northeastern Mexico, was founded by Spaniards and Portuguese in 1575. Twenty years later, 87 converted Tlaxcala Indian families from central Mexico resettled near the town to help Christianize and pacify anarchistic desert tribes. They brought their weaving traditions, and today the *sarape de Saltillo*, a bright-colored woolen blanket, is a universally recognized Mexican icon.

The refreshingly untouristy city of Saltillo feels both old and modern.

Saltillo

105 B3

Visitor Information

Blvd. V. Carranza 8520, Col. Valle Hermoso, Via Ferre 85-B

844/432-3690 or 01800/045-4545 (toll-free within Mexico)

www.ocvsaltillo.com

Although the mile-high city sprawls with suburbs and industrial complexes, its historic center is visually appealing, with buildings in a variety of architectural styles. Brick and stucco homes surround the town's open main square, **Plaza de Armas** (*Hidalgo at Juárez*). Wrought-iron benches face inward to the stone-and-bronze central fountain and outward to the pink-stone **Palacio de Gobierno.**

Behind the state government palace is **Plaza de la Nueva Tlaxcala,** a public square whose eye-catching statue depicts the city's founders: Spaniards, Tlaxcaltecans, and friars. Three blocks northwest, **Plaza Acuña** (*Aldama bet. Allende & Flores*) is surrounded by stores, cafés, and the municipal market, where you can shop for leather goods, Saltillo's colorful sarapes, and locally made pottery.

Facing Plaza de Armas is one of the region's most gorgeous churches, the baroque **Catedral de Santiago de Saltillo** (*tel 844/414-0230*). Built between 1745 and 1800, the base of its Churrigueresque facade is adorned with spiral Solomonic columns covered with images of fruit and flowers.

West of the cathedral, board the **Tranvío Turístico** (*runs Fri.–Sun., $*) at Alameda de Zaragoza park for a guided city tour. You can get off and reboard the trolley four times, or just stay on and enjoy the ride.

On the opposite side of town, the **Museo del Desierto** (*Prol. Pérez Treviño 3745, Parque las Maravillas, tel 844/410-6633, www .museodeldesierto.org, closed Mon., $$*) covers plants, animals, geology, paleontology, and ecosystems, as well as regional Indian cultures and post-conquest history. ∎

Las Pozas de Cuatro Ciénegas

Many think of deserts as barren, lifeless expanses of brown earth and tumbleweeds, but they can be places of surprising beauty. Bubbling out of the desert at Cuatro Ciénegas, hundreds of mineral springs form crystalline pools, lagoons, superficial rivers, and salt marshes lined with sedges and bunchgrass. Wander the adjoining stark white gypsum dunes on your own, or hire a guide. To see the far-flung pools, you'll need your own transportation.

Nestled between two spurs of the Sierra Madre Oriental, the **Area Protegida Pozas de Cuatro Ciénegas** (Pools of the Four Marshes Protected Area) forms a rare desert wetland. These grasslands, scrub forest, gypsum dunes, and mineral springs have been protected since 1995. Hundreds of pools—from 1 to 262 feet (30 cm–80 m) in diameter—are fed by deep subterranean aquifers. Mineral content and the presence of organic materials and algae determine each pool's clarity and color.

Because of its isolation, this unusual desert wetland has a high ratio of endemic fish and reptiles. Of the 16 known fish species, half are found nowhere else. Swimming and snorkeling, permitted in a few areas within 6 to 11 miles (10 to 18 km) of the town of Cuatro Ciénegas, are delightful, especially in the winter, when the water typically reaches 70–82°F (21–28°C).

Mezquites is a slow-flowing river fed by a series of springs, whose depth varies from about 6 inches to 6 feet (15 cm–1.8 m) along the 2.5-mile-long (4 km) stretch that is open for bathing and kayaking. A natural channel connects two crystal-clear blue pools at **Becerra;** unfortunately

at press time it and **Playitas,** used mainly by locals, are closed. The crystal-clear pool at Shurince, shrunken in summer, is part of a larger system of interconnected rivers and a lagoon.

Exposed deposits of gypsum from pools such as Shurince are generally blown west, forming sparkling white dunes that tower above the desert floor. Visit the dunes at Becerra springs *($),* or hire a guide *($$$$$ per group)* at Cuatro Ciénegas's city hall *(municipio).* ■

Cuatro Ciénegas
 105 B4
Visitor Information
✉ Calle Juárez 101A
☎ 01800/201-0480 (toll-free within Mexico)

Snorkeling in the mineral pools at Cuatro Ciénegas is especially pleasant in the winter, when water temperatures reach 70°F–82°F (21°C–28°C).

Monterrey & Environs

Seated in a valley at 1,765 feet (540 m) above sea level, Monterrey is surrounded by the craggy, abrupt peaks of the Sierra Madre Oriental. Dramatic Cerro de la Silla (Saddle Hill), symbol of the city, lies to the west. A modern, independent-thinking city, Monterrey is the third largest in Mexico (after Mexico City and Guadalajara). As a leader of industry, it enjoys the nation's highest per capita income and has one of the highest literacy rates.

With an important university and international commerce, today's Monterrey disavows its insouciant founding.

Monterrey grew slowly, hindered by fierce Chichimec Indian raids, several serious floods in the 17th and 18th centuries, and the Mexican-American War, when the city was occupied by U.S. troops. Construction of railroad lines in 1881 and tax exemptions for industry under President Porfirio Díaz attracted U.S., French, and British as well as Mexican investors. Construction of the Cervecería Cuauhtémoc brewery in 1890 led to the establishment of a glassworks and a foundry. Today, Monterrey's economy is centered around these industries, as well as cement, steel, beverages, glass, financial services, and automotive products.

In the 1980s, 40 central city blocks separating the state and city government buildings were razed to create the 100-acre (40 ha) **Macroplaza,** or Gran Plaza *(bet. 5 de Mayo, Av. de la Constitución, Zuazua, & Zaragoza),* a series of green spaces punctuated with fountains and statues. A great place for relaxing and people-watching, this busy, popular park is surrounded by some of Monterrey's early modern buildings, including the steel-and-glass **Condominio Acero** building and the rust red-colored **Faro del**

Comercio, a 230-foot (70 m) obelisk designed by Luis Barragán (see p. 41), the father of contemporary Mexican architecture.

At the north end of the Macroplaza, at 5 de Mayo, enter the **Palacio de Gobierno** to admire the building's leaded-glass windows honoring heroes of the revolution, as well as its gleaming parquet floors, crystal chandeliers, and other lovely neoclassical elements.

Extending west from the south end of the narrow park is the **Zona Rosa,** a ten-block pedestrian zone with stores, cafés, juice bars, restaurants, and downtown's nicest hotels. At the southeast corner of the park, the adobe-colored **Museo de Arte Contemporaneo de Monterrey** (*Zuazua at Padre Raymundo Jardón, tel 81/8262-4500, closed Mon., $$*) sports architect Ricardo Legorreta's trademark marigold, purple, and pink accents. The museum hosts installation art and other avant-garde exhibits (both permanent and changing), and has a restaurant and café. Admission is free on Wednesdays.

Across the street, the **Catedral de Monterrey** (*Zuazua 1100 Sur, tel 81/8340-3752*) has been rebuilt several times owing to fires and floods; its interior was remodeled in the 19th century in the neoclassical style. Worth noting are five murals in the apse, painted in 1942.

Near the northeast end of the Macroplaza, the **Museo de Historia Mexicana** (*Dr. Coss 445 Sur, tel 81/8345-9898, www.3museos.com, closed Mon., $$*), actually three museums in one, provides a fascinating visual history of the nation, with artifacts, religious icons and clothing, scale models, installations, and illustrative maps. Exhibits of popular art and culture fill the first-floor galleries.

Behind the cathedral, antiques shops, cafés, discos, and bars are cropping up in the restored 19th-century homes of the *barrio antiguo,* an older neighborhood currently in vogue. Within this 15-block area of cobblestone streets and 19th- and early 20th-century houses is one of the city's few remaining examples of secular colonial architecture: **La Casa del Campesino** (*Abasolo bet. Mina & Naranjo, closed Mon.*). Built in the mid-18th century, it contains later murals describing Mexican history in its chapel.

El Obispado (*José Rafael Verger s/n, tel 81/8346-0404, closed Mon., $$*) is one of the few things English writer Graham Greene liked about Mexico. He called it "as beautiful as anything out of the Middle Ages." Originally the summer home of one of the last bishops of the viceregal era, this baroque structure houses the **Museo Regional de Nuevo León.** And while Greene's epitaph seems an exaggeration, the building

INSIDER TIP:

Ladies, you can expect attention. But take it as it is intended: a compliment.

—NINA-NOELLE HALL
National Geographic contributor

Monterrey
105 C3
Visitor Information
Calle Washington 648, Antiguo Palacio Federal Piso 2, Centro
81/2020-6789
www.visita nuevoleon.travel

Centro Cultural Alfa

Visitor Information

✉ Av. Roberto Garza Sada 1000

☎ 81/8303-0002

🕐 Closed Mon

💲 $$

www.planetarioalfa.org.mx

itself—with its sculpted facade and the Chapel to the Virgin of Guadalupe—is more interesting than the period artifacts within.

West & Southwest of Monterrey

West of town, the stately, brick-and-ivy **Cervecería Cuauhtémoc** (*Av. Alfonso Reyes 220 Norte, tel 81/8328-5355, closed Sun.*) offers a free guided tour of its brewery (*by appt. only*) and a sample of the brew in the outdoor beer garden. The adjacent **Salón de la Fama** (*tel 81/8328-5815*) still documents the history of baseball. *"El beis"* was introduced in the late 19th century by people from the United States working in Mexico.

changing exhibits of glass, from the utilitarian and lowly beer bottle to the classiest art glass in a variety of formats.

Southwest of the city, on the road to Parque Ecológico Chipinque (see opposite), the **Centro Cultural Alfa** houses a planetarium, an Omnimax theater, and a science museum. This modern cultural complex also has a gift shop and a restaurant; the entrance price includes one movie. Hours are 3:30 to 8 p.m.

Parque Nacional Cumbres de Monterrey

Surrounding Monterrey, 619,000-acre (250,500 ha) Cumbres de Monterrey actually comprises a series of parks and

---

EXPERIENCE: Taking Medical Matters to Mexico

Bariatric surgery and face-lifts may be the most popular procedures, but these days some folks even travel abroad to get heart surgery or angioplasty. When you consider the cost of medical procedures in the United States and elsewhere, it's no surprise that people in record numbers are heading south of the border for procedures that are therapeutic as well as cosmetic. A root canal in Mazatlán costs about U.S.$150, veneers about U.S.$45 each, and implants about U.S.$65; you can

get your "work" done and spend the rest of the cash on margaritas and manicures as you recover by the pool.

As with any medical procedure, potential patients should make sure their surgeon is board-certified and ask for references. Companies such as **HealthCare Resources** (*www.healthcareresourcespv.com*), in Puerto Vallarta, can help with post-surgical care, arranging long- and short-term nursing, physical therapy, and assistance with meals.

Before it became established as a Mexican sport, northern Mexican teams played against U.S. teams, while those in the Yucatán played against Cubans.

El Museo del Vidrio (*Majallanes 517 at Zaragoza, Col. Treviño, tel 81/8863-1000, closed Mon., $*) has, as its name conveys,

attractions, each with its own administration and agenda. The park's name refers to the jagged peaks that tower over Monterrey, which lies tucked under a blanket of smog in the valley below. As is the case with many Mexican national parks and reserves, only a small portion is developed for tourism, while the rest serves as a buffer to development, a refuge for wildlife, and in this instance a natural aquifer.

Southwest of Monterrey loom the steely green peaks of **Parque Ecológico Chipinque,** about 12 miles (20 km) from the city center. Chipinque's varied topography includes valleys, canyons, mountain peaks, and pine-oak forests. The mammals most often seen are squirrels, gray foxes, and coati. However, white-tailed deer and black bear are also present, as are at least 120 species of birds and 170 of butterflies.

There's camping ($$) by prior arrangement, or go for the day to hike or mountain bike, take short guided walks from the visitor center *(reserve several days in advance),* or scale one of the park's four peaks (with park guides if you wish). The highest summit is **El Copete de las Águilas** (Eagles' Crest), at 7,410 feet (2,260 m); the most frequently climbed and the symbol of the park is **El "M"** (pronounced EH-may). Both are accessed from a mesa near the entrance to **Hotel Chipinque** (see p. 362), a stone-and-timber lodge with a restaurant overlooking Monterrey and a faux-rustic bar. There are also tennis courts, a swimming pool, small spa, and other facilities.

Rock climbers are attracted to the sheer, 984-foot (300 m) walls of **Cañón de la Huasteca** *(Carr. federal Km 40.3 S of Santa Catarina, $),* about 12 miles (20 km) west of Monterrey. These canyons once provided local Indians and Spanish settlers with a refuge from Apache raids. In the municipality of Santiago is **Cascadas Cola de Caballo** *(Carr. Cola de Caballo Km 6 off Hwy. 85, tel 81/8347-1599, $),* an 82-foot (25 m) waterfall named for its resemblance to a horse's tail. A 20- to 30-minute

INSIDER TIP:

Buildings in Monterrey and other cities are decorated with murals. Wander the streets to see all sorts. To some the paintings are graffiti, to others masterpieces.

—NINA-NOELLE HALL
National Geographic contributor

climb from the entrance brings you to the viewpoint; a set of stone steps leads about a third of the way up near the falls, and a dirt path takes you to the summit. Along the last few miles before the park entrance, locals sell wicker furniture, stone carvings, and large ceramic pots.

North of the Cañón de la Huasteca, the **Grutas de García** *(Salida a García, tel 81/8347-1533, $$)* is a series of 50-million-year-old caverns filled with stalactites and stalagmites. A winding, illuminated, 4-mile (2.5 km) path and wooden stairs lead through 16 monumental caves, many with 40-foot-tall (12 m) ceilings. Guided tours are given on the hour between 9 a.m. and 5 p.m. You can also get a bite at the on-site snack shop. ∎

Parque Ecológico Chipinque

Visitor Information

✉ Carr. a Chipinque Km 2.5, San Pedro

☎ 81/8303-2190

www.chipinque .org.mx

Zacatecas

Surrounded by craggy, arid mountains and unusual rock formations, Zacatecas occupies a narrow canyon at 8,900 feet (2,700 m) above sea level. Zacatecos are known for their friendly, open demeanor with a hint of cowboy swagger. If you're lucky, you may happen upon one of the city's traditional *callejoneadas,* festive musical parties that parade through the smaller streets, often accompanied by a mescal-bearing burro.

Zacatecas gets its Náhuatl name from the grasses that make the surrounding areas ideal ranchlands. The city grew quickly after the discovery of a rich vein of silver at Cerro de la Bufa (Wineskin Hill) in 1546, despite uprisings led by the Caxcanes tribe. Financed by silver barons,

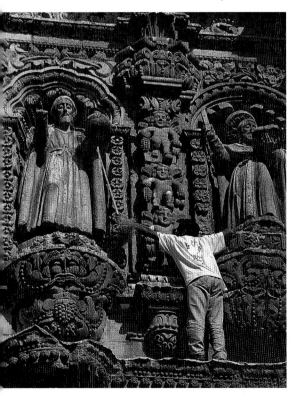

A worker cleans the almost overpowering baroque facade of the Catedral Basílica Menor.

the Dominicans, Jesuits, and Augustinians established headquarters here for evangelizing the north, leaving a legacy of grand churches and seminaries.

The facade of the **Catedral Basílica Menor** *(S side of Plaza de Armas on Av. Hidalgo, tel 492/922-6211)* is a masterpiece of Mexican baroque. Carved of pink sandstone, the church's exterior epitomizes the Churrigueresque style. The interior, sacked during the Reform wars and again during the revolution, is nearly naked. On the east side of **Plaza de Armas,** Zacatecas's rather cheerless main square, stands the 17th-century **Palacio de Gobierno** *(Hidalgo 604, tel 492/923-9511),* with murals of local history adorning its interior.

South of the main square, the beaux arts **Mercado González Ortega** *(Hidalgo & Tacuba, tel 492/922-7990)* was converted from a daily market to a shopping mall with several restaurants, losing none of its splendor. The small **Museo Zacatecano** *(Dr. Hierro 301, tel 492/922-6580, closed Tues., $)* contains naive religious paintings *(retablos)* and Huichol art. Now an auditorium, the nearby **Iglesia de San Agustín** sports a wonderful plateresque facade.

Baroque-style **Templo de Santo Domingo** *(Genaro Codina 227 at Plaza Santo Domingo, tel*

492/922-1083) has a sumptuous interior, with eight Churrigueresque altarpieces; 18th-century paintings decorate the octagonal sacristy. Next door, the **Museo Rafael Coronel** (Ex-Convento de San Francisco s/n, tel 492/922-8116, closed Wed., $) boasts Mexico's largest collection of ceremonial masks (about 6,000) as well as puppets, pre-Hispanic ceramics, and colonial jewelry.

pink-stone aqueduct that served the city until the early 20th century. West of the park is **Museo Goitia** (E. Estrada 102, tel 492/922-0211, closed Mon., $), with 19th- and 20th-century paintings by half a dozen native Zacatecos.

For a city view, drive or hike to **Cerro de la Bufa.** A **museum** (tel 492/922-8066, closed Mon., $), chapel, and rotunda com-

Zacatecas
🗺 105 B2
Visitor Information
✉ Av. Hidalgo 403
☎ 492/922-1757
www.turismo zacatecas.gob.mx

Folk Remedies

Mexicans depend on many simple yet effective home remedies to cure common ailments. Aloe vera gel straight from the leaves of the succulent make a soothing night cream and works for burns, too. Flax seeds soaked in a little water and then chewed, relieve constipation. Nopal cactus juice is good for ulcers, high blood pressure, and high cholesterol. The juice of a raw (peeled) potato neutralizes acid produced by gastritis; water of the

coconut drunk on an empty stomach each morning is said to prevent intestinal parasites (bichos). Chile peppers are also said to discourage bichos from establishing a base camp amid the intestinal flora. Papaya seeds are yet another folk remedy for getting rid of intestinal parasites. Start with one and add one each day until the 12th day, then start counting backward. When you reach one seed again, your parasites should be gone.

Housed in a 17th-century Jesuit seminary, **Museo Pedro Coronel** (Av. Fernando Villalpando at Plaza Santo Domingo, tel 492/922-8021, closed Thurs., $) has an extensive international art collection that includes works by Georges Braque, Salvador Dalí, and Marc Chagall, as well as African, Indian, and Asian art. The **Museo de Arte Abstracto Manuel Felguérez** (Calle Colón at Seminario s/n, tel 492/924-3705, closed Tues., $) displays the modern abstract art collection of the museum's namesake.

Parks southwest of the town center include **Parque Alameda** (Villalpando at Av. Torreón) and **Parque Enrique Estrada** (González Ortega at Manuel M. Ponce), which has a fine view of the

memorate the battle in which Pancho Villa's División del Norte ousted government forces in the Revolutionary War (see p. 32). Or take the 2,100-foot (640 m) aerial tram, or *teleférico* (tel 492/922-5694, $), from **Cerro del Grillo.** From here you can descend into **"El Edén"** mine (Jaime Dovali off Av. Torreón, tel 492/922-3002, $$), productive for more than 350 years. There's a popular disco ($$$) here after 10 p.m., Thursday to Saturday.

Six miles (10 km) southeast of Zacatecas, the **Museo Virreynal de Guadalupe** (Jardín Juárez Oriente s/n, tel 492/923-2386, $$), a former Franciscan monastery, houses a collection of viceregal religious art. ∎

Reserva de la Biósfera El Cielo

Designated a biosphere in 1986, El Cielo (the Sky) stretches between two spurs of the Sierra Madre Oriental in southwestern Tamaulipas. A dramatic range of elevation (7,218 feet/2,200 m) and a favorable location near the Tropic of Cancer produce vastly distinct ecosystems. The park is a haven for wildlife, while its cloud forest provides a rainwater catchment for the tropical forest and commercial agriculture to the east and southeast.

El Cielo has four distinct ecosystems: tropical rain forest, cloud forest, pine-oak forest, and evergreen forest.

Ciudad Victoria

🅜 105 C2

Visitor Information

✉ Calle Hidalgo s/n, Gómez Farias

☎ 832/236-2002

El Cielo was heavily logged for 30 years from the 1930s, but ecotourism may prove a viable alternative to forestry and a source of much needed income. Today, rustic restaurants and lodgings are available at some of the area's ranches and *ejidos* (community landholdings).

The reserve has a high level of biodiversity. There are 95 species of mammals, about 60 species of reptiles, and 430 of birds.

About two hours from Ciudad Victoria, natural swimming pools at **El Nacimiento,** the source of Río Frío, lures local boys and travelers en route to higher ground. Follow the signs to **La Florida,** one of several restaurants on the riverbank.

A regular bus service is available as far as **Gómez Farías,** where you'll find a handful of humble but comfortable and charming hostels with restaurants. Here you can hire four-wheel-drive vehicles with a driver and guide. If you have a high-clearance vehicle, continue about an hour longer to the tiny hamlet of **Alta Cima,** which hangs above a cloud-forest valley. Hire local guides for day hikes to mountain glens and meadows, and, in season, to waterfalls and streams. You can also arrange for guides and pack animals for longer treks into the reserve. The friendly women at **Restaurant La Fe** prepare simple but filling fare and sell liqueur of local fruits. Adjoining the restaurant are lodgings and a campground.

A four-wheel-drive vehicle is necessary beyond Alta Cima, where the cloud forest scenery is magical; everything, even rocks, seems to be covered with orchids and other mist-loving plants.

At about 4,590 feet (1,400 m) above sea level, **San José** is tucked into a green valley between cloud and pine-oak forest. From here hike to the **Cueva del Agua,** a cave containing a limpid pool. Venture still farther to reach the evergreen forest around **La Gloria,** beyond which you can visit huge **Elephant Rock** and the beautiful waterfalls around **El Amarillo Cave.** ■

More Places to Visit in Northeast Mexico

Parras de la Fuente

One of Northeast Mexico's prettiest historic towns, Parras de la Fuente, in Coahuila state, brings a splash of green to the desert. Secular and religious buildings cluster around the center of town; of note are the **Santuario de Guadalupe** *(Viesca & Ocampo),* with its baroque and neoclassical altarpieces, and the 16th-century **Templo de San Ignacio de Loyola** *(Treviño 103 Sur),* with its small museum of old documents, books, and viceregal-era paintings.

At 4,985 feet (1,520 m), the city and surrounding countryside enjoy a pleasant climate well suited to growing figs, dates, pecans, avocados, and grapes. Here you'll find the continent's first winery, built in the late 16th century. Originally the Hacienda de San Lorenzo, and now **Casa Madero** *(Carr. Paila-Parras Km 18.5, tel 842/422-0111),* the winery continues to produce wine and brandy and offers daily tours and tastings 9 a.m. to 5 p.m. The harvest is celebrated each August with the week-long **Grape and Wine Festival (La Fiesta de la Vendimia).**

🅰 105 B3 ✉ Carr. Parras Paila Km 3 ☎ 842/422-0259

Sierra de Organos

Relatively unexplored, this 9.7-square-mile (25 sq km) region of Zacatecas is named for the resemblance of its huge igneous rocks to the branches of the organ cactus. It's perfect for hiking, rock climbing, and mountain biking, but it's a remote destination should you have an emergency. Fantastic canyon views and rock formations have induced cinematographers to film scenes for more than 50 movies here, including *Caveman* (1981). Cabins *($)* for up to six people each at the park entrance offer kitchens, bedrooms, and bathrooms; inquire here about guided horseback expeditions.

🅰 105 A2

Sombrerete

Sombrerete, in Zacatecas, was once an important producer of lead, tin, mercury, silver, and gold, and the town has some impressive buildings in baroque and neoclassical styles. Visit the 18th-century **Templo de San Francisco,** the **Templo de la Soledad,** and the **Templo de Santo Domingo,** whose main facade is adorned with female caryatid columns. The town's main fiesta, held for two weeks beginning February 2, honors the Virgin of Candlemas.

www.sombrerete.com.mx 🅰 105 A2 ✉ Av. Hidalgo s/n, Los Portales ☎ 433/935-1438

INSIDER TIP:

Near Reserva Biósfera El Cielo's ranger station, you can rent mules to take you to *los ojos de agua* ("eyes of the water") and other nearby springs.

—DR. SERGIO GUEVARA SADA
Instituto de Ecología, A.C.

Tampico

Tampico has merged with Ciudad Madero in the southern extreme of Tamaulipas to form one of Mexico's major seaports and its tenth largest metropolis. Surrounded on three sides by the Gulf of Mexico, the Pánuco River, and a maze of interconnecting lagoons, this area was fought over by pirates, Spanish settlers, and indigenous tribes throughout the 16th and 17th centuries. Today, late 19th- and early 20th-century buildings surrounding **Plaza de la Libertad** show French and English influence, while on the waterfront oil refineries, storage facilities, and tankers

Strange and beautiful basalt rock formations characterize the Sierra de Organos.

have replaced the picturesque structures of former years. Marimba bands entertain on Sunday afternoons in **Plaza de Armas.** In adjacent Ciudad Madero, the **Museo de la Cultura Huasteca** *(Espacio Cultural Metropolitano, Blvd. López Mateos s/n, Col. Obrera, tel 833/210-2217, closed Sun., $$)* has exhibits on Huasteca culture.

🅰 105 D1

Zona Arqueológica La Quemada

About 31 miles (50 km) south of Zacatecas is **La Quemada,** the ruins of an ancient, unknown culture or cultures, with cylindrical, circular, and rectangular ceremonial structures built of stone, rubblework, and brick. Experts believe they were created by an agricultural group, probably between A.D. 350 and 950.

Among the surviving structures is the mysterious **Salón de las Columnas** (Room of the Columns), a series of 6-foot-tall (1.8 m) brick columns. The purpose of the building called the **Pirámide Votativa** (Votive Pyramid) is not clear, but the ball court is similar to those used throughout Mesoamerica. Stone-and-clay roads radiate for more than 100 miles (160 km) from the hilltop site, possibly constructed to link the northern tribes with more militant peoples to the south. There is a small museum on-site that interprets the evidence of the lost culture or cultures. A paved road reaches the site from Highway 54, which leads south out of Zacatecas.

🅰 105 B2 ☎ 492/922-2184 🅢 $$

Chilies 411

Practically every region of Mexico produces *chile,* the fruit that spices the nation's many distinctive dishes. The names of the chilies change with the region and also depend on the state of the chilie. Piquant jalapeño peppers, for example, one of the most popular and ubiquitous, become the smoky-tasting chile chipotle when dried. Northern Mexico produces the mild *chile dulce,* while at the country's opposite extreme, the Yucatán Peninsula is famous for the *habanero,* a fat orange chile that's as hot as the summer sun. Among Mexico's more than 40 varieties of chile, the dried *chile ancho* is brown and leathery, while the dense *serrano* is used green or ripened

to bright red. All are an excellent source of Vitamin C.

Every cook has her favorite salsas—signature sauces that define her kitchen and nourish the family. In addition to salsas, the most popular recipes featuring chiles include *rajas,* strips of chile poblano sauteed with onions and tomatoes and served in tacos or wrapped in tortillas. Waxy poblano chilies are also used to make *chiles rellenos* (chilies stuffed with a spicy meat mixture, or cheese, and batter-fried) or the quintessential Mexican recipe called *chiles en nogada,* the national dish served with pride during September, the month Mexicans celebrate independence from Spain.

Embracing both the mighty Sierra Madre and the Bajío lowlands, with a legacy of baroque and neoclassical edifices and stately plazas

Central Mexico

Dome of the Templo de San Cayetano in Guanajuato

Central Mexico

"Arriba, abajo, al centro, al dentro" ("Up, down, to the middle, to the inside"), a Spanish drinking toast, also describes the colonization of central Mexico. Spurred by the discovery of huge silver deposits in Zacatecas (up), and subsequently Guanajuato (down), Spanish entrepreneurs swarmed "the middle" to extract mineral deposits. Guanajuato became a great mining city, while San Luis Potosí, Aguascalientes, and San Miguel de Allende became important agricultural centers and way stations.

Along with the entrepreneurs came the Catholic Church. Persuaded to give up their nomadic lifestyle, the Pame tribe in the Sierra Gorda built the missions whose mixture of indigenous and classic ecclesiastic imagery is much admired today. Forty years of warfare against the Guayachicilies around San Luis Potosí, however, failed to subdue this Chichimec tribe. Peace was achieved only after Franciscan friars convinced Spain to offer palatable terms for peace, including freedom from paying tribute.

Free-thinking clergy were among the instigators of independence from Spain, an idea conceived in central Mexico. Intellectual and well-spoken, the idiosyncratic priest Miguel Hidalgo y Costilla is considered the father of Mexican independence. Along with Capt. Ignacio Allende and others, Hidalgo plotted the revolution in Querétaro; his famous cry for freedom was rung on the parish bell at Dolores Hidalgo. Both men were captured and executed, losing their lives but unleashing a bloody war.

After independence, mining concerns continued to thrive with an enlarged European market. On the rich plains of the Bajío region, Querétaro merchants amassed great fortunes providing luxury goods and investment capital. Individual fortunes paid for incredible masterpieces of baroque religious and secular architecture, indulging every whim with imported tiles, French furnishings, and goods made locally by talented artisans.

Today the colonial cities of the Mexican heartland merge history, European and *mestizo* culture, and modernity. Stunning churches and palaces—some now housing hotels, restaurants, and museums—line well-tended plazas, and internationally known musicians perform at Guanajuato's Cervantes Festival (see p. 122) and at San Miguel de Allende's classical and jazz events. Posh colonial-era theaters host the opera and symphony, while *callejoneadas* (roving musical parties) snake through the streets. Throughout the region there are many museums, language schools, and an eclectic range of folk and fine art for sale. ■

4▷

Luis Moya

45

3▷ Rincón de Romos

AGUASCALIENTES
Aguascalientes
Calvillo

2▷

70

△
A

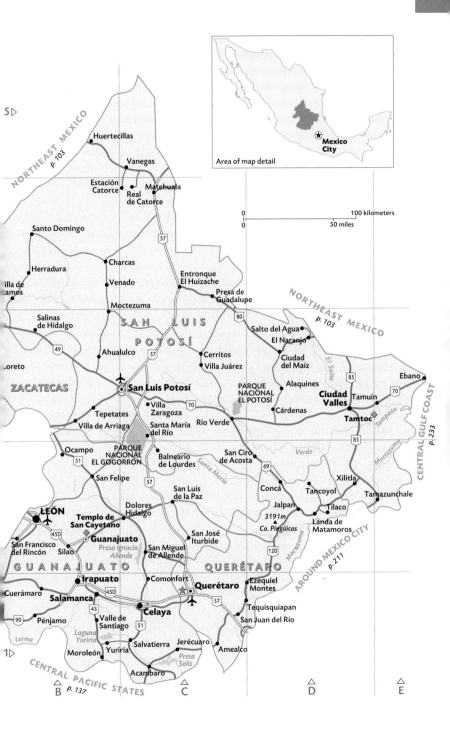

5▷

NORTHEAST MEXICO
p. 103

Huertecillas

Vanegas

Estación
Catorce
Real
de Catorce
Matehuala

Santo Domingo

Herradura

illa de
amos

Charcas

Venado

SAN LUIS

POTOSÍ

Salinas
de Hidalgo

ZACATECAS

49

oreto

Ahualulco

57

Tepetates

Villa de Arriaga

Ocampo

51

San Felipe

PARQUE
NACIONAL
EL GOGORRÓN

LEÓN

Templo de
San Cayetano

San Francisco
del Rincón

Silao

Guanajuato

Presa Ignacio
Allende

GUANAJUATO

Irapuato

45D

Cuerámaro

Salamanca

90

Pénjamo

43

Valle de
Santiago

51

Laguna
Yuriria

Moroleón

Yuriria

Salvatierra

Acámbaro

Presa
Solís

Jerécuaro

CENTRAL PACIFIC STATES

B
p. 137

C

Entronque
El Huizache

Presa de
Guadalupe

80

Moctezuma

57

Cerritos
Villa Juárez

San Luis Potosí

70

Villa
Zaragoza

Santa María
del Río

Río Verde

Balneario
de Lourdes

San Ciro
de Acosta

San Luis
de la Paz

Dolores
Hidalgo

San José
Iturbide

San Miguel
de Allende

Comonfort

Querétaro

QUERÉTARO

Celaya

Ezequiel
Montes

Tequisquiapan

San Juan del Río

Amealco

NORTHEAST MEXICO
p. 103

Salto del Agua
El Naranjo

Ciudad
del Maíz

PARQUE
NACIONAL
EL POTOSÍ

Alaquines

Cárdenas

85

Ciudad
Valles

Tamuín

Tamtoc

85

Verde

Santa María

69

Concá

Tancoyol

Xilitla

Tamazunchale

Jalpan

3191m
Co. Pingüicas

Tilaco

Landa de
Matamoros

120

Moctezuma

AROUND MEXICO CITY

p. 211

El Salto

Ebano

70

CENTRAL GULF COAST
p. 233

Tampaón

Moctezuma

D

E

1▷

Area of map detail

Mexico
City

0   100 kilometers
0   50 miles

Guanajuato

Unlike other cities that radiate in grids from the main plaza, Guanajuato's long, loopy streets intersect at odd angles. A turn in a cobblestone lane may lead to an ancient stairway, a dead end, or one of more than a dozen plazas surrounded by stores, open-air cafés, and rainbow-painted homes. On special occasions *callejoneadas*—movable parties—snake through town, led by student musicians dressed as Spanish troubadours.

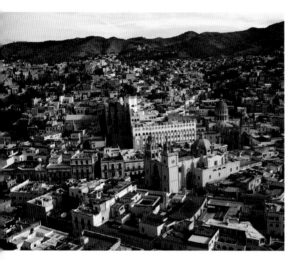

Filled with winding streets and ornate buildings, Guanajuato is one of Mexico's most beautifully preserved colonial cities.

Guanajuato, whose name is derived from a Purépecha Indian word meaning "hill of frogs," begins at the bottom of a gorge, sweeping up the surrounding hills in a tapestry of multicolored dwellings. Most sights are located on or just off extended Juárez and Pocitos streets, both of which change names several times as they follow the ancient riverbed. Tunnels underneath the city divert cross-town traffic, easing mid-city congestion.

Once Mexico's most significant mining town, Guanajuato, capital of its namesake state, has a wealth of magnificent churches,

museums, theaters, and homes—a successful jumble of rococo, Moorish, neoclassical, baroque, and other styles. An impressive example of Churrigueresque architecture is the **Templo de la Compañía de Jésus** *(Plaza de la Compañía near Hidalgo, tel 473/733-9782)*, its fantastic pink-stone facade topped by an elegant neoclassical cupola.

The church originally pertained to the adjacent **Universidad de Guanajuato** *(Lascuráin de Retana 5, tel 473/732-0006)*. Established in 1724 as a Jesuit college, the school is now a major university emphasizing the arts and letters. Leafy **Jardín de la Unión,** the city's social hub, occupies the former atrium of the adjacent 18th-century **Templo de San Diego Alcalá.**

Surrounding the park are restaurants, outdoor cafés, and **Teatro Juárez** *(Calle de Sopeña s/n, at Jardín de la Unión, tel 473/732-0183, closed Mon., $)*, whose sober neoclassical facade belies its luscious interior, with both Moorish and art nouveau elements. One long block southeast is the **Museo Iconográfico del Quijote** *(Manuel Doblado 1, tel 473/732-6721, closed Mon., $)*, where each of the 600 exhibits relates to Spanish author Miguel de Cervantes' Don Quixote or Sancho Panza.

Most of Guanajuato's major sights are found northwest of Jardín de la Unión; many cluster around **Plaza de la Paz** (*Calle de la Paz at Av. Juárez*). Adjacent to the neoclassical green quarrystone **Palacio Legislativo** is the beautiful **Palacio de Justicia** (Supreme Court Building), originally designed by colonial architect Eduardo Tresguerras as the home of Guanajuato's wealthiest mining baron, Count de Rul y Valenciana.

The **Museo del Pueblo de Guanajuato** (*Positos 7, tel 473/732-2990, closed Mon., $*) has a varied collection of secular and religious art highlighting 18th- and 19th-century sculpture, paintings, and decorated utilitarian objects. To the east, the bright yellow **Basílica Colegiata de Nuestra Señora de Guanajuato** houses an eighth-century, polychrome

statue of the Virgin on a silver pedestal. Thought to be Mexico's oldest Christian icon, it was the gift of King Felipe II of Spain.

Family furnishings and photos, the muralist-painter's sketches and finished canvases, and the work of contemporary artists fill the **Museo Casa Diego Rivera** (*Positos 47, tel 473/732-1197, closed Mon., $*), where Rivera was born in 1886.

Soon after its debut as a granary, the **Alhóndiga de Granaditas** staged a rebel success in the War of Independence (see pp. 29–31). It was later captured and used as a fortress by Spanish Royalists, who hung the severed heads of revolutionary leaders in cages from its four corners, where they remained until the end of the war. The structure now houses a **museum** (*Mendizabal*

Guanajuato

⬛ 119 B2

Visitor Information

✉ Plaza de la Paz 14

☎ 473/732-1574 or 1800/714-1086 (toll-free within Mexico)

www.guanajuato .gob.mx

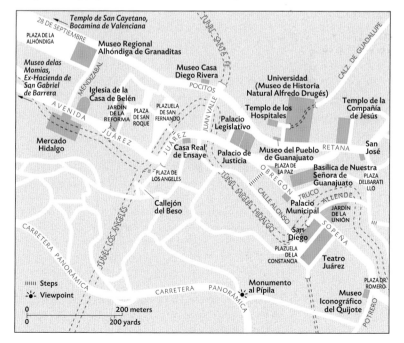

Festival Cervantino

Guanajuato's internationally known Cervantes Festival (*tel 55/5615-9403 ext. 7326 in Mexico City, www.festivalcervantino. gob.mx*) began in the 1950s, when a professor encouraged his students to perform *entremeses*, one-act Spanish plays. The success of these informal productions led to a more organized, annual event.

Seeking to showcase artists across a wide spectrum of genres, the producers contract traditional, folkloric, and avant-garde theater and music ensembles in addition to Chinese acrobats and other world-class acts. Participants have included the Royal Shakespeare Company, the New York Philharmonic Orchestra, and the Black Vampire of Argentina. Today, tens of thousands of spectators attend the two-week event in October, making advance hotel reservations essential.

INSIDER TIP:

Join Guanajuato's frequent *calleoneadas*, musicians and story-tellers, as they parade the streets, attracting spirited crowds.

—CHARLES KULANDER
National Geographic Traveler
magazine writer

6, *tel 473/732-1112, closed Mon., $$*), with murals showing topical regional events as well as history, archaeology, and ethnology exhibits. Nearby is the **Mercado Hidalgo** (*Av. Juárez off Mendizabal*), a busy city market. Designed by French architect Gustave Eiffel in 1910, it is an interesting glass and cast-iron structure.

Lovers of the macabre should visit the **Museo de las Momias** (*Explanada del Panteón, tel 473/732-0639, $$*). Within the mummy museum are more than one hundred former Guanajuato residents, disinterred and displayed in glass cases. A combination of dry atmosphere, unique soil composition, and their descendants' failure to pay cemetery fees permits this ultimate indignity. For just a few pesos more, visit **El Salón del Culto de la Muerte,** next door, with inquisition torture devices and more mummies.

For a breath of fresh air, continue outside town to the **Ex-Hacienda de San Gabriel de Barrera** (*Carr. Antigua a Marfil Km 2.5, tel 473/732-0619, closed Mon., $*). Seventeen fabulous gardens, each in a different horticultural style, grace this restored hacienda. It is now a museum filled with 17th-to 19th-century European art and furnishings.

Perched above the city is the **Templo de San Cayetano,** also known as Templo la Valenciana (*Carr. Dolores Hidalgo Km 2*), built by the Count of Valenciana, a silver baron. The church's beautifully sculpted facade of pink quarrystone leads to an even more dazzling interior with three gilded altarpieces, respectively plateresque, Churrigueresque, and baroque. The adjacent **Bocamina de Valenciana** (*Carr. Dolores Hidalgo Km 5, tel 473/732-0641, $*) is usually visited as part of a tour.

San Miguel de Allende

Some places dazzle, others seduce, but San Miguel de Allende most definitely bewitches. Nothing short of magic explains how a place so full of foreigners remains so endearingly Mexican. Awash with charm, this is a painterly town whose steep, cobblestone streets echo the undulating lines of the surrounding hills. An energetic community of artists produces excellent folk and fine art, in addition to an awesome jazz and blues festival.

Originally a mule train stop along the gold and silver highway, San Miguel later prospered as a market village for surrounding haciendas. The Mexican government wisely declared it a national historic monument in 1926, preventing modern-style buildings from destroying its vintage essence. Since then, its simple but pervasive charms have been luring artists, rat-race dropouts, and students of Spanish.

The **Instituto Allende** *(Ancha de San Antonio 20, tel 415/152-0190, www.instituto-allende.edu. mx)* offers language courses as well as fine arts; the **Escuela de Bellas Artes** *(Hernández Macías 75, tel 415/152-0289)* teaches music, dance, painting, sculpting, and more. Both are located in gracious, two-story, mansions.

Touring the town on foot is most agreeable. A good place to begin is the main square, **Plaza Allende** *(Calles Correo, San Francisco, Portal Allende, & Portal Guadalupe)*, called "el Jardín" by most people. As you negotiate the cobblestone streets and high sidewalks, you'll pass many churches, cozy cafés, and beautiful old homes—most well preserved, some deliciously decrepit. To gain entry to some of the town's mansions and lovely gardens, join

a Sunday **house and garden tour** by bus *($$$$$)*, organized by the **Biblioteca Pública** *(Insurgentes 25, tel 415/152-0293)*. Two-hour guided historical walking tours *($$$$)* depart Monday, Wednesday, and Friday at 9:45 a.m. from La Parroquía on the main plaza.

The city's most cherished icon is the 19th-century Gothic Revival exterior of **La Parroquía de San Miguel Arcángel** *(S side of Plaza*

San Miguel de Allende

 119 C2

Visitor Information

✉ Calle Canal bet. Reloj & Hidalgo, facing plaza

☎ 415/152-0900

www. turismosanmiguel .com.mx

A vibrant courtyard in San Miguel de Allende

Museo de la Casa de Ignacio Allende

✉ Cuna de Allende 1

☎ 415/152-2499

🕐 Closed Mon.

💲 $

La Gruta Hot Springs

✉ Off road leading to Dolores Hidalo, about 5 miles (8 km) outside San Miguel

☎ 415/152-2530

Allende), which untrained local stone cutter Cerefino Gutiérrez is supposed to have designed after looking at postcards of French Gothic cathedrals. The many-steepled church is meant to honor the town's patron saint, the Archangel Michael.

San Miguel's other five-star church is the **Oratorio de San Felipe Neri** (Insurgentes at Loreto), a few blocks northeast of the main

INSIDER TIP:

Visit San Miguel de Allende's social heartbeat, el Jardin, and take a dip in La Gruta Hot Springs.

—PAM GROUT
National Geographic author

plaza. In the west transept, the **camarín de la Virgen de Loreto** (dressing room) is an extraordinary, eight-sided baroque alcove with three impressive altarpieces.

The birthplace of independence hero Ignacio Allende (1779-1811), at what is now the **Museo de la Casa de Ignacio Allende,** is also worth a visit. The museum's

display of colonial-era furnishings complements its 19th-century style with baroque influences.

But what draws tens of thousands of visitors to San Miguel are the city's seemingly endless array of events, many in English. Lectures on spiritualism and fiction writing take place in lovely venues around town. Backgammon fans toss the dice at the public library's **Café Santa Ana** while choral groups practice next door. And there are dozens of fine arts galleries. Check the weekly *Atención* newspaper (*www.atencionsanmiguel. org*) for listings.

In San Miguel's many stores you will find outstanding utilitarian and decorative handicrafts—including tinwork, textiles, blown glass, papier-mâché, and jewelry—with design and technical innovations.

Outside town, visit the public cactus gardens at **El Charco del Ingeniero** (*0.5 mile/1 km out of town, tel 415/154-4715, www. elcharco.org.mx, $*) or one of the many hot-water springs that have been channeled to form pools and spas. Most are en route to Dolores Hidalgo (see p. 136); you can get details from the San Miguel tourism department. ■

Vegetarians in Mexico

Although eating meatless may be a challenge in carnivorous Mexico, vegetarians won't starve. Northern Mexico is especially known for its meat dishes, but tacos and other dishes can be ordered with potatoes or beans as well as guacamole and delicious salsas. Be aware that although *carne* translates as "meat," it is also shorthand for *carne de res*, or

beef. Stress that you don't want *pollo* (chicken), *puerco* (pork), or *productos animales* (animal products). Watch out for *asiento* (pork lard), which may be spread on otherwise meatless snacks. Mexico grows a huge variety of tropical fruits that can be made into juices and *licuados* (smoothies). And be sure not to miss the cactus-pad salads!

Querétaro & Environs

Located in Mexico's Bajío region, Querétaro's wealth of productive farmland made it one of New Spain's most important cities. Since its founding in 1531, the city has figured in political dramas—from plotting independence from Spain to signing the Treaty of Guadalupe Hidalgo, ceding half the country to the United States in 1848. Despite Querétaro's industrial status, its center has baroque churches, historic buildings, and worthy museums.

The Templo de San Francisco (built 1540–1550) overlooks Jardín Zenea, Querétaro's pleasant hub.

Plans to throw off colonial rule were nurtured in the **Casa de la Corregidora** on the north side of dignified **Plaza de Armas** (*Avs. Pasteur & 5 de Mayo*). Here Doña Josefa Ortiz de Domínguez, the wife of the Spanish-appointed *corregidor* (mayor), conspired with Miguel Hidalgo, Ignacio Allende, and other intellectuals. *La corregidora* was later executed. You can explore the interior courtyards of the grand home, which now houses state government offices.

On the plaza's west flank, admire the baroque facade of the 18th-century **Casa de Ecala,** built of sculpted quarrystone and effusively decorated with Talavera tiles.

The city's hub is congenial **Jardín Zenea** (*Avs. Corregidora, 16 de Septiembre, Juárez, & Madero*), a few blocks to the west, where elderly couples get up to dance when the band strikes up on weekend afternoons. Nearby, the dome of the 16th-century **Templo de San Francisco** is

Querétaro

119 C1

Visitor Information

Pasteur Norte 4

01800/715-1742 (toll-free within Mexico) or 442/238-5067, 888/811-6130 (from U.S. & Canada)

www.queretaro .travel

Museo de Arte de Querétaro

 127

✉ Allende Sur 41 at Pino Suárez

☎ 442/212-2357

🕐 Closed Mon.

decorated with imported Spanish tiles. Within the adjoining former monastery, the **Museo Regional de Querétaro** *(Corregidora 3 Sur at Madero, tel 442/212-2031, closed Mon., $$)* houses 17th- to 19th-century furnishings and paintings.

A few blocks north, the 19th-century **Teatro de la República** *(Juárez at Calle A. Peralta)* has seen

INSIDER TIP:

Bernal's Peak near San Sebastián Bernal is said to be an energy point for UFOs.

—ERIC RAMIREZ BRAVO
National Geographic field researcher

its share of real-life drama. The formal signing of the Constitution of 1917 took place here; and Mexico's short-term emperor, Maximilian of Habsburg (see p. 31), was sentenced at the Teatro to die by firing squad in 1867. Today, the neoclassical venue hosts plays and concerts; visitors are welcome to look inside.

The severe early 17th-century facade of the **Iglesia de Santa Clara** *(Madero at Allende, tel 442/212-1777)* belies an extravagant baroque interior. Eduardo Tresguerras (1759–1833), a talented Bajío native, sculpted the adjoining **Fuente de Neptuno** (Neptune Fountain) in 1797. Nonguests can explore the elegant sitting room and bar of the **Casa de la Marquesa** *(Madero 41 at Allende, tel 442/212-0092),* noted for its Mudejar influences and extensive tilework. The

Museo de Arte de Querétaro resides in a fabulous late-baroque building, originally an Augustinian monastery. The museum's extensive collection consists primarily of 16th- to 18th-century paintings from Mexico and Europe. Note the expressions on the faces of the caryatid columns in the monumental inner courtyard.

A Middle Eastern influence can be seen in the **Iglesia y Convento de Santa Rosa de Viterbo** *(Arteaga at Ezequiel Montes, tel 442/212-1691),* with its Mudejar-style cupola and odd inverted flying buttresses adorned with gargoyles. Inside the church are six baroque altarpieces of gilded wood, a lovely pulpit inlaid with ivory, ebony, and silver, and an 18th-century pipe organ.

After the fall of the Second Empire in 1867, Maximilian of Habsburg was executed by firing squad on **Cerro de las Campanas** *(Morelos at Tecnológico)* on the city's west side. An **Expiatory Chapel,**

built by the Austrian government in 1901, commemorates the site. Near the top of the Hill of Bells, a statue of Benito Juárez rises over a wonderful view.

On the opposite side of the city, monks carry on with their devotions despite the distraction of guided visits to their early 17th-century monastery, the **Convento de la Santa Cruz,** considered the site of a miracle. Legend recounts that the Apostle James (Santiago, patron saint of Spain) appeared on a white horse to urge the Spaniards to victory over the Otomí. Behind the church you can see part of the 18th-century 4,000-foot (1,200 m) **aqueduct,** a marvel of 74 sandstone arches.

Thirty-three miles (54 km) north of Querétaro is the little colonial town of **San Sebastián Bernal,** with deep yellow and ocher-red buildings and flagstone streets. People from surrounding cities flock here on weekends to enjoy the town's slow pace, eat food from casual restaurants, and to buy souvenirs like wool sweaters and lace tablecloths. X-treme types come for the rock climbing: outside town is **la Peña de Bernal,** the world's third largest monolith (1,150 feet/350 m).

Less than an hour's drive southeast of Querétaro, **San Juan del Río** (visitor information, Av. Juárez at el Templo del Santuario) is a prosperous market town, known for its baskets, wood carvings, palm furniture, and semiprecious gems, especially amethysts, Mexican opals, and topaz.

Tequisquiapan (tel 414/273-0295, www.tequis.info), north of San Juan (visitor information, Plaza Hidalgo, Andador Independencia 1), is smaller and more picturesque. Swimming pools with restaurants cluster outside town. Sarapes, wicker baskets, and other handicrafts are available. In late may or early June is the **Fiesta del Queso y del Vino.** ■

Convento de la Santa Cruz

🄰 127

✉ Independencia at Felipe Luna, Barrio de Santa Cruz

☎ 442/212-0235

🕐 Closed Mon.

$ Donation

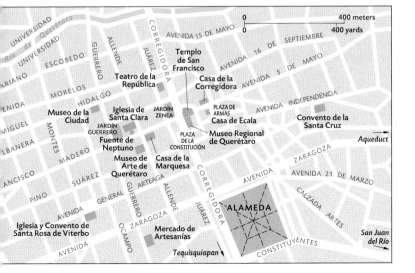

Las Misiones de la Sierra Gorda Drive

Between 1751 and 1768, five Franciscan missions were built amid the Sierra Gorda, a rugged range heading northeast of Querétaro toward Ciudad Valles, San Luis Potosí. Led by Fray Junípero Serra, Franciscan monks attempted to catechize the Pame (a Chichimec tribe). The unusual mission churches exemplify Mexican baroque style and combine Christian didactic symbols with indigenous sensibilities.

The drive along mountain roads is curvy yet beautifully scenic, ascending through a semi-arid landscape to mountain escarpments and valleys peppered with pines.

Misión de Jalpan ❶ *(tel 441/296-0033),* perches on a high bluff northeast of Querétaro. It is 73 miles (118 km) away, driving first east on Highway 45 and then northeast on Highway 120. The first mission built (1751–1758) in this isolated region, Jalpan is the best base for

Young visitors rest on the steps outside Jalpan mission.

persons who are planning to stay overnight, because it has the most hotels and restaurants. On the mission's facade, statues of the revered Virgin of Guadalupe and the Virgin of Pilar symbolize the equal importance of Mexico and Spain. Near the bottom of the facade, note the double-edged symbolism of the two-headed eagle (a Habsburg icon) devouring a snake (a well-known Aztec icon).

NOT TO BE MISSED:

Misión de Jalpan • Misión de Concá • Landa • Tilaco

The adjacent **Museo Histórico de la Sierra Gorda** *(tel 441/296-0165, closed Mon. & 2–4 p.m.)* has artifacts from the Pame, Chichimec, Purépecha, and monastic cultures.

From Jalpan head northwest on Highway 69 toward Río Verde. After about 25 miles (40 km) you will come to **Misión de Concá ❷**, at the entrance to town. Although both the town and adjoining mission are located in Arroyo Seco (Dry Riverbed) township, thermal springs abound. The striking orange-and-red-ocher facade of this church, the smallest in the Sierra Gorda, is notable for detail that mimics the foliage of the semitropical valley in which it sits. The profuse decoration and the rather heavy-handed sculptures show the involvement of the region's indigenous artisans. Crowning the facade is a Trinity, rarely seen in Mexico.

Return to Jalpan and continue on Highway 120 to **Misión de Landa de Matamoros ❸**, its elaborate facade resplendent with carved saints tucked within niches. The drive is about 37 miles (60 km) total. The last mission church to be built, Landa is also the most intact. All together within this compound are a church, cloister, open chapel, atrium, and four *posas,* or corner chapels.

Drive north for 6 miles (10 km). Take a right turn and follow this road for another

6 miles (10 km) to **Misión de Tilaco** ④. As at Jalpan, sculptures of Saints Peter and Paul flank the wide portal. Above, the images of St. Joseph and the Virgin on the second level symbolize familial devotion. Near the top of the facade, a multitude of angels flies up toward a fabulous garden.

Returning to Highway 120, continue northeast to the left-hand turnoff to **Misión de Tancoyol** ⑤ (tel 429/293-3718). Drive about 10 miles (16 km) through the forested valley of Tancoyol (meaning "place of coyoles," a regional fruit). This mission's facade is decorated with Franciscan saints and symbols, although two of the interior columns are crowned with a jaguar and a character with Indian features.

Back at Highway 120, return to Querétaro or make the shorter drive to **Ciudad Valles,** in the Huasteca region of San Luis Potosí (via Highway 85). The second route will take you past **Xilitla** ⑥ and the open-air sculptures of Scottish eccentric Edward James (see p. 136).

All of the missions open daily at 7 a.m. and close around sunset.

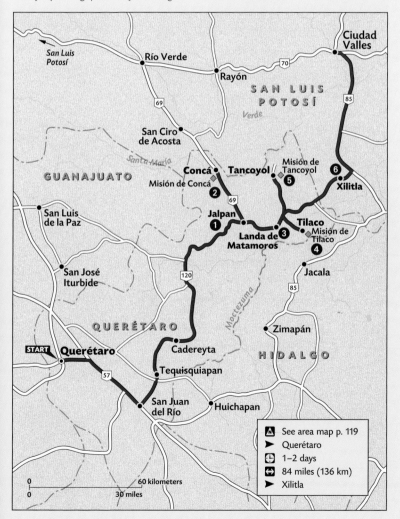

- See area map p. 119
- ► Querétaro
- ⊕ 1–2 days
- ⇄ 84 miles (136 km)
- ► Xilitla

San Luis Potosí

In the mid- and late 16th century, the discovery of rich veins of silver in neighboring Zacatecas and Guanajuato flamed the Spanish desire for precious metals. They struck silver at Cerro de San Pedro but established the city of Real San Luis Minas de Potosí (now San Luis Potosí) some 8 miles (5 km) away. The large mineral deposits petered out fairly quickly, but by then San Luis was firmly established as a center of ranching and commerce.

The Capilla de Aranzazú, within the Museo Regional Potosino, is a chapel unique for its second-story location.

Once the most important city in northern Mexico, San Luis Potosí was capital of a huge region encompassing not only today's states of Nuevo León and Coahuila but also Texas and Louisiana. The city maintains its sense of tradition with a wealth of urban colonial and republican-era buildings in its historic center. Many are neoclassical, and a number of baroque churches have been remodeled with neoclassical interiors. Now home to a million people, San Luis enjoys a brisk, sunny climate with little temperature variation. More then 90 percent of its visitors are nationals.

Potosinos are proud of their cuisine. Specialties include *enchiladas potosinas* (a cornmeal and chili mixture filled with cheese, fried, and garnished with fresh onions) and *tacos Camila* (tortillas filled with cheese, lightly fried, and buried under a medley of vegetables). The city is also known for its *queso de tuna,* a caramelized treat of condensed cactus juice.

Unpretentious restaurants serving the local fare are found on and around the main square, popular **Plaza de Armas,** also called Jardín Hidalgo *(bet. Los Bravo, Zaragoza, Othón, & 5 de Mayo).* Upscale cafés and restaurants line Avenida V. Carranza west of **Plaza de los Fundadores.** Also on this busy street is the **Casa de la Cultura** *(Av. V. Carranza 181, tel 444/813-2247, closed Mon., $),* built in the 1920s as an elegant mansion in the English neoclassic style. The cultural center doubles as a museum with Mexican and European religious art, regional handicrafts, and pre-Hispanic artifacts. Along with the new **Centro de las Artes de San Luis Potosí** *(Calzada de Guadalupe 705, Col.*

Julian Carrillo, tel 444/137-4100), it offers concerts, film festivals, and other events. The latter, in the city's former penitentiary, is worth a look for the amazing architectural rehabilitation project.

Several blocks east, **Museo Federico Silva** *(Alvaro Obregón 80, tel 444/812-3848, closed Tues., $)* displays one of the most important collections of contemporary sculpture in all of Latin America.

You can probably find regional handiwork cheaper elsewhere, but **La Casa de los Artesanos** *(Av. V. Carranza 540, tel 444/814-8990)* has all the state's typical folk art and souvenirs in one place and pays fair prices to artisans.

North of Plaza de Armas, Calle Hidalgo is closed to traffic for several blocks leading to the

1005, tel 444/815-0769), built in the shape of the Latin cross, shows a mixture of late-baroque and neoclassical styles. Its high altar has a painting of the Virgin of Guadalupe by Jesús Corral.

On the southwest side of the city, **El Laberinto de las Ciencias** *(Blvd. Antonio Rocha Cordero s/n, Parque Tangamanga I, tel 444/210-0108, $$)* opened in 2008. Among this museum's fantastic indoor-outdoor exhibits are a musical cactus garden and an aluminum tube that shoots daily newspaper headlines in sprays of water. There's an interactive kids' room, too. Also in Parque Tangamanga are jogging and cycling paths, mountain-bike trails, and the city's open-air theater.

About 30 miles (48 km) south

San Luis Potosí

🅰 119 C3

Visitor Information

✉ State tourism office, Manuel José Othón 130, Centro

☎ 444/812-9939 or 01800/343-3887 (toll-free within Mexico)

✉ Muncipal tourism office, Palacio Municipal, Jardín Hidalgo

☎ 444/812-2770

www.visitsanluis potosi.com

EXPERIENCE: Riding the Range

San Luis Potosí state has programs aimed at introducing travelers to its varied landscapes. Among these adventures are horseback rides to archetypical Mexico, a few paces off the beaten path.

In the Altiplano region, local men lead reasonably priced horseback expeditions to explore the dry mesas and plateaus around the former mining town of **Real de Catorce** and **Guadalcázar** *(information*

for both: tel 488/882-5005). Not all of the cowboys speak excellent English, but that's part of the fun.

In the central region *(tel 487/871-6359),* horseback-riding treks access **La Cathedral caves** and the swimmable **Laguna La Media Luna** outside Río Verde. For more information, contact the State Tourism Board *(tel 444/812-9939)* or visit *www. visitsanluispotosi.com* (Spanish only).

---

municipal market, **Mercado Hidalgo.** South of the plaza, the neoclassical **Caja de Agua** is an unusual monument to public works. Built in 1832, this water storage tank was used by city residents until the 1900s.

Farther south along Avenida Juárez, 18th-century **Santuario de Guadalupe** *(Calz. de Guadalupe*

of the city lies **Santa María del Río,** a town dedicated to weaving exquisite shawls of silk (or nowadays, synthetic materials). This region is also known for its hot springs. **Balneario de Lourdes,** 12 miles (20 km) southeast of Santa María, has medicinal alkaline waters, a restaurant, and hotel.

(continued on p. 134)

San Luis Walk

San Luis Potosí was afforded city status in 1656, but many of its important buildings were constructed in the 18th and 19th centuries. Throughout the historic center are baroque, neoclassical, and structures built during the presidential era of Porfirio Díaz (1877–1911), who commissioned many buildings in the European style.

The city's limestone buildings range from pink and peach to gray and pale yellow.

Begin your walk at **Plaza de los Fundadores,** at Avenidas V. Carranza and D. Carmona. At the northwest corner, visit the late 16th-century **Capilla de Loreto** ❶, its facade graced with a baroque portal. Inside is one of Mexico's few surviving Jesuit altarpieces. Walk east on Obregón, past the rectory of the **Universidad Autónoma,** in a former Jesuit monastery.

Cross the square diagonally and head east on Av V. Carranza to **la Plaza de Armas** ❷ (*Jardín Hidalgo*), surrounded by historic buildings and shaded by magnolia trees. Note the sober neoclassical lines of the **Palacio de Gobierno,** which occupies the square's west flank. This state government building twice housed the interim government of Benito Juárez during the French occupation (see p. 31).

Taking a clockwise turn around the square, you will pass the oldest house in the city, **Casa**

NOT TO BE MISSED:

Templo del Carmen • Museo Nacional de la Máscara • Templo de San Francisco • Capilla de Aranzazú

Virreina, built in 1736. Now an excellent restaurant, it was once the home of Mexico's only female vicereine, Francisca de la Gandara. On the northeast corner of the square is the 19th-century **Palacio Municipal** *(closed Sat.–Sun.).*

The imposing baroque **Catedral** ❸ *(tel 444/812-2439)* dominates the square's southeast corner. Note the Carrara marble statues of the Apostles adorning the facade. The neoclassical altars and Byzantine decorations inside were added in the 19th century.

A few blocks farther east on Calle Manuel J. Othón is the baroque **Templo del Carmen** ❹ (tel 427/273-3564), its Churrigueresque facade nearly as ornate as the cathedral in Zacatecas (see p. 112). Inside are impressive side altars; the main altar, designed by architect Eduardo Tresguerras (1759–1833); and the **camarín de la Virgen,** a baroque chapel whose gold altarpiece is crowned with a giant scallop shell. Within the former convent, the **Museo del Virreinato** (tel 444/812-5257, closed Mon., $) shows colonial treasures.

Facing lovely **Plaza del Carmen** on its southeast side is the neoclassical **Teatro de la Paz** (Villerías 205, tel 444/812-5909, closed Mon.), built during the Porfiriato era. The French neoclassical building at the south end of the plaza houses the telegraph office and the **Museo Nacional de la Máscara** ❺ (Villerías 210, tel 444/812-3025, closed Mon., $), which now displays hundreds of ceremonial masks.

Walk south to Avenida Universidad. Turn right and walk several blocks to **Plaza de San Francisco,** also known as Jardín Guerrero.

Cross the long, rectangular plaza to the pink-stone 17th-century **Templo de San Francisco** ❻ (tel 444/812-4246). Note the Franciscan emblems and saints on the baroque facade. Ask permission to see the lovely Churrigueresque sacristy, with paintings by Miguel Cabrera, Antonio de Torres, and Francisco Martínez. Below the main dome, a ship-shaped crystal chandelier alludes to the evangelical travels of the order's founder, St. Francis of Assisi.

Behind the church, the former Franciscan monastery contains the **Museo Regional Potosino** ❼ (Plaza de Aranzazú, tel 444/814-3572, closed Mon. $), with pre-Hispanic artifacts and colonial-era statues and furnishings. Within the museum, the 18th-century **Capilla de Aranzazú** is a chapel unique for its second-story location and covered atrium.

Ⓜ	See area map p. 119 C3
▶	Plaza de los Fundadores
⊕	0.8 mile (1.3 km)
⟷	4 hours
▶	Capilla de Aranzazú

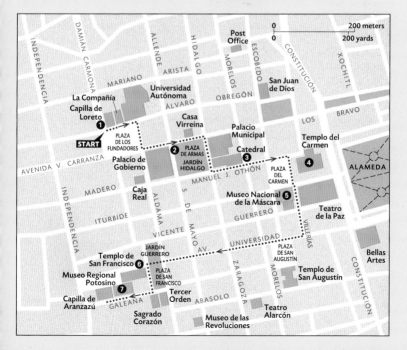

Real de Catorce

🗺 119 C4

Visitor Information

✉ Constitución 27

☎ 488/882-5005

Real de Catorce

This nearly abandoned town, isolated amid the arid mountains and high desert of the Sierra Madre Oriental, attracts only the most curious or solitary of travelers, as well as pilgrims who come to venerate a miraculous effigy of St. Francis of Assisi. Rarely seen in town, Huichol Indians scour the surrounding hills in search of sacred peyote, a hallucinogenic plant used in mystical rituals throughout the year.

During its productive years between the late 18th and early 20th centuries, Real de Catorce built impressive private homes for its nearly 40,000 citizens. Many are now crumbling into ruins, while

tower. Tucked in a side altar, its image of St. Francis of Assisi is said to have miraculous powers, attested by the hundreds of naive ex-votos (paintings giving thanks for blessings received) on display. Thousands of pilgrims descend on the town each year to celebrate the October 4 holy day associated with the Franciscan Order's founder.

Other structures of note are the stone *palenque,* or cock-fighting arena, sometimes used as an amphitheater, and the **bullring** (both from the late 18th century), as well as the dilapidated **Casa de la Moneda,** the former mint.

Real de Catorce's clear, starry nights—a consequence of the

EXPERIENCE: Bring Your Camera

Mexico is a wonderful place for a camera, with its varied geographies, plant life, and animals, its colorful people and brilliant light. Even in small Real de Catorce, photography holds an honored place. Cristino Rodríguez Hernández of **Willys de México** (*tel 488/882-6108*) leads 4WD tours, in Spanish only, through spectacular high desert, with a chance to photograph historic religious sites as well as nature.

Photography workshops are offered throughout the country. **National Geographic Expeditions** (*www.*

nationalgeographicexpeditions.com) hosts a seven-day Day of the Dead workshop in Oaxaca, featuring one of its renowned photographers; another workshop is taught in beautiful San Miguel de Allende (see pp. 123–124). Each fall **Santa Fe Photographic Workshops** (*www.santafe workshops.com*) offers one-week courses in San Miguel. And **Baja Expeditions** (*www. bajaexpeditions.com*) organizes a one-week cruise that includes instruction in the techniques specific to capturing wildlife images in the harsh sunlight of Baja and the Sea of Cortez.

---

others house modest restaurants, hotels, and modern businesses.

It doesn't take long to complete the tourist circuit. The simple stone church, the **Parroquia de la Purísima Concepción,** is built in the traditional Latin cross format, with a single sturdy bell

town's elevation at 9,042 feet (2,756 m) above sea level—are one of its most captivating attractions. For something a little more physical than stargazing, rent a horse through one of the hotels or restaurants and make an excursion outside town.

Aguascalientes

The capital of one of Mexico's smallest states was originally conceived as a defensive way station between regional silver mines and Mexico City. Farms and ranches sprang up around it to supply the mining towns, and today the city serves them as a commercial center. North of town lie its namesake hot springs and the San Marcos Winery, where the region's grapes are turned into brandy.

Aguascalientes is especially popular during **Feria Nacional de San Marcos** *(mid-April–mid-May),* celebrated since the early 19th century. It has parades, concerts, fireworks, bullfights, and livestock expos, with special festivities on the feast day of St. Mark, April 25. Events are at the fairgrounds in the **Jardín San Marcos** and **ExpoPlaza,** connected by pedestrian-only Calle Pani.

With its and historic buildings, **Plaza de la Patria** recalls the city's colonial past. On the plaza, Aguascalientes' oldest church (1575), the **Catedral Nuestra Señora de la Asunción** *(tel 449/915-1052),* has endured several renovations. Ask to see the 18th-century paintings by Miguel Cabrera.

Aguascalientes's state government palace (Palacio de Gobierno) resembles many of the government buildings in Spain.

Behind the cathedral is the **Museo de Historia Regional** *(V. Carranza 118, tel 449/916-5228, closed Mon., $$).* Across the plaza, the lovely **Palacio de Gobierno** *(tel 449/915-1155)* contains murals by Chilean Oswaldo Barra Cunningham, a protégé of Diego Rivera.

East of the plaza, the **Museo de Aguascalientes** *(Zaragoza 507, tel 449/915-9043, closed Mon., $)* exhibits paintings of Aguascalientes native Saturnino Herrán (1887–1918). Across the street, admire the stained-glass windows of the cupola at the **Templo de San Antonio** *(Pedro Parga*

& Zaragoza, tel 449/915-2898).

Near the central plaza, the **Museo de Arte Contemporáneo** *(P. Verdad at Morelos, tel 449/915-7953, closed Mon., $)* has a permanent collection of young, prize-winning artists. The affiliated **Centro El Obraje** *(Juan de Montoro 222, tel 449/994-0074, closed Mon.–Fri. 2 p.m.–4 p.m. & weekends, $)* exhibits work from the attached printmaking studio.

See the work of local political cartoonist José Guadalupe Posada (1852–1913) at the **Museo José Guadalupe Posada** *(Díaz de León, Jardín del Encino, tel 449/915-4556, closed Mon., $).* ∎

Aguascalientes

🅰 118 A2

Visitor Information

✉ Palacio de Gobierno, Plaza de la Patria

☎ 449/910-2088

More Places to Visit in Central Mexico

Dolores Hidalgo

Mexico's War of Independence officially began in this town, then known as Dolores. On September 15, 1810, Father Miguel Hidalgo y Costilla launched the movement that resulted 11 years later in freedom from Spanish rule (see p. 30). **Casa Hidalgo** *(Morelos 1, tel 418/182-0171, closed Mon., $),* the priest's former home, is now a museum with war artifacts and historic documents. Visit the baroque church, **Nuestra Señora de los Dolores,** on the main plaza, where the priest first sounded the alarm. The town's distinctive tiles can be seen adorning the better hotels and restaurants throughout Mexico; tiles and pottery can be purchased locally. Dolores is also known for its ice cream.
🗺 119 C2 ☎ 418/182-1164 ✉ 25 miles (40 km) N of San Miguel de Allende; 30 miles (48 km) N of Guanajuato

La Huasteca

Encompassing parts of San Luis Potosí, Veracruz, Tamaulipas, and Hidalgo states, La Huasteca is named for the cultural group that lives in this region of secluded valleys and wild mountains, lakes, forests, and steaming coastal plains. A good base for exploring the region is **Ciudad Valles,** San Luis Potosí's second largest city.

Little visited by tourists, La Huasteca has a variety of natural attractions. Caves await enterprising spelunkers, sheer rock walls tempt climbers, and opportunities for rafting, kayaking, hiking, and bird-watching abound. Cloud-forest conditions prevail in the **Reserva de la Biósfera Abra-Tanchipa,** a 51,890-acre (21,000 ha) biosphere surrounding Ciudad Valles. Abundant rainfall creates lush forests and feeds fabulous waterfalls such as **Tamul, El Salto,** and **Minas Viejas,** where tropical trees sprouting wild orchids surround crystal-clear pools tinged green or blue.

Towns such as **Tancanhuitz** and **Tamazunchale**—with large Huastec

populations—can be visited on Sunday market day, to sample local delicacies, buy crafts, and perhaps listen to a *huapango,* regional music accompanied by violins, flute, *jarana* (small guitar), harp, and rhythm instruments.
🗺 119 D3 ✉ Hidalgo 18, Ciudad Valles ☎ 481/383-2459

INSIDER TIP:

Although native vegetation in central Mexico is sparse, you'll find eucalyptus trees from Australia along the roadways and African calla lilies bordering the canals.

—MARAEL JOHNSON
National Geographic author

Xilitla

Near the Querétaro border and the missions of the Sierra Gorda, **Las Pozas** is a fantastic garden of sculptures built by surrealist poet Edward James (1907–1986). The wealthy eccentric exchanged Edwardian Britain for *peyote*-inspired projects in the Mexican highlands. With friend and mentor Plutarco Gastelum and a group of local artisans, the Scot occupied more than 30 years of his life creating an 80-acre (32 ha) dreamscape. About three dozen surrealist concrete structures—some 100 feet (30 m) tall—lose themselves in the equally fascinating tropical forest. At the site are a waterfall and a series of clear pools for bathing. In the nearby town of **Xilitla,** Gastelum built James an equally odd house, now a unique bed-and-breakfast—**Hotel El Castillo** *(tel 489/365-0038, $$).* On Sundays visit Xilitla's open-air market, or take in a church service in the temple, all that remains of the 450-year-old Augustinian monastery.
www.xilitla.org 🗺 119 D2 ✉ Las Pozas: 3 miles (5 km) outside Xilitla 💲 $$

Lush and humid, with miles of untrammeled coast, small cities full of understated charm, posh beach resorts, and some of the country's best folk art

Central Pacific States

A close-up of Huichol Indian yarn art

Central Pacific States

Sharing a swath of coast and the foothills and mountains that rise abruptly beyond it, central Pacific Mexico has a multitude of distinctly different destinations. Manzanillo calls itself the "sailfish capital of the world," Puerto Vallarta is a fast-growing beach resort brimming with art galleries, and Michoacán's undeveloped coast is the playground of surfers and locals.

There are boutique hotels on isolated bays and beaches, lazy fishing villages on mangrove lagoons, and Acapulco, with its all-night salsa clubs. Inland are straight-laced Guadalajara, land of mariachis and tequila, funky Colima, and whitewashed Taxco, looking like a misplaced Mediterranean village.

Indigenous people are not found here in great numbers. The largest population is the Nahua-speaking people of Guerrero. In Nayarit, mountain-dwelling populations of Huichol, though small in number, maintain their cultural identity and religious practices. Shamans cure the sick and perform magic rituals, while everyday citizens are guided by an ancestral wisdom. Mirroring Huichol daily activities are playful, naive-looking figurines that their ancestors left in the area's unique shaft tombs (buried at the bottom of vertical passageways) beginning around 250 B.C.

Soon after the fall of Tenochtitlán (see pp. 27–28), the Spanish conquerors fanned out in search of further adventure, bringing to bear the usual influences, including widespread death by disease. The Indians suffered especially violent treatment at the hands of conquistador Nuño Beltrán de Guzmán, whose reign of terror stretched from Sinaloa to Guadalajara. Individuals were branded and sold as slaves, and hundreds of villages burned.

Those Indians who survived disease and injustice took to the hills. After de Guzmán was dispatched to a Spanish jail, Bishop Vasco de Quiroga lured the Purépecha back to their villages in today's Michoacán. He built as many hospitals as churches, and schooled indigenous artisans in useful trades.

Today, Michoacán is one of Mexico's leading producers of fine crafts, including copper cookware, wooden furniture, pottery, and elegant lacquerware. The Huichol produce fabulous yarn paintings, masks, and beaded objects for ritual use and for sale to a growing body of collectors. Throughout the region, but especially in Michoacán and Guerrero, ritual masks and elaborate costumes are used during celebrations that incorporate elements of both pre-Hispanic and Catholic ritual. ■

NOT TO BE MISSED:

Mariachi music, the heartbeat of Guadalajara **151, 155**

Sampling true tequila **154, 155**

Volcán de Colima, the most active volcano in North America **159**

Shopping for Purépecha crafts **163**

Day of the Dead festivities on the island of Janitzio **164**

San Juan Parangaricutiro, a town buried in lava **167**

Watching the cliff divers at Acapulco and having a drink overlooking the bay **170–173**

Taxco silver shops **174**

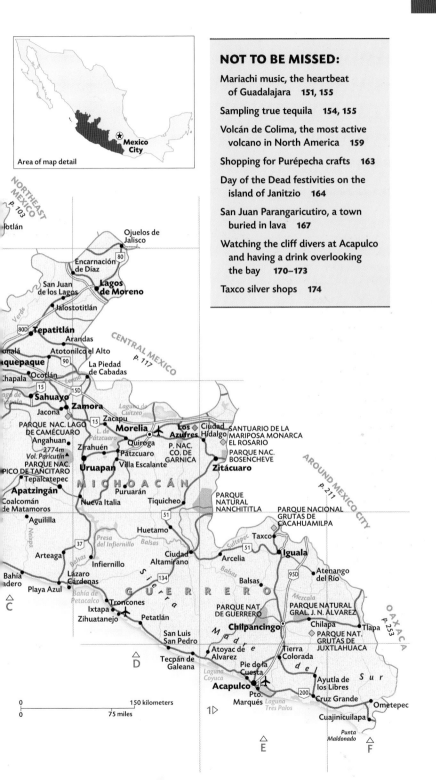

Area of map detail

Mexico City

0   150 kilometers
0   75 miles

Tepic

Tepic is the capital of the small state of Nayarit, which produces much of the country's tropical fruits and tobacco. It's a crossroads of agriculture and commerce where farmers come to town to buy supplies and sell their produce. In the foothills at 2,950 feet (900 m) above sea level, it is significantly cooler than the coast.

Tepic
🔺 138 B4
Visitor Information
✉ Av. México
   at Calzada
   del Ejército
   Nacional
☎ 311/214-8071
**www.visitnayarit
.com**

Huichol men in white cotton trousers and embroidered tunics sell their handicrafts in front of the cathedral. Along with their close relatives, the Cora, they fled to the mountains to escape the cruel Nuño de Guzmán in the 16th century (see p. 138). Many women of both groups still wear their colorful traditional clothing.

Many Huichol men and women still wear traditional clothing.

Tepic isn't touristy. Accordingly, prices are inexpensive. Aside from the usual government buildings with murals, and churches, folks visit **el Museo Casa de los Cinco Pueblos** (*Av. Mexico 111 at E. Zapata*), which displays and sells clothing and handicrafts representative of *mestizo* culture as well as the state's four indigenous groups: Cora, Huichol, Tepehuano, and Mexicanero.

Housed in a restored 18th-century mansion is the **Museo de Antropología e Historia** (*Av. México 91 Norte at Zapata, tel 311/212-1900, closed Sun., $*). It displays pre-Hispanic artifacts, regional folk art, and colonial religious paintings.

Several lovely lakes are within an hour's drive of Tepic. Off the toll road to Guadalajara is the deep, crystalline crater lake **Laguna Santa María del Oro.** Here you can swim with locals, fish, camp, explore the lake by boat (*boats for rent, $$$$*), have a picnic, or simply enjoy a walk around the lake taking in the breathtaking views of the surrounding mountains. There's a boat ramp for ski boats.

A turnoff just before the town of Santa María leads to **Laguna de Tepeltitic,** smaller and shallower than Laguna Santa María del Oro but surrounded by a lovely forest. ∎

The Riviera Nayarit

Along with federal grants and corporate funds, Nayarit state is investing in tourism infra-structure along some 99 miles (160 km) of coast between San Blas and Nuevo Vallarta. Beaches that have traditionally attracted escapists from Puerto Vallarta are now being developed, but for the time being the lifestyle is still laid back, the pace is relaxed, and palm-fringed beaches beckon.

Families enjoy a day of sunbathing and boating at Rincón de Guayabitos on the Riviera Nayarit.

About an hour north of Tepic (see opposite), coastal **San Blas** has been anathema to mass tourism for years, in large part due to its *jejenes* (or no-see-ums). While these biting gnats can be fierce, their reputa-tion—which far exceeds the menace—has at least served to keep developers from thinking twice. For the time being, San Blas's miles of solitary beaches have been spared high-rises and private developments.

An important port during the colonial era, sleepy San Blas is today headquarters for birders and beach bums who avoid fancy resorts. At this writing there is but one elegant hotel, and just enough restaurants and amenities to entertain a dedicated following. For many the highlight of their vacation is a boat trip *(El Conchal Bridge, entrance to San Blas, $$$$)* up Estero San Cristóbal to **La Tovara** freshwater spring. Herons, egrets, turtles, alligators, and other aquatic fauna haunt

Riviera Nayarit
 138 B4
**www.rivieranayarit
.com**

San Blas

⚐ 138 B4

Visitor Information

✉ Canalizo at Sinaloa, Presidencia Municipal

☎ 323/285-0005

www.visitsanblas
.com

Paradise Village

☎ 322/226-6770 (from Mexico) or 800/995-5714 (toll-free in U.S.)

www.paradisevillage
.com

mazelike canals of mangroves. After an hour-long ride, you'll have an hour to swim in the spring before the return trip.

San Blas's closest beach is **Playa Borrego,** which terminates in an estuary. This beach is especially infamous for its no-see-ums (ward off with DEET-based repellent, cover-up clothes or by avoiding sunrise and dusk). To the south, **Las Islitas** is a lovely stretch of beach punctuated by rocky coves. Here you can lounge in a hammock or play a game of dominoes under a *ramada* (palm-thatch, open-sided structure). The bay is backed by jungle-clad mountains and the beach is long and unadorned. Farther round the curve of the bay

short string of seafood restaurants on the soft white sand. Next stop is **Rincón de Guayabitos.** On lovely Bahía de Jaltemba, this soft sand beach is the haven of Mexican families on vacation and Canadian snowbirds. Its streets are loaded with small hotels and nearly identical informal restaurants, grocery stores, and bathing suit shops.

Lo de Marcos is for the moment a somnolent seaside town geared mainly to Mexican families. South of the town proper, twin beaches **Las Minitas** and **Los Venados** are nice for fishing and bathing in the calm waters. Not 10 miles (16 km) south, **San Francisco** is a growing beach community more often called by its nickname, San Pancho. For a small town it has a disproportionate number of fine restaurants. Designed as a company town (mango processing) by former president Luis Echevarría, San Pancho has wide, straight streets and a pretty beach. Swimming here is dicey, as the waves are not gentle, and there's an undertow.

Just beyond a headlands on a lovely cove, **Sayulita** has been coming into its own for decades. The narrow streets, muddy and rutted during summer rains, support increasing traffic but the town's attitude is nearly as kicked back as ever. This is surfer heaven, as there are lefts and rights, shore and reef breaks, and lots of inexpensive restaurants. As up and down the coast, boats pulled up on the beach are available for impromptu surfing safaris, turtle- or dolphin-watching expeditions, or fishing trips. On a hill outside of town proper, **Haramara** is a lovely yoga retreat.

Punta de Mita, at the northern

EXPERIENCE:
Surfing in Sayulita

In Sayulita, Nayarit, there are several options for learning to surf . . . and several different surf spots as well. There's a right break directly off the main beach that's good for beginners and a faster left just north of town across the river. **Costa Azul resort** (tel 800/365-7613, www.costaazul. com) offers packages and individual lessons. On the main beach, **Patricia Southwood** (tel 329/291-2070) has boards for rent as well as lessons at reasonable prices. **Via Yoga** (www.viayoga.com) workshops combine vinyasa yoga with surf lessons.

Haramara

✉ 16 Tamarindos, Puerto Vallarta

☎ 329/291-3558 or 888/494-3688 (toll-free in U.S.)

www.haramara
retreat.com

toward the small fishing village of Santa Cruz is **Playa Los Cocos,** shaded by palms, and **Bahía Matanchén,** once a surf mecca but less awesome since hurricanes altered the ocean floor.

Another hour south, **Playa Chacala** is rarely crowded and offers a

Traveling with Children

Traveling in Mexico with kids is kind of like walking your dog in Central Park—an ideal way to meet people. Mexicans adore children and will instantly gravitate to the traveling gringo family. Few people enjoy intercity bus rides, with the dilapidated vehicles, but most children enjoy intra-city bus rides. All but second-class buses have bathrooms. Beach destinations have water parks, as do inland sites, many of them fed by warm springs. Fresh fruits are abundant, and there's no lack of such universal kid-pleasers as pizza, quesadillas, burgers, and fries.

tip of Bahía de Banderas, has been sealed off from the hoi polloi and is now the exclusive domain of high-rollers. Entry to the exclusive resort complex—home to the Four Seasons and St. Regis Resorts, as well as boutique hotels and private residences—is strictly for guests. Facing the complex, **El Anclote** is still a kicked-back beach with seafood restaurants (more expensive now), cheaper hotels, and surfboard rentals.

The southernmost stop on the federal government's Escalera Naútica program of private marinas—from Baja down the Sea of Cortez—**La Cruz de Huana-caxtle** is ripening from a green fishing village to something more sophisticated. Although the town retains a simple charm, land prices have skyrocketed and development around the 400-slip marina has begun. Just south, burgeoning **Bucerías** has a good deal more experience with tourism. Strung out between Highway 200 and its 3-mile (5 km) beach, this town doesn't look appealing from the road; however, it boasts many good restaurants, bars, and plenty of home rentals, the latter snapped up by wintering snowbirds. There is a small but growing number of hotels. Overlooking the wide, flat,

grainy sand beach—which heads south nonstop to Nuevo Vallarta—are plenty of restaurants serving up fresh fish and cold lemonade.

The most established tourism enclave on the coast, **Nuevo Vallarta** was developed for tourism in the 1980s. Just north of the Ameca River, it has mainly all-inclusive hotels, some restaurants, and a long beach. At the south end, **Paradise Village** resort has a large marina and a plaza with shops.

Nuevo Vallarta
▲ 138 B4
Visitor Information
✉ Regional office of Nayarit State tourism board, Av. Cocoteros s/n at Club de Playa Nuevo Vallarta (bet. Marival & Gran Velas hotels)
☎ 322/297-1006
www.visitnayarit.com

Surfing the Pacific's warm waters

Puerto Vallarta

Puerto Vallarta sits on Bahía de Banderas, one of the biggest bays in the world. Although it had no permanent settlements until the mid-19th century, the bay was charted and used for hundreds of years as a rest stop for pirates, priests, the military, and other sailors. Once an idyllic village with white-sand beaches, Puerto Vallarta is now a savvy tourist mecca with a string of high-rise hotels marching up and down the bay.

Puerto Vallarta
🗺 138 B4
Visitor Information
✉ Juárez at Independencia, Palacio Municipal
☎ 322/226-8080

Puerto Vallarta became an overnight star with the highly publicized romance of Elizabeth Taylor and Richard Burton during the filming of John Huston's *Night of the Iguana* in 1963. (The film starred Burton and Ava Gardner; Taylor tagged along.) And it hasn't stopped growing or attracting vacationers since, the original town having expanded to cover much of 25-mile (40 km) Bahía de Banderas.

The resort specializes in galleries and shops selling fine art and handicrafts, including objects made by the mountain-dwelling and spiritually attuned Huichol. Some galleries focus on the crème de la crème of folk art from the states of Oaxaca, Chiapas, and Michoacán.

The heart of the old city is **Vallarta Vieja,** where buildings are painted white by government decree. Capped in rust-colored roof tiles and draped in bright fuschia-pink bougainvillea, sunlight-dappled houses stagger up palm-covered hills. From there, the **Río Cuale** descends to divide the Old Town into north and south sectors. Pedestrian and automobile bridges both cross the river and access **Isla Río Cuale,** a slip of an island where restaurants, shops, and the small **Museo del Cuale** *(closed Sun.)* are surrounded by gardens and brushed with the best breeze in town. Below the Insurgentes Street bridge, a sprawling handicrafts market sells mainly mass-produced souvenirs.

A few blocks north of the river, **Plaza Principal,** or Plaza de Armas *(Zaragoza, Morelos, Iturbide, & Juárez),* is surrounded by the city hall and the open-air **Los Arcos amphitheater,** which often hosts concerts. The seawalk, or *malecón,* stretches north and

Puerto Vallarta's emerald green hills back up to beautiful azure mountains.

south from the main square, itself fronted by bars, shops, and restaurants. The malécon is a great spot at sunset, when the sun glints on a dozen bronze sculptures along its length.

New development lies north of town. First is the **Zona Hotelera,** an untidy string of high-rise hotels. Most rent water toys along their contiguous beaches, not quite as attractive since Hurricane Kenna replaced some of the sand with rocks. Farther north is **Marina Vallarta,** an enclave of resort hotels and condos surrounding a 380-slip marina, a popular yacht club, and an 18-hole golf course. This development is a favorite among boaters, although its beaches aren't among Vallarta's prettiest. Fishing charters and day cruises depart from the **Maritime Terminal.**

Those who want to be close to the party scene congregate in downtown Vallarta. Near the Río Cuale, **Olas Altas** and **Playa de los Muertos** beaches, just south of the river, are popular with tourists, locals, and vendors selling mangoes carved to look like flowers, grilled fish on a stick, *sarapes,* and most everything else.

The coast highway continues south of downtown, past pretty **Playa Conchas Chinas** and other sandy white beaches scalloped between rocky coves. The hills are sprinkled with luxury homes as the road continues to **Mismaloya,** where *Night of the Iguana* was filmed. Although the enormous Hotel Mismaloya has appropriated much of this once pristine cove, it's still a pretty beach with colorful fishing

---

EXPERIENCE:
Connecting with Locals through the Arts

One way to meet local people is to take a class through a city-sponsored program. In most cases, language shouldn't be a problem; if your Spanish isn't perfect the teacher may speak English, or another student will. In Puerto Vallarta, **Centro Cultural Cuale** (*Cuale Island, S end of downtown, tel 322/223-0095*) has a lovely setting and offers classes for adults and children for about U.S.$10 a month. Study folkloric dance, ballet, theater, painting, sculpture, printmaking, or a musical instrument. **La Biblioteca Los Mangos** (*Francisco Villa 101, Col. Los Mangos, tel 322/224-9966*) also offers courses. The bimonthly English-language magazine *Bay Vallarta* lists courses throughout the area.

---

boats in the adjoining lagoon. An inland road leads to **El Edén,** with a 12-line canopy tour and seafood restaurant, above the rushing Río Mismaloya.

From Mismaloya, divers and snorkelers can hire skiffs to **Los Arcos,** a protected underwater park just offshore, or to secluded beaches farther south. Closest is jungle-lined **Boca de Tomatlán,** also accessible by car or bus.

The beaches beyond Boca de Tomatlán are accessible only by boat. Sandy **Playa Las Animas** offers beach toys for rent. **Quimixto** offers good snorkeling. Both have small restaurants. **Yelapa** is a Mexican Shangri-La where simple restaurants on the sandy beach face the deep bay. Tour boats descend on these lovely beaches daily, so come early or late to avoid the large crowds. ■

La Costalegre

La Costalegre covers the 280-mile (450 km) stretch between Puerto Vallarta and Manzanillo. Exclusive resorts operate on a few of the idyllic beaches, and continued development is inevitable. But for the moment, roads lead to simple fishing villages, rocky coves perfect for snorkeling, and long bays. Manzanillo, the Pacific's most important industrial port, combines commercial fishing and shipping with excellent billfishing and low-key tourism.

Whitewashed buildings overlook Manzanillo Bay, part of La Costalegre's coast.

Barra de Navidad
🗺 138 B3
Visitor Information
✉ Jalisco 67
☎ 315/355-5100
www.costalegre.com

Twenty-seven miles (44 km) south of Puerto Vallarta, the quaint colonial village of **El Tuito** is opening its doors to tourism. Visitors can have a bite at one of the informal restaurants facing the large, pretty plaza. A packed dirt road leads to three tiny coastal hamlets: **Tehuamixtle, Mayto,** and **Villa del Mar,** all of which only recently received electricity. Restaurants and hotels are very basic; visitors come for the long, pristine beaches here at **Cabo Corrientes.** The drive takes about an hour; there are two buses a day from El Tuito.

Another 50 miles (80 km) from El Tuito, the solitary **Playa Chalacatepec** lies down a 5-mile

(8 km) packed dirt road. There's a fish camp and some tide pools among the rocks, but no services. About 14 miles (23 km) south, beautiful **Perula** sits on Chamela Bay. Boat owners charge ($$$$$) for fishing and will take groups to **Pajarera** or **Isla Cocinas** for diving, snorkeling, or sightseeing. Under a protected headlands, this is a good place to swim.

Chamela Bay curves to the south; at the other end, **Playa Negrita** has places to snorkel, swim, and fish. There's a place for RV camping, and Bahía Chamela has some humble hotels. A few miles down the road, **El Careyes** (www.elcareyesresort.com) offers gorgeous rooms and a full-service spa.

About 20 miles (30 km) brings you to beautiful **Bahía de Tenacatita,** with restaurants on the beach and fishermen bringing in the day's catch. Of the bay's long, walkable beaches—where boats can be rented—**La Manzanilla** is the most developed. Rentals and vacation homes line the beach; the town has shops, art galleries, and some of the area's best hotels.

Just before the Colima state line is gorgeous **Bahía de Navidad** (Christmas Bay). At its northern end, the small resort town of **San Patricio Melaque** has a good swimming beach. A clutch of thatch-roofed, open-air eateries crowd around the west end of the beach. Many Guadalajara families vacation here on long weekends and holidays, including a week-long celebration for the town's patron, St. Patrick.

You can walk several miles along the sandy beach to **Barra de Navidad,** a funky little village strung out along a sandbar extending into the bay. Thatch-roofed restaurants serve up spicy shrimp, fresh fish, and cold beers.

Fishing charters are available from private operators as well as the local co-op, the **Sociedad Cooperativa de Servicios Turísticos** *(Av. Veracruz 40),* which also takes passengers on bay cruises or across the lagoon to seafood restaurants at Isla Navidad. Multiple fishing tournaments are held in January, late May, September, and November. The town honors its patron, St. Anthony of Padua, in the week preceding June 13.

South of Barra de Navidad the highway enters Colima state and passes near, but not along, the coast to **Bahías Manzanillo** and **Santiago.** The bays are divided in two by the Santiago peninsula, a short spit of land on which sits **Las Hadas** resort, opened in 1974 and showcased in the movie *10* (1979). The famous and rich have moved on to more exclusive resorts.

Unlike Ixtapa and Cancún, **Manzanillo** is a real city and a busy port. Instead of a row of restaurants and hotels, its attractions are found here and there along the bay and scruffy downtown, located at the far eastern point of the bay. Despite the industrial flavor, this rather unattractive resort does have its admirers: mainly sun-starved Canadians, Mexican families, and deep-sea anglers who come for the big game fish.

Manzanillo
138 B3
Visitor Information
✉ Blvd. Costera Miguel de la Madrid 875A
☎ 314/333-2264

EXPERIENCE: You Can Dance, You Can Jive

Dancing is an essential part of any Mexican celebration, so learn the steps and join in. **The Coco Loco Café** *(Ave. Lazaro Cardenas 1316, tel 314/333-2528)* in Manzanillo is a great place to pick up a few salsa steps. The dance lesson is complimentary; stay after for the house salsa band. In Puerto Vallarta, Al and Barbara Garvey *(tel 322/222-8895, www. tangobar-productions.com)* teach tango. They meet once a week at **J. B. Salsa Club** *(Blvd. Francisco M. Ascencio 2043, in hotel zone, tel 322/224-4616)* for practice sessions and for hosting *milangas,* which are tango dance parties. In similar cities and towns across the country you should be able to find places to learn the fun dances of Mexico.

In & Around Guadalajara

Guadalajara is the Mexican's Mexico—an archetype of idealized Mexican culture. It's the home town of mariachi music, the romantic ballads performed by large bands of uniformed musicians playing harps, violins, guitars, and soulful trumpets. This is the land of tequila soirees and of plantations of blue agave from which tequila is made. On Sunday afternoons, elegant equestrians known as *charros* perform stylized feats of showmanship.

Plazas and pedestrian malls surround the cathedral in historic Guadalajara.

Guadalajara (Arabic for "river of stones") was moved several times before a final site was chosen near the west end of the 5,400-foot (1,645 m) Valle Atemajac, 300 miles (480 km) northwest of Mexico City. Several earlier settlements of the same name failed owing to drought and Indian attacks. Once established, the seat of western colonial government soon also became a capital of agriculture and ranching.

As Mexico's second largest city, Guadalajara embraces mainstream, as well as Mexican, culture, with four 18-hole golf courses and three soccer teams, a zoo, a planetarium, and a large convention center. Many visitors come to shop. Residents from surrounding haciendas and rural communities buy everything from lizard-skin boots and spurs to plows. City folk scour shops and galleries for the region's famous handicrafts: leather clothing, handblown glassware, wood-and-pigskin *(equipal)* furniture, handcrafted and factory tableware, and home accessories of tin, wrought iron, pewter, papier-mâché, and copper.

Many of these modern

handicrafts are found in the art-driven satellite villages of Tlaquepaque and Tonalá (see pp. 152–153). In Guadalajara proper, visitors explore the *centro histórico*, a square mile surrounding the cathedral, where historic churches, museums, and shops line pedestrian malls and fountain-filled public squares.

Centro Histórico

Presiding over Guadalajara's historic district is the majestic **catedral** *(Av. 16 de Septiem- bre bet. Hidalgo & Morelos, tel 33/3614-5504)*, with its yellow-tiled dome and twin spires. Earthquakes and changing fashions have led to many modifications over the years, rendering it Gothic, Moorish, baroque, and neoclassical in style. Its three naves house a dozen side altars; the sacristy is lined with colonial-era paintings.

Plazas surround the cathedral on all sides. To the west is **Plaza Guadalajara,** where guided, one-hour tram tours (in English or Spanish) cover the sights of the historic center *(tel 341/414-0836, daily except Mon. 11 a.m. & 1 p.m., 4 p.m., & 6 p.m., $$$)*. Tours depart from the **Palacio Municipal,** the municipal palace.

Afternoon concerts are held at 6:30 p.m. Tuesday through Friday and Sunday at the art nouveau bandstand on **Plaza de Armas,** which flanks the cathedral to the south. Facing this grace-ful old square is the **Palacio de Gobierno** *(Moreno at Corona, tel 33/3688-1600)*, a baroque government edifice with Chur-rigueresque decorations. Murals by Jalisco native José Clemente Orozco (1883–1949) embellish the stairwell and the congressional chambers upstairs.

Horse-drawn carriages await passengers in front of the **Museo Regional de Guadalajara** *(Liceo 60, tel 33/3614-5257, closed Mon., $$)*. This comprehensive museum

Guadalajara

🅰 138 C4

Visitor Information

✉ Morelos 102, Plaza Tapatía

☎ 33/3668-1600 or 01800/363-2200 (toll-free within Mexico)

www.gdlmidestino .com

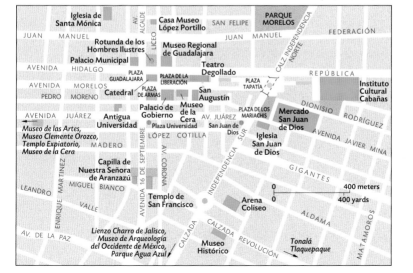

El Museo de las Artes Populares

✉ San Felipe 211
☎ 33/3614-3891
🕐 Closed Mon.
💲 $

occupies the former baroque seminary of San José. Surrounding a typical colonial courtyard are rooms with archaeological and paleontological exhibits, including offerings from area shaft tombs and a complete mammoth skeleton. Upstairs are colonial paintings, artifacts of west coast cultures, and other regional history exhibits.

Downtown Guadalajara has many worthy museums. The **Casa Museo López Portillo** *(Liceo 177 at San Felipe, tel 33/1201-8720, closed Mon.)* is a 19th-century home with furnishings typical of an upper-class family (one of this family's sons was the former president of that name). The **Museo Casa Clemente Orozco** *(Av. Aurelio Aceves 27, tel 33/3616-8329, closed Mon.)* houses personal and professional artifacts of the famous muralist, as well as

---

Gay Mexico

As in many things, Mexicans' attitude toward gays is ambiguous. While machismo is prevalent, Mexicans tend to admire those willing to flaunt societal norms. Today even such bastions of conservative society as Guadalajara support gay pride parades, bathhouses, and gay bars. If things aren't as casual as one would hope, there's always Mexico City, where there's something available for everyone, as well as beach towns like Cancún, Puerto Vallarta, and Acapulco, where attitudes are even freer.

---

a huge mural, "Alegoría del Vino" ("The Good Life").

The **Museo de las Artes** *(Juárez 975, tel 33/3134-1664, closed Mon. & bet. exhibitions)* shows temporary exhibits of contemporary art. Not far away, **El Museo de las Artes Populares** occupies a classic two-story, 19th-century house restored in the late 20th century. In addition to rooms for temporary exhibits, this museum has permanent exhibits of Jalisco crafts that are beyond the usual genres. Check out rooms dedicated to *charrería,* music, and cooking implements as well as glass, ceramics, and leather.

Facing the cathedral, **Plaza de la Liberación** is surrounded by imposing government buildings and the neoclassical **Teatro Degollado** *(Degollado s/n at Morelos, tel 33/3614-4773, closed Sun.–Mon.),* inaugurated in 1866 by soprano Angela Peralta. Visit the stunning theater 11 a.m. to 3 p.m. and 4 p.m. to 7 p.m. to see the interior fresco illustrating Dante's *Divine Comedy* among other subjects, or better yet, attend a symphony or opera. More events are held at **Teatro Diana** *(Av. 16 de Septiembre 710, tel 33/3614-7072),* inaugurated in 2005. On the south side of Plaza de la Liberación, Ripley's **Museo de la Cera** *(Morelos 217, tel 33/3614-8487, $$)* has 120 reasonably lifelike wax figures, including depictions of Madonna and a complete mariachi band.

Like Monterrey's Macroplaza (see pp. 108–109), **Plaza Tapatía** was created in the 1980s to incorporate existing churches, government buildings, shops, and public squares into a cohesive entity of green spaces, walkways, sculptures, fountains, and benches. At the east end of the 17-acre (7 ha) public square lies one of Guadalajara's landmarks, the stately **Instituto Cultural Cabañas** *(Cabañas 8, tel 33/3668-1640, closed Mon., $$, free Tues.)*, a World Heritage site where concerts, film screenings, and performances are held. Originally

beyond is **Plaza de los Mariachis** *(Obregón at Av. J. Mina)*, where roving bands in matching silver-studded ensembles serenade clients. Unfortunately, the plaza, and this part of town in general, is now rather seedy. It's better to go to a mariachi bar such as **Casa Bariachi** *(Av. Vallarta 2221 at Calderón de la*

EXPERIENCE: Sing Along at the Mariachi Festival

Mariachi music is quintessential Mexico. Violins, trumpets, harps, and strings conspire to create a festive sound like no other. Born from ranch life, mariachi has a rural heartbeat that's found a place in Mexico's second largest city, Guadalajara.

During a ten-day festival in late August and early September, visitors to the Encuentro Internacional del Mariachi y la Charrería can enjoy not only the music, but also parades, *charreadas* (fancy-dress rodeos), fine art exhibitions,

and mariachi Masses. Festival venues dot the city as well as surrounding municipalities. An opening parade features a thousand musicians from throughout mariachi-rich Jalisco state and also the world, although mainly Mexico.

For more information, see *www.mariachi-jalisco.com.mx* or *vive.guadalajara.gob.mx* (the first is in Spanish only, the second provides information in English, too) or the Guadalajara tourism office at 33/3616-9900.

an orphanage designed by Spanish architect and sculptor Manuel Tolsá, it served this role until the 1970s. More than 50 of José Clemente Orozco's murals adorn the walls and ceilings of this neoclassic building, which has a movie theater and performance venue as well as several dozen linked patios planted with trees. The site museum hosts permanent and temporary exhibits of contemporary art.

Past the modernistic bronze sculpture depicting the Immolation of Quetzalcóatl lies the **Mercado San Juan de Dios** *(Av. J. Mina at Calzada Independencia, tel 33/3618-0506, also known as Mercado Libertad)*. A footbridge connects the enormous city market to the church for which it was named. Just

Barca, tel 33/3616-990), which has shows daily at 3:30 and 9:30 p.m.

Within the city center are several churches of note. **Iglesia de Santa Mónica** *(Santa Mónica 250 at San Felipe, tel 33/3614-6620)* is considered one of Guadalajara's loveliest, its baroque facade graced with a twin portico. South of Plaza de Armas, the **Templo de San Francisco** *(Av. 16 de Septiembre 289 at Prisciliano Sánchez, tel 33/3614-4083)* and the **Capilla de Nuestra Señora de Aranzazú** are all that remain of a 16th-century Franciscan monastery. Note the typical Mexican motif—the eagle and cactus—on the facade of the former, and the gilded Churrigueresque altarpiece inside the latter.

Also south of Plaza de Armas

Museo Regional de la Ceramica

✉ Calle Independencia 237, Guadalajara

☎ 33/3635 5404
www.artesanias.jalisco.gob.mx

Zapopan

🔺 138 C4

Visitor Information

✉ Basílica de Zapopan

☎ 33/3818-2200 ext. 1103

Tlaquepaque

🔺 138 C4

Visitor Information

✉ Morelos 288

☎ 33/3562-7050 ext. 2321

are the **Museo de Arqueología del Occidente de México** *(Calz. Independencia Sur at Av. del Campesino, tel 33/3619-0104, closed Mon., $),* with archaeological exhibits of western cultures, and **Parque Agua Azul** *(Calz. Independencia Sur 973, tel 33/3619-0328, closed Mon., $),* a children's park, which also houses an orchid house, a butterfly pavilion, and an aviary. At the nearby **Lienzo Charro de Jalisco** *(Dr. R. Michel 577, tel 33/3619-3232, $),* families congregate at noon on Sunday for that most *tapatío* (native Guadalajaran) of traditions, the colorful *charreada* (rodeo; see p. 155).

INSIDER TIP:

In June or July, don't miss Guadalajara's National Ceramics Fair. Other months, see the Museo Regional de la Ceramica.

— EDIE JAROLIM
National Geographic Traveler
magazine writer

Zapopan

About 5 miles (8 km) northwest of central Guadalajara is Zapopan, known throughout the country for its diminutive statue of the Virgin of Zapopan. The 10-inch (25 cm) corn-paste statue is said to have cured epidemics and aided Spaniards in battle. After four months of travel among parish churches, the statue is returned to Zapopan on October 12 during the **Romería de la**

Virgen de Zapopan. Hundreds of thousands fill the streets as the Virgin's entourage heads for the baroque **basílica** *(Hidalgo at Zapata),* begun in 1690. It's a lively party with music and folkloric dances, food vendors, mariachis, men on horseback, and kids in costume.

Within the church is **Museo de la Arte Huichol** *(tel 33/3636-4430, closed 1:30–3 p.m., $),* a small shop selling Huichol Indian yarn paintings, beaded masks, and other handicrafts at reasonable prices. Larger than the church itself is the atrium and adjoining **Plaza de las Américas,** surrounded by the flags of North American and Latin American countries.

Tlaquepaque

Once an independent village, the suburb of Tlaquepaque has grown and melted into Guadalajara, but its downtown still charms. Its inhabitants have been making pottery since the time of the Spanish incursion; in the Indian dialect, Tlaquepaque means "place on high clay hills." Traditional Tlaquepaque ceramics are fragile earthenware, although today other genres, including more durable stoneware, have been adopted.

The art of glassblowing was introduced in the 19th century, and today shops sell miniatures and glassware in addition to pottery, textiles, silver jewelry, tin, high-end furniture, and household accessories. Many shops are themselves works of art, housed in gracious, restored mansions.

But Tlaquepaque has more to offer than just shopping. This is a fascinating place to walk: There are restaurants, lively cantinas, B&Bs, and several interesting churches.

Pedestrianized Calle Independencia leads to the main square, **Jardín Hidalgo,** and the 18th-century, neoclassical-Byzantine-style **Santuario de Nuestra Señora de la Soledad** (Prisciliano Sánchez at Morelos). In the next block, the **Parroquia de San Pedro** (Guillermo Prieto at Morelos) was built by the Franciscans in 1813.

Before buying ceramics, take a look at the exhibits and prize-winning contemporary pieces at the **Museo del Premio Nacional Pantaleón Panduro** (Prisciliano Sánchez 191 at Flórida, tel 33/3562-7036, closed Mon.). After a day's shopping expedition, relax at **El Parián** (bet. Independencia, Prieto, Morelos, & Madero), a plaza filled with lively cantinas and open-air restaurants, shops, and strolling mariachis. The town celebrates its annual **Feria de San Pedro Tlaquepaque** during June.

Tonalá

Five miles (8 km) east of Tlaquepaque is Tonalá, a pre-Hispanic regional capital whose Náhuatl name means "place where the sun rises," or "place of the sun." It was also briefly the capital of Nueva Galicia before a dearth of water and other factors forced the settlers to abandon the site. Tonalá produces much of the glass and pottery sold around Guadalajara.

On Thursdays and Sundays vendors line Avenida Tonaltecas at Calle Benito Juárez and surrounding streets in a chaotic tianguis (market) that has taken place since pre-Hispanic times. Throughout

A worker harvests the piña, or heart, of the blue agave plant for making tequila.

the week you'll find shops selling ceramics, blown glass, pewter, and works of papier-mâché, tin, copper, wood, basketry, and iron.

Handicrafts shops can be found on Avenida Tonaltecos and around the *plaza principal* (Juárez, Pino Suárez, López Pajar, & Madero). Surrounding the square are the Gothic-style **Santuario del Sagrado Corazón** (Hidalgo at López Pajar) and the **Parroquia de Santiago Apóstol** (Pino Suárez at Juárez), one of the oldest temples in the Atemajac Valley. Named for the town's patron saint, the Apostle James, this is the site of festivities in the days preceding July 25, when local men don masks and costumes to perform regional dances.

The **Museo Regional de Tonalá** (Ramón Corona 73, tel 33/1200-3936, closed Sat.–Sun., $) showcases regional skills with ancient and newer ceramic pieces. It's closed after 3 p.m.

Tonalá
138 C4
Visitor Information
Av. Hidalgo 21
33/1200-3913 or 3914

Tequila

🗺 138 C4

Visitor Information

✉ Ramón Corona 33

☎ 374/742-0012

Chapala

🗺 138 C4

Visitor Information

✉ Av. Madero 407

☎ 376/765-3141

Tequila

The pleasant town of Tequila, about 35 miles (56 km) north-west of Guadalajara, sits under an extinct volcano of the same name. Fields of blue agave shimmer in a spiky azure haze around the town. The heart of the agave, or *maguey,* is used to make tequila in its various forms. Unique not just to Mexico but to the region, true tequila can be made only in Jalisco and four other states.

Larger distilleries such as **Sauza** and **José Cuervo** give tours, but it's best to arrange ahead of time. Across from the José Cuervo factory, the **Museo Nacional del Tequila** (*Calle Ramón Corona 32, tel 374/742-0012, $*) has photos and exhibits of tequila-making. For an excursion from Guadalajara, take the Saturday **Tequila Express** (see below)**.** The train arrives at **Amatitán** and the **Hacienda San José del Refugio,** a 10,000-acre (4,000 ha) family-run agave plantation of eight million plants and a distillery producing Herradura tequila, which

sets industry standard for efficiency and cleanliness.

Lago de Chapala

About 25 miles (40 km) south-east of Guadalajara lies Mexico's largest natural freshwater lake, Lago de Chapala. Its agreeable climate, tree-lined promenades, and surrounding mountains convinced President Porfirio Díaz to establish a vacation home here. Later discovered by Canadian and U.S. expats, its three principal towns now house thousands of foreign residents. Deforestation of the surrounding woods and erosion have sullied the lake, and water hyacinths and pollution from Río Lerma cause problems.

In the principal town, **Chapala,** Mexican families stroll and shop for folk art on weekends. In the 1920s, D. H. Lawrence (1885–1930) penned his first novel, *The Plumed Serpent,* in a house on Calle Zaragoza. Restaurants lining the lake-shore serve typical *charales* (fried fish) and tequila accompanied by *sangrita,* a chili, tomato, and orange juice chaser invented here.

Ajijic, about 5 miles (8 km) west of Chapala, is a growing town whose red-tiled adobe houses and narrow cobblestone streets began attracting artists and writers in the mid-20th century. Galleries and stores sell fine art, handicrafts, and designer clothing. Week-long festivities lead up to the town's patron saint's day on November 30, with celebrations at the **Iglesia de San Andrés,** on the north side of the town plaza. Smaller villages surround the lake, including **San Juan Cosalá,** with thermal pools, a restaurant, and accommodations. ∎

EXPERIENCE:
The Tequila Express

One of the easiest and most pleasant ways to explore tequila country is a Saturday train trip to Amatitán, Jalisco. Departing from Guadalajara, the tour passes through blue agave fields en route to **Hacienda San José del Refugio** for a tour of modern and ancient processing techniques. Visitors sample tequila straight up and in cocktails along with appetizers and later a buffet lunch with entertainment by mariachis and folkloric dancers. For tickets and information see *www.tequilaexpress.com.mx* or call 33/3880-9090 or 01800/503-9720.

Tapatío Traditions

The traditions of tequila, charros, and mariachis are quintessentially Guadalajaran while at the same time generating the broader Mexican persona. In the nostalgic musicals of the 1940s, film stars Pedro Infante and Jorge Negrete personified the Mexican "everyman." When dressed as charros in fine felt hats and elegant dress they crooned songs of unrequited love, romance, and machismo.

Another seeming contradiction is that Guadalajara, long Mexico's second largest city, maintains a provincial atmosphere. The typical *tapatío* (Guadalajara native) is traditional and Catholic, and like all Mexicans, intensely loyal to his region and family. Famous tapatíos—including muralist and painter José Clemente Orozco and writers Juan Rulfo and Agustín Yáñez—are greatly esteemed and their works often quoted.

Guadalajarans are also immensely proud of the national drink, tequila. Made from blue agave, *agave tequiliana Weber,* a relative of the lily, true tequila can be distilled only in Jalisco as well as designated areas of Nayarit, Guanajuato, Tamaulipas, and Michoacán. The better tequilas contain 100 percent blue agave, although only 51 percent is required.

The first agave-derived drink was *pulque,* a mild beer fermented and drunk throughout pre-Hispanic Mesoamerica. The Spaniards took the process further, distilling the fermented brew. When plants are 8 to 12 years old, the heart, or *piña,* weighing up to 120 pounds (55 kg), is extracted, shredded, and cooked for six to eight hours. The resulting *aguamiel* is fermented and distilled—usually twice. White tequila is unaged; *reposado* is aged for at least two months in wooden barrels; and *añejo* is aged at least a year in oak barrels.

If tequila is the unofficial national drink, *charrería* is the official national sport—so decreed by presidential edict in 1933. Charros perform feats of equestrian skill similar to those of a rodeo, but with more finesse. Teams of six to eight compete in the pan-shaped ring, the *lienzo charro,* performing *suertes* (moves) that range from steer-throwing, bull-roping,

A *charro* demonstrates his roping skills.

and riding to changing horses at a dead run. *La escaramuza charra* is an elaborately choreographed and colorful women's event. Requiring fine mounts, expensive, brocaded outfits, and silver spurs, charrería is a sport for the wealthy.

Mariachis add ambience to the *charreada.* The name is thought to be a corruption of the French word *mariage,* meaning "wedding," as the five-piece bands often played at society weddings during the 19th century. Originally featuring two violins, a harp, and *jarana* and *vihuela* (types of guitar), these bands played romantic ballads popular after Mexican independence. Trumpets, now an integral part of most mariachi bands, were added in the 1930s.

All of these traditions can be experienced at the **Encuentro Internacional del Mariachi y la Charrería** (see p. 151) held at the end of August and beginning of September; and in October at the **Fiestas de Octubre,** a month of art, performances, and music of all kinds.

Colima & Environs

For those weary of flashy beach resorts and cities with countless colonial landmarks, Colima is a delightful retreat. The small state capital is among the safest cities of its size in Mexico, and the downtown area is alive with semitropical greenery. Colimenses take great pride in their city, which is alive with museums, art galleries, music, festivals, and even magic supply shops. Nearby towns provide a glimpse into a gentler, even less frenetic era.

Behind these vulcanologists looms Volcán de Colima, North America's most active volcano.

Founded by the Spaniards in 1527, Colima has been repeatedly rocked by earthquakes, leaving few colonial buildings intact. However, the townspeople have taken advantage of their misfortune by transforming whole city blocks into impeccably manicured parks. No fewer than eight elegant green spaces grace the urban center, providing both a feeling of luxuriant openness and a plentiful supply of oxygen.

The city's elevation of 1,800 feet (550 m) above sea level makes it cooler and less humid than the coast, just 28 miles (45 km) away. Most days a welcome breeze blows down from the mountains backing the city, while between July and October, afternoon and early evening rain showers freshen the air. Rain or shine, Thursday evenings find families and friends at the central plazas enjoying eclectic live music ranging from mariachis and romantic ballads to modern rock.

In the heart of the city are three plazas. **Plaza Principal** *(Reforma bet. Madero & Hidalgo)* is dominated on the east side by the 18th-century **Catedral Santa Iglesia** (Reforma 21, tel 312/312-0200) and the adjacent **Palacio de Gobierno** (tel 312/312-4360), whose inner courtyard is decorated with murals depicting Mexican history. Directly behind the cathedral lies the **Jardín Quintero,** with **Parque Núñez,** an enormous flower garden, four blocks east at the corner of Madero and Juárez. Within walking distance of these plazas are hotels, restaurants and cafés, shops, banks, and a handful of notable museums.

The **Museo Universitario de Artes Populares** (Barreda at Gallardo, tel 312/312-6869, closed Mon. & 2–5 p.m., $) has exhibits of popular art, regional textiles, masks, and pre-Hispanic artifacts, including beguiling ceramic figures of short-legged, pot-bellied tepezcuintle dogs, once greatly esteemed (and eaten) by local inhabitants. Its gift shop sells wonderful reproductions of pre-Hispanic pieces. Similar exhibits can be found at the smaller **Museo de Historia de Colima** (Portal Morelos 1, on plaza, tel 312/312-9228, closed Mon., $). Next door, the **Sala de Exposiciones de la Universidad de Colima** (tel 312/312-9228, closed Mon.) presents temporary exhibits of modern art. Perhaps the best permanent collection of fine art can be found in the **Pinacoteca Universidad** (V. Guerrero 35, tel 312/312-2228 ext. 15, closed Mon.). The work of local painters is housed in three exquisite mansions linked by courtyards filled with green plants.

One block south of the plaza principal, the **Teatro Hidalgo** (Hidalgo at Morelos, tel 312/314-8283) stands on land given to the city by revolutionary hero Miguel Hidalgo (see p. 30), once a priest in the city. Built between 1871 and 1883, the neoclassical theater hosts concerts, plays, and operas.

Half a mile (1 km) northeast of the city center, the **Casa de la Cultura** (Calz. Galván Norte at Ejército Nacional, tel 312/313-0608, closed Mon.) is a modern cultural

Colima

138 C3

Visitor Information

Palacio de Gobierno, Hidalgo at Reforma

312/312-4360 or 01800/505-7130 (toll-free within Mexico)

www.visitacolima.com

Festivals

Three large festivals take place each year around Colima. The rustic **Feria de San Felipe de Jesús** is celebrated in the first two weeks of February in Villa de Álvarez, a community 3 miles (5 km) north of the city center. Events include horse parades, bullfights, and regional foods. Taxi drivers dressed in drag parade through town, snatching unsuspecting men from the crowds.

More commercial (and sober) is the **Feria de Todos Santos** (late Oct. & early Nov.), which takes place on the enormous fairgrounds just east of Colima. On offer for participants at the event are rides, food, cultural attractions, and regional handicraft exhibits.

During the **Fiesta de la Virgin de Guadalupe** (Dec. 1–12), downtown Colima is lined with food stalls, live music events are offered nightly, and there are parades and other entertainments. Women, children, and babies dressed in regional costume file solemnly in and out of the cathedral, paying homage to the Virgin.

complex housing a theater and a library. Its most important asset, however, is the **Museo de las Culturas del Occidente** *(tel 312/313-0608 ext. 15, closed Mon.)*, which has an excellent display of pre-Hispanic ceramic pottery. One block south, **Parque Piedra Lisa** *(Calz. Galván at Aldama)* is famous for its volcanic rock, whose top protrudes from the ground. It is said that those who slide on it will form a lifelong connection with the city.

of the use of metallurgy, point to an immigrant population. It's a small site and can be explored in less than an hour.

Comala is a picture-postcard *pueblo* of bright white buildings with red-tile roofs 6 miles (10 km) north of Colima. Its main attraction is its plaza, with trees shading park benches, a bandstand, and a plain but pretty church. On weekends Colimenses gather in colonnaded restaurant-bars serving local delicacies.

Magic or Realism?

Colima has a keen interest in mysticism and a number of shops peddling potions and powders for performing white and black magic. This preoccupation with the spirit world reflects the locals' belief that near Colima exists a portal to another dimension, kept wide open by the active shaman community of Suchitlán (3 miles/5 km NE of Colima). Wizards there are said to transform themselves into animals upon a large stone etched with ancient carvings of female genitalia.

Buildings of all ages are reputedly haunted, including a hotel, a hospital, and a café. Ghostly apparitions are taken seriously; some victims report being groped or sexually assaulted by invisible assailants. Although a belief in witches is held throughout Mexico, the exchange of paranormal experiences is a pastime particularly enjoyed by Colimenses.

Around Colima

North of the capital are several sites worth visiting. Named for mythical beings thought to live in arroyos (dry washes), **Zona Arqueológica El Chanal** *(3.5 miles/6 km down rock road at end of Calle V. Carranza, closed Mon., $)* has a number of images related to the rain god, Tlaloc. This Postclassic site was probably the largest pre-Hispanic city in the state of Colima, with ceremonial plazas, altars, and a few ball courts. Ceramicware unlike that produced elsewhere in the region, as well as evidence

Favorite dishes include *sopes* (grilled rounds of masa smothered with spicy chicken or pork with onions). During the **Fiesta de la Virgin de Guadalupe** *(Dec. 1–12)*, vendors sell locally grown and roasted coffee and hand-carved furniture.

Five minutes outside Comala, by way of the enchanting Camino a Nogueras roadway, is **Hacienda de Nogueras,** a former plantation housing the **Museo Alejandro Rangel** *(tel 312/315-6028, closed Mon., $)*, comprising a chapel, locally made furniture, and more of Colima's famous ceramic dogs.

A small, attractive restaurant *(open sporadically)* offers regional specialties such as *pollo en pipian,* chicken in a pumpkin-seed and peanut sauce.

Six miles (10 km) north of Comala, the town of **Suchitlán** is famous for its carved ritual masks, used during Semana Santa (Holy Week) celebrations. Just outside town is a small slope in the road, the *zona mágica.* On this slope, stationary vehicles and even water seem to defy gravity and run uphill. The interesting phenomenon remains unexplained.

Fourteen miles (22 km) north of Colima is lovely **Laguna la María** *(tel 312/320-8891),* a placid green lake surrounded by coffee groves. It offers rowing as well as a rustic hotel and restaurant.

Just 5 miles (8 km) beyond the lake, twin volcanoes are the main attraction at **Parque Nacional Volcán de Colima. Volcán de Colima** (also called Volcán de Fuego, meaning "fire

volcano") stands at 12,989 feet (3,960 m) and has erupted nine times in the last four centuries. Activity beginning in January 1999 produced shooting sparks, lava, and other breathtaking pyrotechnical displays clearly visible from Colima. Such activity makes a visit to the volcano and its dormant partner, the **Volcán de Nevado** (meaning "snowy volcano"), impossible. If and when the activity subsides, check with the tourist office for maps and tours of the area.

Colima residents enjoy the low-key restaurant-bars of nearby Comala.

Morelia

Established by Spain in 1541, Morelia—originally called Valladolid after the Spanish city—grew slowly in the 16th and 17th centuries, and much of its architecture is subdued 18th-century plateresque. The city's wide avenues and expansive plazas are American in character rather than European. These, along with its many restored convents and monasteries, give Morelia—the capital of Michoacán state—a dignified demeanor.

Morelia is home to many churches and monasteries, including the Church of Guadalupe.

Flanked by two squares, the superb three-nave sandstone **catedral** *(Av. Madero at Juárez),* built between 1660 and 1744, blends neoclassical elements and a baroque facade whose carved columns and panels create a chiaroscuro effect. The magnificent 4,600-pipe German organ is celebrated each May during the **Festival Internacional del Órgano.** Locally crafted and characteristic of pre-Hispanic Purépecha art, the cathedral's 16th-century Christ in one of seven lateral chapels is made of a paste of pulverized cornstalks and orchids.

Catercorner from the cathedral, the **Palacio de Gobierno** *(Av. Madero 63, tel 443/317-7805)* was originally a seminary where radicals José María Morelos (1765–1815) and Melchor Ocampo (1814–1861), both instruments of the independence movement (see pp. 29–31), were schooled. Its stairwell and second floor are covered in 1970s-era murals of regional history by

Michoacán artist Alfredo Zalce (1908–2003).

Zalce's work and that of other contemporary artists can be seen at the **Museo de Arte Contemporáneo** *(Av. Acueducto 18, tel 443/312-5404, closed Mon.)*, east of the city center. The restored Porfiriato-era house is within leafy **Bosque Cuauhtémoc.** En route to the park you'll pass the 250-arch **acueducto,** which once supplied fountains throughout the city center with drinkable water.

Bearing straight ahead instead of right past the aqueduct brings you to **Calzada Fray Antonio de San Miguel,** a two-block pedestrian mall connecting to the **Santuario de Nuestra Señora de Guadalupe.** The church's interior received a lavish redecoration in the early 20th century, with molded clay designs combining art nouveau and baroque elements.

Morelia has more than its share of religious buildings, and many today serve secular purposes. The **Conservatorio de las Rosas** *(Santiago Tapia 334, tel 443/312-1469, closed Sat.–Sun.)*, is home to an internationally known boy's choir. The adjoining **Templo de las Rosas** has been totally restored. Once a Carmelite convent, the huge **Casa de la Cultura** *(Av. Morelos Norte 485, tel 443/313-1059, closed Sun.)* hosts classes and cultural events and houses the **Museo de las Máscaras,** with more than a hundred traditional carved wooden masks.

Showing typical Franciscan restraint, the **Templo y Ex-Convento Franciscano** *(Fray Juan de San Miguel 129 at Humboldt, tel 443/312-2486)* has a simple plateresque facade. Within the old monastery is the government-run folk-art museum and store, the **Casa de las Artesanías.**

Born and educated in the city, hero of the War of Independence (see p. 30) José María Morelos y Pavón has several museums dedicated in his honor, including the **Museo Casa de Morelos** *(Av. Morelos Sur 323, tel 443/313-2651, $)*, showing personal and war memorabilia. A few blocks away, an eternal flame burns in the backyard of the hero's birthplace, the **Museo Casa Natal de Morelos** *(Corregidora 113, tel 443/312-2793)*; the main house contains a historical library and several Alfredo Zalce murals.

Also worth visiting is the **Mercado de Dulces** *(Calle V. Farías at Santiago Tapia)*, a sweets market. Here you will find *ate* (an aspic-like paste made with fruit puree and eaten with soft white cheese),

INSIDER TIP:

Try the enchiladas at restaurants in Morelia's city center.

—ERIC RAMIREZ BRAVO
National Geographic field researcher

crispy fried *buñuelos* sprinkled with sugar and cinnamon, sweet *empenadas*, and other local treats. The **Museo Regional Michoacano** *(Allende 305, tel 443/312-0407, closed Mon., $)*, in an 18th-century palace that once belonged to Emperor Agustín de Iturbide's father-in-law, has paintings and regional artifacts. ∎

Morelia
 139 D3
Visitor Information
✉ Av. Madero 63, Palacio de Gobierno
☎ 443/317-7805 or 1800/830-5363 (toll-free within Mexico)
www.turismo michoacan.gob.mx

Pátzcuaro & Environs

Drowsing in the mountain sunshine at 7,131 feet (2,170 m) above sea level, Pátzcuaro has long been a center for indigenous culture and folk crafts, possibly since the mid-16th century, when the region's capital was moved from Pátzcuaro to Morelia. Whether for its native crafts, mountain air, or the almost total lack of modern construction, this lakeside town is probably the most often visited of any in Michoacán state.

Fishing with traditional butterfly nets is now done mainly for tourists.

Pátzcuaro was the first capital of the Late Postclassic Purépecha kingdom (1200–1521), located in the hilly central part of today's Michoacán. On the southern shores of **Lago de Pátzcuaro,** its inhabitants fished, hunted, and gathered food, and, unlike most Mesoamericans, forged metal tools. Admired as fine craftsmen, they produced brilliant copper utensils, feather work, and *maqueado,* decorated gourds from which Aztec nobles drank their bitter chocolate. They were excellent warriors as well, resisting absorption into the ever expanding Aztec Empire.

The Purépecha were undoubtedly amazed at the annihilation of their enemy at Tenochtitlán by the Spaniards, with their Indian allies and superior weapons. King Tzimtzincha-Tangaxuan II readily accepted the terms of peace set forth by Hernán Cortés, swearing fealty to the Spanish crown and accepting Christian baptism.

However, the king's fealty made little impression on the brutish conquistador Nuño Beltrán de Guzmán, who as a representative of the colonial governing body, *la real audiencia*, tortured and hanged the Indian sovereign. The persecution, slavery, and torture that de Guzmán inflicted on the local Indians was so excessive—even by 16th-century standards—that he was finally sent to a Spanish prison for the rest of his life.

After institution of a second, more benevolent audiencia, the task of regaining the Indians' trust was given to don Vasco de Quiroga. The Spanish judge was ordained a priest and named bishop in 1536. By the time of his death 30 years later, "Tata Vasco" ("Grandpa Vasco") had built as many hospitals and schools as churches, and given many towns a craft or vocation to ensure their prosperity.

The tradition of fine craftsmanship continues to this day, and Michoacán has some of Mexico's finest decorative and utilitarian art. Traditional gourd decoration incorporated techniques introduced from Asia. Other arts include weaving, embroidery, metalsmithing, and ceramics, especially tableware.

You can purchase and watch regional crafts being made at the **Casa de los Once Patios** *(Madrigal de las Altas Torres near Lerín, tel 434/342-4753)*, within a former convent. Another place to view regional crafts is the **Museo de Artes Populares** *(Enseñanza at Alcantarilla, tel 434/342-1029, closed Mon., $)*, a pleasing colonial structure that once housed the Colegio de San Nicolás. At the rear is a typical Purépecha wooden dwelling.

Named for its benevolent Spanish benefactor is large **Plaza Vasco de Quiroga** *(Portales Hidalgo, Morelos, Matamoros, & Guerrero)*. (Street names change at the square.)

Different from most Mexican main squares, it is surrounded by houses (now hotels, restaurants, and shops) instead of municipal buildings and churches. One block away is the more intimate **Plaza Gertrudis Bocanegra** *(Mendoza, Libertad, Iturbe, & La Paz)*, named for a heroine of the War of Independence. Facing the plaza on the north side, the **Biblioteca Gertrudis Bocanegra** *(tel 434/342-5441, closed Sun.)* is an unassuming library with an intricate mural of regional history by architect, painter, and muralist Juan O'Gorman (1905–1982).

Pátzcuaro
🅰 139 D3
Visitor Information
✉ Ahumada 9-B
☎ 434/342-1214

EXPERIENCE: A Crash Course in Woodcarving & Spanish

From their tiny town on the north shore of Lake Pátzcuaro, the ladies of Santa Fe de la Laguna (28 miles/47 km from Michoacán's capital, Morelia) teach visitors about Purépecha culture. Proud of their pre-Hispanic roots, the women of Ateshiru Co-op offer cozy lodgings ($–$$) and traditional meals ($$) in their homes around the plaza. Affiliated artisans give workshops in wood carving or ceramics by the day or week. The government has invested hundreds of thousands of dollars in rural and cultural tourism programs that produce income for worthy towns outside the tourist meccas. For more information, contact Michoacan state tourism office *(tel 443/317-8052 ext. 149)*.

Pátzcuaro's attraction lies more in popular culture than in ornate churches. The devout regularly visit the **Basílica de Nuestra Señora de la Salud** *(Árciga at Serrato)*. Housing the corn-paste Virgin of Health, it is located away from the main square.

Día de los Muertos (Day of the Dead) is a living communion with deceased relatives that is celebrated throughout the region. Because of massive international interest in the festivals of neighboring Janitzio (see below), the Pátzcuaro tourism delegation has created a program of cultural events taking place in the week or so surrounding the celebration, October 31 to November 2.

a lookout point in one raised arm. Steps from the ferry landing are lined with diminutive souvenir shops and two-table restaurants. Of the lake's five islands, only tiny, less touristy **Yunuén** has accommodations. Rent a room for 2, 4, 8, or 16 people *(tel 434/342-4473, $ for a double).* Boats leave for all the islands from Pátzcuaro's wharf *(10 min. N of town center, Muelle General, tel 434/342-0681).* Boats

Regional Dances & Masks

Indigenous cultures throughout Mexico, but especially in Tlaxcala, Guerrero, and Michoacán, celebrate feast days and festivals with regional dance. Donning masks and sometimes elaborate costumes, the townspeople replay traditional roles that survived the Conquest and, in some cases, were modified by it. Universal themes are the conquest of good over evil and the vanquishing of invaders.

Wooden masks representing Spaniards, or "Moors," are painted white, bright pink, or more realistic flesh tones; they are sometimes "two-faced." Tlaxcala masks have glass eyes that open and close when a string is pulled. Animal masks may incorporate horns, whiskers, teeth, claws, and pelts to make them more realistic. Some of the country's most impressive masks are made in the village of Tocuaro, about 6 miles (10 km) west of Pátzcuaro.

The Lake Region

Inquisitive souls should consider a trip into the rolling countryside, where many villages and small towns are known for their folk art. The lake district is also known for its many colorful religious celebrations, involving masked and costumed dancers, locally made instruments, and traditional songs.

One of the best known and most visited islands is **Janitzio,** Lake Pátzcuaro's largest, where evocative Day of the Dead celebrations have been much publicized and massively visited by outsiders. Atop the cone-shaped island is an imposing, blocklike statue of War of Independence hero José María Morelos *($),* with

($$) depart every 15 minutes or so for Janitzio, on demand for Yunuén and the smaller islands, in which case fewer than four passengers must split the cost of the trip among themselves.

A 55-mile (88 km) road circumvents the lake. On the eastern shore are **Ihautzio** and **Tzintzuntzan,** two Purépecha towns that shared power with Pátzcuaro before the Spanish Conquest. Tiny Ihuatzio is little visited except for its partially excavated Purépecha ruins. Tzintzuntzan's name means "place of the hummingbirds" in Purépecha, a language related to no other in Mexico.

Tzintzuntzan makes for a nice day or half-day excursion from

Pátzcuaro. Walk along cobbled streets and dirt paths to the lakeshore. The crafts market sells woven straw objects, pottery, and wood carvings. Across the street, the **pre-Hispanic ceremonial site** *(Carr. 15 at entrance to Tzintzuntzan, $)* consists of a large platform supporting five *yácatas,* stepped pyramids joined to circular structures originally faced with sheets of volcanic stone. The excavated buildings have yielded burial sites, presumably of Purépecha kings.

Behind the crafts market is a large religious complex built by the Franciscans. Passing olive trees in the open atrium, you'll come to **Templo de San Francisco,** whose wall decorations and painted wooden ceiling are currently under restoration. Tzintzuntzan comes alive for Easter week, Day of the Dead, and Christmas *pastorelas* beginning December 16.

Named for the 16th-century bishop who dedicated his later life to the local population, **Quiroga** was an important crossroad before the conquest. Today it's a commercial hub. A candlelight procession on the first Sunday in July marks the **Fiesta de la Preciosa Sangre de Cristo** (Festival of Christ's Precious Blood).

Just a mile (1.5 km) beyond Quiroga, **Santa Fe de la Laguna** (see "Woodcarving & Spanish," p. 163) specializes in ceramics, especially candelabra. The free-standing cross in the atrium of the **Templo de San Nicolás** is typical to Michoacán state. The town celebrates its fiesta on September 14 with fireworks and local dances.

On the far west side of the lake, **Erongarícuaro** lies surrounded by mixed forests, and like other area towns, has chilly winters and warm, rainy summers. A U.S.-owned store makes painted wooden furniture in a huge variety of styles and motifs, including commissioned work.

About 10 miles (16 km) south of Pátzcuaro is **Santa Clara del Cobre,** where artisans produce hand-hammered copper tableware and other decorative items. Santa Clara is to copper what Taxco is to silver: a town full of brilliant metalwork. Well worth a visit is the **Museo Nacional del Cobre.**

Southwest of Pátzcuaro off Highway 120, **Zirahuén** is a small town on a lake of the same name. Smaller and deeper than Lake Pátzcuaro, Lago Zirahuén is surrounded by pine-oak forests. Known for its music and dance, the town celebrates especially Easter week and the Day of the Holy Cross (May 3). ∎

Museo Nacional del Cobre

- ✉ Morelos 263 at Pino Suárez
- ☎ 434/343-0254
- 🕐 Closed Mon.
- 💲 $

Once a year, on the Day of the Dead, family graves are cleaned and decorated with candles and flowers.

In & Around Uruapan

Regarded by some as Pátzcuaro's less popular neighbor, Uruapan makes a good base for visiting the region. Its elevation at 2,000 feet (610 m) below Pátzcuaro gives it a subtropical climate that supports lush vegetation and year-round flowers. An enchanting national park within the city center, one of the country's largest craft fairs, and a nearby lava-covered ghost town are just three reasons to visit this untouristed market town.

Only the church's upper facade protrudes above the lava that engulfed Parangaricutiro in 1943.

The Purépecha lived here centuries before Father Juan de San Miguel arrived from Spain and founded the city in 1533. He built a chapel, market, and school, but also instated a feudal system that reduced the Indians to serfs. Under the *encomienda* system, Uruapan prospered as an important agricultural center and today is renowned as the avocado capital of the world.

The city is laid out in a grid, at the center of which is the *plaza principal.* On the north side of the plaza stands the Mudejar and plateresque **La**

Huatápera *(Jardín Morelos s/n),* the original hospital erected by Father Juan in the 16th century. Today it houses the **Museo de los 4 Pueblos Indígenas** *(tel 452/524-3434, closed Mon.),* displaying an impressive array of crafts from around Michoacán state, including a collection of the beautiful cedar lacquerware for which Uruapan is famous.

Behind La Huatápera, the city's **market** sprawls along Calle Constitución, where the locals sell produce, cheeses, and a variety of crafts, including lacquered trays, gourds, and boxes, and wooden furniture. During Semana Santa (Holy Week), the main square is converted into a huge crafts market with beautifully carved guitars and violins from nearby Paracho on sale.

On either side of La Huatápera, the exteriors of the **Templo de la Inmaculada** and the **Templo de San Francisco** are fine examples of plateresque architecture constructed of local *cantera* (quarrystone).

INSIDER TIP:

A short walk from the city center leads to the river's edge, where you'll find waterfalls, lush vegetation, and Uruapan's most gen-teel neighborhoods.

—MARAEL JOHNSON
National Geographic author

About six long blocks west of the main plaza (a 15-min. walk), at the end of Calle Independencia, lies **Parque Nacional Eduardo Ruíz** *(Calz. Fray Juan de San Miguel s/n, tel 452/524-0197, $).* A model of landscape architecture, this magical park follows the Río Cupatizio for just over half a mile (1 km). Within this limited space are shady stone paths, terraced banks, bridges, waterfalls, and an explosion of flowers. A rainbow is said to form in the mist of the river every day.

Uruapan is a great base for exploring the region's charming and original churches. The under-choir at **Cochuco** is painted with terrific naive scenes full of pre-Hispanic icons. **Nurio** is said to have the best naive paintings; visit on Sunday for the best chance of entering. **Pomacuarán,** just a few miles away, has a vaulted ceiling covered in vibrant paintings. Drive or hire a taxi.

More dramatic is a visit to the buried village of **San Juan Parangaricutiro,** where in 1943 the 8,400-foot (2,560 m) **Volcán Paricutín** began its geologically rapid ascent in the middle of a farmer's field. The volcano spewed lava for eight years, forcing 4,000 people to evacuate. Today, only the upper facade of the church is visible. To get there, take a bus to **Angahuan** *(NW of Uruapan),* where you can rent a horse to San Juan Parangaricutiro or to Volcán Paricutín itself *($$$$$),* 6 miles round-trip. Angahuan has a restaurant and rustic accommodations. Sturdy shoes are recommended. ∎

Uruapan
▲ 138 D3
Visitor Information
✉ Juan Ayala 16
☎ 452/524-7199

Lucha Libre

Along with soccer, Mexicans get passionate about wrestling. *Lucha libre* was popularized in the 1930s with stars like Tarzan López; today's heavies have names like El Hombre Eléctrico (Electric Man) and Dr. Wagner. Masked and unmasked men in a variety of sizes and shapes may fight individually or on teams. Those fans who can't visit one of Mexico City's two arenas get all they need on TV. For more info about lucha libre, visit *www.cmll.com.*

Ixtapa & Zihuatanejo

Zihuatanejo was a pre-Hispanic settlement and an important port in the early days of the Spanish colony; modern Ixtapa was, about 35 years ago, just a coconut plantation—one of a handful of resorts developed by the Mexican government in the early 1970s. Today the two places are marketed together, pronounced in a single breath that encompasses 15 miles (24 km) of some of the Pacific coast's most scenic beaches.

Vacationers relax under individual palm-thatch umbrellas at Isla Ixtapa.

Ixtapa

📍 139 D2

Visitor Information

✉ Paseo de las Gaviotas 12

☎ 755/553-1270

www.ixtapa-zihuatanejo.org

After a decree in 1561 pronounced Acapulco to be New Spain's only official Pacific port, **Zihuatanejo** diminished in importance. Following centuries of obscurity, the village was connected to the outside world once again by the construction of Highway 200 in the 1960s.

Today Zihua's dirt roads have been paved, and folk-art shops and international restaurants lure vacationers from the tree-shaded but sultry streets. Still a working fishing town, it has several elegant boutique hotels on the bay. Other hotels are up on the bluffs above the beaches or in the friendly

downtown area. A pedestrian promenade connects downtown, which fronts the main beach, **Playa Principal,** to **Playa La Madera,** a pretty and accessible beach equally popular with travelers and picnicking families.

Taxis are the easiest way to reach **Playa La Ropa** (Clothing Beach), with good restaurants, gentle surf, and water sports equipment for rent.

Water taxis (*$$ round-trip*) from the main dock in Zihuatanejo access **Playa Las Gatas.** Named for once-prevalent nurse sharks (not cats), Las Gatas is perfect for snorkeling and swimming. Rustic cafés serve soft drinks and ceviche, beer and snacks, and, except during inclement weather and low season, water-sports concessions rent wave runners and other toys.

Located on a shallow, open bay, the beaches at **Ixtapa** are largely unprotected from the surf. The hotel zone parallels **Playa del Palmar** for several miles, with access to hotel restaurants and bars and water-sports rentals. The somewhat narrow beach slopes down to the water. Across the street are boutiques, pharmacies, and more restaurants. An inexpensive taxi ride between the two towns takes about 10 minutes.

More isolated beaches can be found at Ixtapa's northwest end, past the surf spot at **Escolleras** and the Marina Ixtapa, a 620-slip marina and yacht club. Here also is the **Club de Golf Marina Ixtapa** (tel 755/553-1424). West of the marina are several more lovely beaches. Beyond Punta Ixtapa, **Playa Quieta** is a tranquil beach with a remodeled Club Med hotel. Rent a horse ($$$$$) for an early morning or late afternoon jaunt on the beach at **Playa Linda.**

Farther north, **Playa Larga** is great for long walks, although strong riptides discourage even serious swimmers. There are several restaurants and **Puerta Paraíso** (tel 755/553-0979, www .puertaalparaiso.com.mx), a beautiful boutique hotel.

From Playa Linda pier, water taxis ($$ round-trip) access popular **Isla Ixtapa,** where you can dive or snorkel, lounge on the beach, or dine at the adjacent restaurants. On the far side of the small island, quiet **Playa Carey** has no facilities.

Fishing co-ops near the pier in Zihuatanejo offer deep-sea fishing for dorado, marlin, yellowfin tuna, roosterfish, and sailfish. The May tournament is gaining popularity.

Snorkel and dive trips can be arranged through several operators, including **Carlo Scuba** (Playa Las Gatas, tel 755/554-6003, www.car loscuba.net). Play golf at the 18-hole **Club de Golf Ixtapa Palma Real** (Blvd. Ixtapa s/n, tel 755/553-1163), and explore regional history at the minuscule **Museo Arqueológico de la Costa Grande** (Plaza Olaf Palme, tel 755/554-7552, closed Mon., $).

About 14 miles (22.5 km) south of Zihuatanejo lies luscious **Barra de Potosí.** Thatch-roofed restaurants on the beach provide hammocks where you can while away

INSIDER TIP:

Even during Easter Week the long beaches at Troncones, 25 minutes north of Ixtapa, are fairly uncrowded.

— FERNANDA GONZÁLEZ
National Geographic Traveler magazine editorial director, Mexico

the day. During the dry season, boats tour the adjacent lagoon. Half-day tours ($$$$$) are available through Ixtapa or Zihuatanejo tour operators, or you can get there by taxi or city bus. The scenery along the way is lush and beautiful.

About the same distance north of Zihuatanejo is **Troncones,** a surfing beach with inexpensive and moderately priced hotels and house rentals. ∎

Zihuatanejo

⬛ 139 C2

Visitor Information

✉ Paseo de las Gaviotas 12, Ixtapa

☎ 755/553-1270

www.ixtapa-zihuatanejo.org

Acapulco

Deliciously self-satisfied, the aged port city of Acapulco remains a major resort destination for foreign honeymooners and Mexicans cutting loose on annual vacations. Trendy restaurants serve international and haute Mexican cuisine, while friendly seaside bistros pile on fresh shrimp and Acapulco-style ceviche. Still among the hippest in Mexico, the city's many discos play live and canned music until the roosters crow in the surrounding hills.

A dazzling view of Acapulco Bay from one of the city's exclusive hilltop neighborhoods

Acapulco's balmy weather ranges from hot to hotter, and summer rains (June–Oct.) exacerbate the heat instead of diminishing it. As the humidity rises, hotel prices fall, but the trade-off is high. Throughout the year, myriad species of flowering trees produce brilliant blossoms. Tropical fruits—including mango, papaya, and watermelon—appear as fresh drinks or as salads served with a squeeze of lime and a sprinkle of powdered chili. On Thursdays, tradition calls for a late, leisurely lunch of *pozole*–hominy soup served with raw onions, avocado, and oregano.

Although Jet Skis, water skis, diving and snorkel equipment, and other water toys are offered by the hotels crowding Avenida Costera, this area tends to be the most polluted part of the 4-mile (7 km) bay—especially during the rainy season. Beaches on or near the points, such as **Playa Caleta** and **Playa Puerto Marqués,** are the cleanest. If you're hesitant about swimming, consider sport-fishing for sailfish or dorado, playing tennis, or golfing at one of the city's four 18-hole courses.

Acapulco became absolutely hip and happening in the 1960s, when sybaritic Hollywood stars partied in private homes and exclusive restaurants above downtown, before the "scene" marched unequivocally east. Today, nostalgic Acapulqueños stop by for a sunset cocktail at the once-glamorous **Hotel Flamingos** bar, above **Playitas.** The coast road winds through neighborhoods of older homes, shops, and restaurants to **La Quebrada,** where cliff divers hurtle themselves more than 15 stories into a rocky cove below. Dives ($) are usually performed at 1, 7:30, 8:30, 9:30, and 10:30 p.m.

The road continues to twin coves of coarse sand at **Playa Caleta** and **Playa Caletilla,** lined with informal restaurants and water equipment concessions. Separating the two beaches is

corresponding snack shops. During the coolest hours of the day, climb the hill to the **lighthouse** for a sweeping view.

From Playa Caleta, Avenida Costera Miguel Alemán (usually simply called "la Costera") curves past the Yacht Club to downtown Acapulco. Once the center of tourist attention, it is now left mostly to the locals, who hang out at the laid-back **zócalo.** The cathedral of **Nuestra Señora de la Soledad,** built in the 1930s, combines art deco and Moorish elements with no great success.

At the oceanfront *malecón,* or seawalk, cruise ships disgorge their passengers to haggle at **Mercado de Artesanías** (*Velázquez de León near 5 de Mayo),* a 350-stall flea

Acapulco

 139 E1 & pp. 172–173

Visitor Information

✉ Av. Costera Miguel Alemán 38-A, Fracc. Costa Azul

☎ 744/484-8555

EXPERIENCE: Bodysurfing Competitions

Along the southern Pacific coast in Guerrero state, bodysurfers compete in **El Torneo Internacional de Bodysurf** (tel 755/113-6621 cell, www.mantabodysurfclub. com, Spanish only) at Playa Las Escolleras, between Ixtapa and Zihuatanejo. (Bodysurfers use their body instead of a fiberglass or foam surf board.) The second-annual event in April 2008 drew about 40 competitors from surrounding

states as well as from Italy and California. Free for competitors and spectators, the event includes a reggae concert after the awards ceremony.

The **Cuija Open** (tel 744/485-6428 in Acapulco) takes place at Pie de la Cuesta, north of Acapulco. The inscription fee (about U.S.$19) includes lodging for international participants. There's a cash prize for places one through four.

Mágico Mundo Marino (tel 744/483-9344, $$), a theme park with a sea lion show, waterslides, and a restaurant. From Playa Caleta, a ten-minute boat ride ($$) or a longer glass-bottom boat tour takes you to hilly **Isla de la Roqueta,** a lovely little beach that's nice for swimming; umbrellas and chairs on the sand provide shade if you buy from the

market. "Booze cruises" ($$$$$) offer afternoon and evening cruises with food, shows, meals, or swimming in addition to drinks.

Constructed in 1615 to protect the Manila galleons from pirates, Acapulco's **Fuerte de San Diego** was destroyed by earthquake in 1776. The fort was rebuilt of stone with a surrounding moat. The excellent **historical museum** (tel 744/482-3828, closed Mon., $$) holds permanent exhibits as well as temporary cultural expositions. About a block away, don't miss the **Museo de las Máscaras** (Hornitos at Morelos, tel 744/486-5577), with more than 400 of Guerrero state's traditional masks as well as equally colorful wood carvings.

Just a few miles northeast of downtown Acapulco is **Sitio Arqueológica Palma Sola** (tel 744/486-1514, open 8 a.m.–4 p.m.). English- and Spanish-language signs along the half-mile (1 km) uphill path explain the meaning of the some 18 petroglyphs created by the Yope people who once inhabited the area. Take a cab ($) from Parque Papagayo, on Acapulco's main highway.

Approximately 50 minutes from

Acapulco, recently discovered **Tehuacalco** (in Chilpancingo, southern Guerrero) has the remains of a ball court, pre-Hispanic residences, and a temple.

Locals and visitors fill the eateries lining **Playa Hornos,** or spread their picnics along the shore. Across the street, trees and coconut palms shade children's amusement rides, snack shacks, and dusty soccer fields in the large but neglected **Parque Papagayo.** Pools and waterslides lure visitors to **Parque Acuático CICI** (Av. Costera Miguel Alemán at Cristóbal Colón, tel 744/484-4035, $$$).

Between placid **Playa Icacos** and the Hyatt Regency hotel lies a less-than-scenic proliferation of hotels, restaurants, drugstores, souvenir shops, discos, and car rentals.

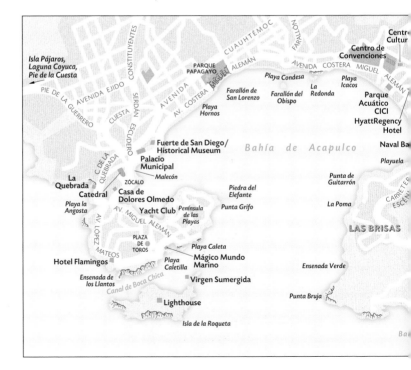

Ambulant Vendors & Haggling

Dealing with ambulant vendors can be annoying; a parade of mobile *sarape* sellers interrupts the peace of an idyllic beach. But a low-overhead salesperson can offer bargain prices. Some vendors charge way more than their goods are worth, however, while others ask a price near the actual value. When in doubt, politely offer 50 to 60 percent of the asking price and work up from there. Don't quibble about the price of inexpensive trinkets unless the amount in question would affect your well-being more than that of the seller.

Concessions line the beach, with drinks and snacks served under palm-leaf shades.

The coast highway's name changes to **Carretera Escénica** as it winds east toward Acapulco's newer developments. Perched high above the ocean on either side of the highway, the exclusive palaces and hotels of **Las Brisas** are blessed with ocean breezes. From here enjoy splendid views of the bay, which positively sparkles at night. Many of the resorts on the cliff side of the highway have elevators or steep stairways to semiprivate beaches.

Investors began construction of a huge $300 million resort spa and convention center called Mundo Imperial about 7.5 miles (12 km) outside of downtown. Il Foro performance venue opened in 2008; other parts of the complex were scheduled for a later opening.

Farther east, a number of high-rise hotels lining calm **Bahía Puerto Marqués** rent water toys, while horses wait for riders at long **Playa Revolcadero.** Near the airport, sip a tropical drink from a seaside cabana at **Barra Vieja,** or take a boat ride around the lagoons of adjoining **Laguna Tres Palos,** a small fishing village.

Twenty-two miles (35 km) northwest of downtown, mangroves line freshwater **Laguna Coyuca.** Eat at one of the beach shacks, arrange a lagoon tour with a visit to **Isla Pájaros,** or water-ski. The long beach at nearby **Pie de la Cuesta** is a favorite for horseback riding and hammock lounging in simple thatch-roofed restaurants. Both Laguna Coyuca and Pie de la Cuesta are wonderful spots to watch the sun set. ■

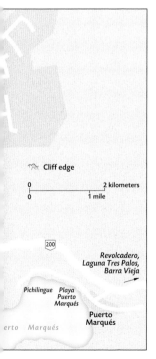

Cliff edge

0   2 kilometers
0   1 mile

200

Revolcadero,
Laguna Tres Palos,
Barra Vieja

Pichilingue   Playa
Puerto
Marqués

Puerto
Marqués

erto   Marqués

Taxco

Sun-splashed Taxco winds up and down narrow, cobblestone streets. U.S. expatriate William Spratling, who started Taxco's first silversmithing workshop, called it the "Florence of Mexico," but it's more like a Mediterranean village. By city ordinance, its white-painted facades crowned with red-tile roofs rise no more than three stories above street level.

The Iglesia de Santa Prisca rises above Taxco's center.

Most of Taxco's sights lie on or near pretty **Plaza Borda,** where patent-leather grackles voice urgent calls from the trees. Streets radiate like spokes, surrounded by handsome two- and three-story buildings housing restaurants and silver shops.

Facing the plaza are the **Museo de la Platería** *(Plaza Borda 1, tel 762/622-0658, closed Mon., $),* a small, privately owned silver museum, and the **Centro Cultural Casa Borda** *(Plaza Borda 1, tel 762/622-6634, closed Mon.),* offering art classes, cultural performances, and changing exhibits.

The original Taxco was inhabited by Thalhuica Indians, who paid tribute to their Aztec overlords in gold and silver. After the conquest, the Spaniards established mines at the site of present-day Taxco (El Nuevo, or New Taxco), relocating workers and engineers from the old city, now known as Taxco el Viejo.

Although silver was mined for centuries and artisans in nearby Iguala were known for their gold-smithing, it was American William Spratling (1900–1967) who established the first silver workshop, Las Delicias, in 1931. Today, about 80 percent of the population is involved in silversmithing, and the Ministry of Tourism estimates there are some thousand silver shops, with additional vendors selling at the **Saturday market** *(Av. de los Plateros s/n, near Flecha Roja bus terminal).*

The unequivocal star of this silver city, however, is gold-drenched **Iglesia de Santa Prisca** *(Plaza Borda 1),* paid for by mining entrepreneur don José de la Borda. The ornate pink quarrystone church is dedicated to the obscure, 12th-century Roman martyr Santa Prisca.

The temple is said to hold

23 tons (21 tonnes) of gold and, except for the lighting, almost everything is original. The 256-pipe organ—which took six months to bring piece by piece by mule from Veracruz—is still played occasionally. The narrow church's 12 gold and polychrome altarpieces create a dizzying feeling of excess. Dozens of saints lean out in high relief from the exuberant main altarpiece, dedicated to the Virgin of the Immaculate Conception.

The left side chapel was built for the town's indigenous population. Note the unusual crucifix, with the Christ figure's arms above the head, nails in the wrists instead of the hands, and the feet nailed separately to the cross. Sometimes referred to as "the Michelangelo of Mexico," Miguel Cabrera (1695–1768) executed most of the church's paintings.

As you face Santa Prisca, the city's wonderful **market**—a twisting warren of stalls—is a block to your right. On Thursdays, vendors here and throughout the city sell *pozole,* hominy soup served with a plate of condiments. Other regional foods include *cecina taxqueña* (thin pieces of marinated beef) and barbecued goat. Author John Dos Passos and William Spratling claimed to have invented the lime and tequila concoction "la Berta" at **Berta's** bar. The cantina claims a secret ingredient—but it's basically tequila, soda, and lime.

A portion of Spratling's collection of pre-Hispanic art is shown at the **Museo Spratling** (*Porfirio Delgado 1, tel 762/622-1660, closed Mon., $*). Although poorly labeled and displayed, it

is worth a look. Of more interest is the nearby **Museo de Arte Virreinal** (*Juan Ruíz de Alarcón 12, tel 762/622-5501, closed Mon., $*), which presents traveling exhibits along with a collection of religious art and liturgical objects. The beautifully restored 17th-century building has exposed ceiling beams, whitewashed walls, baked earth tiles, and great cityscapes.

For an even greater view, climb the street behind town to **Templo de Guadalupe,** or take the aerial tram from Los Arcos, near the visitor center on Avenida de los Plateros, to **Club de Campo Monte Taxco** (*tel 762/622-1300*). For a fee, you can play tennis or golf, or swim in the pool. Alternatively, sip a drink at the bar, and enjoy the view—on a clear day you'll have a lovely view of Taxco and the surrounding hills. ■

Taxco
△ 139 E2
Visitor Information
✉ Avenida de los Plateros 1
☎ 762/622-2274

Parque Nacional Grutas de Cacahuamilpa

About 19 miles (30 km) from Taxco is Mexico's largest system of underground caves. Guided tours (**tel 762/622-2274,** $$) leave hourly 10 a.m. to 5 p.m., following a 1.2-mile (2 km) lighted path past stalactites, stalagmites, and rock formations. The entire system comprises about 10 miles (16 km) of tunnels and 20 caves. Minibuses leave from the Taxco bus depot; if you are traveling by car, take the marked turnoff from Highway 55.

More Places to Visit in Central Pacific Mexico

Lagos de Moreno

Lagos de Moreno is a prosperous place, and one little visited by foreign tourists. Stately churches of rose-colored limestone and a handful of colonial-era private homes surround its plazas. Located 50 miles (82 km) southeast of Aguascalientes, this small city in the central highlands of Jalisco appears to belong in a more distant era. Visit the baroque **Parroquia de la Asunción** (*Hidalgo at the main plaza*), the parish church and the sober but elegant **Rinconada de las Capuchinas** (*Miguel Leandro Guerra at Mariano Azuela*), a former convent with a museum and cultural center. www.lagosdemoreno.gob.mx 🄰 138 D4 ✉ Hidalgo 230 ☎ 474/746-5622

Los Azufres

About 1.5 hours east of Morelia, near the city of Ciudad Hidalgo, off Highway 15, lies an area of natural hot springs called Los Azufres.

Spas here offer different levels of service, but most have restaurants, changing rooms, and one or more pools; some have campgrounds and offer massage or other services. For a more natural retreat with few services, head for **Churritaco.** The spring's sulfurous 104°F (40°C) waters are said to benefit the skin. 🄰 138 D3

INSIDER TIP:

Pescado a la talla **is a delicacy eaten along Mexico's Pacific coast from Acapulco to Ixtapa. The fish is baked with spices, lime, and cilantro. Try it mild, not too hot.**

—FERNANDA GONZÁLES
National Geographic Traveler *magazine editorial director, Mexico*

EXPERIENCE:
Polo by the Pacific

Look at San Pancho, so young and yet so sophisticated! Built in the 1970s near Punta Mita north of Puerto Vallarta as a company town (mango processing), San Pancho (officially San Francisco) has more than its share of good restaurants, and now, **La Patrona Polo Field** (*tel 322/297-2334, www.polovallarta. com*), too. During the season (November through June), people from as far as Mexico City show up, dressed to the nines. Watch polo practice from the restaurant-jazz bar Tuesday through Friday. Or mingle with the players after the game on Saturday, a day spiced with various other entertainments. If you want to go beyond watching matches, join the club for polo lessons and horseback riding, or just take a day course to learn the basics of the sport.

El Santuario de la Mariposa Monarca el Rosario

The transvolcanic mountain range in eastern Michoacán is the winter home for the monarch butterfly. The butterflies migrate up to 3,100 miles (5,000 km) from Canada and the Great Lakes. After resting throughout the winter, they mate. The males die; the females prepare for the return journey beginning in early or mid-April.

El Santuario de la Mariposa Monarca el Rosario is the better of two wintering sites open to the public. In a good year the monarchs blanket oyamel trees (a type of spruce). Visit late November through March. Park entrance is relatively inexpensive (*$$*), but the excursion is more interesting with a knowledgeable guide. Recommended are the state-licensed, English-speaking guides of **Movisa** (*tel 443/312-8723, Morelia*) or **Viajes Maruata** (*tel 443/324-2120*), who lead long day tours from the capital. Call for more information. 🄰 139 E3

A wealth of cultural attractions and a cosmopolitan character, breathing history in its art, artifacts, and architecture

Mexico City

Mexico City architecture reflects old and new.

Mexico City

Mexico City is a lot like the little girl from the nursery rhyme: When she's good, she's very, very good, but when she's bad, she's horrid. Despite the considerable dangers and annoyances, el D.F. (short for Distrito Federal, or Federal District) is a fascinating mélange of the hip and the historic. Today this capital city represents the epitome of the country's *mestizaje,* or blending of Indian and European cultures.

To the good, theater, dance, and musical performances—everything from marimba to Mozart—are held in dozens of theaters throughout the city. Mariachi musicians in matching, silver-studded ensembles croon romantic tunes in historic Plaza de Garibaldi. Upscale boutiques, cutting-edge art galleries, and sidewalk cafés line the main streets in Polanco, la Zona Rosa, la Condesa, Roma, and other diverse neighborhoods. Trendy restaurants in la Condesa serve carpaccio and decaf espresso, while down the street, family-run stands sell tamales and tacos.

On the down side, several million cars crowd into the 570-square-mile (1,475 sq km) city,

Mexico City

Area of map detail

spewing tons of contaminants into the air each year. At 7,400 feet (2,250 m) above sea level, the megalopolis of some 22 million people is ringed by volcanic mountains that trap the pollution—although the situation has improved dramatically in recent years. Visitors must be on the lookout for petty thieves, and there's an established protocol for hailing a legitimate cab.

When the Mexica (pronounced meh-SHEE-ka; see pp. 184–185) first wandered into the bowl-shaped Valle de Anáhuac (Valley of Mexico) from the north, they met people of learning: the cultured descendants of the Toltec tribe, with an accurate calendar and elaborate religious rituals. The Mexica, or Aztec, founded

NOT TO BE MISSED:

Templo Mayor, the great pyramid of Tenochtitlán **186–187**

Admiring the fine murals at the Palacio de Bellas Artes **190**

Visiting the shrines and temples to the Virgin of Guadalupe, at la Villa de Guadalupe **192–193**

An afternoon stroll through popular Chapultepec Park **194–195**

Museo Nacional de Antropología, Mexico's best collection **198–201**

Shopping in San Ángel **204–205**

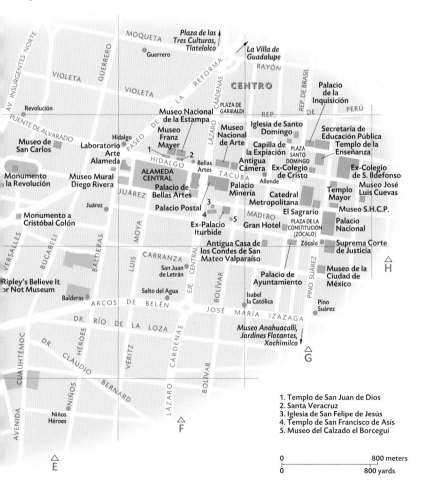

1. Templo de San Juan de Dios
2. Santa Veracruz
3. Iglesia de San Felipe de Jesús
4. Templo de San Francisco de Asís
5. Museo del Calzado el Borceguí

the conquest, the Spaniards built their new capital, Mexico City, from the ruins of Tenochtitlán and filled in the lake.

South and southwest of the historic center, the villages of Coyoacán and San Ángel—which predated the Spanish conquest and even the building of Tenochtitlán—have over the years retained their identities. Between the two towns are at least half a dozen captivating plazas surrounded by baroque churches, cobbled streets, and brightly painted homes. On weekends local artists and antiques dealers sell their wares at inexpensive prices, while an excellent assortment of the country's handicrafts are sold daily in boutiques and shops.

Xochimilco, one of the southernmost villages on former Lake Texcoco, has produced much of the region's plants and cut flowers since pre-Hispanic times. On Sundays lively groups of friends and families climb aboard *trajineras*—covered punts decorated in plastic flowers—for a leisurely cruise along Mexico City's last remaining system of canals and *chinampas,* or waterborne gardens. ■

Tenochtitlán on Lake Texcoco and, after rubbing elbows with their civilized neighbors for 200 years, amazed the Spanish conquistadores with their ingenious city of broad avenues lined with brightly painted palaces and temples. After

EXPERIENCE: Shop Where the Locals Sell

Shopping in Mexico—away from department stores—is generally intriguing. Ask around to find the local *tianguis*, an indigenous word for a daily or weekly market where vendors bring produce, crafts, and even animals for sale and barter. You can practice your Spanish, purchase folkloric art from the region, and interact with local people.

Mercado de la Ciudadela *(Calle Baldera & Enrico Martinez)* is one of Mexico City's best known markets, featuring handicrafts from around the country. Help keep it open—there have been efforts recently to shut it down—and keep the artisan tradition alive. While there you can visit nearby Ciudadela Park.

In other parts of the country, federal- and state-run shops offer crafts at fair prices to artisans while purchasers have the opportunity to select from the cream of traditional crafts as well as support the local people. An example is **Casa de las Artesanias del Estado de Michoacán** (www.casadelasarte sanias.gob.mx), which runs excellent stores in Morelia, Michoacán

(Ex-convento de San Francisco, tel 443/312-1248) and San Miguel de Allende, Guanajuato *(Salida a Celaya 69, tel 415/152-3448)*.

In addition are craft co-ops like Oaxaca's **MARO** *(Calle 5 de Mayo 204, tel 951/516-0670)*, which offers excellent prices and encourages local artisans to continue ancient and more modern crafts traditions.

Centro Histórico

Cosmopolitan and chaotic yet eager to please, downtown D.F. is a synthesis of ancient and modern Mexican culture. Administrative offices, prominent homes, and churches replaced the palaces and temples of the dispossessed Mexica in the nucleus of the new city. Having weathered the centuries and the region's intermittent earthquakes, many still fulfill their original purposes; others house bookstores, jewelers, museums, and restaurants.

A good place to begin exploring the city is the 10-acre (4 ha) *zócalo,* or central plaza, built from the rubble of Tenochtitlán. Officially called **Plaza de la Constitución,** it is the world's second largest square. On the north side of the square, the **Catedral Metropolitana** *(tel 55/5510-0440),* the first cathedral in New Spain, was ordered to be built by Hernán Cortés, but later razed and replaced with the present church, finished in 1813. The dignified baroque facade is dominated by twin 18th-century bell towers.

Inside, worshippers pray at the cathedral's five principal altars and 14 side chapels, much of the exuberant craftsmanship hidden behind tooled wooden bars. Dusky light filters through small stained-glass windows to illuminate the dazzling **Altar de los Reyes,** a gilded wood altarpiece in Churrigueresque style, which took nearly 20 years to complete.

Also Churrigueresque is the intricate facade of the adjoining mid-18th-century parish church, **El Sagrario,** covered in an army of carved saints. **La Piedra del Sol,** the 24-ton (22 metric ton) Aztec "calendar" stone now seen in the Museo Nacional de Antropología (see pp. 198–201), was discovered in El Sagrario's courtyard.

Mexico's cherished "dark-skinned Virgin" is fêted in the capital city's *zócalo*

The east side of the zócalo is dedicated to the **Palacio Nacional** *(tel 55/5999-2800).* Originally the official residence of the colonial viceroys, the palace later held the presidential offices. Today, it houses various state departments, but visitors come to see the Diego Rivera murals highlighting Mexican history and culture. Hire an English-speaking guide *($$)* at the foot of the stairwell.

On the second floor are scenes from pre-Hispanic life. Smaller panels pay tribute to the rubber tree, corn, cacao, and the agave plant. The last mural on the second floor shows the

Centro Histórico

🅰 179 F3/G3

Visitor Information

✉ Av. Nuevo León 56, Col. Hipódromo

☎ 55/5553-1901

🚇 Metro: Insurgentes

www.mexicocity .gob.mx

By night historic downtown, dominated by the Catedral Metropolitana, regains an air of refinement.

Ex-Colegio de San Ildefonso

🅰 179 G3
✉ Justo Sierra 16
☎ 55/5702-6378
🕐 Closed Mon.
💲 $

mestizaje of Mexico, the blending of indigenous and Spanish blood and cultures. Cortés is shown as a hideous, syphillitic man; behind him, his mistress, La Malinche (see sidebar p. 206) holds a green-eyed *mestizo* baby.

One block south, in the **Suprema Corte de Justicia** *(Pino Suárez 2, tel 55/5522-1500)*, José Clemente Orozco's mural, "La Justicia" ("Justice"), hangs over the main interior staircase.

On the south side of the plaza, the tiled exterior of the **Palacio del Ayuntamiento** (Municipal Palace) depicts the coats of arms of Mexico City, Coyoacán, Christopher Columbus, and Hernán Cortés.

Naturally, some of the city's finest architecture stems from its religious past. Built in 1588 as a Jesuit seminary, the **Ex-Colegio de San Ildefonso** was remodeled during the early 18th century but maintains its original baroque and neoclassical facade. Inside, dark orange walls and stone porticos surround a large central patio shaded by giant magnolias. Now owned by the National University, the museum and cultural center hosts events and temporary fine arts exhibits. Murals by José Clemente

INSIDER TIP:

Festival del Centro Histórico is in March. Enjoy free concerts.

—LUZ MARIA MEJIA
National Geographic field researcher

Orozco are along three stories at the building's north end range.

Nearby, the striking, ultra-baroque interior of the narrow **Templo de la Enseñanza** *(Donceles 102, tel 55/5702-1843)* is a dazzling display of Spanish colonial wealth. Vacated during the Reform Laws, the late 18th-century convent church was declared a national monument in 1931 and once again functions as a place of worship.

One block north, the interior patios of the neoclassical **Secretaría de Educación Pública** *(Av. República de Argentina 28, tel 55/3601-1000)*, or Ministry of Education, are covered with murals. Diego Rivera painted nearly 200 panels between 1923 and 1928, notably "La Maestra Rural" ("The Rural Teacher") and "La Liberación del Peón" ("The Peasant's Liberation")—common themes for the socialist painter. The singular "Patriots and Parricides," by Siqueiros, decorates the stairwell near the República de Brasil street entrance.

One of Mexico's oldest squares, the **Plaza Santo Domingo** (*República de Venezuela at Brasil*) shelters the **Portal de los Evangelistas,** a colonnade where *evangelistas* (public scribes) have traditionally clacked away on ancient typewriters, completing job applications and "Dear John" letters for the unschooled. A few continue to perform this function.

At the north end of the plaza, native red *tezontle* (volcanic rock) contrasts with the white-stone Corinthian columns on the facade of the baroque **Iglesia de Santo Domingo** (*tel 55/5529-3906*). It was built in the early 18th century after floods and earthquakes ruined the first Dominican monastery in New Spain, dated 1527. Inside, note the neoclassical high altar created by Manuel de Tolsá. All that remains of the original structure is the small **Capilla de la Expiación,** or Chapel of Atonement, with its rococo altarpiece.

The Dominican-led Inquisition was aimed as much at purging political rivals from the colony as in pursuing heretics. A tribunal was established in 1521 in rented buildings surrounding the Plaza de Santo Domingo. Built 200 years later, the more permanent **Palacio de la Inquisición** (*República de Brasil 33 at Belisario Domínguez*) across the street was purchased in 1854 by the National University and now houses the Museum of Mexican Medicine.

But there's more to Mexico City than murals and museums.

Visit one of the many quirky bars downtown—some no doubt built of quarried limestone blocks from dismantled Aztec edifices. Admire the European-style window displays of delis and chocolate shops, and check out the national pawn shop facing the cathedral. Enjoy incredible pastries from **Pastelería Ideal,** then wander upstairs to see replicas of their wonderful cake collection. Take in a soccer game at one of D.F.'s major stadia (Estadio Azteca, Azul, or CU at the university); or how about some *lucha libre* (see sidebar p. 167)? The Coliseo wrestling stadium is right downtown on Calle República de Cuba. ∎

Pastelería Ideal

✉ Calle 16 de Septiembre 16
☎ 55/5521-2233
🚇 Metro: Bellas Artes

Business Decorum

Although Mexicans are friendly and outgoing, they're also rather formal, so inquire about the weather or other pleasantries before launching into business. Mexicans value subtlety and courtesy above punctuality and efficiency; voicing irritation or complaints won't win friends. The Latino schedule may be leisurely but rarely extremely late. If you speak Spanish, use the polite form of address *(usted)* with waiters, bellmen, and other strangers. Although most of your business associates will speak excellent English, speak slowly and clearly. Using basic phrases such as *"por favor"* (please) and *"gracias"* (thank you) demonstrates goodwill.

A Brief History of the Mexica

The Mexica, or Aztec, arrived in the bowl-shaped Valle de Anáhuac (Valley of Mexico) in the late 13th century. They were a poor and barbarous people—with no formal religion, calendar, or system of writing—who wandered south from a place they called Aztlán.

Human sacrifice in Mesoamerica

Initially reviled and briefly enslaved by more powerful city-states in the valley, the Mexica fled in 1322 to the uninhabited wetlands at the edge of Lake Texcoco, where they founded Tenochtitlán on an island on the lake. Just 50 years later they began their rapid rise to power with a strategic marriage into the royal family of Culhuacán, their former masters.

With the ascent of Itzcóatl to the throne in 1427, there began a systematic conquest and absorption of the established lakeside cities, including Coyoacán, Xochimilco, and Atzcapotzalco—the latter providing access to important freshwater springs at Chapultepec. Through warfare, intimidation, strategic alliances, and a ruthless political agenda, the Mexica extended their domain throughout Mesoamerica. From their first king, they began to reinvent their own history and genealogy in a more favorable light, even claiming lineage back to the god-king Quetzalcóatl.

Although governed during its early years by a representative council of elders and speakers, Tenochtitlán soon developed a ruling oligarchy, the *pipiltin*. Most people lived in servitude, subject to laws governing such minutiae as what they ate, drank, and wore. Meanwhile, the extravagant lifestyle of the pipiltin necessitated a constantly expanding empire enriched by plunder and the labor and taxation of subject states. These divergent living standards are reflected in the folk belief of the time that after death nobles were regenerated as gems, beautiful birds, or fluffy white clouds, while commoners became weasels, dung beetles, and skunks.

Few peoples except the Purépecha of Michoacán and some of the fierce Chichimec tribes to the north were able to repel the Mexica war machine. The conquered paid dearly both in tribute and in victims for the sacrificial slab. The Mexica's principle god, Huitzilopochtli (Southern Hummingbird, the god of war), grew in power as the empire grew. Initially an insignificant local deity, the hummingbird demanded human sacrifice on an incredible scale, feasting on hearts and blood from captured warriors, scofflaws, and other unfortunates.

By the time a Spanish expedition under Hernán Cortés arrived on Mexico's east coast in 1519, Tenochtitlán was feared, respected, and hated almost as much by its allies as by its subject states and enemies. Only this far-flung hostility made possible one of history's most amazing conquests (see p. 26–29). Another important factor was timing. According to legend, Quetzalcóatl had sailed eastward five centuries before, promising to return in the year 1 Reed. Cortés's

Moctezuma's historic first meeting with Cortés

arrival in that very year (a 1:52 probability) convinced the Mexica ruler, Moctezuma, of the god's return. A priest, poet, and philosopher, Moctezuma had been chosen king in 1502 based on his courage in battle, sagacity, and clarity of mind. Ironically, it was his indecision and unwillingness to acknowledge and engage the enemy that led to the downfall of the Mexica Empire, and ultimately, to the conquest of Mesoamerica.

Templo Mayor

Until the Spanish Conquest, el Templo Mayor, or great pyramid of Tenochtitlán, was the site of coronations, dedications, human sacrifice, and other civic and religious events. Today, a partial reconstruction of the pyramid allows you to appreciate its building stages, as well as view several surviving rooms and temples. Although the ruins themselves are interesting, it's in the well-designed museum that you'll really get a feel for life in Tenochtitlán.

Tzompantli (skull rack), with stucco representations of the skulls of sacrifice victims

Twin temples atop the Templo Mayor pyramid were dedicated to the two most important gods: the southern temple, painted red, housed the war god Huitz-ilopochtli; to the north was the blue shrine of Tláloc, god of rain and fertility. Still visible on the Tláloc temple are vertical black and white stripes and circles representing rain, eyes, and sky. Before it, a statue of Chac Mool, messenger to the gods, received the hearts of sacrificial victims.

Within the structure, thou-sands of priests and their acolytes lived and worshipped, accessing apartments and shrines through labyrinthine corridors of polished stone. Each ruler modified or enlarged previous structures. At the excavation's northern extreme, the **Eagle Warrior Room** was the exclusive enclave of that respected military order.

The first four galleries are dedicated to Huitzilopochtli. **Gallery One** has a scale model of the Templo Mayor. In **Gallery Two** you will see votive offerings as well as objects used in sacrifice and self-sacrifice. Among these

INSIDER TIP:

For lunch while visiting the *zócalo* or Templo Mayor, stop at Pepe's Tacos de Canasta (*Seminario at Moneda*). Tacos cost only 50 cents, and they may be stuffed with potatoes, green mole, beans, adobo sauce, or *chicharrón*.

—LISA OVERHOLTZER
National Geographic field researcher

are the flint knives used to open the chest cavity of sacrificial victims, and needles of filed eagle bones with which the nobles bled their earlobes, genitals, arms, and tongues in penitence and purification rituals. **Gallery Three** houses objects traded or paid in tribute from some of the Mexica's 370 subject towns, including fine gold filigree and turquoise jewelry from Oaxaca, and carved shells from the Caribbean and Pacific coasts.

Large statues, stelae, and the life-size, ceramic statues that guarded Huitzilopochtli's temple form the core of **Gallery Four.** Perhaps most impressive is the huge circular stone with relief carving of the moon goddess Coyolxauhqui, whose discovery by city workers in 1978 precipitated the temple's excavation. According to legend, Huitzilopochtli sprang fully armed from the womb of the earth goddess Coatlicue in order to protect her from his 400 siblings, including Coyolxauhqui.

(Coatlicue had been impregnated by a feather while sweeping, and her children were outraged over her mysterious and unseemly pregnancy.) Huitzilopochtli beheaded the moon goddess, and the others fled to the sky, where they became stars. In addition to explaining the demise of the moon each month, this legend undoubtedly helped to establish the fledgling god Huitzilopochtli during the early days of the kingdom by relating him to the venerated earth goddess Coatlicue.

Galleries Five to **Eight** are dedicated to Tláloc. In the first of these is a reproduction of the original wall decoration on the rain god's temple. Also exhibited are figures and images associated with Tláloc, including the frog, eaten by the Mexica as a ritualistic food. **Galleries Six** and **Seven**

Visiting the Museum

Signs are in Spanish, but an excellent English-language audio tour ($$) is also available. Guided Spanish-language tours are offered Tuesday through Friday; call 55/5542-4949 for an English-speaking guide.

are dedicated to the area's flora and fauna, and agriculture. The last of the main galleries describes the end of the Aztec era and the introduction of Christianity and Hispanic rule. Don't miss the last two galleries, near the exit, with fascinating exhibits regarding the cult of death. ■

Templo Mayor

🅰 179 G3

✉ Calle Seminario 8, NE corner of *zócalo*

☎ 55/5542-4943

🕐 Closed Mon.

💲 $$

🚇 Metro: Zócalo

www.templomayor. inah.gob.mx

A Walk In & Around Historic Parque la Alameda

Originally created for everyone, Alameda Park, its grassy esplanade punctuated with trees and fountains, became a fenced and elitist park during the presidency of Porfirio Díaz. Today, as intended, it attracts all manner of people and is surrounded by historic churches, museums, and the lovely Palace of Fine Arts. To the east, the Madero neighborhood, named for revolution hero Francisco I. Madero, has seen an influx of revenue and extensive restoration of its historic buildings.

Begin your walk at the Sanborns flagship venue in **Casa de los Azulejos ❶** *(Madero 4 at La Condesa, tel 55/5512-7824)*, one of the few nonhotel restaurants open at 7 a.m. This was a popular restaurant during the Mexican Revolution, when it hosted Pancho Villa, Emiliano Zapata, and their troops. The building's exterior is entirely covered in Puebla-style tiles; José Clemente Orozco's intriguing mural "Omnisciencia" (1925) graces the interior stairwell.

Directly across Calle Madero is the **Templo de San Francisco de Asís** *(Madero 7, tel 55/5518-4690)*, originally a Franciscan monastery begun in 1524 under the patronage of Hernán Cortés. Remodeled several times, the surviving Church of St. Francis of Assisi presents an excellent example of Churrigueresque design, especially in the facade and the main altar—the latter completely reconstructed in the 1940s. Next door is the lovely, 18th-century **Iglesia de San Felipe de Jesús ❷**, dedicated to Felipe de las Casas Martínez (1572–1597), the first Mexican saint. Its interior is covered in large, extraordinarily beautiful paintings of saints, while the high ceiling gives the small, French neo-Gothic church the illusion of space.

NOT TO BE MISSED:

Palacio de Bellas Artes • Parque la Alameda • Museo Mural Diego Rivera • Museo Franz Mayer

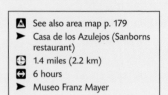

- ⓜ See also area map p. 179
- ► Casa de los Azulejos (Sanborns restaurant)
- 🕒 1.4 miles (2.2 km)
- ⏱ 6 hours
- ► Museo Franz Mayer

A Sanborns restaurant now occupies the Casa de los Azulejos (House of Tiles).

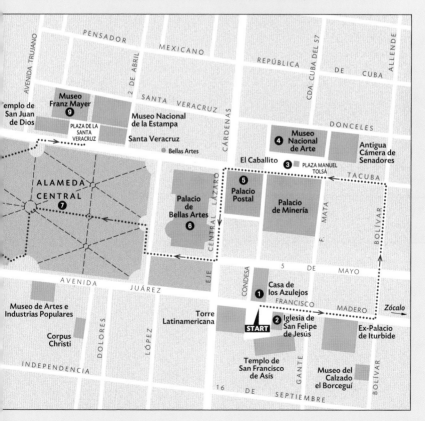

PENSADOR MEXICANO

AVENIDA TRUJUANO

2 DE ABRIL

REPÚBLICA

CDA. CUBA DEL 57

DE CUBA

ALLENDE

Museo Franz Mayer **9**

SANTA VERACRUZ

CÁRDENAS

DONCELES

Templo de San Juan de Dios

PLAZA DE LA SANTA VERACRUZ

Museo Nacional de la Estampa

Santa Veracruz

● Bellas Artes

Museo Nacional de Arte **4**

Antigua Cámera de Senadores

El Caballito **3** PLAZA MANUEL TOLSÁ

TACUBA

ALAMEDA CENTRAL **7**

CENTRAL LÁZARO

Palacio de Bellas Artes **6**

Palacio Postal **5**

Palacio de Minería

F. MATA

BOLÍVAR

EJE

AVENIDA JUÁREZ

5 DE MAYO

CONDESA

Casa de los Azulejos **1**

FRANCISCO

MADERO

Zócalo

Museo de Artes e Industrias Populares

DOLORES

LÓPEZ

Torre Latinoamericana

START

Iglesia de San Felipe de Jesús **2**

Ex-Palacio de Iturbide

Corpus Christi

INDEPENDENCIA

Templo de San Francisco de Asís

GANTE

Museo del Calzado el Borceguí

BOLÍVAR

16 DE SEPTIEMBRE

One block east (toward the *zócalo*) on the same side of the street is the **Palacio de Iturbide** *(Madero 17, tel 55/1226-0120, closed Sat.–Sun.)*, an 18th-century baroque building of volcanic stone. Now a Banamex bank office, it is open to the public during temporary exhibitions of its fine art collection. Emperor Agustín de Iturbide occupied the luxurious home for a few short years until his exile in 1823.

Named for its poplars, Parque la Alameda abounds in ash, pine, and jacaranda trees.

Turn left at the next corner, Bolívar, and walk two blocks to Calle Tacuba, where a number of colonial buildings, including the **Biblioteca del Congreso de la Unión** *(Tacuba 27)*, have received face-lifts. Walk east on Tacuba to Calle Mata and the **Plaza Manuel Tolsá ❸**, named for the Spanish architect and sculptor (1757–1816) who in 1803 created the **Estatua Ecuestre de Carlos de Borbón.** The statue, which most people call **El Caballito** (referring to the mount rather than the Spanish sovereign), now stands in the center of the plaza. Presiding over the square is the **Museo Nacional de Arte ❹** *(Tacuba 8, tel 55/5130-3405, www.munal.com.mx, closed Mon., $)*, home to a permanent collection of Mexican art from the 16th to mid-20th century. The wrought-iron-and-brass staircase, baroque lamps, and painted ceiling are based on turn-of-the-20th-century European design.

Across the street, the **Palacio de Minería** *(Tacuba 5, tel 55/5623-2982, closed Sat-Sun., & university holidays, $)*, also designed by Tolsá, is one of the city's best examples of neoclassical architecture and now houses the Engineering School of the National University (UNAM). Next door, the distinctive, plateresque-style **Palacio de Correos ❺** *(Tacuba 1 at Eje Central, tel 55/5510-2999, closed Sat. & Sun. afternoon)*, with its facade of pinkish-yellow quarrystone, was designed by Italian architect Adamo Boari at the beginning of the 20th century. Philatelists and lovers of old books can take the staircase to the third-floor post office library. Major renovations that took place in 1999 to 2000 have rejuvenated its Moorish, Gothic, Venetian, and Renaissance interior design elements.

Cross busy Eje Central to examine another of Boari's creations, the exquisite **Palacio de Bellas Artes ❻** *(Av. Juárez & Eje Central, tel 55/5512-1410 or 2593, museum closed Mon., $)* on the east flank of Parque la Alameda. President Porfirio Díaz commissioned the art nouveau–style, Carrara marble palace in 1904, but construction was interrupted by the revolution. The art deco interior was completed in 1934 by Mexican architect Federico Mariscal. Murals on the second floor include "Mexico Today" (1952) and "Birth of Our Identity" (1953) by Rufino Tamayo. On the third floor are José Orozco's "La Catársis" (1935), David Siqueiros' "New Democracy" (1945), and Diego Rivera's "Man, the Controller of the Universe" (1934), a reproduction of the painting commissioned for the Rockefeller Center and destroyed the following year because of its socialist content. There's no charge to view the art on the first floor or to visit the bookstore, giftshop, or restaurant located there.

From the fine arts palace, head into **Parque la Alameda** ❼, created in the early 17th century. It was expanded in the 1900s to include the former Plaza del Quemadero, where the politically incorrect were burned at the stake during the Inquisition. Numerous monuments and fountains give character to the park. About halfway down Avenida Juárez you'll see the **Juárez Hemiciclo,** a monument of pale Italian marble, Doric columns, and roaring lions honoring statesman and president Benito Juárez. Across Avenida Juárez and a bit west of the monument are a visitor information booth (*Juárez 64 at Revillagigedo, tel 55/5518-1003*) and a Sheraton Hotel with convention center and excellent restaurant.

Cross Calle Dr. Mora at the west end of Parque la Alameda. At the rear of the Plaza de la Solidaridad, the **Museo Mural Diego Rivera** ❽ (*Colón at Balderas, tel 55/5510-2329, closed Mon., $*) houses Rivera's elaborate 1947 mural "Sueño de una Tarde Dominical en la Alameda" ("Dream of a Sunday Afternoon in the Alameda"), which was moved here after

the Hotel del Prado was irreparably damaged in the 1985 earthquake. A schematic identifies the historical and allegorical characters in the mural; there are portraits of Rivera, Frida Kahlo, Sor Juana de la Cruz, the Habsburg emperors, and many others.

Reenter Parque la Alameda, walking east. At the metal-roofed bandstand, cross busy Hidalgo at Trujano and continue half a block east to **Plaza de la Santa Veracruz,** named for the Church of the True Holy Cross, on the east side of the square. Occupying part of the adjoining former hospital is the **Museo Nacional de la Estampa** (*Hidalgo 39, tel 55/5510-4905, closed Mon., $*), with rotating exhibits from its permanent collection of early lithographs and linoleum prints, as well as visiting print media shows.

On the west side of the square is the baroque **Templo San Juan de Dios.** Next door, the **Museo Franz Mayer** ❾ (*Av. Hidalgo 45, tel 55/5518-2267, closed Mon., $$*) houses the fabulous applied arts collection of German-born financier Franz Mayer (1882–1975). The galleries surrounding a beautiful central courtyard are full of 16th- to 19th-century Mexican utilitarian and decorative art objects. A separate gallery shows European Renaissance paintings.

Mexican Idioms & Slang

When traveling, it's nice to try to fit in a little by tossing out a word of slang (or two) or an idiomatic expression. Here's a list of some that you might find occasion to use on your travels. For a larger list of slang and idiomatic expressions, see *www.mexicoguru.com*.

Porfis [POR-fees]	Please
No sea malito [no SAY-a mah-LEE-to]	Be an angel
Si fuera tan amable [see FWEH-ra tahn a-MAH-blay]	If you'd be so kind
¡Chin! [cheen!]	Darn!
chela [CHAY-la]	beer/brewski
Sale [SAH-lay]	That's fine. That's cool. I agree.
¡Híjole! [EE-ho-lay!]	Son of a gun!
¡Órale! [OR-a-lay!]	Great! Right on!
¡Aguas! [AHG-was]	Look out!
¿Qué húbole? [kay OO-boh-lay?]	What's up?

North of Centro Histórico

North of the historic center, two sites offer pre-Cortesian ruins, colonial churches, and a modern 20th-century cathedral. The main pyramid at Tlatelolco, a contemporary of Tenochtitlán, once had adjoining temples honoring the gods Tláloc and Huitzilopochtli. Farther north, la Villa de Guadalupe honors the Virgin of Guadalupe, whose miraculous appearance on Tepeyac Hill led to the conversion of tens of thousands of Indians to Catholicism.

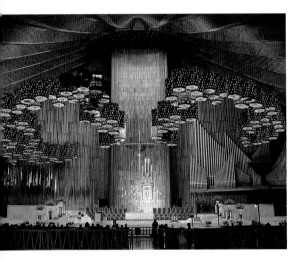

The new basilica is one of many temples honoring the Virgin at la Villa de Guadalupe.

Tlatelolco

🔺 179 F4

Visitor Information

✉ Av. Lázaro Cárdenas at Flores Magón

 Metro: Tlatelolco

Tlatelolco

Tlatelolco was established in 1338 by a dissident group who left Tenochtitlán to build their own city near the northernmost part of Lake Texcoco. Although allied with the Tenochcan kings, the people of Tlatelolco refused to accept their sovereignty but were finally subjugated in 1473 by Axayácatl. An important center for merchants and traders, this city served as the most important Aztec market.

Visitors today can see the reconstructed ruins of Tlatelolco, the last stand during the siege that brought down the Aztec Empire.

As was customary, the **Iglesia de Santiago Tlatelolco,** completed in 1609, was built with stones from the dismantled pyramids. Indian peasant Juan Diego, who witnessed the apparition of the Virgin of Guadalupe in 1531 (see below), was baptized here at the baroque font, with its shell motif characteristic of St. James the Apostle. To the right of the church, the former Franciscan monastery was the first college to tutor Indians of noble birth, teaching history, philosophy, and Latin.

Most Mexico City residents remember Tlatelolco as the site of a massacre of student demonstrators by government troops just before the 1968 Olympic Games. Although there is no official death toll, up to several hundred young demonstrators were killed during a political rally. A simple monument on the north side of the temple acknowledges the tragedy.

Don't miss David Alfaro Siqueiros's mural "Cuauhtémoc Against the Myth," combining sculpture with fresco work. It is in the Tecpan building, at the far side of the quadrangle behind the church and monastery, at the site of Cuauhtémoc's former palace.

La Villa de Guadalupe

Every Mexican schoolchild knows the story of Juan Diego,

to whom the Virgin of Guadal-upe is said to have appeared on three occasions at Tepeyac Hill. When Bishop de Zumárraga asked the Chichimec Indian for proof of the miracle, the Virgin showered Juan Diego with roses. Returning to the bishop with his precious cargo wrapped in his cloak, Diego found that the roses had disappeared, replaced by an image of the Virgin.

An estimated 15 million people make the pilgrimage to Tepeyac each year, many on December 12, the Virgin's feast day. The new, round **Basílica de Nuestra Señora de Guadalupe** (tel 55/5577-6022) was built between 1974 and 1976 to accommo-date the faithful. The imposing interior of the structure features an undulating, wood-slat ceiling, modern stained-glass windows, a floor of polished Mexican onyx, and a main altar of Carrara marble. The basilica's most important

icon, Juan Diego's cloak with the Virgin's image clearly visible, sits up high at the back of the church behind the main altar.

An annex of the old basilica houses the **Museo de la Basílica de Guadalupe** (tel 55/5577-6022 ext. 137, closed Mon., $), with reli-gious paintings as well as offerings and ex-votos left by the devout.

Beyond the T-shirt vendors and painted ponies stands the 18th-century **Capilla del Pocito,** built at the site of a miraculously appearing spring. This lovely round baroque chapel has a dome of blue-and-white Talavera tiles and exterior walls of tile, quar-rystone, and volcanic rock. Inside, the walls of the tiny chapel are covered with little angel scenes in pastel colors. The holy well for which the temple is named is now dry. At the top of Tepeyac Hill, the **Capilla de las Rosas** denotes the spot of the Virgin's first alleged appearance. ∎

La Villa de Guadalupe
- 179 G4
- Plaza de las Américas 1
- 55/5748-2085
- Metro: La Villa-Basílica

EXPERIENCE: Go on a Pilgrimage

Catholic devotion leads millions of Mexicans on pilgrimages each year, and you, as well, can join journeys to the sacred sites. In the heartland, ranchers by the hundreds clatter down the cobble-stone streets of colonial towns in multiday horseback pilgrimages. Fathers and sons bicycle to mountain shrines, and old ladies wend their way to old stone churches. Pilgrimages escalate during town feast days, making advance hotel reservations necessary. You can join any of many feast-day pilgrimages, or, to avoid crowds, go in the off-season—pilgrimage sites are prepared for pilgrims at any time.

The most venerated Mexican saint is its dark-skinned patron, the Virgin of Guadalupe; her shrine is at **Las Villas de Guadalupe,** a few miles north of downtown Mexico City (see map p. 180). The second most popular is Our Lady of San Juan de los Lagos, whose sacred site is about 75 miles (121 km) north of **Guadalajara** (see pp. 148–154). Faithful from all over also visit Jalisco's Virgen of Zapopan (part of Guadalajara; see p. 152); and el Santo Niño de Atocha (Holy Child of Atocha) in **Fresnillo,** Zacate-cas. Other popular saints include the Virgen de Juquila, in Oaxaca state; the Virgen del Rosario de Talpa, Jalisco; Nuestro Señor de Chalma, in Mexico state; el Señor de Carácuaro, in Michoacán; and the Virgen de la Salud in Pátzcuaro, Michoacán.

Bosque de Chapultepec, Paseo de la Reforma, & Environs

Bosque de Chapultepec once provided drinking water for the Aztec nation and housed the royal hunting preserves, vacation palaces, and gardens. Today a source of much needed oxygen, the 2,000-acre (800 ha) park has a zoo and a castle, an elegant restaurant on a swan-dotted lake, and nearly a dozen museums. Bisecting the park and connecting it to the historic center is elegant Paseo de la Reforma, a legacy of the ill-fated Emperor Maximilian.

The Angel of Independence dominates the Paseo de la Reforma in the heart of Mexico City.

Bosque de Chapultepec

The **Monumento a los Niños Héroes** marks the eastern entrance of the park *(Metro: Chapultepec)* and the spot where six young cadets leapt to their deaths rather than surrender to U.S. troops during the Mexican-American War. Here, biking and jogging trails wend their way around monuments, fountains, and most of the park's museums. Lovers embrace beneath the pines, palms, and jacarandas, or converse on wooden park benches. With lots of possibilities for inexpensive family entertainment, the park becomes quite crowded on weekends, especially Sundays, the traditional day for family outings.

The two-story **Museo de Arte Moderno** *(Paseo de la Reforma at Gandhi, tel 55/5211-8729, closed Mon., $)* exhibits the country's most important 20th-century artists, temporary displays, and sculptures of aluminum, stone, bronze, iron, and ceramic in a rambling garden. There is a small but excellent shop and a well-stocked bookstore.

Across the street, the **Museo Rufino Tamayo** *(Paseo de la Reforma at Gandhi, tel 55/5286-6519, closed Mon., $, Metro:*

Chapultepec) houses the international contemporary art collection of Oaxaca painter and sculptor Rufino Tamayo (1899–1991), including works by Picasso, Miró, Fernando Botero, Andy Warhol, and others. To the west lies the fabulous **Museo Nacional de Antropología** (see pp. 198–201).

Just beyond the modern art museum is the **Castillo de Chapultepec,** begun in 1785 as a retreat for Spanish viceroys but interrupted by the War of Independence. Perched on a small hill, the building was finished as a military academy and remodeled by Emperor Maximilian of Habsburg and again by president Porfirio Díaz. Since 1939, it has housed the **Museo Nacional de Historia** *(tel 55/5061-6200, closed Mon., $),* whose historical displays and period furnishings are enhanced by the wonderful murals of Juan O'Gorman, José Clemente Orozco, and David Alfaro Siqueiros (see p. 202).

From the castle, walk or board the miniature tram *($)* to the free **Zoológico de Chapultepec** *(tel 55/5553-6263, closed Mon., Metro: Auditorio or Chapultepec),* with a petting zoo and pony rides. Reasonably large, open-air enclosures house about 250 different species, about half of them native to Mexico and a good number endemic. Nonnatives include a pair of superstar Chinese pandas.

Midway through the park, west of Avenida López Mateo, are several child-friendly attractions. The **Feria de Chapultepec** *(tel 55/5230-2121, closed Mon., www.feriachapultepec.com.mx, $–$$$,*

Metro: Constituyentes)—an amusement park with roller coasters, a rowing lake, a restaurant, and a coffee shop—appeals to both young and old. During February or March, the *Swan Lake* ballet is performed on an island on **Lago Menor;** the rest of the year, resident swans abide a less theatrical existence on nearby **Lago Mayor,** interrupted only by people in rented rowboats.

Paseo de la Reforma

Connecting the park and Avenida Juárez, Paseo de la Reforma was once lined with gracious mansions and flowering trees. Today, monumental sculptures decorate the major traffic circles, while busts of Mexico's heroes line both sides of the street. Closest to Parque Chapultepec is **Diana la Cazadora** *(at Río Misisipi),*

Bosque de Chapultepec

178 B1/B2

Paseo de la Reforma, across from Museo Nacional de Antropología

55/5286-3850

Metro: Chapultepec, Auditorio, or Constituyentes

a nude bronze statue that was clothed for 25 years from 1942 owing to a burst of civic modesty. Today the Roman huntress is once again as artist Juan Fernando Olaguíbel (1896–1971) intended.

A graceful, bronzed, winged figure (commonly called "*el angel*," or "The Angel") sparkles atop a 120-foot-tall (36.5 m) Corinthian column at the **Monumento a la Independencia** *(at Av. Florencia)*. The monument was erected in 1910 to honor the heroes of the War of Independence, whose sculptures in Italian marble are found near the base.

A classic bronze statue on a stone pedestal honors the last Mexica emperor, **Cuauhtémoc** *(at Av. Insurgentes)*. Its base is carved with scenes of the ruler's capture and subsequent torture by Spanish conquistadores. Four friars surround Christopher Columbus at the **Monumento a Cristóbal Colón** *(at Av. Morelos)*, representing the evangelization of the Americas.

Just a few blocks southwest of Parque la Alameda, on Avenida Juárez, is the metal, yellow-painted sculpture **"Cabeza de Caballo."** The modernistic, 90-foot (28 m) piece is the work of Chihuahua sculptor Sebastián (1948–), who studied at the San Carlos Academy.

Around the Park

North of Chapultepec lies **Polanco,** a mix of well-to-do

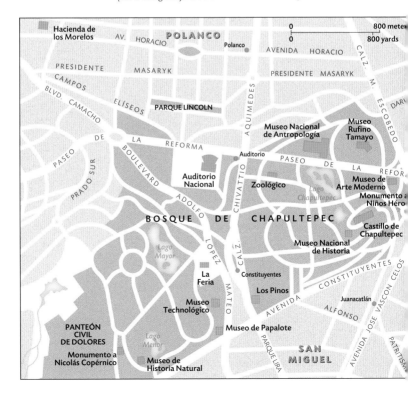

houses behind high garden walls, businesses in high- and low-rise buildings, hotels, foreign embassies, and restaurants. It was developed in the 1940s when the extensive grounds of **Hacienda de los Morales** (see p. 372) were divided and sold. Chic cafés and restaurants become packed during peak hours, especially along the main thoroughfare, Presidente Mazaryk, and adjacent streets.

The traditional favorite for fine dining and nightlife is the **Zona Rosa,** or Pink Zone, a pie-shaped piece of real estate bordered by Avenida Insurgentes, Paseo de la Reforma, and Chapultepec. The compact neighborhood, now a gay hangout, is a mélange of two-

story shops, Internet cafés, strip bars, and boutiques interspersed with high-rise buildings. It is also relatively easy to negotiate on foot—especially because of the handful of pedestrian-only streets. For some light laughs, visit **Ripley's Believe It or Not Museum** or the affiliated **Museo de Cera** (*Londres 6, Col. Juárez, tel 55/5546-7670, daily, www.museodecera.com/mx $$*), where revolutionaries and rock-and-roll stars are re-created as life-size wax statues.

Ripley's Believe It or Not Museum

 179 E2

✉ Londres 4, Col. Juárez

☎ 55/5546-3784

$ $$

www.ripleys.com

INSIDER TIP:

For exercise, note: On Sundays, Paseo de la Reforma is blockaded for walking, jogging cycling and rollerblading.

—NINA-NOELLE HALL
National Geographic contributor

Luring shoppers and diners from the Zona Rosa are two neighborhoods to the south: **La Condesa** and **Colonia Roma.** The former is especially known for its hip and trendy restaurants, cafés, and nightspots, many in restored art deco buildings for which this part of the city is famous. East of Avenida Insurgentes, the wealthy built lovely homes in Colonia Roma during the first half of the 20th century. The neighborhood declined when residents moved to more fashionable areas such as Lomas de Chapultepec, but is currently experiencing a renewed gentrification. ∎

Museo Nacional de Antropología

The spacious National Anthropology Museum was built in 1964 and received a serious, $13-million restoration in the late 1990s. This remodel improved lighting, added English language signage for some exhibits, and provided space for 2,000 new artifacts. Touch-screen computers in most galleries provide a wealth of information, although in Spanish only.

Finds in the Mexica room include the Aztec sun stone.

The remodel did not change the basic structure of the complex of buildings, designed and built by architect Pedro Ramírez Vázquez, and called "one of the most satisfying in modern Mexico" and "an incomparable example of institutional architecture" by author and photographer Hans Beacham in his book *The Architecture of Mexico: Yesterday and Today* (1969).

Four large buildings surround a central courtyard, whose open space is nearly half covered by an enormous aluminum canopy supported by a single column faced in carved stone. From the top of the support, an unusual structural element, water splashes down to the patio floor in a refreshing juxtaposition of art, architecture, and precipitation.

In 12 huge exhibition halls surrounding the ground-floor courtyard is Mexico's finest archaeological collection, devoted exclusively to pre-Hispanic civilizations. After breezing through the first three rooms in a sort of crash course in anthropology, visit the remaining rooms in any order, as they are organized according to region. Since the collection is so large, it makes sense to concentrate on the cultures that interest you most. Choose from Preclassic, Teotihuacán, Toltec, Mexica (Aztec), Oaxaca, Gulf Coast, Maya, northern Mexico, and western Mexico.

INSIDER TIP:

The Aztec calendar is perhaps the museum's most famous highlight, but don't miss the re-creation of Pakal's tomb or the jade mask of the Zapotec bat god.

—BARBARA A. NOE
National Geographic editor

Spectacular and varied archaeological treasures along with photographs, paintings, dioramas, and reproductions of murals and temples create a satisfying portrait of pre-conquest civilizations. The lack of information in English is a drawback for many (resolved to some degree by using the English-language audio tour or by hiring a guide). In most salons, informative video presentations in English and Spanish run consecutively.

If you have an interest in pre-Hispanic cultures, one day will probably not be sufficient for studying all the exhibits. Consider dedicating several mornings or afternoons to the museum, visiting other attractions in Parque Chapultepec, or wandering adjacent neighborhoods when the scope and grandeur of the exhibits begin to overwhelm you.

Behind many of the galleries you'll find outdoor patios and gardens sheltering stone sculptures and stelae, reconstructions of houses, and other fascinating, alfresco, large-scale exhibits. In the Maya room, don't miss the full-size reproduction of the royal tomb from the Temple of the Inscriptions at Palenque, Chiapas, and, in the **back garden,** reproductions of the murals of Bonampak and a Chenes-style temple from Hochob, Campeche.

The museum has too many fabulous pieces to name, but you must not fail to see the following: **Teotihuacán**

Museo Nacional de Antropología

178 A2/B2

Paseo de la Reforma at Gandhi, Bosque de Chapultepec

55/5553-6243

Closed Mon.

$$

Metro: Auditorio

www.mna.inah .gob.mx

EXPERIENCE:
Mexico City Off The Beaten Track

If you're looking to see beyond the surface and learn about the cultural, architectural, and historical riches that Mexico City has to offer, contact **Journeys Beyond the Surface** (*tel 55/1745-2380, www.travelmexicocity.com. mx*). With a master's degree in Community Development, coordinator Mojdeh Hojjati (born in the U.S. of Iranian parents, but has lived nearly 20 years in Mexico) tailors tours to the tastes of individuals or small groups. She can arrange for guides in Spanish, English, or other languages and organize wonderful, off-the-beaten-track tours to small pottery villages, markets, museums, or other places of interest to travelers, educators, and scholars of all kinds.

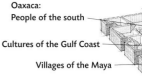

Upper Floor

Oaxaca:
People of the south

Cultures of the Gulf Coast

Villages of the Maya

The Northeast

The Nahuas

gallery—reproduction of Tepantitla murals; **Toltec gallery**—Atlante sculptures and mother-of-pearl-encrusted warrior (both from Tula); **Mexica gallery**—24-ton sun stone, statue of earth goddess Coatlicue,

INSIDER TIP:

Pre-order your tickets to avoid long lines at the museum. Avoid Sundays when large crowds take advantage of free admission.

—LUZ MARIA MEJIA
National Geographic field researcher

and the pregnant monkey vessel of polished obsidian (the museum's most costly piece—once stolen but later recovered); **Oaxaca gallery**—jade bat god mask, Mixtec jewelry, and reproduction of Monte Albán's Tomb 104; **Gulf Coast gallery**—colossal stone head (Olmec), large-scale female warriors and goddesses; **Maya room**—funerary mask and regalia from Pakal's tomb, Palenque, clay figurines from Jaina, and Chac Mool from Chichén Itzá.

The ethnology exhibits on the second floor are

Ground Floor

similarly arranged by region and cultural group. Dioramas and glass-cased exhibits show ceremonial and everyday clothing, as well as masks, pottery, baskets, musical instruments, toys, and the items of daily life among Mexico's diverse ethnic populations. ■

Coatlicue, the Aztec earth goddess

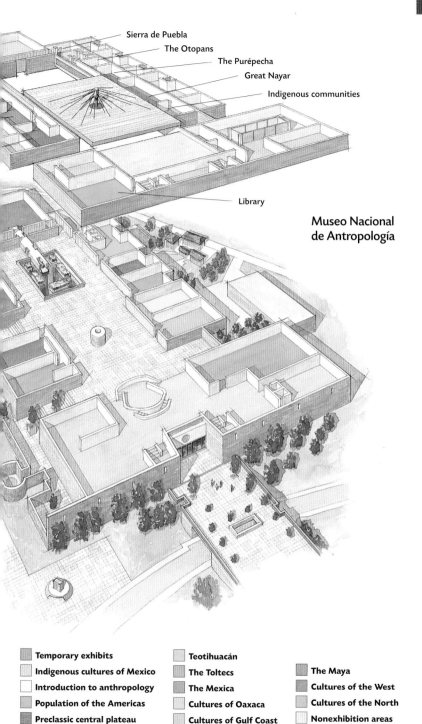

Sierra de Puebla
The Otopans
The Purépecha
Great Nayar
Indigenous communities

Library

Museo Nacional
de Antropología

Temporary exhibits
Indigenous cultures of Mexico
Introduction to anthropology
Population of the Americas
Preclassic central plateau

Teotihuacán
The Toltecs
The Mexica
Cultures of Oaxaca
Cultures of Gulf Coast

The Maya
Cultures of the West
Cultures of the North
Nonexhibition areas

The Mexican Mural School

Following conquest and colonization, Mexico began to adopt European values and artistic styles. After the revolution, nostalgic Mexicans living abroad spawned an artistic and political movement venerating indigenous people and the working classes. They integrated the intellectualism of Marxism and the romanticism of the Spanish Civil War with a desperate passion for their native Mexico. Many artists participated, but the "Big Three" were Rivera, Siqueiros, and Orozco.

The mural movement flourished between 1920 and 1970, especially in the early days under the patronage of prominent philosopher and education minister José Vasconcelos. Although the muralists' radical political views seemingly conflicted with the agenda of the conservative, pro-business administrations of the period, the Mexican government became their patron, and huge public spaces their canvases. The murals' nationalistic content and socialistic spirit to some degree substituted for actual revolutionary measures, constituting a sort of political and artistic placebo for the masses. Working within the system, the artists spoke their piece and pursued their art, while the government seemed to support both the arts and radical politics.

Best known outside Mexico is the allegorical work of **Diego Rivera** (1886–1957). Showing artistic talent from an early age, he entered Mexico City's prestigious San Carlos Academy at the age of ten. After years of experimentation and travel through northern Europe, Paris, and Russia, Rivera developed an unequivocal style. Favoring a palette of deep pastels, he painted rounded, nearly neckless, brown-skinned folk wearing seamless trousers. The simple themes and engaging designs he chose were meant to inspire and educate the common people he almost religiously portrayed in his art. Both Rivera and fellow muralist **David Alfaro Siqueiros** (1896–1974) were members of the Mexican Communist Party. Siqueiros' work, known for its experimental and innovative technical character, is moody—often violent and chaotic—with strong, bold colors.

The murals of **José Clemente Orozco** (1883–1949) were influenced by his early work as a caricaturist, although in later years his simple yet stirring style became more expressionistic. The work of all three men centered on social ills and human suffering—especially that of their compatriots.

Less well known than the Big Three, architect and painter **Juan O'Gorman** (1905–1982), a Coyoacán native, produced realistic murals and paintings in exquisite color and detail. The work of internationally proclaimed Oaxaca impressionist muralist, painter, and sculptor **Rufino Tamayo** (1899–1991) was taken less seriously at the time because of its lack of direct social commentary. Fermín Revueltas, Alva de la Canal, Fernando Leal, and Miguel Covarrubias are among others who contributed to the wealth of murals in Mexico City.

Viewing the Murals

Below is a partial list of places in Mexico City where these masterpieces can be found.

La Alameda: Museo Mural Diego Rivera (see p. 191); Palacio de Bellas Artes (see p. 190)

Bosque de Chapultepec: Museo Nacional de Historia (see p. 195)

Universidad Autónoma Nacional de México (UNAM): Biblioteca Central, Estadio Olímpico, and Rectoría (see p. 207).

Zócalo, on or near: Ex-Colegio de San Ildefonso (see p. 182); Palacio Nacional (see p. 181); Secretaría de Educación Pública (see p. 182); Suprema Corte de Justicia (see p. 182)

Father Hidalgo is the centerpiece of this Orozco mural depicting oppression.

South of Centro Histórico

Skirting the eastern edge of Chapultepec Park near the Zona Rosa, 18-mile-long (29 km) Avenida Insurgentes continues south past the World Trade Center, the Plaza México (the world's largest bullring), and a stunning Diego Rivera mural decorating the curved facade of the Teatro de los Insurgentes. After a few more miles, it reaches San Ángel and neighboring Coyoacán, two charming towns absorbed by ever growing Mexico City.

Shoppers browse at one of Mexico City's ubiquitous daily markets.

San Ángel

🅰 178 D1

Visitor Information

✉ Av. Revolución at Madero (Casa de la Cultura)

🚌 Bus: San Ángel bus from Av. Insurgentes at Paseo de la Reforma

San Ángel

San Ángel is so pretty that it's been declared a national historic monument. Called Tenanitla before the Spanish Conquest, this town of cobblestone streets and colonial- and Republican-era homes is anchored by two pleasing squares, **Plaza de San Jacinto** and, one block away, **Plaza del Convento.** Shoppers and vendors fill the former on Saturdays, when the weekly crafts market, **Bazar del Sábado** (*Plaza San Jacinto 11, tel 55/5616-0082*), spreads under the pines, cedars, and yucca trees shading the plaza.

Also on Plaza de San Jacinto is the simple 17th-century church for which the square is named and the **Casa del Risco** (*Plaza San Jacinto 15, tel 55/5616-2711, closed Mon.*), an 18th-century residence housing an art museum and cultural center. In the main courtyard, you can't miss the unusual fountain, encrusted with mirrors and shells, as well as European and Mexican ceramic tiles, plates, platters, and cups. Temporary exhibits fill the ground-floor halls, while on the second floor, the permanent collection consists of 15th- to 19th-century European and Mexican paintings. The adjacent **library** *(closed Sun.)* has 31,000 volumes related to international law, Mexican history, and criminology.

Just across busy Avenida Revolución, it's a pleasure to prowl around the cloisters and chapels of the **Museo del Carmen** *(Av. Revolución 4, closed Mon., $, Metro: Quevedo),* a museum of primarily religious paintings and artifacts. The former Carmelite monastery, with its magnificent domes of Talavera tiles and exquisite gilded altarpiece in the first-floor chapel, is every bit as interesting as the museum exhibits.

INSIDER TIP:

The San Ángel Inn in San Ángel is old and famous; Zapata and Pancho Villa dined and signed a pact here.

—NINA-NOELLE HALL
National Geographic contributor

Items of contemporary art from a permanent collection are shown in rotation in the modern, low-ceilinged, glass and aluminum **Museo Carrillo Gil** *(Av. Revolución 1608 at Av. Altavista, tel 55/5550-6284, closed Mon., $).* In addition to paintings by the Big Three of the Mexican Mural school (see p.

202), there are oils, pen and ink, gouache, and pencil drawings by lesser-known artists.

A short uphill walk along Avenida Altavista brings you to the **Museo Casa Estudio Diego Rivera y Frida Kahlo** *(Diego Rivera 2, tel 55/5550-1518, closed Mon., $, Metro: Viveros),* a boxlike modern house on steel stilts designed and built by architect and artist Juan O'Gorman (see p. 202). Frida Kahlo and her husband, Diego Rivera, occupied these two houses separated by a catwalk. The first two-story building held Rivera's gallery and, above, his studio. Kahlo both lived and worked in the house behind. The museum has a small collection of the artists' photographs, letters, documents, and personal effects, as well as sketches and paintings by their contemporaries.

Coyoacán

About 2 miles (3 km) from San Ángel is equally engaging Coyoacán, home to artists and journalists from Mexico and elsewhere. If you're walking, stop at the **Parque de la Bombilla** *(Av. Insurgentes Sur at La Paz),* where joggers follow meandering trails under willow, pine, ash, and avocado trees. On weekends kids kick balls and practice tai-chi, and peanut and cotton-candy vendors appear. During the week it's less lively, but you will have space to admire the **Monumento al General Alvaro Obregón,** dedicated to the post-Revolution-era president assassinated in 1928 during the Cristero Revolt (see p. 32).

Coyoacán
 178 D1
Visitor Information
✉ Jardín Hidalgo 1
☎ 55/5658-0221
🚇 Metro: Coyoacán
**www.coyoacan.df.
.gob.mx/turismo**

San Ángel Inn
✉ Diego Rivera 50 &
    Altavista
☎ 55/5616-1402
www.sanangelinn.com

East of the Parque de la Bombilla is the **Museo Nacional de la Acuarela** *(Salvador Novo 88, tel 55/5554-1801, Metro: Quevedo)*. Donated by watercolorist Alfredo Guati, the collection includes a variety of styles of gouache and watercolors.

Calle La Paz intersects with **Avenida Francisco Sosa,** lined with carefully maintained homes, many of them restored colonials, as well as shops, ice-cream parlors, restaurants, and bars. This is the main street of Coyoacán, a prosperous city when the Mexica first arrived in the Valley of Mexico. It was soon swallowed and digested by the more powerful newcomers. Hernán Cortés also made his

little remains of the original building except the facade and the pilgrim's archway. Inside, its stained-glass windows portraying Franciscan saints illuminate the large, single-nave church and elaborate main altar.

Cafés, restaurants, boutiques, and bookstores surround adjacent **Jardín del Centenario** *(Carrillo Puerto & Centenario)*, and, on weekends, vendors, locals, and tourists mill about. As in San Ángel, artists sell oil and acrylic paintings, framed etchings, and other works at reasonable prices.

About five blocks north of the plaza is the **Museo Frida Kahlo** *(Londres 247, tel 55/5658-5778, closed Mon., $$, Metro:*

La Malinche

In a rust-red, two-story house on the southeast side of Plaza la Conchita, in Coyoacán, Hernán Cortés is said to have installed his interpreter, mistress, and the mother of his son Martín: la Malinche. Called Malintzin in Náhuatl and doña Marina by the Spaniards, the young woman was apparently sold as a slave to noblemen, who gave her, along with others, as a gift to Cortés.

For the Spaniards, la Malinche proved an invaluable interpreter, adviser, and even military strategist who well understood their enemy. Although her motivations and actions are not really known, this controversial and important historical figure was branded a traitor to the indigenous people. In modern Mexico, *un malinchista* is a person of questionable patriotism or cultural loyalty.

headquarters in Coyoacán after the Spanish Conquest. The sunny yellow structure mistakenly cited as his home, the **Palacio de Cortés** *(Jardín Hidalgo 1)*, houses city government offices and a visitor information booth.

Presiding over the opposite side of the square is the **Templo de San Juan Bautista** *(Jardín Hidalgo 8, tel 55/5554-6376)*. Constructed in the 16th century,

Viveros). Self-taught artist Frida Kahlo (1907–1954) was born and died in this cornflower blue house. She began to paint during convalescence from a bus accident suffered as a teenager, adopting a deliberately naive style full of Mexican icons and imagery. Her intensely personal canvases, generally smaller-format oil paintings, reflected her constant physical pain and the mental anguish

A storyteller draws a crowd in Coyoacán.

brought on by her inability to conceive and husband Diego Rivera's philandering. Underestimated artistically during her lifetime, this independent woman has become something of a feminist folk hero. In addition to her illustrated diary, love letters, and hand-painted body cast are about a dozen of her paintings; the furnishings and decorations form a fabulous folk-art collection. The front rooms have changing exhibits pertaining to the lives of Kahlo and Rivera.

Five more blocks north and east bring you to the **Museo Leon Trotsky** (*Río Churubusco 410, tel 55/5658-8732, closed Mon., $, Metro: Coyoacán*). The house where the exiled Russian revolutionary lived contains his documents and personal effects. A friend of artists Kahlo and Rivera, Trotsky was assassinated by Spaniard Ramón Mercader in 1940. The former communist leader had survived at least one other attempted murder in which the muralist David Siqueiros, an ardent Stalinist, was allegedly involved.

Latin America's largest and oldest university, the **Universidad Autónoma Nacional de México,** or UNAM (*Av. Insurgentes Sur s/n, tel 55/5622-6470, Metro: Copilco or Universidad*), was founded in 1553. Originally occupying different buildings throughout the city, the 800-acre (320 ha) campus was established south of San Ángel in the 1950s. On campus, don't miss Juan O'Gorman's stunning mosaics, which cover all four sides of the Biblioteca Central (Main Library). Nearby, David Alfaro Siqueiros' glass-mosaic mural, "The People for the University, the University for the People," covers the north wall of the Rectoría, or Administration Building, while other dramatic murals cover the south wall and the tower.

Directly across Avenida Insurgentes Sur, Diego Rivera's high-relief, natural stone mosaic on the exterior of the **Estadio Olímpico** (Olympic Stadium) depicts ancient and modern sports. ∎

Xochimilco

Famous since pre-Cortesian times for its flowers, Xochimilco is the last place you can see the remains of the system of canals and artfully engineered garden plots that once threaded Lake Texcoco. This laid-back town (its name means "place of flowers") also has a lovely old cathedral and one of the country's best museums.

Xochimilco

🗺 179 G2

Visitor Information

✉ Calle del Pino 36, Barrio San Juan

☎ 55/5676-0810

About 9 miles (15 km) southeast of downtown Mexico City, Xochimilco is best known for its *trajineras* (punts) that float the canals, these days sporting artificial flowers. The scene is festive on weekends, when families party and picnic as they wind down from the working week. There are several docks in the main part of town; boats departing from **Embarcadero Celada** (55/5676-8879), on the west side, tour the **Parque Natural Xochimilco** ecological reserve, created in 1993. You also can tour the reserve's botanical gardens on foot.

The tree-shaded monastery of **San Bernardino de Siena** was built by Franciscans in the late 16th century. It has a sweet, classical-style facade and, inside, a spectacular main altarpiece. From downtown Xochi, plant and flower lovers head just outside

INSIDER TIP:

Saturday night is very festive in Xochimilco's floating gardens, with colorful punts, maria-chi bands, and hustling beer vendors. Nothing is quite like it.

— NINA-NOELLE HALL
National Geographic contributor

town to **Bosque de Nativitas** (Bus: Route 36), with a large, inexpensive plant market year-round.

No trip would be complete without a visit to the fabulous **Museo Dolores Olmedo Patiño** (Av. México 5843, tel 55/5555-1016, closed Mon., $$, tren ligero: La Noria). Señora Olmedo collected works by friend and protégé Diego Rivera and colleagues, as well as Mexican folk art and more than 600 pre-Hispanic pieces. Have a bite to eat in the glass-walled café, set amidst a garden of cactuses and purple-flowered jacarandas. ■

Decorated punts glide along the town's canals, often followed by floating food vendors and musicians.

More Places to Visit in Mexico City

Antigua Casa de los Condes de San Mateo Valparaíso

Now housing Banamex offices, this building is one of the city's best examples of 18th-century civic architecture. Note the corner tower with the image of the Virgin of Guadalupe and the family coat of arms on the building's facade. Inside is an unusual double spiral stairway, designed to be used by both servants and their masters without the two groups having to meet.
🅰 179 G3 ✉ Isabel la Católica 44 at Carranza ☎ 55/5225-6088 🕐 Closed Sat.–Sun. 🚇 Metro: Isabel la Católica

Cuicuilco

Located within sight of Xitle volcano, which destroyed the city in about A.D. 300, the Cuicuilco archaeological site is considered the oldest in the Valley of Mexico, dating from the Preclassic era. The most important structure is a rare, circular, four-layered pyramid with an interior altar, discovered in 1922. The in situ museum displays photographs of the excavation and artifacts found there, including stelae and the figure of Huehueteotl-Xiuhtecuhtli, the god of fire portrayed as an old man.
🅰 178 D1 ✉ Av. Insurgentes Sur s/n at Periférico, Col. Ysidro Favela ☎ 55/5606-9758 💲 $ 🚇 Metro: Universidad

Monumento a la Revolución

Initiated by president Porfirio Díaz to house legislative offices, this huge art deco building was finished instead as a tribute to the fallen in the Mexican Revolution. Inside is the **Museo Nacional de la Revolución,** containing documents, photos, and memorabilia from that war.
🅰 179 E3 ✉ Av. Juárez at La Fragua, Plaza de la República, Col. Tabacalera ☎ 55/5566-1902 🕐 Closed Mon. 💲 $ 🚇 Metro: Revolución

Museo Anahuacalli

This unusual-looking museum has room to display only 2,000 of its 55,000-piece collection of pre-Hispanic art donated by Diego Rivera. Represented are cultures from Guanajuato (Rivera's home state), the Valley of Mexico, and Teotihuacán, but especially the Pacific states of Colima, Nayarit, and Jalisco. The black volcanic rock and onyx building was designed by Rivera and inspired by pre-Hispanic structures.
🅰 179 G2 ✉ Calle del Museo 150, Col. San Pablo Tepetlapa ☎ 55/5617-4310 🕐 Closed Mon. 💲 $ 🚇 Metro (tren ligero): Xochipingo

Museo de la Ciudad de México

Built of red volcanic stone in the 16th century, this elegant house was redone in the baroque style several hundred years later. It is now a museum of history and culture, offering pre-Hispanic pieces, several rooms of period furnishings, and salons for temporary fine art and cultural exhibits. Note the carved wooden doors, imported from the Philippines, and on the courtyard fountain, a *nereda,* or female figure with three tails. Musical performances are held periodically.
🅰 179 G2 ✉ Pino Suárez 30 ☎ 55/5542-0487 🕐 Closed Mon. 💲 $ 🚇 Metro: Zócalo

Museo del Calzado el Borceguí

Latin America's only museum dedicated to shoes has 15,000 exhibits. These include historic shoes (Napoleonic- and Louis XV–era shoes, Chinese slippers, NASA moon boots); folk art representing shoes; and 175 pairs of celebrity shoes. This fascinating museum is connected to the store of the same name, established in 1895 and specializing in comfortable and orthopedic shoes.
🅰 179 F3 ✉ Bolívar 27, 2nd floor ☎ 55/5512-1311 🕐 Closed Sat.–Sun., & midday 🚇 Metro: Allende

Museo de la Caricatura

Housed in the 18th-century Ex-Colegio de Cristo, this is the only museum in Mexico to showcase the work of Mexican cartoonists. Featuring work from the country's most famous illustrator, José Guadalupe Posada, this interesting museum explains the history of protest through this unique artform.
🏔 179 G3 ✉ Donceles 99 ☎ 55/5702-9256 💲 $ 🚇 Metro: Zócalo

Museo José Luis Cuevas

Artist José Luis Cuevas's erotic etchings are rather incongruously housed in the cloister of this 16th-century former convent, a lovely building declared a national monument in 1932. Cuevas's 26-foot-tall (8 m) bronze "La Giganta" dominates the central patio, while smaller statues and paintings line the passageways. On Sundays, the museum often hosts performances of theater, dance, and music.
🏔 179 G3 ✉ Calle Academia 13 ☎ 55/5542-6198 🕐 Closed Mon. 💲 $ 🚇 Metro: Zócalo

Museo S.H.C.P.

The first-floor galleries are a bit barren and disappointing, but those on the second floor of this former archbishop's palace are more interesting. These include the "paid-in-kind" collection, acquired through the Mexican system that allows artists to pay income tax in artwork rather than pesos, as well as "hereditary estates" handed down to artists' heirs.
🏔 179 G3 ✉ Antiguo Palacio del Arzobispado, Moneda 4 ☎ 55/9158-1243 💲 $ 🚇 Metro: Zócalo

Museo de San Carlos

Just a few blocks northeast of the Monumento a la Revolución is this lovely if restrained neoclassical mansion. Diego Rivera and other greats were educated in this former academy of fine arts. Today, its important collection of 15th- to 19th-century European paintings includes Spanish Gothic panels and renaissance, Mannerist, baroque, neoclassical, romantic, and symbolist works.
🏔 179 E3 ✉ Puente de Alvarado 50, Col. Tabacalera ☎ 55/5566-8085 🕐 Closed Tues. 💲 $ 🚇 Metro: Revolución or Hidalgo

Plaza de Garibaldi

Five blocks north of the Palacio de Bellas Artes, elegantly uniformed mariachi bands arrive each evening to vie for customers in this famous square. There's no shortage of local color, including taco vendors and pickpockets. Bars and small restaurants facing the plaza run the gamut from cantinas full of maudlin men crooning over a bottle of tequila to live-music dance clubs. It's especially spirited on November 22, the feast day of Santa Cecilia, patron saint of music, with fireworks, folk dancing, food, crafts, and, of course, mariachis.
🏔 179 F4 ✉ Av. Lázaro Cárdenas at Honduras 🚇 Metro: Garibaldi

Poliforum Cultural Siqueiros

David Alfaro Siqueiros's "The March of Humanity" covers both exterior and interior surfaces of this 12-sided structure, built specifically for the project. On Saturday and Sunday afternoons, a Spanish-language sound-and-light show enhances the relief and sculptural elements of the unusual mural. *(English-speaking groups by appt.)* The space doubles as a venue for cultural events.
🏔 178 D1 ✉ Insurgentes Sur 701 at Filadelfia ☎ 55/5536-4520 💲 $ 🚇 Metro: Chilpancingo

Sala de Arte Público Siqueiros

Just before his death, Siqueiros donated his home and its contents to the government, which now displays his finished and unfinished work, including drawings, paintings, sketches, and the mural "Maternity." A second-floor gallery exhibits changing contemporary art.
🏔 178 A2 ✉ Tres Picos 29, Col. Polanco ☎ 55/5545-5952 🕐 Closed Mon. 💲 $ 🚇 Metro: Auditorio

Missions and cathedrals, haciendas, archaeological ruins, and markets where Otomí and Nahuatl languages are still spoken

Around Mexico City

A fabulous baroque interior

Around Mexico City

Most of the major cities of the central plateau, around the Valle de Anáhuac (Valley of Mexico), were pre-Aztec centers. At the time of the Spanish Conquest they were held in the vicelike grip of the Triple Alliance—Tenochtitlán, Texcoco, and Tlacopan. An exclusive spa for Aztec nobility, Cuernavaca still attracts the rich and famous. And, as we continue to do today, priests and nobility made pilgrimages to Teotihuacán.

Tepoztlán's isolated valley setting made it a popular retreat in the 1960s and 1970s.

Civilization flourished in the river valleys, plains, and semitropical lowlands surrounding the crescent-shaped Valley of Mexico. So close to the defeated Teno-chtitlán and the new capital, Mexico City, the central plateau was promptly carved up by the Spanish crown. Among the cities Hernán Cortés received from King Carlos V of Spain were Toluca and Cuernavaca, today capitals of México and Morelos states. As a reward for being Spain's indispensable allies during the Aztec campaign and beyond, Tlaxcala enjoyed privileges denied the majority of the conquered peoples.

Unlike the Maya, whose great culture was nearly 500 years past its prime at the time of the Spanish Conquest, and the nomadic northern tribes, indigenous culture in the central plateau was in full flower in the 16th century. Skilled indigenous artisans and European craftsmen together produced some of Mexico's most intriguing architecture. Inspired by their desire to convert the local people and glorify God, the Spaniards built magnificent cathedrals and far-flung mission churches; Indian craftsmen enthusiastically embraced the baroque style. In Puebla, gilded and polychrome sculpted plasterwork combined with Talavera tiles adorn myriad churches and private palaces to create an exuberant architecture unique to the state. The monastery murals at Ixmiquilpan, Hidalgo, have unusual native imagery: jaguars, Aztec eagles clutching snakes, and violent battle scenes among warriors.

Forming a tight circle around Mexico City, the states of Hidalgo, Tlaxcala, Puebla,

Morelos, and México are today influenced by their proximity to the capital. Now highly industrialized, the state of México surrounds the Distrito Federal, or D. F., on three sides and has benefited from the accessibility to banks, transportation, and the powers-that-be. Most of the capital cities of these states are industrialized yet preserve outstanding churches and colonial buildings. ∎

Area of map detail

Cuernavaca

Since pre-Hispanic times Cuernavaca (from the Náhuatl for "wooded valley") has been much admired. Its temperate climate and generous rainfall make it well suited for growing both agricultural products and ornamental plants. In early April, the Feria de la Flor (Flower Fair) beckons with music and garden shows, while outside the city, rivers and more than 40 spas and water parks lure those looking to commune further with nature.

A Cuernavaca plaza, with fountain, balconies, and iron street lamps

Cuernavaca

🅰 213 B2

Visitor Information

✉ Av. Morelos Sur 187, Colonia Las Palmas

☎ 777/314-3872

www.morelostravel .com

In spring, Cuernavaca blossoms—even if the *guayaba* trees that gave locals their nickname, *guayabos*, are now few and far between. In the large plaza, people stroll past the plain millennium clock, installed for the year 2000 but already looking half a century old. On the east side, the formidable **Palacio de Cortés** (*Av. Leyva 100, tel 777/312-8171, closed Mon.*) has interior murals by Diego Rivera. Inside the palace is the **Museo Cuauhnáhuac** (*Av. Morelos 278, tel 777/318-6498, closed Mon., $*), which has displays of colonial art as well as archaeological and historical exhibits.

The **Ex-Convento de la Asunción** (*Av. Morelos at Hidalgo,* tel 777/318-4590) has a huge atrium designed to hold many potential Indian converts. Its ornate altarpieces were removed in 1959, unveiling wall murals of Mexican San Felipe de Jesús's martyrdom in Japan. Further evidence of the "new Catholicism" is seen in its modern stained-glass windows, a resurrected Christ (instead of a crucifix), and the popular **mariachi Mass,** held Sunday mornings at 8.

Not to be missed is the **Museo Robert Brady** (*Nezahualcóyotl 4, tel 777/318-8554, closed Mon., $*), home of the wealthy American collector and expatriate of the same name. Throughout this fabulous house are a thousand pieces of fine and folk art from Mexico and throughout the world, placed in inspired juxtaposition.

Stroll through the landscaped grounds of **Jardín Borda** (*Av. Morelos 271 at Hidalgo, tel 777/318-1050, closed Mon., $*), established by the Taxco mining tycoon José de la Borda. The mansion here later became the summer home of Emperor Maximilian. Visit the site museum (*$*), with exhibits from the emperor's reign. Music or other cultural events are sometimes held in the garden. For more live entertainment, head for the hipper cafés and cantinas around **Plazuela del Zacate** (*Galeana at Hidalgo*). ∎

Xochicalco

From its perch on a series of low terraced hills, the Place of the House of Flowers archaeological site covers 60 acres (25 ha), most of which are still unexcavated. The fortified city, which flourished between A.D. 700 and 900, was discovered during the Mexican Revolution, when according to legend, Gen. Emiliano Zapata noticed bullets ricocheting off the grassy hill he was defending. Upon investigation, the "hill" turned out to be a buried pyramid.

The site spreads down from its high point at the **Plaza Ceremonial.** Facing this sacred square is Xochicalco's most important structure, the **Templo de Quetzalcóatl,** richly adorned in bas-relief carvings of the god. Different types of calendars carved on the pyramid's walls have led to speculation that Zapotec, Maya, and Gulf Coast tribes met together at Xochicalco to discuss astronomy or to synchronize their calendars.

Below, the **Plaza de la Estela de Dos Glifos** (Two Glyph Stelae Square) was a large grassy meeting place with a stele carved with the date 10 Sugarcane 9 Reptile Eye. Still farther down the hill, the I-shaped ball court is considered to be one of the first built on the central plateau and has been influenced by Maya design.

Twice a year (May 14–15 & July 28–29) at the **underground observatory,** when the sun is at its zenith, a hexagonal shaft of light appears on the floor of the cave. It enters through a hole bored 26 feet (8 m) through solid rock. There are also the ruins of a cistern and a *temescal* steam bath.

The **site museum** includes pottery and examples of hieroglyphic writings; headsets (*$$*) are available with information in English and other languages. Light and sound shows Friday and Saturday (*$$$$*) include museum entrance; for an additional fee, round-trip transportation is provided from the tourism kiosk of Cuernavaca's Plaza de Armas (see opposite). ■

Xochicalco
- 213 B2
- 24 miles (38 km) SW of Cuernavaca via Hwy. 95
- 737/374-3090
- $$

Pre-Hispanic Place-names

Look at a map of central Mexico and you'll get a glimpse of the country's pre-Hispanic roots. Although some indigenous words were corrupted or changed by the Spaniards, others indicate a place's unique characteristics.

In many cases, both indigenous and Spanish words form compound place-names, such as Oaxaca de Juárez, the capital of Oaxaca state, and Santo Tomás Xochimilco, one of its suburbs. You may encounter places whose names contain some of the following Náhuatl words in your travels through the heart of Mexico.

Nahuatl word:	Example:
Cal/Calli (house)	*Xochicalco* (Place of the House of Flowers)
Xochi (flower)	*Xochimilco* (Place of Flowers)
Tepec (hill)	*Tehuantepec* (Hill of Jaguars)
Teo (god)	*Teotihuacán* (Place Where They Become Gods)

Ruta del Volcán Popocatépetl Drive

The Franciscans, Dominicans, and Augustinians divided up the area that now forms tiny Morelos state. Heading clockwise from Cuernavaca lies a necklace of monasteries established soon after the Spanish Conquest. This route through the foothills is especially dramatic in winter, when snowcapped Popocatépetl and slumbering Iztaccíhuatl appear, giving the route its nickname, "the Volcano Monasteries."

Cuernavaca's Franciscan **Ex-Convento de la Asunción ❶** (see p. 214) is dedicated to the Virgin of the Assumption. State and federal grants have funded restoration of many paintings, some by renowned colonial artists.

From Cuernavaca, drive about 16 miles (26 km) east on Highway 95D to Highway 115. Follow Highway 115 in the direction of Cuautla to **Tepoztlán ❷**, where you can buy handicrafts and *amate* (bark paper) at the weekend market. In 1550, Dominican friars ousted the god of pulque, Ometochitli, from his temple and used the stones to build the **Convento de**

NOT TO BE MISSED:

**Tepoztlán • Tlayacapan
• Yecapixtla**

Nuestra Señora de la Natividad ❸, located on the town's main plaza. Today the town blends Christian and pre-Hispanic rituals, especially during Mardi Gras and the celebration of Our Lady of the Nativity on September 7.

Around the church's plateresque doorway are symbols of the Virgin: the sun, moon, and eight-pointed stars. Dominican symbols include the foliated cross, fleur-de-lis, and torchbearing dogs. From the cloister, there are views of the seamed hills of the Sierra Tepozteca, where remnants of a pre-Hispanic pyramid, **Tepozteco,** can be reached after an hour's hike.

Continue about 20 miles (32 km) toward Cuautla to **Oaxtepec ❹** *(tel 735/358-0101),* once a retreat for the lords of Xochimilco and the Emperor Moctezuma, and now home to one of the state's largest water parks. Some historians call it "Tenochtitlán's granary," as its orchards and fields were an important source of food for the Aztec capital. Oaxtepec's 16th-century **Convento de Santo Domingo** is surrounded by a variety of ancient trees. Throughout the adjoining monastery are monochrome paintings of Dominican saints.

From Oaxtepec, head north on Highway 142 for about 6 miles (10 km) to **Tlayacapan ❺** *($)*, whose **Convento de San Juan Bautista** is characterized by its simplicity.

Families enjoy the bustling Tepoztlán market.

START
① **Cuernavaca**

95D

115 115D

Convento de
Nuestra Señora
③ de la Natividad
● **Tepoztlán**
②

PARQUE NACIONAL
EL TEPOZTECO

Tepozteco

160

M O R E L O S

Sierra *Tepozteca*

Yautepec

Convento
de San Juan
Bautista ⑤
●**Tlayacapan**

Convento de
Totolapan

142

160 *Yautepec*

2

●**Oaxtepec** ④
Convento de
Santo Domingo
Convento de
Atlatlahuacan

115

🅰 Also see map p. 213
► Cuernavaca
🕐 80 miles (128 km)
↔ One day
► Cuernavaca

Cuautla

10

Convento de
San Juan Bautista
●**Yecapixtla**
⑥

Cuautla

0   8 kilometers
0   4 miles

160

The church's pale facade is crowned with an *espadaña,* a row of small bells in individual arches. Within the refectory museum are a half dozen wooden, polychrome statues, and within the private chapel there are paintings of Augustinian saints, friars, and the four Evangelists.

Drive east on Highway 2 for 6 miles (10 km) past basalt bluffs to the neglected **Convento de Totolapan.** This Augustinian monastery was once virtually covered in paintings. Continue on the same road, which curves south to the **Convento de Atlatlahuacan,** about 9 miles (14 km). A huge, crenelated atrium encloses the former Augustinian monastery; the cloister contains portrayals of early saints. Dedicated to St. Matthew, the church has a blue nave full of

saints and folk altars tucked in candlelit niches.

Continue south on Highway 2, turning right onto Highway 115 toward Cuautla, and left after about 3.5 miles (6 km) onto Highway 10 to **Yecapixtla** ⑥. A slave market during pre-Hispanic times, this town later became a regional Augustinian priory. At the back of the **Convento de San Juan Bautista** stands **Cortés's Palace,** where the conqueror sometimes stayed. The church's renaissance facade has a rose window and a plateresque portal. Inside, note the Augustinian insignia of the ornate Isabelline pulpit. Head back to Highway 115, continue south, and then turn west on Highway 160 to return the 39 miles (62 km) to Cuernavaca.

In & Around Cholula

Cholula (Place of Flight) is thought to have been established by supporters of Quetzalcóatl fleeing religious persecution. Today home to the Universidad de las Américas, Cholula and surrounding villages have some of Mexico's most stunning churches. Forced to abandon the Quetzalcóatl cult, indigenous artisans built inspired churches. Combining pre-Hispanic and European motifs and techniques, they created an eloquent, irrepressible baroque.

Nuestra Señora de los Remedios church sits upon the Gran Pirámide de Tepanapa, Mesoamerica's largest pyramid and focal point of Cholula archaeology.

At the dawn of the 16th century, Cholula was a powerful city and an important commercial center under the dominion of the Aztec. Despite the advice of his Tlaxcala Indian guides, Hernán Cortés stopped here for ten days during his initial march to Tenochtitlán. Upon learning of a plan to slaughter and sacrifice his troops, he ordered a massacre of soldiers and citizens after delivering a speech discouraging idolatry and human sacrifice. The Cholulans' resounding defeat reinforced Cortés's image as an all-seeing superior being.

Within just two years, the Aztec capital had been conquered and the Spaniards set about reinventing Cholula in European fashion, replacing Quetzalcóatl's temples with Christian churches.

Abandoned since late Postclassic times, Meso-america's largest pyramid, the **Gran Pirámide de Tepanapa** (Av. Morelos at Calle 6 Norte, tel 222/500-9622, $), was probably just too big to dismantle. The huge structure of sun-dried adobe bricks was constructed in distinct phases over a thousand-year period (roughly 300 B.C.–A.D. 700).

Unlike other archaeological sites, Tepanapa is accessed exclusively through a 5-mile (8 km) honeycomb of tunnels. Enter on your own, or hire a guide ($$$$) at the entrance. A small site museum displays period pottery and a cutaway model showing the different layers of the pyramid. Perched on top of the 230-foot (70 m) structure is the **Iglesia de Nuestra Señora de los Remedios.** On a clear day, the late 16th-century church affords a superb view of the city and Popocatépetl and Iztaccíhuatl volcanoes.

Brightly painted restaurants and shops surround Cholula's large main square, **Plaza La Concordia** *(Blvd. Miguel Alemán at Morelos),* some tucked into the arcade on the west side. On the east side lies the entrance to the **Convento San Gabriel** *(Calle 2 Sur at Morelos),* built by the Franciscans on the site of a pre-Hispanic temple. Inside the monastery is the fascinating **Capilla Real**—modeled after the great mosque of Córdoba, Spain—a maze of columns and colonnades topped by 49 domes.

Just a few miles south of Cholula are two famous "Indian baroque" churches, unique for their blend of European and Indian elements. Said to have been designed and executed entirely by native people, the church at **Santa María Tonantzintla** is one of the hemisphere's most astonishing artistic accomplishments. Every inch of the interior is covered in polychrome and gilded, sculpted plaster ornamentation: cherubs (some with Indian faces), flowers, fruit, vines, saints, rosettes, and scrolls. On columns on either side of the main altar, look for mirrors representing respectively wisdom, morality, truth, and humanity.

Less than a mile (1.5 km) farther south is the astonishing **San Francisco Acatepec church,** its fabulous tiled facade a breathtaking barrage of bright yellow, blue-and-white flowered, green, and unglazed brick-red tiles.

An English-style manor house built by colonials and updated by an archbishop of Oaxaca, **Ex-Hacienda de Chautla** *(Carr. 190, 2.5 miles/4 km from San Martín Texmelucan, tel 248/481-1141, www.amatzcalli.com/cha.htm)* can be toured. On its lovely grounds is a lake for bass fishing; there are also camping facilities, cabins, a restaurant, and boats for rent.

INSIDER TIP:

Cholula, with its bars and clubs, is the best place in the area to go for nightlife.

—ERIC RAMIREZ BRAVO
National Geographic field researcher

Less than 10 miles (16 km) to the northwest of Cholula, **Huejotzingo** is home to an ancient **Convento Franciscano** *(closed Mon., $)* built between 1529 and 1570. See the cloister, kitchen, and charming chapel, and in the adjoining church admire the beautiful plateresque altar. Huejotzingo is known for its wool *sarapes* (blankets), sold at the outdoor Saturday market, and for its boisterous carnival celebrations. ∎

Cholula

🗺 213 C2

Visitor Information

✉ 12 Oriente at 4 Norte

☎ 222/261-2393

www.vivecholula.com

Popocatépetl & Iztaccíhuatl

Only 50 miles (80 km) southeast of Mexico City loom active Popocatépetl and its slumbering companion, Iztaccíhuatl. At 17,802 feet (5,426 m) and 17,343 feet (5,286 m) respectively, these giants are outpeaked only by Pico de Orizaba, in Veracruz. The subject of legends and an object of worship since the reign of Quetzalcóatl, Popocatépetl has erupted at least 36 times, the last major event being in A.D. 820.

Although Popo and Izta (as they are affectionately called) are both classified as stratovolcanoes, Izta has long been dormant and has no crater. Popo, on the other hand, began to rumble and quake in 1993, with belches and explosions of gas, ash, and rocks. The next year, 25,000 people were evacuated from vulnerable villages when ash and red-hot rocks began to rain down its snowy slopes.

According to legend, Popoca was a poor but valiant youth in love with Mixtli, the lovely daughter of Tizoc, lord of Mexico. Popoca went to battle in hopes of gaining the rank of Caballero Aguila, or Eagle Warrior, thus meriting marriage to the princess. Imagining her beloved's death and her own marriage to the most ambitious and cruel of her suitors, Mixtli killed herself. Returning triumphant from battle and finding his lover dead, Popoca laid the princess's body atop a high mountain, hoping the snow would revive her. He remained by her side with his smoldering torch, and so the pair gave shape to Popocatépetl (Smoking Mountain) and Iztaccíhuatl (Sleeping Woman).

More than just a fairy tale, Popocatépetl and Iztaccíhuatl figure in modern-day religious ritual. Many villagers consider them to be living beings—simultaneously mountains, humans, and gods. They refer to the pair as "don Gregorio and doña Rosita," who bring rain and fertility to their fields. For the corn-planting season, local rainmakers conduct prayers at sacred sites on both volcanoes, one within a mile (1.6 km) of Popo's crater.

However, Popo is now closed to mountaineers. Still open is the technically more challenging Iztaccíhuatl. Both are accessible from Paso de Cortés, 10.5 miles (17 km) off Highway 115. The pass is named for the Spanish conquistador, who is said to have first glimpsed the city of Tenochtitlán from here.

EXPERIENCE: Climbing the Volcanoes

Mountainous Mexico offers challenges for expert and intermediate climbers. Extinct **Nevado de Toluca** (14,954 feet/4,558 m above sea level), near Toluca, 50 miles (80 km) west of Mexico City, attracts nature-starved city dwellers to its lower slopes on weekends. A climb to the peak rewards with a beautiful crater lake and, on clear days, a view of dormant **Iztaccíhuatl** (17,132 feet/5,222 m).

Nicknamed Izta, this mountain offers a variety of technical climbs and day hikes. Izta's more challenging Ayoloco glacier route offers practice on snow and ice: a good warm-up for Pico de Orizaba.

Called Citlaltépetl (Star Mountain) by the Aztecs, **Orizaba** (18,490 feet/5,636 m), between Veracruz and Pueblo, is Mexico's tallest peak. You can join **Alaska Mountain Guides** (www.mountainguides international.com) expeditions January to March and October to December.

Mexican adventure tourism companies lead rock climbing, rappelling, and canyoneering expeditions. The Mexican Association of Adventure Tourism and Ecotourism (www.amtave.org) gives location and activity recommendations.

Puebla

The city of Puebla was established in 1531 in a green valley surrounded by three of Mexico's tallest volcanoes—Pico de Orizaba, Popocatépetl, and Iztaccíhuatl. Located within the geologically active Ring of Fire, the region is periodically rocked by wall-jarring earthquakes, but civic pride ensures that Puebla's precious historic buildings and gorgeous churches are quickly restored.

Although established early on by the Spaniards as a center of agriculture and trade, Puebla soon diversified to manufacture textiles, glass, and ceramics. To the Moorish-inspired motifs in blue and white imported from Talavera, Spain, indigenous and *mestizo* craftsmen added earthy reds, oranges, and greens. Tiles, used in conjunction with effusively carved plasterwork (often painted and gilded) and other baroque ornamentation, created a unique architectural style seen throughout the capital and surrounding towns.

It's not just the architecture of Puebla that overwhelms the senses. *Poblano* chefs use the huge variety of chilies grown in the region to create many distinctive recipes. Traditionally prepared around Independence Day, *chiles en nogada* are poblano peppers stuffed with a sweetmeat mixture, smothered in walnut cream sauce, and garnished with pomegranate seeds. Prepared using bitter chocolate, nuts, sesame seeds, and chilies, *mole poblano* is a complex sauce served over turkey, chicken, or pork.

The sunny yellow kitchen where mole was allegedly first concocted can be found in the **Ex-Convento de Santa Rosa,** a nunnery confiscated during

Brickwork as well as decorative tiles embellish Puebla facades.

the Reform and now housing the **Museo de Arte Popular Poblano** *(Calle 14 Poniente at 3 Norte, tel 222/232-7792, closed Mon., $).* The museum showcases folk crafts from throughout the state, including masks and inlaid furniture. In the Ex-Convento de Santa Mónica, the **Museo de Arte Religioso** *(18 Poniente 103, tel 222/232-7792, closed Mon., $)* shows, in addition to paintings and other more traditional exhibits, an unusual display: the preserved heart of the convent's founder.

Puebla

🅰 213 C2

Visitor Information

✉ Calle 5 Oriente 3

☎ 222/246-2044

www.sectur.pue .gob.mx

Catedral de la Inmaculada Concepción

✉ 16 de Septiembre at 3 Oriente

☎ 222/232-2316

Surrounding the shady **Plaza Principal** (Juan de Polofox y Mendoza, 3 Oriente, 2 Sur & 16 de Septiembre) are many impressive buildings, including the French neoclassical-style **Palacio Municipal** (Portal Hidalgo 14, tel 222/405-5000). At the plaza's northeast corner, the redbrick, sculpted-plaster, and tile facade of the **Casa de los Muñecos** is as fascinating as the colonial paintings within the **Museo Universitario** (2 Norte 2, tel 222/229-5500, closed Mon., $).

Opposite is the impressive **Catedral de la Inmaculada Concepción,** with its severe twin towers and massive interior containing five naves and 14 side

INSIDER TIP:

Be sure to try *chiles en nogada* in Puebla between July and September. These peppers stuffed with nuts and dried fruit are a unique regional specialty.

—KATHERINE AMATO
National Geographic field researcher

chapels. The main altar, by colonial master Manuel Tolsá, is of gold, marble, and smoky onyx.

Behind the cathedral, the **Casa de la Cultura** (Calle 5 Oriente 5, tel 222/242-1966, $) comprises a theater, art galleries, and a concert hall. Inside the House of Culture is the **Biblioteca Palafoxiana,** named for the Bishop Palafox, who donated his large personal library. The collection now numbers more than 40,000 tomes. Another local philanthropist donated the pre-Colombian artifacts, European and American colonial art, and 20th-century Mexican art found at the **Museo Amparo** (Calle 2 Sur 708 at Av. 9 Oriente, tel 222/229-3850, www.museoamparo.com, closed Tues., $).

North of the cathedral, the **Iglesia de Santo Domingo** (5 de Mayo at 4 Poniente, tel 222/242-3643) houses the city's most ornate chapel. Dedicated to Our Lady of the Rosary, the **Capilla del Rosario** is a mind-bending baroque surfeit of decorated gilt plasterwork. A few doors down, the **Museo Bello y Zetina** (5 de Mayo 409 at 6 Oriente, tel 222/232-4720, closed Mon. & Jan.), the lavishly decorated former home of one of Puebla's wealthy families, is a good example of secular opulence.

The 18th-century **Casa del Alfeñique** (4 Oriente 416 at 6 Norte, tel 222/232-0458, closed Mon., $)–named for the similarity of its ornately carved plaster facade to a popular sugar candy of the same name—houses a museum of colonial and pre-Hispanic artifacts. In the same neighborhood, crafts stalls sell *alfeñique* and other typical candies, in addition to factory-made Talavera pottery, at **El Parián** (2 Oriente & 6 Norte), on the old **Plaza San Roque.** You can buy local artwork from workshops at the **Barrio del Artista** (6 Oriente & 6 Norte) and **Callejón de los Sapos** (Calle 4 Sur near Av. 7 Oriente), two lively shopping districts. ■

Tlaxcala & Cacaxtla

Most people visit lively and historic Tlaxcala to see the fabulous pre-Hispanic murals at Cacaxtla. Surrounding the fountain-filled plaza, patio restaurants serve regional specialties under the arched colonnade. Shops sell folk art, including carved wooden canes, striped *sarapes*, and colorful Carnival masks used throughout the region. Proud of both its Spanish and indigenous ancestry, the town's motto is "Heritage of Two Cultures."

Tlaxcala's colorful parish church of San José

Both the tiny state and its capital city are named for the Tlaxcaltecans, whose hatred for the Aztec made them Hernán Cortés's trusted Indian allies. Relatively well treated for their loyalty, the Tlaxcaltecans voluntarily resettled in places as far-flung as Santa Fe, New Mexico, and San Cristóbal de las Casas, Chiapas, to aid converting reluctant indigenous groups.

Tlaxcala boasts the first permanent church in New Spain. The Franciscan monastery **Ex-convento de San Francisco,** at Plaza Xicotencatl, was built from the stones of a pyramid to the rain god Tláloc. The sacristy holds the baptismal font where the four lords of Tlaxcala were baptized before Cortés marched on Tenochtitlán; the cloister now houses the **Museo Regional de Tlaxcala** *(tel 246/462-0262, $),* with pre-Hispanic and colonial artifacts and paintings.

Many of the 16th-century buildings surrounding **Plaza de la Constitución** preserve the lower portions of their original facades, giving the square a historic

Tlaxcala

 213 C2

Visitor Information

✉ Av. Juárez 18 at Lardizábal

☎ 246/465-0900 ext. 7 or 01800/509-6557 (toll-free within Mexico)

www. descubretlaxcala .com

Basílica de Nuestra Señora de Ocotlán

✉ Pocito de Aqua Santa, Carr. a Santa Ana Chiautempan

☎ 246/462-1073

uniformity. On the northwest corner, the **Parroquia de San José** has been decorated in brick and Talavera tiles after several remodels. The brick and rococo plaster **Palacio de Gobierno** *(tel 246/465-0900)* graces the plaza's north side. Throughout the state government building's interior, complex murals describe the city's indigenous roots and historical events. The **Museo de Artes y Tradiciones Populares** *(Emilio Sánchez Piedras 1, tel 246/462-2337, closed Mon., $)* shows samples of pulque (fermented cactus liquor) and regional weaving and masks.

INSIDER TIP:

For the best tamales and *atole* in Tlaxcala— and maybe all of central Mexico—go to Tamales Agus at Avenida Juárez 25.

—LISA OVERHOLTZER
National Geographic field researcher

On the east side of town, the 18th-century **Basílica de Nuestra Señora de Ocotlán** was built at the site of several miraculous appearances of the Virgin Mary within a pine forest *(ocotlán);* its stunning interior took indigenous artist Francisco Tlayotehuanitzin more than 20 years to complete. The octagonal **Camarín de la Virgen** (Virgin's Dressing Room) is completely engulfed in gilded and polychrome angels, saints, flowers, and garlands. At nearby **Capilla del Pocito de Agua Santa** (Chapel of the Holy Spring), pilgrims purchase

red-clay vessels for carrying off some of the site's sacred water. Outside the city center are more than a dozen old **haciendas** used for agriculture, or cattle or bull raising. Check with the tourism office to see which offer tours, meals, and/or lodgings.

The ruins of a fortified city at **Cacaxtla,** 12 miles (19 km) southwest of Tlaxcala *(tel 246/416-0000, $$),* contain what are arguably Mexico's most important pre-Hispanic murals, discovered only in 1975. Closed for restoration for nearly a year, the site reopened in April 2008. A combination of Classic lowland Maya painting style and non-Maya hieroglyphics led scholars to believe the murals were painted by Gulf Coast émigrés, the Olmeca-Xicalanca, who flourished between the mid-seventh and tenth centuries.

The site is dominated by an enormous building whose adobe walls, corridors, and open courtyards were covered in stucco and decorated with complex murals. The largest, about two thirds intact, depicts warriors dressed as jaguars, apparently in the act of sacrificing rival bird-warriors. Less bellicose murals show images related to trade and fertility.

Most tours to Cacaxtla stop at **Xochitécatl,** a mile (1.6 km) north *(free with Cacaxtla admission),* where pepper trees sprout on an unusual spiral pyramid of compacted sand covered in stone. Related to fertility, this structure may have been dedicated to the wind god Ehécatl. Both Cacaxtla and Xochitécatl have site museums. ∎

EXPERIENCE: Celebrate Day of the Dead

For Mexicans, Day of the Dead is a pleasant if sometimes emotional time of remembrances. Both spiritual and upbeat, it's a way of honoring loved ones now gone to the grave. Day of the Dead most likely has roots in a Celtic pagan holiday called Samhain, celebrated at the end of the growing season. Over centuries the holiday took new forms and meaning under Spanish Catholicism, then altered yet again with the sensibilities of Native Americans.

Traditions vary by region, but the most colorful celebrations are in the countryside, especially in central and southern Mexico. In San Luis Potosí, Michoacán, Chiapas, and other states, trails of marigold petals lead souls from the street to the family home and altar. An arch over the altar may be twined with marigolds, symbol of this season, called *cempasúchil* in the Nahuatl tongue. Moving in the breeze, cut-paper flags attract a spirit's attention as well.

Mexico's fascination with death manifests in the family-oriented Day of the Dead celebration.

Covered in a white cloth signifying purity, the altar has a glass of water to slack the thirst of the soul after its long journey from the afterworld. Favorite drinks of the departed—whether mescal or Diet Coke or fruit juice—are there, as are favorite foods. Also tobacco, if the soul enjoyed it in the flesh. Among the candles and the photo or likeness of the deceased are peanuts and fruit, incense, more flowers (primarily marigolds and coxcombs), and for the children, sweets. This is the time of year to buy egg-based *pan de muerto* (a bread for the holiday) and sugar skulls in the marketplace.

Children's souls are thought to return on November 1, *el día de los angelitos* ("Day of Little Angels," or All Saints' Day). In many regions the celebration begins the evening before. Loved ones may simply clean the gravesite, perhaps repainting the tomb or headstone and leaving fresh flowers. Some families have a picnic on the grave, bringing the favorite foods of their loved one. Roving musicians entertain, flower sellers set up at the cemetery entrance. In other communities, families spend the entire night in the graveyard, lighting the grave with candles. Flares and noisy rockets guide the souls to Earth. The spirits of deceased adults are thought to begin arriving late on November 1; their day is November 2, All Souls' Day.

The best known ceremonies are those of tiny **Janitzio island** on Lake Pátzcuaro, Michoacán, and towns like **Xoxo** outside of Oaxaca city. But away from these now-commercialized celebrations are thousands of towns and villages carrying on their unique version of the ancient traditions. Author and editor Mary J. Andrade has traveled extensively in Mexico and her blog, Day of the Dead Blog: A Celebration of Life *(www.dayofthedeadblog.com)*, has information concerning celebrations throughout Mexico.

Hidalgo State

A microcosm of Mexico's heartland, tiny Hidalgo state is a patchwork of haciendas, arid plains, mines, and 16th-century monasteries. Worked since before the Conquest, the silver and gold mines in Pachuca and the surrounding hills still contribute significantly to the economy, augmented by the manufacture of textiles, cement, and other products. The streets winding through this hilly city meet at small plazas fronted by modern and neoclassical buildings.

Sunlight warms the pinnacles of El Chico National Park.

Pachuca
🅰 213 B3
Visitor Information
✉ Av. Madero 702 at Pino Suárez
☎ 771/717-6400 or 01800/718-2600 (toll-free within Mexico)
www.hidalgo.travel

Pachuca

The old city of Pachuca radiates from the rather severe **Plaza de la Independencia** *(Matamoros at Allende),* surrounded by a mix of 20th-century buildings. The neoclassical **Reloj Monumental,** an imposing clock tower with an eight-bell carillon, dominates the square. Built just prior to the revolution, its marble statues represent Liberty, the Constitution, Reform, and Independence.

Southeast of the plaza, the fortress-style **Templo y Ex-Convento de San Francisco** *(Arista & Hidalgo, tel 771/715-2965)* began as a Franciscan monastery. It has seen many uses in its more than 500-year history, including as stables and a jail; the church is still in use today.

Within the former monastery is the **Teatro de la Ciudad** *(tel 771/714-0764),* built by the Spanish inventor of the "patio system" for amalgamating silver using quicksilver. Inside, the **Museo de la Fotografía** *(tel 771/714-3653, closed Mon.)* has changing exhibits of historic photos from the adjoining **Fototeca Nacional.** The National Photographic Archives offers a reproduction service of its 900,000 images, many from the revolution.

Pachuca is located at the northern extreme of the Valley of Mexico, just 56 miles (90 km) northeast of Mexico City. Beyond rises the Sierra Madre Oriental, and en route lies **Mineral Real del Monte,** 7 miles (11 km) northeast on Highway 105, a charming old mining town that has seen ups and downs over the centuries. After a violent miners' strike, the mine was sold to an English consortium, which went bankrupt 25 years later. During its brief tenure, the British firm used miners from Cornwall—who brought soccer and their traditional meat pies, or pasties (called *pastes* in Mexico), a delightful treat now adapted and filled with meat, tuna, potatoes, or sautéed peppers. The tombstones of the English buried in the town graveyard face Britain.

Huasca

A few miles beyond and off Highway 105 lies Huasca, a charming town of cobblestone streets and brightly painted buildings. A smaller road leads from Mineral Real del Monte to the mining town of **Real del Chico** and the adjacent **Parque Nacional El Chico** (tel 771/715-0994), with well-marked hiking and mountain-bike trails through pine, oak, and juniper forest. On weekends city dwellers flee to the 6,670-acre (2,700 ha) park to fish, rock climb, or simply enjoy the mountain air. There are restaurants, pastie shops, and a nice hotel; camping is permitted.

Actopan

About a half hour away, Actopan, 23 miles (37 km) north of Pachuca on Highway 85, celebrates its weekly market each Thursday. Right in the center of town, the **Templo y Ex-Convento San Nicolás** ($), begun by the Augustinians in 1548, is one of Mexico's most admired buildings. Note the well-proportioned plateresque facade and the barrel vaulting above the **capilla abierta** (open chapel), with its trompe l'oeil coffered ceiling.

Most remarkable, however, are the **murals.** Many are renditions of illustrations from medieval books vividly painted in blue, brown, ocher, and red. The Apocalypse scenes in the open chapel are among the finest in Mexico. Painted over in layers of whitewash after the Council of Trent—a church edict set forth in the 16th century banning profanity, nudity, and apocalyptic themes in sacred art—they have only recently been uncovered.

Throughout Hidalgo state are more than a dozen important **former monasteries,** built in the 1600s near the largest Náhua and Otomí centers. The Franciscans produced more modest houses of worship in the west, while the Augustinians took the east and built more slowly and lavishly (see pp. 216–217). ■

EXPERIENCE:
Build Needed Homes

Many of Mexico's people live in inadequate housing, and they lack the economic means for the huge effort needed to make new homes. Habitat for Humanity Mexico works in 17 Mexican states and invites volunteers to improve conditions by helping its mission of creating housing solutions and of inspiring community development and investment. Trips for constructing homes that involve volunteers usually last about nine days. Visit www.habitat.org/gv or call 800/422-4828, ext. 7530 (from the U.S.) for more information on how to get involved, trip dates, and prices.

Teotihuacán

Rising above a gold, grassy plain to the northeast of Mexico City are the ruins of the first true metropolis in the Western Hemisphere. It outlived its contemporary, imperial Rome, and was the greatest city in the Americas until the Mexica (Aztec) built Tenochtitlán nearly 700 years later. The Mexica elite made frequent pilgrimages to the ruins of Teotihuacán and gave the city its Náhuatl name, meaning "where men become gods."

While Europe stumbled through the Dark Ages, Teotihuacán's culture shone like a beacon around Mesoamerica.

Scholars today know very little about the people who constructed this magnificent city, or why they abandoned it just a few centuries after it reached its golden age, roughly A.D. 200 to 500. Theories include overpopulation, rampant disease, internal power struggles, and rebellion of the masses. Systematic burning of ceremonial buildings points to the purposeful destruction of the city.

At the height of its power, however, fine palaces and temples adorned with bas-relief sculptures and brilliant murals lined **Avenida de los Muertos** (Avenue of the Dead), a broad, straight avenue paved with volcanic stone, set with dazzling mica, and aligned with the stars. Its leaders excelled in architecture and astronomy, and had a well-developed religious system. An extensive commercial network extending to the Petén region of Guatemala was probably initiated in the first century A.D.

Today, many of the ceremonial buildings lining Avenue of the Dead have been partially reconstructed, although without their colorful stucco facades. At its southern end stands **La Ciudadela,** the compound of plazas and temples that formed Teotihuacán's administrative and ceremonial center and also the principal secular royal palace for generations of unknown kings.

La Ciudadela is dominated by the **Templo de Quetzalcóatl,** which honored the Plumed Serpent, worshipped as the god of water, the dawn, and agriculture. Although fanged serpent sculptures originally covered the lower level, those on three sides were pulled down not long after its inauguration. The intact west wall is impressive, with rows of stone serpent heads interspersed with images of Tláloc and feathered shells.

At the far extreme of the 2.5-mile (4 km) avenue is the **Pirámide de la Luna** (Pyramid of the Moon), a royal funerary monument with tombs dating back to the first century A.D.; the oldest of these may be that of the founder of the royal dynasty. Just over a hundred tall, narrow steps lead to the summit, where you will be rewarded with a view of the Avenue of the Dead, sacred **Cerro Gordo** (Fat Hill) to the north, and lonely plains dotted with prickly pear cactuses and pepper trees. The pyramid has six layers of construction; in contrast, the Pyramid of the Sun was built mostly during a single phase.

Smaller, related structures are symmetrically arranged on both sides of the Avenue of the Dead; the most impressive is the **Palacio de Quetzalpapálotl.** Within the building's rooms, open patios, and antechambers are some well-preserved murals. Square stone pillars in the interior patio are decorated with low-relief sculptures of the building's namesake, the Feathered Butterfly, while the temple below is adorned with a fascinating sequence of quetzals, sea-shells, and Tláloc masks.

Across the avenue, the **Pirámide del Sol** (Pyramid of the Sun), the third largest pyramid in the world, squats like an immense behemoth. Although its base is nearly as broad as that of the Great Pyramid at Giza, at 213 feet (65 m) tall it is less than half the height of the Egyptian pyramid. Underneath the tremendous structure winds a honeycomb of tunnels and caves, which the Aztec considered the birthplace of the world. Although the four-level, 244-step pyramid has more than twice as many steps as the Pyramid of the Moon, it is slightly easier to climb as the steps are shorter. Thousands of people converge on the structure near dawn each spring equinox hoping to receive a supercharge of celestial energy.

In addition to its ceremonial and commercial functions, 8-square-mile (20 sq km) Teotihuacán was, at its apogee, home to approximately 175,000 people. Neighborhoods of one-story dwellings had shared patios and kitchens, with private apartments for each family. East of the Pyramid of the Sun, several restored apartment complexes with vivid if fractured murals can be visited. The most impressive are those at **Tepantitla,** whose mural depicting the rain god Tláloc in his paradise is re-created at the Museo Nacional de Antropología, in Mexico City (see pp. 198–201).

To get the most out of your visit, spend the preceding night at the Hotel Villas Arqueológicas Teotihuacán (book in advance; see p. 374) within the archaeological zone itself and take advantage of

INSIDER TIP:

Try to spend a whole day at Teotihuacán. But amenities are scarce. Bring sunscreen, an umbrella, and plenty of water.

—NINA-NOELLE HALL
National Geographic contributor

the site's 7 a.m. opening time—only available at Gate 1. (There are three other entrances.) Otherwise, take a day trip from Mexico City by limo, bus, or licensed taxi. Near the Ciudadela entrance are a restaurant, a bar, and a warren of souvenir stalls, while the site museum and botanical gardens are located near the Pyramid of the Sun. ∎

Teotihuacán
- 213 B3
- 30 miles (48 km) NE of Mexico City
- 594/956-0276

Tepotzotlán

The church and former seminary at Tepotzotlán, masterpieces of Mexican baroque, are reason enough to visit, but housed within the lavish complex is perhaps the country's finest colonial art museum. Tepotzotlán itself, with a population of fewer than 50,000 and just 72 miles (115 km) northeast of Mexico City, is a breath of fresh air after the congested capital.

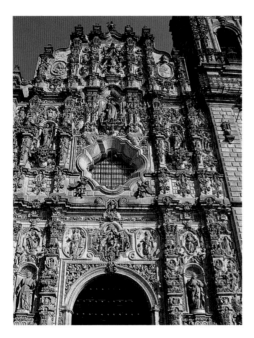

Carvings of saints, angels, and floral and shell motifs cover San Francisco Javier's limestone facade.

Tepotzotlán
🗺 213 B3
Visitor Information
✉ Av. Benito Juárez 1
☎ 55/5876-8068

The Franciscans were the first to arrive, soon followed by the Jesuits at the end of the 16th century. A generous bequest allowed the order to build the **Seminario de San Martín,** a seminary for young indigenous noblemen, the **San Francisco Javier** novitiate, and a language school to teach priests Náhuatl, Otomí, and Mazahua.

The lovely **Iglesia de San Francisco Javier** we see today is the result of an intensive remodel of the facade, belfry, and altarpieces almost immediately after the church was completed. Its complex Churrigueresque facade cannot prepare you for the church's impressive interior. Within the church one gilded, intricately carved altarpiece leads to the next; there are five on each side in addition to the ebullient main altar.

Three fascinating rooms lie to the right of the nave. The **Casa de Loreto** is a re-creation of the home of the Virgin Mary, said to have been miraculously transported to Loreto, Italy, after the Muslims invaded the Holy Land. The **Relicario de San José,** richly decorated in paintings and gold, houses Jesuit relics. Last is the octagonal **Camarín de la Virgen,** the dazzling "dressing room" of carved plaster reserved for the statue of Our Lady of Loreto.

In the adjoining edifice, the **Museo Nacional del Virreinato** (tel 55/5876-2771, closed Mon., $$) has a fantastic collection of three centuries of colonial and folk art: paintings, jewelry, ecclesiastic accoutrements, porcelain, ivory statuettes, and other treasures. Don't miss the **Capilla Domestic,** a chapel covered floor to ceiling in gold leaf and carved polychrome stucco. More exhibits are located on the second story; on the lower level are the kitchen, pantry and cold room, and the gift shop. ■

More Places to Visit Around Mexico City

Malinalco

Subjugated by the Mexica, or Aztec, just 50 years before the Spanish Conquest, Malinalco is a ceremonial center carved into living rock. Its **main temple** is entered through the "mouth" of a large fanged serpent. Within is a circular room decorated with relief sculptures of eagle and jaguar motifs; it is believed to have been dedicated to warriors of those cults. There are 426 steps to the few restored buildings, but you're rewarded with a wonderful view over the town. The site is about a mile (1.6 km) from Malinalco (Place of Grass Blossom), which is a popular weekend escape from Mexico City. Its **Iglesia del Divino Salvador** is its main attraction; in the adjacent Augustinian monastery are many fine frescoes in its cloister.

🔺 213 B2

Tepoztlán

An hour south of Mexico City and just east of Cuernavaca, Pre-Hispanic Tepoztlán attracts travelers with a bohemian spirit. Some come to climb the sandstone peaks looming over town and so visit a Late Classic temple dedicated to the minor local deity Ome Tochtli (Two Rabbit), god of intoxication. It is a wonderful hike for the reasonably fit. Traditional market days in Tepoztlán are Wednesdays and Sundays; at the former you'll see mainly produce, while the larger Sunday market has handicrafts as well. The market fills the plaza in front of **la Iglesia de la Natividad** (Church of the Nativity). Adorning the portal to the churchyard, a mural made entirely of legumes

INSIDER TIP:

Possession of artifacts or fossils in Mexico or any attempt to export such items without a permit is a serious criminal offense that can include jail time.

—LOREN DAVIS
National Geographic field researcher

Monastery Routes

Two groups of Augustinian monasteries are found in eastern Hidalgo: one in the north, in the rugged Sierra Alta, the other on the dry plains called El Mesquital.

Padres set out to convert the Otomí in the sierra in 1537, establishing **Atotonilco el Grande** (today in poor condition) and **Molango**, a rustic mission with a breathtaking valley view. The best of the group is the **Monasterio de los Santos Reyes** in Metztitlán. One of Mexico's finest fortress monasteries, it has the region's only surviving original high altarpiece. There is a wonderful view of the subtropical river valley from the terraced atrium, said to be built on an ancient temple to the moon. The town's name means "moon in the middle."

The plains group consists of **Actopan** (see p. 227), **Epazoyucan, and Ixmiquilpan.** Built on a hill associated with the rain god, Tláloc, Epazoyucan's monastery is best known for its magnificent 16th-century frescoes. Ixmiquilpan's murals are unique for their many vivid battle scenes and unrestrained indigenous imagery and iconography.

Just outside the ruins at Teotihuacán is **Acolman,** built from the stones of a temple dedicated to Quetzalcóatl and noted for its fine plateresque facade.

and seeds depicts village iconography with pre-Hispanic and post-conquest themes. For a delicious meal *(Fri.–Mon.)*, Tepoztlán foodies recommend **La Diferencia** *(Isabel La Católica 3, tel 739/395-1371, $$)*, for its worldly recipes (including crêpes suzettes and superb fondues) and its untouristy atmosphere. If you're in town midweek or prefer Mexican fare, eat at **Antojitos Erika** in the main market. For an overnight stay, check out Las Golondrinas *(tel 739/395-0649, www.lasgolondrinas.com.mx, $$$)*, a quaint but not cutesy, European-style B&B just outside town. For budget digs a block from Tepoztlán's plaza, there's clean, bright, reliable Posada Paraíso *(Buenavista 10, tel 739/395-2553, $)*.

🅰 213 B2

INSIDER TIP:

Most people visiting archaeo-logical sites near Mexico City go to the Templo Mayor and Teotihuacán. If you have the time, go to Tula as well, where the crowds are lighter and the souvenirs are cheaper.

—LISA OVERHOLTZER
National Geographic field researcher

Tula

Founded by the Spaniards around a Franciscan monastery in the early 16th century, Tula was in a previous incarna-tion the pre-Hispanic capital of the Toltec culture, also called Tollan. Descendants of Chichimeca "barbarians" from the north es-tablished Tollan as the center of an impor-tant alliance of city-states. King Topoilzin, later associated with the god Quetzalcóatl (who abhorred human sacrifice), was forced to flee around A.D. 987 by enemies devoted

to the fierce god Tezcatlipoca, or Smoking Mirror. Under the rule of the latter faction, Tula became a powerful city. It was once thought to have influenced or invaded Chichén Itzá because Chac Mool statues have been found there and because of the similarity of the sites' architectural styles and artifacts (see pp. 338–342). However, Tula is now considered to have been a link along an Itzá trade route stretching north to Paquimé and south to the Yucatán and Central America. At its height between A.D. 900 and 1150, it was destroyed by invaders from the north—most likely by the Chichimec from which it was descended.

The archaeological site is perched on a promontory about a mile (1.6 km) outside of Tula. The excavated portion of the city—one of the largest in Early Postclassic Meso-america, covering 5.4 square miles (14 sq km)—consists of several ball courts, pyramids, and temples. The most important building excavated so far is **Pirámide B.** Its temple roof was supported by four tall pillars in the form of Toltec warriors, called Atlantes. One of the four on-site is a reproduction; the origi-nal is at the Museo Nacional de Antropología in Mexico City (see pp. 198–201.) Bas-relief sculptures on the outer walls depict coyotes, jaguars, eagles devouring hearts, and compos-ite creatures thought to represent Quetzal-cóatl. At the **site museum** note the statue of Chac Mool, the reclining messenger god brought north from the Yucatán Peninsula.

🅰 213 B3 ☎ 771/718-4489

Valle del Bravo

About 90 miles (145 km) west of Mexico City, Valle del Bravo is a whitewashed, red-roofed town with popular restaurants and galleries surrounding the main plaza. The town, overlooking **Laguna Avandaro,** an artificial lake with water sports, is visited by wealthy *defeños* (Mexico City residents) escaping the capital.

🅰 213 A2

Home to Mesoamerica's first true civilization, an area where irrepressible jungle still smothers hundreds of archaeological sites

Central Gulf Coast

Jade figurines, found at La Venta, near Villahermosa

Central Gulf Coast

Rain forests, rivers, and ruins attract adventurous travelers to Tabasco and Veracruz, which form a thin curve of land cupping the Gulf of Mexico. The central Gulf coast contains vast lowland plains and, in odd juxtaposition, the country's highest volcanic peak: snowcapped Pico de Orizaba. Its people are as exuberant as its landscape, famed for their spicy cooking, lively dances, and sentimental songs.

More than 40 rivers etch the landscape of Veracruz, creating endless marshy swamps, which frustrated the Spanish conquistadores in the 16th century. The state's coastal plains stretch 424 miles (684 km) along the oil-rich Bay of Campeche, although its beaches are not conducive to swimming and sunbathing. Waterfalls streak the Sierra Tuxtla in the north, while the Río Tonalá creates a natural border between Veracruz and Tabasco to the south. In both states, plantations cover valleys and plateaus in a lush green checkerboard.

Though its hot, humid, and often bug-ridden terrain is far from welcoming, the Gulf coast has a rich pre-Hispanic history. Mesoamerica's first known civilization, the

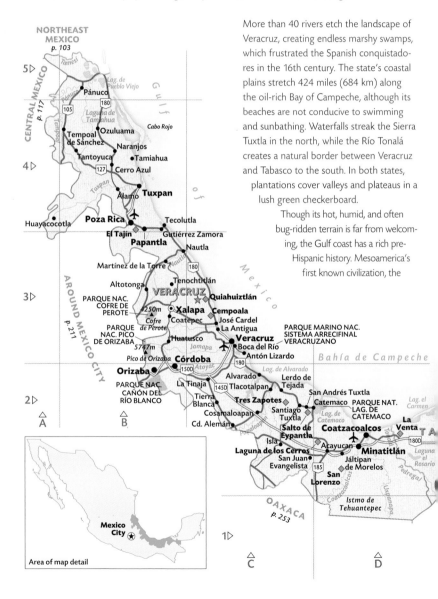

Shady Plaza de Armas is the main square in the coastal city of Veracruz.

Olmec, flourished in this region between 1200 and 400 B.C. Many remote Olmec sites have been uncovered in Tabasco and Veracruz. Veracruz boasts Mexico's second most important archaeology museum iand one of its most intriguing archaeological sites, El Tajín.

History buffs follow the Ruta de Cortés, a journey of conquest that began with the Spaniard's arrival in 1519 and ended two years later with the fall of Tenochtitlán. Adventure travelers struggle up steep trails to the summit of Pico de Orizaba, raft the Ríos Antigua and Filobobos, and explore the jungles around Lake Catemaco, while culture buffs are content to wander the port city of Veracruz, haunting the dungeons of San Juan de Ulúa, dancing in the lively Plaza de Armas, or feasting on seafood. ∎

NOT TO BE MISSED:

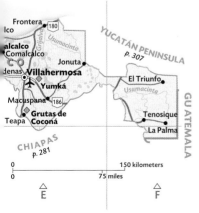

p. 307

El Tajín

Surrounded by emerald green hills, El Tajín must have been resplendent at the height of its influence, when stuccoed pyramids painted bright blue and red surrounded the city's great plazas. Although abandoned for around 800 years, the uniformity and density of its construction, the fascinating bas-relief carvings, and the tropical setting still make this a breathtaking site, worth the effort to find.

Small figurines may have originally occupied the 365 niches of El Tajín's most outstanding pyramid.

Archaeologists aren't sure who built this ceremonial and residential city, which was established during the Early Classic period but reached its height between 800 and 1150 A.D. Its pyramids were built in the *talud y tablero* style found at Teotihuacán (see pp. 228–229). This distinctive style consists of slanted walls *(taludes)* capped with overhanging vertical panels *(tableros)*. By about A.D. 1200 the site had been abandoned, having been burned —possibly by the Chichimec (see

pp. 25–26) to the north.

The site was named by the Totonac of northern Veracruz, who believe that the 12 ancient ones, or *Tajín,* live here and cause rain. The jungle-clad city was not discovered until the late 18th century. Restoration is ongoing; to date about 45 of the structures have been restored.

The ball game served as a ceremonial staging ground of good versus evil in order to assure continued prosperity. The 17 **ball courts** unearthed thus far at El Tajín are ample proof of the importance of sacrifice and auto-sacrifice (such as bloodletting) in this society.

Near the entrance, the **Grupo Plaza del Arroyo** comprises four stepped pyramids surrounding a large plaza. Beyond are four ball courts. Although many of El Tajín's ball courts have bas-relief carvings, the most intricate and well-preserved panels decorate the **Juego de Pelota Sur.** Scenes show the god of death witnessing men preparing for war (the ball game), and the final outcome: ritualistic death for the loser. Central panels on the east and west sides show the god of rain piercing his penis in a ritual self-sacrifice to produce the intoxicating drink *pulque.*

Just to the north, a large number of buildings cluster around the magnificent **Pirámide de los Nichos,** named for its 365 deeply recessed niches. This stocky structure has a single steep stairway on the east side. The step-and-fret pattern at the top is repeated on many other structures, including **Edificios 5** and **12,** to the right and left, respectively.

Farther north, the buildings in **Tajín Chico** were most likely the residences of elite citizens. Note the Maya arch on the south side of **Edificio A** and the remnants of murals on **Edificio C. Edificio de las Columnas** has carved columns with narrative scenes of rituals practiced by the ruling elite. Three of the columns from the Building of the Columns can be found in the modern **site museum.** Other items typical of Classic Veracruz civilization, which predominated along the Gulf coast plain, include ritual objects associated with the ball game: yokes (u-shaped stones, probably replicas of players' belts); *palmas* (objects that hung from the belt); and *hachas,* possibly used as scoring devices.

Established in 2000, **Cumbre Tajín** *(tel 01800/823-2000, toll-free within Mexico, www.cumbretajin .com.mx)* is a five-day celebration featuring music of various genres from around the world, indigenous dances and rituals, and other events. ∎

El Tajín
- 234 B4

Visitor Information
- 10 miles (16 km) SW of Poza Rica
- 784/881-2727
- $$

Mesoamerican Leap of Faith

Adjacent to the site museum, the Voladores de Papantla perform a strange flying ritual for the benefit of visitors. Dressed in elaborate costumes—decorated with sequins, beads, and fringe, and with headdresses encrusted with mirrors and plastic flowers—five Totonac men climb to the top of a slim, 100-foot (30 m) pole.

Inspired by the music of flute and drum performed by their leader, the other four men dive backward off the platform, completing precisely 13 revolutions before landing on the ground. The number of revolutions totals 52, the number of years in an important Mesoamerican religious cycle. The group usually performs at the request of a tour guide, or when enough people congregate.

Xalapa & Environs

At 4,680 feet (1,427 m) above sea level, Veracruz's hilly capital city of Xalapa (also spelled Jalapa) was once an important stagecoach stop between Mexico City and the port of Veracruz. Today this university town is one of Mexico's most entertaining capitals, offering art cafés, theater, dance troupes, a fine symphony orchestra, and a world-class anthropology museum. Set on a series of verdant terraces, it is also filled with pretty parks and lakes.

Xalapa's heart is **Parque Juárez** *(Enrique between Revolución & Clavijero)*, a small but well-groomed garden overlooking the city. Within the urban park, **El Agora** *(tel 228/818-5730, www.agora.xalapa.net, closed Mon.)* houses an art gallery, theater, and cinema; it's also the place to find out about the city's many cultural performances, including state orchestra and ballet folkloric shows.

Veracruz's oldest city, Xalapa, has an interesting mix of colonial and modern buildings.

Catercorner from the plaza, across Calle Revolución, the 18th-century **catedral** is remarkable for its unusual sloping nave. Walk a few blocks east to see **Callejón del Diamante** *(bet. Calles Enriquez & Juárez)*, one of the city's many alleyways, this one with charming typical restaurants, cafés, and shops.

For most, the highlight of a stay in Xalapa is a visit to the **Museo de Antropología** *(Av. Xalapa s/n, tel 228/815-0920, closed Mon., $$)*. This modern masterpiece, imitating the city's terraced cityscape, consists of nine staggered platforms surrounded by gardens. The collection is dedicated to Veracruz's three most influential indigenous cultures: the Huastec, Totonac, and Olmec—the latter considered the mother of Mesoamerican culture.

Among the thousands of exhibits are massive stone heads carved by the Olmec, a bone-filled burial ground, carved jaguars, were-jaguars (half-man, half-beast), murals, jade masks, and ritually deformed skulls. An enormous model re-creates the ruins of El Tajín (see pp. 236–237).

Five blocks southeast of Parque Juárez, large, circular **Parque los Berros** *(Miguel Hidalgo at Díaz Mirón)* is named for the watercress that once grew here. This favorite gathering place of Xalapeños (people from Xalapa) for nearly two centuries is a quiet retreat from the city and has served as a backdrop for the novels of local author Sergio Galindo.

Two blocks south, **La Zona de los Lagos** is Xalapa's most popular spot for a Sunday outing; paths meander around a series of lakes surrounded by a wooded canyon. Overlooking the lake at the western entrance to the park is the handsome, 19th-century **Centro Cultural de los Lagos** *(Paseo de los Lagos, tel 228/818-0704)*, showing changing exhibits of arts and crafts.

Venture outside the city to admire the lush countryside. (If you visit between November and March, bring a thick sweater and a raincoat—the light but constant rain known as *chipi-chipi* can be chilling.) The beautiful **Jardín Botánico Francisco Javier Clavijero** *(Antigua Carr. a Coatepec Km 2.5, tel 228/842-1827, $)* displays more than 1,500 varieties of flora found throughout Veracruz. It features a small arboretum, a large pond with aquatic plants, and a winding, shady path through a riot of greenery.

About 7 miles (12 km) farther south is colonial **Coatepec.** Enjoy coffee, an ice cream, or a shoeshine in **Parque Hidalgo** and then wander in **Iglesia de San Jerónimo,** its dark red face in dramatic contrast to the ocher-yellow bell tower. Inside, admire the many lovely saints in niches on both sides of the single nave.

Just past Coatepec, lovely little **Xico** is also worth a visit. The town's unusual patron saint

is Mary Magdalene. On July 19, the saint's feast day, townspeople decorate the main street with elaborate "paintings" of colored sawdust, and the church facade is decorated with plants from the forest outside town. Another lovely Xico tradition takes place on January 17, when local people bring their pets and favorite farm animals to church to be blessed.

Xico is also known for its coffee and artisan wines, which you can try at stands lining the

INSIDER TIP:

Xalapa has a really good archaeological museum and a pleasant climate. And it is close to some of the best outdoor recreational activities in Mexico.

—JAMES DION
National Geographic Center for Sustainable Destinations

entrances to the **Cascada de Texolo,** just a few miles out of town. The 132-foot (40 m) waterfall was featured in the movie *Romancing the Stone* (1984).

Six miles (10 km) east of Xalapa lies **Hacienda Lencero** *(Carr. a Veracruz Km 10, tel 228/812-8500, closed Mon., $)*, a 16th-century estate-turned-inn once owned by Gen. Antonio López de Santa Anna (see p. 30). Now a museum of 19th-century furnishings, it has a pretty chapel and extensive gardens surrounded by cool-climate trees, plus a small, spring-fed lake.

Xalapa
⚑ 234 B3
Visitor Information
✉ Enriquez s/n, 2nd floor, across from Parque Juárez
☎ 228/842-1214
www.veracruz turismo.com.mx

Veracruz

Vibrant Veracruz is a busy port with a lively attitude, and visitors are either charmed or repelled by the city's extremes. The climate is hot and sultry, the beaches less than appealing, and the downtown a crowded, cacophonous urban jungle. But those who love Veracruz do so with a passion—entranced with the rhythm of marimbas, the scent of salt air, and the whirl of heel-stomping fandango dancers in the main plaza.

The Fuerte de San Juan de Ulúa, which defended Veracruz in three wars, is now a museum.

Prisoners at the **Fuerte de San Juan de Ulúa** *(Av. San Juan de Ulúa s/n, closed Mon., $)* had a less favorable view of the city. Built between 1535 and 1692, the gray-stone fortress served as a defense against pirates and the French and United States naval invasions of Mexico. But the fort is more famous as a brutal dungeon where disease, famine, and flooding awaited those who crossed the dreaded Puente de los Suspiros (Bridge of Sighs) into Ulúa's dank cells. For more than three centuries, religious and political prisoners were tortured here. In 1915, Venustiano Carranza claimed Ulúa as a presidential residence—surely a deterrent to anyone seeking that office. The complex is now a museum well worth touring with

a knowledgeable guide.

Shipyards and commercial docks line the waterfront east of Ulúa to the pleasant **Paseo del Malecón,** a delightful seaside walkway reminiscent of the *malecón* in Havana. In fact, visiting Cubans feel very much at home in Veracruz, where the *danzón,* a highly disciplined dance that originated in Cuba, is widely popular.

Plaza de Armas

Several times a week, the band plays and locals dance at the city's main square, Plaza de Armas *(Avs. Independencia, Zamora, Lerdo, & Zaragoza).* The crowded plaza, shaded by laurels and lacy royal palms, is a natural meeting place for city dwellers. Musicians and dancers often perform on the center stage.

Fronting the plaza are the 17th-century **Palacio Municipal** and the 18th-century **Catedral de Nuestra Señora de la Asunción,** topped with a tiled dome. Travelers immune to the never-ending parade of vendors have a drink or a snack at **Los Portales,** a block-long colonial-era building at the south side of the plaza. In the evenings, there's always music—xylophone, rock, or salsa, and sometimes all of the above simultaneously—at lively indoor-outdoor cafés.

Elderly gentlemen sip cups of *lechero,* a frothy mix of coffee and steamed milk, at the popular **Gran Café de la Parroquia** (*Av. Gómez Farias 34, across from malecón, tel 229/932-2584*). The huge place is always packed with local people and closes only for a few hours between 1:30 and 6 a.m.

Museums & Attractions

Several museums highlight the city's tumultuous history. The **Museo de la Ciudad** (*Zaragoza 397 at Esteban Morales, tel 229/989-8873, closed Tues., $*) devotes considerable space to Carnaval, celebrated since the mid-19th century. **Cañonero Guanajuato** (*Plaza Banderas s/n, Boca del Río, tel 229/200-2238, closed Mon., $*), a floating naval museum aboard a retired gunboat, has a café and restaurant on deck. The **Museo Agustín Lara** (*Blvd. Ruíz Cortines s/n, Boca del Río, tel 229/937-0209, closed Mon., $*) honors one of Mexico's most famous musicians and the composer of boleros, including "María Bonita" and "Veracruz," which play over the museum's sound system.

The city's beaches are generally bleak. The best are located south of town at **Playa Mocambo** and **Boca del Río.** Those interested in local sea life might want to avoid swimming altogether in favor of a visit to the **Acuario Veracruz** (*Blvd. Manuel Ávila Camacho at Av. Xicoténcatl, tel 229/931-4376, www.acuariodeveracruz. com, $$*), where a series of galleries displays different marine domains. The doughnut-shaped **Main Gallery** houses Gulf coast species, while in the **Freshwater Gallery** are specimens from Mexico's lakes, lagoons, and rivers. In the **Reef Exhibit,** sea horses and sea stars, eels, and octopuses cruise outcrops of slow-growing coral.

For a guided visit (via headset, in English or other languages), hop aboard a **Circuito Turístico** (*tel 229/928-9169, $$$*), which also serves as transportation to the aquarium, Augustin Lara Museum, beaches, and downtown venues. You can get on and off more than once; board at the post office or any stop. ∎

Veracruz

◿ 234 C3

Visitor Information

✉ Blvd. Adolfo Ruíz Cortines 3497, World Trade Center, 2nd floor, Boca del Río

☎ 229/923-0391

www.veracruz turismo.com.mx

EXPERIENCE:
Cleanse Your Spirit

Mexico is a magical country and it's no surprise that shamanism as well as super-stition is active. Both city and country folks have the likes of palms and tea leaves read. In addition to saying prayers to saints, individuals may visit *curanderos* (healers) who might use herbs or a chicken to remove negative vibes. *Hueseros* repair bones using prayer, herbs, and chiroprac-tic-style maneuvers. Spiritual healers don't advertise, so ask hotel personnel (includ-ing housekeepers and waiters) or use other contacts to find bona fide spiritual advisors in the cities and towns you visit.

Drive: Arrival of the Conquerors

Searching for a route to the East, 16th-century Spanish fleets found instead a fascinating new land. Gifts of gold from friendly Indians inspired future expeditions, but in 1519, when Hernán Cortés led a third voyage, the Indians came prepared for battle. The Spaniards' horses and superior weapons made up for their small numbers, and a shipwrecked Spaniard and an Indian noblewoman—speaking Spanish, Mayan, and Náhuatl between them—were key to the Spanish success.

Begin the drive in **Quiahuiztlán** (pronounced qwea-wheat-ZLAN) **❶**, 43 miles (70 km) north of Veracruz. Strategically placed atop Cerro de Bernal and terraced for defensive purposes, it was nonetheless successfully invaded by the Toltecs and then the Aztecs. Today, much of the ruined city ($) remains unexcavated. Most impressive for visitors are several dozen tombs, built in the style of miniature Aztec temples, which have yielded ceramic vessels decorated with geometric and animal motifs. On a clear day, you can see the cove where the Spanish ships anchored.

Head about 3 miles (5 km) down to the coast to visit the site, today a tiny fishing village of fewer than 200 people. Although there are no vestiges, this is where Cortés established the first garrison at **Villa Rica de la Vera Cruz** (Rich City of the True Cross). There's a broad beach of fine, dark sand and a couple of rustic huts, where cold beer, coconuts, juice, and simple fish dishes are sold.

Drive south along Highway 180 about 21 miles (34 km) to the ruins of **Cempoala ❷**. This was a prosperous city that amazed the Spaniards with its gleaming plaster palaces surrounded by gardens and orchards. Anxious to shrug off the yoke of their Aztec overlords, this Totonac kingdom allied with the Spaniards, providing crucial aid to Cortés. An important urban center surrounded by waterways and supported by agricultural fields, Cempoala today has temples to the gods of rain, the sun, and the moon.

NOT TO BE MISSED:

Quiahuiztlán • Cempoala
• Veracruz • Boca del Río

Spanish Stronghold

Continue south on Highway 180 for 13 miles (21 km) to **La Antigua ❸**. Here the Spaniards built shelters and housed a contingency of soldiers while others marched inland to Tenochtitlán. During the early years of the Conquest, this was the main entry and exit port for Spanish trade. Through most of the 1500s, treasures reaped by the Spanish from the Americas, as well as goods from Asia via Manila in the Philippines, passed along these streets to ships awaiting winds for Havana, Cuba, and then Cádiz in Spain. When Veracruz was moved south to its present location around 1600, this city became La Antigua Veracruz (meaning "the former Veracruz"), and later simply La Antigua.

Visit **La Ermita del Rosario** (*Av. Independencia s/n*), Mexico's first Catholic chapel, and the **Casa de Cortés,** the ruined Spanish headquarters, draped in vines and fig trees. Note that the building is made of river stones, brain coral, and bricks that were carried from Spain as ships' ballast. Down the street, the **Templo del Buen Viaje** (Church of the Good Trip) provided a prayer stop en route to the port of Veracruz, about a day's journey away.

Cruising on to Veracruz

Keep south on the coast highway to **Veracruz.** Enjoy the vibrancy and jumble of this 400-year-old city (see pp. 240–241). Then motor down a few miles to **Boca del Río ❹**, which was another stop along the conquerors' route. Thirty years ago it was just a simple fishing village at the mouth of the Río Jamapa; today it has business-oriented hotels and several museums. On weekends, Veracruz families spend long lunches at the lively riverside restaurants, serenaded by local musicians. (The restaurants are open, although less lively, throughout the week.)

⚠ See also area map p. 234
➤ Quiahuiztlán
🕐 50 miles (80 km)
↔ A full day (plus time in Veracruz)
➤ Boca del Río

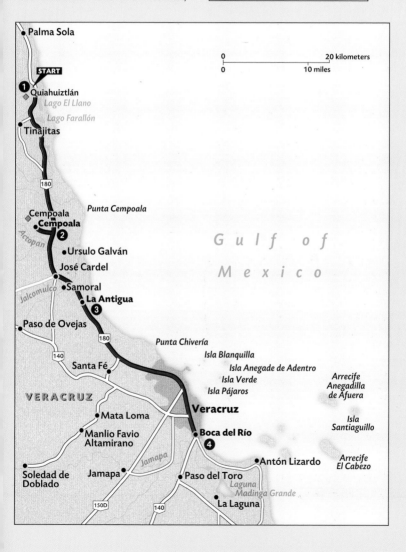

Córdoba & Environs

Founded to protect colonial trade caravans, Córdoba and Orizaba lie in the foothills of the Sierra Madre Oriental, separated by the luxuriant Río Metlac ravine and with miles of hiking trails. From here, the intrepid can assault Mexico's highest peak, Pico de Orizaba, as well as the extensive caves and caverns of the Sierra de Zongolica.

Córdoba
🅼 234 B2
Visitor Information
✉ Palacio Municipal
☎ 271/717-1700 ext. 1778

Orizaba
🅼 234 B2
Visitor Information
✉ Av. Colón Poniente 230
☎ 272/726-2222

For centuries Córdoba thrived on wealth from vast sugarcane plantations maintained by legions of black slaves. Today the city is relatively large and modern. Historic buildings surround pretty **Parque 21 de Mayo,** where the **Iglesia de la Inmaculada Concepción** has a priceless gold altarpiece.

The city's most popular attraction is the **Portal de Zevallos,** a lovely arcade where people meet over locally grown coffee or refreshing mint juleps. A few miles west of town, **Fortín de las Flores,** famous for its greenhouses and private gardens, is best visited during the **Fiestas de Mayo.** The area between Córdoba and Xalapa offers many opportunities for adventure tourism, including the country's best rivers for whitewater rafting (see p. 251).

Small, industrial **Orizaba** is nonetheless a pleasant city, retaining some colonial and neoclassical architecture. Facing the main square is the old town hall, an art nouveau iron building which served as the Belgian pavilion at the 1889 World Exhibition in Paris. It was purchased from Belgium, shipped across the seas and reassembled here in 1894. The "new" **Palacio Municipal** *(Av. Colón Poniente 230),* an attractive neo-Gothic building, has a large mural by José Clemente Orozco.

Housed in a lovely colonial structure, the **Museo de Arte del Estado** *(Av. Oriente 4 bet. Calle Sur 23 & Calle Sur 25, tel 272/724-3200, closed Mon., $)* shows paintings and graphic art.

Dominating all other peaks in Mexico is dormant **Pico de Orizaba,** which rises to 18,490 feet (5,636 m). Its Náhuatl name, Citlaltépetl, means "star mountain." Amateurs can hike the trails along the lower slopes, but only experienced hikers should attempt the summit. ∎

The Green Angels

Since the 1970s, the Angeles Verdes (Green Angels) have provided roadside service to distressed travelers on federal and toll highways. They typically work from 8 a.m. to 8 p.m. and patrol major highways twice daily. On major holidays they are available around the clock. If you're stranded, call 078.

Drivers carry gasoline and motor oil, as well as spare tires and parts for minor repairs; most speak English. They can administer first aid and also carry maps and brochures of the region. There's no charge for these services, but motorists must pay for gasoline, oil, and parts. Tip the driver as you see fit.

Tlacotalpan

On the banks of the wide Río Papaloapan is Tlacotalpan, named a World Heritage site for its beautiful location and well-maintained pre-revolution buildings. During the colonial period, this important port and shipyard received schooners and side-wheel steamships that imported European goods and exported tobacco, exotic woods, cotton, and sugarcane.

Tlacotalpan's colonnades provide shade from the tropical heat.

The town declined in importance with the completion of competing railroad lines and the advent of the revolution. However, it maintains an air of seductiveness lost in more modern cities. Lining the streets are imposing mansions with ancient red-tile roofs, their Arabesque-style portals brightly painted in kelly green and cobalt blue, coral, and sunshine yellow, with accents in contrasting colors. Open doorways offer a glimpse of cool patios and ornate front rooms, while the colonnades provide welcome shade.

Visit the **plaza principal,** with its lacy, Mudejar-style bandstand, and the parish church, the **Parroquia de San Cristóbal,** which has beautiful altarpieces of carved wood. The **Museo Jarocho Salvador Ferrando** *(Manuel M. Alegre 6, closed Mon., $)* exhibits the paintings of the local artist, as well as furnishings and artifacts from the 19th century.

Tlacotalpan vigorously celebrates its patron saint, the **Virgen de la Candelaria,** from January 31 to February 9. The first three days see musical parades on horseback and **El Encuentro de Jaraneros** (Meeting of the Revelers), when young and old perform the physically challenging regional dance, the *jarana,* accompanied by harp and guitar. On February 1 there is bull-running and more dancing, while on the saint's feast day, February 2, her icon is serenaded by mariachis during a festive river parade of boats. ∎

Tlacotalpan

▲ 234 C2

Visitor Information

✉ Palacio Municipal, Plaza Zaragoza

☎ 288/884-2050

Los Tuxtlas & Catemaco

Rising abruptly from sea level to about 5,000 feet (1,500 m), Los Tuxtlas mountain range lies in an area of great natural beauty and contains a range of ecosystems, including the continent's northernmost tropical rain forest. However, expanding cattle ranches and farms have dramatically reduced the forests. Today, the region's most visitor-oriented town is Catemaco, in a forested lakeshore setting.

Olmec Laguna de los Cerros, at the edge of the Tuxtlas Mountains

Los Tuxtlas

🅰 234 C2

www.tuxtlas.com

Los Tuxtlas

Santiago Tuxtla, located 140 miles (225 km) south of Veracruz, is a commercial hub for the area. While not particularly geared to tourists, this pleasant, traditional foothill town has some impressive and photogenic old mansions. Lively equestrian events, some dating back to medieval Spain, are held during July festivities honoring the city's patron saint, the Apostle James.

In the main square, **Parque Juárez,** is the **Cabeza de Cobata,** the largest of the colossal Olmec heads discovered so far and the only one with its eyes closed. The **Museo Regional Tuxteco** (*Parque Juárez, tel 294/947-0196, $*) exhibits other Olmec artifacts, including some from the Tres Zapotes site, 8 miles (13 km) away. One of Mesoamerica's oldest cities, Tres Zapotes was where the first giant Olmec stone head was discovered, in a farmer's field, in 1860.

San Andrés Tuxtla, 9 miles (14.5 km) east, took Santiago's place as regional capital in the 19th century. Today it is primarily known as a cigarmaking center with the colorful celebration, **Feria de la Primavera,** held in May.

About 7.5 miles (12 km) outside town off the road to Catemaco is **Salto de Eyipantla,** a wide, roaring waterfall. Little kids will guard your car while their older brothers lead you down the sometimes slippery slope to a viewing area and a jumble of open-air kitchens.

Just a mile or two outside town, **Laguna Encantada,** on the edge of **Los Tuxtlas Biosphere Reserve,** is suitable for birding and swimming and has a humble restaurant. Folks there can guide you to more remote **Poza de la Reina,** an idyllic natural pool, and **Cola del Caballo,** a waterfall resembling a horse's tail. Both are located in the hills above the northeast shore of **Laguna de Catemaco.**

Catemaco

About 7 miles (11 km) east of San Andrés, Catemaco hugs the west shore of Mexico's third largest natural lake. The languid town has quite a reputation among Mexicans and foreign visitors for its large number of *brujos* (witches) and *curanderos* (healers). People throughout Mexico—including the middle and upper classes—consult purveyors of the magic arts to cure ills from lumbago to broken hearts and *mal de ojo,* the evil eye. Catemaco's notoriety in a

country full of such practitioners is due in part to its annual witches' convention, to which the public is not invited.

Perhaps its reputation as the land of shamans attracted movie moguls to film *Medicine Man* (1992) here. Some location work was done at **Proyecto Ecológico Nanciyaga** (*tel 294/943-0199, www.nanciyaga.com, $*), a privately owned, 100-acre (40 ha) nature preserve on the north shore. You can visit it as part of a short lake tour arranged in Catemaco, but it's also fun to rent one of the little wooden cabins and spend the night. *Temazcal* sweat-lodge ceremonies can be arranged in advance. Visitors can take a mud

INSIDER TIP:

Los Tuxtlas Biosphere Reserve in Veracruz is ignored by most tourists. Hire a ride from Catemaco to Montepio to explore the rain forest or enjoy the isolated beaches.

—KATHERINE AMATO
National Geographic field researcher

bath and rinse off in a crystalline spring or rent a kayak or rowboat for cruising the lake. Adjacent to Nanciyaga, La Jungla campground is also set in the tropical jungle. These and other natural areas surrounding the lake hide a large number of resident and migratory bird species. ∎

San Andrés Tuxtla
△ 234 C2
Visitor Information
✉ Palacio Municipal, Madero 1 Altos
☎ 294/947-9300 ext. 606

Los Tuxtlas Biosphere Reserve
www.tuxtlas.com/ biosfera

Catemaco
△ 234 C2/D2
Visitor Information
✉ Palacio Municipal, Av. Carranza
☎ 294/943-0016
www.catemaco.info

Villahermosa

With its wilting tropical heat deflected off a cityscape of modern cement, glass, and concrete structures, there's physically not much to recommend Villahermosa, Tabasco's capital. However, those who spend a day or two here usually develop an odd affection for this business-oriented city filled with seafood restaurants, several excellent anthropology museums, and a pedestrian-only zone with a good mix of hotels, cafés, and small museums.

Basalt stone heads are now considered monumental portrait-sculptures of Olmec leaders.

Founded during Cortés's 1519 exploration, the regional capital was later relocated to its present, more easily defended, site and renamed Villahermosa. The city evolved as a distribution center for rubber, cacao, dyewood, coffee, and bananas. Today, Villahermosa sprawls along both banks of the wide, navigable Río Grijalva, and unlike many other Mexican cities, few of the most visited sites are clustered around the main square. Taxis are the easiest way to negotiate the city.

Just a block away from the river, **Plaza de Armas** *(bet. Calles Guerrero & Independencia*

at Martínez Escobar), the city's pleasant if unexciting main plaza, is surrounded by the white neoclassical **Palacio de Gobierno** and the odd-looking **Templo de la Concepción**, a mid-20th-century church with Gothic-style elements.

Behind the state government building, north of the main plaza, lies a pedestrian-friendly zone called the **Zona Luz**, a brick-paved area of art galleries, shops, cafés, and ice-cream stands created in the 1970s. The **Museo de Historia de Tabasco** *(Juárez at 27 de Febrero, tel 993/312-6344, closed Mon.)*, a museum of the state's history within the Casa de Azulejos, is in an early 20th-century building featuring a tiled facade and eclectic architectural elements.

Southwest of the historic center you will find **CICOM,** a large complex with a popular restaurant, museum, public library, and important theater. The latter, modern **Teatro Esperanza Iris,** was inaugurated in 1981 and named for a well-known Villahermosa singer and actress. The theater hosts the National Ballet as well as concerts, folkloric shows, and other performances.

The important **Museo Regional de Antropología Carlos Pellicer Cámara** (*Carlos Pellicer 511, tel 993/312-6344, closed Mon., $$*) is within the same complex. The anthropology museum gives great attention to the Olmec civilization, which thrived in the Middle Preclassic period (approximately 1200–400 B.C.). On the first floor are galleries for temporary exhibitions and a room for the monumental

pieces of Maya and Olmec origin. The second floor contains exclusively Olmec and Maya displays, two important cultures that shared a common border around the Tabasco lowlands. Exhibits from these cultures include ceramic and carved stone pieces, such as small jade figurines of mythical were-jaguars—half-human, half-jaguar babies with cleft heads.

The museum tour is best started on the third floor, where maps show the distribution and evolution of civilization throughout Mesoamerica. There are Preclassic pieces from the central plateau and funerary masks, jewelry, and ceramics from Classic-era Teotihuacán. Totonac and Huastec cultures are represented with figurines, "smiling face" figures, and wheeled toys. Typical of Classic Veracruz civilization are the axes, yokes, and *palmas,* ritual artifacts inscribed with bas-reliefs that are related to the ball game.

Villahermosa
235 E2
Visitor Information
Paseo Tabasco 1504
993/310-9700
www.visitetabasco.com

EXPERIENCE: Sampling the Source of Chocolate

Before the Spanish brought sugar by way of their Caribbean possessions, indigenous Mesoamericans drank a hot, frothy drink of chocolate and chili. The base of this bitter but exhilarating drink was cacao, grown in abundance in tropical Tabasco.

The Spanish promptly established cacao plantations, converting the former growers and merchants to slaves. Tabasco still produces the bulk of the nation's crop. Some of the old haciendas have been restored, with modern factories cranking out chocolate and inviting guests to tour. Mainly these are near Comalcalco, 35 miles (56 km)

from Villahermosa; make reservations in advance.

Fábrica CACEP (*tel 933/337-6176, www.cacep. com*) offers tours ($$) of its Hacienda José María, outside Comalcalco. See the orchards and the old and modern chocolate-making processes; visit the shop and 1910 house. For a reasonable price (*about U.S.$65 for two adjoining rooms*), spend

the night at the hacienda. Nineteenth-century **Hacienda La Chonita** (*tel 933/312-0085, www.haci endalachonita.com*), on a lake south of Comalcalco, has kayaks, bikes, and a temascal steam hut as well as tours. In downtown Comalcalco, **Hacienda La Luz** (*Calle Leandro Rovirosa Wade s/n, tel 993/139-5692*) also offers tours and a museum.

On the west side of town, the **Tabasco 2000** complex has a cultural center, shopping mall, convention center, and planetarium. Also within this vast complex are the City Hall, or Palacio Municipal, and the luxurious Camino Real Hotel. The tourist information center is located nearby.

At the south end of **Laguna de las Ilusiones** is the **Parque Museo La Venta** *(Av. Ruíz Cortines at Laguna de las Ilusiones, tel 993/314-1652, closed Mon., $$)*, where more than 30 large Olmec sculptures sit amid tropical foliage.

INSIDER TIP:

In the state of Tabasco, it's well worth your while to take a tour of one of the chocolate-making factories. You'll learn the whole process from tree to wrapper.

—ERIC RAMIREZ BRAVO
National Geographic field researcher

Located on a 2-square-mile (5 sq km) island within a coastal swamp near the Río Tonalá, **La Venta,** 43 miles (70 km) to the west, rose in importance with the decline of the San Lorenzo settlement, where more colossal heads have been found than anywhere else. San Lorenzo was violently overthrown, and its monuments defaced, around 1200 B.C., after which La Venta apparently reigned as the center of Olmec influence. Now thought to have been a residential as well as ceremonial city,

La Venta produced a cone-shape clay pyramid 110 feet (33 m) tall, the largest of its period in Mexico. Found at the site were a group of 16 small jade figures and an unusual mosaic of serpentine blocks and ground and colored clays that formed a geometric jaguar mask—now on display at **La Venta Museum.** When petroleum was first exploited at La Venta, many of these priceless Olmec treasures were transferred to this specially designed museum in Villahermosa. (Other artifacts can be found in the Xalapa and Mexico City anthropology museums.)

Hire an English-speaking guide, or take a self-guided tour (exhibits are labeled in English and Spanish). There's also a small zoo *(closed Mon.),* with spider monkeys, reptiles, and some of the region's larger mammals. A winding path continues past Olmec "altars" (now thought to be thrones), stelae, and jaguar-boys. The huge basalt heads with characteristic full lips and wide noses are considered monumental portrait-sculptures of Olmec leaders.

Ten miles (16 km) east of Villahermosa at Dos Montes is **Yumká** *(Ranchería Las Barrancas s/n, tel 993/356-0115, www.yumka. org, $$),* a 250-acre (100 ha) park. During one-hour guided tours, visitors walk about half a mile (1 km) through a section of tropical rain forest and across a hanging bridge, and then take a half-hour tram ride through the savanna, ending at a children's playground, restaurant, and gift shop. There is a small additional charge for a boat trip through the lagoon. ■

EXPERIENCE: Adventure Tourism

For those seeking an active holiday, Mexico does not disappoint. There are plenty of adventure sports opportunities on offer in out-of-the-way places throughout the country.

With its abundant rainfall and more than 40 rivers, Veracruz is Mexico's premier rafting destination. One of the most thrilling excursions is a kayak or raft descent of Río Pescados, between Xalapa and Veracruz. Winding through deep canyons dressed in semitropical vegetation, the river encompasses 35 Class III and IV rapids. The Río Antigua offers Class III and IV rapids during the wet season only, roughly July to November. And a few hours north of Xalapa, the Río Filobobos (Class II and III) provides access to the ruins of El Cuajilote and Vega de la Pena (A.D. 200–900), recently discovered in the lush jungle.

For rock climbing, rappelling, spelunking, as well as rafting, visit the La Huasteca region. Comprising parts of San Luis Potosí, Hidalgo, Tamaulipas, and Veracruz states, this is a land laced with waterfalls that form grottos and crystalline turquoise pools edged in lacy ferns. Adventure outfitters such as **Eccosports** *(tel 55/5644-3775 in Mexico City, or tel 279/832-3559 in Jalcomucho, Veracruz, http:// eccosports.com.mx)* offer trips in the area.

Around Monterrey in the northeast are the Matacanes and Hidrofóbia Rivers, each affording opportunities for rappelling, hiking, scrambling, and exploring underground rivers and caves. The **American Canyoneering Association** *(www. canyoneering.net)* provides information for those who wish to venture here.

Between Monterrey and Saltillo in Cumbres de Monterrey National Park, the boxy limestone canyons of Cañón de la Huasteca draw the attention of rock climbers. Characterizing the arid, rugged terrain are such sheer cliffs as the 1,000-foot-high (300 m) Torre Diablos and 1,640-foot (500 m) Pico de Independencia.

Northwest of Mexico City, in Querétaro, rock climbers can scale one of largest monoliths in the Americas, Peña de Bernal. At 8,284 feet (2,525 m) above sea level, the summit perches atop a 157-foot-high (48 m) *arête*.

Running across the country south of Mexico City are some of the country's most notable mountains, attracting adventurous climbers. The impressive peaks include Pico de Orizaba, the country's highest at 18,490 feet (5,636 m). Iztaccíhuatl provides a variety of climbs along many routes, while La Malinche, at 14,636 feet (4,461 m), is a warm-up ascent for first-timers. (See also "Climbing the Volcanoes," p. 220.)

If you are interested in adventure tourism, contact the not-for-profit **Mexican Association of Adventure Tourism and Ecotourism** (AMTAVE, www.amtave. org). Their website is a good source for information on activities and tour operators. In addition, **Río y Montaña** *(Guillermo González Camarena 500 PB, Santa Fé, Mexico City, tel 55/5292-5032, www .rioymontana.com)* leads white-water trips, biking, trekking, and climbing adventures around the country.

Sea kayakers enjoy calm waters on the Sea of Cortez.

More Places to Visit on the Central Gulf Coast

Comalcalco

The ruined city of Comalcalco (meaning "place of baked clay, or bricks") lies about 35 miles (56 km) northwest of Villahermosa. Due to a lack of suitable local stone, builders made their temples and pyramids of oven-baked bricks of sand, crushed shells, and clay. Occupied since the first century A.D., this Chontal Maya city (the westernmost of any known Maya site) saw the height of its civilization in the Late Classic period, as did Palenque (see pp. 290–293) and Yaxchilán (see pp. 302–303). Almost two dozen of its nearly 300 structures have been restored, including a ball court, palaces, and temples.

🅰 235 E2 💲 $

Costa Esmeralda

This 13-mile (21 km) stretch of coastline between **Nautla** and **Tecolutla** consists of flat, often lonely sand beaches, bathed by the Gulf's murky waters. The beaches are lined with palms and interspersed with estuaries. Tecolutla is more geared to visitors, with moderately priced hotels and restaurants serving fresh sea bass, oysters, and *huachinango* (red snapper).

🅰 234 B3/B4

Wild Tabasco

To explore a less touristy corner of Mexico, head for rural Tabasco. Due south of Villahermosa (*en route to Tuxtla Gutiérrez, Chiapas via Hwy. 195),* **Teapa** is a good base for exploration. The municipal seat has a picturesque square and several 18th-century churches. A few miles east of Teapa, cave enthusiasts marvel at the eight roomy caverns of **Grutas de Coconá,** while serious spelunkers with gear crawl through **La Cueva de las Canicas,** named for its marble-like calcite deposits.

A bit farther east, the municipality of **Tacotalpa** offers several ecological reserves.

Swim in the natural pool formed by **Agua Blanca** waterfall, in the park of the same name, or explore lighted caves and practice spelunking or rappelling. The reforested, 67-acre (27 ha) **Kolem-Jaá ecopark** *(tel 993/314-3192, www.kolemjaa.com.mx)* has tent camping, cabins, self-guided trails, horseback riding, mountain biking, and other activities, with equipment provided. Nearby **Tapijulapa** is a popular weekend escape for Villahermosans who enjoy its riverfront location and humble but picturesque houses. On the hill above town, visit the 17th-century chapel to the Apostle James.

East of Villahermosa, towards Palenque, the **Río Usamacinto** and its tributaries form canyons and waterfalls in the municipality of Tenosique. Near the town of **Santo Tomás** are the lovely green sinkholes (cenotes) **Ya Ax Ha** and **Aktun Ha.** The county seat, **Tenosique** is the best base for organizing fishing, rafting, rappelling, and caving expeditions, but don't expect your hosts to speak fluent English.

🅰 235 E2

Tuxpan

Tuxpan, a port city 7 miles (11 km) in from the sea on the river of the same name, has sandy beaches and luxuriant river scenery. Archaeological finds show this site to have been continuously occupied between the Preclassic and Postclassic periods (see pp. 23–26). Locally excavated artifacts preserved in the **Museo de Arqueología** *(tel 783/834-6180, closed Sun.)* include pieces found at the ancient Huastec city of Tabuco, across the river. Known for their outgoing personalities, the townspeople celebrate spring carnival in May, and, in preparation for the feast day of the patron saint, the Virgin of the Assumption (August 15), a country fair.

🅰 234 B4 ✉ Av. Juárez 20 ☎ 783/835-2647 ext. 125

From Tehuantepec to Tuxtepec, a region characterized by
a distinctly indigenous and idiosyncratic flavor

Oaxaca

Alebrijes are carved and painted
wooden creatures.

Oaxaca

The state of Oaxaca forms the elbow of a geographic arm extending south and east to embrace the indigenous heart of Mexico. Dozens of fractured ranges lead to isolated high valleys draped with mist, where tiny hamlets are accessible only on foot or by burro. Despite a deep devotion to the Virgin, many Oaxaqueños observe pre-Christian rituals and believe in the existence of *nahuales,* shape-shifting wizards.

Oaxaca counts 570 municipalities, more than any other state. Physical isolation contributes to traditionalism; each village does things its own way. Trique women in mountain villages weave cherry-colored *huipiles* (loose, calf-length dresses) with bright bands of color; near the border with Guerrero, Amuzgo women create brocaded designs for their fine cotton huipiles. During *las velas,* traditional parties in the Isthmus of Tehuantepec, Zapotec women proudly don fancy stiff lace headdresses and petticoats with flowing skirts, and short, brightly embroidered velveteen huipiles.

Of the state's 15 major ethnic groups, the Zapotec and Mixtec are the largest, occupying both coastal and mountain regions. Their ancestors built the large ceremonial centers whose ruins dot the central valleys today. Grandest of all, Monte Albán was a contemporary of Teotihuacán, in central Mexico, reaching its peak of civilization during the Classic period. Its stone-lined ball courts and well-proportioned pyramids overlook Oaxaca,

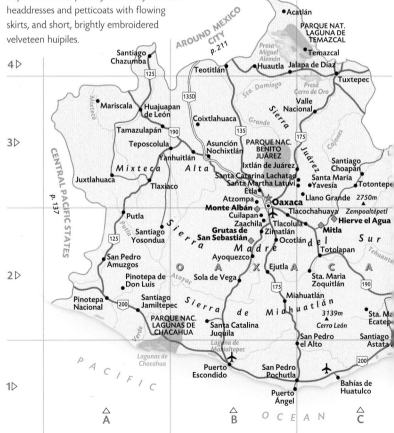

the capital city, which stretches out in the valley below.

The city of Oaxaca is a delightful base for exploring the region. People crowd the *zócalo,* or main plaza, sipping coffee in the outdoor cafés that surround the bandstand where lively marimba bands play. The historic center is peppered with carefully restored architectural treasures, including the sumptuous Santo Domingo church and former monastery, the latter home to Oaxaca's wonderful regional museum. Excursions to magnificent churches and monasteries surrounding the city reveal the extraordinary wealth and aesthetic sensibilities of the Dominican Order in the 16th and 17th centuries.

Oaxaca's 320-mile (515 km) Pacific coast is another important tourist destination. Hotels are popping up along the beautiful bays of

Chilies are a staple food and a source of Vitamin C.

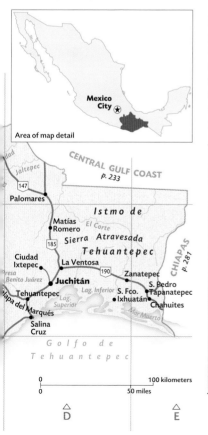

Area of map detail

Huatulco, one of the smallest of Mexico's planned seaside resorts. Puerto Escondido, a world-famous surf spot, has natural beauty and casual restaurants and hotels. Outside the tourist destinations, fishing villages and inland towns lure adventurous travelers with annual religious festivals and unusual folk art, including masks, pottery, and textiles. ∎

NOT TO BE MISSED:

Oaxaca

It's said that if you sample *chapulines,* a highly seasoned local delicacy, you're sure to return to Oaxaca. But more of a draw (and less of an acquired taste) than its famous fried grasshoppers is the colonial heart and multiethnic soul of the capital city itself. Baroque churches of locally mined stone glow in the semitropical sunshine; at an elevation of 5,085 feet (1,550 m), Oaxaca enjoys warm weather most of the year, rarely getting too hot or cold.

The café patios along the *zócalo* are a great start to the night.

The towns and villages surrounding the capital produce an astonishing variety of quality folk art. The Zapotec towns of **Teotitlán del Valle** (see p. 266) and less famous **Santa Ana del Valle** have been making hand-loomed wool *tapetes* (rugs) for centuries. Other crafts—including smoky black pottery from San Bartolo Coyotepec and carved wood figures from Arrazola—are more recent innovations. These and many more fine handicrafts are sold in upscale shops on and around **Calle Alcalá,** a pedestrian-only street north of the *zócalo.*

If you enjoy bartering and have the time, check the fixed prices in the shops first, then head to **Abastos** or **Benito Juárez markets,** where you'll find a lesser selection of handicrafts (but a big "slice of life") along with everything from vice grips to love potions that double as floor polish. Head into the surrounding countryside, to the towns where the items are produced, for some serious bargains and a glimpse of rural life.

While folk art is an important element of Oaxacan culture, the city also has an impressive fine arts scene and lots of cultural activities to keep visitors and residents entertained, including theater at several venues downtown for bargain prices, and live music in bistros as well as in more formal venues like the **Casa de la Cultura** *(González Ortega 403). (See www. oaxacacalendar.com for current listings.)* The city also hosts an annual international film festival, and free art films are shown most nights at **Cinema El Pochote** *(Av. García Vigil 817, tel 951/514-1194, www.elpochote. blogspot.com).*

Excellent museums also demonstrate the city's commitment to arts and culture. The **Museo de Arte Prehispánico Rufino Tamayo** *(Av. Morelos 503, tel 951/516-4750, closed Sun. after 3 p.m., Tues., & 2–4 p.m., $)* displays the private collection of Oaxacan abstract painter, muralist, and sculptor Rufino Tamayo (1899–1991), donated to the state in 1975. About 2,000 pieces representative of pre-Cortesian Mexico are well displayed in a restored colonial home in the heart of downtown. The **Museo de Arte Contemporáneo de Oaxaca,** or **MACO** *(Alcalá 202, tel 951/514-2818, www.museomaco.com, closed Tues., $),* housed in an even more imposing colonial residence, offers interesting temporary exhibits in a variety of media.

Several more museums have opened in the last few years, including the wonderful **Museo del Palacio** *(S side of zócalo, tel 951/501-1662, closed Mon.),* with rotating cultural exhibits in the lovely former municipal palace. Just three blocks away, **Museo de los Pintores** *(Av. Independencia 607 at García Vigil, tel 951/516-5645, closed Mon., $)* shows contemporary works of art.

If the city's 27 historic churches are considered works of art, one of the most cherished is the **Basílica de Nuestra Señora de la Soledad** *(Av. Independencia 107 at Galeana, tel 951/516-7566),* built in the late 17th century to honor Oaxaca's patron saint, Our Lady of Solitude. Oaxacans petition the Virgin for favors, making special pilgrimages culminating on December 18, her feast day. Visit the **church's museum** to see gifts left by devotees—from plastic flowers and severed braids to naive ex-votos (pictorial expressions of thanks) painted on wood or tin. The basilica is on the site of a garrison maintained by the Aztec, who controlled the region in the 15th century. ∎

Oaxaca

🗺 254 B3

Visitor Information

✉ Av. Juarez 703

☎ 951/502-1200

www.aoaxaca.com

EXPERIENCE: Learning on Foot

Town life in Mexico is often best seen by walking around. In some places, guides can help you to the right streets, all the while spinning out local history. In Puerto Escondido, **Oaxaca**, Gina Machorro leads two-hour walking tours *(tel 954/582-0276, $$$$$)*, discoursing on the different peoples and foods, and stopping at an herb shops and chocolate factory.

San Miguel de Allende's tourism department leads historical walking tours *($$$)* Monday, Wednesday, and Friday mornings departing from La Parroquia on the main plaza at 10 a.m. (A Sunday home & garden bus tour *($$$$)* leaves from the public library at Insurgents 25.)

Mérida's English Library, in Yucatán state, has a home-and-garden walking tour *($$$$$)* Wednesdays at 9:45 a.m. Free historical tours depart Monday through Saturday at 9:30 a.m. from the municipal palace *(Calle 62 between 61 & 63).*

A Walk Around Historic Oaxaca

Oaxaca has many interesting and historic sites radiating from its lovely main plaza, a tranquil, traffic-free place marking the end of this walking tour. On pedestrian-only Calle Alcalá, shops and restaurants occupy crayon-box colored, two-story buildings erected soon after the city was founded by the Spanish in the 16th century.

Locals enjoy Calle Alcalá, a pedestrian-only stretch in Oaxaca City.

Begin at the **Arcos de Xochimilco ❶**, south of Calzada Héroes de Chapultepec on García Vigil. The arches of this 18th-century stone aqueduct shrink as the 985-foot (300 m) structure stretches south toward downtown. Individual arches now provide access to modest apartment dwellings.

Walk several blocks south along García Vigil to **Iglesia del Carmen Alto ❷**. The church hosts a lively fair for the feast day of the Virgin of Carmen (July 16), which initiates the **Guelaguetza,** an annual festival of dance and music with roots in pre-Hispanic tradition. Across the street is the **Museo Casa de Benito Juárez ❸** *(García Vigil 609, tel 951/516-1860, closed Mon., $),* the historic house where Oaxaca's revered statesman lived as a youth in the early 19th century.

Return across the street and down the steps of Plazuela del Carmen to Oaxaca's **Calle**

NOT TO BE MISSED:

Templo y Ex-Convento de Santo Domingo • Museo de las Culturas de Oaxaca • Mercado Benito Juárez • catedral • zócalo

Alcalá and the **Templo y Ex-Convento de Santo Domingo ❹**, home to the **Museo de las Culturas de Oaxaca** *(Calle Alcalá at Calle Constitución, tel 951/516-9741, closed Mon.).* Walk east along Calle Constitución to Calle Reforma. Half a block north on Reforma, stop in at the stamp museum, **Museo de Filatelia de Oaxaca** *(Calle Reforma 504, tel 951/516-8028, www. mufi.org.mx, closed Mon.).*

Return south along Calle Constitución and go left on Cinco de Mayo one and a half blocks

INSIDER TIP:

The food in Oaxaca is amazing. Be sure to try Oaxacan cheese, sausage, chocolate, and, of course, grasshoppers. Also, sip a shot of mescal, and eat the worm if you dare.

—KATHERINE AMATO
National Geographic field researcher

to the **Ex-Convento de Santa Catalina** (now a hotel), home to the nuns of the Immaculate Conception until the Reform Laws of 1859. Continue several blocks to admire the belle époque **Teatro Macedonio Alcalá,** a theater and dance venue on the corner of Cinco de Mayo and Avenida Independencia.

Continue south; the street's name changes from Cinco de Mayo to Armenta y López. Turn right on Colón. Two blocks west (Colón becomes Las Casas), enter the **Mercado Benito Juárez** ❺, established in 1892. Here find locally made blocks of chocolate (for delicious, cinnamon-laced hot cocoa), string cheese, and piles of fresh vegetables and exotic fruits as well as some clothing and handicrafts. Walk through diagonally and come out the southwest side.

Cross Aldama to the **Iglesia San Juan de Díos** ❻ (Aldama at 20 de Noviembre). Although unimpressive, Oaxaca's first church is dear to its people. The original adobe-and-thatch temple was christened in 1526; the present structure replaced it in the mid-17th century.

A few steps to the south, the next doorway leads to the **Mercado 20 de Noviembre,** originally a hospital for the adjoining convent. Today it's jammed with informal eateries serving chicken soup and beef stew. Women sell sweet and savory breads from bins and large wicker baskets. This is also the place to buy mescal and hot, cinnamony cocoa.

Exit the market and walk north along Miguel Cabrera. Continue to the attractive main plaza, the *zócalo*. At the back of the neoclassical **Ex-Palacio de Gobierno** ❼, on the south

side of the square, a colorful, two-story mural summarizes Oaxaca history. Cross the square to the 16th-century **catedral** ❽, on the adjoining plaza, **La Alameda,** dedicated to the Assumption of the Virgin Mary.

The *zócalo* is the finest place in the city to rest and refresh yourself. An unannounced remodel in 2005 enraged citizens. However, it still looks much the same, and the many nonstop cafés under the plaza's shady porticos are as popular as ever.

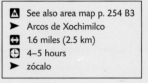

- ⚠ See also area map p. 254 B3
- ► Arcos de Xochimilco
- 🔁 1.6 miles (2.5 km)
- ⏱ 4–5 hours
- ► zócalo

Oaxaca's Dominican Monasteries

The spiritual conquest of New Spain was launched after the Spanish army under Hernán Cortés literally flattened Tenochtitlán (the site of present-day Mexico City). Franciscan friars were the first ecclesiastics to arrive, establishing themselves throughout populous central Mexico. A few years later, the Dominicans headed south of Mexico City.

Oaxaca's Santo Domingo church

Frequently criticized for the exorbitant sums spent on their temples, the zealous Dominicans imported skilled designers from Europe. Working with equally talented local craftsmen, priest-architects blended renaissance motifs with Gothic and Mudejar elements of the Spanish plateresque school. Even the thick buttressed walls and stocky towers—intended to help withstand the area's earthquakes—don't detract from the rich embellishment and the high quality of locally quarried stone. The Dominican preoccupation with aesthetics is evident in the unique architectural design, elaborate altarpieces, and fine paintings in a chain of monasteries stretching from Puebla to Guatemala, many of them in Oaxaca state.

Churches were vandalized after the Reform Laws of 1859 expelled the religious orders. The **Iglesia y Ex-Convento de Santo Domingo,** one of the first and most intoxicating of

INSIDER TIP:

Santo Domingo is overwhelming in its baroque magnificence. A sense of power and wealth exudes from every inch.

— OLIVER SACKS

Neurologist, author, and National Geographic writer

Oaxaca's church-monasteries, suffered considerable damage during a stint as an army barracks. Today it has been scrupulously refurbished at great expense. The church's narrow *retablo* facade, elaborately carved in four tiers and flanked by two majestic bell towers, is in transitional Renaissance style, with traces of baroque. Inside, bright white stucco honeycombed in gold and polychrome relief extends to vaults, domes, and niches. In fact, every inch of the dazzling interior is covered in high-spirited, Puebla-style decoration. The genealogy of the order's founder, Santo Domingo de Guzmán (ca

1170–1221), spreads seductively if naively in a grapevine motif across the underchoir at the temple's entrance. On the right side of the church, the abundance of scrolls, angels, and arabesques decorating the **Capilla del Rosario** (Rosary Chapel) nearly drowns the saints and apostles portrayed.

The two-story, white limestone cloister of the adjoining monastery is home to the **Museo de las Culturas de Oaxaca** *(Alcalá at Constitución, tel 951/516-9741, closed Mon., $$).* The first floor houses temporary exhibits, an excellent book shop, and the **Biblioteca Francisco de Burgos,** a library with more than 20,000 historical tomes. Walk up the double baroque staircase to the second floor, its doorways and ceiling richly decorated in the lavish Puebla style. Ten former monastic cells now exhibit artifacts representative of regional culture from the prehistoric to post-Revolutionary times; an additional 14 galleries are organized by theme, including ceramics, music, and medicine. Gallery 3 houses the invaluable treasures excavated

Oaxaca

🗺 254 B3

Visitor Information

✉ Murguía 206

☎ 951/516-0123

20th-century Artists & el Tequio

El tequio, Zapotec for "the burden," refers to the obligation to contribute to the community, a custom practiced since the days of Monte Albán (see pp. 264–265). Francisco Toledo, a successful modern painter and graphic artist from Juchitán, in the Isthmus of Tehuantepec, takes this obligation seriously. He has funded or contributed his seemingly limitless energy toward many cultural endeavors in Oaxaca, among them the creation of the Instituto de Artes Gráficas, a wonderful

graphics art library and museum, a Braille library, Mexico's first stamp museum, and a papermaking workshop in Vistaher-mosa, Etla (north of Oaxaca).

Fellow artist Rudolfo Morales, who died in 2001, was equally active. Between the two, they formed **los Amigos de Monte Albán,** a nonprofit organization working to preserve Monte Albán, and dedicated a good deal of time and money toward the restoration of Oaxaca's priceless Dominican monasteries.

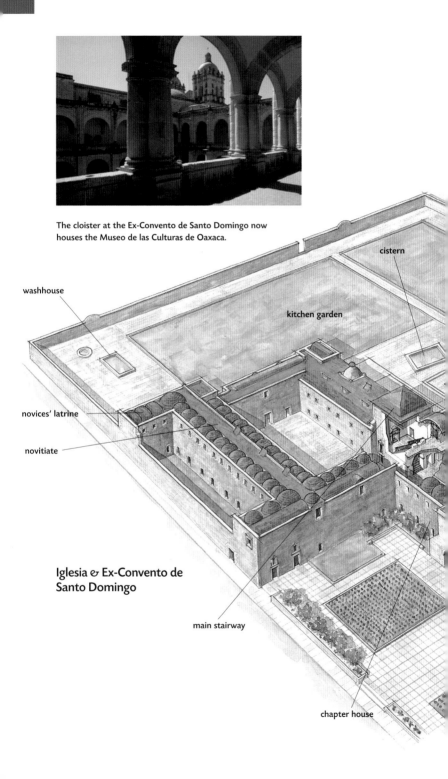

The cloister at the Ex-Convento de Santo Domingo now houses the Museo de las Culturas de Oaxaca.

cistern

washhouse

kitchen garden

novices' latrine

novitiate

Iglesia & Ex-Convento de Santo Domingo

main stairway

chapter house

from the tombs at the Zapotec site of Monte Albán (see pp. 264–265), including gold, silver, shell, and jade jewelry. Tours of the **botanical gardens** are usually given in English *(Tues., Thurs., & Sat. 11 a.m., $$$)*. One-hour tours in Spanish *($$)* are given daily at 10 a.m. and 12 and 5 p.m.

Other monasteries in the Valley of Oaxaca include **Cuilapan,** which is on the road to **Zaachila** (see p. 270); **Tlacochahuaya,** with an outstanding 1620 pipe organ (see p. 266); and the **Iglesia del Santo Cristo** at Tlacolula de Matamoros (see p. 268). In the Mixteca Alta region north of Oaxaca, **Yanhuitlán** was recently restored using many original construction techniques. Of note are its elegant plateresque "door within a door" on the north portal and the stunning main altarpiece. Farther on are **Coixtlahuaca,** once the site of a temple to the god Quetzalcóatl; and **Teposcolula,** whose open chapel is said to be the loveliest in Oaxaca. ■

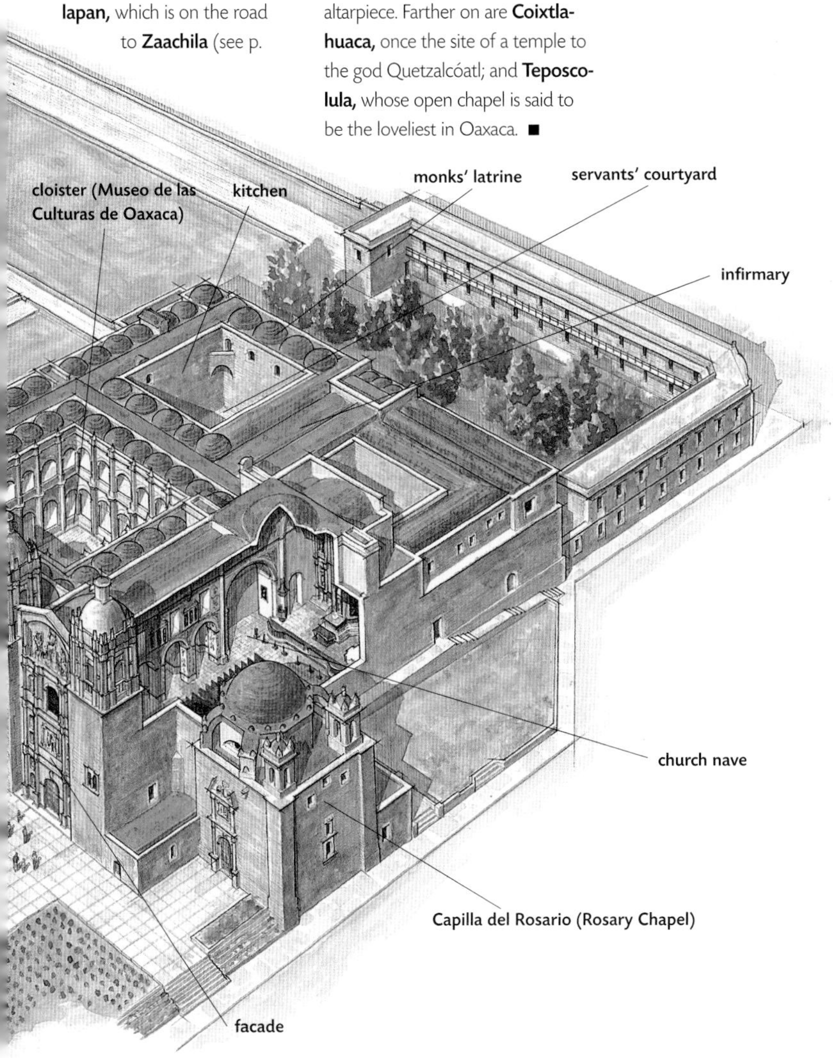

cloister (Museo de las Culturas de Oaxaca)

kitchen

monks' latrine

servants' courtyard

infirmary

church nave

Capilla del Rosario (Rosary Chapel)

facade

Monte Albán

A millennium before the arrival of the Spaniards in 1521, the Zapotec city now known as Monte Albán was flourishing. Sweet-smelling copal incense wafted from gracefully designed, precisely aligned temples. Architects contrived cisterns to collect rainwater and built a specialized irrigation system. Trade flourished; busy open-air markets sold local goods and imported jade beads, stone implements, metal, minerals, and pigments.

Monte Albán, perched on a hill overlooking three valleys, was among the most advanced cities of its time.

colonial Oaxaca centuries later, the wealthiest and most influential families lived closest to the central plazas.

Although the Zapotec were the principal architects of this remarkable city, the original inhabitants may have been Mixe-Zoques from the isthmus, or even relatives of the Olmec of Veracruz. The Zapotec (or one of their predecessors) first inhabited the site about 500 B.C., and for reasons unknown abandoned it after around 12 centuries of continuous settlement.

A hundred or more years later, the Mixtec made the site into an elaborate cemetery. The dead were buried in rectangular and cross-shaped tombs decorated with glyphs, murals, or sculptures, and accompanied by offerings made of ceramic, shell, or precious metals. More than 220 burial sites have been discovered and explored. The most fabulous, **Tumba 7,** yielded more than 500 pieces of gold, amber, and turquoise jewelry, as well as other exquisite articles of jade, silver, crystal, and finely sculpted bone. Most of the artifacts are on display at the Museo de las Culturas de Oaxaca in downtown Oaxaca.

Today, several of these tombs are open to visitors, including **Tumba 104,** located on the

Animals were domesticated, deer and other beasts and birds were hunted in the surrounding valleys, and hillsides were terraced and planted with crops and fruit trees. Society was stratified, with warlords, warriors, priests, and bureaucrats among the upper class. Artisans and craftspeople lived and worked in separate districts, according to their craft. There was no central ruler; control was probably shared among families with a common ancestor. As in

northwest perimeter of the site. Note the god of corn, Pitao Cozobi, embedded at the top of the facade. Inside are multicolored frescoes showing important people in ceremonial dress. The carved slab in the antechamber originally sealed the tomb.

At either extreme of the **Gran Plaza,** once the heart of the city, are the **Platforma Norte** and the **Platforma Sur,** each with stone steps flanked by wide balustrades. Buildings were generally made of irregularly shaped stones cemented with mud, and then covered with facing stones and layers of stucco; newer buildings were superimposed on older ones. **Estructura I,** in the center of the Gran Plaza, is a typical Zapotec construction. Single or double scapulary panels at the top of buildings (the latter evident on **Edificio H)** symbolized the sky, or the jaguar's jaw.

The earliest inhabitants built structures of monolithic block walls, some plain, others with elaborate bas-relief sculptures. One of the best known examples of the latter is the **Galería de los Danzantes,** on the west side of the plaza. It is engraved with large figures depicting slain enemies and the rulers of defeated towns. Their names and those of their towns are inscribed on or alongside their mutilated corpses in Zapotec hieroglyphics. **Estructuras K, L, and IV Sur** were among the first constructed. In **Estructura H,** the tomb of five young men yielded one of the greatest Zapotec works of art—a jade mask of the bat god. The skeletons were also adorned with breastplates, necklaces,

earflares, pearls, and shells, now in the Museo Nacional de Antropología (see pp. 198–201).

At the plaza's northeast corner, the *juego de pelota,* or ball court, is representative of those in the region. This I-shaped court is flanked on both sides by sloping, stepped walls, and, unlike those in central Mexico and the Yucatán, shows no evidence of ball hoops.

There's a well-stocked gift shop and bookstore, and a restaurant with an excellent view of the

Monte Albán

- 254 B2
- 6 miles (10 km) SW of Oaxaca
- 951/516-1215
- $$

EXPERIENCE: Amaranth For Health

Puente a la Salud Comunitaria *(tel 951/518-6642, www.puentemexico.org)* is a nonprofit working in rural Oaxaca to advance the nutrition and livelihood of poor families through the cultivation of amaranth. Rich in nutrients, this grain is native to the region, uses relatively little water, and makes a valuable commercial crop. You can participate by performing office tasks such as fund-raising or working in-country to train farmers in natural and organic farming practices. You might also assist community health workers promote this nutritious food within impoverished villages. A limited number of paid and volunteer positions are available.

valley. Buses depart approximately on the half hour from the travel agency across from the **Hotel Ribera del Angel** *(Calle Mina 509, 5 blocks SW of zócalo, tel 951/516-6175, $).* The small surcharge for staying beyond three hours is worthwhile for those who want to examine the site and museum thoroughly. Full tours *($$$$$)* are another option. ∎

Mitla Drive

East of Oaxaca along Highway 190 lie four archaeological sites, several 17th-century Dominican monasteries, the world's fattest tree, and Zapotec towns backed by the sun-baked Oaxaca hills. Smoky blue mountains form a persistent backdrop, seemingly rising from the stubby cornfields along either side of the highway.

About 8 miles (13 km) southeast of Oaxaca, the pride of tiny **Santa María el Tule ❶** on Highway 190 is its 2,000-year-old *ahuehuete,* or Montezuma cypress tree. Wider than it is tall, the gnarled tree towers above the 17th-century church at its side. Local imagination has found figures in the bark and limbs of the 138-foot-wide (42 m) tree as incongruous as the derrière of Mexican actress and violinist Olga Breesky, the face of Jesus, and a turkey. Behind the church, open-air kitchens serve up local specialties.

Four miles (6.5 km) farther along, turn right toward **Tlacochahuaya ❷**, a small Zapotec village with a picturesque plaza and adobe houses surrounded by stone hills and cornfields. Completed in the early 17th century, the town's Dominican church and monastery perch on the base of the pre-Hispanic temple mound that provided building materials. Covering the interior walls and vaulted ceiling are stylized vignettes of cherubs and flowers rendered in red, gold, blue, and green by indigenous artists. Don't miss the meticulously restored pipe organ, built in 1620, in the choir loft.

Return to the highway and after about a mile (1.6 km), turn right onto a dirt road to **Dainzú.** Evidence suggests that this terraced Zapotec city was a contemporary of Monte Albán, and was inhabited some time after 300 B.C. Look for bas-relief carvings of ball players with jaguar faces along the lower section of **Edificio A,** the remains of a step-platform structure.

Another mile (1.6 km) farther along the highway is the turnoff to prosperous **Teotitlán del Valle ❸**, famous for its hand-loomed Zapotec rugs. Purists prefer undyed wool or natural dyes such as the increasingly rare

NOT TO BE MISSED:

Santa María el Tule • Tlacochahuaya • Tlacolula • Mitla

cochineal, a cactus parasite, but most rugs these days are made of wool or synthetic fibers tinted with commercially produced dyes. Some people make a pilgrimage to Teotitlán simply to lunch at **Tlamanalli** *(Av. Juárez 39, tel 951/524-4006, closed Mon., $$$)*, a Zapotec

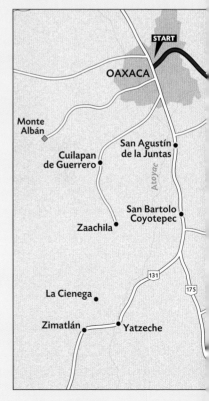

The 2,000-year-old *ahuehuete* tree at Santa María el Tule

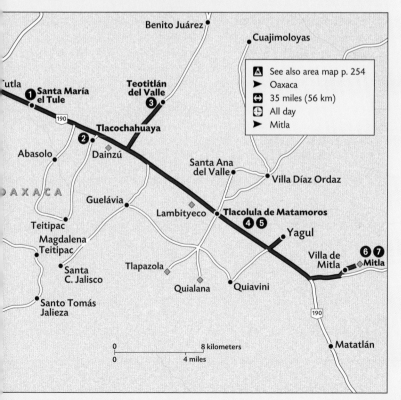

Benito Juárez

Cuajimoloyas

Tutla

① Santa María el Tule

Teotitlán del Valle ③

190

Tlacochahuaya

Abasolo   **② Dainzú**

Santa Ana del Valle

Villa Díaz Ordaz

Guelávia

Lambityeco   **Tlacolula de Matamoros**

④⑤

Teitipac   Yagul

Magdalena Teitipac

Santa C. Jalisco   Tlapazola   Villa de Mitla **⑥⑦ Mitla**

Santo Tomás Jalieza   Quialana   Quiavini

OAXACA

See also area map p. 254

► Oaxaca

↔ 35 miles (56 km)

🕐 All day

► Mitla

190

Matatlán

0 _____ 8 kilometers
0 _____ 4 miles

restaurant of some renown. It's only open between 1 and 4 p.m.

Continue along Highway 190 about 5 miles (8 km) to the ruins of **Lambityeco** *($)*, an important salt-mining center abandoned about A.D. 750 in favor of Yagul, to the southeast. The interior panels of the altar in the **Estructura 195** are decorated with figures and symbols of the city's leading lords and ladies. Note the two identical masked figures of Cocijo, god of rain, thunder, and lightning on **Estructura 190;** each holds a water vessel in the right hand and a lightning bolt in the left.

INSIDER TIP:

When near Oaxaca, if you go to Hierve el Agua (see p. 280) or spend a day at the Mitla ruins, you can find comfortable overnight accommodations at Don Cenobio's in Mitla *(www. hoteldoncenobio.com)*. **They have a lovely garden.**

—GARY FEINMAN
National Geographic field researcher

Back on the highway, continue just a mile (1.6 km) to **Tlacolula** ❹, where women in distinctive flowered headscarves and plaid skirts preside over the busy Sunday market. A smaller market is held throughout the week. Within the **Iglesia del Santo Cristo,** the town's 17th-century Dominican church is the **Capilla del Rosario** ❺, or Rosary Chapel, a stunning example of gilded plasterwork and polychrome relief. Note the fine detail on the wrought iron of the choir grille and pulpit.

Continue southeast along the highway a few miles to **Yagul** *(tel 951/516-4828, $)*, a fortified Zapotec city built on a hilltop for defense. The discovery of more than 30 tombs confirms that this was a residential area; inhabitants were customarily buried underneath the doorway of their homes. The **Palacio de los Seis Patios**

may have served as a principal residence.

After another 3 miles (5 km), a short detour off Highway 190 takes you to the impressive ruins of **Mitla** ❻ *(tel 951/568-0316, $)*, whose name comes from the Náhuatl word *mictlán*, meaning "land of the dead." The Zapotec shifted their base to this ceremonial city—and to other centers such as Zaachila, Cuilapan, and Lambityeco—about the time Monte Albán was abandoned (A.D. 700–800). They called the city Lyobaa, meaning "place of rest" or "burial place," and built tombs both above and below ground. As at Monte Albán, Mitla was taken over by the Mixtec after it was abandoned by the Zapotec around the 11th century. It was still in use when the Spaniards arrived.

The site consists of five groups of buildings once guarded by a fortress on a nearby hill. Of the two that have been excavated, the more exceptional is the **Grupo de las Columnas,** where long masonry halls surround a central plaza. In the first complex, the **Templo de las Columnas** is named for the six enormous pillars that originally supported wooden beams and a large, flat roof. From this structure, enter the **Patio de las Grecas** ❼, named for the intricate step and fret stone mosaics that adorn its walls. Mitla's almost uniformly geometric decoration reflects the Mixtec influence. As in the Puuc region of the Yucatán, the area's fine limestone made possible such artistic achievement. Unlike those found throughout Mesoamerica at the time, the Mixtec designs lack beasts, gods, and human figures. The narrow rooms surrounding the patio were most likely tombs, and the site itself home to the high priest of the Zapotec nation and his retinue as well as visiting royalty and soldiers.

The **Grupo de la Iglesia** is what remains of a similar structure disassembled to build the 16th-century **Iglesia de San Pablo Apostol,** named for Mitla's patron saint, the Apostle Paul. Some evidence of this shared heritage can be seen on the stones forming the church's exterior walls. Behind the church, several small structures with decorated lintels and patios are all that remain of the original building.

Towns Around Oaxaca

Surrounding the capital, towns large and small produce the folk art that fills the shops in downtown Oaxaca. Some are prosperous, such as Teotitlán del Valle, whose internationally known weavers have built imposing two-story homes. Others remain poor, with packed dirt streets and fields of corn and alfalfa. Zapotec is still spoken in many homes where traditional arts—especially weaving, ceramics, and carving—continue to be practiced.

Although the Spaniards conquerors introduced new methods of production, the local people have maintained many of their ancestors' forms and techniques. The Spaniards also restricted metalsmiths to working with nonprecious metals, and craftsmen today produce beautiful work in stamped and molded tin. Symbols such as crosses and saints are juxtaposed with scorpions, birds, frogs, and other traditional icons.

Due west of Oaxaca, dusty **Atzompa** squats in the shadow of Monte Albán. It is famous for its green-glazed tableware, unique, unglazed crosses in contrasting tones of clay, and *muñecas bordadas* "embroidered dolls." The late Teodora Blanca designed 2- to 3-foot (0.75–1 m) female figures, some studded with elephant heads, lizards, and other zoomorphic figures. Artisans along the town's streets will show you their wares if available, but most of the finest work is found in Oaxaca's shops.

The scene is quite different in **Arrazola,** where family workshops double as showrooms for colorful *alebrijes,* carved and painted wooden creatures ranging from miniatures to monsters more than several feet long.

San Martín Tilcajete, like Arrazola, produces fantastic

Part of the Y-shape Oaxaca Valley, as seen from the heights of Monte Albán

painted wood figures. Some artisans specialize in devils, others in barroom drunks; the majority make fanciful animals as well. **La Unión Tejalapan** produces wonderfully naive wooden statuettes, including endearing crèches and funky farm animals. Rarely visited by tourists, the town is spread over a series of dry rolling hills, and most artisans sell to shops in Oaxaca.

South of Oaxaca along Highway 175 are several historic towns, including **San Bartolo Coyotepec** *(7.5 miles/12 km from Oaxaca),* famous for its black pottery.

Oaxaca

🅰 254 B3

Visitor Information

✉ Av. Juárez 703

☎ 951/516-4828

Overnight firing of the unglazed pottery in pit kilns produces lustrous patinas from gunmetal gray to sooty black. Shop at the town's co-op, across from the pretty parish church, or wander through town and check the individual artisans' showrooms.

Another 7.5 miles (12 km) south brings you to **Santo Tomás Jalietza,** where the town's open-air cooperative sells belts, table runners, and other goods made on traditional backstrap looms. The same distance again brings you to **Ocotlán,** known for its fine machetes and knives, the latter sometimes carved with picaresque sayings. The restored Dominican monastery and church on the town plaza are well worth exploring. The former has a wonderful museum showing the unique work of benefactor and local hero, the artist Rudolfo Morales (1925-2001), and of the Aguilar sisters, whose bright ceramic female figures have become Oaxaca icons. Ocotlán is also known for its mescal minero.

Wooden carts driven by oxen or horses trundle along the road leading into **Zaachila,** surrounded by the rolling hills of the Zimatlán valley. Early Thursday mornings, locals arrive at the **animal market** on the outskirts of town to barter for shrieking piglets, big-eyed baby burros, and other farm animals. In the town center, the traditional market remains in full swing until mid-afternoon. Visit one of the two pre-Hispanic tombs excavated so far, as well as the appealing 18th-century church dedicated to the Virgin of Juquila.

La Sierra Norte

Oaxaca state promotes "rural tourism," providing access to mountain towns—and the surrounding countryside—with

Selling bread on the streets of Ocotlán

Market Towns

These market towns serve local communities, not tourists, but offer a chance to purchase local produce and folk art.

Monday Miahuatlán, 62 miles (100 km) south of Oaxaca on Hwy. 175

Tuesday Ayoquezco, 93 miles (150 km) south of Oaxaca on Hwy. 131; Atzompa (see p. 269)

Wednesday San Pedro y San Pablo Etla, 12 miles (19 km) north of Oaxaca off Hwy. 190; Zimatlán, 15.5 miles (25 km) south of Oaxaca off Hwy. 131

Thursday Zaachila, 9.5 miles (15 km) south of Oaxaca on Hwy. 175 West

Friday Ocotlán, 20.5 miles (33 km) south of Oaxaca on Hwy. 175 East; San Bartolo Coyotepec (see p. 269); Santo Tomás Jalietza (see p. 270)

Saturday Mercado de Abastos, Oaxaca (see p. 256)

Sunday Tlacolula (see p. 268), east of Oaxaca on Hwy. 190

no hotels. This program offers a look at real, rural Oaxaca. Adventurers should set out with open minds, inquisitive hearts, and a Spanish-English dictionary.

About an hour and a half (40 miles/66 km) north of Oaxaca city, **Llano Grande** *(tel 200/125-7541)* is known for the friendliness of its inhabitants and the beauty of the surrounding pine-oak forests. This 19th-century town has magnificent vistas and impressive biodiversity for excellent bird-watching. During Holy Week, Mass is celebrated at **Yaa Tini,** an overlook outside town. This is good mountain-biking country; bring your own or rent one in town.

Endemic orchids abound in the cloud forests around **Ixtlán de Juárez** *(tel 955/553-6075),* an area with multiple ecosystems. Within the township of the same name, locals from **Santa Martha Latuvi** *(tel 200/125-7108)* teach visitors about herbal medicines, regionally brewed firewater, and breadmaking. Founded as a mining hacienda, **Santa María Yavesía** *(tel 951/553-6042)* is surrounded by primary forest (great for birding) and offers lodging with local

INSIDER TIP:

Around Oaxaca you'll find fine woven products: woolen rugs in Teotitlán del Valle, belts in Santo Tomás Jalietza, and embroidered goods near Mitla.

—GARY FEINMAN
National Geographic field researcher

families, as well as camping. Closer to the capital city of Oaxaca at 6,888 feet (2,100 m) above sea level, the town of **Santa Catarina Lachatao** *(tel 951/514-8271)* has cobblestone streets, red-tile roofs, and a 16th-century church.

Guides, meals, and accommodations for these destinations are available; call the phone numbers above or the regional tour operator **Sierra Norte** *(tel 951/514-8271, www.sierranorte .org.mx)* for reservations or more information. Bring warm clothing (many towns are more than 9,000 feet/2,700 m above sea level) and comfortable walking shoes. ■

EXPERIENCE: Learn to Cook Mexican Cuisine

Mexican cuisine is among the most varied and unusual of the Americas. New World ingredients like chocolate, maize, chilies, and turkey (not to mention grasshoppers and ant eggs) are combined with those supplied by the Spanish invaders, including sugar and wheat. The country's varied geography lends itself to regional variations of cooking that take advantage of a bounty of tropical fruits, seafood, and northern beef.

Oaxaca state contributes substantially to the Mexican culinary lexicon. On her ranch outside the city of Oaxaca, Susana Trilling of **Seasons of My Heart** *(tel 951/508-0469, www. seasonsofmyheart.com,)* offers one-day, long weekend, and one-week cooking classes and regional culinary tours. Susana sometimes travels to San Miguel de Allende, where she is guest lecturer at **La Cocina** *(tel 888/407-3168 in U.S., www.mexicocooks. com)* cooking school. Owner Kris Rudolph specializes in healthy versions of classic Mexican dishes and offers market tours as well as hands-on cooking classes.

To learn exotic dishes of the Yucatán peninsula, visit Chef David Sterling's **Los Dos Cooking School** *(www. los-dos.com)*, in Mérida. Chef David shares not just the dining tables of this restored colonial mansion with his clients, but the rooms beyond: The school doubles as a charming B&B. Also offering lodgings are Jon Jarvis and Estela Salas Silva, in the state of Tlaxcala. Their **Mexican Home Cooking** *(tel 246/468-0978, http:// mexicanhomecooking.com)* school offers cooking and baking classes with optional archaeological trips.

Cocinar Mexicano *(tel 777/317-9769; 866/779-4430 in the U.S., http:// cocinarmexicano.com)* offers a workshop in Mexico City for chefs and culinary professionals only, including meals at some of the capital's top restaurants and Q&A with their chefs. For the general public, they offer specialized, multi-day workshops in picturesque towns outside the capital. Participants learn to create special foods for Day of the Dead, Christmas, or Candlemass. Sunday cooking classes in Tepoztlán hook participants up with local women specializing in cooking traditional dishes and making tortillas.

For those with an appetite for learning Spanish as well as Mexican dishes, some language schools offer cooking classes as part of the language curriculum. Two are **Veracruz Language School** *(http://www.veracru zspanish.com)* and **Querétaro Language School** *(www. queretarolanguageschool.com/ cooking.htm)*.

Cities throughout Mexico celebrate their cuisine with festivals. Two are in Puerto Vallarta. Guest chefs arrive during the **International Gourmet Festival** *(www. festivalgourmet.com)* each November. During **Restaurant Week** (actually two weeks long) during the latter part of May, nearly three dozen of Puerto Vallarta's top restaurants offer prix-fixe meals at discounted prices. For information on either call 322/222-2247.

Shelling corn for *masa* (dough) at a Cocinar Mexicano workshop

Oaxaca's Coast

Oaxaca's coast arcs east to west, from the border with Guerrero to Chiapas, as if tracing a line along the bottom half of a shallow bowl. Zapotec and, to a lesser extent, Mixtec are found up and down the coast; Zoques and Mixes make their home around the isthmus. Cultures blend, but in many cases, indigenous peoples speak their own languages and continue many of their great-grandparents' traditions.

Pinotepa Nacional

About an hour from the coast, Pinotepa Nacional is not a stop on the tourist trail, but it's an important commercial center. Until well into the 20th century, Pinotepa women wore nothing above the waist except a plain white cotton shawl. Many today still wear striking straight wrap skirts of naturally dyed red, purple, and lilac stripes whose pattern varies subtly from one village to the next.

The predominantly Mixtec men throughout the municipality perform elaborate dances at Carnaval, Easter, and major feast days, using masks and story lines passed down over generations. Working around scripts whose meanings have faded with time, dancers don masks of rabbits, dogs, and two-faced Spaniards.

There are no tourist accommodations outside Pinotepa Nacional. Visitors may be asked to contribute toward the musicians' refreshments. Be respectful and ask permission before taking photos.

Pinotepa de Don Luis, 15 miles (24 km) northeast of Pinotepa Nacional, vigorously celebrates both Carnaval and Semana Santa (Holy Week), the former climaxing on the Sunday before Ash Wednesday.

A view of the coast near Bahías de Huatulco in southern Oaxaca state

Parque Nacional Lagunas de Chacahua

Bird-watchers should check out the coastal lagoons and mangrove swamps of 35,000-acre (14,164 ha) Parque Nacional Lagunas de Chacahua, about halfway between Pinotepa Nacional and Puerto Escondido. Boat tours are especially rewarding during the winter months, when migrating birds arrive.

The park entrance is about 17 miles (27 km) along a fairly good dirt road off Highway 200. You can get here on your own via the town of Río Grande or book a tour in Puerto Escondido through **Viajes Dimar** (Av. Pérez Gasga 905, tel 954/582-0737, $$$$$).

The same operator runs full-day tours to **Laguna de Manialtepec,** a 10-mile-long (16 km) mangrove lagoon less than 10 miles from Puerto Escondido. In the rainy summer season the Río Manialtepec forms an estuary, which birds—including anhingas, parrots, jacanas, and herons—find especially attractive. In winter you will see the migratory species.

Puerto Escondido

Coastal tourism doesn't gain much of a foothold until Puerto Escondido, connected directly to Oaxaca City by Highway 131 as well as via Pochutla (Hwy. 175). Surfers were the first travelers to discover this small town, whose name means "hidden port." Until a paved road was completed in the 1970s, they bumped for miles down a bad dirt road to attack some of the world's best waves. Today they can fly in on major

airlines for the surf competitions held each summer and mid-November, the latter coinciding with the town's fiesta, a lively month of cultural events, sportfishing championships, and a beauty pageant; traditional dances are also performed. A

INSIDER TIP:

La Crucecita, Huatulco, in Oaxaca state, is a new town with old Mexico charm. The coastline is pristine and protected, and much of the surrounding area is within a nature preserve.

—JON CHURCH
National Geographic contributor

major festival honoring la Virgen de la Soledad culminates on December 18, when local fishermen take their patron saint on an oceangoing procession that sets out from the main beach.

Although it caters nonstop to outsiders, Puerto Escondido maintains its identity. The main tourist drag, a four-block-long pedestrian promenade nicknamed *el adoquín* (the paved road), slows down only during the hottest hours at midday and sudden downpours. But the mix of foreign and national visitors is nice, the prices are reasonable, and seafood is served from open-air eateries right on the sand. By noon, fishermen are disgorging their catch at **Playa Marinero,** the town's most central beach.

Some boats transport sunbathers to nearby **Puerto Angelito** and **Playa Carrizalillo,** two secluded coves where simple seafood shanties serve up fried fish, ceviche, beers, and sodas. You can walk or bike the dirt trail to these beaches or take a cab.

Private homes, hotels, and restaurants are cropping up on the hills farther west at **Carrizalillo** and **Rinconada** neighborhoods; **Bacocho** is more established with a few of Puerto Escondido's fancier hotels, discos, condos, and private homes. But it feels deserted compared to el adoquín and **Playa Zicatela,** where surfers search for swells or talk shop in palm-thatch restaurants. Sipping a sunset cocktail at one of the many restaurants and bars facing Zicatela Beach, or from the wide green lawn at Hotel Posada Real, at Playa Bacocho, is highly recommended.

For a pre-Hispanic experience, visit **Villas Temazcalli** (*Via Temazcalli 3, tel 954/582-1023*). Throwing aromatic water on hot coals, which are replenished from the outside by a trap door, produces cleansing steam. The traditional-style sweat lodge also offers massage and both personal and ceremonial steam baths on a cliff above Zicatela beach. After you emerge—purified, relaxed, and exfoliated—you can sip a cup of tea and gaze at the ocean below. **Hotel Aldea del Bazar** (*Av. Benito Juárez s/n, Bacocho, tel 954/582-0508*), at Bacocho, also has a temazcal.

Puerto Ángel

Once the state's most important port, Puerto Ángel, 51 miles (83 km) southeast of Puerto Escondido, is a sleepy town with a small naval base. Rocky headlands rise on either side of the secluded bay, and basic hotels, restaurants, and homes straggle up the hills and canyons. In 1997 Hurricane Pauline dealt this small community—along with others throughout Oaxaca and Guerrero states—a very nasty smack.

Here you can watch the fishermen haul in their catch and explore the area's beaches. If you want to swim close to town, the cleanest beach is **Playa Panteón,** on the west side of the bay; otherwise, hire a fisherman to take you to **Playa la Boquilla,** a quiet beach on a pleasant cove a few minutes away.

The most famous beach in the area is **Playa Zipolite,** about 4 miles (6 km) away, where

Puerto Ángel
◭ 254 B1

EXPERIENCE:
Celebrating the Sea with Local Fishermen

Throughout the centuries, the sea has brought bounty but also tragedy to Mexican fishermen. Many towns and villages fête their patron saint as they petition for a safe year on the sea. On December 18, fishermen of Puerto Escondido, **Oaxaca**, honor the state's patron saint and protector of fishermen, la Virgen de Soledad. Join the parade from the town's church to the bay and help send the statue of la Virgen out to sea to bless the fish. Finish by celebrating with dancing and fireworks. Other maritime celebrations include Dia de la Marina (Navy Day) in **Puerto Peñasco** and **Guaymas** on June 1, and similar celebrations from **Ixtapa** to **Zihuantanejo** on May 2, both of which joyously celebrate the people's connection to the sea.

Oaxaca's Spectacular Festivals

Even the humblest village celebrates its patron saint, sometimes spending the greater part of the annual budget on week-long festivities. Local men lead parades; close behind, young beauty queens ride on floats. Shrieking with delight, crowds scatter before *los toros,* reed towers spitting dangerous firecrackers and wielded by zealous young men. Most impressive of all, everyone joins the party.

Zapotec women from the Isthmus of Tehuante-pec in party mood

Throughout the state, pre-Cortesian beliefs overlap iconoclastic Christianity to produce rituals as intoxicating as a shot of pure cane liquor. This is literally the case in the eccentric **Paso y Credo,** a solemn religious procession in which the men of Pinotepa de Don Luis (see p. 273) march from dusk to dawn around the town, taking a ritualistic sip of liquor about every third step. In an Easter week celebration, the town's men and boys, their bodies painted white with purple icons and slogans, fight a mock battle representing their ancestors' attack on invading Spaniards.

Other traditions, including the **Día de los Muertos** (Day of the Dead, or All Souls' Day), demonstrate not a clash, but a blending of New and Old World traditions. Near the end of October, villagers and city dwellers through-out the region begin rejuvenating family graves: weeding, cleaning headstones, painting crosses

and crypts. From the evening preceding **All Saints' Day** (November 1), families begin to entice deceased children—*los angelitos,* or little angels—to the graveside with candles, favorite foods, and (in true Mexican style) loud rockets. As throughout Mexico, Oaxacans relieve gloominess with exuberant partying, and piety is tempered with *picardía,* a mischievous irrever-ence. Altars—some humble, others lavish—are arranged with traditional sugar-candy skulls embellished with Day-Glo colors, along with yellow-orange *cempasúchil* (marigolds), peanuts, and *pan de muerto* (sweet bread decorated with skulls). The rituals continue through **All Souls' Day** (November 2) to honor deceased adults.

Even unequivocally Christian celebrations have a unique Oaxaca flavor. On **Viernes Santo** (Good Friday), purple-robed penitents in long, pointed hoods perform a solemn proces-sion through downtown Oaxaca in **el Desfile del Silencio,** the Silent Procession. On a more lighthearted occasion, mongrels wearing glasses, cats in glossy capes, birds in beribboned cages, and box turtles in the grubby hands of young owners crowd the courtyard at La Merced church on August 31 for the **Blessing of the Animals.**

The Christmas season brings nonstop celebrations, including *las calendas,* in which celebrants dance from church to church hold-ing baskets of offerings on their heads. One of Oaxaca's most unusual traditions is **La Noche de Rábanos** (Radish Night), held December 23. To compete in this classic secular Yule tradi-tion, growers fashion sophisticated tableaux out of carved radishes, toothpicks, and moss.

For more Oaxaca festivals, see "Entertain-ment & Activities," p. 389.

topless sunbathing is accepted. Here and in adjacent **San Agustanillo,** industrious locals have set up informal thatch-roofed restaurants and basic lodgings along the wide, palm-studded, sandy beaches, while the kids peddle *pescadillas* (grilled fish in a flour tortilla), and sodas and beers in buckets of rapidly melting ice. San Agustanillo is popular with bodysurfers, and some enterprising local usually has body boards for rent.

Nearby **Mazunte** is another beautiful, wild beach. Here you can visit **el Centro Mexicano de la Tortuga** (*Domicilio Conocido, www .centromexicanodelatortuga.com, closed Mon.*). Take the obligatory guided tour to see the turtles in large tanks and learn about the conservation of Mexico's seven marine turtle species and several freshwater species. Involving local people in the project provides them with economical alternatives to poaching endangered turtles and their eggs. Until recently, selling turtle meat, oil, and eggs was a viable business venture, and collecting eggs at least continues illegally.

Huatulco

There's no doubt that Huatulco, about 31 miles (50 km) northeast of Puerto Ángel, has abundant natural beauty and charm. Nine lovely bays with dozens of pel-lucid coves and lagoons crowd its 21-mile (35 km) coastline. Clear water and plenty of rocky coves make for great snorkeling, and swimming is pleasant year-round. There's no shortage of sunshine or palm trees, and the rugged mountains of the Sierra de

Miahuatlán looming just beyond the beach only make the scene more intimate.

Huatulco's coastline first attracted the attention of FONATUR, the Mexican tourism development board, in the 1960s. Construction began in the 1980s, and since then, the once innocent Mixtec fishing village has received a significant makeover. Buildings here are limited to six stories, 70 percent of the development's land has been set aside as an ecological reserve, and mid-range and economical hotels are built along with the exclusive five-star resorts. The original plan was scaled back after the economic slump of the mid-1990s: The new plan calls for 1.2 million visitors per year by 2020.

The first bay developed, scenic **Bahía Tangolunda** has reached its maximum density of six resorts. Located here are the Quinta Real, Camino Real, Dreams, and a few other five-star hotels and the area's only **18-hole golf course** (*tel 958/581-0059*). Concessions rent sailboards, catamarans, and other water toys. You can get PADI dive certification, rent diving gear,

Huatulco

🗺 254 C1

Visitor Information

✉ Blvd. Benito Juárez s/n, Bahía Tangolunda

☎ 958/581-0486 or 0176

http://huatulco .magazzine.net

Cascades

Huatulco has more than beach; the bays' backdrop of lush mountains offer their own attractions. Notable are the Copalitilla Cascades, a long series of pools and waterfalls cours-ing through thick jungle, which is itself remarkable for birds and butterflies. Explore on your own or take a package tour.

**Istmo de
Tehuantepec**
🅰 255 D2

or book a snorkel tour through
Action Sports Marina *(tel
958/581-0055).* **Playa Consuelo**
and **Playa el Arrocito** are small
beaches on Tangolunda, the
former accessible only by boat.

Bahía Santa Cruz has also
been developed, with moderately
priced hotels, shops, a cruise ship
pier, and several plazas surrounded
by cafés. At the southern end of
the bay, the underwater preserve
at **Playa La Entrega** attracts

INSIDER TIP:

**Soak up the rays and
promote ecotourism at
the Centro Mexicano
de la Tortuga research
facility. Visit some
of the region's endan-
gered sea turtles.**

—PAM GROUT
National Geographic author

divers and snorkelers. Sportfishing
or bay tours can be arranged at
the Marina Santa Cruz, through
**La Sociedad Cooperativa Tan-
golunda** *(tel 958/587-0081),* or
through **Bahías Plus** *(Carrizal 704,
La Crucecita, tel 958/587-0216)* or
other operators.

Bahía Chahué, the largest of
the bays, has a day spa, a marina
for private yachts, a beach club,
and the largest parking lot ever
seen—right out in the middle of
nowhere ("If you build it, they
will come..."). En route to La
Crucecita, Chahué's few hotels,
restaurants, and bars are located
haphazardly here and there a
short walk from the beach.

About a mile (1.6 km) inland
from Bahía Chahué, **Crucecita** is
a pleasing, custom-built town with
restaurants, a relatively lively night
scene, and budget and mid-range
hotels within a few blocks of the
main square. Other services include
banks, a post office, and a market.

A popular day trip into the lush
coastal mountains is a tour of one
of the **coffee plantations** established by European immigrants in
the 19th century. Tour operators
can also arrange day trips to the
Centro Mexicano de la Tortuga
at Mazunte, **Bahía Manialtepec,**
and **Lagunas de Chacahua.**

Istmo de Tehuantepec

Of the three principal cities in
the Isthmus of Tehuantepec,
only commerce-oriented **Salina
Cruz** is on the water, and hotels
throughout the region are bare
bones. Neither **Juchitán** nor
Tehuantepec is terribly scenic—
they are sweltering hot and
often dusty. Those who visit are
inexorably drawn by the strength
of the culture and the lively,
witty people who live here, most
descendants of the Zapotec. Travelers often stop off here en route
to Chiapas, or to experience *las
velas,* exuberant celebrations held
throughout the region between
April and September—mainly in
May. Town life centers around
the main plaza and the market,
the latter presided over by
women in short *huipiles* (loose
calf-length dresses) and billowing,
ankle-length skirts. In Juchitán,
visit **Casa de la Cultura** *(Jose F.
Gómez, 1 block from plaza),* which
displays 20th-century art and
archaeological pieces. ■

EXPERIENCE: Cultural Mexico: Up Close & Personal

What better place than Oaxaca to immerse yourself in Mexican culture? Descendants of Mixes and Mixtecs, Zapotecs and Triquis and Chatinos, Oaxacans manifest some of Mexico's most fascinating cultures. Fortunately there are a number of excellent, bilingual tour operators who facilitate non-mainstream tourism.

In the rolling hills outside Oaxaca city, **Casa Sagrada** (*tel 951/516-4275, www.casa sagrada.com*) offers cultural immersion masquerading as the perfect family vacation. At their ranch just outside the Zapotec rugmaking town of Teotitlán del Valle, they offer horseback riding for experienced and novice riders, as well as yoga retreats, *limpias* (spiritual cleansings), massage and acupuncture, and many other experiences and activities. Their diminutive Oaxacan burros can carry a picnic lunch or a bundle of firewood for an evening campfire under the stars. For cooking enthusiasts, bilingual guides lead half-day and weeklong cooking classes and market tours.

Traditions Mexico (*tel 951/571-3695, www .tradionsmexico.com*) started off as Manos de Oaxaca, offering tours to remote Oaxacan villages where potters produce simple yet beautiful traditional pottery. Over the years the offerings have expanded, but tour size has remained small. Today's tours include photography and culinary trips, but the emphasis is on local crafts, including weaving and pottery. Tours (*7–9 days*) visit rural townships, and participants should enjoy the rustic and the remote.

Study Zapotec weaving (backstrap and floor looms); or learn how natural dyes are produced from sea creatures and cactus-eaters (the bright red dye cochineal, or carmine, comes from a scale insect that attacks the nopal cactus). Most of all, enjoy interacting with the artisans who follow the ancient ways.

My Mexico Tours (*tel 831/476.9693 in the U.S., www.mymexicotours.com*) leads more traditional tours that still focus on the cultural and culinary side of things, with tours to Chiapas, Michoacán, and the central highland cities of San Miguel de Allende and Guanajuato, as well as Oaxaca. Tour groups are small, roughly eight to ten people, allowing for a more personal and authentic experience that opens the door to a Mexico tourists rarely see.

Valente Nieto Real, making black pottery in San Bartolo Coyotepec

More Places to Visit in Oaxaca

Grutas de San Sebastián

An interesting excursion from Oaxaca is a trip to the underground caves at San Sebastián. Local youths guide you through the 1,300-foot-long (400 m) cave, which has five chambers measuring 65 to 230 feet (20–70 m) in height. Bring a strong flashlight, and comfortable walking shoes for exploring the cave and the gentle hills of the surrounding countryside. The caves are located 52 miles (84 km) southwest of Oaxaca City.

🗺 254 B2

INSIDER TIP:

A beautiful place to watch an Oaxaca sunset is the rock outcropping behind the Yagul ruins, 21 miles (35 km) east of Oaxaca city (see p. 268).

—GARY FEINMAN
National Geographic field researcher

Hierve el Agua

Spectacular mineral falls get folks out of the city and onto the top of this mountain with wonderful, arid views. On weekends, especially in hot weather, families stake out prime spots under the few shade trees close to these dramatic, cold-water pools. On weekdays, it's not unusual to find yourself alone in the dry, scrubby landscape, where a looping trail leads into the canyon for excellent views of the site's unique formations. Buses make the 50-mile (80 km) trip several times a day from the second-class bus station. The site has a parking lot and restrooms. A half dozen clean cabins used to offer overnight lodgings, but squabbles between rival villages make an overnight stay unreliable.

Salina Blanca has a smaller mineral falls. About 1.5 hours from Oaxaca near the town of San José de Gracia, the town offers small restaurants, rental of tents and camping equipment, and guides for touring the semi-arid river scenery.

🗺 254 C2 ☎ 951/502-1200

San Pedro Amusgos to la Mixteca Alta

A few shops selling the finely embroidered *huipiles* (loose calf-length dresses) for which the Amuzgo women are known cluster along Highway 125 as it passes **San Pedro Amusgos,** 32 miles (51 km) north of Pinotepa Nacional (see p. 273). The town celebrates its namesake saint, St. Peter, on June 29 with a colorful procession, and again for the Fiesta de la Virgen del Rosario on the first Sunday in October.

The highway snakes through the Mixteca Alta region on its way to the capital, passing faded but engaging **Tlaxiaco,** once a strategic Aztec garrison and the site of one of Oaxaca's first Dominican monasteries. The feast of the Virgin of the Assumption is celebrated the days leading to August 15.

🗺 254 A2/A3

Shrine of the Virgin of Juquila

Every year hundreds of thousands make a pilgrimage to pray at the shrine of la Virgen Morena de Juquila (the dark-skinned Virgin of Juquila), some coming part or all of the way on foot. The object of adoration is a diminutive statue. According to legend, when fire destroyed much of the village, the statue was unharmed, its skin darkened.

Santa Catalina Juquila, a simple town surrounded by mountains, has a fresh, cool climate and plenty of no-frills hotels to accommodate the pilgrims. On the days preceding the saint's day, December 8, there are religious and cultural festivities, including a dawn rosary, processions, and later food, music, dance, and, of course, fireworks. The town is located 123 miles (198 km) from Oaxaca city on Highway 135.

🗺 254 A3

An isolated region of jungle-draped pyramids, breathtaking scenery, and one of Mexico's most synergistic versions of Catholicism

Chiapas

Flower motif on the church at San Juan Chamula

Chiapas

To speak of Chiapas is to speak of the Maya, the largest Native American group north of Peru. About a quarter of Chiapas's people speak an indigenous tongue, and the highland Maya alone have four distinct languages. Owing in large part to centuries of governmental neglect, indigenous communities carry on a traditional way of life. And corn remains the staff of life; planting and harvesting the grain, and cooking daily tortillas, are activities bound by ritual and blessed with devotion.

Most locals, like these Tzotzil men from San Juan Chamula, still dress traditionally.

The early 16th-century Spanish conquest of Chiapas was particularly swift and brutal. Discouraged by the lack of gold and other riches, the conquerors established San Juan Chamula as a slave market and inflicted other atrocities. Distance from the regulatory *audiencia* (see p. 28) in Mexico City meant little or no meddling in their affairs. Even by the day's standards, treatment of the Indians was beyond harsh, and Bishop Bartolomé de las Casas eventually persuaded the Spanish crown to revoke many of the Spanish-held land holdings.

Unlike the Aztecs, the Maya at the time of the conquest were far removed from their golden age (A.D. 250–900), when great cities such as Palenque and Yaxchilán flourished. Among the most advanced civilizations of the world at that time, the Classic Maya achieved great heights in mathematics, astronomy, architecture, and the arts.

Today, Chiapas is one of Mexico's most rural states, its economy based on fishing, forestry, and agriculture. Coffee, cotton, bananas, and cacao are among its most important exports, and subsistence agriculture is widely practiced. Mostly mountainous, Chiapas shares a fringe of tropical lowlands with neighboring Tabasco, Campeche, and Guatemala. The state capital and transportation hub, Tuxtla Gutiérrez, lies on a central plain surrounded by plateaus. Little visited by foreign tourists, the Pacific coast is a

NOT TO BE MISSED:

series of estuaries and fishing villages accessed almost exclusively by rural roads. Following a multimillion-dollar renovation, Puerto Madero was transformed in 2006 to Puerto Chiapas, designed to accommodate large cruise ships filled with eager tourists.

Abundant rain produces waterfalls, lakes, and the *selva úóona,* one of North America's last remaining rain forests. This endangered land is home to the small Lacandón tribe (for which it is named), who fled Spanish encroachment in their Yucatán homeland. Until a few generations ago, this forest-dwelling people worshipped at the jungle-shrouded ruins of Bonampak. Today, this and other archaeological sites, only partially rescued from the

surrounding jungle, are among the state's most powerful tourist magnets. Its other big draw is San Cristóbal de las Casas, a colonial city whose abundance of traditional culture and indigenous handicrafts attracts droves of visitors. ■

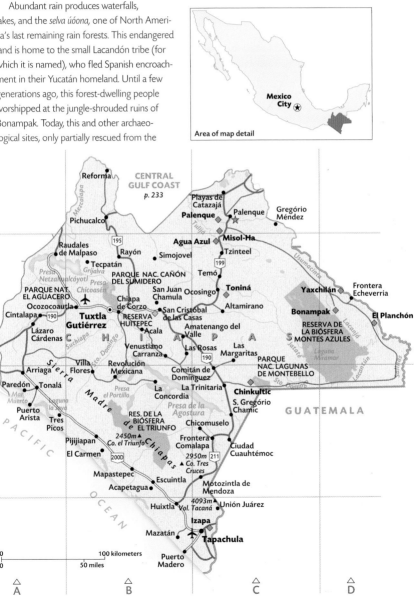

Mexico City

Area of map detail

Tuxtla Gutiérrez & Environs

Tuxtla means "place of many rabbits" in Náhuatl, and Gutiérrez refers to Joaquín Miguel Gutiérrez, who championed Chiapas's union with Mexico in 1824. This large, hot metropolis replaced San Cristóbal de las Casas as the state capital in 1892 after San Cristóbal sided with the Royalists during the War of Independence. Tuxtla is an important commercial and distribution center for coffee, tobacco, and other locally produced products.

Tuxtla's main thoroughfare, Avenida Central, divides the sprawling main square, **Plaza Cívica.** Surrounding this central plaza are the post office, modern **Catedral San Marcos,** and several government offices.

More attractive is **Parque de la Marimba** (*Av. Central at Calle 8 Poniente*), a shady square where couples dance to live marimba music daily, 6 to 10 p.m. If you're not a dancer, grab a folding chair and enjoy the band.

Although it is actually a government-run folk-art shop, the **Casa de las Artesanías** (*Blvd. Belisario Domínguez 2035, tel 961/602-9800, closed Sun.*), northeast of the *zócalo*, seems more like a handicrafts museum with an ethnographic museum at the rear.

The capital's principal attraction is the peaceful, well-laid-out **Zoológico Miguel Álvarez del Toro** (*Calz. Cerro Hueco s/n, tel 961/614-4765, closed Mon., $*), about 5 miles (8 km) southeast of downtown. The zoo gives a great overview not just of Chiapas's native animals, which are the only species represented, but also of its plant life. A small museum, store, and restaurant complete the complex. Catch a minivan from Calles 1a Oriente and 7a Sur, downtown.

About 9 miles (14 km) east of Tuxtla Gutiérrez is **Chiapa de Corzo,** a takeoff point for boat trips along Cañón del Sumidero (see opposite). At the time of the Spanish invasion, the bellicose Chiapaneco tribe dominated

Hire a taxi in Tuxtla Gutiérrez for a tour along the rim of Cañón del Sumidero.

the region, having established themselves around 1300. They fought with Maya towns for control of local salt mines and cacao fields, and generally made life so unpleasant that the Maya allied themselves with the Spaniards.

As soon as the Spaniards had dispatched the Chiapanecos for whom the state is named, they enslaved their former Maya allies. A Spanish settlement established in Chiapa de Corzo in 1528 was soon abandoned for the fresher, mosquito-free climate at what is now San Cristóbal de las Casas (see pp. 286–287).

The main square is crowned by **La Pila,** an octagonal fountain (1562) said to have been inspired by the diadem of Spain's Queen Isabella. Adjacent to the 16th-century Ex-convento de Santo Domingo, one block south of the plaza, the **Museo de la Laca** (*tel 961/616-0055, closed Mon.*) shows lacquered gourds made in the town, as well as other lacquered objects from around the world. If you're around in January, don't miss the *parachicos,* inimitable free-for-alls where men dressed as women take over the streets.

One street from Chiapa de Corzo's main plaza, motorboats depart for tours (*$$$$*) of the impressive **Cañón del Sumidero.** This steep-walled canyon was created millions of years ago by the wild **Río Grijalva,** which was tamed by the construction in 1981 of the Chicoasen Dam. Rocky red walls rise as high as 3,280 feet (1,000 m) above the brownish-green river. With luck you'll spot hawks, egrets, kingfishers, crocodiles, and other animals.

Within the canyon, the Ixcaret Group has created **Parque Sumidero** (*Av. Independencia s/n, Barro San Miguel, tel 961/128-8894, www.sumidero.com, $$$$$*), with a swimming pool and natural areas, and adventure activities at additional cost. It's expensive, so if you go plan to spend the day.

Eighteen miles (30 km) from Tuxtla via Ocozocoautla is **Sima de las Cotorras** (*tel 968/689-0289, e-mail: simadelascotorras@gmail.com*), an unusual 295-foot-by-525-foot (90 m by 160 m) chasm. Hire a local guide for rappelling or bird-watching, but

If you happen to be near Tuxtla Gutiérrez in mid-January, take a trip to nearby Chiapa de Corzo. The costumes and celebrations during the Feria de Enero are spectacular.

—KATHERINE AMATO
National Geographic field researcher

the real show is at sunset, when hundreds of birds fly in and out. To see this seasonal event, it's easiest to stay at the rustic but pleasant on-site cabins (*$, tent camping also allowed*) and get up with the chickens, or in this case, the *cotorros* (a type of parrot). Or just come for a few hours in the afternoon; help stimulate the ecotourism project by having a snack at the restaurant. ∎

Tuxtla Gutiérrez
🗺 283 B3
Visitor Information
✉ Blvd. Belisario Domínguez 950, Edificio Plaza de las Instituciones, 4th floor
☎ 961/617-0550 ext. 35012 or 1800/280-3500 (toll-free within Mexico)
www.turismochiapas.gob.mx

Chiapa de Corzo
🗺 283 B3
Visitor Information
✉ Av. Domingo Ruiz I
☎ 961/616-1013

San Cristóbal de las Casas

Surrounded by magnificent pine-covered peaks, San Cristóbal accepts its beauty with the naiveté of a child. Simple homes in a range of bright colors line cobblestone streets, and even the hordes of foreign backpackers don't diminish the city's cozy, exotic appeal. At 6,890 feet (2,100 m) above sea level, the climate is conducive to sweaters and jeans, while wood smoke perfumes the chilly evenings.

The colors of the cathedral's facade represent the four directions in the Maya world view.

After an intense but fruitless resistance by the Chiapaneco Indians, the city of Villareal de Chiapa de los Españoles was established in 1528 by Spaniard Diego de Mazariego. It was later renamed San Cristóbal de las Casas in honor of its patron, St. Christopher, and its protector, Dominican monk Bartolomé de las Casas (1474–1566). As the first bishop of Chiapas, de las Casas fought to improve the lives of indigenous men, women, and children under the devastating *encomienda* system (see p. 28).

The Spaniards organized the new town in barrios, each with its own church, patron saint, and industry. Today, tradition-minded townspeople retain neighborhood loyalties, visiting **La Merced** for sweets and wax religious figures, and **Guadalupe** for wooden toys, candles, and leather. The best fireworks are still found in **Santa Lucía.** These neighborhoods are a few blocks west, east, and southeast of the *zócalo*, respectively.

The physical and social nucleus of the city, the **zócalo,** officially Plaza 31 de Marzo, is surrounded by arcaded stores and restored mansions—now banks, bars, hotels, and restaurants. On the west flank is the courtly neoclassic **Palacio Municipal,** while to the north stands the **catedral,** built in the 16th century and later remodeled in the baroque style. Stylized floral details decorate its unusual facade.

North and west of the zócalo, two museums have excellent displays of local minerals. **El Museo de Jade** (Av. 16 de septiembre 16, tel 967/678-2550, www.eljade. com, $) has reproductions of pieces valued and traded among many Mesoamerican cultures. **El Museo de Ambar** (Calle Diego de Mazariegos, adjacent to La Merced, tel 967/678-9716, closed Mon., $) has a gift shop as well as exhibits and information about this oft-imitated fossil resin.

Two churches perched above the city provide good views and an energizing, if short, uphill walk. The **Templo de Guadalupe** (end of Real de Guadalupe) is on the west side. The **Templo de San Cristóbal** (Hermanos Domínguez at Ignacio Allende) is higher up and has a better view, but opens only on Sundays and for the feast of the town's patron, St. Christopher.

Solomonic columns and other baroque elements fancify the lovely, intricate facade of the **Templo y Ex-Convento de Santo Domingo** (Av. Lázaro Cárdenas s/n). Inside, note the graceful, gilded wood altarpieces and carved pulpit. Filling the church's extensive open-air atrium is a market of regional crafts. Within

the adjacent former monastery, **Sna Jolobil** (see p. 385) sells intricate pieces of brocade and other hand-loomed textiles.

A few blocks north is the living, labyrinthine **mercado municipal** (Av. General Utrilla at Nicaragua). The daily market is especially vivid on Saturdays, when Tzeltal and Tzotzil men and women arrive dressed traditionally in brilliant garments, the women's braids woven with jewel-toned ribbons.

Another home-turned-museum is **Na Bolom** (Av. Vicente Guerrero 33, tel 967/678-1418, www.nabolom. org, closed Mon., $$). Longtime Chiapas residents Swiss photojournalist Trudy Blom and her husband, Danish archaeologist Franz Blom, for decades welcomed students, researchers, and Lacandón Indians into their home. The obligatory tour provides insight into this unique guesthouse, restaurant, botanical garden, and library. Tours ($$$$$) depart daily at 10 a.m. for San Juan Chamula and Zinacantán. ∎

San Cristóbal de las Casas

⚠ 283 B3

Visitor Information

✉ Av. Miguel Hidalgo 2

☎ 967/678-6570 or 967/678-0665 (Palacio Municipal)

Museo Sergio Castro

If you want to learn more about local weaving and culture, visit the Museo Sergio Castro (Guadalupe Victoria 38, tel 967/678-4289, $). Art historian Sergio Castro gives nightly lectures and slide shows about weaving and shows his considerable collection. He speaks various languages, so call when you hit town to schedule a visit on the appropriate night.

Maya Villages Around San Cristóbal

Religion, spirituality, family, and duty are the threads from which everyday life in Chiapas is woven. Ceremony and custom pervade daily ritual, and even the elaborate designs woven painstakingly into textiles have special significance. Culturally and sometimes physically isolated from mainstream Mexico, the Tzotzil and Tzeltal villages around San Cristóbal maintain ancient traditions as they deal with the interference of well-meaning outsiders.

The Chamula are a large and relatively prosperous group of Tzotzil-speaking people that have their municipal seat in **San Juan Chamula,** about 7 miles (11 km) from San Cristóbal. Most women and girls in San Juan wear distinctive, hairy, black-wool wrap skirts held in place by wide cotton belts, and short-sleeved, blue or white blouses lined with decorative trim. Traditional menswear consists of white cotton trousers and shirt, with a fleecy wool cloak for warmth.

The physical and spiritual center of this traditional town is its enchanting **church,** dedicated to St. John the Baptist. The beauty of the church's facade would move all but the most hopeless philistine. An arched doorway—decorated with rows of stylized flowers in sea green, vivid violet, hot pink, gold, and blues—contrasts soulfully with the simple lines of the bright white facade.

The church offers no formal services and has no pews. Seated on the floor amid fragrant pine needles and powerful copal incense, worshippers chant prayers while lighting rows of tiny candles. Lining the walls are Catholic saints dressed in clothing respectfully woven by the local women. Taking photographs or video recordings inside the church is both strictly forbidden and severely punished with fines and/or jail sentences.

Visitors to town must register at the tourist office, pay a small fee to visit the church, and get a short but stern admonition

A colorful Sunday market occupies the plaza in front of San Juan Chamula's church.

EXPERIENCE: Going 'Round with the Experts

Some folks just want to be entertained on tour, but others with the need or desire for accurate, up-to-date information require more of their guides.

MayaSites Travel Services (*tel 877/620-8715 in U.S., www.mayasites. com*) counts on the services of archaeologists with plenty of field experience (as well as a Ph.D.) to lead custom tours to Maya archaeological sites. Guides include Christopher Powell, who trained in Maya archaeological studies out of the University of Texas at Austin—associated for decades with excavations in Mexico—and Lilia Lizama Aranda, a Yucatán native.

For those lovers of archaeology who actually want to get their hands dirty,

the website of the **Archaeological Institute of America** (AIA; *tel 617/353-9361 in U.S., www.archaeological.org*) lists volunteers opportunities for students and aficionados.

National Geographic Expeditions (*tel 888/966 8687, www.national geo graphicexpeditions.com*) organizes ventures to Mexico (as well as other parts of the world) accompanied with world-class field experts and scholars.

Affiliated with the Smithsoian Institution, **Smithsonian Journeys** (*tel 877/338-8687 in U.S., www.smithsonianjo urneys.org*) also runs specialty tours to Mexico, tending to focus on art, architecture, and archaeology.

---

about church protocol. Visit San Juan Chamula on Sunday, when vendors fill the church square, or during a holiday celebration.

About 5 miles (8 km) away, **Zinacantán** is a Tzotzil town whose inhabitants are known for their flowers. Lilies, chrysanthemums, gladioli, and roses grow in their fields and gladden their altars. They can be purchased at the town's small Sunday market, although many growers sell them wholesale in the steamy lowlands. Embroidered flowers adorn the women's bright blue shawls and the thinly striped pink shirts of the men.

Sights in Zinacantán include the **Iglesia de San Lorenzo** (*Isabel la Católica at 5 de Febrero, $*) and the adjacent **Museo Sna Tsotz Levetik,** a traditional building with utilitarian and decorative items.

A half-day guided tour ($$$) is an excellent way to visit

Zinacantán and San Juan Chamula and can be arranged through Na Bolom (see p. 287) or with **Alex and Raul** (*tel 967/678-3741, e-mail: alexyraultours@yahoo.com.mx*). Guides usually visit specific families and arrange weaving demonstrations. They also know what can be photographed; except for children begging, the indigenous people in Chiapas do not appreciate being photographed. Area tour operators also offer horseback riding tours to San Juan Chamula ($$$$).

A dramatic drive through the mountains due north of San Cristóbal brings you to **San Pedro Chenalhó,** set in a pretty river valley. The Sunday market day is a celebrated rural ritual and reason enough to visit.

Equally rewarding in terms of mountain scenery is a drive to the Tzeltal village of **Tenejapa,** set in a pretty river valley 17 miles (27 km) northeast of San Cristóbal. ∎

San Cristóbal de las Casas

⧉ 283 B3

Visitor Information

✉ Av. Miguel Hidalgo 2

☎ 967/678-6570 or 967/678-0665 (Palacio Municipal)

Palenque

More than just an awesome archaeological site, Palenque has one of the region's last remaining patches of evergreen tropical forest. Epiphyte-draped trees surround graceful pyramids topped with delicate temples, glowing the color of rich cream in the tropical sun. Small rivers crisscross the site, and trails through unexcavated portions of the 4,400-acre (1,780 ha) reserve lead to parties of squawking parrots and shrieking howler monkeys, where silent Jesus Christ lizards and snakes slink under damp fallen leaves.

The geometric stone ruins of Palenque stand in stark contrast to their jungle surroundings.

Its exuberant tropical setting and harmonious, graceful archi-tecture make Palenque magic. Corbeled vaults permit larger doorways, giving the buildings a refined appearance enhanced by delicate roof combs, mansard roofs, and T-shaped windows evocative of the wind god, Ik. Of all the Maya sites, Palenque is among the most elegant, mysterious, and accessible.

Accessibility was the key to Palenque's initial success. Built on a natural terrace overlooking the floodplain of the Río Usumacinta, the city served as the center of trade between the Petén region,

the highlands of Chiapas, and the Grijalva Valley. Knowledge and ideas as well as trade goods flowed along the wide Usuma-cinta, especially during the Late Classic era (A.D. 600–800), when Palenque flourished. Under leaders such as Pakal the Great and his oldest son and successor, Chan Bahlum, Palenque joined Calakmul, Tikal, and Copán as one of the most influential kingdoms of the lowland Maya.

Large panels throughout the city were commissioned to illustrate the royal dynasty and its accomplishments. A dearth of suitable stone in the region explains the use of exquisite bas-relief carvings, in limestone and stucco, in lieu of the stelae favored elsewhere in the Maya world. Many of the carvings were ordered by Chan Bahlum, who traced his lineage back 11 gen-erations, beginning with a mythic ruler nicknamed "Lady Beastie."

Among the most stellar examples are the three elaborate stucco panels found within the **Templo de las Inscripciones,** containing about 620 glyphs. Royalty in elaborate feathered headdresses stand on monster masks; each holds a representation of the god K'awil, one of three gods worshipped as mythic ancestors. Access to the temple is now forbidden; you'll have to be satisfied with reproductions in the site museum. To the right, as you enter the site, the **Temple of the Skull** can still be climbed.

The monumental Temple of the Inscriptions was commissioned by Chan Bahlum's father, Pakal the Great (also called Kan-Hanab-Pakal II), as his royal tomb. Unveiled by Mexican archaeologist Alberto Ruz Lhuillier in 1952, this tomb is to date Mexico's most elaborate burial site. Sixty-six narrow steps lead deep within the pyramid to the crypt, where portraits of prior sovereigns decorate the walls in stucco relief.

Still bearing traces of red paint, the sarcophagus's 5-ton (4.5 metric ton) lid of intricately carved limestone depicts Pakal's descent into the underworld. Near the top, a bird symbolic of the heavens perches on the sacred ceiba tree. The crypt's contents, including Pakal's remains and rings, necklaces, ear spools, and a funerary mask in a mosaic of jade, with eyes of obsidian and shell, are displayed at Mexico City's Museo Nacional de Antropología (see pp. 198–201).

Across the Río Otolum is the **Grupo de la Cruz.** In 1998, finds in Temple 19 revealed a previously unknown ruler, Uc-Pakal-Kinich, as well as possible liaisons with rulers at Copán, in present-day Honduras. Surrounding a large plaza, the group takes its name from cross-like images found in the **Templo de la Cruz Foliada.**

Within its sunken courtyard, several sets of carvings depict captured enemy rulers in various poses of submission and mutilation. Depicting a holy ceiba tree decorated with cornstalks, the stone panel shows ruler Chan Bahlum's ascent to power.

At the north end of the plaza, five tiers lead to the large **Templo de la Cruz,** which also displays the World Tree motif. Its roof comb, one of the highest in Palenque, is in excellent condition. Here, panels depicting the royal ancestors emphasize their role as mediators between heaven and Earth.

On the west side of the plaza, themes of war and sacrifice dominate the well-preserved **Templo del Sol,** where the face of the jaguar-man god peers from a Maya war shield.

INSIDER TIP:

Be wary of public transportation in the Palenque area. Drivers will try to charge you double the normal cost if they think you are a tourist.

—KATHERINE AMATO
National Geographic field researcher

Back across the river, the **Palacio** served the royal family as both ceremonial and living quarters. The complex of vaulted galleries and rooms surrounding interior courtyards was built and added to over many centuries.

On the west steps, glyphs heralding the birth of Pakal the Great are among the site's earliest, while its unusual, four-tiered tower (possibly an observatory) was built

Palenque
🄰 283 C4

Visitor Information
✉ Carr. Catazaja–Palenque Km 27.5 at Calle Dr. Manuel Velasco Suárez, Plaza Chula Vista, Local 2
☎ 916/345-0356

just before the city's disintegration.

Northeast of the Palace, divergent paths enter the jungle shade, a welcome respite from the intense tropical sun. After crossing **Río Murciélagos** (Bat River), a right-hand path leads to **Grupo C,** a half dozen small temples surrounding a central plaza. The

left-hand path leads to **Grupo Murciélagos** (Bat Group), a residential complex for Maya nobles, and to a series of cascades forming the **Baño de la Reina** or Queen's Bath.

East of the Río Otolum, the four-

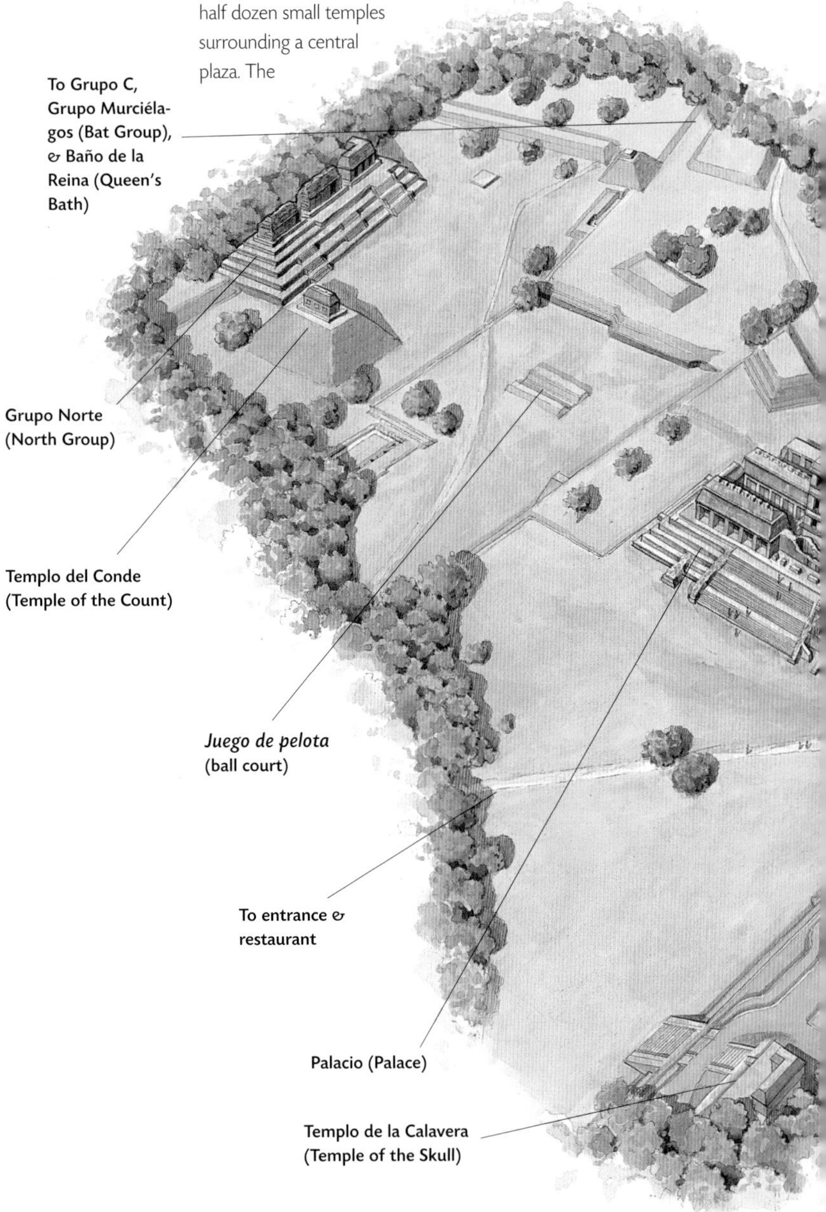

To Grupo C, Grupo Murciélagos (Bat Group), & Baño de la Reina (Queen's Bath)

Grupo Norte (North Group)

Templo del Conde (Temple of the Count)

Juego de pelota (ball court)

To entrance & restaurant

Palacio (Palace)

Templo de la Calavera (Temple of the Skull)

tiered **Templo del Conde** (Temple of the Count) was named for the 19th-century German eccentric who set up housekeeping here. Nearby is a compact *juego de pelota* (ball court), as well as the **Grupo Norte,** whose plazas and temples were among the last constructed before the city's demise.

Retreat to the restaurant for a meal or cool drink during the hottest hours of the day. The air-conditioned **site museum** *(closed Mon.),* where your ticket stub gains entrance at no additional cost, is located at the main entrance but at least half a mile (1 km) down the road. You can access it from the archaeological zone by taking the *andador ecológica* (ecological path) past the Groups Bat and C. Excellent exhibits are labeled in English, Spanish, and Tzotzil. Among the museum's collection is the **Palace Tablet,** an intricate stone relief detailing the lineage of Palenque's rulers. Shuttles *($)* make a loop between the ruins, hotels along the highway, and town. ■

Templo de la Cruz (Temple of the Cross)

Templo de la Cruz Foliada (Temple of the Foliated Cross)

Templo del Sol (Temple of the Sun)

Río Otolum

Palenque

Templo de las Inscripciones (Temple of the Inscriptions)

Templo de la Reina Roja (Tomb of the Red Queen)

Drive: Palenque to Parque Nacional Lagunas de Montebello

This route follows the Pan-American Highway (Hwy. 199) between Palenque and Parque Nacional Lagunas de Montebello. The highway climbs out of the tropical jungle to rolling hills and lush valleys around Ocosingo before continuing to the evergreen mountains around San Cristóbal de las Casas. From this endearing colonial city, the route descends slightly to end at the Guatemalan border.

An aerial view of the ruins of Toniná

Recommended places to stay overnight as you make this magnificent drive are Palenque, San Cristóbal de las Casas, and either Comitán de Domínguez or the elegant Parador Santa María, near Chinkultic and the Lagunas de Montebello.

After visiting the ruins at **Palenque ❶** (see pp. 290–293) drive south along Highway 199 for about 14 miles (22 km) to see the 130-foot (40 m) waterfall at **Misol-Ha** (*$*), most impressive when swollen with late summer and fall rains. Swim in the pool at the base of the waterfall, or explore the cave behind the falls, which leads to a subterranean pool. The site has restrooms, basic camping facilities, cabins (*www.misol-ha.com;misol-ha@palenque.com.mx, $*), and a simple restaurant.

About 25 miles (40 km) to the south, follow a dirt road for several miles to the

NOT TO BE MISSED:

Palenque • Agua Azul • Toniná
• San Cristóbal de las Casas • Parque
Nacional Lagunas de Montebello

extraordinary falls of **Agua Azul ❷** (*$$*). Surrounded by exuberant tropical vegetation, the river plunges into a rocky gorge, forming hundreds of frothy white falls and, during the dry season, crystal-clear pools that give the site its name: blue water. Hike down the canyon to bathe in a series of lovely interconnected pools or up from the parking lot to take advantage of lots of different views. Some people feel the multitude of stands selling crafts detracts from the experience; others enjoy the shopping opportunity as well as the informal cafés selling regional treats.

Continuing south, the highway curves and climbs past vistas of patchwork fields and farms, abandoning the sometimes oppressive lowlands for the refreshing climate around the Ocosingo Valley, with mixed broadleaf vegetation and many species of birds. Little-visited by tourists, **Ocosingo** is a pleasant, fairly prosperous mestizo town.

A detour of about 6 miles (10 km) southeast of Ocosingo on a paved road brings you to the important but little-known ruins at **Toniná** ❸ *(919/670-9589, $)*, which flourished at the beginning of the tenth century, around the time Palenque was being abandoned. Here, one of the tallest pyramids of the Maya world rises 230 feet (70 m) above the Grand Plaza, commanding an awesome view of the valley and the mountains to

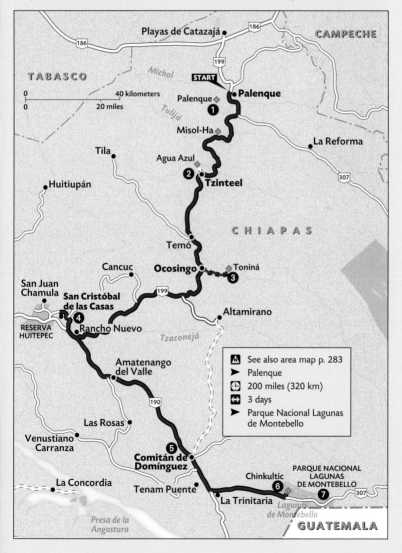

For crystalline water, visit Agua Azul in the dry season.

the south. Most likely the city's Mayan name, which means "big house of stones," refers to this massive pyramid.

Construction of this structure took place over more than a thousand years. Successive generations built new palaces and temples; to date, 4 of the former and 13 of the latter have been identified throughout the seven-level pyramid. In 1992, the remarkably well-preserved **Mural of the Four Suns** was discovered on the sixth level. The 13-foot-long (4 m) stucco painting represents a Maya codex describing the four distinct eras of creation. Crowning the structure are the **Temple of the Prisoners** and the **Temple of the Smoky Mirror.** Near

the base of the pyramid lies the **sarcophagus** of one of the city's last rulers, Tzotz-Choj. Entrance to the small but worthwhile **site museum** *(closed Mon.)* is included in the price.

Return to Highway 199, and continue west for 70 miles (112 km) along this and Highway 190, passing cattle ranches, small farms, and coffee plantations, to **San Cristóbal de las Casas ❹** (see pp. 286–287). After your visit to this engaging city, return to Highway 190 (the Pan-American Highway) and head southeast toward the Guatemalan border.

After about 22 miles (35 km), look for the Tzeltal village of **Amatenango del Valle** on the right. You'll spot the entrance to this pottery-making town by the traditional and more modern clay pots and animal figures along the highway. The traditional method of producing the town's decorative and utilitarian vessels is under an open-air wood fire. Amatenango's women spend their time building pots instead of weaving, so they must buy the cloth for their *huipiles* (dresses). They still find the time to embroider the blouses with designs in red and yellow.

Continue south another 25 miles (40 km) to **Comitán de Domínguez** ❺ *(visitor information, Calle Central Benito Juárez 6, Plaza Principal, tel 963/632-0244)*, a wonderful small city built by the Spaniards as a commercial and transportation hub. Today the city serves the same function for Tzeltal Indians and mestizos in outlying ranches.

If you're interested in Mexican history or simply like republican-era edifices and antiques, it's worth a look at the **Casa-Museo Dr. Belisario Domínguez** *(Av. Belisario Domínguez 35, tel 963/632-1300, closed Mon., $)*. The medical doctor and Chiapas senator was a revolution hero whose frank and unflattering assessment of the Huerta administration led to his assassination in 1913. Dr. Domínguez was born in this gracious house in 1863; preserved here are his instruments, pharmaceuticals, and other medical paraphernalia as well as photographs, documents, and letters that date from the Mexican Revolution.

Other sights of interest in Comitán are the **Catedral Santo Domingo de Guzmán** *(1a*

Av. Oriente Sur, on main square), the **Iglesia San Caralampio** *(Calle Norte Oriente 2a at Av. Oriente 4a, tel 963/632-0673)*, and the **Museo de Arte Hermila Castellanos** *(Av. Central Sur 51, tel 963/632-2082)*, with an excellent collection of contemporary Mexican art.

Beyond Comitán, it's less than 6 miles (10 km) to **Tenam Puente** *($)*, a large but unremarkable archaeological site. Built on a strategic hilltop location, this religious center and residential area flourished during the Classic and Early Postclassic periods, after the Maya had abandoned cities such as Palenque.

Continue along the Pan-American Highway, detouring after 4.5 miles (7 km) onto the road marked "Lagunas de Montebello." Twelve miles (19 km) down the road, a left-hand dirt road leads to **Chinkultic** ❻ *($)*, a Maya city that was abandoned just a few hundred years after reaching its apogee during the Late Classic period (A.D. 600–900). Not many structures have been restored on this site, but there's an incredible view from the top of the main pyramid—a rather steep climb from the park entrance. Swim in the *cenote azul* (the sinkhole is a bit hard to find; ask the park guard), or visit the ball court, less impressive since its bas-relief sculpture was moved to the Museo Nacional de Antropología in Mexico City (see pp. 198–201).

The last stop of the journey is **Parque Nacional Lagunas de Montebello** ❼ (see pp. 298–299), where more than a dozen lakes of various hues can easily be seen from different viewpoints.

Rules of the Road

Mexican roads are generally in good condition, but cobblestone roads in colonial towns like San Cristóbal de las Casas can be tough on a vehicle's shocks. Difficulties also arise in the rainy season, when potholes form and dirt roads to some beaches, archaeological sites, and small towns may become impassable. Although expensive, it's safer and faster to take toll roads whenever possible.

The most important road signs you should look out for are:

Curva peligrosa—Dangerous curve
Disminuye su velocidad—Slow down
No rebase—Do not pass
No rebase con raya continua—Don't pass with solid line
Puesto de control militar—Military checkpoint
Topes/vibradores—Speed bumps

Parque Nacional Lagunas de Montebello

Lagunas de Montebello, Chiapas's only national park, comprises 14,880 acres (6,022 ha) of temperate forest along Mexico's southern border with Guatemala. Lakes of different hues are sprinkled throughout the park like translucent marbles flung down by a tempestuous giant. Oxides cause the lakes to take on different shades; some glow a deep green, others are emerald, steel gray, greenish blue, violet, or pale blue.

One of the more than 50 lakes of the Parque Nacional Lagunas de Montebello

Because of weeds growing on the lake bottom and occasional drownings over a period of many years, locals do not recommend swimming in the majority of these lovely lakes. (Bear in mind that Mexicans are generally not avid swimmers.) However, even they deem a few lakes safe, and others can be toured on log rafts, rowboats, and pedal boats. The most accessible lakes have nearby parking lots and food and soda stands attended by local women eager to prepare you a simple meal or, at the very least, sell you a bag of chips and a drink.

Local young men wait at the park entrance, ready to hop in

your car and give you a lake tour for an appropriate tip. Just beyond the entrance gate, the paved road forks. The left-hand road leads to the **Laguna Encantada** (Enchanted Lake); half a dozen lakes can be appreciated as a slice of water in the distance.

INSIDER TIP:

Even if your skills are basic, try Spanish every chance you can with locals. They'll love you!

—NINA-NOELLE HALL
National Geographic contributor

At the far end of the road, hike around large **Laguna Bosque Azul,** take an inexpensive rowboat tour, or rent a pedal boat. Boys offer hour-long horseback excursions in the forest, where you can see native birds, a small cave, and two sinkholes. There is a parking lot as well as a simple restaurant.

To visit the southern lakes, return to the park entrance and take the right fork toward Tziscao, about 7.5 miles (12 km) distant. First you will come to large **Laguna de Montebello** (a ten-minute walk down a dirt road), which is recommended for swimming. Park right at the broad lakeshore, where locals rent out their horses and sell snacks.

Continue toward Tziscao. A signed road leads to a cluster of five lovely lakes, **Cinco Lagunas,** which can be viewed from the lookout point. (This group is about a 30-minute walk from the main road.) Farther along the paved road, deep-blue **Lago Pojoj** lies down a steep road. The last of the park's major lakes is **Tziscao,** named for the community along its eastern shore.

The **Hotel Tziscao** (*tel 963/633-5244, $*) offers rather musty cabins, camping, and a restaurant for guests. You can swim at the sandy beach or take a rowboat trip around the lake. Motorboats are not permitted on Montebello's lakes.

Chiapas Amber

Chiapas is one of a handful of places in the world to produce amber, fossilized resin of the guapinol tree. It takes millions of years to produce this lustrous material, which is extracted from mines. Ranging in color from yellow to red in 30 different hues, amber may contain insects, bubbles, or tiny leaves or debris. Amber is thought by some to extract *malas vibras* (bad vibes) from the body, making it valuable as jewelry.

The lake district is about 37 miles (60 km) southeast of Comitán, where you can pick up a map at the tourist office. The best way to tour the park is by car. If you choose to take a bus or taxi, these can easily be found in Comitán. Buses access both Laguna Bosque Azul and Tziscao; you can alight at any point in between. ∎

Parque Nacional Lagunas de Montebello

🅰 283 C2

Visitor Information

✉ Primera Avenida Poniente Sur #3 Comitán

☎ 963/632-4047, 963/632-8253, or 01800/280-3500 (toll-free within Mexico)

The Maya Calendar

The Maya and the Aztec shared the same 260-day ceremonial calendar (Tzolkin in Maya or Tonalamatl in Náhuatl), a ritualistic almanac used for astrological prophecies as well as decision-making in daily affairs. Each day was ruled by several lords whose personalities influenced the day, much as the sun, moon, and planets affect daily life according to astrologers.

Together, the monkey glyph, the god's head, and the skull mean 16 days.

The Tzolkin, or sacred calendar, was a cyclical calendar of 260 days. As with our days of the week, its 20 named days followed each other in endless succession. Combined with each day was a number from 1 to 13, for a total of 260 days, such as 2 Ahau or 8 Eb. Each day was ruled by the lord of its name and of its number. The number 13 was lucky, so both the 13th day and days paired with the number 13 were often auspicious.

Maya mathematicians also devised a 365-day solar calendar, which they knew to be only an approximation of the Earth's solar orbit. This calendar, called the Haab, consisted of 18 periods of 20 days each (totaling 360), plus five unlucky days at the end of the period, called Uayeb. The days between the end of one "year" and the beginning of the next were, according to Maya astronomers and priests, extremely unstable and dangerous, as they pertained to neither one year nor the other. The two calendars were then meshed, like two cogs of unequal size, to form the Calendar Round, which permitted a deeper level of both practical and spiritual interpretation. Crops were planted, battles waged, and rulers crowned on the most auspicious dates. The cycle repeated every 52 years.

As these cyclical calendars eventually repeated themselves, they were not useful in recording the date of historical events. For this reason the Maya invented the Long Count, a calendar based on multiples of 20. The most basic unit was a day (called a *kin*, or sun), followed by a *uinal* (20 days), a *tun* (360 days), and so on. Think of it as expressing a date this way: "It happened 5 centuries, 8 decades, 3 years, 2 weeks, and 4 days ago."

Throughout the Classic era, dates carved on thousands of stelae throughout the Maya world precisely recorded birth, death, marriage, ascension to power, and decisive battles, providing today's scientists with many clues about ancient Maya history. According to this manner of reckoning, Creation occurred in the year 0.0.0.0.0., which Maya expert Sir Eric Thompson (1898–1975) interpreted as August 11, 3114 B.C. Most scholars still agree. Its ceremonial date is 4 Ahau 8 Cumku.

Fascinated by mathematics as both a scientific tool and an art, the ancient Maya played endlessly with numbers, had a place-value system of counting, and invented the concept of zero (perhaps adapting an earlier Olmec idea). Using simple observation and their advanced mathematical knowledge, they calculated the orbit of Venus and other planets nearly as precisely as astronomers do today.

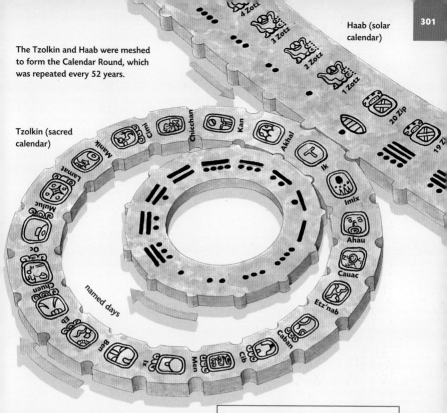

The Tzolkin and Haab were meshed to form the Calendar Round, which was repeated every 52 years.

Haab (solar calendar)

Tzolkin (sacred calendar)

named days

The unlucky five-day Uayeb comes at the end of the Haab.

Month glyphs of the Haab

Pop

Uo

Zip

Zotz

Zec

Xul

Yaxkin

Mol

Ch'en

Yax

Zac

Ceh

Mac

Kankin

Muan

Pax

Kayab

Cumku

Uayeb

The numbers

•	• •	• • •	• • • •
1	2	3	4

▬	▬ •	▬ • •	▬ • • •
5	6	7	8

▬ • • • •	▬▬	▬▬ •	▬▬ • •
9	10	11	12

▬▬ • • •	▬▬ • • • •	▬▬▬	▬▬▬ •
13	14	15	16

▬▬▬ • •	▬▬▬ • • •	▬▬▬ • • • •	◉
17	18	19	0

The Maya system of counting was based on 20 "digits," literally ten fingers and ten toes. The numbers 0–19 could be written either with head glyphs or using a place-value system based on five. A dot represented 1; a bar, 5; and a seashell or similar glyph, the placeholder 0. These numbers could be written horizontally or vertically. For example, the number 20 would be: • ◉

Yaxchilán & Bonampak

Both Yaxchilán and Bonampak flourished in the Late Classic era. As it did for other Maya centers in eastern Chiapas, the luxuriant Lacandón rain forest supplied their needs, while the wide Río Usumacinta and its many tributaries facilitated transportation. Today, these and other protected enclaves form a tiny buffer against deforestation in the threatened Lacandón rain forest and an untouristy destination for lovers of Maya lore.

Carved lintels, stelae, and vine-draped buildings characterize Yaxchilán.

Yaxchilán

🅰 283 D3

Visitor Information

☎ 916/617-0550 (Tuxtla Gutiérrez) or 01800/280-3500 (toll-free within Mexico)

Yaxchilán

Their jungle location is part of the allure of these two remote archaeological sites. Towering mahogany trees host vines and blossoming epiphytes, creating a home for colorful toucans, parrots, flycatchers, orioles, and tanagers. Vampire bats hang in the damp chambers of ruined limestone palaces, centipedes creep along moist green walls, mosquitoes suck your blood.

Although Yaxchilán is more extensive, and its setting more lush, both sites have a wonderful, wild, "lost in the jungle" feel.

About 118 miles (190 km) southeast of Palenque, Yaxchilán was built on a terrace at a large bend in the Río Usumacinta. Howler monkeys roar from the tops of enormous ceiba trees, held sacred by the Maya as the Tree of Life. The humid tropical air seems to have eased the rigid poses of temples, palaces, and stelae, which blend with—but don't completely succumb to—the pervasive rain forest.

Enter the site through Building 19, or **el Laberinto** (the Labyrinth), named for its maze of small rooms. The upper story consists of a central hall annexed by a series of rooms; narrow stairways lead to subterranean chambers. The facade, originally covered in molded and painted stucco, gives way to remnants of roof combs above a wide cornice. This and other vine-draped, gray-green buildings that inspired the name "Place of Green Stones" face the broad, grassy **Gran Plaza.** Among these are a steam room **(Edificio 14)** and an I-shaped *juego de pelota,* or ball court.

Graceful roof combs and upper facades with remnants of beautifully worked figures in stucco and stone are among Yaxchilán's most impressive elements. The large number of intricately carved lintels and stelae tells tales of conquest and ceremonial life: Epigraphers have identified glyphs symbolizing ascension to power, birth dates, and marriage. Among the most impressive lintels are those found on Buildings 12, 16, and 22. **Stele 11,** moved to the Gran Plaza from several miles away, is the site's pièce de résistance. The larger figure represents Yaxchilán's most important ruler: Pájaro Jaguar, or Bird Jaguar.

South of the Gran Plaza, stairs lead up to the **Gran Acrópolis,** which commands a fantastic view of the site. Here you will find the well-preserved **Edificio 33,** with its headless sculpture

of Pájaro Jaguar, to whom the building is dedicated. The temple's elaborate roof combs are intact, but its fabulous lintel is now at the British Museum in London. Short walks through the jungle bring you to the **Acrópolis Sur** (where **Edificio 40** has traces of original murals) and the **Acrópolis Pequeña,** with excellent bas-relief lintels in **Edificios 42** and **44.**

Bonampak

A less important center under the jurisdiction of Yaxchilán, Bonampak *($$),* to the south, was established around the year A.D. 600 near the Río Lacanjá, a tributary of the Usumacinta. The first outsiders to visit were two Americans working for the

INSIDER TIP:

Visit an archaeological site early. The heat in the afternoon can be very uncomfortable, especially if you're in Chiapas or Oaxaca.

—KATHERINE AMATO
National Geographic field researcher

United Fruit Company, who in 1946 convinced a Lacandón Indian to reveal the site of devotional rituals.

The highlight of a visit to Bonampak is the murals of the **Templo de las Pinturas** (Temple of the Paintings). Although the recreation at Mexico City's Museo Nacional de Antropología (see pp. 198–201) shows the murals with their original, brilliant colors

Bonampak

283 D3

Visitor Information

Carr. Catazaja–Palenque Km 27.5 at Calle Dr. Manuel Velasco Suárez, Plaza Chula Vista, Local 2

916/345-0356 (Palenque)

and bold outlines, the fading scenes viewed in situ still convey a wondrous force. In the first room, the royal family exults in its heir apparent, while musicians entertain. Above the doorway, the lord of Bonampak, Chaan Muan, is resplendent in embroidered loincloth, jaguar-skin skirt, jade collar, and headdress of quetzal feathers.

Violent battle scenes dominate the second room. A captive kneels in supplication before Chaan Muan, while others are tortured and humiliated. A prisoner slumps in exhaustion on the temple steps. In the third chamber, victory is celebrated with elaborate ritual. Elite women perform a bloodletting of the tongue, while lords in grand costume execute a graceful dance.

These murals rank among the finest of Classic Maya art. Attention was paid to expression, foreshortening makes perspective realistic, and each panel is a harmonious triumph of composition. The murals, dated 790, seem to be the last work done at the site. Chaan Muan and his bride from

Bonampak's powerful murals date from the end of the eighth century A.D.

Yaxchilán, Lady Rabbit, may have been the last rulers at Bonampak. No evidence has been found that the baby boy so proudly presented in the temple paintings was ever crowned.

Other temples and palaces on the Gran Plaza and adjoining **Acrópolis** can be explored with the help of a guide waiting just inside the entrance. Guide service is optional, but with luck you'll get an English speaker or, if you speak Spanish, a loquacious Lacandón Indian eager to relate the tales of their forefathers—sometimes strangely interwoven with Bible stories introduced by missionaries. Even visitors with cars must make the trip from the site parking lot to the entrance with a Lacandón driver ($); it's an obligatory contribution to the community.

Long overland day tours from Palenque visit both sites; a 30-minute boat trip from Frontera Corozal (where comfortable tourist accommodations are available) completes the journey to Yaxchilán. Tours in small aircraft can be arranged from Ocosingo, San Cristóbal, Comitán, and Palenque through **Servicios Aereos San Cristóbal** (tel 963/632-4664, www .serviciosaereossancristobal.com). You'll fly over waterfalls and have the thrill of landing right at the archaeological sites.

Bring mosquito repellent, water, sunscreen, and a wide-brimmed hat. This close to the border, it's also wise to bring your passport or international identification and tourist card. Fer-de-lance and other poisonous snakes are found here, so watch where you put your hands and feet. ■

More Places to Visit in Chiapas

Reserva de la Biósfera El Triunfo

Located in the Sierra Madre de Chiapas, El Triunfo Biosphere Reserve was established in 1990. Most of its 494,000 acres (200,000 ha) constitute a buffer zone; approximately one-fifth of this region of mountains, valleys, and plains has been designated federal land. Pine, mixed, and low tropical forests are home to several species of endangered cats; rare quetzal birds hide in the cloud forest.

Permission to enter the reserve must be obtained a week in advance, and visits are advisable only during the dry season (mid-Nov.–mid-May). The park entrance is about 115 miles (184 km) south of Tuxtla Gutiérrez via Angel Albino Corzo. The only accommodations are a rustic lodge, though camping is permitted.
🗺 283 B2 ☎ 961/611-3891 or 961/611-3975

INSIDER TIP:

The ecolodge Las Guacamayas in the Lacandón rain forest is great for ecotourists. The accommodations are very nice.

—KATHERINE AMATO
National Geographic field researcher

Reserva de la Biósfera Montes Azules

Together with Calakmul Biosphere Reserve and the Petén region of Guatemala, Montes Azules represents the largest remaining virgin rain forest north of the Amazon Basin. The 818,000-acre (331,000 ha) reserve, whose name means "blue mountains," changes significantly in elevation, from near sea level at the Río Lacandón, in the south, to around 5,250 feet (1,600 m) in the more mountainous west. The varied topography produces

swamps, lakes, rivers, evergreen and tropical rain forest, palm forest, and pine and oak forest. Of the 3,000 plant species, there are 320 species of orchids alone. It is best to visit January through September.

Services within the park are limited. The town of Emiliano Zapata is working to establish ecotourism and offers lodgings in communal cottages. Guided camping trips of four days or more take you to **Laguna Miramar,** the largest lake in the Lacandón rain forest, with excellent hiking, snorkeling, and canoeing. It is possible to get to Lake Miramar by road (about five hours from Ocosingo) or by small plane, a thrilling 30-minute ride via **Servicios Aereos San Cristóbal** (see p. 304).

Near the park's southern border is **Centro Ecoturístico Las Guacamayas** or **Ara Macao** *(Reforma Agraria, tel 664/134-1137)*, a community-run ecotourism lodge. Comfortable cabins with wide porches are located on the right bank of the Río Lacandón, where you can swim, fish, or travel upriver over a series of small smooth-rock falls within the reserve. Local guides lead hikes into the surrounding forest, where there are harpy eagles, hawks, yellow-throated toucans, and the endangered red macaw for which the reserve is named. It's about five hours south of Palenque along federal and state highways to the town of Reforma Agraria; charter small planes in Comitán.
🗺 283 C3/D3

Reserva Huitepec

On the east slope of 8,860-foot (2,700 m) Volcán Huitepec, one of the highest mountains in the Chiapas range, is Huitepec *(closed Mon., $)*, a 335-acre (135 ha) nature reserve. Oak forest prevails at the lower elevations; higher up are cloud forests cloaked in epiphytes and ferns. Many of the 300-plus plant species have been used for generations by local Maya for medicinal and religious purposes. Trekkers may see foxes, armadillos, flying squirrels, and raccoons, but more easily spotted are some of the reserve's 60 resident bird species. You can wander the forest trails on your own or arrange a Tuesday or Thursday guided visit through **Pronatura** (see sidebar p. 73), based in San Cristóbal de las Casas *(Pedro Moreno 1 at Juárez, Barrio Santa Lucia, tel 967/678-5000, www.pronatura-sur.org).*

⚠ 283 B3

Tapachula

Most people visit Tapachula as the gateway to Guatemala, but this is a friendly (if hot and humid) city with several interesting sights in the surrounding countryside. Maya stelae and artifacts can be seen at the **Museo Regional del Soconusco** *(8a Av. Norte 24 between 1a & 3a Poniente, tel 962/626-4173),* or you can see them in situ at the **Izapa** *(Carr. a Talisman s/n, $),* a spread-out archaeological site about 15 minutes outside town. About half a mile (1 km) from the entrance is **Grupo F,** the best restored, with altars and ball court in addition to pyramids and stelae. Northeast of Tapachula and a stone's throw from Guatemala, the town of **Unión Juárez** makes an excellent base for mountain excursions. Bring your bathing suit and take an agreeable alpine walk to the **Cascadas de Muxbal,** where a waterfall in a narrow gorge forms a pretty pool. Mountaineers can make an overnight assault on 13,400-foot (4,085 m) **Volcán Tacaná.** About 7 miles (11 km) outside town, the working coffee plantation of **Centro Ecoturístico Santo Domingo** *(Municipio Unión Juárez, tel 962/627-0055, www. centroecoturiscosantodomingo.com, $)* was built by early 20th-century German immigrants using imported materials. The chalet-like structure has recently been restored and has a coffee museum, guest rooms, and a restaurant serving regional food.

⚠ 283 C1 ✉ Calle Octava Norte 20, Antiguo Palacio ☎ 962/625-5409

EXPERIENCE: Bunk Down in the Country

If you're willing to leave the road well-traveled, Chiapas offers excellent first-hand encounters with nature, man, and beast. The following ecotourism ventures provide income for local people and co-ops and take you far from the large groups of tourists at Palenque and San Cristóbal de las Casas.

Northwest of Tuxtla Gutiérrez en route to Tabasco, **Rancho del Lago del Rey Nezahualcoyotl** *(Carr. de Cuota a Ocozocuautla Km 136.6, tel 967/678-2550, www .ranchochiapas.com)* has cabins perched above its enormous namesake dam. Río La Venta provides fluvial visits to caves and rock formations.

In southern Chiapas, beautiful **El Chiflón** waterfalls *(www.chiflon* *.com.mx)* are less visited than Misol-Ha and Agua Azul. Although most folks visit just for a few hours, there are cabins among the trees. At the rustic landing where boats depart for Yaxchilán archaeological site, **Escudo Jaguar** *(Frontera Corozal, www.escudojag uarhotel.com)* has snug little thatch-roofed cabins and a nice restaurant overlooking the river. The people of this town are Tzeltal Maya. At one of the few Lacandón villages near the Bonampak ruins, **Campamento Río Lacanjá** *(tel 967/674-6660 in San Cristóbal, www .ecochiapas.com)* offers a glimpse of rural life. Simple, pleasant rooms share a veranda and a small restaurant. The taciturn staff offers guided hikes to wild places.

All of the above accommodations are less than $60 a night.

Lovely beaches and intriguing Maya ruins connected by two-lane highways on a peninsula as flat as a tortilla

Yucatán Peninsula

A street scene in convivial Campeche

Yucatán Peninsula

Throughout the Yucatán Peninsula, rural towns doze in the shadow of white-washed 16th-century monasteries. Each of the peninsula's three states—Quintana Roo, Campeche, and Yucatán—has scores of archaeological sites shrouded in jungle. Visitors can go deep-sea fishing and fly-fishing, snorkel along the world's second largest reef, and dive in underground rivers or in one of thousands of sinkholes. No place in Mexico has so much variety in so compact an area.

Warm water and the Palancar reef bring cruise ships and solo travelers to Cozumel island.

NOT TO BE MISSED:

The Yucatán Peninsula is a land without lakes or rivers, yet is covered in tropical forests. Rainwater filters through the porous subterranean limestone shelf to create an extensive underground river system. Sinkholes (*cenotes* in Spanish, *dzonot* in Maya) form when this thin layer of limestone collapses, revealing deep green pools or shallow turquoise lagoons. More than 2,000 have been discovered in the state of Yucatán alone.

Water was sacred to the ancient Maya, who worshipped the rain god Chac. Respected mathematicians, astronomers, and architects, the Maya built fabulous cities during the Classic era (A.D. 250–900). Cosmology, history, celestial events, and community achievements were recorded in the *Chilam Balam*—a living document added to until the 19th century. The Maya also covered stelae and other stone monuments in phonetic hieroglyphs. Luckily, many survived to be examined, but most of the Maya books were burned by Franciscan monks.

The Yucatán is an amalgam of distinct cultures. It is mainly Maya and

Spanish, but waves of Lebanese, French, and other immigrants came as well. Its unique cuisine combines the region's famous citrus fruits, honey, and fiery habanero chilies with saffron, annatto, capers, prunes, and other unusual flavors.

Festivals reflect the diversity too. Hanal Pixan (All Souls' Day) is celebrated in Mérida, Campeche, and throughout the countryside by preparing regional foods and altars for the dead. Campeche and Cozumel are known for their pre-Lenten carnivals. ■

Mexico City

Area of map detail

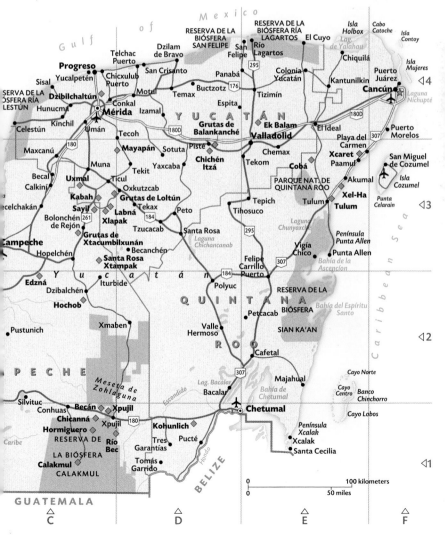

Quintana Roo

Quintana Roo became a state in 1974, shortly after the Mexican government baptized Cancún. It didn't take long for both entities to swell beyond all expectations. The state contains wildly popular vacation destinations, significant Maya ruins, and a coastline that exceeds all superlatives.

Cancún's pristine beaches lure tourists from around the world to its resorts.

Quintana Roo's semitropical climate is perfect most times of year. The Caribbean washes beaches from Cancún to Chetumal, on the border with Belize. Scrubby jungle covers most of the limestone terrain. Subterranean rivers flow through caves and into cenotes, enormous wells of cool, dark water. Tropical fish swim in underwater reserves, while sea turtles lumber ashore on summer nights to lay their eggs.

However, hurricanes do blow through between September and November. In recent years,

hurricanes carted off much of Cancún's sugar-white sand, which has been replaced with inferior sand from elsewhere.

Cancún attracts most of the state's visitors. Travelers with adventure in mind explore the Riviera Maya—the coastline between Cancún and Tulum, although old-timers bemoan what they call the "Cancún-ization" of this area.

The second longest chain of coral reefs in the world runs between Quintana Roo's mainland coast and the islands of Cozumel and Isla Mujeres. Sections of the reefs are littered with wrecked galleons from the 19th century and earlier. The coral they destroyed has grown back; the same can't be said for that crushed by modern cruise ships. Cozumel has become a major cruise port, much to the dismay of marine biologists.

The southern coast of Quintana Roo, long the provenance of small dive lodges and private homes, is now called the Costa Maya, which includes the coastline south of Sian Ka'an and inland jungles dotted with restored Maya archaeological sites in both Quintana Roo and Campeche. Majahual, the largest town between Punta Allen and Campeche, has become a cruise port, with ships calling at a modern terminal at Puerto Costa Maya. Development plans include golf courses and resort hotels. Some of Quintana Roo's most precious attributes have been preserved in nature parks or enhanced in resorts, but continued growth is inevitable.

Cancún

The nouveau riche of the resort world, Cancún lacks culture but is rich in real estate. The aquamarine sea laps the shores of the offshore island's northern coast and inland lagoons, while slapping more energetically the beaches along the east-facing Caribbean. Sultry days drift into warm evenings, when breezes ruffle coconut palms.

Designed in 1970 and developed by government agencies and private investors, Cancún now draws 3.5 million visitors a year and has the second busiest international airport in Mexico. It lacks the depth of resorts such as Acapulco and Puerto Vallarta, both of which grew rapidly but naturally out of existing villages. But for those with cash to spend, the all-inclusive resorts offer a wide variety of activities. Most of the larger beachfront hotels rent aquatic equipment, including body boards, snorkeling gear, sailboards, and personal watercraft, and many offer fishing, diving, kite-surfing, and skin-diving tours, party boats, and other such activities (see p. 316).

Cancún has large shopping malls and boutiques, although fewer open-air markets. Discos rock well into the morning, and (continued on p. 316)

Cancún

309 F4

Visitor Information

✉ Av. Tulum 26 at Coba

☎ 998/881-2745

www.cancun.info

La Feria del Cedral

In the mid-19th century, the Maya—virtual slaves in their own land—rose up against their Spanish and mestizo overlords. Today descendants of the Maya who fled to the island of Cozumel hold an annual festival thanking God for his help. Following a dawn prayer vigil on April 23, daily devotional prayers, or novenas, lead up to Day of the Holy Cross, May 3. On that day, female descendants of the founders perform *la danza de las cabezas de cochino* (Dance of the Pigs' Heads), representing an offering to God (and, for the less religiously inclined, an amazing photo opportunity). The festival has expanded over the years to include horse races, rodeos, cultural events, and live music.

Riviera Maya Drive

Dubbed the Riviera Maya, the coast along Highway 307 is full of diversions. Divers head for spooky cenotes (sinkholes) and caves or sunlit coves teeming with tropical fish; beach bums choose between bikini and beer hangouts or secluded stretches of untrammeled sand; sightseers climb pyramids; shoppers browse through folk-art boutiques; and everyone eats at least one meal of fresh fish a day.

Xcaret Eco Theme park combines the nature, culture, and archaeology of the Riviera Maya.

In the 1980s, Highway 307 had only two lanes. Pickups and buses lumbered along at a leisurely pace, sharing the asphalt with villagers lopping off roadside branches with machetes for fuel. A few signs pointed the way to campgrounds and small hotels on white-sand beaches. The highway is now four lanes wide, and hulking motor coaches whiz past idle wanderers in VW bugs. Bold entryways announce the presence of theme parks; more modest signs lead the way to special haunts.

NOT TO BE MISSED:

Playa del Carmen • Xcaret • Paamul • Tulum

Puerto Morelos ❶, 22 miles (36 km) south of Cancún, remains a sandy beach town, but it's growing, with a new marina and more sophisticated restaurants and shops. A coral reef littered with shipwrecks shelters

Río Lagartos

Gulf of Mexico

Isla Holbox

RESERVA DE LA BIOSFERA RÍA LAGARTOS

El Cuyo

Chiquilá

Isla Contoy

Colonia Yucatán

START
Cancún

Puerto Juárez

Tizimín

Kantunilkin

Laguna Nichupté

YUCATÁN

Leona Vicario

180D

307

X-can

181

El Ideal

① Puerto Morelos

Tres Reyes

Punta Bete
Xcalacoco

Punta Maroma

Valladolid

③ Xcaret

Playa del Carmen ②
Playacar

Paamul ④

San Miguel de Cozumel

Puerto Aventuras

Akumal

PARQUE NATURAL DE QUINTANA ROO

⑤ Xel-Ha

Isla Cozumel

Tulum

◆ Tulum ⑥

QUINTANA ROO

307

CARIBBEAN SEA

295

Vigía Chico

Punta Allen

Bahía de la Ascensión

184

Felipe Carrillo Puerto

⑦

RESERVA DE LA BIÓSFERA SIAN KA'AN

Bahía del Espíritu Santo

307

Cafetal

🅜 See also area map p. 309
▶ Cancún
🕐 80 miles (130 km)
↔ 3 hours to 3 days
▶ Tulum

0   40 kilometers
0   20 miles

the coastline from surf, but the water close to shore can be grassy and murky. Several luxurious, secluded spa resorts claim patches of jungle and sand north and south of town, while small budget hotels and dive shops in town cater to travelers seeking something more laid-back. Vehicles bound for Cozumel line up at the ferry dock south of town, and rumors fly of a cruise port or major marina for the town.

Dirt and paved roads lead from Highway 307 to resorts, nature parks, and secluded hideaway beaches. The Tides, and other exclusive luxurious retreats are found at **Punta Maroma.**

Playa del Carmen ❷, 6 miles (10 km) south of Punta Bete, has long been the main stop between Cancún and Tulum. In just a few decades, it has grown from a small town without telephones into a bustling city of more than 100,000 inhabitants. Banks, supermarkets, auto supply stores, and budget hotels line Avenida Juárez, the entrance to town from Highway 307, and Constitució, which is north of Avenida Juárez and easier to drive. A steady stream of trucks and taxis

INSIDER TIP:

Consider a side trip to the Maya town of Filipe Carrillo Puerto and learn about the 18th-century rebellion of the Maya against the Spanish.

—JAMES DION
National Geographic Center for Sustainable Destinations

golf course and private houses and condos spread about manicured lawns dotted with small Maya ruins. All-inclusive hotels face white-sand beaches in Playacar; some are a long walk from town. Parrots and macaws are among two hundred birds that inhabit the open-air natural setting aviary at **Xaman-Há** *(tel 984/873-0593, $$$)* in Playacar.

Travelers with time constraints can immerse themselves at **Xcaret ❸** *(tel 984/873-2643, www.xcaret.com, $$$$$),* five minutes south of Playa del Carmen. Spend a full day to get the most out of the steep admission; note that some activities and rental gear cost extra. You

---

Quick Method for Converting Kilometers to Miles

One kilometer is the equivalent of 0.621371192237334, or approximately six-tenths, of a mile. While you are on the road in Mexico, you may not have a calculator with you. In order to make a rough conversion of kilometers to miles, divide the number of kilometers by 10 and then multiply by six. For example, if you wanted to find the equivalent of 40 kilometers, you would divide 40 by 10 then multiply the result (four) by six to see that 40 kilometers equals roughly 24 miles. This result is extremely close to the exact measurement of 24.854847689493358 miles.

---

continues to the pier, where ferries depart for the island of Cozumel. International restaurants, excellent folk-art shops, and small hotels line Avenida 5. In Playa del Carmen you can arrange for diving, boating, and archaeological tours, or just drowse in a hammock. The south side of town gives way to **Playacar,** a development with an 18-hole

can visit the bat cave, botanical garden, and butterfly pavilion, float down an underground river with natural skylights, snorkel in the saltwater lagoon, hike through caves, ride horses, eat at one of five restaurants, nap on the sand, or get married. The dinner show is a captivating blend of ancient Maya stories and old Mexican folkloric dances.

Once you've passed Xcaret, the traffic thins out around **Paamul** ❹, the antithesis of a theme park. Turtles and humans like to burrow into this little haven, the former digging nests in the sand, the latter booking a few nights of rest and recreation at a modest hotel. The water is calm, snorkeling and diving are satisfactory, and the restaurant serves homemade tacos and fresh fish.

Those who require more amenities head for **Puerto Aventuras,** a planned resort with

jungle, where spider monkeys hang out, to spooky dark caves filled with stalactites and stalagmites. A milky green cenote (sinkhole) seems to glow within one cave. **Xel-Ha** ❺ *(tel 998/ 884-7165, www.xelha.com, $$$$$),* the coast's first ecopark, has been revived by the Xcaret team. Mature tropical trees shade pathways leading to an aquamarine cove; there are many land and water activities. Tulum bus tours often stop here. Come early to appreciate it. Scuba divers and snorkelers can explore

The marine lagoon at Xel-Ha

hotels, condos, a 250-slip marina, and a nine-hole golf course. Stop by the **Museo Pablo Bush Romero,** named for the region's most famous scuba diver. Exhibits cover early scuba gear, the reefs, and booty from shipwrecks. Divers tend to congregate at nearby **Akumal,** where Romero was headquartered in the 1920s. Hotels, cabanas, and private homes line the cove here.

Walking through the five-million-year-old caverns and caves at **Aktun Chen** *(tel 984/109-2061, www..aktunchen.com, $$$$$)* is otherworldly. Guides lead visitors through the

cool freshwater underground rivers and wells at **Hidden Worlds Cenotes** *(tel 984/115-4514, www.hiddenworlds.com.mx, $$$$$).* The jungle-shrouded property includes several cenotes and bat caves linked by rough, rutted roads.

The Riviera Maya route ends at the town of **Tulum** ❻ (see pp. 320–321), whose ruins are famous and very crowded with day-trippers. Once barely a blip on the map, Tulum has grown significantly. The road ends at the **Reserva de la Biósfera Sian Ka'an** ❼ (see pp. 320 & 321), a fitting reminder of the Quintana Roo coast as it used to be.

Cozumel

▲ 309 F3

Visitor Information

✉ Calle 2 Norte
299-B

☎ 987/872-7636

**www.islacozumel
.com.mx**

Cozumel
Association of
Dive Operators

☎ 987/872-5955
or 987/872-
5966 (fax)

Hotel Na Balam

☎ Calle Zazil-Ha
118 Playa Norte

☎ 998/770-0279
or 0058

www.nabalam.com

restaurants offer international, regional, Mexican, and California cuisine. Upscale spa-oriented resort hotels claim beaches away from the action, and Miami-style clubs and restaurants cater to sophisticates. The quarter-mile-wide (0.5 km) island has five golf courses, with another five at exclusive hotels along the Riviera Maya to the south and one off-shore, on Cozumel.

Perhaps more exciting for culture lovers are the dozens of well-restored Maya ruins found throughout the peninsula. Tulum (see pp. 320–321) and Chichén Itzá (see pp. 338–341) are two

INSIDER TIP:

Hotel Na Balam on Isla Mujeres is a little known laid-back oasis with lush gardens. It also offers yoga classes and has wonderful beach vistas.

–PAM GROUT
National Geographic author

and three hours' drive, respectively, from Cancún. Rent a car or take a tour to visit these or less touristy ruins, or to snorkel in sinkholes, dive the peninsula's underground rivers, or visit historic cities such as Izamal in Yucatán state. Cancún is a convenient base for day trips south along the coast and a good point of departure for tours.

Islands & Diving

The world's second longest chain of coral reefs lies just beneath the Caribbean's crystalline surface and stretches from the northern tip of the Yucatán Peninsula to Belize. Divers can access the reefs from Isla Mujeres, Cancún, and the Quintana Roo coast, but their mecca is Isla de Cozumel.

Maya women once traveled from the mainland to **Cozumel** to honor Ixchel, the goddess of fertility. Today's pilgrims arrive by plane or by ferry from Playa del Carmen, 12 miles (19 km) west, to worship the reefs. Underwater visibility of 80 to 100 feet (23 to 30 m), water temperatures around 80°F (26°C), a 67,133-acre (27,170 ha) marine reserve, and dozens of competent dive operators all enhance Cozumel's reputation.

Divers float along gardens of white, lavender, and pink corals and sponges beside blue angelfish, and yellow butterflyfish; snorkelers see much the same at **Parque Chankanaab** *(tel 987/872-2940, www.cozumelparks.com, $$$$$)*, where shallow reefs shelter more than 60 species of fish.

Island life centers around the town of **San Miguel,** where jewelry and souvenir shops line the streets. Walk a few blocks inland to find family-run folk art shops and casual restaurants. The island's oldest hotel, La Playa, houses the **Museo de la Isla Cozumel** *(tel 987/872-1475, $)*, with exhibits on the reefs and local history.

The island's longest road curves along the southern tip to the wild windward side, where waves and winds batter limestone coves. Turnoffs lead to beach clubs with restaurants and all the water toys you could want. **Mr. Sancho's** *(Carr. Costera Sur Km 15,*

EXPERIENCE: Save the Turtles

Mexico's shores are home to seven of the world's eight marine turtle species: olive ridley, Kemp's ridley, black, green, loggerhead, leatherback, and hawksbill. But beach development threatens many of them with extinction. Furthermore, although Mexico banned consumption of turtle meat and eggs in 1990, old habits die hard. In recent decades, private and government organizations have sprung up to protect the turtles whose numbers have dwindled.

Different species nest at different times of the year, but generally in summer and fall. Hauling themselves up onto the beach, females deposit clutches of 50 to 120 round, white, leathery eggs that incubate in 45 to 60 days. Once the newborn turtles hatch and crawl to the surface of the sand, they must evade predators such as crabs and seabirds as they make their way to the sea. About one in a thousand makes it to adulthood.

Olive ridley hatchlings make their way to the sea.

On the Caribbean, **Centro Ecológico Akumal** *(tel 984/875-9095, ceakumal.org)* has programs for education and protection of the loggerheads and green turtles of the area. Turtle season (nesting and hatching) is May through October, but divers and snorkelers can spot these graceful giants in the turquoise sea year-round. Akumal is about 56 miles (90 km) south of Cancún, between Playa del Carmen and Tulum. Volunteers are accepted for conservation programs, and the usual fee for a visit to the center and nighttime walk is U.S.$10.

On the Pacific, many hotels in Puerto Vallarta and Costalegre have programs protecting turtle eggs. Biologists excavate the eggs as soon as they are laid, transferring them to secure corrals on the beach. Late summer through fall, hotel guests can help repatriate the hatchlings to the sea, improving their chances of survival. Participating hotels include the CasaMagna Marriott (see p. 368), Dreams Puerto Vallarta (see p. 368), Four Seasons Punta Mita *(tel 329/291-6000)*, Westin *(tel 322/226-1100)*, and Velas Vallarta *(tel 866/847-4609 from U.S.)*, among several others.

Open Air *(tel 322/222-3310, e-mail: openair@vivamexico.com)*, in addition, leads nighttime tours to watch females lay eggs or—at the end of the season—guide their tiny progeny to the ocean. Similar tours are part of the program at **Ecotours de México** *(tel 322/222-*

6606, www.ecotoursvallarta.com); **Vallarta Adventures** *(tel 322/297-1212, www.vallarta-adventures.com)*; and **Wildlife Connection** *(tel 322/225-3621, www.wildlifeconnection.com)*. Cost is about U.S.$50 per person.

North of Puerto Vallarta in San Pancho (also known as San Francisco), in Nayarit, **Grupo Ecológico de la Costa Verde** *(tel 311/258-4100, www.project-tortuga.org)* holds educational presentations and accepts long-term volunteers to monitor and protect turtle populations.

In Baja California, **Baja and Beyond Tours** *(tel 619/328-9814 in U.S., www.beyondbaja.com)* leads more expensive, multiday trips to a turtle conservation camp north of Los Cabos.

Isla Mujeres
🗺 309 F4

Visitor Information
✉ Av. Rueda
   Medina 130
☎ 998/877-0307

www.islamujeres
.com.mx

tel 998/112-1933, www.mrsanchos
.com) offers horseback riding,
swimming pools, restaurants,
bars, and endless water activities.
There's no admission fee, but
you must eat or drink. **Playa San
Francisco** is more laid-back, with
hammocks swinging under palms
on a quiet beach.

Near the southern tip of the
island, **Faro Celarain Eco Park,**
also known as **Parque Punta
Sur** (tel 987/872-2940, $$$), has a
beach that's good for snorkeling,
but is a bit pricey for beach access
plus a look at the lighthouse and
nautical museum.

In summer, biologists usually
set up camp at **Punta Morena** to
protect the eggs of nesting
sea turtles from poachers. The
windward coast's first hotel,
Ventanas al Mar (www.ventana
salmar.com.mx), is an idyllic escape
located on the site of the biolo-
gists' original headquarters.

Inland are the ruins of **San
Gervasio** (Carr. Transversal, tel
987/872-2940, $$), a ceremonial

manta ray

lookdow

center occupied from
A.D. 300 to 1500. About
a dozen of its more than
300 buildings have been
restored, including
a temple honoring the
goddess Ixchel.

Divers and escapists favor **Isla
Mujeres,** a 5-mile-long (8 km) limestone shelf 8 miles (11 km) northeast of Cancún. Blacktip and nurse
sharks often doze in 80-foot-deep
(24 m) underwater caves. Experts
believe a lack of carbon dioxide and
an overabundance of oxygen from
underwater springs puts the sharks
into this somnolent state.

Scattered reefs along the
island provide more typical
underwater sights. **Coral Scuba
Center** (Av. Matamoros 13, tel
998/877-0061) offers trips to the
shark caves. With its reefs not far
below the water's surface, **Man-
chones Reef** is good for beginners.
Snorkelers head for **El Garrafón**
(Carr. a Garrafón, tel 998/193-3360,
www.garrafon.com, $$$$$), an under-
water reserve restored in 1999 by
the people who created Xcaret (see
p. 314). The least expensive expedition is U.S.$69 and includes lunch,
drinks, use of installations, kayaking,
and transportation from Cancún.
Canopy tours and other activities
cost more.

The waters off Isla's main beach,
Playa Norte, are more suitable for

El Garrafón reef, Isla Mujeres

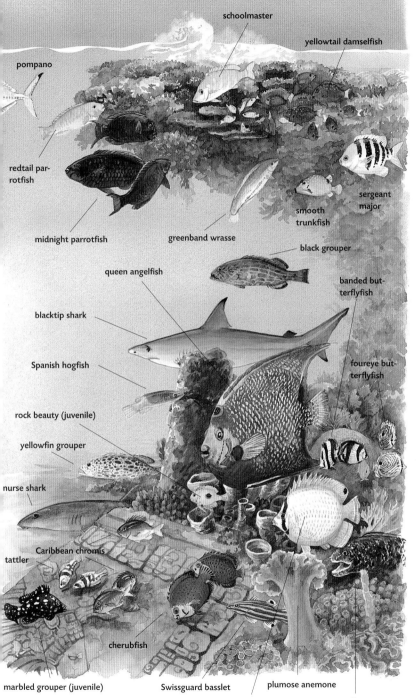

schoolmaster

yellowtail damselfish

pompano

redtail par-
rotfish

sergeant
major

smooth
trunkfish

midnight parrotfish

greenband wrasse

black grouper

queen angelfish

banded but-
terflyfish

blacktip shark

Spanish hogfish

foureye but-
terflyfish

rock beauty (juvenile)

yellowfin grouper

nurse shark

Caribbean chromis

tattler

cherubfish

marbled grouper (juvenile)

Swissguard basslet

plumose anemone

spotfin butterflyfish

spotted moray

EXPERIENCE: Exploring Sian Ka'an

Serving as a model of sustainable development in sensitive tropical ecosystems, Sian Ka'an operates using ecologically responsible systems, including waste management, rainwater collection, and solar and wind power. Any revenue earned through tourism is used to fund further programs within the reserve. What this means is that you can feel free to explore this idyllic land, at the same time feeling that you're giving back.

CESiaK Ecological Center (tel 984/871-2499, www.cesiak.org) provides employment for local fishermen, who lead birding, fly-fishing, and cultural excursions. Full-day tours offer an opportunity to explore several Maya sites combined with a float (wearing a life vest but without inner tube or boat) downriver, snorkeling, swimming in a cenote, walking, and bird-watching. CESiaK also offers rustic lodgings in fully furnished tents.

Bird-watchers and archaeology buffs can enjoy boat tours with **Eco Colors** (tel 998/884-3667, www.ecotravelmexico. com), an eco-friendly company that conducts day and night trips through the park's lagoons and canals. They offer biking, birding, trekking, snorkeling, and archaeological tours.

Tulum
- 309 E3
- 984/206-3150
- $$

Reserva de la Biósfera Sian Ka'an
- 309 E2/E3

Visitor Information
- 998/884-3667

www.ecotravel
mexico.com

swimming than snorkeling, and there are several *palapa* (thatched-roof) bars and restaurants. The town is a few streets with more restaurants, hotels, and shops; bare feet and bathing suits with cover-ups are acceptable in almost all establishments.

Tour agencies on Isla Mujeres offer bird-watching and snorkeling trips to **Isla Contoy,** 19 miles (30 km) north. Undeveloped and protected as a national wildlife park, the island is home to around a hundred species of birds. Visitors are not allowed to spend the night on the island; dedicated bird-watchers should hire a boat captain to take them to Contoy at dawn, when the birds are most active.

Tulum & Sian Ka'an

An alabaster limestone castle sits atop a grassy bluff overlooking the Caribbean Sea at **Tulum.** Six hundred years ago, Maya sailors relied on beams of light from the castle's windows as they made their way to shore

through treacherous reefs.

Tulum may be the most popular archaeological site on the Maya circuit; it's certainly the most accessible. Busloads of tourists arrive every morning from Cancún, which is 80 miles (130 km) to the north. Visitors walk or take a jitney bus to the ruins and must follow prescribed paths when inspecting the 60 or so buildings. You can no longer climb to the top of **El Castillo,** and only those with a vivid imagination can picture the city in its prime.

Between A.D. 1100 and the Spanish Conquest, Tulum was a trading center, possibly ruled by a wealthy merchant class. Its citizens worshiped the Descending God, whose portrait can be seen above the doorway of the temple of the same name. This upside-down god may represent the Bee God, an important deity in a region known for its honey. Paintings in the **Templo de los Frescos** depict Maya gods and goddesses.

The Spanish explorers who survived shipwreck below Tulum in 1511 found a busy commercial center whose buildings were painted various bright colors. Two of the sailors stayed at Tulum. One, Gonzalo Guerrero, married a Maya woman and fathered the first *mestizo* children on the peninsula. He helped the Maya fight off Spanish invaders in 1517, but by the end of the century Tulum was a ghost town.

Though Tulum was the only major site right by the sea, the Maya lived and worked all along the Quintana Roo coast. Engineers built an elaborate system of canals dotted with shrines in the mangrove lagoons just south of Tulum. Their work is protected in the 1.3-million-acre (516,110 ha) **Reserva de la Biósfera Sian Ka'an,** 2 miles (3 km) south of Tulum at the southern end of the Riviera Maya, the last remaining expanse of undeveloped land on the Caribbean coast. Declared a UNESCO World Heritage site in 1987, this unique ecosystem of mangrove swamps, freshwater lagoons, ocean beaches, grasslands, and dune environments also supports a population of some 2,000 humans, as well as hundreds of species of birds and animals.

The majority of its residents, most of Maya ancestry, live around the community of **Punta Allen** at the tip of the 22-mile-long (35 km) Punta Allen Peninsula. Chicle harvesting is no longer allowed within the reserve, which occupies about one-third of Mexico's Caribbean coast. Sustainable fishing is a source of income for local men, however; they fish for spiny lobster, shark, and tarpon. A couple of fishing lodges are open to visitors, who can fly-fish for tarpon, snook, and bonefish.

A dirt road runs the length of the long Punta Allen Peninsula. The drive can take three hours, so bring plenty of fresh water, snacks, and a spare tire. A couple of small hotels and restaurants in Punta Allen fulfill basic needs. On summer nights, sea turtles haul themselves ashore to lay their eggs on area beaches.

More than 350 species of birds have been spotted in the Sian Ka'an lagoons. Boats that penetrate the huge biosphere glide past birds, turtles, and solitary Maya ruins, as guides describe the history and ecology of Sian Ka'an ("birth of the sky" in Maya).

Amigos de Sian Ka'an *(tel 998/8806024 in Cancún, www. amigosdesiankaan.org)* is a private nonprofit organization that works closely with park officials. ∎

Tulum was a thriving commercial city when the first Spaniards arrived.

More Places to Visit in Quintana Roo

Chetumal

Few visitors make it as far as Chetumal, the capital of Quintana Roo. But it has its charms; the peaceful city faces Chetumal Bay, where manatees hide in secret coves and herons fly along the shore. Hotels and restaurants are aimed at business travelers and those crossing into Belize. The excellent **Museo de la Cultura Maya** (*tel 983/832-6838, closed Mon., $$*) is a must-see for archaeology buffs.

🏛 309 D1 ✉ Av. 5 de Mayo at Carmen Ochoa de Merino, 1 block from beach

Cobá

Cobá rises from dense jungle about half an hour's drive from the coast. The archaeological site covers more than 80 square miles (210 sq km) and may have been the largest city on the peninsula. Only 5 percent of the structures have been restored, and visitors wander through steamy heat to climb 120 steps up the majestic pyramid of **Nohuch Mul.** The frequent squawks of wild parrots and the rare rustling of the branches by squirrel monkeys break the silence. Remains of a ball court, small pyramids, and temples lie at the end of barely cleared trails. Many ornate stelae, carved with life-size depictions of kings and queens and lengthy hieroglyphic texts, stand amid the vegetation. Carry plenty of water and a map obtained from the rangers at the entrance. Sights are spread out; you can rent bicycles to get around.

🏛 309 E3 ✉ Carr. a Cobá, 30 miles (48 km) W of Tulum 💲 $

Kohunlich

This little-visited Maya site may contain more than 200 structures; up until now only a handful have been restored. The most impressive is the **Pirámide de los Mascarones,** where 6-foot-tall (2 m) bas-relief masks in stucco from the Early Classic era (ca A.D. 300– 450) are said to portray the sun god. Visit also the acropolis and remnants of residences, as well as a ball court. The area is popular with adventure travelers and escapists.

🏛 309 D1 ✉ 42 miles (67 km) W of Chetumal on Hwy. 186 💲 $

Laguna Bacalar

Fed by freshwater and saltwater streams and springs, Laguna Bacalar, 25 miles (40 km) north of Chetumal, is Mexico's second largest lake, often called the Lake of Seven Colors for its varying shades of green and blue. The shores are lined with vacation homes, *balnearios* (bathing resorts), restaurants, and a few hotels. It's a good base for those wishing to explore remote Maya ruins in the interior.

🏛 309 D2

Majahual & Xcalak

The 40-mile-long (64 km) **Península Xcalak** is the last undeveloped haven on the coast (except for Sian Ka'an). But the coastline and nearby jungles of southern Quintana Roo (or Costa Maya) are slated for development. Cruise ships come to Puerto Costa Maya, a terminal north of Majahual, the coast's largest town. Tour buses ply the roads between the coast and Maya archaeological sites in the jungle. A 30-mile-long (48 km) paved road runs south of Majahual to the fishing community at Xcalak.

Reefs line the coast offshore, but the pièce de résistance is **Banco Chinchorro,** a 24-mile-long (38 km) reef littered with shipwrecks. Boat captains in Xcalak and at the hotels take divers to Chinchorro when the seas are calm. **Costa de Cocos** (*www .costadecocos.com),* a hotel with cabanas on the sand, has a dive shop. It also offers charter fishing expeditions.

🏛 309 E1/E2

Campeche

Maya ruins dot the state of Campeche. Calakmul lies deep within Mexico's largest remaining rain forest, while Edzná, the best known pre-Hispanic site, is less than an hour's drive from the capital city, Campeche. Dozens of other archaeological sites throughout the small state are easily reached along flat, two-lane roads with minimal traffic. The city of Campeche, with its wonderfully restored colonial buildings, makes an excellent base for area excursions.

The temples at Hochob have elements of both Río Bec- and Chenes-style architecture.

Campeche may be the country's most languorous capital city. Traffic trundles along slowly within the compact historic district, once enclosed by a hexagonal wall to protect its citizens from pirate attacks. Today, pedestrians stroll the recently refurbished *malecón*, while businessmen discuss oil prices over long lunches at their favorite restaurants.

Campeche's west-facing beaches along the eponymous bay don't attract many foreign tourists, but wading birds fish in the shallow, warm waters off

soft-sand, grass-strewn beaches at pretty Seybaplaya, and small cities such as Champotón attract hunters and sports fishers. Highway 186 heads inland from service-oriented Escárcega to access the ruins at Xpujil, Becán, and Chicanná before continuing east to the Yucatán coast. The most adventurous travelers explore the jungles of Calakmul Biosphere Reserve, where hundreds of Maya ruins lie unexcavated.

A road heading north from Xpujil makes it possible to continue to the Chenes-style ruins

Campeche

309 C3

Visitor Information

✉ Av. Ruíz Cortines s/n, Plaza Moch-Couloh

☎ 981/127-3300

www.portal.camp .gob.mx

around Hopelchén, passing en route some of the Maya dwellings still used in the countryside. Round or oval houses of thick adobe walls and high thatch roofs, usually painted white but occasionally plain adobe or a startling sky blue, provide the tradition-minded Maya inhabitants with a cool respite from the impressive peninsular heat.

City of Campeche

Once completely walled to fend off marauding pirates, the unique and relatively isolated city of Campeche retains a quiet, 17th-century elegance unmatched by other colonial cities. Since 1987, hundreds of structures have been restored in delicious tones of pale yellow, earthen brown, celery and dill green, deep gold, and ocher red, transforming Campeche into a living museum of colonial- and republican-era architecture.

Founded in 1540 by Francisco de Montejo, Campeche gained importance as a port through which gold and silver passed en

route to Spain. This wealth did not escape the notice of pirates, who for nearly two centuries besieged the city, sometimes inflicting wholesale massacres. In 1686, the Spanish crown finally took adequate preventive measures. The city was entirely walled, but it was only after twin forts were erected that the pirate attacks finally ceased.

Today, the old city, **Viejo Campeche,** is a compact zone measuring five blocks by nine. Although the walls that once coddled the city in a hexagonal cocoon have largely been destroyed, the seven bastions, or *baluartes,* are mostly intact; those that were demolished have been rebuilt. The two original entrances that once allowed the only access to the city still stand.

The land gate, **Puerta de Tierra** (*Calle 18 across from Calle 59),* provides a dramatic background for a sound and light show (*$$*) featuring dancers and musicians. The schedule varies depending on the season, but there are performances most

Sacred Cenotes

The Yucatán peninsula is made of porous limestone, which when it cracks and collapses forms sinkholes, or cenotes. Water was held sacred by the Maya, the rain god Chac was a principal deity. Offerings were left in caves, also considered holy; sacrificial victim were tossed in ceremonial wells, like that at Chichén Itzá, to ensure adequate rainfall.

Today snorkelers pay top dollar to swim underground at Xcaret (see p. 314); divers favor Dos Ojos, connected by an underground river. More accessible,

pricewise, is the diminutive green cenote at Dzibalchatún, near Mérida, and Ik Kil, a massive and beautiful pond at Pisté. Very swimmable Cenote Zaci is right at the edge of downtown Valladolid.

Ask the locals about more remote sites such as cenotes Azul and del Pato outside Champotón, Campeche. From Hacienda Cuzamá, southeast of Mérida, you can ride in horse-drawn buggies that follow the old henequen railway lines, transporting you to three beautiful cenotes in the countryside.

weekend evenings at 8 p.m. The sea gate, **Puerta del Mar** *(Calle 8 at Calle 59)*, is now just a large commemorative arch two blocks from the seawall.

Within the compact city center, the neoclassical **Catedral de la Concepción Inmaculada** *(Calle 55 at Calle 10)* incorporates renaissance elements. The pièce de résistance is the brilliant Holy Sepulcher of carved ebony covered in miniature stamped silver angels and icons tucked in the small, interior museum.

The cathedral stands on the north side of the *plaza principal.* Unlike the main squares in other Mexican cities, Campeche's tranquil park hardly ever seems busy—the majority of townsfolk are found strolling the seaside walkway, the *malecón,* in the evening. The plaza livens up on weekends, however, when the surrounding streets are closed to cars and the symphony orchestra plays in the central bandstand.

Wandering around the city is one of the most pleasant things to do in Campeche. For those who prefer to ride, daily **tram tours** *($$)* also depart from the main plaza. They offer three different routes but no set schedule.

At the outskirts of the historic center is Campeche's spiffy *mercado municipal (Av. Circuito Baluartes between Calles 51 & 55).* Except for fine "Panama-style" hats and some woven goods, Campeche is not known for its crafts, but this organized warren of locally grown produce and other everyday items is nonetheless a fascinating place to shop. The surrounding area is full of

shoe stores and other shops.

Located in strategic defensive positions at both ends of the city are Campeche's two historic forts. The completion of imposing **Fuerte San Miguel** *(Av. Escénica s/n)* in 1771 finally put an end to pirate raids. At the south end of the city, this hilltop fort now contains the city's best museum, the **Museo de la Cultura Maya** *(closed Mon, $)*. Housed here are pre-Hispanic artifacts from

INSIDER TIP:

Attend Campeche's Sunday festival and sample *machacado,* a local dessert mixture of fruit, milk, and ice.

— LUZ MARIA MEJIA
National Geographic field researcher

throughout the state, including quite a few of Jaina island's statuettes portraying people of various stations and professions (see p. 331), and half a dozen spectacular jade funerary masks discovered at Calakmul.

Northeast of the city center, at **Fuerte San José** *(Av. Francisco Morazan s/n),* is the **Museo de Armas y Barcos** *(closed Mon., $)*, which has a small collection of 18th-century weapons, religious art, manuscripts, and model ships.

Several of the bastions that once punctuated the city's hexagonal walls also house small museums. **Baluarte San Carlos** *(Calle 8 at Calle 65, closed Mon.)* houses a simple city museum. The **Museo de las Estelas** *(closed*

Edzná

⚑ 309 C2

Visitor Information

✉ 28 miles (45 km) SW of Campeche

☎ 981/811-1314 (INAH)

$ $$

Mon., $) of the **Baluarte de la Soledad** *(Calle 8 at Calle 57),* on the south side of the main plaza, exhibits a collection of carved Maya stelae and artifacts.

Within the thick walls of **Baluarte Santiago** *(Calle 8 at Calle 49, $)* is a small botanical garden, and **Baluarte de San Pedro** *(Calle 51 at Calle 8)* is a shop selling crafts of local design and material.

INSIDER TIP:

Highway 186 in Campeche is flanked by Mayan ruins. Though hard to reach, they are infinitely rewarding to adventure seekers.

—ELAINE GLUSAC
National Geographic writer

Edzná

A regional capital between A.D. 400 and 1000, Edzná enjoyed its greatest period of influence in the Late Classic era (A.D. 600–900). Its population dwindled slowly after 1000, finally disappearing at the end of the Postclassic period around 1450. Its appeal lies in the symmetry and monumental character of its structures and in the well-designed layout of the city center.

Located at a crossroads and trade route between the northern Yucatán Peninsula, the southern lowlands, and Ah Kin Pech (today's Campeche city), Edzná shows the influence of several architectural styles. Classic-era carved stelae, many still on site, are common to the southern lowlands, as are roofcombs and corbeled arch roofs. The most telling element of the Puuc style is the complex and symbolic stone mosaics adorning the temple facades.

Unique to Edzná, however, was its vast system of irrigation. Construction began in 200 B.C. without beasts of burden, metal tools, or the wheel. During the rainy season, when the wide river valley often flooded, water was collected and redirected to a multitude of reservoirs via canals.

The excavated buildings cluster in the vicinity of the main plaza, **Plaza Principal,** and the adjacent **Gran Acrópolis.** South of the former are the well-restored *juego de pelota* (ball court) and the **Templo Sur.** The temple surmounting this five-level structure appears to be of a different style and was probably added during the Late Classic period.

The site's largest and most impressive building is the **Templo de los Cinco Pisos** (Five-story Temple), located on the Great Acropolis. Sanctuaries on each level are accessed via a central staircase; the tiny temple at the top is crowned by the remnants of a roof comb. A solar phenomenon occurs each year at the planting season *(May 1–3)* and again at harvest *(Aug. 7–9).* On these days, the sun enters the normally dark interior to illuminate the face of Itzamná, the sky serpent-creater deity, on a stele within. (The stone remains, but the carving is gone.)

Some of the site's oldest

structures have been found on the **Pequeña Acrópolis,** south of the Great Acropolis. Each of the four buildings seated on this raised base faces one of the cardinal directions. West of this acropolis is the **Templo de los Mascarones,** with its modeled plaster masks of the rising and setting sun god on the east and west flanks, respectively. Campeche tour operators offer transportation *($$$$$)* to sound and light shows Friday and Saturday nights. The show *($$$)* begins at 8 p.m. in the summer and 7 p.m. in the winter.

north. Within the reserve and easily reached by highway are the Maya ruins of Xpujil, Chicanná, and Becán. Hormiguero, Calakmul, and other remote sites require a bit more effort.

Covering more than 1.7 million acres (723,185 ha), Calakmul provides a refuge for nearly a hundred species of mammals, including some of Mexico's endangered felines, such as the puma and jaguar. There are 235 known bird species, including toucans, parrots, macaws, and peninsula natives such as the ocellated turkey.

Reserva de la Biósfera Calakmul

309 C1

The Templo de los Cinco Pisos, Edzná's largest structure, was originally faced with stucco and paint.

Reserva de la Biósfera Calakmul

Mexico's largest remaining tropical forest, this slightly elevated spine on the flat back of the Yucatán Peninsula forms an ecological link between the tropical rain forests of Guatemala's Petén region and the drier, shorter forests to the

Despite its protected status, the biosphere is threatened by forestry and colonization. Immigrants from Tabasco, Veracruz, and Chiapas have settled along the fringes in various waves since the 1950s, bringing slash-and-burn agriculture, ranching, and hunting. The nonprofit Pronatura Península de Yucatán, directly involved in park management, works with communities in reforestation and in developing sustainable industries such as handicraft production and rural tourism.

When the municipality of Calakmul was formed in 1996, the town of Xpujil became its seat of government. Highway 186 bisects the park at this tiny town, which has a few restaurants and basic hotels, a regional bus service, and a phone, Internet, and fax service. The two-lane highway stretches east and west, connecting Chetumal, the capital of Quintana Roo, with Escárcega—a major crossroads and regional supply center for Campeche state. Heading north from Xpujil, a paved road leads to Hopelchén, the Chenes region, and to the state of Yucatán.

Visitors can book tours out of Campeche or hire a guide through the Chicanná Ecovillage Resort near Xpujil. All of the archaeological sites are open

Becán was once the capital of the Río Bec area, but like other sites nearby remains largely unrestored.

daily from 8 a.m. to 5 p.m. and charge admission ($).

As they are within a few miles of each other and just off the highway, Chicanná, Becán, and Xpujil can be explored in a day or half day. These sites combine elements of the Chenes architectural style (most notably their zoomorphic "mask" doorways), prevalent in northern Campeche, with the Río Bec style, typified by twin lateral towers topped by false temples, rounded corners, and false stairways.

Chicanná is a small site whose Mayan name means "house of the snake's mouth." Occupied during the Late Preclassic period, it reached its peak during the Late Classic, when it may have served as an elite community dependent on nearby Becán.

Brown-and-white pea birds shriek as you cut through a small forest of sapodilla trees to Chicanná's main plaza, around which several ruined buildings are grouped. Typical of the site's Chenes-style structures, the facade of **Estructura II** forms an enormous mask representing the creator god Itzamná. The principal doorway represents the god's open mouth; above it, carved stones depict fangs, nose, and crossed eyes. Along the sides of the building, vertical rows of stone-mosaic Chac masks were once covered in stucco and bright red pigment. These elements and themes are repeated on many of the site's structures.

Becán, less than a mile (1.6 km) away, served as the capital of the Río Bec area. A long moat built during the earliest days of settlement enclosed the site's largest and tallest buildings and various plazas, an inner city reserved for the elite.

Coiled in front of **Estructura III** are the remains of a round altar representing the feathered serpent god, Kukulcán (called Quetzalcóatl by the Toltec and others to the north). A dank, dark, bat-lined tunnel penetrates **Estructura VIII,** leading from the building's base on the south side to the east side at the second level. From the top of this pyramid you can see the Temple of the Three Towers at Xpujil, about 5 miles (8 km) to the northeast.

Named for a plant that grows abundantly in the area, **Xpujil** (Cat's Tail), like Chicanná and Becán, flourished in the Late Classic era and combines Chenes and Río Bec architectural styles. Built-in benches such as those found in **Estructuras III** and **IV** suggest the buildings were living quarters.

About 14 miles (23 km) southwest of Xpujil, **Hormiguero** (Ant Hill) was named for the looters' tunnels that researchers found snaking through the site in 1933. Three distinct groups of buildings (North, Central, and South) are surrounded by clusters of dwellings. The Río Bec style predominates, typified by the side towers with rounded corners and false stairways of **Estructura II,** in the South Group. The tropical forests surrounding the ruins are interrupted by pastures, savannas, and marshes. Half-day excursions can be arranged in Xpujil.

Río Bec refers to a group of at least 18 ceremonial structures so spread out that archaeologists are unsure if they belonged to a single community. Hire a guide in Xpujil to take you on a hiking tour to this little-visited site on the Bec River.

Calakmul is located deep within the reserve, about 37 miles (60 km) off Highway 186. Troops

of monkeys chatter in the trees, and the site has a lovely, lost and alone feel. Since the road was paved in 1993, it's generally quite easy—although slow going on the potholed road—to access the archaeological site.

Discovered in 1931 by U.S. botanist Cyrus Lundell, this extensive city—built on a flood-plain and once near a large fresh-water lake—is related stylistically to habitations in the nearby Petén region of Guatemala. Calakmul was continuously inhabited for more than 1,500 years, from the Middle Preclassic period (500–300 B.C.) to the Late Post-classic era (A.D. 1200–1521).

The site apparently had several periods of growth and success. For 500 years it was the capital of a kingdom called Cabeza del Serpiente (Serpent's Head), uniting such lowland cities as Dos Pilas, Naranjo, and Caracol. After the death of its leader Jaguar Claw and a significant defeat to Tikal in

Guatemala, Calakmul appears to have strengthened relations with its northern neighbors of the Río Bec area, and buildings such as **Estructura V** show the influence of the Río Bec style. During this time a great number of stelae were carved and erected. The city declined in importance, and after A.D. 1000 was used almost exclusively as a ceremonial center.

Hopelchén, Hochob, & Dzibilnocac

Directly east of Campeche City is the small but important town of Hopelchén. Mennonites from surrounding farms come here to sell their homemade cheese and purchase supplies. They generally wear traditional farmer clothing and still speak the Low German dialect of their ancestors. South of town are Hochob and Dzibilnocac, two small archaeological sites demonstrat-

Two-week Carnival Is Twice the Fun

Campeche's carnival (Mardi Gras) is perhaps the oldest in Mexico, but it's mostly overlooked by foreign tourists. Beginning with the ritual burning of "Mal Humor" ("Bad Mood"), it's two weeks of parades, costume contests, dances, pop and rock concerts, and great firework displays. Weary participants are theoretically ready for the sober period of Lent, initiating on Ash Wednesday.

ing the Chenes-style architecture of the region.

Due north of Xpujil is Hochob, 9 miles (14 km) from Dzibalchén off the Dzibalchén-Chencho road. To date, a plaza and four buildings have been excavated, seated on an artificially leveled hill. The giant mask facades of the **Palacio del Este** (East Palace) and **Palacio Principal** (Main Palace), both on Plaza I, provide examples of one of the most important elements of Chenes architecture. The former building has a zoomorphic figure; the latter, the sun god Itzamná, whose squinting eyes appear above the doorway. Chac masks adorn the edges of the Main Palace, and the remains of roof combs can be seen.

Behind the palace, several cavities in the ground are all that remain of an ancient irrigation system. The false stairways and towers crowned by false temples on **Estructura III,** also on the first plaza, are typical of Río Bec style.

North of Dzibalchén along a paved secondary road, the ruins at Dzibilnocac are found in the town of Iturbide. Although platforms, pyramid bases, palaces, and vaulted chambers are strewn throughout the site, only one building has been excavated. Combining various architectural elements, the three-story **Templo Palacio** (Estructura I) has the false stairways and temple-topped towers characteristic of the Río Bec style. Well-preserved Chac masks adorn the top temple. The site was a midsize ceremonial center between about A.D. 250 and 900, but was inhabited as early as 500 B.C. ■

More Places to Visit in Campeche

Campeche's Coast

Although Campeche is not known for its beaches, a drive down the coast holds pleasant surprises. One of the prettiest stretches of beach is found around **Seyba-playa,** an unpretentious fishing town about 20 miles (32 km) south of Campeche. The narrow beach, lined with brightly painted skiffs, heads north about a mile (1.6 km) to **Payucán,** where herons and sandpipers stalk their prey in shallow waters. Another hour south is **Champotón,** the largest town between Campeche and the unattractive oil town of **Isla del Carmen.** It was in the bay at Champotón, now named **Bahía de la Mala Pelea** (Bay of the Evil Fight) that the Maya soundly defeated the Spaniards for the first time. The unremarkable yet pleasant coastal city of Champotón is a center of hunting and fishing expeditions.

308 B2

Grutas de Xtacumbilxunaan

Near the Yucatán border, the Grutas de of Xtacumbilxunaan are a series of underground limestone chambers with interesting formations. The ancient Maya held these and other caves sacred as a link between this world and the next. If you're driving north from Hopelchén, it is worth the short detour off Highway 261 to visit the caves. Visitors walk through the cham-bers as lights are projected on the rocks; headphones with narration in English translate the taped dialogue. The site is closed on Mondays.

309 C3 ☎ 981/816-1782 💲 $$
🕐 Closed Mon.

Northern Campeche

Between Campeche city and Yucatán state, Highway 180 passes a series of small towns. Sixteenth-century **Hecelchakán,** 37 miles (60 km) north of Campeche, is admired among Campechanos for its *cochinita pibil* (baked pork seasoned with achiote), sold at informal eateries in the main square. **Isla Jaina** (just offshore) is not open to the public, but its famous statuettes can be seen in Hecelchakán's **Museo Arqueológico del Camino Real** (*closed Mon., $*). About 15 miles (24 km) beyond, it's worth stopping in **Calkiní** to see the cloistered **Clarisa convent church,** with its beautiful carved pulpit and main altarpiece.

Just before the Yucatán border is **Becal,** the birthplace of the famous *jipis,* straw hats varying from very fine, expensive "Panama hats" (a misnomer that annoys Campechanos no end) to colorful, floppy, coarse models to use at the beach. The hats are produced in cellars beneath residents' homes, where humidity keeps the palm fiber supple.

309 C3

Yucatán

At the top of the peninsula, pie-shaped Yucatán is the flattest state, with the poorest soil and the least rainfall. Here the tropical forest is low, dense, and scrubby. Hot year-round, it is particularly sultry during the rainy months of late summer and fall, when biting bugs are at their worst. December through February is the coolest time of year, when locals wear enormous jackets, while visitors in cotton shirts still manage to break a sweat.

Chichén Itzá is one of Yucatán's most studied and fascinating sites.

While its beaches are not the white-sand and turquoise-water variety of the Riviera Maya, an isolated coastline offers cheaper prices and an opportunity for discovery. Celestún and Río Lagartos lure bird-watchers, and nearby Isla Holbox is a haven for escapists. Coastal infrastructure is limited but growing; accommodations outside Mérida (with the exception of some stellar five-star boutique hotels) are generally basic. Development of the northern coast was scrapped after Hurricane Isidore, much to the delight of purists and dedicated beach bums.

Yucatán's main draw is its Maya ruins. Despite the pressure of busloads of visitors, Chichén Itzá remains among Mexico's top archaeological sites. Strategically placed throughout the large site are Mesoamerica's largest ball court, a sacrificial sinkhole, and stepped pyramids covered in bas-reliefs.

Yucatán's other antique jewel, Uxmal, is one of a half dozen excavated sites forming the Puuc Route, a loop of archaeological sites south of Mérida. In the same area of low, rolling hills are unassuming towns with lonesome Franciscan monasteries, orange-scented markets, and loads of appeal for the inquisitive traveler.

Once dedicated to corn and cattle, and later to sugarcane and then sisal fiber, the peninsula's haciendas were sold and subdivided during post-revolutionary land reforms. Today, many have been transformed into luxurious, rural hotels and restaurants.

Mérida

Little in Mérida reminds you of its past as one of the most important ceremonial cities in the Postclassic Maya world: T'ho (meaning "fifth place"). Some vestiges remain of its days of wealth and European elegance. Forged by indigenous labor under the brutal hacienda system, tempered with Maya resilience and sense of self, and enriched by the contributions of immigrants, Mérida is *mestizo*, but different from anywhere else in Mexico.

Unlike Tenochtitlán, which was felled in a four-month siege (see p. 27), T'ho resisted the invaders for 15 years. The resolute Maya first battled Francisco Montejo (el Adelantado) and later his son, Montejo el Mozo, who finally prevailed in 1542.

Today, Mérida is a city of more than 734,000 people. Hotels are clustered in historic downtown, with the fanciest highrises along **Prolongación de Paseo Montejo.** Restaurants range from air-conditioned bistros with French menus to fan-cooled terraces and outdoor cafés. Horse-drawn

Mérida

🅰 309 C4

Visitor Information

✉ Teatro Peon Contreras, Calle 60 between Calles 57 & 59

☎ 999/924-9290

www.merida.gob .mx.turismo

EXPERIENCE:
Sundays with the Locals

When planning your time in the Yucatán area, make sure to spend at least one Sunday *(Domingo)* in Mérida; few places in Mexico are as dedicated to free cultural events. On Sunday, the city closes several miles of downtown streets to traffic so that pedestrians and cyclists can breathe freely. Kids, parents, and grandparents take to the streets to enjoy free concerts, clowns, and comedians. On the main plaza *(bet. Calles 60 & 62, 61 & 63)* is a stage and seating. Along Calle 60 to Hidalgo and Santa Lucia Parks are food and crafts vendors, roving clowns and musicians, and other free, live entertainment from 9 a.m. to 9 p.m.

---

carriages compete with cars, cabs, and diesel-belching buses on downtown streets. Restored churches and theaters are scattered among modern one- and two-story structures—some charming, others crumbling.

Many second- and third-generation buildings surround the city's cultural and civic heart, the *zócalo,* or **Plaza Mayor** *(bet. Calles 60 & 62, 61 & 63).* Now a bank, the **Casa de Montejo** *(Calle 63, S side of plaza)* is one of the city's finest examples of secular plateresque architecture, although

Dzibilchaltún
🔺 309 C4
💲 $

Oxkintok
✉ Accessible from town of Maxcanú, 38 miles (62 km) S of Mérida on Hwy. 180

only the facade is original. Note the Montejo family crest above the grilled balcony.

Across the plaza to the east, the original church has been incorporated into the **Catedral San Ildefonso** (Calle 60 at Calle 61), begun in 1561 and added to over the centuries. Inside, 12 columns support the ribbed vaults over the nave of the Spanish Romanesque interior. Left of the main altar, the **Cristo de las Ampollas** (Christ of the Blisters) is a reproduction of the original statue, said to have survived an all-night fire with only discoloration and blisters.

INSIDER TIP:

To avoid the throngs of tourists at places like Uxmal and Chichén Itzá, rent a car and visit Oxkintok. It's open to the public and only an hour from Mérida.

—SCOTT HUTSON
National Geographic field researcher

Next door, the **Museo de Arte Contemporáneo** (Calle 60 bet. Calles 63 & 61-A, tel 999/928-3258, closed Tues.) was originally the bishop's residence and now houses temporary exhibits on its second floor.

Some Mexican cities are lonely on Sundays, their streets empty except for visitors in search of a meal. Not so Mérida, where everyone seems to stroll the city center, showing off their best clothes. Beginning Saturday

evening, the *zócalo* and adjoining plazas, mercifully closed to traffic, become venues for free folkloric dance performances, crafts and antiques bazaars, and impromptu street theater (see "Sundays with the Locals," p 333). Get a schedule of events at the tourism office.

The free **Museo de la Ciudad** (Calle 56 No. 529A bet. 65 & 65 A, tel 999/923-6869, closed Mon. & weekends after 2 p.m.) is located within the former post office. Permanent exhibits recount the city's history from pre-Hispanic times to the modern era; temporary shows exhibit the work of local artists.

Mérida's sultry climate can be oppressive. The town snaps out of its heat-induced torpor after sundown, when evening breezes ruffle the palms in **Parque Santa Lucía** (Calles 60 & 55). On Thursday evenings at 9 p.m., musicians play while young men and women perform regional dances. On Saturdays from 8 p.m. to midnight, tourists and locals gather in and around El Remate park for **Noche Mexicana** (Paseo de Montejo & Calle 47), an outdoor festival of music, dance, and local crafts. Just up the street is the **Palacio Cantón**—a stately mansion of Carrara marble, ornate columns, and Italianate beaux arts details—housing the **Museo de Antropología e Historia** (Calle 43 & Paseo de Montejo, tel 999/923-0557, closed Mon., $). Although the museum's anthropology collection is limited, the early 20th-century mansion itself is worth the admission. The source of some of the museum's artifacts lies 10 miles (16 km) north of Mérida at the Maya city of **Dzibilchaltún**.

Most of the site's 8,000 structures are unexcavated, but the lovely jade sinkhole for swimming and the ruined Catholic and Maya buildings make it a worthwhile excursion.

Charming as Mérida is, its buses and cars create significant pollution. The wooded areas, boating lake, children's playgrounds, and small zoo at **Parque Centenario** (Av. Itzaes bet. Calles 59 & 65), at the city's western boundary, provide a refreshing escape from urban overload. The **Ermita de Santa Isabel** (Calles 66 & 77, open 4–7 p.m.) is another peaceful refuge, with a pre-Hispanic altar. Also known as Our Lady of the Successful Journey, the church was once a stopping place for travelers. Today 3 miles (5 km) of streets between here, the main plaza, and up to Paseo Montejo are closed to traffic on Sunday; bicycles are rented at the main plaza.

At its founding, Mérida's core was reserved for the elite, surrounded by Indian towns and later mixed and mestizo neighborhoods. Each enclave was a world within itself, its social life centered around the parish church. These barrios still have active churches and lively markets, and make an interesting detour from the main tourist routes.

Visit **Barrio de Santiago,** in the northeast sector, on Tuesday evenings between 8:30 and 11 p.m., when 1940s-era bands play in the park facing the **Templo de Santiago Apostle** (Calles 59 & 72). Closest to the main plaza is **Barrio San Juan,** with a 16th-century church (Calles 69 & 62). About eight blocks southwest of the main square, the **Barrio de San Cristóbal** welcomed Lebanese and Italian immigrants in the 19th century. Its church (Calles 50 & 69) has a sober yet impressive interior decorated with images of the Virgin of Guadalupe (see pp. 192–193).

Northwest of the city center, **La Mejorada** was once separated

Begun in 1561, Mérida's cathedral—with its restrained Renaissance facade—is the oldest in mainland America.

from San Cristóbal by a hill, demolished during the War of Independence. The lovely old former Franciscan monastery (Calles 59 & 50) now houses a school of architecture and the **Museo de la Música** (closed Mon.).

Mérida makes a logical base for trips throughout the region, as it has a central location and good services. There are casual B&Bs and five-star hotels with full amenities, and loads of restaurants serving Yucatecan, Mexican, and

EXPERIENCE: Fêting Friends with Feathers

Each November, along with a number of migratory species, beginning and veteran birders flock to Mérida and Uxmal for the **Yucatan Bird Festival** (*www.yucatanbirds .org.mx*). During the four-day November event you can go to lectures, workshops, and exhibitions in Mérida, then birding expeditions into the field. There are children's programs, a photography contest, and bird counts.

The Yucatán is rich in birds with nearly 550 species from 75 families; a favorite is the Caribbean flamingo. You can see aquatic birds at beaches and lagoons near Mérida and Uxmal, or land species at old haciendas, archaeological sites, and other picturesque venues.

international cuisine. There are plenty of shops, too. Choose from Panama-style straw hats, wonderful hammocks, tropical clothing, or the locally made anise and honey liqueur, Xtabentun.

Around diminutive Yucatán state are a dozen restored haciendas (see *www.merida.gob.mx* for a complete list in Spanish). Some, like **Hacienda Petec** (*tel 999/911-2600, www.haciendapetec.com*) can be rented by the week by private parties; others offer their guests pricey but elegant accommodation and restaurants.

About 15 minutes north of Mérida, **Hacienda Xcanatun** (*tel 999/941-0213, www.xcanatun .com*) has lovely rooms, a restaurant, and a spa. About the same distance southeast of Mérida, **Hacienda Teya** (*tel 999/988-0800, www.haciendateya.com*) hosts business meetings and has a popular restaurant.

Coast & Coastal Reserves

While Quintana Roo attracts sybarites and scuba divers, Yucatán's coast draws slightly more introverted types, such as fishermen and birders. Away from the crowds, natural reserves at Celestún and Río Lagartos create a safe haven for birds, endangered marine tortoises, and other animal and plant species. And between these two reserves, Maya and mestizo villages languish under the tropical sun.

With just over 50,000 inhabitants, **Progreso** is a vacation village for Meridians during the hottest summer months. Some travelers find it an interesting port city with a wide beach and calm water; to others, it's a tumble of cement and stucco buildings without much charm. Calle 19 hugs the coast, lined with seafood restaurants and simple cafés. Progreso's original stone pier has been expanded (twice) in a successful effort to lure cruise ships. When they dock here six times a month in high season, vendors sell crafts along the *malecón*.

If Progreso doesn't float your boat, explore the coast. **Yucalpetén,** about 4 miles (6 km) to the west, attracts many commercial vessels, and a marina for yachts has several sportfishing boats. Just 1.8 miles (3 km) farther, **Chelem** has restaurants and small hotels on the beach, and fishermen offer lagoon tours (*$$*).

The only significant stretch of beach road in the state is the 50 miles (80 km) between Progreso and Dzilám de Bravo, to the east. A two-lane highway passes salt flats used since pre-Hispanic times, and grassy dunes line the beach, accessed by sandy roads leading off from the highway. Meridians take weekend getaways in tranquil **Chicxulub Puerto,** a fishing village just east of Progreso. Straddling the coast here is the huge 112-mile-wide (180 km) **Chicxulub Crater,** created by a meteorite about 65 million years ago and discovered in the 1940s by petroleum geologists. Its impact is thought to have created the peninsula's sinkholes (and possibly polished off the dinosaurs). Other small fishing villages dot the coast, including **San Crisanto,** where local men take visitors through the mangroves (*$*) to visit crystalline cenotes (sinkholes). Look for the excursion office *(tel 999/926-0236)* across from the town baseball field. Bring a bathing suit and, if you have them, binoculars for birds.

West of Mérida, **Sisal** was once the state's first important port but lost out to deeper Progreso in the latter part of the 19th century. Although it is a pleasant fishing village today with a nice beach, tourists are often drawn instead to neighboring **Celestún,** 60 miles (90 km) west of Mérida. From here small boats cruise the estuary and mangrove forests of the **Reserva de la Biósfera Ría Celestún** in search of water-fowl, migratory shorebirds, and especially coral-colored flamingo colonies tens of thousands strong. At the edge of the estuary sits Celestún, a quiet town geared for day-trippers from Mérida and backpackers used to rustic accommodations. Three-hour birding tours *(most flamingos sighted* *Aug.–early Feb.)* include a visit to a freshwater spring (ask for time to swim) and to a forest of petri-fied trees.

Directly north of Valladolid on the north-central coast is **Reserva de la Biósfera Ría Lagartos,** another wildlife sanctuary. Its long, highly saline estuary attracts white ibises, great white herons, snowy egrets, and flamingos. You can arrange three-hour bird-watching tours *($$$$$ per boat)* or fly-fishing outings at **Restaurant Isla Contoy** *(Calle 9 No. 105 at Calle 14, tel 986/862-0452, www.riolagartosex peditions.com).* Pelicans roost in the mangroves, and herons stalk fish among their roots.

Also great for fishing and relaxing is **Isla Holbox** (Mayan for "dark hole"), just over the Quintana Roo state line. There are eight ferry crossings per day *($$)* at

Progreso

 309 C4

Visitor Information

✉ Casa de la Cultura Calle 80 No. 176 at Calle 25

☎ 969/935-0104

The state of Yucatán has miles of solitary beaches.

Chiquila. Most hotels will arrange fly-fishing for snook, tarpon, and bonefish, and ocean fishing for grouper and snapper (both $$$$$). The season is April–July, although ocean fishing continues year-round. Other popular pastimes are horseback riding, kayaking, and—from summer to fall—swimming with whale sharks.

Chichén Itzá

With competition from Uxmal, the most architecturally intriguing and majestic Maya site on the Yucatán Peninsula is Chichén Itzá. Its earliest structures, including an ornate circular observatory, date to the Classic era (A.D. 250–900) and echo the native Maya architectural details of the Puuc region south of Mérida. Its famed Castillo was constructed during the Terminal Classic or Early Postclassic period (A.D. 900–1200).

Unlike the vine-shrouded sites of Palenque and Yaxchilán, Chichén Itzá has an almost militaristic appearance. Murals and stelae depict warriors, battles, and human sacrifice, belying the long-held image of the Maya as a pacifist people. More than 30 meticulously reconstructed buildings rise above artificial platforms, while hundreds of other structures lie crumbling in scrubby jungle. The site sprawls over more than 39 square miles (100 sq km), of which only about 3.5 square miles (9 sq km) may be visited: Grupo Central, Grupo Norte, and Old Chichén (Grupo Sur).

Chichén's oldest structures are located in the southern part of the site, an area first settled by the Maya around A.D. 400. It was already deserted when the Itzá peoples from the south arrived in the eighth century and began constructing a major city. Also known as the Chontal Maya or Putún, the Itzá were a seafaring people from what is now Tabasco state. The fact that they were considered interlopers or at least outsiders is evidenced by the fact that their Maya name means "those who speak our language badly."

The buildings once thought to

EXPERIENCE:
Herald an Equinox in the Land of the Maya

The ancient Maya were adept mathematicians, astronomers, and architects who worshiped the sun, stars, moon, and other natural phenomena. Some of their most important temples were designed to create a symbolic light show at the equinox. At Chichén Itzá's **Kukulkán temple**, you can join thousands of people to celebrate the equinox; the movement of the sun causes a serpent-like shadow to slither down the pyramid, after several hours touching a sculpted snake's head at the temple's base.

To witness an equinox light spectacle at **Dzibilchaltún,** 8 miles (14 km) north of Mérida, get up before dawn. As the sun rises, watch it shine through opposite windows of The Temple of the Seven Dolls.

Either equinox displays these phenomenon, but generally the spring has a better record of cloudless skies.

have been Toltec-inspired dominate the **Grupo Norte,** where pyramids and temples were constructed atop existing structures around the tenth century. More than 35,000 people lived in the area in the 11th century, when Chichén Itzá was a major religious and commercial center. But by 1250, the site was again deserted.

Archaeologists long believed the Toltec of Tula, 600 miles (965 km) to the west (see p. 232), conquered the Maya of Chichén Itzá in the Early Postclassic period (around A.D. 900) and imposed their beliefs and symbols. However, it is now generally accepted that the reverse is true: Chichén Itzá actually influenced Tula, not by conquest but by example. Turquoise found in Chichén Itzá was traded from the Oasis America people of today's Arizona, and gold was imported from as far south as Costa Rica.

The confusion springs from the similarity of carvings, architectural styles, and symbols found at both Chichén Itzá's Grupo Norte and Tula, or Tollan. One of the most significant similarities is the presence of the feathered serpent god, called Kukulcán by the Maya and Quetzalcóatl by the Toltec and other groups. The serpent is particularly important at the **Castillo,** also called Pirámide de Kukulcán, Chichén Itza's most famous structure. Built atop an earlier temple, the pyramidal building has four stairways with a total of 365 steps, corresponding with the number of days in the solar calendar. A square temple at the top is believed to honor Kukulcán.

Thousands of onlookers are

At Chichén Itzá, with Caracol standing in the middleground, and, beyond, the temple to Kukulkán, the feathered serpent

drawn to Castillo during the spring and fall equinoxes, normally March 21 and September 21. On these days, the sunlight hits the pyramid in such a way as to create a snake-shaped shadow wriggling down the steps to meet the head of a serpent carved at the base. The phenomenon gives testimony to the Maya's incredible skill at mathematics and astronomy.

Chichén Itzá holds many examples of human sacrifice. Near the Castillo is the **Tzompantli,** a platform lined with stone carvings of human skulls. (A similar wall can be found at Tula.) Adjacent to this structure is the *juego de pelota,*

Chichén Itzá

🄰   309 D3

✉   Hwy. 180, 72 miles (116 km) E of Mérida

☎   999/942-1400

💲 $$$

or ball court. The traditional ball game had a religious and political significance unknown to most people today. It was a one-on-one game playing a victorious ruler against his defeated enemy—the loser would be sacrificed by being

Spanish Conquest.

A dirt trail leads from the ball court to the **Cenote de los Sacrificios,** a deep natural well into which sacrificial victims may have been tossed. Mexican diver Pablo Bush Romero first investigated the well;

A statue of Chac Mool at Chitzén Itzá's Templo de los Guerreros

rolled down from the top of the pyramid, his arms and legs bound tightly behind him, to smash on the ground below. The fight was fixed, of course, so that the conquering ruler could defeat the captive—a symbolic defeat of evil and darkness by light and life, and a reenactment of the creation of the world. In order to ensure his success, the conquering ruler would starve the other player for several weeks before the game and, if he still had too much spirit, break one of his arms or legs before the match. Evidence of this ritual ball game is seen in Mixtec hieroglyphics, Maya codices, and oral reports from eyewitnesses during the early years of the

Jacques Cousteau followed. Both found human skeletons and jade and gold figurines in the murky depths, further demonstrating the Maya belief in human sacrifice.

Back at El Castillo, rows of carved stone pillars called the **Mil Columnas** front the **Templo de los Guerreros** (Temple of the Warriors), where a few bits of murals decorate the walls. More murals of a battle scene line a wall at the nearby **Templo de los Jaguares.** One of the site's largest statues of the lesser god Chac Mool sits by this cluster of ruins. The reclining figure holds a flat plate on which human hearts were presented to the gods.

More mysterious and ornate

than the newer section, the Grupo Sur is dominated by the **Caracol** (also known as el Observatorio), named for its snail-like shape. Most likely used as an observatory, the Caracol has two levels of stairways and terraces leading to a circular tower with windows facing the four cardinal directions. The Maya were keen astronomers, and studied the cycles of the moon and stars to calculate the passage of time. Their knowledge was particularly important in Yucatán, where crops had to be planted to benefit from the area's limited rainfall.

The Puuc style of architecture is most evident at the **Casa de las Monjas,** whose name, the Nunnery, was given by the Spanish. Elaborate friezes front the crumbling staircase and window frames at the top of the long structure. Beside the Nunnery, **la Iglesia** (meaning "the Church," another Spanish reference) is also elaborately decorated with ornate carvings of animals and latticework designs. A somewhat overgrown trail leads from the Nunnery to **Chichén Viejo** (Old Chichén), where the Itzá let loose their imaginations on structures covered with masks of Chac, bas-reliefs of jaguars and gods, and delicate latticework designs. Some structures are barely visible beneath the ever encroaching jungle brush and vines.

Anyone even remotely fascinated by the Maya should spend at least one night by the ruins. There are several moderately priced hotels and restaurants in the nearby town of **Piste,** but it's worth the splurge to stay closer to the site. Archaeologists who worked here in the early 20th century stayed at Hacienda Chichén; both it and the Hotel Mayaland have their own entrance to the ruins. You can then rest up before returning for the nightly sound-and-light show, included in the price.

Uxmal & La Ruta Puuc

The Mayan word *puuc* describes not only the "hill country" in south-central Yucatán and northeast Campeche, but also the Late Classic cities that flourished here and the architectural style that defines them. Between A.D. 200 and 1000, more than a hundred settlements prospered throughout this small region. With few cenotes, or sinkholes, the land

Please Drink the Water

Although you should heed the caveats about consuming water in Mexico, some drinks are worth trying. While you must make sure that bottled water has been used to prepare any local drink, *agua fresca* or *agua de sabor* (fruit drink) is a delicious alternative to chemically laden sodas. Instead of lemonade try orangeade, with fewer calories than straight juice. Taking advantage of local produce, enjoy deliciously refreshing watermelon water *(agua de sandía)* or *agua de jamaica,* a refreshing drink made throughout the country with hibiscus flowers (not the ornamental type).

Uxmal

▲ 309 C3

☎ 999/944-0033 (INAH in Mérida)

could sustain these settlements only after northward-migrating people devised *chultunes* (water tanks), in which to store water for the dry months. They later created hydraulic systems.

With the demise of the Classic southern lowlands cities such as Tikal, the Puuc flourished between A.D. 800 and 1000 in what Mayanists call the Terminal Classic period. This was a period of intense and uncharacteristic political cooperation among cities, many of which were connected by *sacbéob,* or white roads. In classic Mesoamerican fashion, the great religious centers were abandoned after reaching their height of civilization. Theories include overpopulation, depletion of resources, disease, and increased warfare, but the real reason remains a mystery.

INSIDER TIP:

Uxmal attracts fewer tourists than Chichén Itzá, but it's still a good idea to visit in early morning or late afternoon to avoid crowds.

—DEAN ARNOLD
National Geographic field researcher

Puuc-style architecture is admired as one of the most harmonious and well-proportioned of the Maya world. It is noted for its stone-mosaic facades, veneer masonry, small relief columns, and hook-nosed Chac masks on the facades and corners of buildings. In

a land of uncertain rainfall and no surface rivers, the rain god Chac was an important deity. Walls are often smooth below, while the upper facades are decorated with elaborate geometric shapes. The "false arch," a Maya innovation, reached its most refined at the Palace of the Governor, at Uxmal.

Walled Uxmal, 48 miles (78 km) south of Mérida on Highway 261, was a favorite of 19th-century explorer John Lloyd Stephens, who visited several times with traveling companion and artist Frederick Catherwood. Capital of the Puuc region, Uxmal (meaning "thrice built") was founded around A.D. 800 and reached its peak of civilization under Lord Chac, who reigned between about A.D. 900 and 950. Its name refers to three distinct phases of construction. Considered the most lovely of the Puuc cities, it has been extensively restored but, compared to other major sites in Mexico, little studied.

Rising 125 feet (35 m) above the forest, the **Casa del Adivino** (Pyramid of the Magician) is also called the House of the Dwarf; supposedly it was built by a dwarf hatched from a tiny egg. The tall structure's unusual elliptical base, rounded corners, and harmonious design make it one of the most admired buildings in Mexico—of any age. Steep staircases on either side lead to the temple at its crown, which is decorated with icons of the planet Venus, the sun, flowers, and serpents. This and other buildings are dramatically lit during nightly narrated sound-and-light shows in Spanish *($ for English-language headset).*

The name Uxmal (meaning "thrice built") refers to the site's three separate phases of construction.

Just beyond, the **Casa de las Monjas** (The Nunnery) is a quadrangle of four large, low palaces surrounding an open courtyard. The building was named by the Spaniards, who thought its 74 vaulted chambers resembled monastic cells. Covering the palace's upper interior are intricate carvings of Chac masks and serpents interspersed with latticework designs. Also within the central group are the *juego de pelota,* or ball court, and the **Casa de las Tortugas,** named for the turtles decorating the cornice (much blurred by the passage of time). The more recently restored **Cuadrángulo de los Pájaros** was named for a repeating avian pattern above the doorways.

Cited as one of the most beautiful representations of Puuc-style architecture, the magnificent **Palacio del Gobernador** was built around A.D. 900 on a stepped platform. It seems to have served as both the residence and the administrative center of the ruling elite. The palace's horizontal plane is, on the east face, interrupted by perhaps the most refined false arches in the Maya world. Its frieze is covered in an intricate geometric mosaic composed of 20,000 carefully cut stones forming Chac masks.

The excellent travertine limestone found in the region was largely responsible for the success of Puuc-style carvings at Uxmal, epitomized in the Governor's Palace. This fine-grained limestone, ranging in color from yellow to red, can be cut into thin plates and polished to a high luster. Only around Mitla, in Oaxaca state (see p. 268), is such a high grade of stone found, and the Mixtec of Mitla also produced intricate and exacting mosaics.

Just about 13 miles (22 km) to the southeast, **Kabah** was connected by a sacbé to Uxmal. To the east are the greatest number of restored structures, including the impressive **Palacio de los Mascarones** (Palace of the Masks), elaborately decorated with six tiers of Chac masks, each an inlaid stone mosaic. Walk around to the back of the building to see the giant warrior sculptures wearing loincloths and beaded necklaces.

Nearby **Sayil** (meaning "home of leaf-cutter ants") is one of the oldest Puuc cities. The most

INSIDER TIP:

Ticul is known for its pottery. You can join a pottery workshop, particularly if you pledge to purchase something.

—DEAN ARNOLD
National Geographic field researcher

important structure at this site is the three-story **Gran Palacio,** considered along with the palace of Uxmal to embody classic Puuc architecture. Containing more than 90 rooms, it must have housed the city's ruling elite. **Xlapax,** just a few miles away, is a small site and not much reconstructed. As with Sayil, its palace is decorated with masks of the rain god.

Labná (Old House) is about the same distance farther on. Although inhabited as early as the first century A.D., its most noteworthy construction is the Late Classic ceremonial arch, inscribed on the west facade with representations of thatch houses and stylized snakes. One of the best surviving examples of its type, the arch may have served commemorative purposes, or perhaps it was placed at the end of a sacbé.

The highway now loops north toward the caves of Loltún (see opposite) to the **Ruta de los Conventos,** a series of monasteries built from the beginning of the 16th century for the catechism of the indigenous population. While the churches and adjoining convents have lost much of their glamour, this route returns to Mérida passing typical Maya and mestizo towns. To visit the churches, arrive in the morning or late afternoon, as many are closed between noon and 4 p.m. En route, visit the fruit market in the friendly little town of **Oxcutzcab,** famous for its sweet oranges *(chinas).*

East of Oxcutzcab, the late blooming Maya city of **Mayapan** gained importance around the time of Chichén Itzá's demise; some scholars believe Chichén was conquered by Mayapan. Mayapan lacked the excellent craftsmanship and site design of other Puuc cities, and had few important temples and no ball court. The 5-mile-long (8 km) wall, averaging nearly 20 feet (6 m) thick, suggests a fortified city. Mayapan appears to have been sacked around 1440. With its demise, the Puuc alliance was disbanded and fighting broke out among the region's cities. Soon after, the Spaniards arrived.

Visit the Ruta Puuc as a day trip out of Mérida or Ticul, or as a more leisurely two-day tour. The latter has the added advantage of an overnight stay at one of several pretty hotels right at the ruins of Uxmal. If you choose a day trip, buses *(Calle 69 bet. Calles 68 & 70)* make the circuit daily from Mérida; they make 30-minute stops at the minor sites, with 1.5 hours at Uxmal (\$).

More Places to Visit in Yucatán

Ek Balam

Rising to importance during the Terminal Classic era, between A.D. 800 and 1000, Ek Balam, which means "black jaguar," was a contemporary of the more well-known site at Uxmal (see pp. 342–344). Today the small set of ruins at Ek Balam is growing increasingly popular with tour groups. The site is both easy to get to, off a two-lane highway approximately halfway between Valladolid and the town of Tizimín, and, as it's quite compact, easy to explore.

Archaeologists aren't sure whether the double ring of walls surrounding the city served a defensive or a more symbolic purpose—or perhaps both. Within their crumbled remains are a freestanding arch, ball court, and other buildings constructed in the Chenes style. By far the most impressive building is the acropolis, which was added to by successive rulers and is known to contain at least one royal tomb. Marvelous, well preserved, detailed, high-relief carvings of warriors surrounded by detailed iconography are the pièce de résistance of this magnificent former palace-cum-mausoleum.

🅰 309 E4 🆂 $

Grutas de Balankanché

Just a few miles northeast of Chichén Itzá, the Caves of Balankanché were used by the pre-Hispanic Maya for sacred ceremonies. The outer caves were long known to locals, and a sealed chamber with ancient artifacts was discovered in 1959. The pottery shows it was used for religious ceremonies during thousands of years by Preclassic, Classic, and Postclassic civilizations. In the Terminal Classic period, the Maya rain god, Chac, was replaced with Tláloc, worshipped throughout Central Mexico. Many representations of Xipe Totec, god of spring and regeneration, have also been found.

It's awesome to see the urns, some decorated with relief "faces," in situ. Open daily 9 a.m. to 5 p.m.; guided tours leave on the hour, and it doesn't much matter whether it's in English, Spanish, or French. The caves themselves are the show. Don't forget to tip the guide.

🅰 309 D3 🆂 Tours $$

Grutas de Loltún

Eleven miles (17 km) northeast of Labná along the Ruta Puuc are the Grutas de Loltún, one of the peninsula's most extensive cave systems. The caves were first inhabited by nomadic hunter-gatherers between 9000 and 3000 B.C., who left evidence of their presence in the form of stone tools. Much later, in the Classic period, the caves were used as a source of water by local inhabitants. Water vessels in both the Mayapan and Chichén Itzá Postclassic ceramic styles have been excavated. The Maya revered five physical features:

La Mordida

La mordida (literally, "the bite") is a tradition as old as Mexico itself. Pay a small fee to ease transactions; pay a large bribe to buy your way out of major problems. Mexico is changing, however, and knowing when or where to offer a bribe can be tricky. Foreigners are most likely to encounter the situation on the road. Real or imaginary traffic violations usually disappear by asking the cop in question if he can pay the fee for you. If you feel unjustly ticketed or prefer not to encourage bribery, you can follow the cop to the police station. However, most people want the situation to be resolved as quickly and painlessly as possible.

trees, rocks, mountains, mountain passes, and earth openings—cenotes and caves, which were considered holy because they presented a transition between the physical and spirit worlds.

Guided tours lead through a series of passageways to chambers of various sizes, some with prehistoric paintings or fantastic stalactites and stalagmites. Tours in English depart at 11 a.m. and 2 p.m.; in Spanish at 9:30 a.m., and 12:30 and 3:30 p.m. Guides work for tips only, so don't forget the gratuity.

◭ 309 C3 ⑤ $$

Izamal

An important religious center for millennia, friendly Izamal continues to welcome travelers. The bustling small town's star attraction is the **Convento de San Antonio de Padua,** built from the stones of a pyramid to the god of the heavens, Itzamná, on which it sits. Light-and-sound shows, in Spanish only, show on Tuesday, Thursday, and either Friday or Saturday nights at 8:30. Izamal makes a good base for those who avoid larger cities. Pony traps can be rented on the square for a tour of town, including a stop at the **Pirámide Kinich Kakmó,** all that remains of this once royal Maya city. The horse-drawn carriages are also useful for visiting artisans shops; drivers know the way to home workshops where hammocks, jewelry, embroidery, and other crafts are offered for sale.

◭ 309 D4

Izamal was a pilgrimage site in the pre-conquest era.

Valladolid

Although it is the Yucatán's second largest city—about a two hours' drive from both Cancún and Mérida—Valladolid has the feel of a small town. In 1847 this colonial-era agricultural center was the scene of the War of the Castes, during which the repressed Maya rose in revolt to massacre large numbers of Spanish residents. Worth visiting are the **catedral,** on the *plaza principal,* and the large, 16th-century **Ex-Convento San Bernardino,** three blocks southwest. Outside town, you can visit holy **Cenote Dzitnup,** where light filters through a tiny hole in the ceiling to illuminate the green-blue underground spring or, right at the edge of town, large and lovely **Cenote Zací.** Valladolid also makes an alternative base for visiting the ruins of Chichén Itzá or the north coast.

◭ 309 E3

Travelwise

The Virgin of Guadalupe

TRAVELWISE

PLANNING YOUR TRIP

When to Go

When you visit depends on what you want to do and see, budget constraints, and your tolerance for wet, hot, or humid weather. Mexico is a large and geographically diverse country, its microclimates dictated by altitude and latitude. June through October is the wettest time, and if you don't mind late afternoon showers—which in Mexico City clear the air—consider booking your vacation during this low season to avoid the crowds and get cheaper hotel and air rates. Rain may put a damper on beach vacations, however, and late September and October are hurricane season along the Gulf and south/central Pacific coasts (and, less frequently, in Baja). Baja California and the northern deserts are extremely hot in the summer, although diehard fishermen brave the heat for the excellent fishing. Highland cities are hottest March through May, just before the rainy season, while the tropical regions of southern Mexico are hot year-round but even hotter, muggier, and more bug-ridden during the rainy season. If you want to avoid both the rainy season and the high season, chose late spring (after Easter) or late fall.

High season is late November (Thanksgiving) to Holy Week (Semana Santa), with especially high hotel rates during Christmas, New Year, and Easter. Mexicans as well as foreigners frequently travel during these holidays, and reservations should be made well in advance.

Those interested in Mexican culture might want to plan their vacation around the country's many colorful fiestas, including the weeks preceding Christmas, Easter, Day of the Dead, pre-Lenten Carnaval, and many others. See "Festivals & Fiestas" (pp. 18–19), regional chapters, and "Entertainment & Activities" (pp. 386–389) for specific suggestions. In Mexico, a city or village's saint's day is always cause for celebration. For example, places named San Juan will celebrate on the feast day of St. John, June 24; San Miguel de Allende celebrates its patron, the Archangel Michael, the days preceding September 29. Check with the government tourist office (see individual entries) for more information about specific local festivals.

What to Take

Although Mexicans today are less formal than before, city dwellers are fashionable and businesspeople dress for success. Except on the more casual coast, Mexican women rarely wear shorts, and men are not seen shirtless except on the beach. Bring lightweight, comfortable clothing for tropical climes, plus a sweater or light jacket. Women should also bring slacks and at least one dressy outfit, men a light sports jacket. Much of Mexico consists of mountains and high plateaus, and while hot during the day can get chilly at night. Comfortable walking shoes are essential for archaeological sites, cobblestone streets, and long walks. A lightweight, long-sleeved shirt prevents mosquito bites, as does an insect repellent containing deet.

As well as the usual—documents and money—take sunscreen, sunglasses, and a hat as the sun is fierce. A small English–Spanish phrasebook is useful. Campers or trekkers should include iodine tablets and filters to purify water if bottled water is unavailable.

Entry Formalities

A visa is not necessary for entry into Mexico for citizens of the United States, Canada, the U.K., Ireland, Australia, New Zealand, and much of Western Europe. You will need a passport along with a tourist card (tarjeta de turista), which can be obtained at embassies, travel agencies, and border crossings; they are also distributed during international flights. Minors also need a notarized letter of permission from one or both guardians not accompanying the child. U.S. and Canadian citizens can stay up to 180 days with a tourist card.

Drugs, Narcotics, & Weapons

To avoid problems, prescription drugs should be brought in their original containers. Drugs such as marijuana and cocaine are illegal, and penalties for drug offenses are strict.

Bringing weapons or ammunition to Mexico is illegal; importing either of these carries huge fines and the possibility of a jail term. Hunters must obtain permits and ID cards to import and transport firearms temporarily; it's best to make arrangements through an authorized wildlife outfitter club, such as a hunting lodge.

Pets

U.S. visitors may bring a dog (or cat) if they provide a pet health certificate signed not more than 72 hours before, and a certificate showing that the animal has been vaccinated against rabies and other contagious diseases.

Vaccinations & Disease

No inoculations are required for Mexico, but a current tetanus booster is recommended, as is a hepatitis A and/or B inoculation along with a typhoid shot. For travel to rural lowland areas, consider an antimalarial drug or protect yourself against insect bites with a good insect repellent and adequate clothing/mosquito nets. The Center for Disease Control has a website (www.cdc.gov/travel/camerica.htm) with information about local conditions and health-related issues.

HOW TO GET TO MEXICO
By Airplane
Major airlines serving Mexico from the United States and Canada include:
Mexicana, tel 800/531-7921
Aeroméxico, tel 800/237-6639
American, tel 800/443-7300
Continental, tel 800/523-3273
United, tel 800/241-6522.

Mexico City's Benito Juárez Airport is the connecting hub for flights throughout central and southern Mexico. If your destination is an international airport, your luggage need not pass customs in Mexico City. Confirm arriving and departing flights within 72 hours of flying. In Mexico City, use only official airport taxis, which you prepay within the terminal.

By Boat
Many companies offer cruises to Mexico. Ports of call include Ensenada, Cabo San Lucas, Mazatlán, Puerto Vallarta, Manzanillo, Zihuatanejo/Ixtapa, Huatulco, and Acapulco on the west coast. Caribbean cruises berth at Progreso, Cozumel, Cancún, Playa del Carmen, and Puerto Costa Maya on the Riviera Maya.

By Bus
From the U.S., Greyhound Lines (tel 800/231-2222) can book travel to most of the major cities in Mexico through agreements with Mexican bus lines.

By Car
If you drive into Mexico, buy Mexican auto insurance. Policies issued in the United States do not cover liability within Mexico. Some cover damages, but be sure to check. One-stop insurance offices abound near the busiest border crossings and will issue policies by the day, week, or year. Some also help prepare paperwork for a Temporary Car Importation Permit, which is required when driving beyond the border zone (less than 16 miles/25 km into Mexico, Baja California and Baja California Sur exempt). These forms can be submitted or filled out at the Mexican customs office, at the border. The fee is about $20; use a major credit card and you'll avoid paying a cash bond (tedious, time-consuming, and much more costly) based on the value of the car. If you do not return the vehicle prior to the specified date (up to 180 days) you will suffer large, variable fines and possible impounding of the vehicle. The permit allows multiple reentries during the specified time period. Keep several copies of your permit in different places, as leaving the country without it is problematic.

Also required is proof of ownership of the vehicle, the original vehicle registration or lease contract, proof of Mexican insurance, and a valid driver's license (from your country of origin). You can do the paperwork before reaching the border at a Mexican Consul office, although this isn't really necessary.

TRAVELING AROUND MEXICO
By Air
Mexicana de Aviación and its subsidiary, Mexicana Click Aerocaribe (tel 800/531-7921 in U.S.; 01800/502-2000 toll-free within Mexico), Aeroméxico and Aeromar (tel 800/237-6639 in U.S; 01800/021-4010 toll-free within Mexico, www.aeromexico.com.mx & www.aeromar.com.mx), and Aviacsa (tel 01800/006-2200, www.aviacsa.com) are the primary Mexican airlines. Volaris (www.volaris.com.mx) serves Mexico City and 22 other destinations within Mexico.

By Bus
Buses are ubiquitous in Mexico; where there is a road, you'll find a bus to rumble down it. If available, always book first class (primera) or deluxe. Not only do these buses have air-conditioning, bathrooms, and movies, they also make fewer stops.

The larger towns have modern bus stations, known as the central camionera or central de autobuses, where tickets can usually be purchased in advance. Only second-class buses may be available to rural areas or tiny hamlets. Some are air-conditioned, although rarely efficiently, and they stop whenever a passenger wants to board or descend, lengthening travel time.

It's a good idea to bring snacks, bottled water, and toilet paper. Some long-distance buses stop at restaurants. Check with the tourist information office to make sure the route is safe before booking overnight trips; some routes are discouraged by the U.S. State Department and other foreign government agencies. Robberies, while not frequent, do occur on the most touristed routes, where robbers can be assured of dozens of cameras and other expensive gear. Intercity buses are cheap and frequent, but unpleasantly crowded during rush hours.

By Car
Roads vary greatly in Mexico, with the expensive cuota, or toll road, being the best maintained, fastest, and safest. The libre, or free roads, are usually fine, although in rainy climates potholes can be a problem.

Use extra caution when driving in the countryside, as farm animals may wander onto the road. Don't drive at night, and ask about the condition of roads in each region before you set out. In general, observe speed limits and parking regulations, and watch for speed bumps *(topes* or the less destructive *vibradores)* as you enter and leave towns.

Remember that posted speed limits and distances are in kilometers. The usual speed limit on highways is 100 kph (60 mph); within towns it is 30 to 40 kph (19–25 mph). Many road signs use symbols, not words, but a few important translations are as follows: *Circulación,* with an arrow, means "one-way traffic" (very common in towns); No rebasar or No rebase means no passing; and Ceda el paso means yield right of way. On highways, Mexican drivers often use their left-turn signals to indicate that the car behind it is free to pass.

All gas stations are franchises of the government-owned oil company, PEMEX, and sell three types of fuel: Magna (unleaded), Premium (super), and diesel. As a rule of thumb, fill your tank when it's half full or as often as possible when traveling to a remote area. Many stations are not open at night. It's customary to tip the attendant a few pesos (also to make sure he resets the counter to zero before fueling).

Rental Cars

Rental cars can be expensive in Mexico, and drop-off rates are high. You'll find substantial savings by booking before your trip and shopping around, especially on Internet consolidators. Smaller, locally owned companies are sometimes cheaper than international companies such as Hertz, National, and Budget, but their cars may be not be well maintained. Rental companies require

you to leave a signed credit-card voucher as a guarantee. Ask whether IVA (value-added tax) is included in the quoted price, what insurance is provided, and what the deductible is. Some credit card companies provide coverage at no extra cost.

For day trips, consider hiring a taxi instead of renting a car. Ask the hotel manager or tourist office for a recommendation, or negotiate with a cabby you find helpful and friendly. The price will be about the same (less if you are a good bargainer) as renting a car, and you won't have to worry about driving in unfamiliar areas or parking. Often you'll also get an informal Spanish lesson or an English-speaking "tour guide" who is happy to tell you all about his native city.

By Ferry

Auto and passenger ferries connect Baja California Sur and mainland Mexico. Travelers intending to ferry their vehicles from Baja to Sonora or Sinaloa must obtain a Temporary Car Importation Permit (see "How to Get to Mexico by Car" p. 349), at the international border. The Santa Rosalía ferry serves Guaymas, Sonora *(tel 622/222-0204),* twice weekly. The cost for the ten-hour crossing runs about $50 (depending on accommodations) for passengers; about $225 for vehicles (substantially more for trailers and motor homes). Several ferries per week connect La Paz to Topolobampo, Sinaloa *(tel 668/862-1003).* The ferry landing is at Pichilingue, 10 miles (16 km) to the north; the ticket office is in La Paz at 5 de Mayo 502, *(tel 612/123-0208).* Prices for the daily, five-hour La Paz–Mazatlán ferry are about half as much as for Topolobampo or Guaymas. Reservations are essential, especially during holidays; make them well in advance and confirm at least ten days before departure.

On the Caribbean coast, passenger ferries and hydrofoils connect Playa del Carmen to Cozumel, just offshore, leave on the hour; vehicular ferries depart from nearby Puerto Morelos *(tel 987/872-0950).* Passenger ferries are more frequent, inexpensive, comfortable, and hassle free than the car ferry; you can rent a car, moped, or electric golf cart in Cozumel. Daily passenger ferries connect Puerto Juárez, just north of Cancún, to Isla Mujeres.

By Train

Other than the exceptional train ride through the Copper Canyon on the Chihuahua al Pacífico Railway (see pp. 90–91), train travel is not available.

TRAVELING IN MEXICO CITY
By Car

Even if you have driven your own car to Mexico, park it when you get to Mexico City and take radio cabs or the metro; the quagmire of this city's streets is best left to the locals. If you must drive, be aware that a city ordinance to reduce smog dictates which days of the week cars may circulate; this system is based on the last number of the car's license plate. Foreigners as well as locals are subject to substantial fines for infractions. For information, check at a gas station or online at *www.mexicocity.gob.mx.*

By Bus

Mexico City is well served by a comprehensive yet inexpensive bus service. Routes may or may not be posted at bus stops and may be available at tourist offices. One of the routes most used by tourists connects Chapultepec Park to the Zócalo via Paseo de la Reforma, Avenida Juárez, and Calle Madero. If possible avoid traveling during rush hours, as buses at that time are packed and traffic can be maddeningly slow. If you must ride on a crowded bus, follow the safety advice given in the Metro section below.

For destinations outside Mexico City, there are four major terminals. Check with the concierge or tourist office before making a long trip to the wrong bus station. Generally, Terminal Central del Norte *(tel 55/5689-9745, www.centraldelnorte.com)* serves points north; TAPO *(tel 55/5522-5400)*, points to the east; Terminal Sur, also known as Tasqueña *(tel 55/5689-9745)*, points to the south; and Terminal Central Poniente *(tel 55/5271-4519)*, points to the west.

By Metro

The subway system in Mexico City is extensive and inexpensive. Beyond the city center, *el tren ligero* is a sometimes aboveground line reaching into suburbs such as Xochimilco. Metro maps are available at most stations and at tourist offices. Most lines operate from 5 or 6 a.m. to midnight. Weekday rush hours are 6–10 a.m. and 5–8 p.m.; during these hours separate cars are available for women and children to prevent them being squashed against men. While subways can be extremely crowded, negotiating the system can save you from traffic jams on the congested city streets above. Beware of pickpockets and mashers. Hold purses, cameras, and backpacks tightly, and carry currency in a money belt or hidden front pocket.

By Taxi

Mexico City taxis have received a lot of bad press in the last couple of years, and with good reason. Robbing passengers at gunpoint was the crime du jour around the turn of this century. Using radio cabs instead of roving cabs reduces risk; ask your concierge for a recommendation. It's reasonably safe to grab a street cab following these precautions. The cab should be white plus only one color (usually orange or green); license plate number must be painted on the back and side of the car (and be an official taxi plate with colored stripe). Street cabs are usually a fraction of the cost of a radio cab. Both of these types negotiate their fee; taxis de sitio (associated with a hotel, place, or site) are metered.

Taxis are often unmetered and it's best to establish a fare ahead of time. Tipping the driver is not customary. Outside Mexico City, few cab-related robberies have been reported.

By Tram

Narrated tram rides on Turibus *(tel 55/5553-1901 or 55/5518-1003, $$$$$)* provide a safe, economical, and convenient (if not exactly expedient, given D.F.'s traffic situation) way of accessing major sites. It's an on-again, off-again service that lets passengers get off to see the sights and reboard to continue the tour. Daytime routes *(9 a.m.–9 p.m. Mon.–Sat., $$$$, tickets sold on board)* are Historical Center to Chapultepec, with almost two dozen stops including Parque Chapultepec, La Condesa, La Alameda, Zócalo, Monumento a la Revolución, among others; and the Southern Circuit from La Condesa to Tlalpan, including stops at la Plaza de Toros México, Frida Kahlo museum, Cuicuilco archaeological site, San Angel, among others. Buses also run daily to Teotihuacán from Auditorio Nacional at 9 a.m.; Angel de la Independencia, 9:15 a.m.; Glorieta de Colón, 9:30 a.m.; and Catedral Metropolitana at 9:45 a.m..

PRACTICAL ADVICE
Communications
Mail

Although your mail will eventually get to its intended destination, service from Mexico takes from three days to a month to reach the United States. Courier service is available in most cities, but don't count on overnight service; be sure to ask how long the delivery will take. MexiPost is the government-run competition for private couriers such as DHL and FedEx. Some rural Mexicans still rely on the telegraph service, found at (or next door to) post offices, which are generally open Monday to Friday 9–6 (although some close at 3), Saturday 9–noon.

Telephone, Fax, E-mail, & Addresses

To call or fax Mexico from the United States or Canada, dial 011-52 and then the area code followed by the number. For long-distance calls within Mexico, dial 01, area code, and number. For toll-free calls within Mexico, dial 01-800 and the number.

All towns and cities have seven-digit phone numbers with three-digit LADA (area code), with the exception of Guadalajara, Monterrey, and Mexico City, which have eight-digit numbers and two-digit area codes. This phone system was totally revamped in early 2000, and lots of locals and even some printed material still refer to five- or six-digit numbers of old.

Making international calls from Mexico can be expensive. Some public phones are owned by private companies that charge exorbitant rates; if in doubt, dial 0 and ask the operator for international rates before placing a call. (If he or she refuses to tell you, by all means hang up and use a standard public phone.) Most hotels add a high service charge for international calls, and not all have direct-dial phones or Internet modems. Many pharmacies and newsstands sell prepaid LADATEL phonecards (20, 50, or 100 pesos) for use with public phones; there are few remaining coin-operated phones. LADATEL phonecards work for calls outside Mexico (make sure to use the 100-peso card). For international calls, dial 00 plus the country code (1 for Canada and the United States; 44 for the United Kingdom).

Most towns have at least one private fax service, which may charge by the minute or by the page. Cities small and large have cybercafés where you can connect to the Internet. Some offices do not have fiberoptic lines, and connections can be slow; try to visit during off-peak hours for a faster connection. Internet cafés generally charge a reasonable $2 to $4 per hour.

While most street addresses in Mexico have both street name and number, some properties in small towns—or on large boulevards—are labeled simply by street name and "s/n": shorthand for sin número, meaning "without number." Whenever possible, a cross street or other reference is added. Properties along highways (carreteras) are often addressed simply by their distance in kilometers along the highway in question—for example, "Carr. Trans-peninsular Km 19.5." In the case of streets, with the exception of those that are numbered, the designation "Calle" rarely appears in front of the name on maps or in written addresses.

Conversions

In general, the metric system is used. Temperatures are in centigrade, distances in kilometers, and so on.

Electricity

Mexico's electrical system operates on 110 volts AC, with outlets taking two-flat-pin rectangular plugs. Bring adapters for any appliances with three-prong plugs, and a power-surge protector for laptop computers. If a power outage or brownout occurs while you are using your computer, shut the computer down right away.

Etiquette & Local Customs

Mexicans are very polite and very friendly, but not overly casual with strangers. Use the formal address usted instead of the informal tú when addressing people you don't know, especially in the smaller towns, away from tourist enclaves, and with elders.

When asking directions, be aware that many Mexicans find it embarrassing or impolite to decline to help, even when unsure of the address you are seeking. As they may inadvertently send you in the wrong direction to save face, ask directions often and request landmarks. Also, they rarely give specific street names, although with prompting these may be provided.

It is considered disrespectful to enter churches in skimpy clothing, and to sightsee during services.

Language Study

Spanish-language courses are offered by private institutes and those attached to universities throughout Mexico. Some are intensive courses focusing on grammar; others offer cultural classes (for example regional cooking, handicrafts, or archaeology) or intercambios, casual one-on-one conversations with a compatible Mexican who wants to practice his or her English and help you with Spanish. Programs generally run from two to four weeks (or more), and students can stay with families or arrange to rent apartments or hotel rooms. Some families rent rooms to several students at a time; those committed to full immersion should ask for a family that hosts only one student at a time. You can get information, listings, and links to language schools throughout Mexico on www.worldwide.edu.

Liquor Laws

The legal drinking age is 18 years, although identification is rarely checked. The sale of alcohol is prohibited on election days.

Media

Newspapers & Magazines

Most Mexican reporters rely on stipends from the people or government offices they cover, making impartiality impossible. The newspaper most openly critical of the government is Reforma; that and the left-leaning La Jornada are the largest circulating nationals. For those who do not read Spanish, larger cities carry the English-language daily The News, while towns with many English-speaking residents publish their own small weekly or monthly papers. In hotels, airports, and newsstands in larger cities, foreign periodicals such as Time, Newsweek, and U.S. News and World Report are sold along with women's magazines. The Sanborns chain of restaurant/bookstores is a great source of magazines, books, and periodicals about Mexican culture.

Television & Radio

Many more Mexicans get their information from radio and television than from newspapers. In addition to two government-run television channels, there are a half dozen private networks. The largest (and most influential), Televisa, has a lineup of Mexico's universally popular evening soap operas. Cable television is available throughout most of the country; hotels geared to foreign tourists usually have satellite or cable TV.

Money Matters

The Mexican monetary unit is the peso. Bills come in denominations of 20, 50, 100, 200, and 500 pesos. Always keep a supply of coins and smaller-denomination bills, especially in non-touristy areas, as change can be hard to come by. U.S. dollars are accepted in border cities and at major resorts, although you get a better deal using pesos. Keep a supply of small bills for tipping.

Canadians and other foreign travelers will avoid headaches by bringing traveler's checks and cash in U.S. dollars. You can change money at a bank, but a *casa de cambio*, dedicated exclusively to this activity, is usually faster, has longer, more convenient hours, and offers the same or only slightly lower rate. Check exchange rates online at *www.xe.com*.

Automatic Teller Machines (ATMs, or *cajeros automáticos*) are ubiquitous throughout Mexico. Have a backup of cash or traveler's checks so you won't be stranded if an ATM is broken or out of money. With ATMs you get an excellent exchange rate, but service charges apply. Avoid using ATMs at night or in isolated locations. Credit cards also give a good exchange rate. MasterCard, Visa, and, to a lesser extent, American Express are the most commonly accepted, although mainly at tourist-oriented hotels and restaurants.

The value-added tax, called IVA, is ignored by some stores, restaurants, and even hotels; most will add IVA if you ask for a receipt.

National Holidays

Banks, state offices, and many other businesses close on the following holidays. Check ahead before arriving at museums or other tourist destinations. (See also "Festivals & Fiestas," pp. 18–19, and "Entertainment & Activities," pp. 386–389.)
Jan. 1 New Year's Day (Año Nuevo)
Feb. 5 Constitution Day (Proclamación de la Constitución)
March 21 Benito Juárez Day (Natalicio de Benito Juárez)
May 1 Labor Day (Día del Trabajo)

Sept. 16 Independence Day (Día de la Independencia)
Nov. 20 Revolution Day (Aniversario de la Revolución Mexicana)
Dec. 25 Christmas Day (Navidad)

Opening Times

It is difficult to generalize about opening hours in Mexico, as they vary from region to region. In industrialized areas, government and business offices usually adhere to a 9 a.m.–5 p.m. schedule (but some close at 3 p.m.). In hot climates, however, they may close for two to four hours in the middle of the day, reopening from 4 or 5 until 8 (others do not reopen in the afternoon). Although open until 3 or 5 p.m., banks may exchange money only in the morning, although this schedule isn't common these days. Theaters and museums normally close on Mondays. Standard store hours are 9 a.m. until 7 or 8 p.m., with a possible siesta break in between. Remember, especially in tropical climates, to assume there will be a siesta break between approximately 2 and 4 or 5 p.m. This even applies to churches. Movie theaters give discounts on Wednesdays.

Photography

Digital photography is widely used today. In most destinations you can download photos from your digital camera to a CD if needed; those traveling with laptops can download to their memory sticks. Black-and-white and slide films are hard to come by, so bring your own. When purchasing film, check the expiration date.

Think twice about photographing people in regional costume; either be very discreet or ask permission.

Places of Worship

About 90 percent of Mexicans are Catholics; in the most historic cities and towns it seems there is a church on every corner. Remember that while these churches may seem like fabulous museums, they remain places of worship. Short shorts and skimpy tops are frowned upon (or forbidden), and men should remove their hats. Avoid sightseeing during Mass.

Tourist offices and hotels can provide a list of the most interesting churches in town, some of which offer mariachi or guitar Mass. Most cities and towns also have at least one Protestant (often Evangelical) church.

Safety

Common sense is your most valuable weapon against crime while traveling in Mexico. Be cautious, but not paranoid. Street crime was uncommon until 1994, when the peso devaluation resulted in increased poverty and hence crime. Leave expensive jewelry at home, and don't flash wads of money or fancy cameras. Most hotels have room safes or a safe in the lobby—use them. Hold onto handbags and daypacks tightly; beware of criminals who might cut the pack open with a razor.

Mexico City unfortunately requires extra caution. Although compared to the size of the population, taxi muggings are not common, the safest options to prevent entering a renegade cab are using hotel taxis, carrying the number of a reliable dispatch company with you, or asking a shop or restaurant to call you a taxi. Taxis at official taxi stands (*sitios de taxi*) are also safe. (See also "Traveling in Mexico City By Taxi" p. 351.) For current safety information, contact the U.S. State Department's website at *www.travel.state.gov/ mexico.html.*

The police in Mexico are underpaid, and graft and corruption are commonplace throughout both government and commercial bureaucracies. Although efforts are being made to eliminate *la mordida* (the bite), this form of small-time bribery continues (see "La Mordida," p. 345).

If you are a victim of a minor crime, consider that the criminal justice system is woefully ineffective, and decide according to your loss (and the hassle involved) the benefit of reporting it to the police. It's worth asking at the tourist office if there's an office to resolve travelers' difficulties such as theft or unsatisfactory service. By all means, if you are the victim of a serious or violent crime, report it to your embassy or nearest consular office at once.

Time Differences

Most of Mexico is on Central Standard Time (CST), one hour less than Eastern Standard Time (EST). Baja California Sur, Sonora, Sinaloa, and Nayarit are on Mountain Standard Time (EST minus two hours); Baja California (Norte) is the only state on Pacific Standard Time (EST minus three hours). Daylight saving time was adopted in 1996.

Tipping

Most Mexicans tip little if anything in the more humble places, but it's nice to leave 10 percent anyway. Fifteen percent is customary for good service in tourist-oriented restaurants; always make sure the service is not included on the bill. Cab drivers are not tipped unless they wait while you shop or sightsee, which obviously requires additional payment. Hotel maids are usually given $1 per day, bellboys $1 per bag. Group tour guides should receive at least $1 per person per half day; private guides may be tipped 5 to 10 percent of the tour's price or $10 a day. Gas station and washroom attendants should be given a small gratuity as well.

Rest Rooms

There is much variation in the toilets you will find in Mexico— some good, some very bad, and many without toilet seats or toilet paper. Try to use the rest room at your hotel or in restaurants, cafés, and bars when you stop for refreshments.

Except in tourist-oriented hotels and restaurants, don't throw toilet paper in the toilet, but in the basket provided. As unappealing as this seems to some, it can avoid serious plumbing problems for the proprietor and a nasty overflow for you.

Travelers with Disabilities

Mexico has few accommodations for travelers with disabilities, including ramps and wide doorways, although some progress is being made. The newer hotels are usually the best bet, but advance planning is advised. The Society for the Advancement of Travel for the Handicapped (SATH), 347 Fifth Ave., Suite 605, New York, NY 10016, tel 212/447-7284, has a website at *www.sath.org* with general information and links to other sites.

Visitor Information
Useful Phone Numbers & Websites

English-speaking operators working for the Ministry of Tourism can provide information about weather, holidays, safety, entry requirements, and other aspects of visiting Mexico. They can also recommend hotels and restaurants. Telephone them from the United States or Canada by dialing 800/446-3942. The website, *www .mexico-travel.com,* can help you plan your trip.

The U.S. Embassy in Mexico offers assistance to crime victims; dial 55/5080-2000 (24 hours a day). Visitors of other nationalities should call their embassies

in the event of an emergency (see below).

Consumer Protection in Mexico City, tel 55/5568-8722
Mexican Red Cross, tel 065
The following numbers work throughout Mexico, although not in all towns. For telephone information, call 040; for the police, 060.

EMERGENCIES
Embassies & Consulates

The foreign embassies are all based in Mexico City; although many other cities in Mexico have consular offices.

U.S. Embassy

Paseo de la Reforma 305, Colonia Cuauhtémoc, 06500, México, D.F., tel 55/5080-2000, www.usembassy-mexico.gov.

Canadian Embassy

Schiller 529, Polanco 11580, México, D.F., tel 55/5724-7900, www.canada.org.mx

British Embassy

Río Lerma 71, Col. Cuauhtémoc, 06500 México, D.F., tel 55/5242-8500, www.britishembassy.gov.uk

Health

The most prevalent health problem experienced by travelers in Mexico is intestinal. Gastrointestinal upset may be caused simply by eating food with a different composition from what you are used to. More serious problems result from drinking unclean water or eating improperly prepared fruit or vegetables. The most common disorder is diarrhea (often called *turista,* or Moctezuma's revenge). Although caution is certainly advised, to stop eating at humble establishments makes for a limiting cultural experience, and fancy resorts are in any case not immune to contagion.

As a general rule, drink bottled beverages, including water, and only ice made from purified water. Eat peeled fruit and vegetables, and avoid raw fish or shellfish. If you do contract turista, drink plenty of clean water and rest for a couple days until the symptoms subside. Beware of over-medicating on antidiarrhea remedies. In worst case scenarios, unclean water can lead to salmonella, hepatitis, typhoid, or other serious diseases. If you have a fever or continued severe diarrhea or headaches, seek the advice of a physician.

Air pollution in Mexico City and Guadalajara is severe (especially Dec.–May) and can cause health problems for small children, the elderly, or those with respiratory problems. High altitude can exacerbate the problem (Mexico City sits at 7,400 feet/2,250 m above sea level and is ringed by mountains that trap the smog). To acclimatize, avoid strenuous activity, alcohol, and high-fat foods for one or two days.

Local pharmacies dispense advice as well as over-the-counter remedies (and sometimes prescription meds without a prescription); many can direct you to a doctor. The management at your hotel is also a good source for finding a health-care provider. Get information about the vaccines and health risks at the Centers for Disease Control and Prevention's Travelers' Health website: *www.cdc.gov/travel.*

What to Do in a Car Accident

Unfortunately, Mexican law prescribes that all parties involved in a vehicular accident resulting in physical harm or material damages may be jailed until guilt can be established. For this reason, Mexicans involved in accidents often flee the scene. Obtaining Mexican auto insurance is essential, as it limits liability and, most importantly, it can keep you out of jail (see also "How to Get to Mexico By Car," p. 349). Insurers commonly offer policies from one day to one year for either liability (including medical liability and coverage for passengers, legal aid, bail bond, and towing) or full coverage (above-mentioned services plus theft and collision/property damage).

Baja for Less Mexican Insurance *(tel 800/466-7227 in U.S., www.mexicaninsurance.com)* has a convenient program allowing those who drive into Mexico frequently to keep an open insurance account that can be reactivated just prior to a trip by phone or Internet.

FURTHER READING
Websites & Links
The Mexican government tourism website is *www.mexico-travel.com.* Another website full of excellent information is *www.mexicodesconocido.com.* Mexico Online *(www.mexonline.com)* has travel information and breaking news stories.

Reading List
Distant Neighbors, Alan Riding (Knopf Publishing Group, New York, 1989).

The Hummingbird's Daughter, Luis Alberto Urrea (Little, Brown & Company, New York, 2005).

The Labyrinth of Solitude: Life and Thought in Mexico, Octavio Paz (Atlantic Press, Inc., New York, 1982).

The Mexicans: A Personal Portrait of a People, Patrick Oster (HarperCollins, Publishers, New York, 2002).

Mexico: From the Olmecs to the Aztecs, Michael D. Coe (Thames & Hudson Ltd., London, 1994).

The People's Guide to Mexico, Carl Franz and Lorena Havens (John Muir Publications, Santa Fe, NM, 1995).

The Reader's Companion to Mexico, Ed. Alan Ryan (Harcourt Brace & Company, Orlando, FL, 1995.)

Travelers' Tales Mexico, Ed. James O'Reilly and Larry Habegger (Travelers' Tales, Inc., San Francisco, 1994).

True History of the Conquest of New Spain, Bernal Díaz (Downtown Book Center, 1995).

Viva Mexico!, Antonio Haas (Librería Británica, 1999).

Hotels & Restaurants

While Mexico has some lovely small hotels and plenty of large resorts and business hotels, it doesn't have as many different types of accommodations as some countries. But the major resort destinations and business-oriented cities are represented by world-wide hotel chains, as well as a few Mexican-owned chains. Independently owned hotels run the range of prices, from downright cheap to absolutely upscale. In between are plenty of charming small hotels with prices much more economical than those in the United States, Canada, and Western Europe. The cities most popular with travelers have the greatest range of options.

Restaurants run the gamut from chains such as Sanborns—where kids and other creatures of habit will be comfortable in the plush upholstered booths, with familiar-looking menus—to market stalls and the elegant eateries in exclusive hotels.

Accommodations

Hostels are rare in Mexico, but don't despair: inexpensive lodgings are plentiful. Rural areas not frequented by tourists may have no formal lodgings; if in doubt ask at the city hall (municipio). In states such as Oaxaca and Chiapas, the government has organized communities in areas of great natural beauty or cultural attractions to provide inexpensive lodgings. Financed by the government, these community-run lodgings are an excellent way to visit otherwise inaccessible parts of the country. Information can be obtained at state or municipal tourist offices, which may help make a reservation.

Campgrounds are few, although RV parks are more plentiful, especially along the northern Pacific coast, where snowbirds flock. Camping is usually permitted on public property such as beaches; ask permission to camp on ejido (communally owned) lands or private property. B&Bs and guesthouses are also unusual; most are owned and run by foreigners. But connoisseurs of small, intimate hotels will not be disappointed. Cities such as Oaxaca and San Miguel de Allende have some one-of-a-kind small hotels. And although many rent for hundreds of dollars a night, others that are equally charming can be had for less than $80.

Resort hotels charge resort prices: You'll pay as much for a Sheraton or Westin hotel in Mexico as in First World countries. Also, prices are usually quoted in dollars, so you'll see no savings as the peso fluctuates. Although you'll pay more at these internationally geared hotels, you'll almost always get English-speaking staff, concierge service, swimming pools, smoothly running elevators, in-room safes and minibars, cable or satellite TV, and so on. Most beach resorts have at least a few all-inclusive hotels.

Hotels in business-oriented cities such as Mexico City, Guadalajara, Aguascalientes, and Monterrey may offer secretarial services, business centers, meeting rooms, computer modems, and direct-dial phones. The latter two are not as common as you might think, so if these features are important to you, ask before reserving a room. Many business-oriented hotels offer discounts on weekends (sometimes 50 percent or more) or incentives such as buffet breakfasts. Be sure to inquire about different packages, promotions, and discounts.

Rooms should be reserved well in advance at certain times. Beach resorts such as Cabo San Lucas and Cancún fill up during spring break and holidays (Easter, July and August, and the Christmas season), while hotels in towns with popular celebrations might be booked a year in advance: for example, Taxco's Easter week, Veracruz during Carnaval, or the Christmas season in Oaxaca.

PRICES

HOTELS

An indication of the cost of a double room in the high season is given by $ signs.

$$$$$	Over $300
$$$$	$200–$299
$$$	$120–$199
$$	$60–$119
$	Under $60

RESTAURANTS

An indication of the cost of a three-course meal without drinks is given by $ signs.

$$$$$	Over $35
$$$$	$23–$35
$$$	$15–$22
$$	$8–$14
$	Under $8

Taxes vary by state. Most charge 15 percent tax, which may be augmented by a 2 percent hotel tax. Others have a 12 percent tax. Many of the more humble establishments either don't charge tax or have included it in the price; make sure you ask in order to compare prices accurately. Unless otherwise stated, the hotels listed have private bathrooms and are open year round. Toll-free numbers listed are for making reservations from the United States and Canada (but if the number begins with 01800 it is toll-free in Mexico). In very small towns, domicilio conocido means "known address," and

---

⊞ Hotel   🍴 Restaurant   ① No. of Guest Rooms   💺 No. of Seats   🅿 Parking   Ⓜ Metro   🕐 Closed   🛗 Elevator

indicates there are no street names but anyone can point out the establishment.

Credit Cards

AE American Express, D Discover, MC Mastercard, V Visa.

Restaurants

The midday meal is generally eaten between 2 and 5 p.m., although tourists, some office workers, and farmers eat before then. The set meal (called *el menu del día* in nicer restaurants and *comida corrida* in more humble eateries) is usually a bargain, but often unavailable before 1:30 or 2 p.m. This meal generally consists of soup, a rice or pasta plate, and an entrée, followed by dessert and coffee or tea. A beverage may also be included; *agua de sabor* or *agua fresca* is commonly served. These fruit juice and water drinks range from lemonade to watermelon water.

Antojitos roughly translates as "appetizers," but they can be filling regional specialties such as *memelas,* tacos, or enchiladas (see p. 35). Dinner is traditionally a very light meal, and although restaurants in tourist areas provide full fare, it's generally more expensive than a lavish midday meal. In smaller or less touristy towns, and even some of the larger but less cosmopolitan cities, restaurants may close by 7 or 8 p.m. (Note: restaurants listed as "lunch only" are generally open between 1 and 6 p.m.)

While hotel dining rooms and cafés tend to stay open from morning to late at night, some eateries open for lunch and dinner only. They may close between 5 and 6 or 7 p.m., when the dinner hour begins, and some cafés don't open before 9 or 10 a.m. If you want an early breakfast, check opening hours the day before, or stick with hotel restaurants. Check your bill before tipping, as service may be included. Closings for holidays may

vary, so it is advisable to phone and reserve a table.

L = lunch
D = dinner

In the following selection, towns are arranged alphabetically under each region heading. Hotels are listed under each location by price, then in alphabetical order, followed by restaurants also by price and alphabetical order.

■ BAJA CALIFORNIA

BAHÍA DE LOS ANGELES

🏨 LOS VIENTOS SPA & RESORT

🍴 **$$**

CARR. 1, POBLADO LA VENTANA
TEL 646/178-2614
www.losvientosspaand resort.com
The spa is on-and-off and not everything on the website is available. This pretty hotel, with excellent restaurant, is on the beach.

🛈 15 🅿 🏊 🐴 🍴 ❖ AE, MC, V

CATAVIÑA

🏨 DESERT INN CATAVIÑA

🍴 **$$**

HWY. 1, KM 173, IN CATAVIÑA
TEL 858/454-7166 (IN U.S.) OR
800/336-5454 (TOLL-FREE IN U.S.)
www.desertinns.com
This wonderful and recently refurbished hotel in the middle of the desert is near prehistoric cave paintings. The brick-domed restaurant serves delicio△359
us seafood and international dishes.

🛈 27 🅿 ❖ 🏊 ❖ MC, V

ENSENADA

🏨 LAS ROSAS

🍴 **$$$**

CARR. TIJUANA-ENSENADA
KM 105.5
TEL 646/174-4310 OR

866/447-6727 (TOLL-FREE IN U.S.)
www.lasrosas.com
An aqua-and-pink color scheme pervades this romantic yet family-oriented hotel 10 minutes north of downtown. The pool overlooks the rocky cove on which the hotel perches. There's jazz or blues in the bar, good Mexican and international food in the restaurant, and a full-service spa.

🛈 48 🅿 ❖ ❖ ❖ 🏊 🍴 ❖ AE, MC, V

🍴 EL REY SOL

🍴 **$$**

AV. BLANCARTE 130
TEL 646/178-1601 OR
888/311-6871 EXT. 100 (TOLL-FREE IN U.S.)
www.posadaelreysol.com
Basic but comfortable rooms in the three-story, motel-like hotel face the parking area; a small pool is in the back. But the real star is the 60-year-old, award-winning French restaurant. The extensive menu offers delicious duck a l'orange, and nearly a dozen traditional French pastries.

🛈 52 🅿 ❖ ❖ ❖ 🏊 ❖ MC, V

🍴 CASAMAR

$$-$$$

BLVD. LÁZARO CARDENAS 987
TEL 646/174-0417
The regional seafood is fresh, and the calamari comes with a unique oyster sauce. The staff is friendly, and there's a trio on weekends. If the downstairs looks empty, look upstairs; although it's the smoking section, it has the sea view, and the smoke rarely bothers.

❖ ❖ MC, V

LA PAZ

🏨 POSADA DE LAS FLORES

🍴 **$$$**

ALVARO OBREGÓN 440
TEL 612/125-5871
www.posadadelasflores.com
This little boutique hotel in

🔲 Nonsmoking   ❄ Air-conditioning   🏊 Indoor Pool   🌊 Outdoor Pool   🏋 Health Club   ❖ Credit Cards

a colonial-style house faces the seawalk, and some rooms enjoy excellent sunsets. Wi-Fi and high-speed Internet in rooms and public spaces are included in the price, as are full breakfast and afternoon tea.

🛏 8 ⬛ ⬛ ⬛ ⬛ MC, V

🍴 LAS TRES VIRGENES

$$$$

CALLE MADERO 1141 AT CONSTITUCIÓN

TEL 612/165-6265

Pricey, but worth it for those looking for a special night out. The Mexi-Mediterranean food is creative and yummy; the wine list is good, too.

🕐 Closed L

🍴 LA PAZTA

$$

ALLENDE 36

TEL 612/125-1195

Wonderful, homemade pasta and other Italian dishes are served in this indoor-outdoor trattoria decorated with delightful paintings.

🕐 Closed L & Tues.
⬛ AE, MC, V

LORETO

🏨 COCO CABANAS

$$

TEL 613/135-1729

FAX 613/135-0355

www.cococabanasloreto.com

Comfortable and simply furnished cabins with fully stocked kitchens and covered patios, a short walk to the beach and the main plaza.

🛏 8 🅿 ⬛ ⬛ ⬛ No credit cards

🍴 PACHAMAMA

$–$$

CALLE ZAPATA 3

TEL 613/135-2219

Delicious Argentine food (with international and Mexican dishes, too) in a cheerful setting typical of laid-back Loreto.

🕐 Closed L Tues., & Sept.
⬛ No credit cards

LOS CABOS

🏨 CASA NATALIA

🍴 $$$$

BLVD. MIJARES 4, SAN JOSÉ DEL CABO, 23400

TEL 624/146-7100 OR 888/277-3814 (TOLL-FREE IN U.S.)

www.casanatalia.com

A friendly European couple has created this oasis of international chic. In the palm-shaded restaurant, Mexican ingredients modernize Old World recipes. Room rate includes beach club shuttle and breakfast. Spa services and Wi-Fi for a fee.

🛏 16 🅿 ⬛ ⬛ ⬛
⬛ AE, MC, V

🏨 HILTON LOS CABOS

$$$$

CARR. TRANSPENINSULAR KM 19.5

TEL 624/145-6500 OR 800/445-8667 (TOLL-FREE IN U.S.)

www.hilton.com

In addition to elegant yet accessible rooms with Egyptian cotton sheets and upscale bathrooms, the Hilton (closer to San José than to San Lucas) boasts one of the few swimming beaches. Other pluses: kids- and pets-friendly policies and the sushi bar.

🛏 375 🅿 ⬛ ⬛ ⬛ ⬛ ⬛
⬛ AE, MC, V

🏨 ME CABO BY MELIÁ SAN LUCAS

$$$$–$$$$$

PLAYA EL MÉDANO S/N, SAN LUCAS

TEL 624/145-4444

www.me-cabo.com

Close to the bay, beach, marina, and shops, restaurants, and bars, the ME Cabo Meliá brand is geared toward sophisticates. Rooms vary in size and amenities, but all have earthy decor and furnishings. Arrive early at Yhi Spa to take advantage of the underwater massage chair.

🛏 155 🅿 ⬛ ⬛ ⬛ ⬛ ⬛
⬛ AE, MC, V

🏨 LOS MILAGROS

$$

MATAMOROS 16, CABO SAN LUCAS

TEL 624/143-4566

www.losmilagros.com.mx

This cozy and economical gem in San Lucas is a miracle in expensive Los Cabos. It's a short walk to the beach, the marina, and lots of good restaurants.

🛏 16 ⬛

🏨 TROPICANA INN

🍴 $

BLVD. MIJARES 30, SAN JOSÉ DEL CABO

TEL 624/142-1580

www.tropicanainn.com.mx

Rooms are plain, but there's the pool and the popular restaurant-bar which often has live Cuban or tropical music.

🛏 39 🅿 ⬛ ⬛

🍴 NICK-SAN

$$$

BLVD. MARINA, PLAZA DE LA DANZA, CABO SAN LUCAS

TEL 624/143-4484

(2ND LOCATION, LAS TIENDAS DE PALMILLA, CARR. TRANSPENINSULAR KM 7.5, TEL 624/144-6262)

www.nicksan.com

Locals rave about the fresh seafood here, most conjured by high-energy sushi chefs. Fans return again and again during a one-week vacation.

⬛ MC, V

🍴 LA FONDA

$–$$

AV. HIDALGO AT 12 DE OCTUBRE, SAN LUCAS

TEL 624/143-6926

A varied menu highlights regional favorites from throughout Mexico, from casual fare like tacos and soups to full meals, including some unusual pre-Hispanic dishes. The hacienda-style restaurant itself is very pretty.

🕐 Opens after 1:30 p.m. Closed Sun.

🏨 Hotel 🍴 Restaurant 🛏 No. of Guest Rooms 🪑 No. of Seats 🅿 Parking 🚇 Metro 🕐 Closed ⬛ Elevator

MULEGÉ

⊞ SERENIDAD
⏹ $$
HWY. 2.5 MILES (4 KM) S OF
MULEGÉ, 23900
TEL 615/153-0530
www.hotelserenidad.com
serenidad@mulege.com.mx
Rooms are plain, but the
palm-shaded pool is a popular
hangout, as is the restaurant,
where the food is good and
portions large. This property
has its own airstrip and RV
park. (No restaurant in Sept.)
ⓘ 50 🅿 🅢 🅢 🅰 🅢 MC, V

TECATE

SOMETHING SPECIAL

⊞ RANCHO LAPUERTA SPA
$$$$$
HWY. 2, 3 MILES (5 KM) W OF
TECATE, 21275
TEL 665/654-9155 OR 800/443-
7565 (TOLL-FREE IN U.S.)
www.rancholapuerta.com
Since 1940, the Szekely family
has been offering guests an
increasing array of activities:
hot riverstone massage, European facials, yoga, meditation,
hiking, and ocean loofah-salt glows,
to name a few. Stays at the
3,000-acre (1,210 ha) ranch
are Saturday to Saturday; first-
floor, hacienda-style bungalows
decorated with fine Mexican
handcrafts are set among
luxurious pools and gardens.
Healthful, vegetarian-oriented
meals and shuttle from the
nearby airport at San Diego,
California, are included. Reservations required.
ⓘ 87 🅢 🅰 🅢 MC, V

TIJUANA

⊞ CAMINO REAL
$$$$
PASEO DE LOS HÉROES 10305,
ZONA RÍO
TEL 664/633-4000,

01800/901-2300 (TOLL-FREE
IN MEXICO)
www.caminoreal.com/tijuana
This high-rise retains its fashion-
able and rather conservative air.
The business-oriented prop-
erty is near the Tijuana Cultural
Center and downtown.
ⓘ 250 🅿 🅢 🅢 🅢 🅰 🅥
🅢 All major cards

⏹ CIEN AÑOS
$$$–$$$$
AV. JOSÉ MARÍA VELASCO 1407
TEL 664/634-3039
www.cien.info
Nouveau Mexican cuisine is
presented in this gracious restaurant. Steaks are a specialty,
as is *pollo cien años*—chicken and
potatoes in a spicy, smoky chili
sauce. For dessert, try the flan
with burnt goat-milk topping.
No shorts.
🅿 🅢 🅢 All major cards

TODOS SANTOS

⊞ HOTEL CALIFORNIA
⏹ $$$
JUÁREZ S/N AT MORELOS
TEL 612/145-0525
www.hotelcaliforniabaja.com
The garden-draped hotel
keeps cool via thick walls and
the ocean breezes that bless
Todos Santos. The bar is a local
watering hole; the restaurant is
often recommended.
ⓘ 11 🅢 🅰 🅢 MC, V

⏹ CAFÉ SANTA FE
$$$
CENTENARIO 4
TEL 612/145-0340
The outdoor garden tables of
this Italian café are often filled
with diners from Los Cabos
and La Paz. The café is popular
for its organic salad greens and
homemade pastas.
🕒 Closed Tues. & Sept.–Oct.
🅢 MC, V

■ NORTHWEST MEXICO

ALAMOS

⊞ HACIENDA DE LOS SANTOS
⏹ $$$$
MOLINA 8
TEL 647/428-0222 OR
800/525-4800 (TOLL-FREE IN U.S.)
FAX 647/428-0367
www.haciendadelossantos.
com
This antique-studded property
has a billiards room, a theater,
and its own 19th-century
cantina. Individually decorated
rooms have wood-burning fireplaces; the beds are crisp with
fine linens; and the adjacent
spa has a full-time masseur
and trainer. Children are not
allowed.
ⓘ 25 🅿 🅢 🅢 🅰 🅥
🅢 Most major cards

CHIHUAHUA

⊞ HOLIDAY INN HOTEL & SUITES
$$$
ESCUDERO 702, FRACC.
SAN FELIPE
TEL 614/439-0000
www.holiday-inn.com/
chihuahuamex
Continental breakfast is included in the price of this all-suites
hotel with full kitchens, located
in a residential neighborhood
near the city center. The white,
two-story hotel has a sauna,
whirlpool, business services,
and lots of room amenities.
ⓘ 74 🅿 🅢 🅢 🅢 🅰 🅥
🅢 All major cards

⏹ LA CASA DE LOS MILAGROS
$$
VICTORIA 812, NEAR OCAMPO
TEL 614/437-0693
Sit indoors or out on the
courtyard patio of this restored
adobe hacienda. Popular with
locals and visitors, it offers

light Mexican meals, a festive ambience, and live folk music Thursday to Sunday after 9 p.m.

🕐 Closed L 🏧 🅦 MC, V

DURANGO

🏨 HOTEL GOBERNADOR
🍴 $$

AV. 20 DE NOVIEMBRE 257
TEL 618/813-1919
www.hotelgobernador
.com.mx
Hotel Gobernador has several restaurants and bars, gardens, complimentary airport shuttle, continental breakfast, and Wi-Fi. It's downtown within walking distance of the cathedral and main plaza.

① 100 🅿 🔄 🆂 🏊
🅦 AE, MC, V

EL FUERTE

🏨 HOTEL EL FUERTE
$$

MONTESCLAROS 37
TEL 698/893-0226
www.hotelelfuerte.com.mx
Antiques lean against thick adobe walls and flowering vines hang down from second floor balconies. The restored hacienda is most charming in its welcoming public spaces.

① 30 🅦 MC, V

HIDALGO DEL PARRAL

🏨 HOTEL ADRIANA
$

CALLE COLEGIO 2
TEL 627/522-2570,
01800/543-3525 (TOLL-FREE IN MEXICO) OR 866/317-5966 (TOLL-FREE IN U.S.)
Modest but comfortable and close to the main plaza, this family-friendly hotel offers a covered, guarded parking lot, a restaurant, and free Wi-Fi. There's a computer for customers without laptops and a few exercise machines.

① 56 🆂 🔄 🅦 AE, MC, V

MAZATLÁN

🏨 PUEBLO BONITO
🍴 $$$

CAMARÓN SÁBALO 2121,
ZONA DORADA
TEL 669/989-8900 OR
800/990-8250
www.pueblobonito.com
Flamingos pose on the palm-studded grounds of this low-rise, all-suites beachfront hotel. Rooms have equipped kitchens and furnished outdoor patios. Live music and twinkling candlelight complement Italian and continental cuisine at Angelo's Restaurant.

① 246 🅿 🔄 🆂 🏊 2
🅦 🆂 AE, MC, V

🏨 HOTEL FREEMAN POSADA BEST WESTERN
$$

OLAS ALTAS 79 SUR
TEL 669/985-6060
freeman.grupoposadadelrio
.com
Book an ocean-view room at the this Best Western Freeman, a stone's throw from Old Mazatlán. Avoid small interior rooms. Free Wi-Fi and breakfast buffet. Views also from the bar and pool.

① 120 🅿 🔄 🆂 🔄 🏊
🅦 AE, MC, V

🏨 PLAYA MAZATLÁN
$$

AV. PLAYAS LAS GAVIOTAS 202,
ZONA DORADA
TEL 669/989-0555 OR
800/762-5816 (TOLL-FREE IN U.S.)
www.hotelplayamazatlan.com
Mazatlán's original resort hotel. Nicest of the clean-smelling rooms with tiled floors and private terraces are those overlooking the beach.

① 411 🅿 🔄 🆂 🏊 3 🅦
🆂 AE, MC, V

🍴 LAS LUPITAS
$$$$

BUGAMBILIAS 100
TEL 669/989-2309
Some call it "molecular

cuisine," or Mexican–Mediterranean fusion. We call it pricey for Mazatlán, but well presented. An AAA Diamond Award recipient, Las Lupitas, at Hotel D'Gala in the Zona Dorada, serves Chilean salmon, rack of lamb, osso buco, and tuna tartare in a tasteful, dining room.

🆂 AE, MC, V

🍴 LA PUNTILLA
$–$$

MUELLE LA PUNTILLA
TEL 669/982-8877
Tables are Formica and chairs are the ubiquitous white plastic type, but the large selection of seafood is what makes this restaurant stand out. It's open-sided, under a huge palapa, across from the ferry landing at the point for which it was named.

🕐 Closed D   🆂 Cash only

PUERTO PEÑASCO

🏨 VIÑA DEL MAR
$$

CALLE 1RO. DE JUNIO AT
MALECÓN KINO S/N, COL. EL
PUERTO 83550

TEL 638/383-3600
FAX 638/383-3714
www.vinadelmarhotel.com
There's a beach view from
the restaurant, large pool, and
hot tub. Rooms are simply but
soothingly decorated; suites
have kitchenette or Jacuzzi.
The hotel has a beauty salon
with massage, two bars, and
conference room.
🛈 110 🅿 🚭 ❄ ⚡
❄ MC, V

SAN CARLOS

🏨 HOTEL MARINA TERRA
🍴 $$$
CALLE GABRIEL ESTRADA S/N
TEL 622/225-2020 OR
01800/500-2040 (TOLL-FREE
IN MEXICO) OR 888/688-5353
(TOLL-FREE IN U.S.)
www.marinaterra.com
Pastel-decorated rooms are
desert plain, but there's an fine
view of Tetakawi mountain.
The busy marina is a magnet
for boaters, and the restaurant
bustles during weekend
breakfast buffets. Chocolate
Spa opened in 2009.
🛈 112 🅿 ⚡ 🚭 ❄ ⚡ 2
🏋 ❄ All major cards

SIERRA TARAHUMARA (COPPER CANYON)

🏨 POSADA MIRADOR
$$$$$
ESTACIÓN POSADA BARRANCA
TEL 668/818-7046
(IN LOS MOCHIS), 800/896-8196
(TOLL-FREE IN U.S.)
FAX 668/818-0046
www.mexicoscopper
canyon.com
This log-cabin lodge with
a great canyon view can
arrange horse and walking
tours. Rooms have heating,
fireplaces, and balconies,
but no phone or TV. Meals,
served family-style, are
included in the price. Mainly
geared to groups.
🛈 48 ❄ AE, MC, V

SOMETHING SPECIAL

🏨 COPPER CANYON SIERRA LODGE
$$$
DOMICILIO CONOCIDO,
CUSARARÉ
TEL 800/648-8488 (TOLL-FREE
IN THE U.S.)
www.coppercanyonlodges
.com
About a 15-minute drive from
Creel, this is the area's prettiest hotel and best deal. Three
delicious meals are included
in the price, and served in the
lovely dining room warmed
by a stone fireplace. Rooms
near the forests and waterfall
of Cusararé are cozy, each
with fireplace or potbelly
stove. No electricity adds to
the charm.
🛈 22 🅿 ❄ Cash only

🏨 POSADA DEL OSO
$$$
DOMICILIO CONOCIDO,
CEROCAHUI
TEL 614/421-3372 (IN CHIHUA-
HUA)
www.mexicohorse.com
For birders, hikers, or anyone
eschewing large tour groups,
this family-run lodge is a great
alternative. With an excellent
stable of horses, El Oso is
a great departure point for
canyon jaunts. Family-style
meals and transportation
from Bahuichivo train station
included; great rates for
children.
🛈 21 🅿 ❄ Cash only

🏨 REAL DE MINAS
$$
DONATO GUERRA AT
PABLO OCHOA, BATOPILAS
TEL 649/456-9045
A tiny and tasteful guest lodge
in one of Batopilas's restored
19th-century mansions.
🛈 8 🅿 ❄ Cash only

🏨 MARGARITAS PLAZA MEXICANA
$

ELFIDO BAUTISA S/N,
CREEL, 33200
TEL/FAX 635/456-0245
You can pay more elsewhere,
but you won't improve much
on this comfortable, friendly
lodging in the center of town.
Breakfast and dinner are
included in the room rate.
🛈 25 🅿 ❄ Cash only

■ NORTHEAST MEXICO

MONTERREY

SOMETHING SPECIAL

🏨 HABITA MTY
$$$
VASCONCELOS 150 ORIENTE,
SAN PEDRO GARZA GARCIA
TEL 81/8335-5900
www.hotelhabitamty.com
Like all Grupo Habita hotels,
this brand new Monterrey
property is unique. Here
minimalist decor and vintage
furnishings are combined
with great success. On the
roof are a sleek terrace, two
pools, bar, and solarium; on
the ground floor are restau-
rant, lounge, and business
center. Rooms are set up for
XBox, Wi-Fi, and iPods. Near
upscale malls but about half
an hour from downtown
Monterrey.
🛈 39 🅿 ⚡ 🚭 ❄ ⚡ 2
❄ AE, MC, V

🍴 LUISIANA
$$$–$$$$
AV. HIDALGO 530 ORIENTE
TEL 81/8343-1561
Friendly in a clubby, everyone-
knows-you sort of way,
this downtown restaurant
is elegantly decorated and
rather dark. It's popular for its
meats—including charbroiled
steak and barbecued goat—as
well as international dishes.
🕐 Closed Sun. D ❄
❄ All major cards

🚭 Nonsmoking ❄ Air-conditioning 🛏 Indoor Pool 🏊 Outdoor Pool 🏋 Health Club ❄ Credit Cards

PARQUE NACIONAL CUMBRES DE MONTERREY

🏨 HOTEL CHIPINQUE
$$

MESETA CHIPINQUE 1000, GARZA GARCIA, 66297
TEL 81/8173-1777
www.hotelchipinque.com.mx
Perched above Monterrey in the park for which it is named, this comfortable lodge suits those who like nature, racquet sports, and more. Great night-time view of the cityscape from the restaurant.

🛏72 🅿 🚫 🔄 🏊 📺
🔲 AE, MC, V

SALTILLO

🏨 RANCHO EL MORILLO
🍴 $

PROL. OBREGON SUR AT PERIFÉRICO ECHEVERRIA
TEL 844/417-4078
This pretty, family-owned hotel just outside the perimeter road occupies a former ranch and is surrounded by orchards and gardens. There's yummy Mexican food that's way beyond tacos: like roasted chicken with zucchini soup, rice, and cheese-stuffed pepper. Make sure to call ahead for meal reservations.

🛏14 🅿 🏊 🔲 MC, V

🍴 LA CANASTA
$$

BLVD. V. CARRANZA 2485
TEL 844/415-8050
Tile floors, a low wood-beamed ceiling, roaring fireplaces in each large room, and a mix of antique and modern furnishings make La Canasta a Saltillo tradition for long business lunches. The menu features many *antojitos* (appetizers) and other Mexican dishes.

🅿 🚫 🔄 🔲 All major cards

TAMPICO

🏨 HOLIDAY INN EXPRESS
$$

AV. HIDALGO 2700 AT FRESNO
TEL 833/241-3500 OR
01800/000-0404 (TOLL-FREE IN MEXICO)
www.hiexpress.com
Comfortable rooms are decorated in somber tones. Coffeemaker, hair-dryers, and free Wi-Fi and local calls. Downtown, it's about 4.5 miles (7 km) from the beach. An uninspired breakfast buffet is included.

🛏93 🅿 🔄 🚫 🔄
🔲 All major cards

ZACATECAS

SOMETHING SPECIAL

🏨 QUINTA REAL
🍴 ZACATECAS
$$$–$$$$

AV. RAYÓN 434
TEL 492/922-9104 OR
866/621-9288 (TOLL-FREE IN U.S.)
www.quintareal.com
This glamorous, wonderfully odd hotel was built in a converted 19th-century bullring. Nonetheless, rooms are airy and comfortable with balconies and either bathtubs or spas. The bar occupies the former bullpens; the elegant restaurant, serving international and regional cuisine, offers fantastic nighttime views of the 18th-century aqueduct.

🛏47 🅿 🔄 🚫 🔄
🔲 AE, MC, V

🏨 HOTEL EMPORIO
🍴 $$$

AV. HIDALGO 703
TEL 492/925-6500
www.hotelsemporio.com
A dependable hotel serving vacation and business travelers with free Wi-Fi, gym, restaurant, bar, and business center. Located on the main plaza in a historic old building.

🏨 HOTEL SANTA RITA
$$–$$$

AV. HIDALGO 507, CENTRO
TEL 492/925-4141

www.mexicoboutiquehotels .com/santarita
Behind its early 19th-century facade is a sleek downtown hotel with a contemporary lobby bar and comfortable, sparely decorated guest rooms. There's free Wi-Fi and a 24-hour business center.

🛏35 🅿 🔄 🚫 🔄 📺
🔲 AE, MC, V

▬ CENTRAL MEXICO

AGUASCALIENTES

🏨 HOTEL QUINTA REAL
🍴 AGUASCALIENTES
$$$

AV. AGUASCALIENTES SUR 601
TEL 449/978-5818 OR
866/621-9288 (TOLL-FREE IN U.S.)
www.quintareal.com
Everything about this hotel whispers luxury and tradition. Antique and modern decor mix in public spaces of quarrystone and marble. Rooms with full amenities overlook a colonial-style courtyard, bar, and formal dining room serving a variety of dishes.

🛏85 🅿 🚫 🏊 🔲 AE, MC, V

GUANAJUATO

🏨 LA CASA DE LOS ESPÍRITUS ALEGRES
$$$

EX-HACIENDA DE TRINIDAD 1, MARFIL
TEL/FAX 473/733-1013
www.casaspirit.com
Awash in folk art and antiques, the 16th-century House of the Happy Spirits B&B, several miles outside Guanajuato, has individually decorated rooms with fireplaces. Generous breakfasts served on a covered courtyard are included.

🛏8 🅿 🔲 MC, V

🏨 QUINTA LAS ACACIAS
$$$

PASEO DE LA PRESA 168
TEL 473/731-1517 OR

01800/710-8938 (TOLL-FREE IN MEXICO)
www.quintalasacacias.com
This centrally located, 19th-century, European-style B&B has pretty public spaces, including a library, bar, terraces shaded by greenery, and a Jacuzzi with city view. Individually decorated rooms have a flower-driven Laura Ashley feel.
[i] 9 [P] [&] AE, MC, V

🍴 LA CASA DEL CONDE
$$$
CARR. GUANAJUATO–DOLORES HIDALGO KM 5, LA VALENCIANA
TEL 473/732-2550
The former 18th-century home of the administrator of La Valenciana mine now houses this pretty restaurant. Dishes are regional, Mexican, Spanish, and Italian; eat on the plant-filled patio or inside.
🕑 Closed D. & Sun. [&] MC, V

🍴 POSADA SANTA FE
$$
JARDÍN UNION 12
TEL 473/732-0084
An unbeatable location on the city's liveliest square. The outdoor café-restaurant is a prime people-watching spot.
[&] AE, MC, V

🍴 TRUCO 7
$
TRUCO 7
TEL 473/732-8374
Friendly and down-to-earth describes El Truco, which hums with conversation. The steaks, sandwiches, enchiladas, and other typical Mexican fare are reasonably good and the colorful posters and paintings make for a festive atmosphere.
[&] Cash only

QUERÉTARO

🏨🍴 LA CASA DE LA MARQUESA
$$$$
MADERO 41
TEL 442/212-0092

FAX 442/212-0098
www.lacasadelamarquesa.com
This classy hotel in historic downtown is housed in a 1756 mansion. Suites have antiques, handpainted tiles, and plush rugs. The formal restaurant is offputting to some, but the nouveau Mexican and upscale international dishes lure others to the elegant tables.
[i] 25 [&] [&] AE, MC, V

🏨 HOLIDAY INN QUERÉTARO
$$$
AV. 5 DE FEBRERO 110
TEL 442/192-0202 OR 800/465-4329 (TOLL-FREE IN U.S.S)
www.holidayinn.com.mx
On Highway 57 near both downtown and the industrial zone, this ample three-story property has modern motel-like rooms with balcony, coffeemaker, and other amenities.
[i] 235 [P] [&] [&] [&] [&]
[&] AE, MC, V

🏨🍴 MESÓN DE SANTA ROSA
$$
PASTEUR SUR 17, 76000
TEL 442/224-2623
www.mesonsantarosa.com
Colonial-style furnishings reproduce those of the original, 18th-century inn. The central location and moderate price lure repeat customers. An al fresco restaurant serves Mexican favorites with a modern flair, such as roast kid in pepper and pulque sauce.
[i] 21 [&] [&] AE, MC, V

🍴 EL ARCÁNGEL
$$
GUERRERO NORTE 1
TEL 442/212-6542
This warm mansion-turned-restaurant has lace curtains and small square café tables inside or under a covered patio. Order traditional favorites like squash blossom soup or chicken tacos.
[&] MC, V

SAN LUIS POTOSÍ

🏨 PALACIO DE SAN AGUSTÍN
$$$$
GALEANO 240 AT 5 DE MAYO
TEL 444/144-1900
FAX 444/825-0200
www.palaciodesanagustin.com
This "museum hotel" is full of European art and antiquities. It's centrally located and right around the corner from the church it's named for. Comfortable guest rooms—each unique—have high ceilings and lovely appointments.
[i] 20 [&] [&] [&] MC, V

🏨 PANORAMA
$
CARRANZA 315
TEL 444/812-1777 OR 01800/480-0100 (TOLL-FREE IN MEXICO)
Businessmen and budget travelers have remained loyal over the years to this older respectable property near la Plaza los Fundadores. Enjoy the view from the bar-restaurant.
[i] 120 [P] [&] [&]
[&] AE, MC

🍴 POSADA DEL VIRREY
$$$
JARDÍN HIDALGO 3
TEL 444/812-3280
This converted home of Mexico's first vicereine faces Parque Hidalgo. Popular, it serves regional specialties in a delightful covered courtyard.
[&] AE, MC, V

🍴 LA QUERENCIA
$$
CARRANZA 485 AT BOLÍVAR
TEL 444/151-7999
Come to this informal restaurant-bar for the 99-peso lunch special (chicken, beef, or sausage served with grilled chilies and veggies) or for the trova music offered daily between 3 and 5 p.m. or after 9:30 p.m. Open 9 a.m.

[&] Nonsmoking [&] Air-conditioning [&] Indoor Pool [&] Outdoor Pool [&] Health Club [&] Credit Cards

LA VIRREINA
$$
CARRANZA 839
TEL 444/812-3750
Good food, good service, good everything. Locals and tourists alike flock to this restored mansion in the historical center, for international and regional favorite dishes.
Most major cards

SAN MIGUEL DE ALLENDE

CASA DE SIERRA NEVADA
$$$$
HOSPICIO 42
TEL 415/152-7040 OR 800/701-1561(TOLL-FREE IN U.S.)
www.casasierranevada.com, www.mexicoboutiquehotels.com/sierranevada
Several ancient mansions have been converted as installations for this luxurious hotel. Guest rooms are individually decorated, with lace curtains, antique dressers, and lots of locally made art and handcrafts. In-house is the Laca Spa. No children under 16.
31 P AE, MC, V

CASA CARMEN B&B
$$
CORREO 31 AT RECREO
TEL/FAX 415/152-0844
www.casacarmensma.com
Located just one block from the main plaza, this charming B&B has been in business for decades. Rooms surround the beautiful central patio, with requisite fountain. The price includes breakfast and lunch as well as taxes.
11 Cash only

HARRY'S NEW ORLEANS BAR RESTAURANT
$$$-$$$$
HILALGO 12
CENTRO
TEL 415/152-2645
www.harrysneworleanscafe.com

Harry's is a popular bar with several gorgeous, high-ceilinged dining rooms serving international cuisine. The service is attentive, the bread's great, and the music is eclectic rock. There's a large selection of hot and cold appetizers. Choose from among a number of side dishes; recommended are the super saffron potatoes.
AE, MC, V

CAFÉ DE LA PARRO-QUIA/LA BRASSERÍE
$-$$
CALLE JESÚS 11
TEL 415/152-3161
A downtown colonial beauty, this café offers tasty breakfast foods and lunch. Closing between 4 and 5 p.m., it reopens for dinner as La Brasserie, where ex-pats return for the nightly dinner specials. Stop in at the El Tecolote book seller, which shares the complex.
Closed Sun. (La Parroquia Cafe), Sun. & Mon. (La Brasserie)
Cash only

LOS FAROLES
$-$$
ANCHA DE SAN ANTONIO 28C
TEL 415/152-1849
"The Lanterns" is located within the same building as the venerable Instituto Allende, an enormous stone building once belonging to the Canals, one of San Miguel's founding families. Specializing in grilled food, especially delicious make-your-own tacos.
MC, V

MAMA MÍA
$-$$
UMARÁN 8
TEL 415/152-2063
This longtime favorite features a video bar, live jazz, salsa dancing, and a restaurant that's most impressive at breakfast with outstanding *café de olla*.
MC, V

CENTRAL PACIFIC STATES

ACAPULCO

QUINTA REAL
$$$$$
PASEO DE LA QUINTA 6, FRACC. REAL DIAMANTE
TEL 744/469-1500 OR 866/621-9288 (TOLL-FREE IN U.S.)
www.quintareal.com
This refined hotel features suites with ocean view, satellite TV, mini-bar, and other comforts; some have private pools and dining areas. Perched on the bluffs with a fabulous view of Acapulco Bay. Take a path or elevator to the swimming pools and beach below.
74 P AE, MC, V

FAIRMONT ACAPULCO PRINCESS
$$$$
PLAYA REVOLCADERO S/N
TEL 744/469-1000 OR 800/257-7544 (TOLL-FREE IN U.S.)
FAX 744/469-1016
www.fairmont.com/acapulco
Among the Princess's many

Hotel   Restaurant   No. of Guest Rooms   No. of Seats   P Parking   Metro   Closed   Elevator attributes are the large, airy rooms; immaculate grounds, restaurants, and an endless breakfast buffet. The expensive, sweet-smelling Willow Stream day spa is excellent. Two 18-hole golf courses.

🛈 1,017 P 🔄 🚫 🅱️ 🏊 🎾
🅰 AE, MC, V

🏨 ELCANO
🍴 $$–$$$
AV. COSTERA MIGUEL
ALEMAN 75
TEL 744/435-1500,
01800/090-7500 (TOLL-FREE
IN MEXICO)
www.hotel-elcano.com.mx
A clean, white-and-cerulean-blue theme pervades the cozy rooms, breezy public areas, and outdoor Bambuco restaurant. Fabulous regional favorites with modern touches such as fat shrimp tacos or red snapper grilled with asparagus, shrimp, and clams are served.

🛈 180 P 🚫 🏊 🎾
🅰 AE, MC, V

🏨 ONE HOTEL
$
COSTERA ALEMÁN 16,
COL. COSTA AZUL
TEL 744/435-0470
www.onehotels.com
This new, business-oriented, no-frills hotel has comfortable rooms at great prices. The only amenity is its proximity to the beach. Wi-Fi wired; American-style breakfast is included.

🛈 126 P 🚫 🏊
🅰 AE, MC, V

🍴 BAIKAL
$$$$–$$$$$
CARRETERA ESCÉNICA 1622,
COSTERA
TEL 744/446-6867
Modern, sleek Baikal is still the flavor of the moment. With its awesome view of the bay and fusion menu, it might just stay in vogue for a while.

🕐 Closed L, Mon., May–Nov.
🅰 Most major cards

🍴 MADEIRAS
$$$$
CARR. ESCÉNICA 33, FRACC.
EL GUITARRÓN
TEL 744/446-5636
Sublime international food in a romantic setting with views overlooking Acapulco Bay. The menu offers choices of soup or salad, appetizer (such as octopus in vinaigrette), main course, and dessert.

P 🕐 Closed L 🅰 AE, MC, V

🍴 SR. FROG'S
$$
CARR. ESCÉNICA 28,
FRACC. EL GUITARRÓN
TEL 744/446-5734
www.senorfrogs.com
Best known as a bar with a fine bay view, this member of the Carlos n' Charlie's chain offers *pozole* (hominy soup) on Thursdays, a local tradition. Other favorites include barbecue, nachos, quesadillas, and other kid pleasers.

P 🕐 Open daily from 1 p.m. to 1 a.m. 🅰 MC, V

🍴 EL AMIGO MIGUEL
$–$$
JUÁREZ 31 AT AZUETA,
DOWNTOWN
TEL 744/483-6981
This local favorite off the main square in Old Acapulco is attended by an energetic young staff. Seafood dishes are traditional and tasty. In addition, the original location on the sand serves equally delicious food.

🅰 MC, V

🍴 LA TORTUGA
$
LOMAS DEL MAR 5-A
TEL 744/484-6985
Low-cost lunch specials, combo plates large enough for two, and excellent *tortas* (bread-roll sandwiches) are served in an informal outdoor downtown garden one block off Avenida Costera.

🅰 Cash only

🍴 100% NATURAL
$
BLVD. COSTERA 200
Enjoy soyburgers, many fruit drinks (or beer or wine), healthful salads, or crispy chicken tacos at this unpretentious little chain restaurant. In several locations around town.

🕐 Open from 7 a.m. to 11 p.m. 🅰 AE, MC, V

BARRA DE NAVIDAD

🍴 AMBAR DEL MARE
$$$
AVE. LÓPEZ DE LEGAZPI 158
TEL 315/355–8169
This beach-side bistro offers Mediterranean and French fare. Escargot, ravioli, or pizza are favorites. The vibe is pleasant and the music jazzy.

🕐 Closed L May–Nov., & Tues.–Thurs.

🍴 CASA DE LA ABUELA
$
AV. LÓPEZ DE LEGAZPI 150
You can't get a better cup of coffee in casual little Barra de Navidad than you can here, complete with refills and a delicious homemade cookie. The menu is standard lunch and breakfast fare.

🕐 Closed D, Mon.

BUCERÍAS

🍴 MARK'S
$$$
LÁZARO CÁRDENAS 56
TEL 329/298-0303
www.marksbucerias.com
Yummy food and a cozy beach 'tude that combines great food with attractive atmosphere and sports on the tube.

🕐 Closed L 🅰 MC, V

🍴 DUGARELS
$$
AVE. DEL PACÍFICO S/N
TEL 329/298-1757
New, but possibly the most dependable for standard

Mexican fish dishes and good service. Near the north end of the ocean-facing main street; stroll after on the beach.

COLIMA

🏨 CEBALLOS
$$

PORTAL MEDELLÍN 12
TEL 312/316-0100
www.hotelceballos.com
Built in the 1880s, this lovingly refurbished edifice has been home to three state governors. Unimaginatively decorated rooms have high ceilings; some have small balconies.

ⓘ 54 🅿 🔁 🈂 MC, V

🍴 LOS NARANJOS
$$

BARREDA 34
TEL 312/312-0029
Locals head for this fan-cooled restaurant near Jardín Quintero. The menu features traditional Mexican appetizers and many meat dishes. Open early for breakfast but closes at 8 p.m.

🈂 AE, MC, V

🍴 EL CHARCO DE LA
HIGUERA
$–$$

JARDÍN DE SAN JOSÉ S/N, BETWEEN 5 DE MAYO & TORRES QUINTERO
TEL 312/313-0192
This peaceful outdoor restaurant has a varied menu, offering breakfast, sandwiches, chicken, grilled meats, and *pozole* (hominy soup). Guitar music most weekend evenings.

🈂 MC, V

COSTALEGRE

🏨 EL TAMARINDO
$$$$$

MELAQUE–PUERTO VALLARTA HWY. KM 7.5, CIHUATLÁN
TEL 315/351-5032 OR 800/728-9098 (TOLL-FREE IN U.S.)
www.eltamarindoresort.com

Friendly yet exclusive, this resort's villas and outdoor living areas front pretty beaches and a golf course. There's a spa and lots of outdoor recreation equipment. Although the resort feels isolated, Barra de Navidad is not far away.

ⓘ 28 villas 🅿 🔁 🈂 📺
🈂 Most major cards

🏨 PUNTA SERENA
$$$

KM 20 HWY 200
BAHÍA TENACATICA
TEL 315/351-5427
www.puntaserena.com
An adults-only, all-inclusive property on a cliff high above Tenacatita Bay, this boutique hotel offers a variety of spa treatments, ritual steam baths, and nude sunbathing on the semiprivate beach far below. The rooms are elegant and comfortable, and the clientele tends to be international.

ⓘ 24 🅿 🔁 🈂 📺
🈂 AE, MC, V

GUADALAJARA

🏨 QUINTA REAL
🍴 GUADALAJARA
$$$$–$$$$$

AV. MÉXICO 2727, COL. VALLARTA NORTE
TEL 33/3669-0600 OR 866/621-9288 (TOLL-FREE IN U.S.)
www.quintareal.com
Mostly geared to business travelers and wealthy Mexicans, this luxurious property looks colonial but is actually late-20th century, with all the modern conveniences. All the suites have fireplaces, marble bathtubs, comfortable furnishings, and locally made crafts. Dine on the terrace or indoors on world-class haute cuisine.

ⓘ 76 🅿 🔁 🈂
🈂 Most major cards

🏨 DE MENDOZA
$$

V. CARRANZA 16, CENTRO
TEL 33/3942-5151

www.demendoza.com.mx
A great location, reasonable rates, and a beautiful lobby enliven this five-story hotel near la Plaza Tapatío. Splurge on a suite with roomy bathtub and pleasant balcony.

ⓘ 110 🅿 🔁 🈂 🔁 🏊
🈂 AE, MC, V

🏨 QUINTA DON JOSÉ
$$

REFORMA 139, TLAQUEPAQUE
TEL 33/3635-7522 OR 866/629-3753 (TOLL-FREE IN U.S.)
www.quintadonjose.com
Although nothing fancy, this is the best choice in Tlaquepaque because of its friendly, helpful employees. There's a smallish unheated pool and a Mexican/Italian restaurant. Area tours available at good prices. Free Wi-Fi, international phone calls, and continental breakfast.

ⓘ 15 🅿 🔁 🈂 🏊
🈂 AE, MC, V

🍴 I LATINA
$$$

CALLE INGLATERRA 3128, COL. VALLARTA PONIENTE
TEL 33/3647-7774
We hate to jump on the I (pronounced eee) Latina bandwagon, but this smart restaurant and elegant bar are an essential stop on the Guadalajara nightlife trail. Fusion food, nifty cocktails, and generally a fun crowd.

🕐 Closed L, Mon., & Sun. D

🍴 EL SACROMONTE
$$–$$$

PEDRO MORENO 1398
TEL 33/3825-5447
Treat all of your senses at Sacromonte, particularly known for its service. Icons and candlelit altars provide nighttime ambience in the romantic garden. This is haute Mexican cuisine, with dishes like duck with deep-fried rose petals.

🕐 Closed Sun. 🈂 MC, V

🏨 Hotel 🍴 Restaurant ⓘ No. of Guest Rooms 🔁 No. of Seats 🅿 Parking 🚇 Metro 🕐 Closed 🔁 Elevator

🍽 RÍO SAN PEDRO
$–$$
JUÁREZ 300, TLAQUEPAQUE
TEL 33/3659-6136
Eat on the patio or inside this wonderful old house-turned-restaurant in slow-paced Tlaquepaque. Chef-owner Mayo and his wife Malena are there to insure good service and excellent Mexican and continental food. Open from early until late.
⬡ AE, MC, V

IXTAPA/ZIHUATANEJO

🏨 CLUB MED IXTAPA
$$$$$
PLAYA QUIETA, ABOUT 5 MILES (8 KM) MINUTES W OF IXTAPA'S HOTEL ZONE
TEL 755/553-1000 OR 800/ 932-2582 (TOLL-FREE IN U.S.)
www.clubmed.com.mx
A two-year remodel has brought this Club Med into the 21st century. Activities, most included in the price, include a real-life trapeze and activities for kids of all ages. There's a lovely beach, a full-service spa, and a fun, movie-themed bar.
🛈 298 🅿 ⬥ ⬡ All rooms
🞄 ➰ 3 🔱 ⬡ AE, MC, V

SOMETHING SPECIAL

🏨 TENTACIONES
🍽 $$$$$
CAMINO ESCÉNICA A PLAYA LA ROPA, LOTE 97
TEL 755/554-8383
www.hoteltentaciones.com
A rocky infinity pool separates this cliff-hanging boutique hotel from its patio bar and fabulous, prix-fixe restaurant. The decor is Asian-Mediterranean fusion and so is the food. Chef selects ingredients and prepares daily set meals. Call a day ahead to make reservations, and take what you get. You'll more than likely be pleased with the beautiful bay view as well as the five-course

meal. It's just past Kau-Kan restaurant, up a steep road to the left. Loads of steep steps make it inappropriate for the mobility impaired. Lunch served only to hotel guests.
🛈 4 🅿 ⬡ ⬡ ⬡ AE, MC, V

🏨 VILLAS LAS AZUCENAS
$$
BAJADA DE LOS DELFINES S/N
TEL 755/544-6593
www.lasazucenas.com.mx
We trust you can find the fabulous Casa Que Canta (www.lacasaquecanta .com, $$$$$) on your own. More modest travelers will appreciate Villas's "the Lily": new, clean, cozy digs with kitchenettes 110 yards (100 m) from Playa La Ropa.
🛈 9 🅿 ⬡ All rooms
⬡ Cash only or PayPal

🍽 COCONUTS
$–$$$
PASAJE AGUSTÍN RAMÍREZ 1
TEL 755/554-2518
Order appetizers or a yummy full meal at one of Zihua's oldest and best restaurants. Enjoy the modern continental cuisine under the stars or inside the rooms of this converted old home. There's live romantic music most evenings.
🕐 Closed June–Oct.
⬡ AE, MC, V

LA CRUZ DE HUANACAXTLE

🍽 FRASCATI
$$$–$$$$
AVE. LANGOSTA 10
TEL 329/295-6185
www.frascatilacruz.com
La Cruz's most upscale restaurant, Frascati offers a wide-ranging Italian menu with pizza and pasta dishes as well as meat, seafood, and pesci. The staff is plentiful and helpful, and tables are nicely set.
🕐 No L ⬡ AE, MC, V

MORELIA

🏨 VILLA MONTANA
$$$$
PATZIMBA 201, COL. VISTA BELLA
TEL 443/314-0231
www.villamontana.com.mx
At night, downtown Morelia twinkles as you overlook it from the terrace bar of this lovely oasis of calm. Cottages dot the terraced property; landscaped gardens are peppered with fountains and sculptures. The spa offers the usual treatments, plus chocolate or mezcal.
🛈 36 🅿 ➰ 🔱 ⬡ AE, MC, V

🍽 SAN MIGUELITO
$$–$$$
AV. CAMELINAS S/N, NEAR THE CONVENTION CENTER
TEL 443/324-2399
www.sanmiguelito.com.mx
Slip into the very back room of this converted home. There are hundreds of images of St. Anthony—women in Mexico pray to the upside down icon to get a mate with the promise to set St. Anthony right again if he succeeds. All the rooms are pretty, with lace curtains and thick wooden shutters. And the home-style Mexican food is quite good.
🕐 Closed Sun. ⬡ MC, V

PÁTZCUARO

🏨 MANSIÓN DE LOS
🍽 SUEÑOS
$$$
IBARRA 15
TEL 434/342-5708
www.prismas.com.mx
This colonial mansion, a half block from the main plaza, has been totally restored and nicely decorated. There's often music in one of its two restaurants as well as airport transfer, tour guide service, massage, and a friendly staff.
🛈 12 ⬡ ⬡ ⬡ ⬢ AE, MC, V

⬡ Nonsmoking 🞄 Air-conditioning ➰ Indoor Pool ➰ Outdoor Pool 🔱 Health Club ⬡ Credit Cards

🏨 MANSIÓN DE ITURBE
$$

PORTAL MORELOS 59, 61600
TEL 434/342-0368
www.mansioniturbe.com
Odd but endearing, this creaky, high-ceilinged hotel dominates the Plaza Quiroga. Some of the furnishings and decor have been redone, lightening the antique feel of the massive 17th-century building. Full breakfast is included. All rooms nonsmoking.

🛏 14 **P** 🅿️ 🚭 MC, V

🏨 POSADA DE LA BASÍLICA
$$

ARCIGA 6
TEL 434/342-1108
www.posadalabasilica.com
One of Pátzcuaro's first hotels has tripled its charm (and its price). Rooms have been upgraded with wood floors, nice bed linens, and a spare but modern and pleasing decor. The wonderful woodburning stoves remain. The slow-moving, second-story restaurant has an awesome view of Pátzcuaro's red roofs and the mountains beyond.

🛏 12 **P** 🚭 AE, MC, V

PUERTO VALLARTA

🏨 CASAMAGNA MARRIOTT
$$$$

PASEO DE LA MARINA 455, MARINA VALLARTA
TEL 322/226-0000, 888/236-2427 (TOLL-FREE IN U.S.)
www.casamagnapuertovallarta.com
With its top-notch spa, Asian restaurant, sports bar, and helpful staff, this effort of the international chain is a cut above the competition. Rooms have balconies and most overlook the ocean.

🛏 430 **P** 🅿️ 🚭 🚭 🏊 🏊 AE, MC, V

🏨 DREAMS PUERTO VALLARTA
$$$

PLAYA LAS ESTACAS, CARR. BARRA NAVIDAD S/N
TEL 322/221-5000
www.camino-real-puerto-vallarta.com
This resort has a dizzying number of activities for children, teens, and adults. It is located on a beautiful, sheltered, sandy beach south of downtown PV. Price includes meals, drinks, and entertainment.

🛏 337 **P** 🅿️ 🚭 🚭 🏊 3 🚭 Most major cards

SOMETHING SPECIAL

🏨 HACIENDA ALEMANA
🍴 **$$**

CALLE BASILIO BADILLO 378, COL. E. ZAPATA
TEL 322/222-2071
www.haciendaalemana.com
Lovely studios and suites have warm, modern furnishings and poured cement floors, plus mini-fridge or kitchenette—miraculously stocked daily not just with water, but with champagne! King beds, double-paned windows, and sauna/steam . . . it's all good! The Café Frankfurt *(closed Sept.)* serves really wonderful German food, good enough to please even those not normally impressed with sauerkraut and *bratkartoffeln*. The steamed pork chops are delicious, as is the spätzle.

🛏 12 🚭 🚭 🚭 MC, V

🏨 ELOÍSA
$

LÁZARO CÁRDENAS 179, COL. E. ZAPATA
322/222-6465 OR
322/222-0286
www.hoteleloisa.com
Budget travelers appreciate this well-situated hotel for its large, rectangular rooftop pool and patio and its economical rooms, some with

kitchenette and view, and suites with separate bedroom. It's close to Zona Romántica restaurants and shops, Cuale Island shopping and loitering, downtown PV, and the long beachfront boardwalk.

🚭 MC, V

🍴 RIVER CAFÉ
$$$$

ISLA RÍO CUALE S/N
TEL 322/223-0788
An international menu and a lovely riverside location have made this place endure. Overlooking the Cuale River from the sliver of its namesake island, this restaurant is open all day, but especially recommended for breakfast, and for dinner, when tiny white lights create a romantic ambiance.

🚭 AE, MC, V

🍴 MARISCOS 8 TOSTADAS
$$$–$$$$

CALLE QUILLA AT CALLE PROA, MARINA VALLARTA
TEL 322/221-3124
Don't get carried away ordering off the à la carte menu. Portions are large and

the fresh-as-can-be seafood dishes are filling. There are seafood tostadas and tacos, sashimi and ceviche. The original restaurant (*Calle Río Guayaquil 413 at Calle Ecuador, Col. Versalles, behind Blockbuster videos, closed Sun. & Sept.*) has full seafood plates but isn't nearly as popular as this location, which positively hums with local trade.

🕐 No D 💰 Cash only

🍴 EL ARRAYÁN
$$$
CALLE ALLENDE 344,
AT CALLE MIRAMAR
TEL 322/222-7195
If food could be described as "rustic chic," this would be it: modernized—and much more expensive—versions of classic Mexican dishes. Tables are out on the wide veranda of a simple Mexican house, where the restaurant's namesake tree, *el arrayán*, graces the patio. Los Frijoleros band often entertains on weekends.

🕐 Closed L, Tues., Aug.
💰 MC, V

🍴 TRÍO
$$$–$$$$
GUERRERO 264
TEL 322/222-2196
www.triopr.com
Tasty, innovative Mediterranean dishes with a Mexican flourish have made this restaurant a favorite with the locals. Dishes include rack of lamb served with mint sauce and ravioli, or red snapper with ratatouille and tiny roast potatoes. The venue is warm and charming, like a favorite friend's well-decorated home.

🕐 Closed L 🆒 💰 AE, MC, V

🍴 COMÉDOR DE KAME
$
CALLE GUATEMALA AT
COLOMBIA, COL. 5 AT DICIEMBRE
TEL 322/222-2643
I promised not to reveal this favorite bargain restaurant

... my bad! It was the delicious corn tortillas, just off the griddle, that did me in. In the unassuming living room of the owners' home—complete with crucifix and wandering chihuahua—is served a fixed-price lunch menu with fruit drink, soup, choice of main dishes, and dessert. For breakfast there are items off the tourist radar. Little English spoken, if any; closes at 5 p.m.

🕐 Closed Sun. & D
💰 Cash only

SAN BLAS

🏨 GARZA CANELA
🍴 $$
PAREDES 106 SUR
TEL 323/285-0112
www.garzacanela.com
Run by sisters, this pretty, two-story hotel and its restaurant, El Delfín—serving French, Mexican, and international dishes—is a ten-minute walk from the beach and has a pleasant garden.

ℹ️ 50 🅿️ 🆒 🏊 💰 AE, MC, V

🏨 MIRAMAR PARAISO
$
KM 18 CARR. COSTERA SAN
BLAS–LAS VARAS, BAHÍA
MATANCHÉN
TEL 323/254-9030
www.hotelparaisomiramar
.com
About 20 minutes from San Blas overlooking Matanchén Bay, near the village of Santa Cruz, this former governor's mansion is gorgeous in serene, simple surroundings. There are camping and RV sites, too, as well as a restaurant, bar, and meeting facilities.

ℹ️ 28 🅿️ 🆒 🏊 💰 MC, V

🍴 LA ISLA
$$
CALLE MERCADO AT PAREDES
NO PHONE
A block from the plaza, this seafood restaurant has been around forever, or so it seems.

No wonder: The food is great, and the decorations are quaint, with shells a-go-go. It's a real San Blas institution. Try the flan for dessert.

🕐 Closed Mon. 💰 Cash only

SAN FRANCISCO

🏨 HOTEL CIELO ROJO
$$
CALLE ASIA 6
TEL 311/258-4155
www.hotelcielorojo.com
In San Pancho or for that matter Sayulita, there aren't many hotels. This one is simple yet charming, with *equipale* (pigskin, typical of Guadalajara) tables and chairs, nice Talavera tiles, and fresh paint. Breakfast (and tax) is included in the room price and the onsite restaurant serves organic food. It's about three sandy blocks to the beach.

ℹ️ 8 🆒 🚭 💰 MC, V

🍴 LA OLA RICA
$$$
AV. TERCER MUNDO S/N
TEL 311/258-4123
Yummy international dishes are served in the evenings from this prettily decorated patio/indoor restaurant. At the beach, their new restaurant Mar y Tierra de La Ola Rica (*$$, no dinner, closed Sept.–mid-Oct.*) will serve fish, salads, and burgers.

🕐 Closed Sun., D, & June–Oct. 15

SAYULITA

🏨 VILLA AMOR
$$
PLAYA SAYULITA
TEL 329/291–3010
www.villaamor.com
This aerobically challenging property has lovely views out over the bay, but loads of stairs to the top units. Rooms are simply but inventively decorated and furnished with polished cement floors, pretty

tile work, and glass from Guadalajara. Some have outdoor living space with plunge pool. Rooms have no phones or TV, but you can borrow a bike and a boogie board and head for nearby Los Muertos Beach.

🛏 34 🛋 some 🅿 🚫 MC, V

🍴 CALYPSO
$$$
AVE. REVOLUCIÓN 44
TEL 329/291-3704
One of this surfer town's oldest families operates this second-story restaurant, poised under a huge palapa roof. Order fresh fish, spicy fried squid, or one of several large, inventive salads.

🕐 Closed D, Sun. June–Oct.
🚫 MC, V

🍴 CHOCO BANANA
$
CALLE REVOLUCIÓN AT
CALLE DELFIN
TEL 329/291–3051
Mexicans and foreigners loved this little Canadian-owned burger and breakfast joint long before there was Wi-Fi; today it's more popular than ever. Open to the elements, it's facing the square, a block from the beach, and casual as can be.

🕐 Closes 2 p.m. Sun.
🚫 Cash only

TAXCO

🏨 AGUA ESCONDIDA
$
PLAZA BORDA 4
TEL 762/622-1166
www.aguaescondida.com
You can pay more, but why not save your cash for silver jewelry? Smack in the middle of hilly Taxco, the Hidden Water hotel has terrific views from the rooftop café-bar, a small swimming pool, and average rooms. Massage available, and free Wi-Fi.

🛏 50 🅿 🚿 🚫 Cash only

TEPIC

🏨 FRAY JUNÍPERO SERRA
$$
LERDO 23 PONIENTE AT MÉXICO,
63000
TEL 311/212-2525
www.frayjunipero.com.mx
Right on the main square, this small businessperson's hotel has well-maintained rooms with satellite TV. Ask for a room on the top floor (which will have a great night-time view of the church tower) or for one with a bathtub.

🛏 104 🅿 🛗 🛋 🚫 AE, MC, V

URUAPAN

🏨 HOTEL MANSIÓN DEL CUPATITZIO
$$
CALZADA RODILLA DEL DIABLO
20, COL. LA QUINTA
TEL 452/523-2100
www.mansiondelcupatitzio
.com
At the edge of Parque Nacional Eduardo Ruiz, this old hotel has the feel of a gracious hacienda, with fine views and free Wi-Fi. Fresh flowers enliven the restaurant's atmosphere, which serves mainly regional and Mexican cuisine.

🛏 57 🅿 🚿 🚩 🚫 AE, MC, V

▦ MEXICO CITY

🏨 CONDESA DF
$$$$
AV. VERACRUZ 102,
COL. LA CONDESA
TEL 55/5241-2600
www.condesaDF.com
Sleek and modern, if not warm and fuzzy, at least reasonably welcoming, the Condesa DF is among Mexico City's hippest hotel. Rooms stacked around a central courtyard in the 1920s-era building have minimalist furnishings, iPod docks, DVDs, and generally cool decor. (The same

group's equally stylish Habita Hotel is in Colonia Polanco.)

🛏 40 🅿 🛗 🚫 🛋 🚿 🚩
🚫 AE, DC, MC, V

🏨 CAMINO REAL
🍴 MEXICO
$$$
MARIANO ESCOBEDO 700,
COL. NUEVA ANZURES
TEL 55/5263-8888
www.caminoreal.com
Designed by renowned architect Ricardo Legorreta, Mexico City's low-rise is near Chapultepec Park. There are seven different restaurants, and the hotel is enduringly popular despite the siren's call of newer high-rises in the area. Spread over lots of acreage, it's not appropriate for the mobility impaired.

🛏 713 🚇 Chapultepec
🅿 🛗 🚫 🛋 🚿 🚩
🚫 All major cards

🏨 EMBASSY SUITES MEXICO CITY
$$$
PASEO DE LA REFORMA 69,
COL. TABACALERA
TEL 55/5061-3050 OR 800/
362-3779 (TOLL-FREE IN U.S.)
www.embassysuites.com
A great value and a 20-minute walk from the *zócalo*, this AAA 4-Diamond property has spacious rooms, comfortable beds, and a pleasant staff. The room price includes a cooked-to-order breakfast and evening cocktails. There's an Argentine restaurant.

🛏 160 🅿 🛗 🚫 🛋 🚿 🚩
🚫 AE, MC, V

🏨 SHERATON CENTRO
🍴 HISTÓRICO
$$$–$$$$
JUÁREZ 70, LA ALAMEDA
TEL 55/5130-5300
www.sheratonmexico.com
This Sheraton across from the Alameda park (and near the *zócalo* and Paseo Reforma) is recommended for its ample

rooms, modern business center and meeting rooms, and stunningly sleek architecture and décor. El Cardenal Restaurant is highly recommended for traditional Mexican cuisine.

[1] 457 P ⊕ ⊗ ⊗ ⊡
⊗ Most major cards

🏨 HOTEL MARÍA CRISTINA
$

RIO LERMA 31, COL. CUAUHTEMOC
TEL 55/5703-1212
www.hotelmariacristina
.com.mx
Safe and quiet yet just a block off Paseo de la Reforma, this long-time favorite has nice rooms, a restaurant, bar, and free Wi-Fi. Ask for a room overlooking the garden.

[1] 150 P ⊕ ⊗ ⊗
⊗ AE, MC, V

🏨 HOTEL STANZA
$

ALVARO OBREGÓN 13 AT MORELIA, COL. ROMA
TEL 55/5208-0052
www.stanzahotel.com
Formerly called Parque Ensenada, this is a good budget hotel in Col. Roma, where regentrification is restoring lovely post-war buildings. There's a diner, small gym, and business center.

[1] 132 P 🚇 Niños Héroes
⊕ ⊡ ⊗ MC, V

🍴 IZOTE
$$$$$

PRESIDENTE MAZARIK 513, LOCAL 3, POLANCO
TEL 55/5280-1671
Renowned chef Patricia Quintana produces many innovative nouvelle Mexican dishes at this fine restaurant. Make a meal of the wonderful appetizers, or choose something unusual from the changing menu. In a small strip mall, the milieu is not anything special.

⊕ Closed Sun. D ⊗ AE, MC, V

SOMETHING SPECIAL

🍴 PUJOL
$$$$$

FRANCISCO PETRARCA 245, POLANCO
TEL 55/5545-4111
Recommended as the current best in D.F. by cooking expert Magda Bodin, this cutting-edge but casual Polanco restaurant is not to be missed by gourmands. Things rotate on and off the menu; if you see it, don't miss the unique venison in cocoa crust with three banana sauce. For dinner there's a five-course tasting menu. Chef Olvera's techniques are worldly but his palate is 100 percent Mexican.

P 🚇 Polanco ⊕ Closed Sun.
⊗ AE, MC, V

🍴 PHOTO BISTRO
$$$$

PLAZA CITLALTÉPETL 23-F AT AV. AMSTERDAM, COL. LA CONDESA
TEL 55/5286-5945
This French bistro is one of the most popular in La Condesa, and so gets jam packed on weekends; better to go midweek. Everything on the menu is super. The name refers to the arty photos decorating the walls.

🍴 PRIMOS
$$$$

CALLE MICHOACÁN 168, COL. CONDESA
TEL 55/5256-0950
Here's a trendy restaurant in happening Colonia Condesa that has a little bit of everything, including tapas, steak frites, and a *torta ahogada* (bread roll sandwich drenched in mild sauce) made with duck instead of the usual pork. The kitchen's open daily between 8 a.m. and 11:30 p.m., and they have valet parking.

P ⊗ AE, MC, D

🍴 AZUL Y ORO
$$$

AV. IMÁN BETWEEN PERIFÉRICO & INSURGENTES, UNAM CAMPUS
TEL 55/5622-7135
If traveling at the south end of Mexico City, make a beeline for Blue and Gold, where renowned Chef Ricardo Muñoz, who wrote *Diccionario Enciclopedico de Gastronomia Mexicana*, opened this accessibly priced gourmet restaurant for lucky students and faculty at the University of Mexico. It's on the Cultural Center's second floor. Serves breakfast (exquisite hot chocolate) and closes by 8 p.m. (and 6 p.m. Sunday–Tuesday). No alcohol served.

⊕ Closed university holidays
⊗ Cash only

🍴 LA HACIENDA DE LOS MORALES
$$$–$$$$

VÁZQUEZ DE MELLA 525, COL. POLANCO
TEL 55/5096-3000
Wealthy locals and business executives dine in elegance at this restored 16th-century hacienda on the outskirts of the Polanco neighborhood. Go for the ambience, because the Mexican and international food is average.

🚇 Polanco (plus a short taxi ride) ⊗ Most major cards

🍴 CAFÉ DE TACUBA
$$

TACUBA 28
TEL 55/5518-4950
The third-generation owners have served tacos, fried chicken, and their famous enchiladas in this popular, festive eatery since 1912. The restored mansion is filled with antiques, paintings, hand-painted tiles, and bric-a-brac. Popular with tourists, it's close to Bellas Artes and downtown.

🚇 Allende ⊗ AE, MC, V

CAPICUA
$$–$$$
AV. NUEVO LEÓN 66,
LA CONDESA
TEL 55/5211-5280
www.capicua.com.mx
Delicious (albiet sometimes salty) tapas are served in a minimalist room on the street in this browsable neighborhood. Look for daily lunch specials and a fairly large wine list. There's also one in San Ángel at Av. de la Paz 14B.
🚇 Sonora 🕐 Closed Sun.
⬛ MC, V

FONDA SAN ÁNGEL
$$–$$$
PLAZA SAN JACINTO,
SAN ÁNGEL
TEL 55/5550-1641
Open for all meals, this casual eatery is a welcome retreat in the south of the city. Eat at a café table facing San Ángel's prettiest plaza, or inside in the cool, thick-walled mansion. Call on the head waiter to translate the wide array of choices on the Spanish-language menu. Valet parking.
🅿 ⬛ AE, MC, V

MOSAICO
$$–$$$
MICHOACÁN 10,
NEAR AMSTERDAM,
COL. LA CONDESA
TEL 55/5584-2932
A delicious and varied French and continental menu at reasonable prices means a devoted cadre of repeat customers. The small bistro and adjoining bakery can be packed, due in part to the excellent wine list and charming unpretentious atmosphere.
🚇 Metrobus: Campeche
🕐 Closed Sun. D ⬛ AE, MC, V

SPEZIA
$$
AMSTERDAM 241,
COLONIA LA CONDESA
TEL 55/5564-1367

This Polish restaurant, featuring delightful roast duck, borscht, and grilled trout, is currently very popular with locals. The courtyard and indoor setting are elegant, but diners' dress is studied casual.
🅿 🚇 Chilpancingo
🕐 Closed Sun. D ⬛ AE, MC, V

CARNITAS EL GUERO
$–$$
CALLE XICOTENCATL S/N,
MERCADO DE COVOACÁN
TEL 55/5659-0620
After a visit to the Frida Kahlo museum, take a trip to the Coyoacán market, where you'll find what one well-known foodie calls the best *carnitas* —bites of tender pork served with tortillas and condiments— in all of Mexico. The food is downright delicious, although this dining experience is not recommended for the unadventurous, as it looks a bit hard-core despite the fact that it's clean and safe.
🕐 Closed D ⬛ Cash only

AROUND MEXICO CITY

CHOLULA

🏨 LA QUINTA LUNA
$$$
CALLE 3 SUR 702
TEL 222/247-8915 OR
800/728-9098 (TOLL-FREE IN U.S.)
www.laquintaluna.com
Rooms surrounding a central patio are a refreshing mix of traditional materials and modern design. Just a short walk from city center. Breakfast included; yummy traditional and nouveau Mexican cuisine.
ℹ 6 ⬛ MC, V

🏨 VILLA CHOLULA
$$
CALLE 2 PONIENTE 601
TEL 222/273-7900 OR
888/773-4349 (IN U.S.)

www.villasarqueologicas.com.mx
In Mexico, Club Med properties are found not just at the sea but at some archaeological sites. In the shadow of massive Tepanapa pyramid, this one has smallish but cozy rooms and nice grounds.
ℹ 42 🅿 🏊 ⬛ MC, V

CUERNAVACA

🏨 LAS MAÑANITAS
$$$$
RICARDO LINARES 107
TEL 777/314-1466 OR
888/413-9199 (TOLL-FREE IN U.S.)
www.lasmananitas.com.mx
This restored hacienda is set on immaculate grounds with ponds and fountains; its Orlane Spa has a full range of treatments. Airy suites have antique furnishings, Mexican folk art, and huge tiled bathrooms; request one with a fireplace or large terrace. Innovative and award-winning regional cuisine is served overlooking the garden courtyard.
ℹ 25 🅿 🏊 ⬛ AE, MC, V

LAS ESTACAS
$$

RAYÓN 30, CUERNAVACA
CENTRO, TLALTIZAPÁN
(1 HR. OUTSIDE CUERNAVACA)
TEL 777/312-4412
www.lasestacas.com
Royal palms and semitropical
vegetation shade this luscious
property surrounding the
crystal-clear Río Estacas, once
used for *Tarzan* TV shows. The
many facilities are open to
day-trippers (*$$$$$*), but it's
nicer to overnight in the hotel,
campgrounds, or RV park.
Reservations and transporta-
tion in Cuernavaca.

P 🏊 Ⓢ MC, V

EL CHICO
NATIONAL PARK

EL PARAÍSO
$$–$$$

CARR. PACHUCA–MINERAL DEL
CHICO KM 19
TEL 771/715-5654
www.hotelesecoturisticos
.com.mx
Within El Chico National
Park, this simple hotel offers
outdoor activities as well as
proximity to the small and
picturesque town of Mineral
del Chico. The meal plan is
suggested, as the international
food is truly tasty. Non-guests
need to make reservations.

ⓘ 20 P 🏊 Ⓢ MC, V

PUEBLA

CAMINO REAL
PUEBLA
$$$

CALLE 7 PONIENTE 105
TEL 222/229-0909 OR
800/722-6466 (TOLL-FREE
IN U.S.)
www.camino-real-puebla.com
One of Mexico's earliest convents has been meticulously
restored as a gorgeous inn. Los
Azulejos restaurant serves a
large breakfast buffet (sometimes included in room price);
for lunch and dinner there's

pretty good Mexican and
international fare à la carte.

ⓘ 83 P ⇄ Ⓢ Ⓢ
Ⓢ AE, MC, V

LA PURIFICADORA
$$$

CALLEJÓN DE LA NORTE 802,
PASEO SAN FRANCISCO
BARRIO EL ALTO
TEL 222/309-1920 OR
800/728-9098 (TOLL-FREE
IN U.S.)
www.la purificadora.com
Sporting a stylish, chic, and
somewhat severe interior
design and color scheme, this
hotel occupies a thoroughly
remodeled icemaking factory
from the 19th century. Like all
Grupo Habita properties, it is
cutting edge cool, yet comfort-
able. Well-situated. There's a
Jacuzzi, sauna, free Wi-Fi, and
24-hour room service.

ⓘ 26 P ⇄ Ⓢ Ⓢ 🏊 🎾
Ⓢ AE, MC, V

MESÓN SACRISTÍA DE
LA COMPAÑÍA
$$

CALLE 6 SUR 304 AT CALLEJÓN
DE LOS SAPOS, 72000
TEL 222/242-3554
www.mesones-sacristia.com
Throughout this two-
story boutique hotel antique
furnishings and decorative
elements are punctuated with
more modern regional folk art.
Rooms are snug rustic chic, the
bar has live music on weekends, and the restaurant serves
delicious regional specialties.
Cooking classes teach guests
how to prepare the hotel's
fabulous dishes.

ⓘ 9 P 🕒 Restaurant closed
Sun. D Ⓢ AE, MC, V

FONDA DE SANTA
CLARA
$

AV. 3 PONIENTE 920
TEL 222/246-1919
A welcoming staff comple-
ments the generous helpings

of delicious regional food at
this picturesque, centrally
located inn. Select from a
range of good appetizers; for a
main dish try the *tinga* (shredded chicken in tomato sauce);
then enjoy a pastry for dessert.

Ⓢ MC, V

TEOTIHUACÁN

VILLA TEOTIHUACÁN
$$

PERIFÉRICO SUR S/N,
SAN JUAN TEOTIHUACÁN
TEL 555/836-9020 OR
888/773-4349 (TOLL-FREE IN U.S.)
www.villasarqueologicas
.com.mx
Perfectly situated at the edge
of the archaeological zone,
this low-slung, comfortable
hotel has small rooms typical
of Club Med Arqueológico
properties, plus a tennis court.

ⓘ 42 P Ⓢ 🏊 Ⓢ AE, MC, V

TLAXCALA

MISIÓN TLAXCALA
$$

CARR. TLAXCALA–APIZACO
KM 10, ATLIHUETZIA
TEL 246/461-0000
www.hotelesmision.com
Tlaxcala has few hotels. This
one is 6 miles (10 km) outside
town, but offers peaceful lodgings with Wi-Fi, a spa, Jacuzzi,
and restaurant overlooking the
Atlihuetzia waterfall.

ⓘ 102 P Ⓢ 🏊 🎾 Ⓢ MC, V

PLAZA JARDÍN
$–$$

PORTAL HIDALGO 3
TEL 246/462-4891
Open daily from 7 a.m. until
11 p.m., this portico restaurant
faces the town square. They
specialize in regional and
Mexican fare (try the *molcajete*
or the Tlaxcalan soup with
beans, tortillas, avocado, and
chile) with some steaks and a
few international dishes, too.

Ⓢ MC, V

Ⓢ Nonsmoking Ⓢ Air-conditioning 🏠 Indoor Pool 🏊 Outdoor Pool 🎾 Health Club Ⓢ Credit Cards

■ CENTRAL GULF COAST

CATEMACO

🏨 LA FINCA
$$
CARR. COSTERA 180 KM 147
TEL 294/947-9700
www.lafinca.com.mex
Birders love this three-story
lakeshore hotel surrounded
by greenery. Each room has
a balcony. Although there's
Wi-Fi and the price includes
tax, it seems a bit expensive
given the average rooms and
Catemaco's relative obscurity.
🛏 51 🅿 ⬚⬚⬚ ⬚ 🏊 ⬚ MC, V

🏨 NANCIYAGA
$$
CARR. CATEMACO–COYAME KM
7 (EAST OF HWY. 180)
TEL 294/943-0199
www.nanciyaga.com
For a peaceful and very rustic
retreat, overnight at this New
Age ecological park (*$$*).
Herons wade and crocs snap
outside the microscopic lake-
side cabins. Wander the jungle,
row or kayak on the lake, then
have body mud treatment and
rinse off in the mineral spring.
🛏 11 cabins 🕒 Closed Wed. in
Oct. ⬚ MC, V

VERACRUZ

🏨 GRAN HOTEL
🍴 DILIGENCIAS
$$
INDEPENDENCIA 1115
TEL 229/923-0280
www.granhoteldiligencias.com
Located in the heart of
Veracruz's action facing the
main plaza, this pretty hotel
has double-paned windows
that make guest rooms quiet.
You can watch the action
from the small, chilly pool on
the mezzanine, or the wide
terrace restaurant-bar, which is
insulated by the vendors that

plague those at other restaurants facing the plaza.
🛏 121 🅿 ⬚⬚ ⬚ ⬚ 🏊 ⬚
⬚ AE, MC, V

🏨 HOTEL MOCAMBO
$$
CALZADA RUÍZ CORTINES 4000,
BOCA DEL RÍO, 94299
TEL 229/922-0200
www.hotelmocambo.com.mx
Fabulous and exclusive in the
1930s, this oasis of tropical
calm later faded, but never
lost its charm. Art deco archi-
tecture and the palm-studded
beach still beckon. There are
also sauna, spa, and massage.
🛏 103 🅿 ⬚ 🏊 🏊 ⬚
⬚ AE, MC, V

🍴 VILLA MARINA
$$$
BLVD. AVILA CAMACHO S/N,
NEAR DESEMBOCADURAS DE
HORACIO DIAZ
TEL 229/935-1034
Open 1 p.m. to 1 a.m., Villa
Marina has a great seascape
through its windows, and
serves steaks, regional dishes,
and international favorites.
The specialty, fresh seafood, is
cooked in many styles; waiters
will help translate the Spanish-
language menu.
⬚ ⬚ MC, V

🍴 GRAN CAFÉ DE LA PARROQUIA
$–$$
CALLE 16 DE SEPTIEMBRE AT
MALECÓN
TEL 229/932-2584
This is a legendary Veracruz
coffeehouse facing the
boardwalk (*malecón*). It's
open early (and 'til midnight),
but, as everything is à la
carte, breakfast is no bargain.
Although the food's mediocre,
it's an essential part of any
Veracruz visit.
⬚ MC, V

VILLAHERMOSA

🏨 CENCALI
$$
JUÁREZ 105 AT PASEO TABASCO
TEL 993/315-1999
www.cencali.com.mx
Two-story Cencali abuts Lago
de las Ilusiones; its grounds are
extensive and tropical, with
wandering flamingos. Small
rooms have bathtubs, hair
dryers, and safes. There's a
free airport shuttle. Breakfast
buffet is included.
🛏 160 🅿 ⬚⬚ ⬚ ⬚ 🏊
⬚ AE, MC, V

🏨 HOLIDAY INN EXPRESS
$$
PERIFÉRICO CARLOS PELLECIER
4000, TABASCO 2000
TEL 993/310-4650 OR
01800/000-0404 (TOLL-FREE IN
MEXICO)
These streamlined but comfortable hotels are popping up
around Mexico. Perks include
new construction, comfortable
beds, laundry facilities, unlimited local calls, in-room data
ports, and free Wi-Fi.
🛏 88 🅿 ⬚⬚ ⬚ ⬚ 🏊
⬚ All major cards

🍴 LOS TULIPANES
$$
CARLOS PELLICER 511
TEL 993/312-9217
Try some of Tabasco's unusual
dishes here overlooking the
Río Grijalva. There's a break-
fast buffet Thursday–Sunday
and an extensive Sunday lunch
buffet (*$$$*) 1:30 to 6 p.m.
that's popular with locals.
🅿 🕒 Closed Sun. D & Mon.
⬚ ⬚ AE, MC, V

🍴 HONG KONG
$
5 DE MAYO 343
TEL 993/312-5996
If you're maxed out on Mexican food, head for this Chinese restaurant in the Zona
Luz. It's got all the traditional

🏨 Hotel 🍴 Restaurant 🛏 No. of Guest Rooms ⬚ No. of Seats 🅿 Parking 🚇 Metro 🕒 Closed 🛗 Elevator

favorites and, on weekends, a buffet ($$). Closes at 8 p.m.
🚭 MC, V

XALAPA

🏨 POSADA COATEPEC
$$
HIDALGO 9, COATEPEC
TEL 228/816-0544
www.posadacoatepec.com.mx
This former coffee villa about 4 miles (6.4 km) from Xalapa now houses well-decorated suites with fine accents and satellite TV; antiques grace the bar and lobby. Unfortunately the staff inclines toward rude.
🛈 23 🅿 ⛱ 🚭 AE, MC, V

🏨 MESÓN DEL ALFÉREZ
$
SEBASTIÁN CAMACHO 2 AT ZARAGOZA
TEL 228/818-6351
Diluted washes of bright Mexican colors warm the walls of this restored historic home behind the government palace. Not terribly exciting, but well-situated. Continental breakfast included.
🛈 20 🅿 🚭 AE, MC, V

🍽 LA ESTANCIA DE LOS TECAJETES
$$
AVILA CAMACHO 90, LOCAL 12, PLAZA TECAJETES
TEL 228/818-0732
With a fine view of the leafy park, this strip-mall restaurant puts its own spin on regional dishes. It's popular with locals on weekends; service is slow.
🅿 ⏲ Closed Sun. D
🚭 AE, MC, V

🍽 TRATTORIA TAVOLA
$$
GUADALUPE VICTORIA 66 AT AZUETO, CENTRO
TEL 228/817-8990
www.tavolaxalapa.blogspot.com
The coveted tables are on the patio surrounding a large tree, close to the musicians strum-

ming Mexican jazz and blues. There's mainly pizza, pasta, and salads. Opens at 2 p.m.
⏲ Closed Mon. 🚭 MC, V

▪ OAXACA

HUATULCO

🏨 DREAMS
$$$$$
CALLE BENITO JUÁREZ 4, BAHÍA TANGOLUNDA
TEL 958/583-0400 OR 866/237-3267 (TOLL-FREE IN U.S.)
www.dreamsresorts.com
This lovely all-inclusive offers nice rooms with MP3 players and balcony. Activities seem endless, from volleyball to theme parties to extensive spa treatments.
🛈 421 🅿 ⛱ 🚭 ⛱ 🚭 🏋
🚭 AE, MC, V

🏨 CAMINO REAL
🍽 ZAASHILA
$$$–$$$$
BLVD. BENITO JUÁREZ 5, 70989
TEL 958/581-0460, 800/722-6466 (TOLL-FREE IN U.S.)
www.camino-zaashila.com
Endless stairs at this graceful, plant-drenched beachfront property provide a mildly aerobic vacation. The food and beach are good, and the chaises longues are semi-submerged in the pool.
🛈 120 🅿 🚭 🚭 ⛱ 🏋
🚭 Most major cards

🏨 EDÉN COSTA
🍽 $
CALLE ZAPOTECO S/N, BAHÍA CHAHUÉ
TEL 958/587-2480
www.edencosta.com
The main draw here is the excellent and reasonably priced French restaurant, L'Echalote ($$–$$$, closed Mon.), serving French and Indochinese. The attached hotel, close to the beach, is pleasant; rooms have cable TVs.
🛈 11 🚭 ⛱ 🚭 MC, V

SOMETHING SPECIAL

🏨 MISIÓN DE LOS ARCOS
🍽 $
GARDENIA 902, CRUCECITA
TEL 958/587-0165
FAX 958/587-1904
www.misiondelosarcos.com
This intimate Mediterranean-style hotel is in Crucecita, but vans shuttle to its Santa Cruz Bay beach club. Many rooms have balconies; all have classy, low-key decor. The restaurant serves yummy breakfast as well as Mexican and continental fare, and the gym is good. The Internet café serves coffee and desserts. Prices are low; spring for a garden suite.
🛈 14 🅿 🚭 🏋 🚭 AE, MC, V

🍽 VE EL MAR
$$
PLAYA SANTA CRUZ (S OF PASEO MITLA), BAHÍA SANTA CRUZ
TEL 958/587-0364
At this Huatulco original, you can wriggle your toes in the sand as you order a delicious breakfast, lunch, or dinner. Outdoor tables are under palm-thatch roofs.
🚭 MC, V

OAXACA

🏨 CAMINO REAL OAXACA
$$$$
CALLE 5 DE MAYO 300
TEL 951/501-6100, 800/722-6466 (TOLL-FREE IN U.S.)
FAX 951/516-0732
A converted 16th-century convent on a quiet street in historic downtown, this property is long on charm. The Camino Real Club rooms are larger and offer more amenities. Meals are served in the colonnaded corridor surrounding a central patio; musicians stroll and serenade the diners.
🛈 90 🅿 🚭 🚭 ⛱
🚭 AE, MC, V

🏨 CASA CONZATTI
$$
GÓMEZ FARIAS 218
TEL 951/513-8500 OR
01800/717-9974 (TOLL-FREE IN MEXICO)
www.casaconzatti.com.mx
This quiet little haven downtown was the house of a 19th-century ethnobot-onist for which it's named; his botanical garden is now Conzatti Park. Rooms have coffeemaker, iron/iron-ing board, hair dryer, and safe. The hotel has locally produced art for sale, and a Mexican restaurant.
🛈 45 🅿 ♿

🏨 MARQUÉS DEL VALLE
$–$$
PORTAL DE CLAVERÍA S/N
TEL 951/514-0688
www.hotelmarquesdelvalle.com.mx
This old-fashioned-looking hotel, a colonial original, has received several makeovers and offers three types of rooms (most without air-conditioning) in varying price and comfort levels. The location between La Alameda and the cathedral is great
🛈 95 🔁 📶 ♿ MC, V

🍴 LA BIZNAGA
$$
GARCIA VIGIL 512
TEL 951/516-1800
Full in the evenings with travelers and locals, La Biznaga offers Mexican dishes on its covered courtyard. The sound-track is excellent and the bar well stocked, although service can be slow.
MC, V

🍴 LA ESCONDIDA
$$
CARR. YATARENI KM 7, OFF HWY. TO MITLA
TEL 951/517-5550
Locals flock on weekends and holidays for the regional cuisine. It's even full midweek

as businesspeople and tourists come to the outdoor venue 15 minutes from downtown.
🕐 Closed D 🅿 ♿ AE MC, V

🍴 CAFE ROYAL
$–$$
GARCIA VIGIL 403 AT BRAVO
TEL 951/514-3239
www.ceceo.org.mx/caferoyal
A few blocks up from the *zócalo*, this tiny French bistro offers breakfast, an inexpen-sive daily lunch special (soup, main, and dessert), and such standards as escargot and beef bourguignon.
🕐 Closed Sun. ♿ Cash only

🍴 LA OLLA
$–$$
REFORMA 402
TEL 951/516-6668
Very clean and dependable, the centrally located La Olla creates healthful regional and international dishes. Food is made to order, and a bit slow, but local artwork entertains. Lunch specials 1:30–4 p.m.
🕐 Closed Sun.
♿ Most major cards

PUERTO ESCONDIDO

🏨 QUINTA CARRIZALILLO
$$
FOCAS 5 AT DELFINES, FRACC. LA RINCONADA
TEL 954/582-3564
www.quintacarrizalillo.com
Named for the lovely cove, this hotel is nice and new. It of-fers steam room, airport trans-fers, and massage. Rooms have kitchenettes and coffeemakers, but there's no restaurant.
🛈 11 🅿 📶 ♿ 🏊 🎇
♿ Cash only

🏨 SANTA FE
🍴 **$$**
CALLE DEL MORO S/N, ZICATELA BEACH
TEL 954/582-0170 OR 888/649-6407 (TOLL-FREE IN U.S.)
www.hotelsaftafe.com.mx

This is probably Puerto's nicest hotel, with exuberant gardens, comfortable rooms, and four pools. The surfing is advanced. The ocean-view vegetarian restaurant is a winner.
🛈 77 🅿 🔁 📶 ♿ 🏊 4
♿ AE, MC, V

🍴 GUADUA
$$$–$$$$
CALLE TAMAULIPAS S/N, COL. BRISAS DE ZICATELA
TEL 954/107-9524
www.guadua.com.mx
A classy cabana with a nice beach view, Guadua probably has Puerto's best fine-dining, with delicious fusion dishes. Desserts are inventive, and the bar is très cool. Some nights there's live music.
🕐 Closed L & Mon. ♿ MC, V

🍴 LA VIDA VERDE
$$–$$$
BLVD. JUÁREZ S/N, FRACC. LA RINCONADA
TEL 954/101-5619
The speciality here is pre-Hispanic food, including cactus salad, rabbit in non-spicy chile sauce, and lots of things

wrapped in banana leaves.
🕐 Closed Sun. 💲 Cash only

TEOTITLÁN DEL VALLE

🍴 TLAMANALLI
$$–$$$
AV. JUÁREZ 39
TEL 951/524-4006
Located in Teotitlán del Valle,
this unpretentious, lunch-only,
Zapotec restaurant has been
featured in the *New York Times*
and *Gourmet* magazine. The
Mendoza sisters cook squash
blossom soup, chicken tamales, turkey in mole sauce, and a
few pre-Hispanic favorites.
🕐 Closed D, Mon., & Easter-
time 💲 Cash only

◼ CHIAPAS

COMITÁN

🏨 HOTEL HACIENDA DE LOS ÁNGELES
$–$$
2A CALLE NORTE PONIENTE 6
TEL 963/632-0074
www.hotelhaciendadelosan
geles.com.mx
In 2005 this old mansion was
turned into a fine hotel. The
popular restaurant has live
music Thursday–Saturday
nights, and breakfast and lunch
buffets Friday–Sunday. Junior
suites sleep six; all rooms have
bathtub along with crown
molding and other European-
style decor. Breakfast included.
🛏 25 P 💲💲💲
💲 AE, MC, V

🍴 MATISSE RESTAURANT-BAR
$–$$
AV. NORTE 16
TEL 963/632-7152
International dishes are served
in this pleasant café. It is
popular with local mavens and
businesspeople.
🕐 Closed Mon., Opens 2 p.m.
💲 AE, MC, V

LAGUNAS DE MONTEBELLO

🏨 MUSEO PARADOR
🍴 SANTA MARÍA
$$$
CARR. A LAGUNAS DE MONTE-
BELLO KM 22
TEL 963/632-5116
www.paradorsantamaria
.com.mx
This Independence-era
hacienda—about a 20-minute
drive from the lakes—stands
by its simple but delicious
regional recipes, such as
barbecued chicken with rice
and beef tongue with fried to-
matoes and sherry. Outdated
fabulous rooms are decorated
with period antiques from
different eras. Restaurant
reservations required.
🛏 8 P 💲💲 MC, V

PALENQUE

🏨 CIUDAD REAL
$$
CARR. A PAKAL-NA KM 1.5
TEL 916/345-1315
www.ciudadread.com.mx
This hotel has nicely decorated, comfortable rooms and
a lovely pool. It's not right in
Palenque, but between the
archaeological site and the
town. Has a restaurant.
🛏 72 P 💲💲💲💲 MC, V

🏨 MAYA TULIPANES
$
CAÑADA 6, COL. LA CAÑADA
TEL 916/345-0201
www.mayatulipanes.com
Simply furnished rooms have
TV and screened windows, the
grounds are pleasant, and the
management is friendly. La Cañada is a quiet neighborhood
close to downtown Palenque
and roadside restaurants.
🛏 72 P 💲💲 AE, MC, V

🍴 LAS TINAJAS
$–$$
AV. 20 DE NOVIEMBRE

AT ABASOLO
TEL 916/345-4970
This downtown restaurant got
so popular it had to move to
larger digs, and the place still
fills up with international travelers. Open all day, the house
specialty is *pollo palenque:*
chicken in a special sauce.
💲 Cash only

🍴 RESTAURANT DON MUCHO
$
CARR. A LAS RUINAS S/N
TEL 916/341-8209
This simple, open-sided patio
at the budget digs El Panchán,
is always lively with national
and travelers. There's often
live music, and always generous main courses like the fish
served with pasta, salad, and a
fat slab of garlic toast. They accept Euros, dollars, and pesos.
💲 Cash only

SAN CRISTÓBAL DE LAS CASAS

🏨 CASA VIEJA
$$
MARIA ADELINA FLORES 27
TEL 967/678-6868
www.casavieja.com.mx
Rooms are smallish and some
are dark, but they are quiet
and have free Wi-Fi. Heaters
don't work so well. Sometimes
you can negotiate to get a $
price and/or full breakfast
included, especially if you
pay cash.
🛏 37 💲 All rooms 💲 MC, V

🏨 NA BOLOM
🍴 $$
AV. VICENTE GUERRERO 33,
29200
TEL 967/678-1418
Cozy guest rooms dot the
property, whose organic
gardens provide veggies for
the restaurant. Each room has
a fireplace and is indivdally
decorated with photographs
and art. Meals are family style

in the large dining room, and it's a treat to mingle with visiting artists and archaeologists around a shared table. The recipes are as down-home and wholesome. Dinner reservations are required for non-guests.

🕐 Closed for L 🚫 MC, V

🏨 LA MEDIA LUNA
$
HERMANOS DOMINGUEZ 5
TEL 967/631-5590
www.hotel-lamedialuna.com
Not charming, but cheap and centrally located. Rooms are small but clean, bathrooms tiny. But there's free Wi-Fi and a computer; guests are international and a variety of tours are offered. Ask for a room near the back, avoiding traffic at the front desk.
🛏 14 🚫 MC, V

🍴 RESTAURANT MAGUEY
$$–$$$
AV. GENERAL UTRILLA AT CALLE 28 DE AGOSTO
TEL 967/678-0698
www.hotelcasamexicana.com
This pretty restaurant is in the Casa Mexicana hotel, at the heart of San Cristóbal. It serves tasty Mexican food, mainly from the southern states of Chiapas and the Yucatán. There's an expansive Sunday brunch.
🚫 AE, MC, V

🍴 EL EDÉN
$–$$
CALLE 5 DE FEBRERO 19
TEL 967/678-0085
Hands down the best food in town, combining the Swiss precision of the husband, the Mexican artistry of his wife, and the personal attention of both. Great steaks and margaritas; all the food is wonderful.
🚫 AE, MC, V

TUXTLA GUTIERREZ

🏨 CAMINO REAL
🍴 $$$
BLVD. DR. BELISARIO DOMÍNGUEZ 1195
COL. SANTA ELENA
TEL 961/617-7777 OR
800/722-6466 (TOLL-FREE IN U.S.)
www.caminoreal.com
Tuxtla's nicest hotel belongs to the classy Camino Real chain. It's sleek and modern and integrates pool, green spaces, open bars, and lounge areas in a pleasing way. The gym has sauna, steam, hot tub, and massage. The exceptional 24-hour Azulejos café has a heavenly breakfast buffet, with many items cooked to order.
🛏 210 🍴 🛎 🏊 🍽
🚫 Most major cards

🍴 LAS PICHANCHAS
$$
AV. CENTRAL ORIENTE 837
TEL 961/611-1139
More than a restaurant, it's a culinary and cultural review of Chiapas. Enjoy an afternoon of marimba music (2–5:30 p.m.) or at night, a lively dance troupe (9–10 p.m.) with more music. The cuisine is pure Chiapanecan, with photos on the menu. Or best yet, order the sampler plate.
🚫 AE, MC, V

◼ YUCATÁN PENINSULA

CAMPECHE

🏨 PUERTA CAMPECHE
$$$–$$$$
CALLE 59 NO. 71
TEL 981/816-7508 OR
888/625-5144 (TOLL-FREE IN U.S.)
www.haciendasmexico.com
This lovely member of the Starwood group occupies a block of resuscitated old homes. Rooms and public areas incorporate both traditional and innovative design

elements. Bathrooms blend bright modern paint and fixtures with stone walls and tile floors. Beds are luxurious.
🛏 15 🅿 🛎 🏊 🚫 AE, MC, V

🏨 HOTEL DEL MAR
🍴 $$
AV. RUÍZ CORTINES 51
TEL 981/811-9191
www.delmarhotel.com.mx
Despite its plain appearance and somewhat bland personality, this low-rise hotel is recommended for its many services (car rental, tour desks, business services, and more) and dining options. It's sandwiched between the boardwalk, perfect for a stroll, and the old sea gate leading to the city's heart. Capitán LaFitte's is Campeche's most enduring spot for a late-night drink, dinner, or dance.
🛏 146 🅿 🍴 🛎 🏊 🍽
🚫 AE, MC, V

🍴 LA PIGUA
$$
MALECÓN MIGUEL ALEMÁN 179
TEL 981/811-3365
www.lapigua.com.mx
A seaside theme prevails at this favorite near the north end of town. Renovated in 2005, it maintains the same seaside theme and decor.
🛎 🚫 MC, V

CANCÚN

🏨 LE MERIDIÉN CANCÚN
🍴 $$$$$
BLVD. KUKULKÁN KM 14, ZONA HOTELERA
TEL 998/881-2200 OR
800/543-4300 (TOLL-FREE IN U.S.)
www.lemeridien.com
Public areas and rooms are elegant and restrained, yet the comprehensive European-style spa is inviting. Tasting menus (with optional wines) change monthly at Aioli restaurant.
🛏 213 🅿 🍴 🛎 🏊 🍽
🚫 Most major cards

🏨 Hotel 🍴 Restaurant 🛏 No. of Guest Rooms 🍴 No. of Seats 🅿 Parking 🚇 Metro 🕐 Closed 🛎 Elevator

HILTON CANCÚN GOLF & SPA RESORT
$$$–$$$$
BLVD. KUKULKÁN KM 17,
ZONA HOTELERA
TEL 998/881-8000 OR
800/445-8667 (TOLL-FREE IN U.S.)
www.hiltoncancun.com
This high-rise hotel features tennis, golf, seven pools, spa, beauty salon, and health club offering Pilates and yoga. All of the crisply decorated rooms and suites have ocean views.
🏨 426 P 🔃 🟦 🟦 🏊 7 🎽 🔲 AE, MC, V

EL REY DEL CARIBE
$$
AV. UXMAL AT NADER,
DOWNTOWN
TEL 998/884-2028
www.reycaribe.com
Rooms with kitchenettes crouch among the overgrown gardens surrounding a smallish pool and hot tub. Breakfast included; reiki, massage, and a few other treatments available.
🏨 24 P 🟦 All rooms 🟦 🏊 🔲 MC, V

LA HABICHUELA
$$$–$$$$
CALLE MARGARITAS 25,
DOWNTOWN
TEL 998/884-3158
www.lahabichuela.com
Maya statues, candlelit patios, and splashing fountains create a romantic ambience at this favorite, where couples feast on nouvelle Mexican-Caribbean cuisine such a curried blend of lobster and shrimp.
🟦 🔲 AE, MC, V

THAI
$$$–$$$$
BLVD. KUKULKÁN KM 12,
LA ISLA SHOPPING CENTER
TEL 998/883-1401
When your Thai waitress tells you the house favorites, it's half the gorgeous menu. Green papaya salad, deep-fried fish, pad Thai—all delicious. The trendy bar's huge aquarium has captive dolphins. Overlooking the lagoon, it's lovely but buggy around sunset; ask for or bring insect repellent.
P 🟦 🔲 AE, MC, V

LA CASA DE LAS MARGARITAS
$$$
BLVD. KUKULKÁN KM 12,
LA ISLA SHOPPING VILLAGE,
ZONA HOTELERA
TEL 998/883-3222
www.lacasadelas
margaritas.com
A covered courtyard and second-floor balconies with perky hacienda-style decor. Live music and well-seasoned Mexican dishes.
P 🟦 🔲 AE, MC, V

CASA ROLANDI
$$
PLAZA CARACOL, BLVD.
KUKULKÁN KM 8.5, ZONA
HOTELERA
TEL 998/883-2557
www.rolandi.com
This is one of a series of inspired restaurants serving Italian Lake District fare in an elegant yet unpretentious setting. Fine pastas and carpaccio.
🟦 🔲 AE, MC, V

CHICHÉN ITZÁ

HACIENDA CHICHÉN
$$$
CARR. MÉRIDA–PUERTO JUÁREZ
KM 120
TEL 985/851-0045 OR
800/624-8451 (TOLL-FREE IN U.S.)
www.haciendachichen
.com.mx
The cottages are rustic country elegant, with handwoven bedspreads, wrought-iron bedsteads, and dehumidifiers, but no phones or TV. The ancient chapel is popular with brides and grooms, and the colossal pool beckons even when flecked with leaves from the trees that tower overhead.
🏨 28 P 🟦 🏊 🔲 All major cards

COBÁ

VILLA COBÁ
$$
NEAR ENTRANCE TO RUINS
TEL 985/858-1527 OR
888/773-4349 (TOLL-FREE IN U.S.)
www.villasarqueologicas
.com.mx
Run by Club Med, this simple inn is actually the fanciest place in Cobá. The rooms are a bit stark, but the open restaurant surrounds a swimming pool shaded by deep pink bougainvillea. The hotel has an excellent library and gift shop.
🏨 43 P 🟦 🏊 🔲 AE, MC, V

COSTA MAYA

COSTA DE COCOS
$$
DOMICILIO CONOCIDO, XCALAK
PENINSULA, OFF CARRETERA 307
www.costadecocos.com
Nicely done cabanas on the sand, each with a hammock, prove to be a magnet for snorkelers, fly fishers, and divers. The little village of Xcalak is within walking distance.
🏨 16 🔲 AE, MC, V

COZUMEL

PRESIDENTE INTERCONTINENTAL COZUMEL
$$$$
CARR. A CHANKANAAB KM 6.5
TEL 987/872-9500 OR
800/327-0200 (TOLL-FREE IN U.S.)
www.interconti.com
Vivid magenta and cobalt furnishings set against white walls enhance the tropical feel of Presidente's rooms. Tropical fish swim close to shore beneath El Caribeño restaurant, where guests linger over seafood salad and other fresh fare. There's a full-service spa on-site, and wonderful meals in dinner-

🟦 Nonsmoking 🟦 Air-conditioning 🏊 Indoor Pool 🏊 Outdoor Pool 🎽 Health Club 🔲 Credit Cards

only Alfredo di Roma Italian restaurant. Some guests never leave the grounds.

ⓘ 253 🔲 🚫 🔲 🔲 🔲
🔲 AE, MC, V

🏨 CONDUMEL
$$–$$$
COSTERA NORTE, N OF BLVD. AEROPUERTO
TEL 987/872-0892
This small condo complex is owned by one of the island's top dive-shop operators. Hammocks hang beside the living-room doors that open onto a limestone terrace above blue water. Full kitchens, huge marble bathtubs, and plush mattresses cover all that is needed for a low-key and relaxing vacation.

ⓘ 10 🔲 🔲 MC, V

🍴 GUIDO'S
$$$
RAFAEL MELGAR 23
BETWEEN CALLES 6 & 8
TEL 987/872-0946
www.guidoscozumel.com
This restaurant (and its vine-drenched, open-air central patio) is a local's retreat and must-do for repeat Cozumel visitors. Wood-fire pizzas, Italian seafood dishes, and homemade bread and calzone all but guarantee a great meal.

🔲 Closed Sun. 🔲 AE, MC, V

🍴 LA CHOZA
$$
R. SALAS 198 AT AV. 10 NORTE
TEL 987/872-0958
www.lachozarestaurant.com
Authentic Yucatán cuisine, served on Mexican crockery under a palm-thatch roof. Superb seafood, stuffed chile rellenos, savory marinated pork *cochinita pibil*, and fragrant laced coffee.

🔲 AE, MC, V

ISLA MUJERES

🏨 VILLA ROLANDI
🍴 GOURMET AND BEACH CLUB
$$$$$
FRACC. LAGUNA MAR KM 7
TEL 998/999-2000, OR
800/525-4800 (TOLL-FREE IN U.S.)
www.villarolandi.com
Rates at this all-suites property on a sandy cove include transportation from Cancún and continental breakfast. Suites are modern, with natural materials and bright colors; all have balconies overlooking the beach. The sea-view restaurant has a varied menu of Italian dishes.

ⓘ 35 🚫 🔲 🔲 🔲 AE, MC, V

IZAMAL

🏨 MACANCHÉ
$
CALLE 22 NO. 305
BETWEEN CALLES 33 & 35
TEL 988/954-0287
www.macanche.com
Of Izamal's lodgings, this is definitely the most organic. Plants and trees surround the eclectically decorated, freestanding rooms, and healthful fare is the rule at the family-style restaurant. Full breakfast included. *Temazcal*, spa, yoga, and more.

ⓘ 13 🅿 🔲 🔲 🔲 Cash only

MÉRIDA

🏨 FIESTA AMERICANA
🍴 MÉRIDA
$$–$$$
COLÓN 451 AT
PASEO MONTEJO, 97000
TEL 999/942-1111 OR
800/343-7821 (TOLL-FREE IN U.S.)
www.fiestaamericana.com
Probably the prettiest high-rise hotel in Merida, the Fiesta Americana Mérida, in the high-rent district, has an elegant lobby above a mini-

mall with a bus depot, shops (including Sanborns), and Los Almendros restaurant, which specializes in regional food.

ⓘ 350 🅿 🔲 🚫 🔲 🔲 🔲
🔲 AE, DC, MC, V

🏨 CASA DEL BALAM
$$
CALLE 60 NO. 488 AT CALLE 57
TEL 999/924-8844 OR 800/624-8451 (TOLL-FREE IN U.S.)
www.casadelbalam.com
Neither too big nor too small, this centrally located hotel is on a street full of shops, just two blocks from the main square. Eat or drink in the old-fashioned open courtyard, sit in a rocking chair on the covered corridor outside your room, or just enjoy the pleasant rooms that strike a lovely balance between restored colonial and modern.

ⓘ 51 🅿 🚫 🔲 🔲
🔲 Most major cards

🍴 LA CASA DE FRIDA
$$
CALLE 61 NO. 526
BETWEEN 66 & 66-A
TEL 999/928-2311

🏨 Hotel 🍴 Restaurant ⓘ No. of Guest Rooms 🔲 No. of Seats 🅿 Parking 🔲 Metro 🔲 Closed 🔲 Elevator

www.lacasadefrida.com.mx
Lighter, more modern versions of traditional Mexican meals are making "Frida" as well-known as its namesake. The restored house, offering mainly open patio seating, is decked out in plants, and features plenty of Frida Kahlo images and other paraphernalia of the painter's life.

🕒 Closed Sun., L 🍴 Cash only

PLAYA DEL CARMEN

🏨 SHANGRI-LA CARIBE
$$$$
CALLE 38 BETWEEN AV. 5
& THE BEACH
TEL 984/803-2804,
800/538-6802 (TOLL-FREE IN U.S.)
www.shangrilacaribe.net
Attractive bungalows dot this meandering beachfront property; the nicest ones face the lovely beach. All have twin hammocks. Breakfast and dinner are included in the price, as are taxes.
🛏 107 P 🅰 🌊 2
🍴 All major cards

🏨 BÁSICO
$$$
AVE. 5 AT CALLE 10 NORTE
TEL 984/879-4448
www.hotelbasico.com
Playa's hip and playful hotel makes Wi-Fi and tricycles available to guests. Part of the avante-guard Habita group of hotels, this one has a rooftop lounge facing the ocean and rooms with trademark minimalist decor. Here the theme is beach resort casual meets "industrial chic." Rooms have bathtubs and DVDs; the hotel has a seafood restaurant.
🛏 15 🅰 🔽 🌊 🍴 AE, MC, V

🏨 LUNA BLUE
$$
CALLE 26 NORTE BETWEEN
AVS. 5 & 10
TEL 984/873-0090
www.lunabluehotel.com
This user-friendly hotel is at

the north end of town. There's no pool or restaurant, but you can gets snacks at the chummy bar and go to the beach club a few blocks away. All rooms have a balcony or terrace, a kitchenette or a fridge; some have Wi-Fi access. Adults only.
🛏 18 🅰 🍴 All major cards

🍴 YAXCHE
$$–$$$
CALLE 8 BETWEEN AVS 5 &10
TEL 984/873-2502
www.mayacuisine.com
Possibly the best Yucatán food on the coast Order a traditional Maya dish like *Tikin Xic* (marinated, grilled fish) or one of the chef's inventions, like the *Chac Mool* (shrimp in a tangerine, chile, and tomato sauce). For dessert there's flaming coffee with ice cream.
🍴 MC, V

RIVIERA MAYA

🏨 MAROMA RESORT &
🍴 SPA
$$$$$
HWY. 307 KM 51
TEL 998/872-8200 OR
866/454-9351(TOLL-FREE IN U.S.)
www.maromahotel.com
Set amid a 200-acre (80 ha) jungle preserve, Maroma offers privacy, luxury, and pampering. The spa has a New Age bent, the restaurant serves sublime seafood and delicious Yucatán and Caribbean cuisine, and the guest rooms are truly artistic wonders.
🛏 65 P 🅰 🌊 🍴 AE, MC, V

🏨 CABAÑAS PAAMUL
$$
CARRETERA 307 KM 85, XPUHA
TEL 984/875-1051
www.paamul.com
The beautiful beach and on-site dive shop are the big draws for these simple cabins without TVs or phones. There are campsites and an RV park.
🛏 20 P

TULUM

🏨 ANA Y JOSÉ HOTEL
& SPA
$$$$
CARR. CANCUN-TULUM KM 7
TEL 998/880-5629
www.anayjose.com
This cabana-style hotel remains one of the coast's best hideaways. The restaurant is excellent and the rooms are simple yet comfortable. Some don't face the sea, however, and as Tulum has matured, room prices have risen.
🛏 22 P 🌊 🍴 AE, MC, V

UXMAL

🏨 VILLA UXMAL
🍴 $–$$
CARR. UXMAL KM 76
TEL 997/974-6020 OR
800/258-2633 (TOLL-FREE IN U.S.)
www.villasarqueologicas.com
A friendly, intimate place near the archaeological site. The rooms are comfortable but are less important than the grounds and public spaces, which include a tennis court, pool table, library, and gift shop. None of the guest rooms have TVs. The restaurant serves up a winning combination of local specialties as well as continental cuisine.
🛏 43 P 🅰 🌊 🍴 AE, MC, V

XPUJIL

🏨 CHICANNÁ
ECOVILLAGE RESORT
$$
CARR. ESCÁRCEGA-
CHETUMAL KM 144
TEL 981/811-9192
www.chicannaecovillageresort.com
Comfortable bungalows, each with patio, overlook gardens. The lodge communicates with civilization via radio, but there is a TV in its library.
🛏 42 P 🌊 🍴 AE, MC, V

🚭 Nonsmoking   🅰 Air-conditioning   🌊 Indoor Pool   🌊 Outdoor Pool   🏋 Health Club   🍴 Credit Cards

Shopping in Mexico

Shopping opportunities and items to buy vary greatly by region. Oaxaca, Michoacán, and Chiapas, which have large indigenous populations, produce lovely textiles and simple but excellent pottery, among other items. From the Yucatán come colorful and comfortable string hammocks, fine Panama hats, bright embroidered blouses, and items made of cane and straw.

Mexican handicrafts are not the sole domain of the indigenous artisan. Shops and factories in smaller cities use modern techniques (such as lead-free glazes) in combination with traditional forms and patterns to produce high-quality tableware and a wide variety of household accessories.

Leather goods can be purchased in northern and central Mexico. Leather jackets, belts, briefcases, boots, and shoes are a bargain.

Larger, more cosmopolitan cities have shopping centers that offer good variety. The Sanborns chain sells gifts, music, perfumes, chocolates and pastries, and books and magazines. Cities known for their handicrafts generally have one or two streets lined with boutiques. Virtually every city, town, and village has either a daily or weekly market. Inquire at the tourist office or hotel which is the most colorful *mercado* (also called *tianguis*) and which is the best for whatever you are seeking.

Market shopping often means you are buying from the producer or his family, and it is a fun way to see the countryside and support local artisans. Try to scout a few midtown shops first, to learn of prices and quality. Bartering is expected in marketplaces, although some vendors discourage it. Most, however, will start high, especially with tourists, coming down to half to three quarters of the asking price. It helps to know the value of the item you want to buy.

Markets and small shops generally don't charge tax, and most don't accept credit cards. Now that ATMs are ubiquitous, traveler's checks are less frequently seen, and some vendors refuse them,

especially outside tourist areas. If you're buying large quantities, ask for a receipt to avoid problems with customs in your home country. The larger stores and chains do charge tax, which ranges from 12 to 15 percent Some stores will ship items you buy there as well as items purchased elsewhere. It is illegal to export antiquities, including archaeological artifacts; in any case, most pieces offered for sale at archaeological sites are fakes.

The stores, malls, and markets listed below are among the best-known and most established.

▓ BAJA CALIFORNIA

Baja has few native handicrafts. Shops in tourist enclaves—primarily Tijuana, Rosarito, Ensenada, and Los Cabos—import folk art and ceramics from mainland Mexico. Wineries in the north produce decent wines and brandies.

Shopping Areas

Avenida Revolución, between Calles 2nd and 9th, and down Calle 1 to the U.S. border, Tijuana, B.C. A mixed bag of garish statuettes, bright piñatas, leather wallets and purses, silver, onyx chessboards, and more.

Handicrafts

Artesanías la Antigua California, Av. Obregón 220, La Paz, B.C.S., tel 612/125-5230. Handicrafts from throughout the country.

Malls

Puerto Paraíso mall, on the marina, Cabo San Lucas, B.C.S. A handful of the nicest gift and curio shops in town.

▓ NORTHWEST MEXICO

Handicrafts
Casa de las Artesanías de Chihuahua, Av. Niños Heroes 1101, Chihuahua, Chih., tel 614/437-1292, closed Sun. Regional crafts like Tarahumara dolls, drums, clay pots, and pine-needle baskets.
Casa de las Artesanías de Chihuahua, west side of main square, Creel, Chih. tel 635/456-0080. A subsidiary of the above store; it also sells regional crafts.
Gallery Michael, Camarón Sábalo 19, Mazatlán, Sin., tel 669/916-7816, www.michaelgallerymexico.com. A large collection of well-chosen Mexican crafts. There's a second shop in the tourist district at Av. de las Garzas 18, tel 669/916-5511.

Markets
Mercado de Artesanías, Victoria 506 and Aldama, Chihuahua, Chih. A block-wide store with jewelry and regional crafts.
Mercado Central, between Juárez and Serdán, Mazatlán, Sin. This huge market sells food, along with handicrafts at bargain prices.
Mercado Municipal, between Avs. 20 de Noviembre and 5 de Febrero and Calles Patoni and Pasteur, Durango, Dgo. The place to shop for *sarapes,* leather, and regional sweets.

▓ NORTHEAST MEXICO

Stores here sell cowboy boots, saddles, silver belt buckles, leather jackets, fine straw hats, and Saltillo's *sarapes* (bright striped blankets). Industrial Monterrey has shopping malls.

Handicrafts

El Sarape de Saltillo, Hidalgo Sur 305, Saltillo, Coah., tel 844/412-4889. Lots of sarapes, as well as ponchos, rugs, silver, copper, and pottery.

Leather

Botas Recio, Allende Norte 929, Saltillo, Coah., tel 844/412-1237. Men's shoes, belts, boots, and wallets of exotic leather (such as iguana, sea snake, ostrich, and shark); felt and straw hats.

Malls & Department Stores

Plaza Fiesta San Agustín, Av. Real de San Agustín at Lázaro Cárdenas, Monterrey, N.L., www.plazafiestasasagustin.com.mx. Monterrey's largest mall, with a Sanborns restaurant/bookstore and a theater.

▓ CENTRAL MEXICO

Fine craftsmanship here is a tradition. Dolores Hidalgo is known for hand-painted ceramics and tiles; Guanajuato for glassware; and San Miguel de Allende for housewares and folk art. In San Luis Potosí, buy finely woven silk shawls (rebozos).

Fine Art/Jewelry/ Housewares

Fabrica La Aurora, Camino a La Aurora s/n (continuation of Hidalgo), www.laaurora.com.mx, San Miguel de Allende, Gto. An old cotton mill shelters 49 shops selling antiques, contemporary art, fine furnishings, and jewelry.

Handicraft

Casa del Conde, Carr. Guanajuato–Dolores Hidalgo Km 5, La Valenciana, Guanajuato, Gto., tel 473/732-2550. Imported from elsewhere in Mexico and custom-made housewares of tin, copper, and German silver.
Casa María Luisa, Canal 40, San Miguel de Allende, Gto., tel

415/152-0130. A huge assortment of folk art, carved furniture, and household accessories.

Jewelry

Joyería David, Calle Zacateros 53, San Miguel de Allende, Gto., tel 415/152-0056. Silver and gold jewelry is made on the premises. (Second location at Umarán 26 is open Sun. 11 a.m.–3 p.m.)

▓ CENTRAL PACIFIC STATES

A wide variety of textiles and ceramics are made in Michoacán and Guerrero. Jalisco has excellent folk art, and Puerto Vallarta has shops selling fine art and crafts. Silver jewelry abounds in Taxco.

Shopping Areas

Mercado de Artesanías Turístico, Calle 5 de Mayo, at Paseo del Pescador, Zihuantanejo, Gro. Stands selling souvenirs, including ceramics and silver jewelry.
Plaza Los Patios, Blvd. Ixtapa s/n, Ixtapa, Gro. There are several worthwhile folk-art shops here.
Saturday market, Av. De los Plateros s/n, near the Flecha Roja bus terminal, Taxco. Look for the .925 stamp indicating sterling silver.
Zona Romántica, Col. E. Zapata, Puerto Vallarta, Jal. Highest concentration of folk art shops and fine art galleries. Across the bridge **el Centro,** also has fine shops, though more dispersed.

Handicrafts

Agustín Parra Diseño Barroco, Independencia 158, Tlaquepaque, Jal., tel 333/657-8530. Thirty years' experience building baroque and other period furniture, accessories, frames, and other objects.
Casa de las Artesanías, Ex-Convento de San Francisco, Fray Juan de San Miguel at Humboldt, Morelia, Mich. Two floors of regional artifacts, each stall selling

the craft made in its village.
Casa de los Once Patios, Madrigal de las Altas Torres near Lerín, Pátzcuaro, Mich., tel 434/342-4753).
Galería Tanana, Av. del Palmar 8, Sayulita, Nay., tel 329/291-3889. The not-for-profit Huichol Center for Cultural Survival (www.huicholcenter.org) often has a craftsperson on hand to demonstrate yarn paintings and beadwork at their small Sayulita shop two blocks from the beach.
Plaza de Artesanías, Juárez 145, Tlaquepaque, Jal. A cluster of shops selling regional folk art, blown glass, and pottery.

Malls & Department Stores

La Gran Plaza, Av. Vallarta 3959, Col. Don Bosco, Guadalajara, Jal., tel 33/3563-2900, www.lagranplazafashionmall.com. A modern complex west of town, with a Sanborns, cinema, and many stores and restaurants.
Plaza Bahía, Costera M. Alemán 125, Acapulco, Gro., tel 744/485-6939. A large, air-conditioned mall with bowling alley and shops.
Plaza del Sol, Avs. López Mateos Sur and Mariano Otero, Guadalajara, Jal., tel 33/3121-5950. Huge mall with green spaces, multiplex theater, Sanborns, many boutiques and shops.

Markets

Mercado de Artesanías Tonalá, Av. Tonaltecas at Calle Benito Juárez and surrounding streets. An outdoor pottery and crafts market held Thursday & Sunday.
Mercado de Dulces, Av. Farías at Santiago Tapia, Morelia, Mich. Sells typical sweets of the region.

▓ MEXICO CITY

Fine art galleries are found throughout the city; look in Thursday's *Tiempo Libre* section of *La Jornada* newspaper for show listings. Shopping is particularly pleasant in outdoor weekend markets in Coyoacán and San Ángel.

Shopping Areas
Bazar Sábado, Plaza San Jacinto 11, San Ángel, open Saturday only. Exceptional handicrafts at fair prices within the two-story mansion and in the adjacent plaza.
Mercado de Artesanías Insurgentes, Londrés at Amberes, Zona Rosa. A maze of handicrafts in 225 stalls.
Zona Rosa, bounded by Reforma, Niza, Av. Chapultepec, and Florencia. This compact neighborhood has many shops selling jewelry, leather, antiques, and fine art.

Fine Art & Antiques
Jardín del Arte, Plaza Sullivan, Calle Sullivan near Reforma and Insurgentes. Each Saturday more than a hundred artists exhibit and sell their paintings and sculptures in this city park.

Handicrafts
Centro Artesanal La Ciudadela, Plaza de la Ciudadela at Balderas, tel 55/5510-1828. More than 300 shops selling crafts from all over Mexico.

Malls & Department Stores
Sanborns, Madero 4, Col. Madero, tel 55/5512-1331, www .sanborns.com.mx. This coffee shop/store sells English-language periodicals and books, perfumes, fresh pastries, chocolates, and gifts. (There are dozens more throughout the city.)

Markets
Mercado de Antigüedades La Lagunilla, Libertad between República de Chile and Allende. Sunday outdoor flea market attracts antiques hunters and coin collectors (including pickpockets). Best for Spanish speakers who are

also experienced globe-trotters.
Mercado Xochimilco, Guerrero between Morelos and 16 de Septiembre, Xochimilco. A pleasant covered market (best on weekends) that is less hectic than those downtown.

■ AROUND MEXICO CITY
Shopping Areas
La Calle de los Dulces, Puebla, Pue. Shops sell freshly made *camote* (sweet-potato candy) and other regional treats.

Handicrafts
Mercado de Artesanías El Parían, 2 Oriente at 6 Norte, Puebla, Pue. Covered outdoor market selling souvenirs, sweets, textiles, and inexpensive ceramics.
Mercado de Artesanías, plaza principal, Tepoztlán, Mor. Local handicrafts and those from central and southern Mexico are sold at a Sunday market in the main square.
Tianguis Sabado y Domingo, Plaza Xicotencatl, Morelos at Independencia, Tlaxcala, Tlax. Weekend folk-art market with typical carved wood, embroidered blouses, masks, and peach and pear liqueurs.

Markets
Mercado Cozme del Razo, Hidalgo at Calle 5 Norte, Cholula, Pue. Typical daily market selling handicrafts, fruits, vegetables, and clothing.

■ CENTRAL GULF COAST
While neither Veracruz nor Tabasco is known for its handicrafts, both have modern, air-conditioned shopping centers in their capital cities. The region's few typical souvenirs—including items made of vegetable fiber, woven straw fans, and carved gourds—are sold mainly in hotel and museum gift shops.

Shopping Areas
Zona Luz, between Calle 27 de Febrero, Zaragoza, 5 de Mayo and Madero, Villahermosa, Tab. There's nothing special to buy, but the pleasant pedestrian-only zone has pharmacies, ice-cream stores, and clothing boutiques.

Malls & Department Stores
Plaza Acuario, Blvd. Ávila Camacho s/n, Playón de Hornos, Veracruz, Ver., tel 229/932-8311. Air-conditioned and near the sea, this mall has boutiques and banks but no cinema.
Tabasco 2000, Municipio Libre 7 at Prolongación Paseo Tabasco, Villahermosa, Tab. Marble-lined commercial and shopping center with hotels and restaurants.

■ OAXACA
This state has a wealth of valuable folk art, and the city of Oaxaca boasts many worthy artists and excellent galleries.

Shopping Areas
(See "Market Towns," p. 271.)

Calle Alcalá, between Avs. Independencia and Constitución, Oaxaca. A pedestrian street with many fine shops.

Fine Arts
La Mano Mágica, M. Alcalá 203, Oaxaca, tel 951/516-4275, www .lamanomagica.com. Wool rugs from Teotitlán del Valle, oil paintings, and high-end crafts.
Quetzalli, Constitución 104, Oaxaca, tel 951/514-2606. Excellent contemporary paintings by burgeoning and established artists. There's a café/bar in front.

Handicrafts
Artesanías Chimalli, García Vigil 512, Oaxaca, tel 951/514-2101. A small shop with quality handicrafts; offers shipping.

MARO, Av. 5 de Mayo 204, Oaxaca, tel 951/516-0670. Woman's co-op selling regional clothing, herbed mescal, custom-made textiles, and much more.

Mercado de Artesanías, Calle J.P. Garcia near Zaragoza, Oaxaca. Textiles and clothing exclusively are sold here, including embroidered blouses, shawls, and clothing from Tehuantepec.

Markets

Mercado de Abastos, Periférico between Trujano and Minas, Oaxaca. The state's largest market is a labyrinth of stalls selling cooked food, cut flowers, and just about everything else.

Mercado Benito Juárez and Mercado 20 de Noviembre, Oaxaca. See pp. 256, 259.

▦ CHIAPAS

The Maya have a long tradition of weaving and brocade, kept alive in some towns by local women's co-ops. You'll also find wool clothing, fabrics, wooden dolls, and lots of other intriguing items, many from Guatemala.

Shopping Areas

Amatenango del Valle, 25 miles (32 km) south of San Cristóbal de las Casas. Many of the humble homes in this town sell lovely unglazed pots and pottery birds.

Books, Magazines, & Cards

La Pared, Av. Miguel Hidalgo 2, San Cristóbal de las Casas, tel 967/678-6367, closed Monday. New and used books in various genres, including classic literature, Mexican history, and culture. Most in English.

Taller Leñateros, Flavio A. Paniagua 54, San Cristóbal de las Casas, tel 967/678-5174, www .tallerlenateros.com. Produces handmade stationery, business cards, and books from natural and recycled materials.

Handicrafts

J'pas Jolov003letik, Utrilla 43, San Cristóbal de las Casas. Another great co-op with local woven, embroidered, and brocaded textiles and clothing.

Sna Jolobil, Ex-Convento de Santo Domingo, 20 de Noviembre s/n, San Cristóbal de las Casas, tel 967/678-2646. A women's co-op showcasing top-drawer Maya weaving.

Jewelry

Museo del Ambar, Calle Diego de Mazariegos, adjacent to La Merced, tel 967/678-9716. Has a good collection of amber jewelry, and you don't have to worry about fakes.

Markets

Mercado Municipal, Av. General Utrilla at Nicaragua, San Cristóbal de las Casas. A wonderful warren of candles, copal incense, produce, and hot food; the best market day is Saturday.

▦ YUCATÁN PENINSULA

The Yucatán Peninsula in general (especially in Campeche state) has a surprising dearth of folk art. What you will find are high-quality hammocks, fine Panama-style hats, embroidered *huipiles* (sacklike, lightweight women's garments), dresses, blouses, and pleated *guayabera* shirts in sherbet colors for men. The best shopping is in Mérida and Cancún. Catering to cruise ship passengers, Cozumel also has folk art and lots of high-end jewelry.

Books, Magazines, & Cards

Dante, Calle 17 No. 138-B at Prolongación Paseo de Montejo, Mérida, Yuc., tel 999/927-7676. A good selection of books and a

popular coffee shop.

Fama, Av. Tulúm 105, Cancún, Q.R., tel 998/884-6586. Books on the Yucatán; a large selection of English-language magazines.

Handicrafts

Arte Maya, Calle 23 No. 301, Ticul, Yuc., tel 997/972-1669. Expensive, museum-quality reproductions of Maya archaeological pieces.

El Aguacate, Calle 58 at Calle 63, tel 999/928-6429. Nylon and cotton hammocks in many hues and sizes.

Jewelry & Clothing

Guayaberas Jack, Calle 59 No. 507A, between Calles 60 and 62, 999/928-6002, www.guayaberas jack.com.mx. Excellent selection and service for many styles and colors of men's pleated dress shirts. Also some lovely women's dresses and accessories.

Malls & Department Stores

La Isla Shopping Village, Blvd. Kukulkán Km 12.5, Cancún, Q.R., tel 998/883-5025. 200-plus shops as well as several wonderful restaurants.

Plaza Kukulkán, Blvd. Kukulkán Km 13, Cancún, Q.R. An upscale mall with a new UltraFemme, Louis Vuitton, Cartier, Coach, and other shops in its Luxury Avenue.

Markets

Mercado Municipal, Campeche, Camp, Calle 53 at Baluartes Este. Campeche's main market is one of the Yucatán's cleanest, best organized, and most pleasant for browsing. Surrounded by stores selling shoes and other items.

Entertainment & Activities

Mexicans are dedicated sports fans. Bullfights are popular, and most large cities have at least one bullring; the fights are generally scheduled to coincide with major holidays or festivals. We prefer *charreadas* (Mexican rodeos), a specialty of the northern and central states (see p. 155), while *fútbol* (soccer) and baseball have a nationwide following. Religious holidays are generally lively affairs with food, dancing, and fireworks. Some are specific to a region or village, others are celebrated throughout the country (see pp. 18–19).

The best known Carnaval celebrations take place in Veracruz, Cozumel, Campeche, and Mazatlán but also happen in Guaymas, Sonora; San Juan Chamula, Chiapas; and other towns. Solemn but colorful and engaging celebrations mark Semana Santa, the week preceding Easter. Cities with especially unusual parades or customs include Oaxaca, Oaxaca; Taxco, Guerrero; Suchitlán, Colima; Real de Catorce and San Luis Potosí, San Luis Potosí; Zacatecas, Zacatecas; Zintzuntzan, Michoacán; and Zinacantán and San Juan Chamula, Chiapas.

Día de Muertos, or Day of the Dead, blends Catholic beliefs with local traditions, creating a serious pageant that is also a source of merriment and family bonding. In the Yucatán, families create altars to their departed relatives, spruce up family tombs, and make pit-baked tamales to symbolize the link between the living and the dead. Oaxaca state and Michoacán are known for their rites; although visitors generally flock to the best known towns (Oaxaca, Janitzio), lesser known sites have their own rituals. See www.dayofthedead.com for examples.

December 12, **Fiesta de la Virgen de Guadalupe,** is celebrated with Mass, parades, parties, regional music and dance, fireworks, and other festivities, usually for the week before the saint's day. Celebrations take place at the shrines to the Virgen at La Villa de Guadalupe, north of Mexico City; in Tamazunchale, San Luis Potosí; Tuxtla Gutiérrez and San Cristóbal de las Casas, Chiapas; and in other towns. Most every Mexican town and village celebrates its patron saint in one way or another

Following is a regional listing of Mexico's most important festivals, cultural centers, and activities. Only the most interesting or historically important nightclubs and bars are included. Check with the hotel concierge or tourist information staff, or the local newspaper listings, for other evening entertainment.

■ BAJA CALIFORNIA

Bars
Hussong's Cantina, Av. Ruiz 113, Ensenada, B.C., tel 646/178-3210, www.cantinahussongs.com. Popular for more than a century.

Wineries
See "Wine-tasting in Mexico," p. 37.

Charreadas
Tijuana Tourism Office, tel 664/658-3117 or 888/775-2417 from U.S. Held most weekends, May–September. Venues vary.

Cultural Centers
Centro Cultural Tijuana, Paseo de los Heroes and Mina, Tijuana, B.C., tel 664/687-9600, www .cecut.gob.mx. History, anthropology, and art museums, theater, gift shop, and restaurant.

Festivals
Fiesta de la Vendimia, Ensenada, B.C., tel 646/172-3022, www. fiestasdelavendimia.com. In Aug., wine tastings and cultural events.
Fiesta de San Javier, Misión San Javier, B.C.S., December 3.

Sporting Events
Bisbee's Black and Blue Marlin Tournament, Los Cabos, B.C.S., www.bisbees.com. Three days in October, with a million-dollar purse. Also, the end of July at East Cape.
SCORE Baja 250, 500 and 1000, www.score-international.com. Off-road races in March, May/ June, and October/November, respectively.
Newport Beach-Ensenada Sailing Regatta, www.nosa.org. Held each April for more than 60 years.

Sportfishing
World-class fishing in Bahía de Los Angeles, Los Cabos, the East Cape, La Paz, Loreto, Mulegé, and San Felipe. On the Pacific, fish in Ensenada and San Quintín Bay.

Water Sports
The sheltered Gulf of California (Sea of Cortez) is preferred for **kayaking,** especially around Bahía de Concepción, Loreto, the East Cape, La Paz, and many offshore islands. Pacific coast **sailboarding** sites include Punta San Carlos; Punta Abreojos; and San Quintín, Magdalena, Santa Rosaliita, and Almejas bays; on the gulf, try Bahía de Los Angeles, Punta Chivato, Loreto, and the East Cape.

Diving and **snorkeling** are popular off Cabo Pulmo and Cabo San Lucas. **Surfing** is popular but rentals rare. Northern Baja's best surfing is during the winter.

Baja Expeditions, 2625 Garnet Ave. San Diego, CA, tel 858/581-3311 or 800/843-6967, www.

bajaex.com, is a well-respected company offering island kayaking, wildlife cruises, and scuba diving.

Whale-Watching

The season is from January through mid-April (see pp. 68–69).

◼ NORTHWEST MEXICO
Cultural Centers & Theaters

Centro Cultural de Chihuahua, V. Carranza at Aldama, Chihuahua, Chih., tel 614/429-3596. Music, dance, art exhibits.
Teatro Angela Peralta, Carnaval 1024, Mazatlán, Sin. Folk dances, symphony, theater, and cultural events.

Festivals

La Feria de la Fundación de Durango and la Feria Agrícola, Durango, Dur., two weeks in mid-July. Consecutive fairs celebrate the city's founding and agriculture and ranching. Music, folk dances, horse races, and charreadas.
Festival Cultural de Mazatlán. Two months of free and reasonably priced cultural events in Angela Peralta Theater and other venues, beginning mid-October.
Fiesta de la Fundación del Pueblo, El Fuerte, Sin. Feast honoring the town's founding, Nov. 20. Carnival rides, foot races, folk dancing.
Navy Day, Puerto Peñasco (Rocky Point) and Guaymas, Son., June 1 (see "Celebrating the Sea with Local Fishermen," p. 275).
Ortiz Tirado Music Festival, www.festivalortiztirado.com, last two weeks in January. Classical music festival in Alamos, Sonora.

Sportfishing

Mazatlán, Sin. Sportfishing fleets line the harbor south of town; prices for day charters are similar.

◼ NORTHEAST MEXICO
Cultural Centers & Theaters

Centro Cultural Teatro Garcia Carrillo, Allende at Aldama, Saltillo, Coah. Porfiriato structure hosting concerts and expositions.
Teatro de la Ciudad de Monterrey, Zuazua at Matamoros, Monterrey, N.L., tel 81/8343-4424. Large modern theater.

Festivals

Feria Cultural de Zacatecas, Zac.
Feria Nacional, Zacatecas, Zac. Three weeks of events in September: concerts, bullfights, charreadas, and religious processions.
Fiesta de San Isidro Labrador. Celebrated May 15 in Jalpán, Qto., with fireworks. Mass, music, dance, and a colorful procession.
Fiesta de San Roque, Querétaro, Qto., the days before August 16. Parades, fireworks, and dances.
La Morisma, Zacatecas, Zac., end of August. Festival includes a three-day reenactment of a battle between Moors and Christians, plays, and indigenous dancing.

Fishing

Freshwater fishing (bass, catfish) in Caballero, Méndez, Vicente Guerrero, and other lakes, surfcasting along the coastal lagoons.

◼ CENTRAL MEXICO
Cultural Centers & Theaters

Centro Cultural El Nigromante (or Bellas Artes), Hernandez Macias 75, San Miguel de Allende, Gto., tel 415/152-0289. Arts and crafts classes and cultural events.
Instituto Allende, Ancha de San Antonio 20, San Miguel de Allende, Gto., tel 415/152-0190, www.institutoallende.com.mx. Galleries, library, and theater; offers Spanish-language and art classes.

Teatro de la Paz, Villerías 205, Jardín del Carmen, San Luis Potosí, S.L.P., tel 444/812-2698. Elegant neoclassical theater.
Teatro Juárez, Calle de Sopena at Jardín Unión, Guanajuato, Gto., tel 473/732-0183. Symphony, opera, and more at a lovely theater.

Festivals

Comparsas de San Martin Chalchicuautla, 81 miles (130 km) from Ciudad Valles on Hwy. 85, San Luis Potosí, near Tamazachale, tel 481/381-5735, Nov. 1. Parade and indigenous dance competition. Men dress as women; other themes: death, good, and evil.
Feria del Queso y del Vino, Tequisquiapan, Qto., tel 414/273-0295, www.tequis.info, May/June. Wine and cheese festival; outdoor theater, folk dancing, and concerts.
Feria de San Marcos, Aguascalientes, Ags., tel 449/910-2088, www.feriadesanmarcos.com. Largest and oldest state fair, with dances, bullfights, and fireworks.
Festival Cervantino, Guanajuato, Gto. (see sidebar p. 122), fall. World-class performers here.
Fiesta de San Miguel, San Miguel de Allende, Gto., tel 415/152-0900. Traditional dancing, bullfights, fireworks, and concerts culminating at dawn on Sept. 29.

Nature

Sotano de las Golondrinas, outside Tancanhuitz, east of San Luis Potosí (164 miles/264 km from Ciudad Valle), S.L.P. Cave offers a spectacle of birds arriving and departing at sunrise and sunset.

◼ CENTRAL PACIFIC STATES
Butterfly Migration

Millions of monarchs winter in Michoacán forest sanctuaries (see p. 176).

Cultural Centers
Instituto Cultural Cabañas, Guadalajara, Jal., see p. 151.

Dancing & Shows
Ballet Folklórico, Teatro Dian (see p. 150). Regional dances by university troupe.
Charreadas, Lienzo Charro de Jalisco, Av. Dr. R. Michel 577, Guadalajara, Jal., tel 33/3619-0315. Mariachi music and superior horsemanship on Sundays, noon.
Espectáculo de la Quebrada, Plazoleta de la Quebrada, Acapulco, Gro., tel 744/483-1400 or 744/484-4416. Cliff divers perform throughout the day, and at night to a dinner, dancing, and music spectacle from La Perla Restaurant at El Mirador.
Salon Q, Av. Costera Alemán 3117, Col. Costa Azul, Acapulco, Gro., tel 744/481-0114. Dancing to live music Wed.–Sun. after 10 p.m.

Festivals
Día de San Blas, San Blas, Nay. February 3. The antique statue of San Blas's patron saint accompanies a flotilla of townspeople as the priest blesses the boats and the fishermen; fireworks.
Encuentro Internacional del Mariachi y la Charrería, Guadalajara, Jal., end August/ beginning September. A week of *charro* events and mariachi music.
Feria de la Guitarra, Paracho, Mich., www.feriadelaguitarra.com, Aug. Competitions, concerts, and display of handmade instruments.
Feria de Manzanillo, Colima, end of April to mid-May. The town's anniversary is celebrated with dances, music, and rodeos.
Feria de Michoacán, Morelia, Mich., first weeks of May. Typical state fair, with rides, expos, and cultural and music events.
Feria Nacional de la Cerámica. Usually mid-June. Exhibits, competition, and sale of ceramics in Tlaquepaque, Jal., outside Guadalajara. June 29 is **la Fiesta de San Pedro** (Feast of St. Peter).
Festival Internacional de Organo, Morelia, Mich., tel 443/317-8032, May. International pipe-organ festival held for more than 30 years.
Fiesta de San Antonio Abad, January 17, Taxco, Gro. Pets and domestic animals are dressed in costumes for the priest's blessing at Iglesia de Santa Prisca.
Fiesta de la Virgen de la Salud & La Virgen de la Candelaria in Colima, Col. Nine days of events culminating February 2 (Candlemas). Other events—including masked dances—lead up to this date in Suchitlán, Col., outside the capital.
Fiestas de Octubre, Guadalajara, Jal., tel 33/3585-9954, www .fiestasdeoctubre.com.mx, throughout Oct. Mariachis and charreadas, opera, symphony, and arts exhibits.
Maundy Thursday, colorful processions in Tzintzuntzán, Mich.
Procession of the Virgin of Zapópan, Zapópan (Guadalajara), Jal., Oct. 12. Starting the day before, hundreds of thousands of pilgrims line the road leading to her shrine in the basilica, where the image is reinstated for the holidays.
PV Gourmet Festival, tel 322/222-2247, www.festivalgourmet.com. Ten-day program celebrating food and drink at some of PV's top restaurants. Wine, chocolate, and tequila tastings; wine pairings; cooking demonstrations and lectures; and good food.
Restaurant Week, mid-May. Despite its name, two weeks of reduced price three- or five-course meals at top area restaurants.

MEXICO CITY
Tiempo Libre, www.tiempolibre. com.mx, published in Spanish on Thurs. in the Spanish-language newspaper *Reforma,* lists events and gallery shows, as does the English-language daily *The News.*

Bars
La Guadalupana, Higuera 14, Coyoacán, tel 55/5554-6253, is a traditional watering hole with a mainly masculine clientele.
L'Opera, Cinco de Mayo 10 at Mata, tel 55/5512-8959. Historic cantina with period decor.

Cultural Centers & Theaters
Auditorio Nacional, Paseo de la Reforma 50, Parque de Chapultepec, tel 55/9138-1350, www .auditorio.com.mx. Mostly music and theater events.
Palacio de Bellas Artes, Av. Juárez and Eje Central, Alameda Park, www.bellasartes.gob.mx. Folkloric ballets, symphony, opera, and other performances.
Sala Nezahualcoyotl, Insurgentes Sur 3000, Ciudad Universitaria, tel 55/5622-7113. All types of music and theatrical events.

Festivals
Blessing of the Animals, Coyoacán, January 17. Pets and working animals blessed by monks.
Festival Centro Histórico. The three-week cultural festival each April offers a range of musical performances, flamenco ballet, and guided visits to some of the city's lesser-known cultural sites.
Fiesta de la Virgen del Carmen, San Ángel, July 16. Fireworks, dances, and a traditional fair.

AROUND MEXICO CITY
Cultural Centers
Centro Cultural de Hidalgo, Arista at Hidalgo, Pachuca, Hgo., tel 771/111-4150. Houses the City Theater and school of art, museums, gardens, and plazas.

Entertainment
Free outdoor band concerts Sunday afternoons, Jardín Juárez, Cuernavaca, Mor.

Festivals
Cinco de Mayo, Puebla, Pue., May 5. Colorful parades mark

victorious battle against French. **Fiesta de la Virgen de la Asunción,** Huamantla, Tlax., August 15. Bull-running through the streets for La Noche que Nadie Duerme (The Night When No One Sleeps). **Fiesta de Tepoztlán,** Tepoztlán, Mor., September 8. Dance celebration of conversion to Catholicism. Tepoztlán also celebrates carnival with El Brinco del Chinelo (the "hop dance") and other traditions.

Spas & Water Parks

Morelos state is known for its thermal springs around which water parks (see Las Estacas p. 374) and resort spas have grown; contact Cuernavaca tourist board (tel 777/314-3872) for details or www.morelostravel.com.

■ CENTRAL GULF COAST
Culture

Folkloric ballet and state orchestral performances are held at **El Teatro del Estado,** Ignacio de la Llave at Ávila Camacho, Xalapa, Ver., tel 228/842-1200.

Festivals

Carnaval, Veracruz, Ver., week before Lent. Parades and partying begin with the ceremonial Burning of Bad Humor and climax on Shrove Tuesday (Mardi Gras). **Día de la Candelaria,** Tlacotalpán, Ver., days preceding Candlemas, February 2. A colorful festival with bull runs and riverboats. **Fiesta de Corpus Cristi,** Papantla, Ver., movable feast, usually May or June. Fireworks, parades, cockfights, and traditional dances. **Fiesta de Santiago Apóstle,** Santiago Tuxtla, Ver., July 25. Native dances and fiesta in celebration of patron St. James the Apostle.

■ OAXACA
Boat Tours

Santa Cruz Bay, Bahías de Huatulco. Visit the nine bays, disembarking at one or more.

Festivals

Fiesta de las Velas, Isthmus of Tehuantepec, late spring through early fall, primarily in May. Ancient celebrations honoring religious and secular events. Contact Oaxaca tourist board for dates. **Guelaguetza,** Cerro del Fortín, Oaxaca, generally first two Mondays after July 16. Traditional folk dancing from Oaxaca's seven regions at a hilltop amphitheater. **La Noche de Rábanos,** *zócalo*, Oaxaca, December 23. Making tableaux of carved radishes.

Folk Dancing/ Dinner Shows

Hotel Camino Real, Oaxaca. Folkloric shows in one of the covered stone patios.

■ CHIAPAS
Festivals

Fiestas de Enero, during two weeks of mid-January. Chiapa de Corzo has masked parades, dances, and street festivities.

Celebrations in Zinacantán include **la Fiesta de San Sebastian,** January 20 to 22; Fridays during Lent; Easter; and Carnaval.

San Juan Chamula has colorful fiestas for Carnaval, Easter, and the feast day *(June 22–24)* of its patron saint, St. John the Baptist.

Folk Dancing/ Dinner Shows

Las Pichanchas (see p. 378). Marimba shows and folk dancing.

Tours

Visit villages outside San Cristóbal de las Casas on horse tours through area tour operators.

■ YUCATÁN PENINSULA
Cultural Centers

Casa de la Cultura, Prol. Av. Yaxchilán SM 25, Cancún, Q.R., tel 998/884-8364, www.casa cultura-cancun.gob.mx. Sponsors theater, music, and other activities. **Teatro Peón Contreras,** Calle 60 between Calles 57 & 59, Mérida, Yuc., tel 999/924-9290. Music and dance performances.

Diving/Scuba

Aqua World, Blvd. Kukulcán Km 15.3, Cancún, Q.R., tel 998/848-8327. Full-service aquatic center; game fishing, diving, party boats. **Scuba-Diving-Cozumel,** www .scuba-diving-cozumel.com. Offers dive-related information including diving sites around Palancar reef.

Entertainment

Noche Mexicana, Paseo Montejo at Calle 47 and throughout downtown, Mérida, Yuc., Sat. 7:30 p.m. to 11 p.m. Weekly street party including music, crafts, and food. **Sound and light shows,** after dark at Chichén Itzá, Uxmal, and the Convento San Antonio de Padua, Izamal, Yuc.; also la Puerta de Tierra, Campeche, and Edzná.

Festivals

Fiestas del Equinoxio, Templo de Kukulkán, Chichén Itzá, Yuc., first days of spring and fall. At the equinoxes, a serpent-like shadow descends the pyramid to align with the stone snake's head. **Festival Internacional de Aves,** Held each November in Mérida for exhibits and lectures, a bird-counting contest, dinners, and of course, birding expeditions. **Hanal Pixan,** Mérida, Yuc., the days preceding November 2. Traditional food and altars from around the state for Day of the Dead celebrations. **Otoño Cultural,** Mérida, Yuc., last week of October through first week of November Autumn Cultural Festival with classical music, dance, and art exhibitions.

Language Guide

General
yes *sí*
no *no*
please *por favor*
thank you *gracias*
you're welcome *de nada*
hello, hi *hola*
goodbye *adiós, hasta luego*
good day *buenos días*
good afternoon *buenas tardes*
good evening/goodnight *buenas noches*
OK *está bien/de acuerdo*
today *hoy*
yesterday *ayer*
tomorrow *mañana*
Do you speak English? *¿Habla usted inglés?*
I am from the U.S. *Soy norteamericano/a*
I don't understand *No entiendo*
Please speak more slowly *Hable más despacio, por favor*
What is its/your name? *¿Cómo se llama?*
My name is... *Yo me llamo...*
Let's go *Vamos*
At what time? *¿A qué horas?*

Help
I need a doctor/dentist *Necesito un médico/dentista*
Can you help me? *¿Me puede ayudar?*
Where is a hospital/clinic? *¿Dónde hay un hospital/una clínica?*
Help! *¡Socorro!*

Shopping
I'd like . . . *Quisiera . . .*
How much is it? *¿Cuánto es?*
That's very expensive *Es muy caro*
Do you take credit cards? *¿Acepta tarjetas de crédito?*
size *el talle*
receipt *el recibo/la nota*
bakery *la panadería*
bookstore *la librería*
market *el mercado/tianguis*
pharmacy *la farmacia*
shopping mall *el centro comercial*
supermarket *el supermercado*

Sightseeing
visitor information *información turística*
open *abierto/a*
closed *cerrado/a*
church *la iglesia*
cathedral *la catedral*
country estate *la hacienda*
museum *el museo*
tour *el tour*
town *el pueblo*
city *la ciudad*

In the Hotel
Do you have . . . ? *¿Hay . . . ?*
single room *una habitación sencilla*
double room *una habitación doble*
with/without *con/sin*
bathroom/view *baño/vista*

In the Restaurant
menu *el menú/la carta*
breakfast *el desayuno*
lunch (main meal) *la comida*
dinner *la cena*
check *la cuenta*
takeout *para llevar*
fixed-price meal *el menú del día*
à la carte *a la carta*
vegetarian food *comida vegetariana*

Menu Reader

See also "Food & drink," pp. 34–35.
appetizer *el antojito*
bread *el pan*
soup (broth) *la sopa*
soup (cream) *la crema*
salad *la ensalada*
main course *el plato principal*
vegetable *verdura/vegetal*
rice *(sopa de) arroz*
bean soup *sopa de frijol*
refried beans *frijoles refritos*
dessert *el postre*
spicy *picante*
beer *la cerveza*
coffee *el café*
American-style coffee *café americano*
Mexican-style (sweet) coffee *café de olla*
decaffeinated coffee *descafeinado*
tea *el té*
milk *la leche*
mineral water *el agua mineral*
ice *el hielo*
purified water *el agua purificada*
soft drink *refresco*
lemonade/orangeade *limonada/naranjada*
wine *vino*
apéritif *aperitivo*
Cheers! *¡Salud!*
meat *la carne*
beef *la carne de res*
pork *el puerco*
goat *la cabra/el chivo*
turkey *el guajolote/pavo*
chicken *el pollo*
fish *el pescado*
lobster *langosta*
octopus *pulpo*
shrimp *camarón*
squid *calamar*

INDEX

ILLUSTRATIONS CREDITS

Cover, Raul Touzon/NationalGeographicStock. com; Spine, Richard Cummins/Corbis; 2-3, Tomasz Tomaszewski/NGS Image Collection; 4, Robert Holmes; 9, Larry Dunmire/The Paradise Gallery; 11, Philip Enticknap/Travel Library; 12, Jeffrey Greenberg/Alamy; 13, Mireille Vautier; 15, Justin Guariglia/NationalGeographicStock.com; 16, Radius Images/Alamy; 19, Stuart Franklin/NGS Image Collection; 21, Richard H. Stewart/NGS Image Collection; 22, Gianni Dagli Orti/Corbis UK Ltd.; 25, Robert Frerck/Getty Images; 26, akg-images; 28-29, Louis S. Glanzman/NGS Image Collection; 30, Library of Congress, #LC-DIG-cph-3a10509; 33, Tomasz Tomaszewski/NGS Image Collection; 34, Brian McGilloway/Robert Holmes Photography; 36, Nik Wheeler/Corbis UK Ltd.; 39, Isabella Tree/Hutchison Library/Eye Ubiquitous; 40, Viesti Collection/Art Directors & Trip Photo Library; 42-43, PSHAW-PHOTO/Shutterstock; 44, Dave G. Houser/Corbis UK Ltd.; 47, Charles & Josette Lenars/Corbis UK Ltd.; 51, Danny Lehman/Corbis UK Ltd.; 53, James Davis/Eye Ubiquitous; 54, Tom Bean/Getty Images; 56, Edward Parker/Hutchison Library/Eye Ubiquitous; 58, Robert Holmes/AA Photo Library; 61, Robert Holmes; 62, Robert Holmes; 65, David Muench/Corbis UK Ltd.; 66, Mexico/Alamy; 68, Streano/Havens/Art Directors & Trip Photo Library; 69, Stuart Westmorland/Corbis UK Ltd.; 70, Inti St. Clair/Getty Images; 72, David Sanger; 75, Mireille Vautier; 78, Joanna Pinneo/NGS Image Collection; 80, Flavio Beltran/Shutterstock; 82, Wilbur E. Garrett/NGS Image Collection; 84, Patricio Robles Gil; 85, Lynsey Addario/Corbis; 86, Nik Wheeler; 88, Holger Mette/Shutterstock; 90, Alan Tobey/iStockphoto.com; 93, Macduff Everton/Corbis; 95, Ernesto Rios Lanz/Latinstock Mexico; 96, Robert Frerck/Getty Images; 98, Alan Tobey/iStockphoto.com; 103, Robert & Linda Mitchell; 104, James L. Stanfield/NGS Image Collection; 106, Rick Strange/AA Photo Library; 107, George Grall/NGS Image Collection; 108, Adalberto Rios Szalay/Latinstock Mexico; 112, Robert Francis/South American Pictures; 114, Scott L. Walker; 116, Robert Frerck/Odyssey/Chicago/Robert Harding Picture Library; 117, Bill Perry/Shutterstock; 120, Bill Perry/Shutterstock; 123, Richard Gunion/iStockphoto.com; 125, Danny Lehman/Corbis UK Ltd.; 128, Latinstock Mexico; 130, Rick Strange/AA Photo Library; 132, Adalberto Rios Szalay/Latinstock Mexico; 135, Peter Wilson/AA Photo Library; 137, Diana Dicker; 140, Danny Lehman/Corbis UK Ltd.; 141, Jon Arnold Images Ltd./Alamy; 143, Matthew D'Annunzio/Shutterstock; 144, James Davis/Eye Ubiquitous; 146, InStock/iStockphoto.com; 148, Adina Tovy Amsel/Eye Ubiquitous; 153, Carlos Sanchez Pereyra/Shutterstock; 155, Stuart Wasserman; 156, Roger Ressmeyer/Corbis UK Ltd.; 159, Robert & Linda Mitchell; 160, Rick Strange/AA Photo Library; 162, David Alan Harvey/NGS Image Collection; 165, Isabella Tree/Hutchison Library/Eye Ubiquitous; 166, Robert Frerck/Getty Images; 168, Larry Dunmire/The Paradise Gallery; 170, Kelly-Mooney Photography/Corbis UK Ltd.; 174, Eduardo Peynetti Ruiz/iStockphoto.com; 177, David Sanger; 181, Mireille Vautier; 182, Robert Frerck/Getty Images; 184, Bridgeman Art Library; 185, Bridgeman Art Library; 186, Nik Wheeler; 189, Rick Strange/AA Photo Library; 190, Guy Marks/Travel Ink Photo Library; 192, David Sanger; 194, Steven Allan/iStockphoto.com; 198, Robert Aberman; 200, Carlos Reyes-Manzo/Andes Press Agency; 203, Kelly-Mooney Photography/Corbis UK Ltd.; 204, Carlos Reyes-Manzo/Andes Press Agency; 207, M. Barlow/Art Directors & Trip Photo Library; 208, Nik Wheeler; 211, Robert Frerck/Getty Images; 212, John Mitchell/Alamy; 214, Alexandre Fagundes De Fagundes/Dreamstime.com; 216, John Lander/Alamy; 218, PSHAW-PHOTO/Shutterstock; 221, Stuart Wasserman; 223, Iain Pearson/South American Pictures; 225, Wendy Connett/Alamy; 226, Jonathan Blair/Corbis UK Ltd.; 228, Gary Yim/Shutterstock; 230, Rick Strange/AA Photo Library; 233, Kenneth Garrett/National Museum of Anthropology, Mexico City/NGS Image Collection; 235, Susan Kaye; 236, AM Corporation/Alamy; 238, Chris Sharp/South American Pictures; 240, Richard Gunion/Dreamstime.com; 245, Mireille Vautier; 246, Kenneth Garrett/NGS Image Collection; 248, John Elk III; 251, Charlie Munsey/Corbis; 253, Carlos Sanchez Pereyra/Shutterstock; 255, Kelly-Mooney Photography/Corbis UK Ltd.; 256, Radius Images/Alamy; 258, Gordon Sinclair/Alamy; 260, Robert Frerck/Getty Images; 262, Macduff Everton/Corbis UK Ltd.; 264, Michael Macintyre/Hutchison Library/Eye Ubiquitous; 267, Macduff Everton/Corbis UK Ltd.; 269, Danny Lehman/Corbis; 270, Mireille Vautier; 272, Courtesy Cocinar Mexicano; 273, Felipe González/Shutterstock; 276, David Alan Harvey/NGS Image Collection; 279, Robert Fried/Alamy; 281, Jeremy Horner/Hutchison Library/Eye Ubiquitous; 282, Mireille Vautier; 284, Rick Strange/AA Photo Library; 286, H. Elton/Axiom Photographic Agency Ltd.; 288, Robert Frerck/Robert Harding Picture Library; 290, Ales Liska/Shutterstock; 294, Danny Lehman/Corbis UK Ltd.; 296, Isabella Tree/Hutchison Library/Eye Ubiquitous; 298, Laguna de Montebello, Chiapas/Ricardo Espinosa Orozco/CPTM; 300, Otis Imboden/NGS Image Collection; 302, Fabienne Fossez/ffotograff; 304, Charles & Josette Lenars/Corbis UK Ltd.; 307, Adalberto Rios Szalay/Latinstock Mexico; 308, Larry Dunmire/The Paradise Gallery; 310, Mike Liu/Shutterstock; 312, Susan Kaye; 315, Alison Wright/Corbis UK Ltd.; 317, Irene Chan/Alamy; 318, Mauritius/Photoshot; 318-319, Ann Winterbotham; 321, Chris Caldicott/Axiom Photographic Agency Ltd.; 323, Robert Frerck/Getty Images; 327, Roger Sieber/iStockphoto.com; 328, Robert & Linda Mitchell; 331, Mireille Vautier; 332, Richard A. Cooke III/Getty Images; 335, Larry Dunmire/The Paradise Gallery; 337, Macduff Everton/Corbis UK Ltd.; 339, Larry Dunmire/The Paradise Gallery; 340, Mireille Vautier; 343, Mireille Vautier; 346, Mireille Vautier; 347, Sergio Dorantes/Corbis UK Ltd.

National Geographic
TRAVELER
Mexico

Published by the National Geographic Society
John M. Fahey, Jr., *President
and Chief Executive Officer*
Gilbert M. Grosvenor, *Chairman of the Board*
Tim T. Kelly, *President, Global Media Group*
John Q. Griffin, *Executive Vice President;
President, Publishing*
Nina D. Hoffman, *Executive Vice President;
President, Book Publishing Group*

Prepared by the Book Division
Barbara Brownell Grogan, *Vice President and Editor in Chief*
Marianne R. Koszorus, *Director of Design*
Barbara A. Noe, *Senior Editor*
Carl Mehler, *Director of Maps*
R. Gary Colbert, *Production Director*
Jennifer A. Thornton, *Managing Editor*
Meredith C. Wilcox, *Administrative Director, Illustrations*

Staff for 2010 Edition
Brooke C. Stoddard, *Project Editor*
Kay Kobor Hankins, *Art Director*
Linda Makarov, *Designer*
Mary Stephanos, *Text Editor*
Al Morrow, *Design Assistant*
Michael McNey, Nicholas P. Rosenbach, and Mapping
Specialists, *Map Production*
Richard Wain, *Production Project Manager*
Rob Waymouth, *Illustrations Specialist*
Naomi Linzer, *Indexer*
Bridget A. English, Lise Sajewski, Maura Walsh,
Contributors

Manufacturing and Quality Management
Christopher A. Liedel, *Chief Financial Officer*
Phillip L. Schlosser, *Vice President*
Chris Brown, *Technical Director*
Nicole Elliott, *Manager*
Rachel Faulise, *Manager*

**National Geographic Traveler: Mexico
(Third Edition) ISBN: 978-1-4262-0524-8**

First edition: Edited and designed by AA Publishing
(a trading name of Automobile Association Develop- ·
ments Limited, whose registered office is Norfolk House,
Priestley Road, Basingstoke, Hampshire, England RG24
9NY. Registered number: 1878835).

Area map illustrations drawn by Chris Orr Associates,
Southampton, England
Cutaway illustrations drawn by Maltings Partnership,
Derby, England

The National Geographic Society is one of the world's largest nonprofit scientific and educational organizations. Founded in 1888 to "increase and diffuse geographic knowledge," the Society works to inspire people to care about the planet. It reaches more than 325 million people worldwide each month through its official journal, *National Geographic*, and other magazines; National Geographic Channel; television documentaries; music; radio; films; books; DVDs; maps; exhibitions; school publishing programs; interactive media; and merchandise. National Geographic has funded more than 9,000 scientific research, conservation and exploration projects and supports an education program combating geographic illiteracy.

For more information, please call 1-800-NGS LINE (647-5463) or write to the following address:

National Geographic Society
1145 17th Street N.W.
Washington, D.C. 20036-4688 U.S.A.

Visit us online at www.nationalgeographic.com

For information about special discounts for bulk purchases, please contact National Geographic Books Special Sales: ngspecsales@ngs.org

For rights or permissions inquiries, please contact National Geographic Books Subsidiary Rights: ngbookrights@ngs.org

The Library of Congress has cataloged the first edition as follows:
Onsott, Jane.
    The National Geographic Traveler : Mexico / Jane Onsott.
        p. cm.
        Includes index.
        ISBN 0-7922-7897-6
        1. Mexico--Guidebooks. 2. Mexico--Description and travel. 3. Mexico Tours I. Title.

    F1209 .067 2001
    917.204'836--dc21   2001042784

The information in this book has been carefully checked and to the best of our knowledge is accurate. However, details are subject to change, and the National Geographic Society cannot be responsible for such changes, or for errors or omissions. Assessments of sites, hotels, and restaurants are based on the author's subjective opinions, which do not necessarily reflect the publisher's opinion.

Printed in China

09/RRDS/1

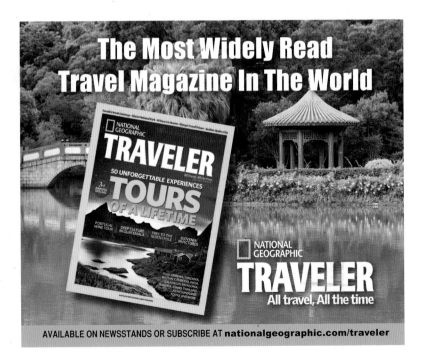